Lecture Notes in Computer Science   16081

Founding Editors

Gerhard Goos
Juris Hartmanis

AF173762

The series Lecture Notes in Computer Science (LNCS), including its subseries Lecture Notes in Artificial Intelligence (LNAI) and Lecture Notes in Bioinformatics (LNBI), has established itself as a medium for the publication of new developments in computer science and information technology research, teaching, and education.

LNCS enjoys close cooperation with the computer science R & D community, the series counts many renowned academics among its volume editors and paper authors, and collaborates with prestigious societies. Its mission is to serve this international community by providing an invaluable service, mainly focused on the publication of conference and workshop proceedings and postproceedings. LNCS commenced publication in 1973.

Davide Taibi · Darja Smite
Editors

Software Engineering and Advanced Applications

51st Euromicro Conference, SEAA 2025
Salerno, Italy, September 10–12, 2025
Proceedings, Part I

 Springer

Editors
Davide Taibi 🆔
University of Oulu
Oulu, Finland

Darja Smite 🆔
Blekinge Institute of Technology
Karlskrona, Sweden

ISSN 0302-9743   ISSN 1611-3349 (electronic)
Lecture Notes in Computer Science
ISBN 978-3-032-04189-0   ISBN 978-3-032-04190-6 (eBook)
https://doi.org/10.1007/978-3-032-04190-6

Preface

These three LNCS volumes contain the papers presented at SEAA 2025, the *51st Euromicro Conference Series on Software Engineering and Advanced Applications*, held on September 10–12, 2025, in Salerno, Italy.

SEAA serves as a long-standing international forum for researchers, practitioners, and students to share and discuss the latest innovations, emerging trends, practical experiences, and ongoing challenges and concerns in the field of software engineering and advanced information technology applications for software-intensive systems.

To address this mission, the 2025 edition of SEAA once again brought together a vibrant community through a diverse program. This year, the conference featured nine specialized tracks, each led by a team of co-chairs. These tracks spanned a wide range of topics and reflected the truly multidisciplinary nature of software engineering research and practice.

This year, SEAA received a record high number of 177 research submissions over nine thematic tracks. Each submission underwent a rigorous single-blinded peer-review process. Every paper was assigned to at least three and up to five independent reviewers, selected based on topic expertise. Reviewers were each asked to evaluate 2–3 papers. They assessed submissions according to criteria such as scientific soundness, originality, relevance to the SEAA community and the track theme, clarity of presentation, and contribution to the field. In cases where reviews yielded divergent scores or conflicting recommendations, track chairs actively moderated discussions to facilitate consensus. Conflicts of interest with the track chairs were further handled by the PC Chairs.

Following this process, a total of 62 full papers (including two vision papers) and 20 short papers were selected for inclusion in the proceedings. The diverse set of contributions reflects the high quality and breadth of work being conducted in the SEAA community.

The final program would not have been possible to complete without the effort, commitment, and invaluable contribution of the track chairs. From managing submissions and overseeing the peer-review process, to assisting in completing the exciting program, the track chairs were central to SEAA 2025's quality and relevance. We express our sincere appreciation to the track chairs as listed below.

1. **Cyber-Physical Systems** (CPS): V. Klös (Carl von Ossietzky University of Oldenburg, Germany), and S. Mubeen (Mälardalen University, Sweden)
2. **Data-and AI-Driven Engineering** (DAIDE): J. Bosch (Chalmers & Gothenburg University, Sweden), and H. Holmström Olsson (Malmö University, Sweden)
3. **Emerging Computing Technologies** (ECT): R. Abreu (University of Porto and Meta Inc., Portugal), A. Janes (Free University of Bozen-Bolzano, Italy), V. Lenarduzzi (University of Oulu, Finland), and S. Ali (Simula Research Laboratory, Oslo, Norway)
4. **Model-Driven Engineering and Modeling Languages** (MDEML): A. Bucaioni (Mälardalen University, Sweden), F. Ciccozzi (Mälardalen University, Sweden), and A. Wortmann (Stuttgart University, Germany)

5. **Software Management: Measurement, Peopleware, and Innovation** (SM): O. Demirors (Izmir Institute of Technology, Turkey), and V. Pontillo (Vrije Universiteit Brussel, Belgium)
6. **Systematic Literature Reviews and Mapping Studies in Software Engineering** (SMSE): S. Swift (Brunel University London, UK), and Mahir Arzoky (Brunel University London, UK)
7. **Software Process and Product Improvement** (SPPI): S. Biffl (Vienna University of Technology, Austria), R. Rabiser (Johannes Kepler University Linz, Austria), and D. Winkler (Vienna University of Technology, Austria)
8. **Software Analytics: Mining Software Open Datasets and Repositories** (STREAM): A. Ampatzoglou (University of Macedonia, Greece), and E.M. Arvanitou (University of Macedonia, Greece)
9. **Practical Aspects of Software Engineering** (KKIO): L. Madeyski, (Wrocław University of Science and Technology, Poland), M. Ochodek (Poznań University of Technology, Poland), M. Staron (University of Gothenburg, Sweden), and A. Zalewski (Warsaw University of Technology, Poland)

We extend our gratitude to the SEAA 2025 keynote speakers—Henry Muccini from FrAmeLab, University of L'Aquila, and Alberto Brandolini from Avanscoperta—for sharing their thought-provoking insights and helping to spark discussions throughout the event. Their talks on LLM-Agent Architectures and the Pitfalls of Remote Work were true highlights of the program.

Finally, we would also like to thank SEAA Steering Committee members for their continued guidance and valuable advice throughout the organization of the conference.

We hope you thoroughly enjoyed Euromicro SEAA 2025 and found it inspiring, insightful, and engaging.

July 2025

Davide Taibi
Darja Šmite

Organization

Program Committee Chairs

Davide Taibi	University of Oulu, Finland
Darja Šmite	Blekinge Institute of Technology, Sweden

General Chairs

Gemma Catolino	University of Salerno, Italy
Carmine Gravino	University of Salerno, Italy

Publicity Chair

Matteo Esposito	University of Oulu, Finland

Proceedings Chairs

Ashley van Can	Utrecht University, Netherlands
Julian Frattini	Chalmers University of Technology and University of Gothenburg, Sweden

Finance Chair

Francesco Leporati	University of Pavia, Italy

Steering Committee

Stefan Biffl	Technische Universität Wien, Austria
Michel Chaudron	Eindhoven University of Technology, Netherlands
Onur Demirors	IzTech, Turkey
Carmine Gravino	University of Salerno, Italy

| Helena Holmström Olsson | Malmö University, Sweden |
| Andreas Wortmann | Stuttgart University, Germany |

Program Committee

Alain Abran	École de Technologie Supérieure, Canada
Shaukat Ali	Simula Research Laboratory, Norway
Rami Almwari	Brunel University London, UK
Mohammad Alshayeb	King Fahd University of PetroleumMinerals, Saudi Arabia
Ahmad Altarawneh	Brunel University London, UK
Sousuke Amasaki	Nanzan University, Japan
Apostolos Ampatzoglou	University of Macedonia, Greece
Areti Ampatzoglou	Aristotle University of Thessaloniki, Greece
Vasilios Andrikopoulos	University of Groningen, the Netherlands
Lefteris Angelis	Aristotle University of Thessaloniki, Greece
Paolo Arcaini	National Institute of Informatics, Japan
Ove Armbrust	Apple, USA
Elvira-Maria Arvanitou	University of Macedonia, Greece
Mahir Arzoky	Brunel University London, UK
Vaibhav Kumar Bajpai	Microsoft, USA
Francesco Basciani	Gran Sasso Science Institute, Italy
Steffen Becker	University of Stuttgart, Germany
Christian Berger	University of Gothenburg, Sweden
Stamatia Bibi	University of Western Macedonia, Greece
Stefan Biffl	TU Wien, Austria
Ilona Bluemke	Warsaw University of Technology, Poland
Florian Bock	Friedrich-Alexander Universität Erlangen, Germany
Marek Bolanowski	Rzeszów University of Technology, Poland
Matthias Book	University of Iceland, Iceland
Jan Bosch	Chalmers University of Technology, Sweden
Ruth Breu	University of Innsbruck, Austria
Alessio Bucaioni	Mälardalen University, Sweden
Alena Buchalcevova	Prague University of Economics and Business, Czechia
Daniel Bujosa	Mälardalen University, Sweden
Piotr Błaszyński	West Pomeranian University of Technology, Poland
Matteo Camilli	Politecnico di Milano, Italy
Jose Campos	University of Porto, Portugal

Gustavo Carvalho	Universidade Federal de Pernambuco, Brazil
Theodore Chaikalis	University of Macedonia, Greece
Panagiota Chatzipetrou	Örebro University, Sweden
Michel Chaudron	Eindhoven University of Technology, The Netherlands
Sophie Chaveli	Brunel University London, UK
Antonio Cicchetti	Mälardalen University, Sweden
Federico Ciccozzi	Mälardalen University, Sweden
Steve Counsell	Brunel University London, UK
Tommaso Cucinotta	Scuola Superiore Sant'Anna, Italy
Wlodzimierz Dabrowski	Warsaw University of Technology, Poland
Maya Daneva	University of Twente, the Netherlands
Juan de Lara	Universidad Autónoma de Madrid, Spain
Onur Demirors	İzmir Institute of Technology, Turkey
Anna Derezinska	Warsaw University of Technology, Poland
Giuseppe Destefanis	Brunel University London, UK
Dario Di Dario	University of Salerno, Italy
Davide Di Ruscio	University of L'Aquila, Italy
Amleto Di Salle	Gran Sasso Science Institute, Italy
Pedro Diniz	University of Porto, Portugal
Arpita Dutta	National University of Singapore, Singapore
Frank Elberzhager	Fraunhofer IESE, Germany
Traecy Elezi	Brunel University London, UK
Christoph Elsner	Siemens AG, Germany
Matteo Esposito	University of Oulu, Finland
Aleksander Fabijan	Microsoft, USA
Daniel Feitosa	University of Groningen, The Netherlands
Sebastian Feld	Delft University of Technology, The Netherlands
Michael Felderer	German Aerospace Center (DLR), Germany and University of Cologne, Germany
Filomena Ferrucci	University of Salerno, Italy
Mariusz Flasinski	Jagiellonian University, Poland
Vahid Garousi	Queen's University Belfast, UK
Marcela Genero	University of Castilla-La Mancha, Spain
Simos Gerasimou	University of York, UK
Christopher Gerking	Karlsruhe Institute of Technology, Germany
Fabian Gilson	University of Canterbury, New Zealand
Görkem Giray	Independent Researcher, Turkey
Krzysztof Goczyła	Gdańsk University of Technology, Poland
Thomas Goldschmidt	Avalara, Germany
Raffaela Groner	Chalmers University of Technology, Sweden and University of Gothenburg, Sweden

Volker Gruhn	University of Duisburg-Essen, Germany
Rong Gu	Mälardalen University, Sweden
Sebastian Götz	Dresden University of Technology, Germany
Tuna Hacaloglu	Atilim University, Turkey and École de Technologie Superieure, Canada
Simon Hacks	Stockholm University, Sweden
Philipp Haindl	St. Pölten University of Applied Sciences, Austria
David Halasz	Microsoft, Czechia
Rachel Harrison	Oxford Brookes University, UK
Sara Hassan	Birmingham City University, UK
Petra Heck	Fontys University of Applied Sciences, The Netherlands
Jens Heidrich	Fraunhofer IESE, Germany
Paula Herber	University of Münster, Germany
Sebastian Herold	Karlstad University, Sweden
Hans-Martin Heyn	Chalmers University of Technology, Sweden and University of Gothenburg, Sweden
Bogumila Hnatkowska	Wrocław University of Technology, Poland
Petr Hnetynka	Charles University, Czechia
Helena Holmström Olsson	Malmö University, Sweden
Frank Houdek	Mercedes-Benz AG, Germany
Zbigniew Huzar	Wrocław University of Technology, Poland
Sami Hyrynsalmi	LUT University, Finland
Martin Höst	Malmö University, Sweden
Zear Ibrahim	Brunel University London, UK
Andrea Janes	Free University of Bozen-Bolzano, Italy
Aleksander Jarzebowicz	Gdańsk University of Technology, Poland
Frank Johnsen	Norwegian Defence Research Establishment (FFI), Norway
Robbert Jongeling	Mälardalen University, Sweden
Marija Katic	University of London, UK
Wiem Khlif	University of Sfax, Tunisia
Michael Klaes	Fraunhofer IESE, Germany
Verena Klös	Universität Oldenburg, Germany
Ayça Kolukısa Tarhan	Hacettepe University, Turkey
Sylwia Kopczynska	Poznań University of Technology, Poland
Piotr Kosiuczenko	Military University of Technology, Poland
Marek Kretowski	Bialystok University of Technology, Poland
Marco Kuhrmann	Reutlingen University, Germany
Supriya Lal	Yelp Inc., USA
Malvina Latifaj	Mälardalen University, Sweden
Valentina Lenarduzzi	University of Oulu, Finland

Zengyang Li	Central China Normal University, China
Peng Liang	Wuhan University, China
Sherlock Licorish	University of Otago, New Zealand
Lech Madeyski	Wrocław University of Science and Technology, Poland
Nazim Madhavji	University of Western Ontario, Canada
Ashley Mann	Brunel University of London, UK
Faisal Maramazi	Brunel University of London, UK
Rui Maranhao	University of Porto, Portugal
Bartosz Marcinkowski	University of Gdansk, Poland
Antonio Martini	University of Oslo, Norway
Jacopo Mauro	University of Southern Denmark, Denmark
Alistair Mcewan	University of Derby, UK
Jorge Melegati	Free University of Bozen-Bolzano, Italy
Emilia Mendes	Aarhus University, Denmark
Andreas Metzger	Paluno and University of Duisburg-Essen, Germany
Judith Michael	RWTH Aachen University, Germany
Jakub Miler	Gdansk University of Technology, Poland
Yoshiki Mitani	SEC and IPA, Japan
Milko Monecke	Technische Universität Berlin, Germany
Maurizio Morisio	Politecnico di Torino, Italy
Saad Mubeen	Mälardalens University, Sweden
Henry Muccini	University of L'Aquila, Italy
Tomi Männistö	University of Helsinki, Finland
Jürgen Münch	Reutlingen University, Germany
Elisa Yumi Nakagawa	University of São Paulo, Brazil
Jerzy Nawrocki	Poznań University of Technology, Poland
Erika Nazaruka	Riga Technical University, Latvia
Michael Neumann	Hochschule Hannover, Germany
Yen Ying Ng	Nicolaus Copernicus University, Poland
Arne Noyer	Ostfalia University of Applied Sciences, Germany
Mirosław Ochodek	Poznań University of Technology, Poland
Marco Ortu	University of Cagliari, Italy
Necmettin Ozkan	Gebze Technical University, Turkey
Claus Pahl	Free University of Bozen-Bolzano, Italy
Oscar Pastor	Universidad Politécnica de Valencia, Spain
Andrzej Paszkiewicz	Rzeszów University of Technology, Poland
Fabiano Pecorelli	Pegaso University, Italy
Rui Humberto Pereira	Instituto Superior de Contabilidade e Administração do Porto, Portugal
Manuela Petrescu	Babeş-Bolyai University Cluj-Napoca, Romania

Aneta Poniszewska-Maranda	Lodz University of Technology, Poland
Valeria Pontillo	Vrije Universiteit Brussel, Belgium
Adam Przybylek	University of Galway, Ireland
Fethi Rabhi	The University of New South Wales, Australia
Rick Rabiser	Software Science at Software Competence Center Hagenberg GmbH and Johannes Kepler University Linz, Austria
Łukasz Radliński	West Pomeranian University of Technology, Poland
Rudolf Ramler	Software Science at Software Competence Center Hagenberg GmbH and Johannes Kepler University Linz, Austria
Adam Roman	Jagiellonian University, Poland
Simone Romano	University of Salerno, Italy
Bruno Rossi	Masaryk University, Czech Republic
Gabriele Rotoloni	Università degli Studi dell'Insubria, Italy
Daniela S. Cruzes	Norwegian University of Science and Technology and Visma, Norway
Mika Saari	Tampere University of Technology, Finland
Małgorzata Sadowska	Politechnika Wrocławska, Poland
Norsaremah Salleh	International Islamic University Malaysia, Malaysia
Slawomir Samolej	Rzeszów University of Technology, Poland
Gleison Santos	Federal University of the State of Rio de Janeiro, Brazil
Zenepe Satka	Mälardalen University, Sweden
Klaus Schmid	University of Hildesheim, Germany
Sibylle Schupp	Hamburg University of Technology, Germany
Asma Sellami	Higher Institute of Computer Science and Multimedia of Sfax, Tunis
Gheorghe Cosmin Silaghi	Babeş-Bolyai University Cluj-Napoca, Romania
Samira Silva	Gran Sasso Science Institute, Italy
Michal Smialek	Warsaw University of Technology, Poland
Michel Soares	Federal University of Sergipe, Brazil
Janusz Sosnowski	Warsaw University of Technology, Poland
Zenon A. Sosnowski	Bialystok University of Technology, Poland
Hassan Soubra	ECE Paris, France
Érica Souza	Federal Technological University of Paraná, Brazil
Luigi Libero Lucio Starace	Università degli Studi di Napoli Federico II, Italy
Miroslaw Staron	Chalmers University of Technology, Sweden
Krzysztof Stencel	University of Warsaw, Poland

Daniel Strüber	Chalmers University of Technology and University of Gothenburg, Sweden, and Radboud University Nijmegen, Netherlands
Jacek Stój	Silesian University of Technology, Poland
Dan Mircea Suciu	Babeş-Bolyai University Cluj-Napoca, Romania
Jakub Swacha	University of Szczecin, Poland
Stephen Swift	Brunel University of London, UK
Kari Systä	Tampere University of Technology, Finland
Tomasz Szmuc	AGH University of Science and Technology, Poland
Marcin Szpyrka	AGH University of Science and Technology, Poland
Davide Taibi	University of Oulu, Finland
Matthias Tichy	Ulm University, Germany
Juha-Pekka Tolvanen	MetaCase, Finland, and University of Jyväskylä, Finland
Adam Trendowicz	Fraunhofer IESE, Germany
Dimitri Van Landuyt	Katholieke Universiteit Leuven, Belgium
Anita Walkowiak	Wrocław University of Science and Technology, Poland
Bartosz Walter	Poznań University of Technology, Poland
Jörg Walter	OFFIS Institute for Information Technology, Germany
Xiaofeng Wang	Free University of Bozen-Bolzano, Italy
Bianca Wiesmayr	Johannes Kepler University Linz, Austria
Dietmar Winkler	Vienna University of Technology, Austria
Emily Winter	Lancaster University, UK
Andreas Wortmann	University of Stuttgart, Germany
Konrad Wrona	NATO Communications and Information Agency, The Netherlands
Włodzimierz Wysocki	West Pomeranian University of Technology, Poland
Andrzej Zalewski	Warsaw University of Technology, Poland
Janusz Zalewski	Florida Gulf Coast University, USA
Jianjun Zhao	Kyushu University, Japan
Zbigniew Zielinski	Military University of Technology, Poland
Darja Šmite	Blekinge Institute of Technology, Sweden

Sponsors

Contents – Part I

Cyber-Physical Systems

Model-Driven Engineering and Modeling Languages

Contents – Part II

**Systematic Literature Reviews and Mapping Studies in Software
Engineering**

Contents – Part III

xxiv   Contents – Part III

xxiv   Contents – Part III

Software Process and Product Improvement

Software Analytics: Mining Software Open Datasets and Repositories

Emerging Computing Technologies

Data and AI Driven Engineering

Feature-Based Versioning for ML-Enabled Product Lines

Matthias Preuner[1], Paul Grünbacher[1]([⊠]), Pedro Luiz de Paula Filho[2],
and Alexander Egyed[1]

[1] Institute of Software Systems Engineering, Johannes Kepler University, Linz,
Austria
paul.gruenbacher@jku.at
[2] Federal Technological University – Paraná, Curitiba, Brazil
pedrol@utfpr.edu.br

Abstract. Components based on Machine Learning (ML) are important for many product lines in the industry today, strongly impacting engineering processes. In particular, engineers need to manage the variability of ML-enabled features in product lines, while at the same time dealing with their continuous evolution, integration, and deployment. MLOps approaches improve the maturity of processes and tools for engineering ML-enabled systems, however, they lack support for feature-based version control, which is essential for product lines. This paper presents an approach providing feature-based versioning for ML-enabled product lines based on the Variation Control System (VarCS) ECCO. Specifically, we present use cases and requirements based on a common MLOps process. We extend ECCO to support Python code and Jupyter Notebooks, two widely used types of artifacts in this domain. We evaluate our approach regarding correctness and performance: the evaluation confirms the extensional correctness of our approach and shows acceptable quality of the intensional checkouts for valid product configurations. Furthermore, the performance is adequate for the investigated use cases.

Keywords: ML-enabled Product Lines · Variation Control Systems · MLOps

1 Introduction

Components based on Machine Learning (ML) and Artificial Intelligence (AI) play an important role in many software product lines, significantly influencing engineering processes. Engineers must manage the variability of ML-enabled features in product lines while handling their continuous evolution, integration, and deployment. In particular, feature-oriented techniques map features to the parts of the artifacts realizing them. These mappings can then be used to compose new variants of the artifacts based on a selection of the desired features [1,4,6]. However, existing approaches to Software Product Line Engineering (SPLE) only partially account for the unique aspects of developing ML-enabled components.

D. Taibi and D. Smite (Eds.): SEAA 2025, LNCS 16081, pp. 3–19, 2026.
https://doi.org/10.1007/978-3-032-04190-6_1

In particular, feature-based version control is crucial for managing variability inherent to ML-enabled product lines and for supporting the ML DevOps process: *(i)* ML algorithms often utilize different pre-trained models, model architectures, or different steps for pre- and post-processing. Similarly, customer-specific training data or labeling may be needed in certain variants only, e.g., for proprietary reasons. In addition, developing ML models involves experimenting with different algorithms, hyperparameters, and datasets. Existing product line approaches allow engineers to compose, refine, and release product variants based on features [17]. However, they lack support for managing the variability of common ML artifacts such as datasets, labels, or training algorithms. *(ii)* ML-enabled product lines are expected to meet the evolving requirements of customers and users over many years. The datasets used for training, the training code and the application code, as well as the trained models of ML-enabled product lines undergo many changes. Engineers thus increasingly adopt DevOps methods [2,7] to put changes into production as quickly as possible using CI/CD pipelines [24]. Such pipelines also greatly benefit from feature-based version control, e.g., for automated testing and deployment of different product variants based on different versions of ML models. However, the field of MLOps [11,15] has received little attention in product line research so far.

In this paper, we thus extend an existing VarCS to support the MLOps process in product lines. In particular, we claim two contributions: *(i)* We extend the VarCS ECCO [12,14], which combines the clone-and-own approach with SPLE, to artifact types common in ML-enabled product lines. *(ii)* We evaluate the tool-supported approach for the identified use cases. Specifically, we investigate research questions regarding extensional and intensional versioning correctness when checking out different product variants, as well as the performance of committing product versions to ECCO.

The remainder of our paper is organized as follows: In Sect. 2 we discuss the background on MLOps, version control systems, and the VarCS ECCO. Section 3 discusses a MLOps process for feature-based versioning, which defines important artifacts and activities for developing our tool-supported approach. In Sect. 4 we describe our multi-language versioning approach, illustrated with a typical engineering workflow. Section 5 presents the research method and results of our evaluation. Section 6 discusses our main findings and threats to validity. Section 7 compares our approach to related work. Section 8 presents conclusions and an outlook on future work.

2   Background

We discuss the background on processes and methods for ML DevOps, version control systems, and the VarCS ECCO.

MLOps aims at bridging the gap between the disciplines of machine learning, software engineering, and data engineering by describing the application of Development and Operations (DevOps) practices to ML-enabled systems. However, it has been pointed out that the definition of MLOps is still vague and it

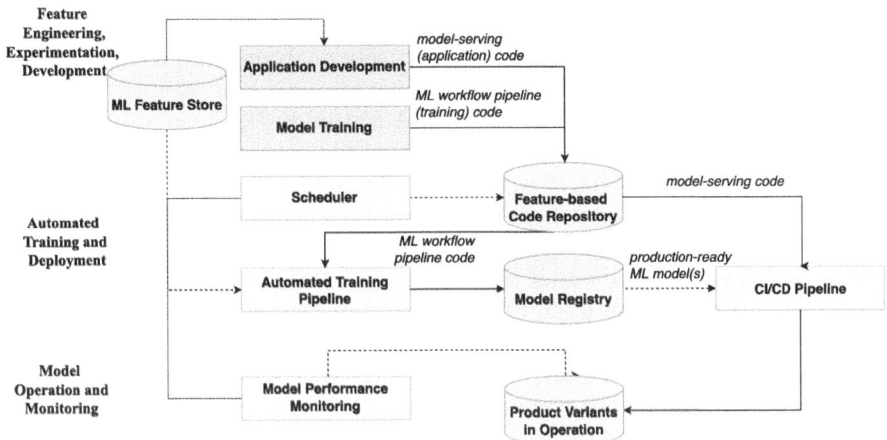

Fig. 1. MLOps workflow for ML-enabled product lines.

remains often unclear how it should be implemented and institutionalized [15]. Kreuzberger et al. provide an overview of the key principles, components, roles, architecture, and workflows of an ML DevOps pipeline based on a literature review, tool assessments, and expert interviews [11]. ML DevOps goes beyond existing DevOps processes and comprises two areas carried out with partially overlapping cycles: *Machine Learning* includes data preparation, the exploratory testing of ML methods and approaches, the training, evaluation and retraining of models, as well as constant monitoring in production. *Application* adopts common DevOps processes known from software engineering to put ML-enabled systems into production.

Version Control Systems (VCSs) manage *versions* of artifacts to enable collaboration among developers in software engineering. A version is either a revision or a variant depending on the intent [5]: *Revisions* are sequential versions superseding previous ones, e.g., when fixing a bug. *Variants* are concurrent versions and co-exist in parallel, e.g., when making customer-specific adaptations in different products. Extensional versioning means the ability to retrieve explicitly created versions by means of a unique identifier, e.g., hashes in Git. Intensional versioning on the other hand means retrieving and constructing new versions not committed as such before, as, e.g., supported by the VarCSs ECCO and SuperMod [14].

ECCO (Extraction and Composition for Clone-and-Own) is a VarCS that supports automatic feature extraction and composition [12,13][1]. It provides extensional and intensional versioning based on features and supports domain-specific languages and artifacts. ECCO thereby overcomes weaknesses of current version control systems for managing product lines, such as using coarse-grained branches to handle fine-grained variants, or determining differences between ver-

---

[1] https://github.com/jku-isse/ecco.

sions in a line-based manner [14]. Specifically, ECCO automatically determines the location of features in artifacts by reactively analyzing and comparing different product versions to identify associations showing how artifact fragments and code snippets implement the features. A feature in ECCO is a subset of an artifact graph describing a part of a committed file, for example, some cohesive or even scattered fragments of code, depending on the kind of artifact [9,12]. The nodes of the graph are labeled with presence conditions defining how artifacts map to features. ECCO can be extended with plugins translating domain-specific artifacts into its internal tree structure, as we demonstrate for MLOps. When committing changes to an ECCO repository, the engineer lists all features affected by the commit. ECCO then updates its artifact tree by modifying the presence conditions accordingly. ECCO also allows one to combine features to create new variants, thereby supporting intensional versioning [5].

3   MLOps for Feature-Based Versioning in ML-Enabled Product Lines

Figure 1 shows artifacts and activities of a MLOps process for ML-enabled product lines, which is based on [11]. The upper part covers activities for feature engineering, experimentation, and development. The activities for model training and application development are shown separately, since the application code and the training code result in different kinds of artifacts, which are developed and maintained independently from each other. The lower part shows the automated training and deployment, including an automated training pipeline and a tool pipeline for deploying and monitoring product variants.

The process relies on several key elements: the *ML Feature Store* contains the data needed to train, evaluate, and test the ML models. The *Feature-based Code Repository* is used to manage the code and algorithms required for the model training process, but also the model-serving code, i.e., the application utilizing the ML model. The *Scheduler* triggers the automated training pipeline, e.g., when new data becomes available in the ML feature store or upon request by another external event. The *CI/CD Component* combines a model with the application, runs different kinds of tests and pushes the ML-enabled product variant to production. The *Monitoring Component* constantly monitors the performance of the *Product Variants in Operation*, allowing to quickly react to performance declines, which could require re-training the model with new data might or lead to new model development.

Feature-Based Versioning. Figure 1 shows two use cases for feature-based version control: *(i)* The first use case concerns the training cycle, and comprises training development, the code repository, the ML feature store, the scheduler, the automated training pipeline, and the model registry. It is triggered after the initial training, whenever the model's performance degrades or when new training datasets become available. It may require the execution of the training pipeline, adaptations of the training code, and finally the creation of a new model to be put into production via the model registry. *(ii)* The second use case focuses on the application in production with embedded ML models. It is similar to a traditional DevOps cycle and assumes a continuous software development process. The CI/CD component triggers a new deployment as soon as changes are pushed to the code repository, or when a new model becomes available in the registry.

We can identify the requirements for feature-based versioning by analyzing the kinds of revisions and variants in these two use cases. The most relevant components affected by revisions and variants are the ML feature store, the code repository, and the model registry. Versioning in the *ML feature store* is needed if new datasets or constraints need to be considered, leading to revisions of the training data. Examples are customer-specific datasets, which may not be shared for proprietary reasons, different image resolutions, or specific data labeling. The *code repository* manages versions of the code needed for the training and the application. Regarding the training code, versions are the result of different revisions and variants of datasets, training algorithms, pre- and post-processing steps, or model architectures. The application code needs to deal with different model versions, as well as variants and combinations of them, in addition to conventional code versions also known from conventional software product lines. The *model registry* stores all trained models including training logs and metadata. It is important that model revisions are tracked and documented, e.g., for legal purposes.

ML Artifacts. Our aim is to support feature-based versioning of ML-enabled product lines in the VarCS ECCO. We focus on the most common file types and programming languages in this domain. Python is the most popular programming language for scientific computing, data science, and machine learning [18] and used by popular ML libraries like tensorflow[2] and scikit-learn[3]. Jupyter Notebooks [22] are common in machine learning projects and support a wide range of scripting and programming languages, most notably Python [10]. They allow online collaboration and easy access to training hardware, e.g., via Colaboratory[4]. Due to their widespread use, Jupyter Notebooks are also subject to research in machine learning [20]. However, Jupyter Notebooks have deficiencies regarding versioning. For instance, they contain metadata and timestamps, which are detected as changes whenever a Notebook is executed. Extensions like JupyterLabGit[5] provide workarounds for committing Jupyter Notebooks to VCSs.

4 Approach

We provide a multi-language adapter for ECCO to support ML engineering. In particular, we enable ECCO to support ML training (Jupyter Notebooks) and applications (Python Code). We further manage code files defining properties of

---

[2] https://www.tensorflow.org.
[3] https://scikit-learn.org.
[4] https://colab.research.google.com.
[5] https://github.com/jupyterlab/jupyterlab-git.

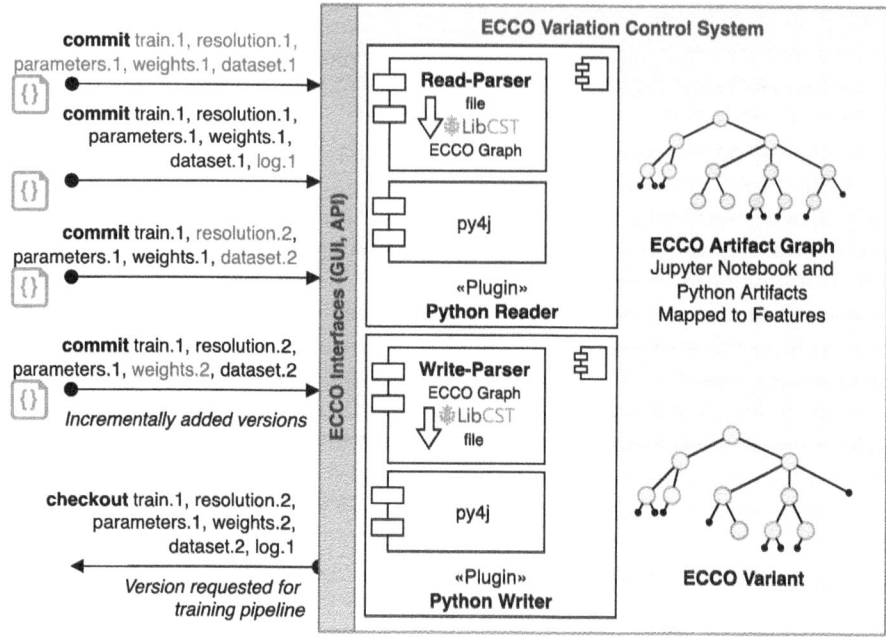

Fig. 2. Multi-language adapter architecture for ML projects.

datasets in the ML feature store in a feature-based manner (via metadata and URI information).

Workflow. ECCO's feature-oriented operations commit and checkout allow users to interact with a single ECCO repository, while the operations clone, fork, and pull allow working with multiple interrelated repositories. Figure 2 shows the architecture of the plugin applied to a Jupyter Notebook training example, which represents our first use case. The engineer in this example incrementally commits four changes, each affecting different features. The newly committed features are shown in red. During the commit, ECCO parses and analyzes the files in the workspace to generate an internal representation in the form of an ECCO artifact tree. This tree is then compared with the current artifact tree to analyze and mark the differences. ECCO detects which snippets of the code (and possibly other artifacts) belong to which feature and which features have changed since the last commit. At the end of a commit step, the plugin provides an artifact tree to the ECCO core, which detects changes between the commits and updates the feature-to-artifact mappings stored in ECCO. After a checkout ECCO returns an artifact tree of the requested variant, which is then used by the plugin to compose the files of that product variant to a workspace. Depending on the use case, the newly generated variant can be used for developing new features, for experimentation in a training pipeline, or for deploying the appli-

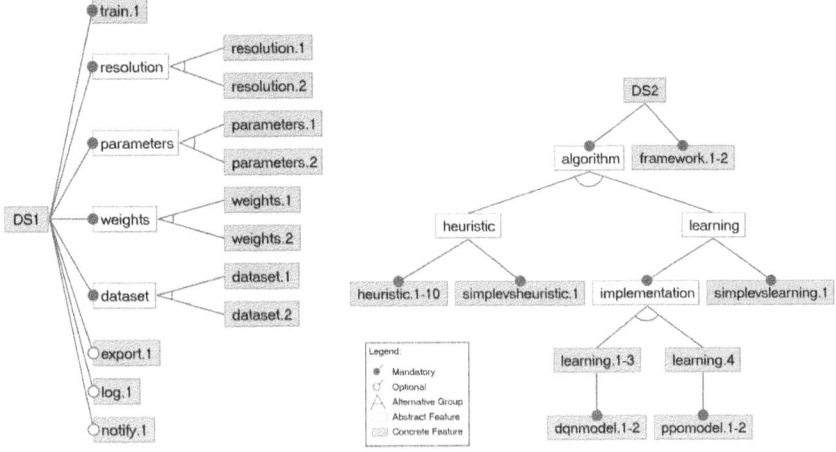

Fig. 3. Feature models for the datasets DS1 and DS2.

cation. In our example, the engineer checks out a variant containing six features and the resulting files are used in an automated training pipeline.

Artifacts. ECCO analyzes artifacts using the abstract syntax tree [3] and thus requires parsers for different domain-specific files or programming languages. ECCO's plugin-based framework allows to add and integrate new artifact adapters. For instance, adapters are available to parse source code [9], plain text files, structured data (XML) [9], images (PNG) or DSLs like LilyPond [8].

Our multi-language plugin supports Jupyter Notebooks and Python files. We used the LibCST[6] library for parsing, since it supports syntax information, comments, as well as code formatting. LibCST is written in Python and the parsing script is integrated with ECCO using Py4J[7]. To handle variability in Jupyter Notebooks we also implemented support for JSON, as the cells of a notebook can contain Markdown text or code. Code cells are parsed by the Python parser. If they contain mixed or non-Python languages, the parser treats them as text and computes differences in a line-based manner.

5   Evaluation

We investigated two research questions:

RQ1–Versioning Correctness. Extensional versioning means retrieving previously committed versions from the repository [5]. In a basic check we investigated if our adapter can read and write correct code. We also investigated if the correctness requirements established in the basic test still hold if an entire

---

[6] https://github.com/Instagram/LibCST.
[7] https://www.py4j.org.

evolution history of different versions is committed to ECCO and then checked out again. Specifically, we assessed for different coding and commenting styles if the adapter correctly identifies code-level differences when analyzing changes to create an artifact graph, and successfully re-composes earlier-committed files.

Intensional versioning is the flexible and fully automated construction of consistent versions in a large version space, where also new combinations of features can be constructed on demand [5]. This means investigating if the adapter correctly generates new variants not committed before from a committed history. In particular, we assessed to what extent our algorithm can create artifact graphs, from which new and syntactically correct variants can be generated.

RQ2–Performance. Execution time is an important aspect of the implemented algorithm, in particular, regarding its use in real-world applications. We also aimed to identify potential performance bottlenecks and areas for improvement. We thus measured the performance of the computationally most expensive task, the commit operation, for the entire dataset and analyzed the execution times of the ECCO commit operation (written in Java) and the multi-language adapter (largely written in Python).

5.1   Datasets

Based on our two use cases we selected two datasets, one covering Jupyter Notebooks and the other one Python code[8]. The preparation started with the creation of feature models after an initial code inspection to identify constraints to exclude clearly meaningless configurations. Based on the feature models we derived the list of all possible variants for the checkouts to be performed for answering RQ1. If a valid artifact graph can be created for a requested variant, our implementation ensures syntactical correctness, as the LibCST library only generates code from valid LibCST graphs.

DS1: Training Project (Jupyter Notebook). The first dataset consists of a version history of seven commits of a Jupyter Notebook created during the training process of a ML model, which was created by an author of this paper not involved in developing the ECCO extensions. It includes commits with features containing the basic training code, resolutions for the training data images, parameter sets for the execution of the model training process, as well as different sizes of the pre-trained models. It also covers optional feature code for exporting the trained model, enabling logging during training, and an email notification when training is finished. Figure 3 shows the feature model for DS1 with a mandatory base feature (*train*), some mandatory features with multiple revisions (*resolution*, *parameters*, *weights* and *dataset*) and some optional features (*export*, *log* and *notify*).

DS2: ML Application Including Trained Models (Python Project). The second dataset comprises the version history of an entire project framework including multiple Python files. The framework provides a machine learning environment

---

[8] https://github.com/jku-isse/ecco-adapter-python-tests.

called Pommerman [19], which allows to implement, train, and test different agents competing against each other. The agents were partially implemented by an author of this paper and another developer [21]. The commit history includes 20 commits of about 35 files per commit covering the evolution from a heuristic non-ML model to a simple ML model, and finally a more advanced model. Training and application code are both part of the framework in this case, as they were developed and improved concurrently. The feature configuration contains the framework code with some improvements (*framework.x*), implementation and training code for a heuristic bot (*heuristic.x*) and a learning bot (*learning.x*) with two different neural network architectures and models (*dqnmodel.x* and *ppomodel.x*). Additionally, the framework allows bots to play against a simple default bot version (*simplevssimple.1*, *simplevsheuristic.1* and *simplevslearning.1*). The feature revisions in the feature model for DS2 are shown in Fig. 3. The model contains the mandatory framework feature and an algorithm, which is either the heuristic or the learning implementation with one of two possible model architectures (*dqnmodel* and *ppomodel*). For each algorithm there is also a game simulation feature (*simplevsheuristic* and *simplevslearning*).

5.2 Research Method

For *RQ1* we first conducted a basic adapter test by committing and sequentially checking out a set of Python files and Jupyter Notebooks and comparing them with their original versions. This allowed us to verify that the output of the parsing algorithm is identical to its input. In the next step we committed the complete commit histories of the datasets to ECCO. Afterwards, we checked out all committed versions again and automatically compared them with the initial input to verify extensional correctness.

We then checked out all possible configurations based on the feature models defined earlier. We used the quality logging of surplus and missing artifacts to compute quality metrics, following [16]. Surplus describes the level of over-determination of artifacts that have been 'learned' multiple times in the same way during various commits, which may lead to code redundancies and ultimately errors when checking out variants. Missing artifacts on other the other hand indicate that ECCO misses code snippets to fully generate the desired variant, i.e., the resulting variants are incomplete. This can happen, e.g., if certain features have always been committed together with others, and a new variant is requested including these features separately. In practice, this can be resolved with an additional commit, which only includes one of these features as part of the configuration, thereby allowing ECCO to correctly determine the feature's mapped artifacts.

Specifically, we took the missing count as a first quality measure and the sum of the missing and surplus artifacts as the second quality measure to compute the quality metrics needed to answer RQ2 (cf. [16]). We normalized the quality measures based on the lowest quality that occurred in the dataset and computed them as follows: $q_{m,ni} = 1 - \frac{missing_i}{max_{i=1...n}(missing_i)}$ represents the normalized quality of variant i (by missing artifacts),

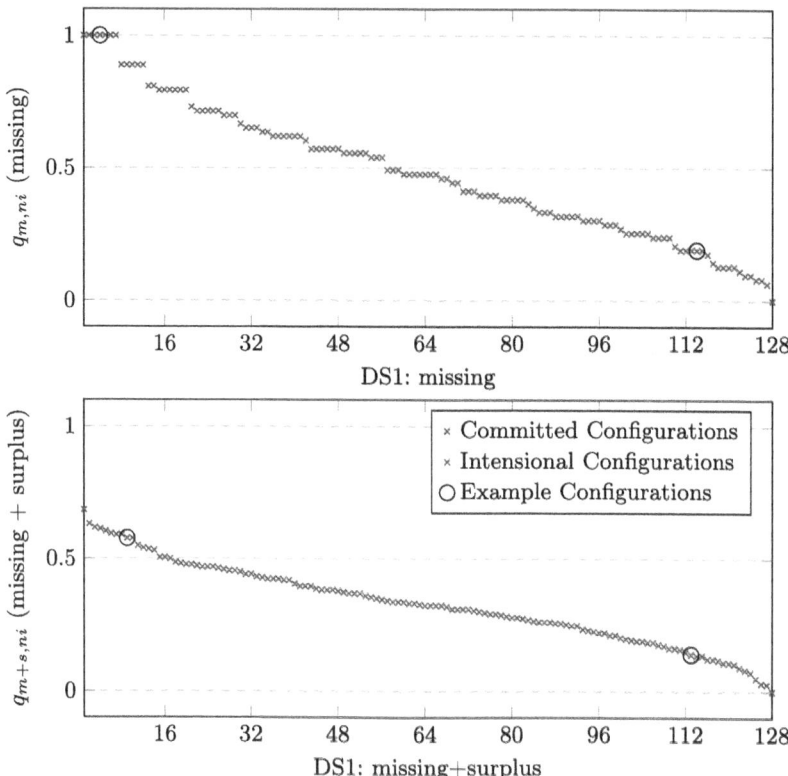

Fig. 4. Versioning correctness (RQ1) for DS1 (variants ordered by quality).

while $q_{m+s,ni} = 1 - \frac{missing_i + surplus_i}{max_{i=1...n}(missing_i + surplus_i)}$ represents the normalized quality of variant i (by missing and surplus artifacts).

Regarding *RQ2* we recorded and analyzed the performance measures during the initial step of committing the entire history. We used the second dataset only in this case, as it contains more files and therefore provides more realistic results. In particular, performance was analyzed with respect to the number of files committed and three significant parts: *(a)* The time spent for the entire Commit (measured in Java); *(b)* The time spent in the Python script (measured in Java); and *(c)* The time spent in the Python script (measured in Python). Warmup effects of the Java virtual machine were taken into account by running an entire commit before starting over with active time measurements.

5.3   RQ1 Results

The automatic unit tests were successful for both DS1 and DS2. This means that regarding extensional correctness the algorithm correctly re-created all files after committing the entire history of both datasets according to the requirements for file correctness.

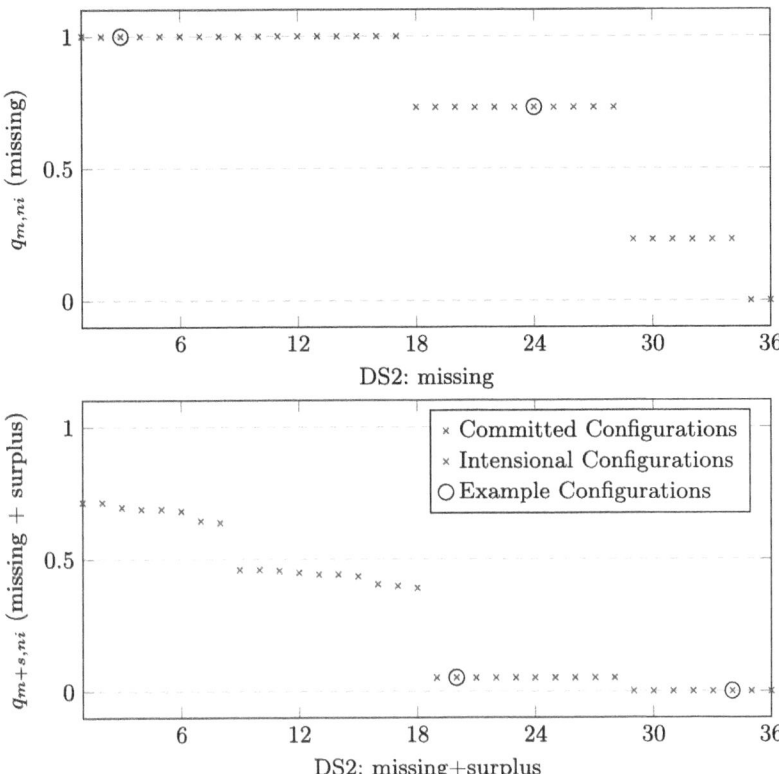

Fig. 5. Versioning correctness (RQ1) for DS2 (variants ordered by quality).

We computed the quality measures $q_{m,n}$ and $q_{m+s,n}$ for each checked-out variant according to the feature model and created a chart sorted by descending quality values. The quality value 1 indicates a variant with no missing or with neither missing nor surplus artifacts. A quality value of 0 is a relative reference value of the lowest quality measured in the entire batch. Since the initial commit configurations are also among the possible checkouts, they are marked separately, as they are expected to have the highest quality.

In total we derived and checked out 128 configurations from the feature model of *DS1*. The quality measure of missing artifacts ($q_{m,n}$) in Fig. 4 shows, that the initial commits are of the highest quality, with no missing artifacts. Other variants show a declining quality down to zero, which was the reference value. For instance, the top-left configuration was already provided as an initial commit and therefore had no missing artifacts. The other example in the bottom right (with rank 114 in quality) is a newly generated variant with 51 missing artifacts. When taking a look at the quality measure of missing and surplus artifacts ($q_{m+s,n}$), we can see that all variants show a certain degree of surplus artifacts, and some newly created variants even have a better quality than the original

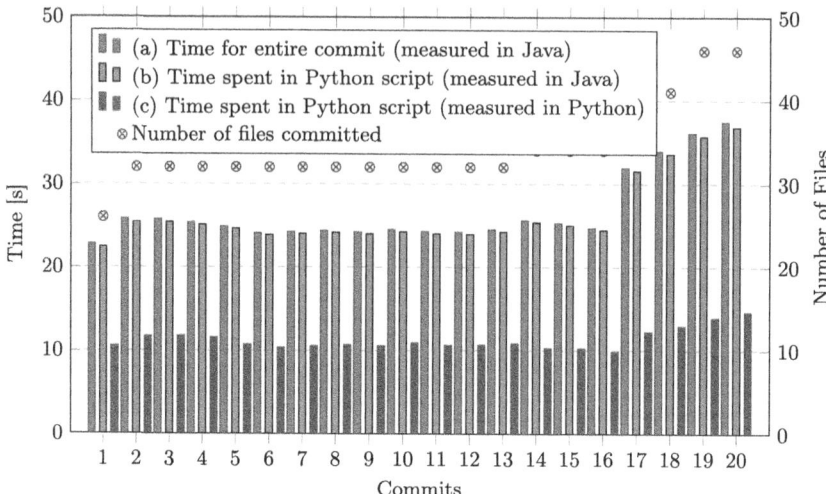

Fig. 6. Commit Time Measurements (RQ2) for DS2.

commit configuration checkouts. Looking at the same example configurations from before, the committed configuration ranks now at position 9 with 94 surplus and zero missing artifacts and some intensional configurations even showing better quality measures. The second example increased its position to 113 with 140 surplus and 51 missing artifacts. From the result of RQ1 we already know, that the checkouts of the original commits are identical to the initial commit repository in terms of code and syntax. We therefore see, that the influence of surplus is not as serious as the influence of missing artifacts.

In total 36 different configurations were checked out based on the feature model of *DS2*. The quality measure of missing artifacts ($q_{m,n}$) in Fig. 5 shows again that the initial commits have the highest quality with no missing artifacts, while the generated variants show a declining quality down to the reference value zero. The example of the committed configuration has no missing artifacts, but a surplus of 262, which puts it at position 20 in the $q_{m+s,n}$ chart. The example of the intensional configuration has 7 missing and 269 surplus artifacts, ranked at 24 for $q_{m,n}$, and at 34 for $q_{m+s,n}$. In this dataset we can see that $q_{m+s,n}$ shows a low quality for some initial commit configurations. A possible reason is the lower number of possible configurations derived from the feature model, which is due to the more linear nature of the evolution history and the absence of optional features.

5.4   RQ2 Results

The commit performance was measured for all 20 commits of DS2 on a machine with an AMD Ryzen 7 6800H and 32 GB RAM. Figure 6 shows these measurements in relation to the number of files of all commits from DS2. As expected, there is a fairly linear relation between the number of files and the commit time. It can be seen, that the time for the entire commit *(a)* and the time spent in Python measured from Java *(b)* are almost identical, meaning that nearly all processing time is spent in Python for reading files, parsing files to LibCST, and then creating the ECCO artifact graph. It is interesting that these steps, measured from within Python, show less than half of the time than measured from Java *(b)*. This difference can be explained by the context switch from Java to Python, i.e., the Py4J environment starting and finishing the Python script. Due to the design of the ECCO framework, this happens once for each file, thereby significantly increasing execution time. When investigating the influence of the number of files on performance we also saw that many files remain unchanged, meaning that performance could easily be improved during the commits.

6   Discussion and Threats to Validity

While determining extensional correctness (RQ1) is straightforward by checking syntactical correctness, checking for intensional correctness (RQ2) is more challenging, as this step often also requires code inspection to determine if the expected output was generated. Similarly to other papers [8,16], we thus used the quality measures for missing and surplus artifacts to determine the overall quality of a checkout. While quality can be defined in terms of missing or surplus artifacts, the level of quality is always a relative value compared to the variant with the lowest-known quality.

Our parsing algorithm uses a generic approach of serializing LibCST nodes, which is flexible towards future changes in the Python programming language as well as the utilized LibCST library. In hindsight, this approach was successful and resulted in a concise and extensible algorithm. However, some effort was needed to take care of corner cases. This is mostly due to the design of the LibCST structure, i.e., how bodies of blocks or try-except-blocks are handled internally, and required some workarounds due to restrictions of LibCST. For each file type, Jupyter Notebook and Python, one specific dataset was used. Even though the datasets DS1 and DS2 contain a lot of Python code, we cannot guarantee that every corner case of coding style and structure has been covered during the correctness checks. More testing and feedback from practical applications of our approach (in particular also the JSON adapter) is necessary to further improve quality.

The datasets for evaluation were created backwards by replaying the evolution history to create the ECCO commits and configurations. This may not fully reflect a practical development environment, which evolves in a forward manner and cannot foresee future developments and changes. So while the datasets are useful to prove the correctness of the algorithms, they may not represent additional challenges faced when using ECCO for active development.

While unique node identifiers are the corner stone of syntax-based parsing of VarCS they also come with a risk. Once an identifier has been defined, e.g., the name of a class, changes of class names due to code refactoring break the evolution history of the ECCO repository, because ECCO can not recognize the previous version of the node. Tracking and handling such kind of changes are needed to avoid shortcomings of the approach in practice, especially when dealing with code files.

The time needed for committing to ECCO is mostly spent for parsing, as shown in RQ3. Currently, ECCO does not determine whether a file has been changed before parsing it, thus increasing the processing time. This could, however, easily be avoided, for example, by generating and comparing hash values of files. Testing was only done on a single system so far (DS2). For that reason performance could not be compared to other implemented adapters. Comparing an implementation with Py4J and additionally with the GraalVM[9] as two Python execution approaches would give more insights into algorithm performance. Our results suggest, however, that Python adapters likely perform worse than adapters written in Java due to the context switch to the Python environment.

7   Related Work

The high importance of ML-enabled systems for the industry is, e.g., demonstrated by the recently released process reference and assessment model Automotive SPICE 4.0 [23], which defines a separate process group for engineering ML-enabled systems in the automotive domain, however, without explicitly addressing issues related to product lines.

The DagsHub tool[10] supports MLOps via a collaborative process to quickly create, manage, and compare experiments. While DagsHubs emphasizes experimentation, the ECCO Python adapter tries to support the process in terms of SPLE and the long term maintenance of the ML models and their performance. Roboflow[11] is another tool for supporting ML projects. It supports labeling and annotating images and provides pre-trained models, which can be used and trained further. It also comes with interfaces to known third party-tools for databases and supports various annotation formats, training frameworks and cloud deployment applications.

ECCO [12] can be extended with plugins translating artifacts into its internal tree structure. This has been done in several domains: The code adapter for ECCO was initially implemented for Java [9]. When parsing programming languages into ECCO, certain aspects, e.g., using class and method names as unique node identifiers come into play, which affect the design and limitations of the algorithm. The granularity of the algorithm determines, to which extend changes are directly being reflected in the ECCO artifact graph. Currently both adapters can recognize changes of a single line and in some cases even smaller chunks. Changes that are to small to be directly recognized, are reflected in a change of the next bigger detectable magnitude, e.g., an entire line. Hinterreiter

---

[9] https://www.graalvm.org.
[10] https://dagshub.com.
[11] https://roboflow.com.

et al. use ECCO to manage mappings between features and their implementation in the DSL IEC 61131-3 [9]. Grünbacher et al. use features managed in ECCO to support the evolution of music artifacts encoded in the DSL LilyPond [8]. The ECCO Python adapter was also developed with the structure and design of the LilyPond adapter in mind. Both adapters rely on a Python environment to execute the parsing algorithm. The Python adapter supports only Py4J for Python execution so far, while LilyECCO additionally allows the use of the GraalVM. Extending that functionality for the Python adapter would allow for further performance testing and a better comparison of both approaches.

8   Conclusions and Future Work

We presented an approach for feature-based versioning and composition of important artifacts of ML-enabled product lines. This is important as versioning becomes ever more important from a development point of view but also from a legal perspective, e.g., when determining which version led to a failure. Feature-based version control can thus foster reproducibility, support informed decisions during development, improve traceability, and allow developers to analyze the impact of changes.

Our evaluation demonstrates the correctness of the extensional versioning for the parsing algorithm, which was verified according to defined requirements. The correctness of intensional versioning was initially manually checked through code inspection and further validated using a quality metric applied to checkouts created via a feature model. This process confirmed the quality of known configurations and highlighted areas where new variants require additional fixes by providing ECCO with more detailed information about features and their interactions. While the performance measurements were satisfactory, they also revealed some architectural drawbacks of the adapter and identified opportunities for improvements. We plan to improve our ECCO ML adapter regarding performance and feature granularity and study its usefulness in real-world ML development processes. The issue of adapter dispatching is another interesting direction: Our adapter processes Jupyter Notebooks, which again may contain different scripting and programming languages. Our results are thus useful for other domains with similarly complex artifacts.

Acknowledgments. This research was supported in part by the JKU Linz Institute of Technology (LIT), the state of Upper Austria [LIT-2023-12-SEE-128], and by the FFG COMET K1 Center "Pro^{2}Future II" (Cognitive and Sustainable Products and Production Systems of the Future), Contract No. 911655. We would like to thank Florian Schmid for sharing the project repository we used to create one of our datasets.

References

1. Apel, S., Batory, D.S., Kästner, C., Saake, G.: Feature-Oriented Software Product Lines - Concepts and Implementation. Springer, Heidelberg (2013). https://doi.org/10.1007/978-3-642-37521-7

2. Bass, L.: The software architect and DevOps. IEEE Softw. **35**, 8–10 (2018)
3. Baxter, I., Yahin, A., Moura, L., Sant'Anna, M., Bier, L.: Clone detection using abstract syntax trees. In: Proceedings International Conference on Software Maintenance, pp. 368–377. IEEE (1998)
4. Berger, T., et al.: What is a feature? A qualitative study of features in industrial software product lines. In: Proceedings of the 19th International Software Product Line Conference, New York, NY, USA, pp. 16–25. ACM (2015)
5. Conradi, R., Westfechtel, B.: Version models for software configuration management. ACM Comput. Surv. **30**(2), 232–282 (1998)
6. Czarnecki, K., Grünbacher, P., Rabiser, R., Schmid, K., Wąsowski, A.: Cool features and tough decisions: a comparison of variability modeling approaches. In: Proceedings of the 6th International Workshop on Variability Modelling of Software-Intensive Systems, New York, NY, USA, pp. 173–182. ACM (2012)
7. Ebert, C., Gallardo, G., Hernantes, J., Serrano, N.: DevOps. IEEE Softw. **33**, 94–100 (2016)
8. Grünbacher, P., Hanl, R., Linsbauer, L.: Using music features for managing revisions and variants of musical scores. Comput. Music J. **47**(3), 50–68 (2023). https://doi.org/10.1162/COMJ_a_00691
9. Hinterreiter, D., Linsbauer, L., Feichtinger, K., Prähofer, H., Grünbacher, P.: Supporting feature-oriented evolution in industrial automation product lines. Concurr. Eng. Res. Appl. **28**, 265–279 (2020)
10. Ingargiola, A., contributors: What is the Jupyter Notebook (2015). https://jupyter-notebook-beginner-guide.readthedocs.io/en/latest/what_is_jupyter.html. Accessed 08 Aug 2023
11. Kreuzberger, D., Kühl, N., Hirschl, S.: Machine learning operations (MLOps): overview, definition, and architecture. IEEE Access **11**, 31866–31879 (2023)
12. Linsbauer, L., et al.: Systematic software reuse with automated extraction and composition for clone-and-own. In: Lopez-Herrejon, R.E., et al. (eds.) Handbook of Re-Engineering Software Intensive Systems into Software Product Lines, pp. 379–404. Springer, Cham (2023). https://doi.org/10.1007/978-3-031-11686-5_15
13. Linsbauer, L., Lopez-Herrejon, R.E., Egyed, A.: Variability extraction and modeling for product variants. In: Proceedings 22nd International Systems and Software Product Line Conference, p. 250 (2018)
14. Linsbauer, L., Schwägerl, F., Berger, T., Grünbacher, P.: Concepts of variation control systems. J. Syst. Softw. **171**, 110796 (2021)
15. Mboweni, T., Masombuka, T., Dongmo, C.: A systematic review of machine learning DevOps. In: International Conference on Electrical, Computer and Energy Technologies, pp. 1–6 (2022)
16. Michelon, G.K., et al.: Evolving software system families in space and time with feature revisions. Empirical Software Eng. **27** (2022)
17. Pohl, K., Böckle, G., van der Linden, F.: Software Product Line Engineering. Springer, Heidelberg (2005). https://doi.org/10.1007/3-540-28901-1
18. Raschka, S., Patterson, J., Nolet, C.: Machine learning in Python: main developments and technology trends in data science, machine learning, and artificial intelligence. Information **11**, 193 (2020)
19. Resnick, C., et al.: Pommerman: a multi-agent playground (2018)
20. Samuel, S., Löffler, F., König-Ries, B.: Machine learning pipelines: provenance, reproducibility and fair data principles. In: Provenance and Annotation of Data and Processes: Proceedings 8th and 9th International Workshop on Provenance and Annotation, pp. 226–230 (2021)

21. Schmid, F.: Applying and evaluating the effect of Deep Q-Learning methods and its improvements in Pommerman (2020)
22. Smajić, A., Grandits, M., Ecker, G.F.: Using Jupyter notebooks for re-training machine learning models. J. Cheminform. **14** (2022)
23. VDA Working Group 13: Automotive SPICE Process Assessment/Reference Model (2023). https://vda-qmc.de/wp-content/uploads/2023/12/Automotive-SPICE-PAM-v40.pdf
24. Yarlagadda, R.T.: Understanding DevOps & bridging the gap from continuous integration to continuous delivery (2018). https://ssrn.com/abstract=3807611

LLMs Based Data Augmentation Techniques for Python Code Refactoring

Vasilica Moldovan[1,2]([✉]) [ID], Rares Patcas[1,2] [ID], and Simona Motogna[1,2] [ID]

[1] Faculty of Mathematics and Computer Science, Babeș-Bolyai University,
Cluj-Napoca, Romania
{vasilica.moldovan,rares.patcas,simona.motogna}@ubbcluj.ro
[2] Babes-Bolyai University, Cluj-Napoca, Romania

Abstract. Refactoring is a crucial software engineering practice aimed at improving code quality. However, detecting and predicting refactoring activities automatically remains a challenging task due to the limited availability of labeled datasets. This study investigates the role of data augmentation techniques in enhancing refactoring detection models. We apply various augmentation strategies to expand training data and assess their impact on model performance. We also discuss validation and balancing of the resulting dataset in order to provide meaningful data for further applied ML techniques. Our findings highlight the importance of data diversity in automated refactoring detection and provide insights into optimizing augmentation strategies for software engineering applications. Experimental results demonstrate that data augmentation improves the robustness and accuracy of refactoring detection models by mitigating overfitting and enhancing generalization.

Keywords: Refactoring · Artificial Intelligence · AI in Software Refactoring · Machine Learning · Data Augmentation

1 Introduction

The size and complexity of current software systems and the methods in which they are developed by teams, that in some cases might be large and geographically distributed, raise concerns for quality both during development and maintenance. Refactoring has been recognized as a key method to control and improve the overall quality [9] and the urge to automate it is of essential interest both for researchers and practitioners. As a consequence, the availability of datasets that can be used off the shelf for refactoring detection, recommendation or prioritization proves its importance.

However, refactoring can be challenging, as it often depends on the developer's experience and subjective interpretation. Numerous studies have been conducted on when a programmer should perform a refactoring process, and the relationship between refactorings and software quality metrics has been widely studied.

© The Author(s), under exclusive license to Springer Nature Switzerland AG 2026
D. Taibi and D. Smite (Eds.): SEAA 2025, LNCS 16081, pp. 20–36, 2026.
https://doi.org/10.1007/978-3-032-04190-6_2

One of the main challenges identified in studies on refactoring and software quality is the issue of data imbalance. Most publicly available datasets contain significantly fewer instances of refactored code compared to non-refactored code, which can hinder the performance and generalizability of machine learning models. In addition, many datasets lack diversity and representativeness in refactoring examples, limiting their usefulness for training robust models. To address this imbalance, it becomes necessary to generate additional data through augmentation techniques. One possible strategy is to augment software quality metrics directly by synthetically generating new metric values. However, this approach may produce unrealistic or inconsistent data that do not correspond to actual code, reducing its reliability and relevance for training or evaluation, and limiting the model's ability to learn meaningful patterns that generalize to real-world refactoring tasks.

A more reliable and effective solution is to augment the refactored code itself. Code-level augmentation introduces greater diversity in structural patterns while ensuring that any derived metrics remain consistent with executable code. This approach allows us to reflect realistic variations in how refactorings are applied across different contexts, which is essential for building models that can generalize beyond narrow or repetitive training examples. It also enables the capture of subtle stylistic and structural differences that are often lost when working only with high-level metrics. Moreover, as presented in Sect. 2, several existing data balancing techniques rely on artificial transformations at the feature level, which can compromise the semantic integrity of the dataset. By contrast, augmenting the code directly avoids these pitfalls and provides a more grounded basis for refactoring analysis.

In this study, we focused on data augmentation techniques that involve code transformation rather than directly augmenting the features. We focused on Python due to its prominence in AI/ML and the limited research on refactoring in this language. Specifically, we analyzed four augmentation approaches: back translation using a different programming language (with Java as the intermediary), back translation from text descriptions, code generation based on existing comments, and code generation from specifications derived using CodeXGLUE on the refactored code.

Our contributions can be summarized in:

- detailed analysis of data augmentation methods on the level of source code
- pipeline of steps to rectify imbalanced datasets
- availability of an augmented, validated and balanced dataset usable for refactoring detection, prioritization, recommendation or other related purposes.

2   Background

2.1   Refactoring, Tools, Related Work to Refactoring Detection

The constant interest given to the refactoring comes from the fact that it represents a key technique to control and improve the quality and efficiency of software systems. Different tools have been proposed and facilities for refactoring have been included in popular IDEs such as Eclipse or IntelliJ. In the context of our study, we used the well known tool **PyRef** [2], designed to detect 9 method-level refactorings in Python projects.

As highlighted in [15], a multitude of research studies addressed the use of AI/ML methods targeting detection, recommendation, prediction or other tasks, such as [16, 19] to mention only a few. This continuing interest deepen the need for reliable datasets.

2.2   Data Augmentation, Methods, Related Work to Data Augmentation on SE

Data augmentation in the Software Engineering domain is an essential subject because it strengthens the foundation of a large variety of research studies by enhancing dataset diversity, mitigating data scarcity, and improving model robustness. In ML applications within SE, such as defect prediction, code summarization, refactoring detection, and bug localization, data augmentation techniques help generate more comprehensive training sets. These techniques include code transformation (renaming variables, modifying control structures), synthetic data generation, and adversarial examples to improve generalization.

There are two primary approaches to perform data augmentation in SE research studies:

– **Feature level**: This involves applying augmentation techniques to features extracted from source code, such as software quality metrics, abstract syntax trees (ASTs), or token representations. Common methods include adding noise, perturbing feature values, or generating synthetic data to enhance model robustness.
– **Source code level**: This approach directly modifies the source code to create diverse training examples. Techniques include code transformations, injecting synthetic bugs, back translation, or generating adversarial examples to improve model generalization.

SMOTE [8], falling under the first category of data augmentation techniques, is one of the most commonly used methods in SE research [7]. Even though SMOTE is not just a data augmentation technique, but a data balancing technique, we consider it as a data augmentation technique because it creates synthetic samples of the minority class by interpolating between existing instances, effectively augmenting the dataset.

The study [7] explores feature-level data augmentation for Software Defect Prediction (SDP), improving the reliability of SMOTE-based oversampling. Traditional SMOTE introduces randomness, leading to inconsistent model performance. To address this, the study proposes stable SMOTE-based methods that systematically select minority instances and interpolation points, reducing variability. Evaluations on 26 datasets and four classifiers show improved consistency and predictive performance. The findings suggest replacing traditional SMOTE with these stable methods for more reliable defect prediction, with future work extending the analysis to additional datasets and classifiers.

In the second category of data augmentation techniques, various approaches can be applied, such as: code translation, where a program is converted from one programming language to another and then back to the original language, or transformed into a textual description and then reconstructed or code generation, which involves creating new code snippets based on predefined patterns or machine learning models. Additionally, rule-based augmentation techniques modify existing code by applying systematic transformations, such as variable renaming, statement reordering, or syntactic variations, to introduce diversity while preserving functionality.

The study presented in [3] uses back-translation, multilingual augmentation, and numeric-aware techniques for improving programming language (PL) translation and summarization using pre-trained language models (PLMs). The results showed that back-translation significantly improved the accuracy, with gains of up to 6.9% and 7.5%, respectively. It enhanced code style adaptation, aligning translations with target language conventions rather than mirroring the source. However, its effectiveness varied, showing smaller gains in Ruby and Java. Despite these improvements, the authors recommend future research on more robust evaluation methods and refining back-translation to better handle divergent code pairs in translation tasks.

Different data augmentation techniques for source code were investigated in [5], including back translation, but instead of programming languages, it used regular languages like English and French. Additionally, it included traditional refactoring operations such as adding dead code, enhancing if statements, renaming methods, and other modifications. The experiments were conducted using Python and Java code. To account for low-resource programming languages, datasets for Ruby and Go were also included. Several deep learning models, such as CodeBERT, GraphCodeBERT, were employed for the following tasks: bug detection, problem classification, authorship attribution and clone detection. The study found that common NLP-based data augmentation techniques are ineffective for code learning, emphasizing the need for specialized methods.

Another data augmentation method for source code was proposed in [26] using program transformation to enhance the generalization capability of deep learning models. The approach involves 18 transformation rules that are proven to preserve program semantics and tested to maintain syntactic naturalness. A Java-based tool, SPAT, was developed to apply these transformations and was evaluated on three important code tasks: method name prediction, code commenting, and code clone detection. The study demonstrates that applying these transformations to training data improves model performance in multiple deep learning models, including Code2Vec, DeepCom, Hybrid-DeepCom, ASTNN, and TBCCD. The results show that augmenting datasets with syntactically natural and semantically equivalent transformations can improve model generalization, though effectiveness may vary depending on the task, model, and dataset.

2.3   Automatic Code Generation, Related Work for B2B Translation

Automatic code generation refers to the process of using artificial intelligence (AI), machine learning (ML), or predefined rules to create source code with minimal human intervention. This method has grown in popularity in software development because it reduces human error, increases efficiency, and automates repetitive coding jobs. With the emergence of large language models (LLMs) such as GPT-4o, Gemini, and Claude, automatic code generation has made considerable strides, enabling developers to easily rework existing code.

The ability to increase the development pace without sacrificing code quality is the main benefit of autonomous code generation. AI-powered technologies can be used by developers to enforce the best coding standards, recommend optimizations, and provide boilerplate code.

There are multiple AI-powered techniques for automatic code generation, for example:

- **Large Language Models (LLMs)** Uses AI (e.g., GPT-4, Codex, Copilot) to generate code from natural language prompts.
- **AI-Based Code Completion** Autocompletes code while typing (e.g., Copilot, Tabnine, IntelliCode).
- **AI-Powered Code Refactoring**   Optimizes and improves existing code (e.g., DeepCode).

These techniques can be effectively utilized for back-to-back translation of code. **Back-to-back translation (B2B translation)** refers to the process of translating code from one programming language into another and back. It can also refer to translating code into a text description and back into code.

Multiple papers approached the back-translation technique. For instance, the study [1] proposed using code summarization and generation to enable back-translation for translating code between languages. They used PLBART, a model pre-trained on coding tasks, and fine-tuned it to convert code into natural language and then generate equivalent code in another language. The method was evaluated on a Java-Python dataset using CodeBLEU and Computational Accuracy, achieving around 64% and over 50% respectively, performing comparably to state-of-the-art systems like TransCoder.

In another study presented in [24], the researchers applied an Iterative Back Translation (IBT) approach to adapt a C++-to-pseudocode model for use with C code, without requiring parallel training data. By converting C code to pseudocode and back, and validating with test cases, the method achieved over 84% success in generating correct C code.

In [6], DeepDebug was presented, a model for automated Python bug fixing. It leveraged a backtranslation approach, where a separate model was trained on bug-fix commits in reverse to learn how to introduce bugs. These synthetic bug-fix pairs were used to augment the training data and fine-tune DeepDebug, which achieved a 53% bug fix rate on the QuixBugs benchmark, a dataset of algorithmic programs with known bugs and corresponding fixes.

The MUFIN technique [23] is another experiment about the back translation of code. Back-translation in MUFIN involved two models: a fixer and a breaker. The fixer tried to correct buggy code, while the breaker intentionally introduced bugs into the correct code. These two models trained each other by taking turns generating training data. The fixer produced corrected code, which the breaker then modified to create new buggy samples. These samples were then used to further train both models. By continuously generating and using these back-translated samples, both models learned to handle a wider variety of coding issues, improving their effectiveness in repairing code.

2.4   Data Balancing

To ensure an efficient training process and achieve high model performance, regardless of the specific task, several key factors must be considered. One critical aspect is the distribution of the dataset, particularly the issue of class imbalance, which can significantly impact model generalization and prediction accuracy. Unfortunately, most datasets used in training are imbalanced, which can negatively affect model performance. To address this issue, data balancing techniques have been proposed as a solution to improve class distribution and enhance model reliability.

Numerous studies have examined this issue, proposing and evaluating different data balancing techniques. One such study is represented by [11], which empirically assessed the performance of the data-preprocessing-level data-balancing techniques, namely: Under Sampling (OS), Over Sampling (OS), Hybrid Sampling (HS), Random Over Sampling Examples (ROSE), Synthetic Minority Over Sampling (SMOTE), and Clustering-Based Under Sampling (CBUS) techniques using six different classifiers and 25 different datasets that had different levels of imbalance ratio (IR). Key findings showed that the "None" and ROSE strategies consistently performed poorly, while other DBT methods (US, OS, HS, SMOTE, and CBUS) generally improved classifier performance. However, the effectiveness varied by classifier. Statistical analyses (Friedman and Nemenyi tests) confirmed significant DBT differences, though Kendall's W showed only partial ranking agreement, indicating DBT impact depends on the classifier and imbalance ratio. The study concluded that while DBT proposed improved classification, future research still being needed.

The data balancing problem has been heavily studied in the software engineering domain. One study that presented a large scale empirical comparison of data balancing techniques for Machine Learning-based code smell detection is represented by [18]. The following data balancing techniques were applied: no balancing, oversampling, undersampling, SMOTE, cost-sensitive classifier, and one-class classifier. Key findings indicated that SMOTE yields the highest accuracy, though its training phase may not always be practical. Avoiding balancing did not significantly reduce effectiveness, while techniques that trained only on the minority class (Cost-Sensitive and One-Class Classifier) and other resampling methods (Class Balancer and Resample) were ineffective. The study also confirmed that structural metrics alone are insufficient for accurate code smell detection, reinforcing prior research that emphasizes the importance of textual and historical metrics. The authors concluded that the studied data balancing methods were inadequate for code smell detection and suggested future work on developing better balancing techniques.

3   Our Approach

Our main objective is to develop a robust data augmentation technique for Python datasets with regards to refactoring and to produce a dataset that is balanced, contains valid code and supports accurate detection for refactoring. As a result, we aim to obtain a consistent dataset suitable to be used in further studies related to refactoring of Python source code.

3.1   Methodology

The approach that we propose is summarized in Fig. 1, describing the pipeline we consider during this investigation: we start by establishing a collection of projects that need to satisfy some inclusion criteria: source code written in Pyhton, the code has been refactored, such that several refactoring types are represented, and it is big enough to offer relevant characteristics. This collection is subject to data augmentation. Our study includes a detailed analysis of different data augmentation techniques with the purposes of determining the most suitable ones for refactoring detection. Since the data augmentation is an automated process, we continue with performing several validation operations such that the obtained code is syntactically correct. We then consider the problem of constructing a balanced dataset, since this was one of the main reasons behind the whole effort, as many existing datasets are unbalanced in terms of refactoring types they expose. Finally, we explore the use of the newly constructed dataset in the problem of detection of refactoring types the source code.

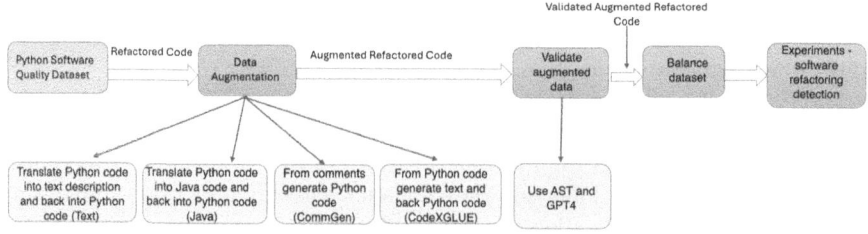

Fig. 1. Pipeline of the proposed study

3.2   Dataset

The **Python Software Quality Dataset** [14] serves as the base dataset for this study on data augmentation of refactorings, providing a diverse set of software quality data, including SonarQube quality metrics and PySZZ bug-fixing commit pairs, which offer insights into software maintainability and defect resolution. While the dataset is not specifically focused on refactoring, it includes 12,301 recorded refactorings detected using PyRef, making it an ideal foundation for augmenting refactoring instances. In this study, we apply data augmentation techniques to expand and balance refactoring types, improving the effectiveness of machine learning models in recognizing and analyzing refactoring patterns.

We focused on the **REFACTORING_RECORD** table, which provides detailed information on detected refactorings. Each entry presents a refactoring or multiple refactoring types, along with the associated commit hash and the line number where the refactoring occurred. To accurately identify the methods affected by these changes, we utilized the GitHub API to retrieve historical versions of the source code and applied a regex-based approach to extract modified function signatures and method bodies. We extracted all the methods affected by the refactoring, presenting them in a pre-commit and post-commit format, ensuring a clear representation of how the code evolved. This method ensured the precise identification of refactored elements, allowing for a more effective application of data augmentation techniques and improving the accuracy of refactoring detection models.

The replication package, which provides the dataset and documentation, is available at: https://figshare.com/s/fd425fb83e3eae915a91.

3.3   Data Augmentation

As presented in Fig. 1, we experimented four different methods to perform data augmentation on the refactored code instances, as described in this section. Specifically, we performed back translations by converting Python code into Java and then back into Python, as well as translating Python code into textual descriptions and then reconstructing the code from those descriptions. Additionally, we generated Python code from the comments present in the original refactored samples and produced textual specifications from Python code before regenerating Python code from those specifications.

Back-Translation from Java. For implementing back-translation through an intermediate programming language, we selected Java as the intermediary language due to the availability of well-trained models for Java code. Additionally, given that the original code was written in Python, Java serves as a structurally distinct yet widely adopted language, facilitating meaningful transformations while preserving the underlying logic. This choice allows us to leverage robust code translation models trained on extensive Java and Python datasets, ensuring high-quality conversions between the two languages. As a model, we used Google's Gemini model, a generative AI system capable of handling complex code translation tasks while maintaining syntactic correctness and semantic equivalence [22]. The translation process was implemented using the Gemini-Pro model (gemini-2.5-pro-exp-03-25), which was configured to process Python-to-Java and Java-to-Python transformations. Given that API-based model invocations are subject to rate limits, safety filters, and response time constraints, we incorporated mechanisms to handle API failures, retries, and response validation. To perform back-translation, refactored Python snippets were translated into Java using the Gemini model, then retranslated into Python to preserve the original logic.

Back-Translation from Textual Description. As for the back-translation from textual descriptions, the process was very similar to the one presented above that performed back-translation using Java as an intermediary programming language. The key difference is that, in this case, instead of translating the code into Java, we first converted it into a natural language description and then reconstructed the Python code from this description. We used the Gemini-Pro model for this task as well, as it has demonstrated strong performance in similar code understanding and generation tasks [22]. To achieve this, each refactored Python block was first processed with a prompt instructing the model to generate a clear and detailed English description of the code, capturing its functionality and intent. This textual description was then used as input for a second model invocation, in which the Gemini-Pro model was tasked with regenerating the original Python function based on the given description.

Generating Python Code from Existing Comments. For this augmentation approach, we utilized OpenAI's GPT-4o model (gpt-4o-2024-08-06) to generate Python code directly from the available textual comments. This model represents a good choice because of its advanced natural language understanding and code generation capabilities, which enable it to accurately interpret textual descriptions and translate them into syntactically correct and semantically meaningful Python code. Additionally, GPT-4o has been trained on extensive datasets comprising both natural language and programming languages, making it well-suited for tasks that require bridging the gap between textual documentation and executable code [10].

Generating Python Code from Generated Comments. The final data augmentation method involved generating text specifications from the refactored code snippets using CodeXGLUE [12], followed by the generation of Python code from these specifications using the GPT-4o model. This approach mirrors the one previously applied for generating code from existing comments. We chose CodeXGLUE because it provides a comprehensive set of standardized benchmarks for code-related tasks, including code summarization, code completion, and code-to-text translation, which are essential for generating meaningful text specifications [12]. By using CodeXGLUE's pre-trained models, we leverage its effective understanding of code semantics, which improves the quality and accuracy of the generated text specifications. The subsequent use of GPT-4o for translating these text descriptions back into Python code capitalizes on GPT-

4o's advanced natural language understanding and its ability to generate syntactically and semantically accurate code from textual inputs.

The reason for which we used both the GPT-4o model and Gemini-Pro is because each model offers distinct advantages suited to different aspects of the translation and augmentation process.

GPT-4o, developed by OpenAI, excels at generating syntactically correct code from natural language, making it ideal for tasks like creating Python code from comments and specifications. Its ability to transform plain English into complex code structures provides flexibility for natural language-to-code tasks, as seen in our work.

On the other hand, Gemini-Pro, developed by Google, excels at translating code between languages like Python and Java, making it ideal for back-translation tasks or language-specific transformations, ensuring high-quality, semantically accurate translations.

The decision to use Gemini-Pro in conjunction with GPT-4o thus allows us to leverage the strengths of both models–GPT-4o for textual-to-code generation and Gemini-Pro for cross-language code translation–ensuring robustness and accuracy in our data augmentation process.

A statistic showing the initial distribution and the new refactoring instances obtained after applying the described data augmentation techniques are presented in Table 1.

It is important to note that not all refactoring instances were successfully translated. Some functions were flagged as unsafe by Gemini during text-to-code translation, highlighting a direction for future work.

Table 1. Dataset Distribution Across Different Sources

Refactoring Type	Text	CommGen	CodeXGLUE	Java	Original
Add Parameter	1516	1746	3734	2141	3956
Rename Method	988	938	2400	1156	2882
Remove Parameter	522	585	1199	681	1304
Rename Class	0	609	1468	0	1767
Extract Method	5	529	823	1	896
Change/Rename Param	318	320	751	417	894
Inline Method	0	30	66	0	76
Change Return Type	129	137	271	199	364

3.4 Validation

In order to ensure that the code was syntactically correct, the **AST (Abstract Syntax Tree) package** was used. AST parses Python source code into a hierarchical tree structure, representing its syntactic elements, making it an effective tool for detecting syntax errors without requiring execution. A key advantage of

AST is its ability to analyze individual functions in isolation, allowing validation of refactored code snippets without needing the full program context. While the AST module verifies the structure and correctness of the given function, it assumes that any referenced classes, methods, or external modules are already implemented and correctly imported. This makes it particularly useful for validating code transformations where dependencies exist but do not need to be explicitly evaluated. The results showed that 90% of the generated code from each augmentation method passed the AST validation, confirming the syntactic correctness of most transformations.

To further ensure the validity of the augmented refactorings, we decided to also validate the generated code using **GPT-4o**. The first validation step involved prompting GPT-4o to analyze whether the meaning of the refactored function remained the same as the original, ensuring that the transformation preserved the intended functionality. In the second validation step, we asked GPT-4o to verify whether the applied refactoring retained its intended type, such as adding a parameter, extracting a function, or renaming a method. This dual-validation approach provided both semantic consistency checks and structural correctness verification, enhancing confidence in the accuracy of the augmented refactoring instances.

We applied the established validation process to all four code augmentation techniques used in our study: Back-Translation from Java (Java), Back-Translation from Textual Description (Text), Generating Python Code from Existing Comments (Comments), and Generating Python Code from Generated Comments (CodeXGLUE). The results of the validation tests are shown in Table 2. Back-Translation from Textual Description achieved the highest scores in both the *Same Spec* (72.40%) and *Refactor Rules* (71.29%) tests. Generating Python Code from Generated Comments showed the lowest performance (29.61%, 52.67%), most likely due to the added layer of abstraction introduced by generating comments with an AI model before code generation, which may have been optimized for fluency rather than functional accuracy.

Table 2. Validation Results of Back-to-Back Code Generation Methods

Method	Valid Syntax	Same Spec	Refactor Rules
Comments	99.75 %	67.24 %	61.30 %
CodeXGlue	99.77 %	29.61 %	52.67 %
Text	98.20 %	72.40 %	71.29 %
Java	98.20 %	63.83 %	63.54 %

3.5   Balancing Data

To address the initial data imbalance, we selected oversampling as the balancing strategy, based on an analysis of the refactoring datasets and available methods. Since refactoring instances are generally scarce, undersampling is not a viable option, as losing information is not acceptable at this stage. Hybrid sampling techniques were not chosen because they typically combine both oversampling and undersampling, which could still result in a loss of valuable minority class instances. Additionally, hybrid methods often introduce complexity in data pre-processing and may lead to inconsistencies in the distribution of refactoring types, potentially affecting model performance and generalization. Given these constraints, we prioritized oversampling to ensure sufficient representation of minority classes while maintaining the integrity of the dataset.

Based on the distribution of the original dataset, the balancing process began by incorporating data generated through the presented augmentation techniques until either the class distribution was equalized or all available augmented data had been used. If the augmented data was insufficient, additional balancing was attempted by randomly duplicating instances of the minority class. However, to prevent excessive duplication, each instance from a minority class was duplicated at most once. This balancing process was applied independently using each of the employed data augmentation techniques: back translation from Java, back translation from text description, code generation from comments found in the original code, code generated from specifications generated using CodeXGLUE from the original code. Hence, the final distributions of the four newly obtained datasets are presented inTable 3.

Table 3. Class Distribution Across Different Refactoring Translation Methods

Refactoring Type	Java	Text	CommGen	CodeXGLUE
Add Parameter	3596	3601	3592	3547
Change/Rename Param	2357	2265	2279	2001
Remove Parameter	2041	1891	1828	3627
Rename Method	3704	3676	3588	3807
Change Return Type	1096	946	962	1244

3.6 Use of Augmented Data in Refactoring Detection

To assess the effectiveness of the proposed data augmentation techniques, we conducted experiments using the dataset introduced in [14], focused on detecting software refactoring processes. We compared model performance across datasets generated by our augmentation methods, the original baseline dataset, and the baseline enhanced with SMOTE for class balancing. The dataset was split into 80% training and 20% testing, with distinct data used for each to ensure proper evaluation and avoid overfitting.

The detection was based on various software quality metrics, including complexity, LOC, LLOC, SLOC, comments, multi, blank, maintainability index, Halstead metrics (H1, H2, N1, N2, vocabulary, length, calculated length, volume, difficulty, effort, time, and bugs) extracted with the Radon tool [20]. Furthermore, we computed Average Cyclomatic Complexity, Weighted Methods per

Class, Response for a Class, and Depth of Inheritance Tree using the Understand tool [21].

We selected the following models for our experiments: Random Forests [17], XGBoost [4], Naive Bayes [13] and SVM [25]. We chose these classifiers because they are well-suited for handling structured data and have been widely used in classification tasks related to software quality analysis. We selected multiple models to better evaluate the effectiveness of data augmentation, as relying on a single model could introduce bias. This approach ensures a more robust assessment of how well the augmented data improves software refactoring detection across different classification methods.

To facilitate the comparison of the applied data augmentation techniques, we ran the models on both the baseline dataset and the baseline dataset augmented and balanced using SMOTE. The results for both the baseline dataset and the SMOTE-augmented dataset are presented in Table 4. The results for the datasets augmented with the proposed data augmentation techniques are shown in Table 5.

Table 4. Model Performance Without Our Data Augmentation

Data Source	Model	Accuracy	Precision	Recall	F1 Score
Original	Random Forest	0.61	0.61	0.61	0.61
Original	XGBoost	0.59	0.60	0.59	0.59
Original	Naive Bayes	0.58	0.62	0.60	0.60
Original	SVM	0.58	0.59	0.59	0.59
SMOTE	Random Forest	0.61	0.61	0.61	0.61
SMOTE	XGBoost	0.58	0.58	0.58	0.58
SMOTE	Naive Bayes	0.62	0.62	0.62	0.62
SMOTE	SVM	0.57	0.58	0.57	0.57

4   Discussion

After analyzing the results, we can conclude that all the proposed data augmentation techniques outperform both the baseline and the SMOTE scenarios, with a significant difference in accuracy (21% for Random Forests, 13% for XGBoost, 13% for Naive Bayes, 20% for SVM) and F1-Score (21% for Random Forests, 13% for XGBoost, 17% for Naive Bayes, 17% for SVM).

The method involving text description generation through CodeXGLUE appears to be the most effective for this task, significantly improving the performance of the Random Forest and XGBoost models, while the code generation from comments method seems to work the best for the Naive Bayes model and the code translation through Java obtained the best results for the SVM model. However, the differences in the computed evaluation metrics across the proposed data augmentation techniques are minimal.

Table 5. Model Performance With Our Data Augmentation

Data Source	Model	Accuracy	Precision	Recall	F1 Score
CodeXGLUE	Random Forest	0.82	0.82	0.82	0.82
CodeXGLUE	XGBoost	0.72	0.72	0.72	0.72
CodeXGLUE	Naive Bayes	0.71	0.82	0.71	0.75
CodeXGLUE	SVM	0.77	0.75	0.77	0.75
Comments	Random Forest	0.78	0.81	0.73	0.75
Comments	XGBoost	0.73	0.77	0.65	0.68
Comments	Naive Bayes	0.75	0.88	0.75	0.79
Comments	SVM	0.78	0.75	0.77	0.76
Java	Random Forest	0.80	0.79	0.80	0.79
Java	XGBoost	0.70	0.71	0.70	0.68
Java	Naive Bayes	0.71	0.77	0.71	0.73
Java	SVM	0.78	0.76	0.76	0.76
Text	Random Forest	0.81	0.81	0.81	0.80
Text	XGBoost	0.71	0.72	0.71	0.69
Text	Naive Bayes	0.66	0.74	0.67	0.68
Text	SVM	0.75	0.75	0.75	0.75

The code translation through text as an intermediate step had the lowest performance among the proposed techniques but still outperformed the baseline and SMOTE-augmented datasets. This suggests that while it introduces some inconsistencies, it retains enough meaningful patterns to improve model learning.

The largest performance gap between the baseline or baseline + SMOTE models and one of the considered data augmentation techniques is observed with the Random Forest model. This suggests that Random Forest benefits the most from the additional variability introduced by data augmentation, likely due to its ensemble nature, which leverages diverse training instances to improve generalization.

On the opposite, the model for which the smallest difference between the performances has been obtained is XGBoost, indicating that it is inherently more robust to variations in the training data.

In order to test the significance of the obtained results, we used the Friedman statistical test followed by the Nemenyi post-hoc test, using the F1-Score values. First, we applied the Friedman test to determine whether there were significant differences between the methods. After ranking the F1-Scores per row and computing the test statistic, we obtained a Friedman test statistic of 14.8529 and a p-value of 0.0110, indicating that at least one data augmentation technique had a statistically different effect, making the Nemenyi test appropriate. We computed the average ranks for each method and applied the Nemenyi post-hoc test for pairwise comparisons. The critical difference was 3.487, meaning only rank differences above this threshold indicate statistical significance. Although

CodeXGLUE achieved the highest rank, the differences among augmentation techniques were not statistically significant, as all p-values were ≥ 0.05. However, all augmentation methods performed notably better than the baseline, reinforcing their effectiveness. Table 6 shows the pairwise p-values.

Table 6. Model Performance With Our Data Augmentation

Data Source	Original	SMOTE	CodeXGLUE	Comments	Java	Text
Original	1.000	0.999	0.086	0.250	0.351	0.408
SMOTE	0.999	1.000	**0.052**	0.170	0.250	0.298
CodeXGLUE	0.086	**0.052**	1.000	0.997	0.986	0.974
Comments	0.250	0.170	0.997	1.000	0.999	0.999
Java	0.351	0.250	0.986	0.999	1.000	0.999
Text	0.408	0.298	0.974	0.999	0.999	1.000

5 Threats to Validity

Similar to [2], we identify potential limitations in this study across construct, internal, and external validity dimensions. One concern related to construct validity is the reliance on LLM-generated code for data augmentation. LLMs often use longer names and extra comments for clarity. They also include more explicit error handling, assuming less about external validations. These traits contrast with concise, context-reliant human code and can cause models to adopt AI-style conventions over practical patterns.

Regarding internal validity, the augmentation process depends on the outputs of non-deterministic APIs such as GPT-4o and Gemini-Pro. These models can yield varying results for identical prompts due to factors like server load or version updates. Although we applied AST-based syntactic validation and GPT-4o-powered semantic checks to mitigate inconsistency, there remains a risk that some augmented samples contain misclassifications.

The study also presents limitations with respect to external validity. All experiments were conducted using Python and based on open-source repositories. This context may not capture the structural complexity, development constraints, or tooling environments characteristic of enterprise-scale software systems, particularly those using statically typed languages.

6 Conclusions

We explored the process of augmenting datasets for software engineering related investigations. Our study enforces the importance of choosing a proper data augmentation technique as different techniques might yield to varying degrees of improvement, but also to follow a well defined process including validation and balancing of the dataset. Through extensive experimentation, we demonstrated that synthetic data generation can enhance model generalizability, leading to more reliable effort predictions. Another important aspect of our approach refers to the object of the augmentation: code based augmentation, instead of feature based augmentation, operates directly on source code, maintaining the structural integrity of programs. It ensures that the augmented data retains meaningful relationships between code elements and making models more robust to unseen refactoring cases.

Future work can focus on using the proposed data augmentation techniques to predict the need for function-level refactoring. The augmented datasets can help train machine learning models to detect code segments that are likely to benefit from refactoring, based on structural and semantic patterns. Another idea can be to apply the refactoring generation techniques to build a plugin that suggests and performs automatic refactorings at the function level. This plugin can be integrated into code editors such as Visual Studio or Cursor to assist developers in improving code quality during development.

References

1. Ahmad, W.U., Chakraborty, S., Ray, B., Chang, K.W.: Summarize and generate to back-translate: Unsupervised translation of programming languages. arXiv preprint arXiv:2205.11116 (2022)
2. Atwi, H., et al.: Pyref: refactoring detection in python projects. In: 2021 IEEE 21st International Working Conference on Source Code Analysis and Manipulation (SCAM), pp. 136–141 (2021). https://doi.org/10.1109/SCAM52516.2021.00025
3. Chen, P., Lampouras, G.: Exploring data augmentation for code generation tasks (2023). https://arxiv.org/abs/2302.03499
4. Chen, T., Guestrin, C.: Xgboost: a scalable tree boosting system. Proc. ACM SIGKDD Int. Conf. Knowl. Discov. Data Min. **10**(4), 785–794 (2016). https://doi.org/10.1145/2939672.2939785
5. Dong, Z., et al.: Boosting source code learning with text-oriented data augmentation: An empirical study (2025). https://arxiv.org/abs/2303.06808
6. Drain, D., Clement, C.B., Serrato, G., Sundaresan, N.: Deepdebug: Fixing python bugs using stack traces, backtranslation, and code skeletons. arXiv preprint arXiv:2105.09352 (2021)
7. Feng, S., Keung, J., Yu, X., Xiao, Y., Zhang, M.: Investigation on the stability of smote-based oversampling techniques in software defect prediction. Inf. Softw. Technol. **139**, 106662 (2021)
8. Fernandez, A., Garcia, S., Herrera, F., Chawla, N.V.: Smote for learning from imbalanced data: Progress and challenges, marking the 15-year anniversary. J. Artifi. Intell. Res. **61**, 863–905 (2018). https://doi.org/10.1613/jair.1.11192
9. Fowler, M.: Refactoring: Improving the Design of Existing Code. Addison-Wesley, Boston, MA, USA (1999)
10. Hou, W., Ji, Z.: Comparing large language models and human programmers for generating programming code. arXiv e-prints arXiv:2403.00894 (2024)
11. Jadhav, A., M. Mostafa, S., Elmannai, H., Karim, F.K.: An empirical assessment of performance of data balancing techniques in classification task. Appli. Sci. **12**(8) (2022). https://doi.org/10.3390/app12083928, https://www.mdpi.com/2076-3417/12/8/3928

12. Lu, S., et al.: Codexglue: A machine learning benchmark dataset for code understanding and generation (2021). https://arxiv.org/abs/2102.04664
13. Maron, M.E.: Automatic indexing: an experimental inquiry. J. ACM **8**(3), 404–417 (1961). https://doi.org/10.1145/321075.321084
14. Moldovan, V.A., Berciu, L.M., Patcas, R.D.: The python software quality dataset. In: 2024 50th Euromicro Conference on Software Engineering and Advanced Applications (SEAA), pp. 395–398. IEEE (2024)
15. Motogna, S., Berciu, L.M., Moldovan, V.A.: Artificial intelligence methods in software refactoring: A systematic literature review. In: 2024 50th Euromicro Conference on Software Engineering and Advanced Applications (SEAA), pp. 309–316 (2024https://doi.org/10.1109/SEAA64295.2024.00055
16. Noei, S., Li, H., Zou, Y.: Detecting refactoring commits in machine learning python projects: A machine learning-based approach. ACM Trans. Softw. Eng. Methodol. **34**(3) (2025). https://doi.org/10.1145/3705309
17. Parmar, A., Katariya, R., Patel, V.: A review on random forest: an ensemble classifier. In: Hemanth, J., Fernando, X., Lafata, P., Baig, Z. (eds.) ICICI 2018. LNDECT, vol. 26, pp. 758–763. Springer, Cham (2019). https://doi.org/10.1007/978-3-030-03146-6_86
18. Pecorelli, F., Di Nucci, D., De Roover, C., De Lucia, A.: A large empirical assessment of the role of data balancing in machine-learning-based code smell detection. J. Syst. Softw. **169**, 110693 (2020). https://doi.org/10.1016/j.jss.2020.110693. https://www.sciencedirect.com/science/article/pii/S0164121220301448
19. Pecorelli, F., Palomba, F., Khomh, F., De Lucia, A.: Developer-driven code smell prioritization. In: Proceedings of the 17th International Conference on Mining Software Repositories, MSR 2020, pp. 220–231. Association for Computing Machinery, New York (2020). https://doi.org/10.1145/3379597.3387457
20. Rubik, M.: Radon: Measure cyclomatic complexity, maintainability index, and halstead metrics in python code (2024). https://radon.readthedocs.io/ Accessed 24 Nov 2024
21. Scientific Toolworks, I.: Understand: Static analysis and code visualization tool (2024). https://www.scitools.com/ Accessed 24 Nov 2024
22. Siam, M.K., Gu, H., Cheng, J.Q.: Programming with ai: Evaluating chatgpt, gemini, alphacode, and github copilot for programmers (2024). https://arxiv.org/abs/2411.09224
23. Silva, A., Ferreira, J.F., Ye, H., Monperrus, M.: Mufin: Improving neural repair models with back-translation. arXiv preprint arXiv:2304.02301 (2023)
24. Sontakke, A., et al.: Knowledge transfer for pseudo-code generation from low resource programming language. arXiv preprint arXiv:2303.09062 (2023)
25. Suthaharan, S.: Support Vector Machine, pp. 207–235. Springer US, Boston, MA (2016). https://doi.org/10.1007/978-1-4899-7641-3_9
26. Yu, S., Wang, T., Wang, J.: Data augmentation by program transformation. J. Syst. Softw. **190**, 111304 (2022). DOIurlhttps://doi.org/10.1016/j.jss.2022.111304, https://www.sciencedirect.com/science/article/pii/S0164121222000541

Empirical Analysis of OpenAI Embeddings for Semantic Code Review Comment Similarity

Robert Heumüller[(✉)] [iD], Theo Langer, and Frank Ortmeier[iD]

Otto von Guericke University Magdeburg, Magdeburg, Germany
{robert.heumueller,theo.langer,frank.ortmeier}@ovgu.de

Abstract. Code review automation is an important area of research given the time and effort required by traditional processes. Evaluating comment generation models requires automated metrics that quantify the similarity between generated and human-authored comments. Prior work has relied on lexical metrics like BLEU and ExactMatches, which fail to capture semantic differences when phrasing varies. Sentence embedding models offer a promising alternative; however, so far there has been no evidence of their superiority in capturing semantic similarity on code review data. In an empirical study with human subjects, we use OpenAI embeddings to assess semantic similarity in review comments. Our analyses show that the embedding-based metric aligns more closely with human annotations than BLEU. Furthermore, our method to support metric choices with empirical evidence may represent a significant advancement in the domain.

Keywords: Code review automation · Semantic similarity · Embeddings · Empirical study

1 Introduction

The field of code review automation has gained significant traction in recent years, with research efforts identifying and formalizing various code review automation tasks. Among these, change quality estimation, comment generation, and code refinement are the most prominent avenues of study [6]. In this paper, we concentrate on comment generation, which has received considerable attention from multiple research groups [6,7,14,15]. This task involves taking a code change, represented either as a *(revision_before, revision_after)* tuple or solely as a *revision_after*, and training a model to generate an appropriate review comment for that change.

Evaluating the performance of models tasked with comment generation typically follows one of two methodologies. The first approach involves subjective evaluation, where human judges assess whether the generated comments are "reasonable" [2,3]. However, the subjective nature of "reasonableness" introduces ambiguity and inconsistency. Consequently, researchers have turned to

D. Taibi and D. Smite (Eds.): SEAA 2025, LNCS 16081, pp. 37–45, 2026.
https://doi.org/10.1007/978-3-032-04190-6_3

using automated similarity metrics to compare generated comments to a human-authored ground truth. The metrics employed thus far have been predominantly lexical in nature, such as *ExactMatches*, *BLEU*, and *ROUGE* [5–7,12,14,15].

As can be easily seen in real-world examples, these metrics often fail to effectively capture semantic similarity. Table 1 illustrates this using pairs of real review comments: one pair is high in perceived semantic similarity but low in lexical similarity (BLEU), and the other exhibits the opposite.

Table 1. Lexical Metrics Fail to Capture Semantic Similarity

Semantic-Similarity	BLEU-4	Candidate	Reference
Very High	12%	"Does it make sense to you to refactor this? See the same code in methods below"	"I am just wondering whether it shouldn't be better to refactor this method with methods below. What do you think?"
Very Low	35%	"There should be an I18n used for this"	"There should be an assertion around this"

Recently, Shuvo et al. proposed using sentence embedding-based semantic similarity as an alternative, which, according to them, should be more effective in quantifying semantic similarity [12]. However, until now, there has been no empirical data supporting this claim. While the results of the aforementioned research demonstrated that the proposed metric could capture relative performance differences between models, we still know little about how well these metrics align with human perception or what their current limitations might be.

Our work aims at bridging this gap by means of an empirical study using OpenAI's current sentence `text-embedding-3-large` [8]. We chose these embeddings as they are easily accessible and represent the state of the art in general-purpose sentence embeddings. We decided against using the embedding model employed by Shuvo et al. [12], because by today's standards, its embeddings are considered to be of low quality[1]. For the lexical metric, we chose BLEU-4 over Exact Matches, as the latter cannot capture any degree of similarity beyond a perfect or no match. Beyond the specific results for OpenAI and BLEU, we emphasize our methodology as a contribution in itself, as it can empirically support metric selection, which was lacking in prior research.

The research questions for this study are as follows:

- **RQ1:** Is OpenAI's `text-embedding-3-large` similarity better aligned with human understanding of semantic similarity than `BLEU`?
- **RQ2:** What are the current limitations of this embedding similarity metrics in its application to code review comment automation?

---

[1] https://huggingface.com/sentence-transformers/stsb-roberta-large.

To answer these questions, three human subjects assessed the semantic similarity of 221 pairs of real-world code review comments that fairly represent the entire value ranges of the BLEU-4 and OpenAI-Embedding metrics.

The findings of our subsequent statistical analyses are:

(1) The embedding similarity is indeed much better aligned with the human assessment of semantic similarity in our data. (2) We identified and discussed examples where the embedding similarity aligns badly with human perceptions. Beyond providing insights into the current limitations of the metric, such examples, could be used to derive superior embedding models by using fine-tuning.

Our work strongly suggests that future research should transition from purely lexical metrics to embedding-based metrics that, as demonstrated, are more capable of quantifying semantic similarity. Further, this presents a promising avenue for future work on one of the major challenges in code review automation research: realistically assessing the performance of generative models. Our data and evaluation scripts are available online for replication and further scrutiny[2].

1.1 Related Work

To the best of our knowledge, this is the first empirical analysis of OpenAI sentence embeddings for assessing semantic similarity in the code review domain, based on human annotations and compared to BLEU, the primary non-binary similarity metric in this context. Related work in machine translation [13] and text summarization [1] have also shown that embedding models effectively capture semantic similarity. While our annotation and evaluation methods are similar, their results cannot be directly applied to code review automation, where both texts and the notion of similarity diverge significantly from general language due to jargon and programming language constructs.

2 Methodology

To investigate the alignment between human-perceived semantic similarity and automated similarity metrics in the context of code review comment generation, we designed an empirical study consisting of five steps: dataset preparation, metric definitions, sampling strategy, human annotation and statistical evaluation.

2.1 Dataset Preparation

Our study is based on the training dataset introduced by Tufano et al. in 2022 [14], which contains more than 134k real-world code review comments associated with code changes, of which we only use the comments. We selected this dataset for its size and wide usage in this domain [7,14,15]. Beyond computing the sentence embeddings for all comments in the dataset using OpenAI's `text-embedding-3-large` model via the OpenAI Batch API, we did no further pre-processing.

---
[2] 10.5281/zenodo.15823944.

2.2   Metric Definitions

We selected two metrics, one common lexical evaluation approach, and a state-of-the-art embedding based alternative.

BLEU-4. is a lexical similarity metric originating from the machine translation domain. It calculates the n-gram overlap between candidate and reference texts individually for different n-gram levels, typically up to four, and averages along this dimension [10]. BLEU was originally intended as a corpus level metric, however, as is common practice in code review automation research, we used it as a sentence-to-sentence similarity metric [14]. Specifically we used *sentence_bleu* from the *sacrebleu* library [11] and lower-cased comments before computation to prevent BLEU from performing worse merely due to different capitalization.

OPENAI-SIM. As recommended, we use the cosine similarity between the OpenAI embeddings review comments as our candidate embedding based metric [9].

2.3   Sampling Strategy

To ensure a balanced evaluation, we sampled pairs of comments based on their similarity scores under each metric. Our goal was to span the entire range of similarity values for both BLEU-4 and OPENAI-SIM.

1. We first sampled 100 comment pairs with BLEU-4 scores uniformly distributed across ten percent bins from $[0, 10)$ to $[90, 100)$.
2. We then similarly sampled an additional 100 comment pairs with uniformly distributed OPENAI-SIM.
3. We computed the missing OPENAI-SIM scores for the BLEU-4 sample and vice-versa.
4. After merging the two sets, we discovered that the *high-but-not-perfect* similarity range, $[90\%, 100\%)$ was underrepresented for both metrics. We therefore explicitly sampled additional pairs to improve coverage.
5. This process yielded a final set of 221 unique comment pairs, annotated with BLEU-4 and OPENAI-SIM scores.

For uniformly sampling both metrics, we used *faiss* indexes as approximate nearest neighbor heuristic to efficiently identify a smaller selection of candidates to sample from. Computing the full pairwise distance matrix is computationally infeasible on standard hardware and random sampling would have taken too long to find enough samples for each bin. For BLEU-4, we used ngram-based bag-of-words vectors for the index, as BLEU is based on ngram frequencies. For OPENAI-SIM, we built the index directly using the dense vector embeddings.

2.4   Human Annotation

To establish a human baseline for semantic similarity, three annotators with varying but relevant backgrounds were tasked with annotating the prepared dataset: (1) A professional software architect with 10 years of industry experience. (2) A post-graduate software engineering researcher. (3) A master's-level computer science student.

Each annotator independently rated the semantic similarity of all 221 comment pairs using a 5-point scale, which we denote as HUMAN-SCORE, and ranging from 0 (no similarity) to 4 (perfect similarity).

To ensure unbiased assessments, all samples were presented in randomized order, and no metric scores were shown to the annotators. The final, combined dataset comprises $3 * 221 = 663$ instances. We also experimented with using the median HUMAN-SCORE for each instance, resulting in a final dataset size of 221. Since this did not impact the results regarding RQ1 and RQ2, we decided to go with the combined dataset to preserve the variability between the annotators.

3   Evaluation

In the following, we evaluate how well the automated similarity metrics BLEU-4 and OpenAI-SIM align with the human annotations (RQ1), and discuss the current limitations of OpenAI-SIM (RQ2). Due to space limitations, we do not include all diagrams and analysis results in this paper. However, additional diagrams and statistical data are available in our replication package.

Metric Distributions: Figure 1 visualizes the distributions of the two automated metrics and the human annotations across the *combined dataset*. While the original sampling strategy ensured approximately uniformity for BLEU-4 and OpenAI-SIM independently, their combination leads to significant skew toward the extremes in the combined dataset, which we explain in the following.

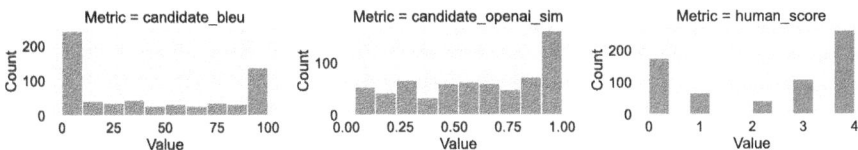

Fig. 1. Metric Distributions in the Annotated Dataset.

For HUMAN-SCORE (Fig. 1, right), one can clearly see a U-shaped distribution. This reflects humans' greater confidence in identifying very high or very low semantic similarity, while "medium" similarity is harder to judge. This is also supported by higher annotator agreement in these ranges[3].

---

[3] Figures are available in our replication package.

Similarly, BLEU-4 (Fig. 1, left) also shows a U-shaped distribution. Due to its purely lexical nature, it assigns very low scores when there is little or no lexical overlap; even in cases where OpenAI-SIM detects some latent similarity. This leads to a large number of instances with near-zero BLEU-4 scores. The opposite end of the scale also sees a concentration of samples, as a proportion of the high OpenAI-SIM pairs are due to almost identical wording, resulting in high BLEU-4 scores as well.

In contrast, OpenAI-SIM (Fig. 1, middle) is skewed primarily toward the high-similarity end. The BLEU-4-based samples in the combined dataset are mostly spread across the full OpenAI-SIM range, except for the very high BLEU-4 region. These pairs are often near-identical and, by extension, also receive very high OpenAI-SIM. This overlap pushes the distribution further toward the upper end.

This skew has analytical implications. Most notably, correlations computed across the combined dataset would be biased by overrepresented regions. To mitigate this, the following evaluations (3) also include multiple resampled subsets with uniform metric distributions.

RQ1 Analysis: To assess the alignment between BLEU-4 and HUMAN-SCORE, we computed Kendall's Tau, a statistical measure of correspondence between rankings. We selected this test because it is more stable for small datasets and tied ranks than alternatives such as Spearman's Rho [4]. Table 2 presents the results. Both BLEU-4 and OPENAI-SIM show significant correlations with HUMAN-SCORE, but OPENAI-SIM demonstrates consistently stronger alignment, as reflected in higher Tau- and lower p-values. A typical significance level in this domain is $\alpha = 0.01$ [14], which is undershot here by several orders of magnitude.

To control for distributional skew, we computed correlation statistics for both metrics on 100 random subsamples, each uniformly distributed across the metric range using 10% bins. As highlighted in Table 2, OPENAI-SIM outperformed BLEU-4 in all cases, even its weakest. Further, removing the extreme 15% of metric values from both ends of the metric distributions also did not change the outcome[3].

Table 2. Kendall's Tau correspondence tests between BLEU-4/OPENAI-SIM and HUMAN-SCORE. Blue: <u>Best</u> uniform resampling results for BLEU-4. Red: <u>Worst</u> uniform resampling results for OPENAI-SIM.

Metric	All Data		Resamp. Min		Resamp. Max		Resamp. Mean	
	p_val	statistic	p_val	statistic	p_val	statistic	p_value	statistic
BLEU-4	2.44e-111	0.66	5.67e-39	0.51	6.38e-28	0.6	3.05e-29	0.54
OPENAI-SIM	8.39e-130	0.71	2.07e-66	0.66	1.56e-58	0.7	4.14e-60	0.68

RQ1 Summary

In our experiments, **OPENAI-SIM** demonstrated statistically significant and stronger correlations with human ratings. These results suggest that its ability to capture semantic similarity of review comments is indeed superior to that of **BLEU-4**.

RQ2 Analysis: To better understand the limitations of OPENAI-SIM, we first visualized the distribution of human scores[3]. While low and high scores revealed clear patterns, the medium range (scores 1 3) exhibited substantial variability, making it difficult to establish a clear semantic partition.

We then analyzed the correlation between OPENAI-SIM and HUMAN-SCORE specifically within this medium range. Here, the correlation weakened, and results from random downsampling showed that statistical significance was no longer consistent across all subsamples.

Digging deeper, to rule out inter-annotator variability as a factor, we repeated the analysis using only instances where (1) two out of three annotators, or (2) all annotators, agreed. Yet even in these cases, a clear semantic mapping across the OPENAI-SIM range remained elusive. This is caused by instances where human annotations consistently indicated strong or perfect semantic similarity, but the metric failed to reflect this. Two such examples are shown below[4]

Candidate	Reference
rename to languages	rename to javaElement
In the live server, there are cases where s is null.	Do we need a null check on s?

In the first example, OPENAI-SIM appears to weigh the difference in concrete identifiers heavily, whereas annotators viewed it as a minor detail. In the second, the annotators correctly identified the strong semantic link between an observed runtime condition and the implied need for a null check, whereas OPENAI-SIM did not capture this.

RQ2 Summary

OPENAI-SIM aligns well with human annotations of high or low semantic similarity, however it struggles with medium-similarity cases; even when annotator agreement is high. Examples of these limitations, such as the metric's stronger weighting of mismatches between identifier names and constants, can be identified using our data.

---

[4] Additional examples are included in our replication package.

4   Threats to Validity

Construct Validity. Our scale for semantic similarity may not fully capture the underlying concept. While annotators struggled with medium-similarity cases, this likely reflects natural human uncertainty, not a flaw in the construct.

Internal Validity. Though sample sizes in our analysis were small, we performed uniform resampling a large number of times and found consistently strong effects with very low p-values. Thus, our findings are likely not due to randomness or sampling bias. Unknown confounding factors may still exist.

External Validity. With only three annotators and a single, albeit well-known and widely used, dataset [14], generalizability may be limited. While other annotators or datasets may introduce some variation, we do not expect the extent of such differences to significantly affect the overall conclusions.

5   Conclusion

In this work, we presented the first empirical study comparing embedding-based similarity to traditional lexical similarity as evaluation metrics for code review automation. Our results show that embedding similarity, specifically, OPENAI-SIM, is more closely aligned with human judgments than lexical metrics, specifically BLEU-4.

Therefore, we recommend that researchers should (at least) include embedding-based metrics alongside traditional metrics when evaluating automated code review systems. Furthermore, our method for identifying cases where metric scores diverge from human judgments offers a practical basis for collecting fine-tuning data to develop more reliable embedding models.

Ultimately, our work and methodology contribute to a shift in evaluation practices, paving the way for more semantically informed and human-aligned metrics in this domain.

Disclosure of Interests. The authors have no competing interests to declare that are relevant to the content of this article.

References

1. Clark, E., Celikyilmaz, A., Smith, N.A.: Sentence mover's similarity: automatic evaluation for multi-sentence texts. In: Proc. ACL (2019). https://doi.org/10.18653/v1/P19-1264
2. Guo, C., Yang, H., Huang, D., Zhang, J., Dong, N., Xu, J., Zhu, J.: Review sharing via deep semi-supervised code clone detection. IEEE Access (2020). https://doi.org/10.1109/access.2020.2966532
3. Gupta, A., Sundaresan, N.: Intelligent code reviews using deep learning. In: Proceedings of KDD (2018)
4. Kendall, M.G.: The treatment of ties in ranking problems. Biometrika (1945)

5. Li, L., et al.: Auger: automatically generating review comments with pre-training models. In: Proceedings of ESEC/FSE (2022). https://doi.org/10.1145/3540250.3549099
6. Li, Z., et al.: Automating code review activities by large-scale pre-training. In: Proceedings of ESEC/FSE (2022). https://doi.org/10.1145/3540250.3549081
7. Lu, J., Yu, L., Li, X., Yang, L., Zuo, C.: Llama-reviewer: advancing code review automation with large language models through parameter-efficient fine-tuning. In: Proceedings of ISSRE (2023). https://doi.org/10.1109/ISSRE59848.2023.00026
8. OpenAI: New embedding models and api updates (2025). https://openai.com/index/new-embedding-models-and-api-updates/
9. OpenAI: Vector embeddings: Which distance function should i use? (2025). https://platform.openai.com/docs/guides/embeddings
10. Papineni, K., Roukos, S., Ward, T., Zhu, W.J.: Bleu: a method for automatic evaluation of machine translation. In: Proceedings of ACL (2002)
11. Post, M.: A call for clarity in reporting BLEU scores. In: Proceedings of WMT (2018). https://doi.org/10.18653/v1/W18-6319
12. Shuvo, O., Mahbub, P., Rahman, M.M.: Recommending code reviews leveraging code changes with structured information retrieval. In: Proceedings of ICSME (2023). https://doi.org/10.1109/ICSME58846.2023.00029
13. Sun, K., Wang, R.: Textual similarity as a key metric in machine translation quality estimation. CoRR (2024). https://doi.org/10.48550/arXiv.2406.07440
14. Tufano, R., Masiero, S., Mastropaolo, A., Pascarella, L., Poshyvanyk, D., Bavota, G.: Using pre-trained models to boost code review automation. In: Proceedings of ICSE (2022). https://doi.org/10.1145/3510003.3510621
15. Zhou, X., Kim, K., Xu, B., Han, D., He, J., Lo, D.: Generation-based code review automation: How far are we. In: Proceedings of ICPC (2023). https://doi.org/10.1109/ICPC58990.2023.00036

Refactoring Detection Across Languages: Leveraging Java-Trained Models for Detecting Class-Level Refactorings in Kotlin

Mohammad Mehdi Afkhami[1] [ID], Iman Hemati Moghadam[2]([✉]) [ID],
Vadim Zaytsev[3] [ID], Mohammad Hossein Ashoori[4] [ID],
and Hossein Bazmandegan[4] [ID]

[1] Yazd University, Yazd, Iran
[2] Eindhoven University of Technology, Eindhoven, The Netherlands
i.hemati.moghadam@tue.nl
[3] University of Twente, Enschede, The Netherlands
vadim@grammarware.net
[4] Vali-e-Asr University of Rafsanjan, Rafsanjan, Iran

Abstract. Automating refactoring detection is an important goal in software engineering, with the potential to significantly reduce development time and costs. However, the complexity of refactoring tasks and the need for language-specific knowledge make the development of general-purpose solutions challenging. While machine learning models have proven effective in detecting refactorings in widely used languages like Java, their applicability to other languages–such as Kotlin–remains largely unexplored, especially due to the limited availability of labeled datasets.

This study investigates the feasibility of zero-shot cross-language refactoring detection by applying machine learning models trained on Java to identify refactorings in Kotlin. We employ *Random Forest classifiers*, originally trained on Java code, to detect *seven* types of class-level refactorings in Kotlin projects. For evaluation, we use RefDetect–an established refactoring detection tool–to extract 2,540 class-level refactorings from approximately 30,000 commits across 10 open-source Kotlin repositories. The Java-trained models are then applied to these projects, and their predictions are compared against RefDetect's results to assess accuracy and generalizability.

Our evaluation shows that the Java-trained models achieve an average F-score of 71% in detecting class-level refactorings in Kotlin. The model demonstrates strong recall (84%), indicating its ability to detect most actual refactorings, but precision is more modest (66%), suggesting a higher rate of false positives. Our analysis shows that model performance is influenced by both the type of refactoring and the characteristics of individual repositories. Refactorings such as *Move Class*, *Extract Interface*, and *Rename Class* consistently yield high F-scores–often above 90%. In contrast, less frequent refactorings like *Extract Subclass* and *Extract Superclass* yield significantly lower F-scores, around 40%. Detec-

D. Taibi and D. Smite (Eds.): SEAA 2025, LNCS 16081, pp. 46–63, 2026.
https://doi.org/10.1007/978-3-032-04190-6_4

tion accuracy for individual refactoring types also differs between repositories, implying that project-specific factors (e.g., code structure and refactoring frequency) influence model predictions. This observed variability highlights the potential benefits of tailoring detection strategies to match the unique characteristics of each project and refactoring type.

Keywords: Software refactoring · Machine learning · Zero-shot · Random forest · Kotlin · Java

1   Introduction

Refactoring restructures a system's codebase or architecture without changing its external behavior, making it easier to understand and modify [19]. Despite its prevalence among developers [21,27,38], refactoring remains error-prone, time-consuming, and often performed by experienced developers [8], making it costly. Effective refactoring requires recognizing its necessity, understanding its applicability, and applying it correctly. While automation aims to address these challenges [2,12,36,50], usability issues persist [7], leading developers to favor manual refactoring [21,48]. Consequently, improving refactoring automation remains an open challenge.

It is important to note that the decision to perform a refactoring is inherently subjective [9,13,25,49]. While objective criteria, such as quality metrics and design defects, provide valuable insights into detecting refactoring opportunities, the developer's judgment on the benefits of applying recommended refactorings remains essential.

Recent advances in machine learning have shown promise in identifying and recommending refactorings [6,14,35], much like human developers. These methods learn from past refactorings to predict future opportunities. By incorporating developer-driven knowledge, they provide more *reliable* and *practical* results in real-world scenarios.

A machine learning-based refactoring prediction pipeline typically involves three key steps: (i) data preparation, (ii) feature extraction and model training, and (iii) prediction. However, the adoption of these steps can be challenging [42].

A major initial challenge in applying machine learning to refactoring detection is the availability of high-quality training data [42,43,46]. In a supervised learning setting, this requires collecting software entities (e.g., classes, methods, fields) that have and have not undergone real-world refactorings, and annotating them with appropriate labels indicating the presence or absence of refactoring [10]. While languages like Java benefit from mature tools such as RefactoringMiner [51] that help extract such data, building large-scale, labeled datasets remains time-consuming and resource-intensive. For instance, Gerling [20] reported spending over 11,500 h–nearly 500 days–on data collection for Java refactoring analysis. However, similar datasets are lacking for other programming languages like Kotlin, which presents a substantial challenge. This scarcity of labeled data can significantly hinder the effectiveness of machine learning models and highlights the need for alternative approaches in data-scarce environments.

The second challenge arises from the difficulty in selecting the most suitable machine learning model and fine-tuning its parameters [42, 46]. This complexity is a key reason why, in practice, simpler models are often preferred [42].

Another challenge lies in the feature selection process, particularly in deciding which metrics to collect during the training phase. Despite various methods proposed to address these feature selection issues, it remains a critical factor that can lead to suboptimal performance in machine learning systems [42, 46].

Finally, one of the most significant challenges concerns the computational resources required for training. The chosen model and the size of the dataset can demand substantial computational power, often exceeding the financial and infrastructure capabilities of many research institutions.

These challenges, when combined, present significant barriers to the effective deployment of machine learning-based refactoring systems, particularly in languages with limited tooling and data availability. To address these challenges, we explore a zero-shot cross-language approach, where a model trained on refactoring data from one language (Java) is *directly* applied to another language (Kotlin) without additional training. This strategy leverages the generalizability of learned code metrics and patterns to make predictions in data-scarce environments, reducing the need for costly dataset construction and model training.

In our study, we build on the work of Aniche et al. [10], who assessed the effectiveness of supervised machine learning algorithms in predicting software refactoring in Java applications. They trained six different models on a dataset of over two million refactorings from 11,149 real-world projects [10]. Their findings indicated that Random Forest was the most effective, often achieving accuracies above 90% in 20 different refactorings at class, method, and variable-levels [10].

Building on this work, we use the *Random Forest* model as the foundation for our transfer learning approach.[1] We begin by extracting relevant metrics from Kotlin projects that align with those used in Java-based models. The Java-trained model is then applied to these metrics to predict refactoring opportunities in Kotlin, enabling knowledge transfer without fine-tuning. This strategy effectively addresses challenges such as limited labeled data, domain variation, and high computational cost by reusing insights learned from Java refactoring data to support Kotlin projects.

To evaluate our approach, we utilized RefDetect [23, 24, 26] to extract refactorings from 10 Kotlin projects, totaling approximately 30,000 commits and identifying approximately 2,500 *class-level refactoring instances* applied in Kotlin classes. We then compared the refactorings detected by the employed machine-learning models with those extracted by RefDetect. In this study, the model was applied to identify seven class-level refactorings, such as Move Class, Extract Class, and Rename Class, among others. This comparison yielded an average F-

---

[1] The Random Forest model is widely adopted for identifying refactoring opportunities, including code smells [56]. It constructs multiple decision trees during training and aggregates their predictions to improve accuracy [56].

score of 71%, showing the effectiveness of our transfer learning-based approach in detecting class-level refactorings in Kotlin using Java-trained models.

This paper makes the following contributions:

- **Zero-Shot Cross-Language Refactoring Detection**: We introduce a zero-shot approach for detecting refactorings across programming languages by applying machine learning models trained on Java to detect refactorings in Kotlin projects without the need for fine-tuning. The approach is evaluated by identifying seven class-level refactoring types in Kotlin.
- **Availability of Dataset and Implementation**: We provide an annotated Kotlin dataset containing over 34,000 refactorings spanning 19 distinct types, extracted from approximately 30,000 commits across 10 Kotlin projects [1]. Additionally, we present the implementation for extracting metrics from Kotlin projects and running the zero-shot refactoring detection model [1], supporting replication and further research.

The paper is structured as follows: Sect. 2 reviews the relevant literature, while the proposed approach is described in Sect. 3. Section 4 presents the empirical evaluation and results. Section 5 outlines the threats to validity, and Sect. 6 provides the conclusions and discusses future work.

2   Related Work

Research on identifying and recommending refactorings has explored various approaches, with significant attention given to heuristic-based methods [3, 36, 37] and machine-learning techniques [4, 11, 46]. Baqais and Alshayeb [12] highlight that search-based refactoring techniques are more prevalent than other approaches. However, recent advancements in machine learning and large language models have significantly impacted the field, demonstrating strong potential in identifying refactoring opportunities, recommending suitable transformations, and assisting in their application [6, 14, 30, 35]. This section provides an overview of relevant research, focusing specifically on machine learning and large language model-based techniques for refactoring identification.

Machine learning techniques have been extensively applied to detect refactoring opportunities, particularly in the area of code smell identification [31, 52, 54, 55]. These methods leverage a variety of features extracted from structural and semantic representations of code, commit history, naming patterns, and other relevant sources to differentiate between smelly and non-smelly code, including common code smells such as Long Methods, Feature Envy, and God Classes [41, 56]. In a recent study, Alazba and Aljamaan [5] demonstrated that combining multiple machine-learning classifiers into a single ensemble model enhances the accuracy of detecting code smells compared to using individual classifiers alone. This approach integrates the strengths of various classifiers to improve detection performance [5].

Although machine learning methods have proven effective in identifying refactoring opportunities, several challenges persist [41, 53, 56]. A key challenge is the difficulty of creating a universal classifier, as different code smells require tailored feature sets [34]. Furthermore, obtaining high-quality labeled datasets remains an obstacle due to problems like poor generalization, inconsistent labeling, class imbalance, and redundancy [53]. Although automated labeling methods generate training data by injecting code smells, these datasets often fail to reflect real-world conditions accurately [33]. Finally, machine learning models often lack interpretability, making it hard to know the rationale behind their predictions [14].

Machine learning models play a dual role, not only in identifying potential refactoring opportunities but also by suggesting suitable refactorings [14,41]. A typical approach involves first detecting code smells and then suggesting appropriate refactorings [31,52]. In contrast, some methods [10,16,39,40] eliminate the code smell detection step and directly predict which specific refactorings should be applied. This approach relies on the idea that common refactorings stem from standard developer practices, with the model trained on a large dataset of past refactorings.

Among the various proposed approaches, Aniche et al. [10] conducted a comprehensive empirical study evaluating supervised machine learning techniques for refactoring prediction, comparing six learning algorithms. Leveraging a dataset of over two million refactoring instances extracted by RefactoringMiner [51], their models achieved high accuracy in predicting 20 refactoring types across class, method, and variable levels–often exceeding 90%, with Random Forest delivering the best performance. Building on this foundation, Leij et al. [28] focused on recommending Extract Method refactorings in Java. In our study, we extend this line of work by applying the *Random Forest* model from Aniche et al. [10] to detect refactorings in Kotlin projects, without additional training on Kotlin-specific data.

Recent studies have explored advanced learning techniques. For example, Cui et al. [16] introduced REMS, a framework that detects Extract Method refactorings using a multi-view code property graph, analyzing code structure to identify patterns and predict refactorings. Following this, Cui et al. [15] developed HMove, a hypergraph learning-based method for recommending Move Method refactorings by modeling complex inter-class dependencies. Both frameworks leverage advanced learning methods to enhance prediction accuracy.

Recent studies [17,18,30,32,44,47,57] highlight the growing role of large language models (LLMs) in improving the detection of refactoring opportunities through the analysis and semantic understanding of code. For instance, Pomian et al. [44] developed EM-Assist, which uses LLM to suggest Extract Method refactorings. By combining LLM recommendations with static analysis, EM-Assist filters out irrelevant suggestions, achieving a recall rate of 53%, a 14% improvement over previous tools. As another example, Dilhara et al. [18] proposed PyCraft, a framework that integrates LLMs with Transformation by Example techniques to enhance code variant generation. PyCraft achieved an impressive F-score of 97%, underscoring the growing potential of LLMs to enhance refactoring tools. Similarly, Cui et al. [17] combine hypergraph neural networks with LLMs to suggest Extract Class refactorings, demonstrating a

44.4% F-score improvement over existing tools and offering more useful suggestions for developers.

Existing methods mainly concentrate on detecting refactoring opportunities within a single language, like Java. However, in a recent study, Sharma et al. [45] applied transfer learning by training models on one language (e.g., C#) and using them to identify code smells in another (e.g., Java). Similarly, Lin et al. [29] developed XCode, which leverages large-scale pre-training across multiple languages such as C#, C++, Java, and Python to detect code clones through shared representations. In another work, Gupta and Singh [22], examine the feasibility of transfer learning to predict code smells on unseen heterogeneous target data. Their method used modified domain invariant transfer kernel learning to transfer knowledge across source and target data sets, achieving notable results for detecting long methods and temporary field code smells. These techniques [22, 29, 45] demonstrate the feasibility of applying transfer learning to predict code smells across different programming languages and datasets. While our approach builds on a similar foundation–leveraging models trained in one language to support analysis in another–it differs in its objective: rather than identifying potential refactoring opportunities, we focus on directly predicting which refactorings should be applied.

3   Proposed Approach Overview

This study explores the extent to which a supervised machine learning model trained to identify refactoring opportunities in one object-oriented language (Java) can effectively predict refactoring opportunities in another (Kotlin). Our approach, outlined in Fig. 1, follows a four-step process. First, Java repositories are analyzed to identify both *applied refactorings* and *non-refactoring instances*, along with *relevant metrics* such as cohesion, coupling, method count, and bug fixes. Second, this data is used to train and evaluate a machine learning model for predicting refactoring opportunities in Java. In the third step, equivalent metrics are extracted from Kotlin projects. Finally, the trained model is applied to these Kotlin metrics to predict refactoring opportunities. While the first two steps, described in Sect. 3.1, build on the work of Aniche et al. [10], the last two steps, detailed in Sect. 3.2, are unique to our approach.

3.1   Training a Model for Java Refactoring Prediction

Aniche et al. [10] developed a supervised machine-learning approach to predict refactoring opportunities in Java. They first built a dataset of over two million refactoring operations from 8.8 million commits across 11,149 Java projects from GitHub, F-Droid, and Apache repositories. Using RefactoringMiner [51], they identified 20 types of refactorings at the class, method, and variable levels. They also extracted over one million non-refactoring instances where entities were modified without refactoring (e.g., adding a new method or field). Additionally, they collected various code (e.g., cohesion, coupling), process (e.g., lines added/deleted), and ownership metrics (e.g., number of authors). This dataset construction represents the first step of our approach, as illustrated in Fig. 1.

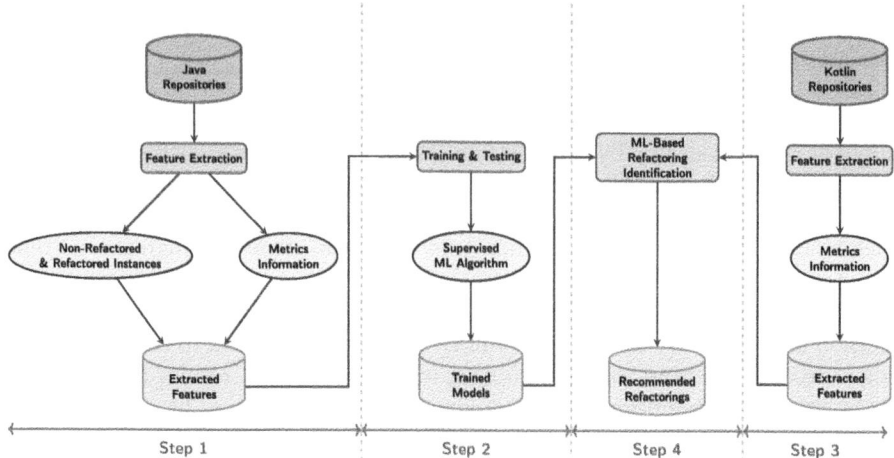

Fig. 1. Approach Overview: Extending Aniche et al.'s Method [10] for Cross-Language Refactoring Prediction in Kotlin.

In the second step, Aniche et al. [10] leveraged the dataset to train and evaluate six machine learning models–Logistic Regression, Naive Bayes, Support Vector Machine, Decision Trees, Random Forest, and Neural Network–for predicting refactoring opportunities in Java. Their results showed that *Random Forest* outperformed the others. They also found that models trained on data from diverse sources (GitHub, F-Droid, and Apache) achieved better performance than those trained on a single dataset. Following these insights, we adopt the *Random Forest* models trained on *heterogeneous* datasets for our predictions.

3.2   Applying the Java Model to Predict Kotlin Refactorings

As illustrated in Fig. 1, the *third step* involves extracting relevant metrics from Kotlin projects to identify their refactoring potential. Notably, we extract the same *source code*, *process*, and *ownership* metrics used during model training [10]. Table 1 summarizes the 44 metrics employed in our analysis.

Finally, in the *fourth step*, as shown in Fig. 1, the optimal model from step two (i.e., *Random Forest* trained on *heterogeneous* datasets), processes the metrics extracted from Kotlin projects (step 3) to identify potential refactorings.

4   Evaluation

In this section, we evaluate the effectiveness of models trained on Java refactoring datasets in identifying refactoring opportunities in Kotlin. We also analyze their strengths and limitations based on the observed results. Our evaluation is guided by the following research question: **To what extent do Java-trained models accurately identify class-level refactoring opportunities in Kotlin projects?**

Table 1. Metrics Collected for Refactoring Prediction at Class-Level [10]

Class-level (total of 44 metrics)

Source Code (37 metrics): CBO, WMC, RFC, LCOM, number of methods, number of static methods, number of public methods, number of private methods, number of protected methods, number of abstract methods, number of final methods, number of synchronized methods, number of fields, number of static fields, number of public fields, number of private fields, number of protected fields, number of default fields, number of final fields, number of synchronized fields, number of static invocations, lines of code, number of return statements, number of loops, number of comparison expressions, number of try catches, number of expressions with parenthesis, number of string literals, number of number constants, number of assignments, number of mathematical operators, number of declared variables, max number of nested blocks, number of anonymous classes, number of subclasses, number of lambda expressions, and number of unique words.

Process (3 metrics): Number of commits, number of bug fixes, and number of previous refactoring operations.

Ownership (4 metrics): Number of authors, number of minor authors, number of major authors, and author ownership.

4.1 Supported Refactoring Types

Our study supports seven class-level refactoring types: MOVE CLASS, RENAME CLASS, EXTRACT CLASS, EXTRACT SUPERCLASS, EXTRACT SUBCLASS, EXTRACT INTERFACE, and the composite refactoring MOVE & RENAME CLASS. Table 1 provides an overview of the 44 metrics extracted to support the identification of these refactoring types.

4.2 Refactoring Dataset

The dataset used in this evaluation, as detailed in Table 2, includes 10 Kotlin projects from our previous study [23]. These projects vary in size and structure, providing a diverse foundation for assessing the model's refactoring detection ability. We enriched the dataset by extracting refactorings from *Kotlin* and *Java* classes in these repositories using RefDetect [23], totaling 29,170 commits and 34,342 detected refactorings–17 times larger than the original dataset [23].

Although our dataset contains refactorings from both Kotlin and Java projects, *we evaluate the model exclusively on Kotlin class-level refactorings*, as evaluating Java cases offers no added insight into our research objective. While the focus of this study is on class-level refactorings, we also extract method- and field-level refactorings from the Kotlin projects using RefDetect [23]. As indicated in Table 1, the metric *number of previous refactoring operations*–used during training–reflects the cumulative count of refactorings applied up to each commit. Accurately capturing this history is essential, as the model leverages past refactoring activity to predict future refactorings.

Table 2. Summary of Kotlin Projects and Detected Refactorings

Repository	#Commits	#Refactorings	Repository	#Commits	#Refactorings
iosched	3,131	4,814	baseRecycler	1,507	1,464
plaid	1,276	1,258	picasso	1,706	2,323
sunflower	576	80	mirai	8,471	8,867
leakcanary	2,285	2,711	architecture-samples	805	998
okhttp	5,693	11,114	shadowsocks-android	3,720	713

In future work, we aim to extend our approach to predict refactorings at the method and field levels. Once integrated, this capability may eliminate the need for external refactoring detection tools, as the models themselves would identify these refactorings and use them to compute the cumulative number of prior refactorings for each commit. However, the success of this extension depends on several factors, which we discuss in Sect. 4.7.

4.3   Feature Extraction

We implemented a feature extraction script to collect metrics from Kotlin source code, as summarized in Table 1. While our extraction process is based on the work of Aniche et al. [10], certain metrics were adapted to accommodate language-specific differences in Kotlin, where direct equivalents were not available. These metrics serve as input features for the model to support refactoring prediction.

4.4   Experimental Design and Performance Evaluation

For each Kotlin project, starting from the first commit, we identify the classes that have changed between consecutive versions and extract their metric information, as detailed in Table 1. Since refactorings are applied only to these changed classes, we focus on extracting metrics for them. These metrics are then input into the model to assess whether class-level refactorings are recommended in each commit. This process continues until the last commit. *For each class-level refactoring type, we employ a separate Random Forest model*, following Aniche et al. [10], where a distinct model is trained per refactoring type.

If the model suggests a refactoring, we compare it with the refactoring dataset extracted by RefDetect. If the refactoring is present in the dataset, it is considered a true positive. On the other hand, if RefDetect identifies a refactoring that the model does not detect, we manually verify its validity. If the refactoring is valid, we classify it as a false negative, meaning the model failed to detect the refactoring. On the other hand, when the model suggests a refactoring that is not found in the RefDetect dataset, we classify it as a false positive. We do not manually validate these suggestions because verifying their validity would be a time-consuming and complex process. The rationale behind this decision is discussed below.

Table 3. Models Performance Across Refactoring Types

Refactoring	Ground Truth (#TP)	Precision	Recall	F-score
Move Class	1,865	0.96	0.96	0.96
Extract Interface	53	0.98	0.85	0.91
Rename Class	280	0.78	0.90	0.83
Extract Class	220	0.83	0.71	0.77
Move And Rename Class	75	0.48	1.00	0.65
Extract Superclass	31	0.28	0.81	0.42
Extract Subclass	16	0.29	0.69	0.41
Overall	**2,540**	**0.66**	**0.84**	**0.71**

In Aniche et al.'s study [10], models are trained to predict if a class will undergo a specific refactoring within a *50-commit window*. As a result, a prediction can occur at any commit within this window, making validation difficult when RefDetect does not detect a matching refactoring. Tracking changes over 50 commits is both time-consuming and error-prone. Moreover, the model's refactoring suggestion lacks detailed context. For example, in *Extract Class* refactoring, the model indicates a split but does not specify the new class's name, which may be determined only in subsequent commits. Additionally, repeated predictions across commits create ambiguity about which commit to evaluate. To ensure consistency, we consider a prediction valid only if the refactoring occurs in the same commit. While this conservative approach may classify some valid predictions as false positives, reducing precision, it does not affect recall, as actual refactorings are reliably detected.

4.5   Experiment Results

We assess the performance of each model using precision, recall, and F-score, standard metrics for evaluating classification accuracy. These measures are reported both per refactoring type and in aggregate. Table 3 presents the results for the seven supported class-level refactoring types, ordered by F-score. The column #TP indicates the number of true positives–i.e., refactorings identified by RefDetect in the Kotlin repositories.

Overall, the classifiers demonstrate strong generalization, capturing most true refactoring instances with an average recall of 84% and a precision of 66%, resulting in an average F-score of 71%. These results highlight a persistent challenge in reducing false positives–while the model effectively detects true cases, it also flags additional, unconfirmed ones. Notably, our *conservative evaluation*, as discussed in Sect. 4.4, treats all unconfirmed predictions as false positives, potentially underestimating the actual precision. A manual inspection of a sample of these cases suggests that some of these predictions could indeed be valid. Therefore, the true precision is likely *slightly* higher than reported in the table.

In terms of individual performance, the model excels with the *Move Class* refactoring, which clearly outperforms the others by offering a well-balanced detection capability. Both *Extract Interface* and *Rename Class* also exhibit robust performance, with *Rename Class* notably capturing nearly all relevant cases–albeit at the cost of precision. *Extract Class* performs at a moderate level, reflecting a balanced detection capacity. Conversely, while the model achieves complete recall with the *Move And Rename Class*, it does so at the expense of precision. The lowest performance is observed for the *Extract Subclass* (0.41) and then the *Extract Superclass* (0.42), suggesting that the model encounters difficulties distinguishing these refactorings.

Notably, some refactoring types demonstrate substantial imbalances between precision and recall, which may reflect the model's bias in favor of aggressive or conservative predictions. For example, *Move And Rename Class* achieves perfect recall (1.00) but at the cost of very low precision (0.48), indicating that while the model detects nearly all true cases, it frequently misclassifies unrelated changes as such. In contrast, *Extract Interface*, and *Extract Class* show a more balanced pattern (the only refactorings with higher precision than recall), suggesting a more conservative but reliable behavior. These disparities underline the need for refactoring-specific calibration, particularly when high precision is critical.

To assess the robustness of our models, we evaluated their performance across different repositories and refactoring types, as shown in Table 4. The results demonstrate strong generalization capabilities, particularly for common and structurally well-defined refactorings such as *Move Class*, *Rename Class*, and *Extract Interface*, which consistently achieved high F-scores across a range of projects. Notably, some medium-sized repositories such as *baseRecycler* and *plaid* achieved near-perfect detection across nearly all supported refactorings. However, this performance is not uniform across all repositories. In more complex or larger-scale projects such as *mirai*–which contains 1,586 identified refactorings– the model's accuracy shows greater variability, particularly for less frequent refactorings. For instance, the F-score for *Extract Subclass* in *mirai* drops to 30, compared to 100 in smaller repositories like *baseRecycler*. This disparity suggests that increasing project size and structural complexity may hinder precise detection, likely due to overlapping changes, diverse coding styles, or ambiguous patterns that challenge the model's assumptions. These limitations are not unexpected, given that the models were trained on Java but applied to Kotlin projects, underscoring the inherent difficulty of cross-language generalization.

Summary of Results for RQ

The Java-trained models effectively identify class-level refactorings in Kotlin code, with an average F-score of 71%. It performs reliably for well-defined and frequent refactorings like *Move Class* and *Rename Class*, and generalizes well across projects. However, performance is less consistent for rare or structurally complex refactorings, such as *Extract Subclass*, and *Extract Superclass*, particularly in repositories with more diverse code patterns.

Table 4. F-score Distribution by Repository and Refactoring Type

Repository	#TP	Extract Class	Extract Interface	Extract Subclass	Extract Superclass	Move and Rename Class	Move Class	Rename Class
sunflower	2	100	—	—	—	—	—	100
architecture-samples	24	67	—	100	100	100	100	94
plaid	170	97	100	—	—	100	100	96
baseRecycler	54	100	100	100	100	100	100	100
shadowsocks	41	73	—	0	38	0	76	45
picasso	9	0	100	100	100	—	100	—
leakcanary	392	90	77	100	89	100	99	94
iosched	223	84	96	0	50	93	99	95
mirai	1,586	45	91	30	33	56	95	75
okhttp	39	94	—	—	—	—	93	92

4.6 Challenges in Refactoring Prediction Evaluation

A key challenge in our study is accurately evaluating refactorings predicted by the model but not included in the ground-truth dataset. This difficulty arises from the inherent uncertainty in prediction-based refactoring detection, particularly regarding the timing and context of changes. The models employed in this study are trained to consider a K-commit window–set to 50 commits [10]–which serves as the timeframe within which refactoring is expected to occur after it is first predicted. The selection of K is a crucial aspect of the model's training process, as outlined in [10]. It ensures that even when the refactoring is delayed within this window, the model's prediction remains contextually valid. However, this also means that verifying predictions becomes challenging, as the refactoring may happen at any point within this K-commit window. Consequently, manual inspection must span a potentially long sequence of commits–an effort that is both time-consuming and error-prone.

The challenge is further compounded by the model's limited contextual output. For instance, in the case of *Extract Class*, the model may indicate that a class should be split but cannot specify the name, location, or structure of the newly created class–details that only become apparent once the refactoring is performed. This lack of specificity makes it difficult to align predictions with actual changes. Moreover, because the model can repeat the same prediction across multiple commits within the window, it becomes unclear how many distinct refactorings are being suggested. For example, if the model predicts five *Extract Class* operations for the same class across a 50-commit window, it is not possible to determine whether it is referring to five separate extractions or the same refactoring reiterated multiple times, especially in the absence of concrete identifiers like the name of the extracted class. Consequently, relying solely on the model's output for definitive refactoring detection can lead to misleading conclusions. In our study, we took a conservative approach by classifying any model-detected refactorings absent from the ground truth as false positives–even though some might indeed be correct.

As a solution, predictions should be treated as informed hypotheses rather than definitive outcomes. To mitigate false positives and enhance our confidence in the results, it is beneficial to cross-validate predictions with outputs from multiple specialized models while also considering the interrelationships among different refactoring types. For example, if the Extract Class model flags a potential refactoring, the prediction gains credibility when supported by related outputs from models such as Move Method or Move Field–which often recommend transferring associated methods and fields to the new class. Conversely, the lack of corroborating signals may point to an erroneous prediction. As another example, an Extract Superclass/Subclass operation is more convincing when accompanied by complementary actions like Pull Up or Push Down, which confirms the intended design changes without relying only on manual checks.

4.7   Challenges in Evaluating the Approach in New Languages

One metric used by our models is *the number of previously applied refactorings* (see Table 1), and our experiments reveal that the used models are highly sensitive to this parameter. This sensitivity makes evaluating the approach to new languages challenging, as a validated dataset of applied refactorings is needed. One might expect that with comprehensive models, we could start from an initial project version, use the models to generate candidate refactorings, and then use them for later versions. However, as discussed in Sect. 4.6, the inherent uncertainty–resulting by the K-commit window—renders this strategy unreliable. Although methods like ensemble modeling, threshold optimization, and enhanced contextual analysis can improve prediction accuracy and help filter out spurious results, these techniques still depend on a ground-truth dataset for proper calibration. Without such a dataset, adapting the approach to a new language remains difficult. Once validated, however, the model can effectively predict refactorings in the target language.

5   Threats to Validity

This section outlines the potential threats to the validity of our study, which may influence the results and their generalizability. These threats include factors related to the selected model, programming languages, refactoring detection tools, dataset characteristics, and validation processes.

A primary concern is that the model, trained on Java code, is used to detect refactorings in Kotlin. While Java and Kotlin have key differences, their similarities may lead to the model performing well on Kotlin but limit its generalizability to other languages. Additionally, the study concentrated on detecting class-level refactorings, which limits the scope of the analysis. Extending the model to also detect method, field, and variable-level refactorings could enhance its applicability. Furthermore, while Random Forest was used in this study, other machine learning models might yield different outcomes.

The model was evaluated on 10 Kotlin projects, which may not fully reflect real-world code diversity. Expanding the dataset to include a broader range of projects is essential for more robust conclusions. Additionally, metric extraction was based on prior work by Aniche et al. [10], with some adaptations for Kotlin. These modifications may introduce inaccuracies due to the absence of direct equivalents for certain Kotlin-specific language constructs not supported in Java. Finally, refactoring detection relied on RefDetect, which reported an F-score of 84% in its original validation [23]. Its limitations may impact the accuracy of detected refactorings, potentially affecting overall model performance. Improving RefDetect or exploring alternatives could enhance reliability.

6   Conclusion and Future Work

This study investigates the use of a machine learning model trained on Java projects to identify refactoring opportunities in Kotlin. We show that *Random Forest* models, trained on diverse Java datasets, can predict class-level refactorings in Kotlin with reasonable accuracy despite language differences. The model performed well with certain refactorings, such as *Move Class*, *Rename Class*, and *Extract Interface*, but faced challenges with others like *Extract Subclass* and *Extract Superclass*. While its effectiveness varied across Kotlin projects, the approach holds promise for cross-language refactoring detection and could extend to other object-oriented languages for automated code refactoring.

In future work, we aim to extend the model to detect method, field, and variable-level refactorings by adapting the model for these predictions. Additionally, we will investigate the model's applicability to other object-oriented languages, including C++ and C#. However, as noted in Sect. 4.7, a key requirement for evaluating the approach across different languages is the availability of datasets containing previously applied refactorings in those languages. Finally, since the model was trained on Java, there is a risk of overfitting to Java-specific patterns, limiting its generalization to Kotlin and other languages. To mitigate this, we plan to fine-tune the model on a *small* dataset to help it better understand the language structure and potentially improve its accuracy. In addition, we will explore ensemble approaches that aggregate outputs from different specialized models, particularly for refactorings that tend to occur together (e.g., Extract Class/SubClass/SuperClass in combination with Move, Pull-Up, and Push-Down refactorings), to further enhance prediction accuracy as discussed in Sect. 4.6.

Compliance with Ethical Standards

Disclosure of Interests. The authors have no competing interests to declare that are relevant to the content of this article.

References

1. Dataset, July 2025. https://doi.org/10.5281/zenodo.15836585
2. Abid, C., Alizadeh, V., Kessentini, M., do Nascimento Ferreira, T., Dig, D.: 30 years of software refactoring research: a systematic literature review. arXiv preprint arXiv:2007.02194 (2020). https://doi.org/10.48550/arXiv.2007.02194
3. AbuHassan, A., Alshayeb, M., Ghouti, L.: Software smell detection techniques: a systematic literature review. J. Softw. Evol. Process **33**(3) (2021). https://doi.org/10.1002/smr.2320
4. Al-Shaaby, A., Aljamaan, H., Alshayeb, M.: Bad smell detection using machine learning techniques: a systematic literature review. Arab. J. Sci. Eng. **45**(4), 2341–2369 (2020). https://doi.org/10.1007/s13369-019-04311-w
5. Alazba, A., Aljamaan, H.: Code smell detection using feature selection and stacking ensemble: an empirical investigation. Inf. Softw. Technol. **138** (2021). https://doi.org/10.1016/j.infsof.2021.106648
6. Alazba, A., Aljamaan, H., Alshayeb, M.: Deep learning approaches for bad smell detection: a systematic literature review. Empirical Softw. Eng. **28**(3) (2023). https://doi.org/10.1007/s10664-023-10312-z
7. Alcocer, J.P.S., Antezana, A.S., Santos, G., Bergel, A.: Improving the success rate of applying the extract method refactoring. Sci. Comput. Program. **195** (2020). https://doi.org/10.1016/j.scico.2020.102475
8. AlOmar, E.A., Peruma, A., Newman, C.D., Mkaouer, M.W., Ouni, A.: On the relationship between developer experience and refactoring: an exploratory study and preliminary results. In: Proceedings of the 42nd IEEE/ACM International Conference on Software Engineering Workshops (2020). https://doi.org/10.1145/3387940.3392193
9. Amal, B., Kessentini, M., Bechikh, S., Dea, J., Said, L.B.: On the use of machine learning and search-based software engineering for ill-defined fitness function: a case study on software refactoring. In: Proceedings of the 6th International Symposium on Search-Based Software Engineering. Springer (2014). https://doi.org/10.1007/978-3-319-09940-8_3
10. Aniche, M., Maziero, E., Durelli, R., Durelli, V.H.: The effectiveness of supervised machine learning algorithms in predicting software refactoring. IEEE Trans. Softw. Eng. **48**(4) (2020). https://doi.org/10.1109/TSE.2020.3021736
11. Azeem, M.I., Palomba, F., Shi, L., Wang, Q.: Machine learning techniques for code smell detection: a systematic literature review and meta-analysis. Inf. Softw. Technol. **108** (2019). https://doi.org/10.1016/j.infsof.2018.12.009
12. Baqais, A.A.B., Alshayeb, M.: Automatic software refactoring: a systematic literature review. Softw. Qual. J. **28**(2), 459–502 (2019). https://doi.org/10.1007/s11219-019-09477-y
13. Bavota, G., De Lucia, A., Di Penta, M., Oliveto, R., Palomba, F.: An experimental investigation on the innate relationship between quality and refactoring. J. Syst. Softw. **107** (2015). https://doi.org/10.1016/j.jss.2015.05.024
14. Chen, X., et al.: Deep learning-based software engineering: progress, challenges, and opportunities. Sci. China Inf. Sci. **68**(1) (2025). https://doi.org/10.1007/s11432-023-4127-5
15. Cui, D., et al.: Three heads are better than one: suggesting move method refactoring opportunities with inter-class code entity dependency enhanced hybrid hypergraph neural network. In: Proceedings of the 39th IEEE/ACM International Conference on Automated Software Engineering (2024). https://doi.org/10.1145/3691620.3695068

16. Cui, D., et al.: REMS: recommending extract method refactoring opportunities via multi-view representation of code property graph. In: Proceedings of the 31st IEEE/ACM International Conference on Program Comprehension. IEEE (2023). https://doi.org/10.1109/ICPC58990.2023.00034
17. Cui, D., et al.: One-to-one or one-to-many? Suggesting extract class refactoring opportunities with intra-class dependency hypergraph neural network. In: Proceedings of the 33rd ACM SIGSOFT International Symposium on Software Testing and Analysis (2024). https://doi.org/10.1145/3650212.3680379
18. Dilhara, M., Bellur, A., Bryksin, T., Dig, D.: Unprecedented code change automation: the fusion of LLMs and transformation by example. Proc. ACM Softw. Eng. **1**(FSE) (2024). https://doi.org/10.1145/3643755
19. Fowler, M.: Refactoring: Improving the Design of Existing Code. Addison-Wesley (1999)
20. Gerling, J.: Machine learning for software refactoring: a large-scale empirical study. Master's thesis, Delft University of Technology, Delft, The Netherlands (2020)
21. Golubev, Y., Kurbatova, Z., AlOmar, E.A., Bryksin, T., Mkaouer, M.W.: One thousand and one stories: a large-scale survey of software refactoring. In: Proceedings of the 29th ACM Joint Meeting on European Software Engineering Conference and Symposium on the Foundations of Software Engineering. ACM (2021). https://doi.org/10.1145/3468264.3473924
22. Gupta, R., Singh, S.K.: A novel transfer learning method for code smell detection on heterogeneous data: a feasibility study. SN Comput. Sci. **4**(6) (2023). https://doi.org/10.1007/s42979-023-02157-6
23. Hemati Moghadam, I., Afkhami, M.M., Kamalipour, P., Zaytsev, V.: Extending refactoring detection to Kotlin: a dataset and comparative study. In: Proceedings of the 31st IEEE International Conference on Software Analysis, Evolution and Reengineering. IEEE (2024). https://doi.org/10.1109/SANER60148.2024.00034
24. Hemati Moghadam, I., Cinnéide, M.Ó., Zarepour, F., Jahanmir, M.A.: RefDetect: a multi-language refactoring detection tool based on string alignment. IEEE Access **9** (2021). https://doi.org/10.1109/ACCESS.2021.3086689
25. Hemati Moghadam, I., Ó Cinnéide, M., Sardarian, A., Zarepour, F.: Model-based source code refactoring with interaction and visual cues. J. Softw. Evol. Process **36**(5) (2024). https://doi.org/10.1002/smr.2596
26. Hemati Moghadam, I., Sleurink, M., Zaytsev, V.: Surpassing threshold barriers: evaluating the efficacy of nature-inspired algorithms in detecting applied refactorings. In: Proceedings of the 10th International Conference on Computer Technology Applications (2024). https://doi.org/10.1145/3674558.3674568
27. Kim, M., Zimmermann, T., Nagappan, N.: An empirical study of refactoring challenges and benefits at Microsoft. IEEE Trans. Softw. Eng. **40**(7) (2014). https://doi.org/10.1109/TSE.2014.2318734
28. van der Leij, D., Binda, J., van Dalen, R., Vallen, P., Luo, Y., Aniche, M.: Data-driven extract method recommendations: a study at ING. In: Proceedings of the 29th ACM Joint Meeting on European Software Engineering Conference and Symposium on the Foundations of Software Engineering (2021). https://doi.org/10.1145/3468264.3473927
29. Lin, Z., et al.: XCode: towards cross-language code representation with large-scale pre-training. ACM Trans. Softw. Eng. Methodol. **31**(3) (2022). https://doi.org/10.1145/3506696
30. Liu, B., Jiang, Y., Zhang, Y., Niu, N., Li, G., Liu, H.: Exploring the potential of general purpose LLMs in automated software refactoring: an empirical study. Autom. Softw. Eng. **32**(1) (2025). https://doi.org/10.1007/s10515-025-00500-0

31. Liu, B., et al.: Deep learning based feature envy detection boosted by real-world examples. In: Proceedings of the 31st ACM Joint European Software Engineering Conference and Symposium on the Foundations of Software Engineering (2023). https://doi.org/10.1145/3611643.3616353

32. Liu, H., et al.: RefBERT: a two-stage pre-trained framework for automatic rename refactoring. In: Proceedings of the 32nd ACM SIGSOFT International Symposium on Software Testing and Analysis (2023). https://doi.org/10.1145/3597926.3598092

33. Liu, H., Jin, J., Xu, Z., Zou, Y., Bu, Y., Zhang, L.: Deep learning based code smell detection. IEEE Trans. Softw. Eng. **47**(9) (2021). https://doi.org/10.1109/TSE.2019.2936376

34. Liu, H., Xu, Z., Zou, Y.: Deep learning based feature envy detection. In: Proceedings of the 33rd ACM/IEEE International Conference on Automated Software Engineering (2018). https://doi.org/10.1145/3238147.3238166

35. Malhotra, R., Jain, B., Kessentini, M.: Examining deep learning's capability to spot code smells: a systematic literature review. Cluster Comput. **26**(6) (2023). https://doi.org/10.1007/s10586-023-04144-1

36. Mariani, T., Vergilio, S.R.: A systematic review on search-based refactoring. Inf. Softw. Technol. **83** (2017). https://doi.org/10.1016/j.infsof.2016.11.009

37. Mohan, M., Greer, D.: A survey of search-based refactoring for software maintenance. J. Softw. Eng. Res. Develop. **6**(1), 1–52 (2018). https://doi.org/10.1186/s40411-018-0046-4

38. Murphy-Hill, E., Parnin, C., Black, A.P.: How we refactor, and how we know it. IEEE Trans. Softw. Eng. **38**(1) (2012). https://doi.org/10.1109/TSE.2011.41

39. Nyamawe, A.S.: Mining commit messages to enhance software refactorings recommendation: a machine learning approach. Mach. Learn. Appl. **9** (2022). https://doi.org/10.1016/j.mlwa.2022.100316

40. Nyamawe, A.S., Liu, H., Niu, N., Umer, Q., Niu, Z.: Feature requests-based recommendation of software refactorings. Empir. Softw. Eng. **25**(5), 4315–4347 (2020). https://doi.org/10.1007/s10664-020-09871-2

41. Nyirongo, B., Jiang, Y., Jiang, H., Liu, H.: A survey of deep learning based software refactoring. arXiv preprint arXiv:2404.19226 (2024). https://doi.org/10.48550/arXiv.2404.19226

42. Paleyes, A., Urma, R.G., Lawrence, N.D.: Challenges in deploying machine learning: a survey of case studies. ACM Comput. Surv. **55**(6) (2022). https://doi.org/10.1145/3533378

43. Polyzotis, N., Roy, S., Whang, S.E., Zinkevich, M.: Data lifecycle challenges in production machine learning: a survey. ACM SIGMOD Rec. **47**(2) (2018). https://doi.org/10.1145/3299887.3299891

44. Pomian, D., et al.: Next-generation refactoring: combining LLM insights and IDE capabilities for extract method. In: Proceedings of the IEEE International Conference on Software Maintenance and Evolution. IEEE (2024). https://doi.org/10.1109/ICSME58944.2024.00034

45. Sharma, T., Efstathiou, V., Louridas, P., Spinellis, D.: Code smell detection by deep direct-learning and transfer-learning. J. Syst. Softw. **176** (2021). https://doi.org/10.1016/j.jss.2021.110936

46. Sharma, T., et al.: A survey on machine learning techniques applied to source code. J. Syst. Softw. **209** (2024). https://doi.org/10.1016/j.jss.2023.111934

47. Shirafuji, A., Oda, Y., Suzuki, J., Morishita, M., Watanobe, Y.: Refactoring programs using large language models with few-shot examples. In: Proceedings of the 30th Asia-Pacific Software Engineering Conference. IEEE (2023). https://doi.org/10.1109/APSEC60848.2023.00025
48. Silva, D., Tsantalis, N., Valente, M.T.: Why we refactor? Confessions of github contributors. In: Proceedings of the 24th ACM SIGSOFT International Symposium on Foundations of Software Engineering. ACM (2016). https://doi.org/10.1145/2950290.2950305
49. Simons, C., Singer, J., White, D.R.: Search-based refactoring: metrics are not enough. In: Proceedings of the International Symposium on Search Based Software Engineering. Springer (2015). https://doi.org/10.1007/978-3-319-22183-0_4
50. Singh, S., Kaur, S.: A systematic literature review: refactoring for disclosing code smells in object oriented software. Ain Shams Eng. J. **9**(4) (2018). https://doi.org/10.1016/j.asej.2017.03.002
51. Tsantalis, N., Ketkar, A., Dig, D.: RefactoringMiner 2.0. IEEE Trans. Softw. Eng. **48**(3) (2020). https://doi.org/10.1109/TSE.2020.3007722
52. Yu, D., Xu, Y., Weng, L., Chen, J., Chen, X., Yang, Q.: Detecting and refactoring feature envy based on graph neural network. In: Proceedings of the 33rd IEEE International Symposium on Software Reliability Engineering. IEEE (2022). https://doi.org/10.1109/ISSRE55969.2022.00051
53. Zhang, F., et al.: Data preparation for deep learning based code smell detection: a systematic literature review. J. Syst. Softw. (2024). https://doi.org/10.1016/j.jss.2024.112131
54. Zhang, Y., Dong, C.: MARS: detecting brain class/method code smell based on metric–attention mechanism and residual network. J. Softw. Evol. Process **36**(1) (2024). https://doi.org/10.1002/smr.2403
55. Zhang, Y., Ge, C., Hong, S., Tian, R., Dong, C., Liu, J.: DeleSmell: code smell detection based on deep learning and latent semantic analysis. Knowl. Based Syst. **255** (2022). https://doi.org/10.1016/j.knosys.2022.109737
56. Zhang, Y., Ge, C., Liu, H., Zheng, K.: Code smell detection based on supervised learning models: a survey. Neurocomputing **565** (2024). https://doi.org/10.1016/j.neucom.2023.127014
57. Zhang, Z., Xing, Z., Ren, X., Lu, Q., Xu, X.: Refactoring to Pythonic idioms: a hybrid knowledge-driven approach leveraging large language models. Proceedings ACM Softw. Eng. **1**(FSE) (2024). https://doi.org/10.1145/3643776

Towards a Service-Oriented Infrastructure for Distributed Systems with Heterogeneous AI Accelerators

Marius Kreutzer[1]([✉])[iD], Maximilian Kirschner[1], and Jürgen Becker[1,2]

[1] FZI Research Center for Information Technology, 76131 Karlsruhe, Germany
{kreutzer,kirschner,juergen.becker}@kit.edu
[2] Karlsruhe Institute of Technology, 76131 Karlsruhe, Germany

Abstract. The increase of heterogeneous AI accelerators, particularly in edge computing, creates significant challenges for building unified and scalable distributed acceleration systems. Existing approaches often lack support for diverse hardware types across multiple nodes, limit scalability, or introduce significant communication overheads. This paper introduces a novel service-oriented infrastructure concept to overcome these limitations, enabling management of distributed, heterogeneous AI accelerators. The proposed architecture features three core modules: a versatile Model Database supporting various formats and artifacts, hardware-specific Runners acting as execution agents, and a central Scheduler for system-aware task allocation. Key contributions include: 1) A conceptual framework for truly distributed, heterogeneous AI acceleration services, contrasting with single-node or vendor-locked solutions; 2) A modular design enabling extensibility and seamless lifecycle management crucial for long-term edge deployments; and 3) A design incorporating direct data communication paths between sources, accelerators, and sinks, aimed at reducing end-to-end latency compared to proxy-based or application-offloading methods by eliminating intermediate hops. The evaluations show advantages in edge scalability, hardware flexibility, built-in failure recovery, and latency advantages over existing solutions, with a reduction of up to 50% in communication-based latency compared to existing approaches. This infrastructure maximizes resource utilization by unlocking access to a diverse, heterogeneous pool of accelerators, providing robust AI acceleration in complex, dynamic environments, particularly at the network edge.

Keywords: Distributed Systems · AI Accelerator · Service-Oriented Architecture

1 Introduction

The rise of diverse AI accelerators, such as GPUs, TPUs, FPGA- and ASIC-based accelerators, has significantly impacted the performance and scalability of

D. Taibi and D. Smite (Eds.): SEAA 2025, LNCS 16081, pp. 64–78, 2026.
https://doi.org/10.1007/978-3-032-04190-6_5

AI workloads, especially in edge systems, with each accelerator offering a unique tradeoff in terms of performance, power efficiency, precision and capabilities [6]. However, integrating these diverse accelerators into distributed systems remains challenging, especially providing a unified interface for low-overhead, system- and hardware-aware AI acceleration [10]. This paper introduces a service-oriented infrastructure concept designed to address these challenges, proposing a unified and scalable solution for distributed AI acceleration. The proposed infrastructure consists of three core modules: the model database, the runner, and the scheduler, each designed to ensure compatibility, scalability, and ease of integration.

The core contributions of this work are centered around a conceptual framework for truly distributed, heterogeneous AI acceleration services, in contrast to single-node or vendor-locked solutions. We present an interoperable architecture based on three key modules the Model Database, Runner, and Scheduler. A key aspect of the design is the inclusion of direct data communication paths intended to reduce latency compared to alternatives. The potential scalability and flexibility is analyzed through qualitative comparisons with existing approaches.

Despite advances in model formats like ONNX, deploying AI workloads in distributed, heterogeneous environments remains plagued by several key challenges that current solutions fail to adequately address. First, many existing frameworks are constrained to a single compute node, limiting multi-node scalability. Second, they often lack true hardware heterogeneity, focusing on a single vendor's ecosystem (e.g., NVIDIA for rCuda and Triton), thereby not utilizing the full range of available hardware accelerators. Third, they provide little to no support for failure recovery in case of an unresponsive compute node or system lifecycle management, for newly introduced hardware, which are all critical for resilient systems. Finally, many powerful solutions are designed for data center clusters, overlooking the specific constraints of edge deployment. These gaps highlight the need for a new architectural concept designed specifically to provide a scalable, resilient, and truly heterogeneous acceleration service. Our proposed service-oriented infrastructure directly targets these challenges. This paper is structured as follows. After this introduction, follows a description of related works in Sect. 2. After this, the concept is described in Sect. 3 and evaluated in Sect. 4. The paper then closes with a discussion of the results and a conclusion in Sect. 5.

2   Related Work

The rapid advancement of artificial intelligence has gone hand in hand with the development of a diverse array of hardware accelerators, each with unique behavior and interfaces. This heterogeneity poses significant challenges for developers and system integrators seeking a universal interface to utilize these distributed accelerators effectively.

Hardware accelerators for the embedded systems market come in many variants: From CPU-integrated solutions with matrix or vector extensions to System-on-a-Chip (SoC) platforms, including offerings from Qualcomm (Hexagon NPU),

NVIDIA (Jetson, DRIVE), and SiMa.ai (MPSoC platform) to add-on accelerators, such as NVIDIA's GPUs, AMD's FPGA platforms, and Tenstorrent's solutions among a large number of other offers by different companies. Some examples even integrate up to 14 different accelerators in a single chip [4], although not all being AI accelerators, highlights the importance of supporting multiple different accelerators.

These accelerators are typically bundled together with accompanying toolchains. The first group of these accompanying toolchains are hardware vendor libraries such as NVIDIA's CUDA, AMD's ROCm, or Qualcomm's QNN. These are bound to a single vendor or even a single product family. Then there are more universal libraries, such as Intel's oneAPI, SYCL, openCL or Vulkan. These generally target a broader subset of hardware devices, but are still limited. Then there are intermediate frameworks, which typically consist of a frontend and different backends. The frontend gives developers a unified interface, while the backend is then able to reproduce the results on different hardware targets, for example, TVM [3], IREE [8], or the Open Neural Network Exchange (ONNX) runtime. While these support most of the common accelerators, more niche accelerators are either not supported at all or are lagging behind the official, vendor-supplied tools. While some toolchains execute their input model file directly on hardware, others first compile it to an intermediate format, specially tailored for the used accelerator. While accelerator runtimes still struggle with fragmentation, the ONNX format has emerged as a universal intermediate format for AI models in response to the limited convertibility between different AI frameworks [1]. ONNX offers a standardized representation for machine learning models, facilitating interoperability between different frameworks and hardware support libraries. The ONNX format is versioned, if new features are required for newer model architectures. While models in the ONNX format can be executed directly through the ONNX runtime, some vendors use the ONNX format as an input format for their own compiler or runtime. This universality across different hardware accelerators highlights the potential of ONNX as a foundational element for a universal AI acceleration concept.

Despite progress in model representation, existing networked approaches to distributed AI acceleration exhibit limitations. PAAM, from Enright et al. [5], addresses real-time AI acceleration within ROS 2 environments but supports only a single compute node with heterogeneous hardware accelerators, limiting multi-node scalability and failure recovery in case of unresponsive or failing compute nodes.

Varghese et al. [11] propose an Acceleration-as-a-Service method for financial applications based on rCuda (remote Cuda), enabling flexible accelerator usage across the system. However, its dependency on CUDA confines its use to NVIDIA GPUs, limiting its effectiveness in environments that require hardware heterogeneity.

NVIDIA Triton is a serving platform that enables serving of different models on a large number of underlying accelerators. A Triton instance is always restricted to a single compute node. And even though Triton supports multiple accelerators on the same node, it is limited to NVIDIA GPUs, CPUs, and AWS Inferentia, a deep learning accelerator developed and deployed by Amazon [7,9]. Seldon Core 2 is one approach to solve the single-node restriction of NVIDIA Triton and offers a way to scale across multiple Kubernetes nodes, but it relies on a single scheduler that first receives all requests and directs them to a suitable Triton instance [2].

These solutions highlight a significant gap in the current state of the art: no current approach effectively encompasses multiple different hardware accelerators across different compute nodes in a distributed system. The limitations of specialized libraries and the constraints of existing networked acceleration frameworks highlight the necessity for a universal infrastructure. Such an infrastructure would need to integrate heterogeneous AI accelerators into a single, unified interface, facilitating scalability, interoperability, and efficient utilization of distributed resources.

In summary, while there are numerous tools and libraries designed to use the power of AI accelerators, their specialization and vendor-specific limitations prevent them from serving as universal interfaces. The emergence of ONNX offers a promising pathway toward partial standardization. Still, the lack of direct runtime support of ONNX across all hardware accelerators indicates a clear need for a new, universal infrastructure that especially targets distributed, heterogeneous systems. Current approaches restrict the system in the choice of accelerators or limit the resources to a single central compute node.

3 Proposed Concept for Distributed AI Acceleration

This section presents the conceptual framework for the proposed system, which is designed to distribute AI workloads across a system of machines equipped with heterogeneous AI accelerators. A general technical overview is given first, including the intended deployment environment and foundational assumptions. The following subsection gives a detailed description of each component. Then, the possible options for metrics and telemetry data for scheduling are detailed, followed by the interactions between these components and the design decisions taken.

The targeted deployment environment consists of multiple different compute nodes, where each node can have one or multiple accelerators. Communication, control, and data are sent through a service-oriented protocol, like ROS2, DDS, or eCAL. Sensors can either be connected to a compute node, which then offers the sensor's data, or the sensor itself offers the data directly through an integrated network connection. The network architecture is shown in Fig. 1. A typical deployment could be in an Industry 4.0 environment, where components have long lifetimes, but changes to the environment are common. Compute nodes could be located centrally, off-site in the cloud or distributed in the factory.

The system architecture allows for dynamic changes to its components after initial deployment. Possible changes include the addition of new models, updates to existing models, or the removal of models, as well as the addition, modification, or removal of hardware accelerators and compute nodes. Recognizing that

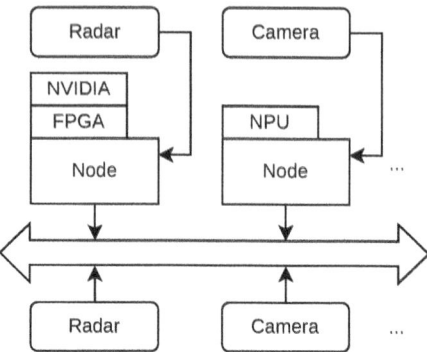

Fig. 1. Block Diagram Showing the Considered Systems with multiple ECUs and Sensors

effective AI processing already demands substantial data flow, it is assumed that sporadically transferring larger model files within the network is feasible. Additionally, the data source (origin) and data sink (destination) for processing results may be distinct from the application initiating the AI acceleration request. Furthermore, it is assumed that accelerators can either directly execute ONNX model files, or that their vendor toolchain can use ONNX as an input format. To support the latter case and broaden hardware compatibility, the system's Model Database manages both original ONNX files and any necessary pre-compiled, accelerator-specific artifacts generated from them.

3.1   Components

The core architecture of the proposed system consists of three primary components: the scheduler, the model database, and the runner. The scheduler serves as the central management module, receiving acceleration requests from applications, and allocating AI tasks to suitable runners based on resource availability and the model's computational requirements. The model database functions as a repository, storing AI models in different variants and performance metrics to support the informed allocation of workloads. Runners operate as hardware-specific execution units, directly interfacing with the scheduler to accept tasks, report status, and provide real-time data on resource usage and execution metrics. Figure Fig. 2 illustrates the interactions among these components, emphasizing data flow and command structure within the system.

Scheduler. The scheduler serves as the central control unit within the system, responsible for managing AI acceleration requests from applications, allocating these requests across available runners, and dynamically re-balancing workloads as needed. The scheduler tracks all acceleration requests and manages their lifetime. A modular, updatable scheduling strategy executes the scheduler's actual decision-making process. The strategy provides two different functionalities to

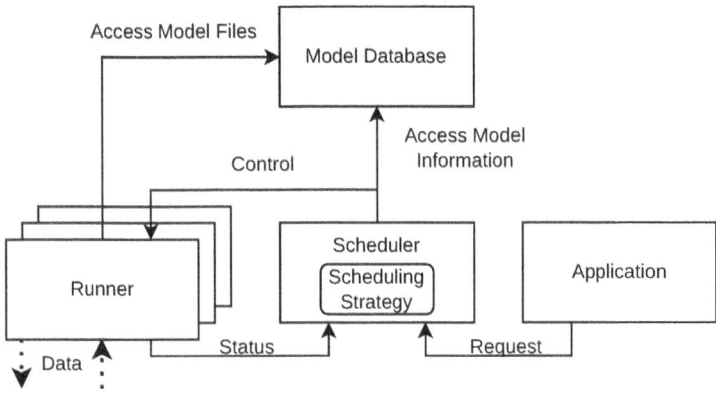

Fig. 2. Block Diagram Showing Interactions of Main Components, Data Movements shown as Dashed Line

the scheduler. First is an incremental placement of a new workload, and second is the global optimization of all existing workloads. The first option is generally preferred, as a global optimization can lead to the transfer of workloads between different compute nodes, resulting in temporary extra compute needs. In both cases, the scheduling strategy is supplied with the complete available system information to enable an intelligent decision. This includes the resource usage and task load of each available accelerator, and information about the available models, such as the different quantizations or prunings, their performance, and precision for the different accelerators. In addition, the application's requirements are also used, such as its preference for faster processing versus higher precision or any upper or lower limits on throughput and latency. A latency-sensitive application might hint at the strategy to prioritize assigning a task to a runner with accelerators known for low inference times, potentially accepting a lower-precision model variant (e.g., INT8) if available and suitable. Conversely, an application requiring high accuracy might lead the strategy to select a runner capable of handling a higher-precision model (e.g., FP16 or FP32), even if it incurs slightly higher latency or utilizes a less power-inefficient accelerator. The core logic for selecting a suitable accelerator is shown in Listing 1.1. First, all currently active runners and details about the requested model are fetched. Then the strategy checks for every quantization option if an accelerator has enough free resources. The implementation of this check depends on the underlying hardware platform, and relevant factors are free memory and compute time. The strategy then selects the best accelerator and quantization based on the preference of the application.

```
# Input: request as req
accelerators = available_accelerators()
model = model_info(req.model)

viable_options = []
```

```
# Find all viable (accel, variant, metric) pairs
for accel in accelerators:
  for variant in model.runnable_variants(accel):
    if resources_available(accel, variant, model):
      metrics = perf_metrics(accel, variant, model)
      viable_options.append((accel, variant, metrics))

if viable_options: return GlobalReSchedule
return select_best(viable_options, req.preferences)
```

Listing 1.1. Scheduler Strategy Pseudocode

Model Database. The model database serves as the central repository for model files accessible to runners. Each model can exist in multiple different variants. These can differ in their quantization, but also in additional post-processing steps, such as pruning. If the same model is trained on different datasets, or for a different purpose, it's considered a seperate model, and not a variant. Models are stored in the ONNX format, with optional pre-compiled artifacts tailored to specific accelerators generated from the original ONNX model file. These pre-compiled artifacts may include fully cross-compiled models for edge-focused accelerators that are not able to execute ONNX models directly or accelerator-specific intermediate representations, such as CUDA artifacts. The model database can receive intermediate model formats generated from runners. In addition to the models itself, the database also stores parameterizable pre- and postprocessing modules. The model database maintains records of the performance metrics reported by the runners, which the scheduler then also utilizes for optimized workload distribution. To ensure consistency and maintain up-to-date execution environments, the model database also manages model versioning and notifies runners of any updates to models.

Runner. Runners function as the execution agents within the system, each dedicated to a specific accelerator to simplify the addition and removal of hardware accelerators. A runner's core responsibility is the communication with the scheduler. This involves registering with the scheduler during startup and continuously reporting the currently executed workloads and the resource usage. When a runner gets assigned an inference task, the runner creates a worker instance specific to the request, similar to spawning a worker thread. This worker instance is then responsible for the lifecycle of a single acceleration request. This starts with retrieving the model in the requested quantization variant from the model database. The worker then establishes direct connections to the data sources and sinks to facilitate direct dataflow. In addition to inference, runners also serve as testing instances. For models with unknown behavior, the runtime characteristics can be measured with randomized input data, with the results being reported back to the model database.

Application, Data Sinks and Sources. While applications, data sinks, and sources are not an inherent part of the proposed concept, they play an integral role and are therefore included. Applications relevant to the concept require some acceleration for the execution of AI models. They can also be data sinks, sources, or both at the same time. In this case, they can also take over parts, or the complete pre- or postprocessing. Data sinks and sources only provide or consume data and have no inherent requirement for AI acceleration.

3.2 Metrics and Telemetry

For the scheduler to make intelligent, system-aware decisions, it must have access to the current system status and model/ accelerator information. This data can be divided into static characteristics and dynamic, real-time telemetry. These metrics, in conjunction with the application-specific requirements outlined in the Scheduler description (Sect. 3.1), form the knowledge base for the system.

Static and Benchmarked Data: This category includes information that is static and is primarily stored in the Model Database or the Scheduler itself. It describes the potential of each model and accelerator:

- Resource Footprint: The required system memory, accelerator memory, and other resources for each model variant and accelerator pair.
- Performance Benchmarks: Pre-measured metrics such as expected latency, throughput, and power consumption for each model variant on a specific accelerator.
- Model Quality: The intrinsic performance of a model variant, such as its mAP score, independent of hardware.
- Accelerator Hardware Capabilities: The total available resources of an accelerator, such as total VRAM or theoretical peak performance

Dynamic Real-Time Telemetry. Each runner provides a periodic status update to the scheduler, containing two key types of information:

- **Committed Workload:** A list of the models currently allocated to the accelerator, along with their agreed-upon performance contracts (e.g., minimum inferences per second).
- **Current Resource Usage:** A snapshot of essential resource metrics, such as currently used system memory and available accelerator memory.

3.3 Interactions

The proposed system's effectiveness relies on interactions between components and deliberate architectural choices. Figure 3 illustrates the core workflow for handling an acceleration request: During the first step, the application submits an acceleration request containing model identifiers, precision requirements, and upper and lower rate limits, as well as optional pre- and postprocessing modules through a standardized service endpoint. The scheduler then generates a

unique identifier to enable lifecycle management. For the next step the scheduler utilizes the scheduling strategy to decide on a runner to execute the model
on. The strategy has access to real-time system information, including accelerator load, model availability, inference metrics for each runner, and the application's quality-of-service preference. After the scheduling strategy has selected
the most suitable runner and quantization variant, taking into consideration the
differences between them, the acceleration request is sent to this runner. During
this step, the runner requests and receives the requested model files from the
model database, as well as any pre- or postprocessing modules. If accelerator-
specific artifacts are available, they are preferred over the ONNX files. The model
database broadcasts any changes in model availability. During the final step, the
runner establishes a dedicated connection to the data sources and sinks. By
skipping unneeded hops for the data, the latency is minimized and the control
and data flow are separated. This is shown in Fig. 3. In the example, the data
source and sink are separate from the application, but the application could
also take one or both of these roles. The separation of control and data flow
also allows for easier deployment of serverless control functions, which have a
potentially lower startup time, but also are often slower during execution. Each
runner updates the scheduler at regular intervals about its status. Included are
the current resource utilization, active instances, and, for each instance, a list
of completed inferences with a timestamp since the last report. If the scheduler
detects any abnormalities or receives no status updates from a scheduler, a fault
is assumed and all impacted instances are then rescheduled to other runners. If
an update for an existing model is added to the database, runners are informed
about the new update. They can then re-fetch the new model and restart the
worker with the updated model.

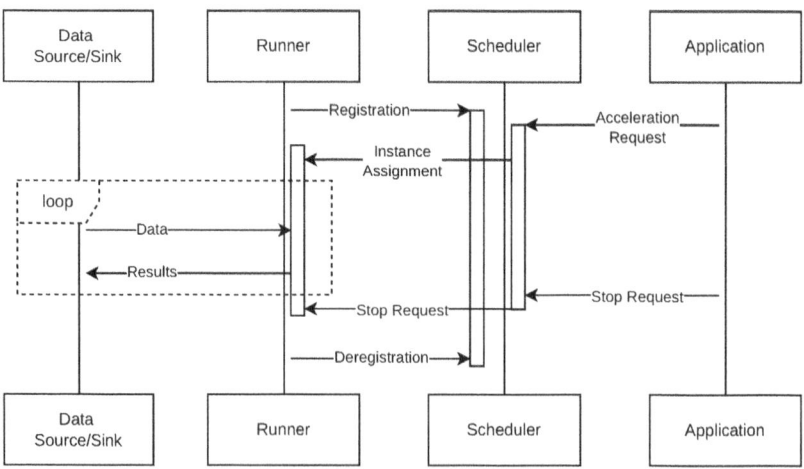

Fig. 3. Sequence Diagram showing Application, Scheduler, Runner, and Data Source/
Sink Interaction

When a new accelerator is introduced to the system or during the initial startup, the runner registers with the scheduler. To enable hardware-specific scheduling, the runner's registration includes the accelerator type. As accelerators of the same family often behave similarly, only differing by their resource configuration, the family is also included in the registration. If new accelerators are introduced, which behave differently to the existing ones, an update to the scheduling strategy is also required. Therefore, the scheduling strategy must be implemented as an exchangeable module, so that any further changes require no other updates to the system. If a hardware accelerator is removed from the system, it unregisters from the scheduler, also causing all instances to be moved to other runners.

4 Evaluation

The evaluation is split into two separate parts. First is an analysis of the benefits of direct source to accelerator to sink communication. This is followed by a qualitative comparison with existing approaches.

4.1 Direct-Path Latency

The direct connection from the data source to the accelerator and then to the data sink promises reduced latency, due to the removal of unnecessary hops in the data path.

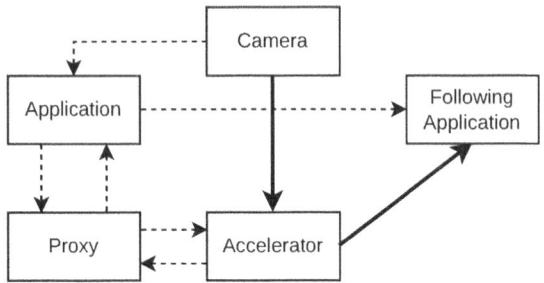

Fig. 4. Comparison of direct communication (solid) and indirect communication (dashed)

Figure 4 shows an exemplary setup, which is used as the model for the communication latency evaluation. All components are independent and connected through a network. The camera is the data source, with the following applications representing the data sink. For the presented approach (direct), the data goes directly from the camera to the application and then to the sink. The dashed lines (Proxy) indicate an approach similar to NVIDIA Triton. First, the application gathers the input data and sends it to the accelerator through a load-balancing proxy. The application is only then able to forward the data to the following applications. The third approach (Offload) is not pictured directly in Fig. 4, but follows the dashed approach, skipping the proxy, so the application is able to offload directly to an accelerator.

Table 1. End-to-End Communication Latency for Different Data Path Options (Full/Reduced Output)

Setup	Mean [ms]	Maximum [ms]	Std Dev [ms]
Direct	40.1/12.5	51.1/15.1	2.653/0.535
Proxy	76.6/25.1	88.5/30.4	3.717/1.086
Offload	47.5/16.8	62.3/25.4	2.802/1.099

This exemplary setup was then simulated by two different computers to measure the communication latencies: a laptop with a Ryzen 7 PRO 7840U CPU and a Raspberry Pi 3B+ connected through a gigabit connection. Each measurement was repeated 1000 times with a 10-measurement warm-up period. To ensure the measurements accurately reflect the simulated system, communication between all simulated components was performed over the network, explicitly avoiding faster on-host IPC. Table 1 shows the measured latency for each of the three setups. The data size is oriented on the input and output size of the YOLOv8 model. Input is given as a 640×640 image in RGB (1.229 MB) and the output either as 2.822 MB if fully sent or 33.6 kB if the output is reduced to only the top 100 detections. The direct data connection shows a 16% reduction for full and a 26% reduction, if reduced, compared to the offloading approach and a 48%, or 50%, reduction compared to the proxy-based approach. It must be noted that this measurement does not take into consideration the actual processing time and any compression that could be applied to either the input or the output, such as JPEG encoding.

4.2 Comparison with Existing Systems

This subsection now moves from direct performance results to an external feature comparison between the presented solution, other existing approaches, and applications directly accessing hardware accelerators. The overview is presented in Table 2. ✓ means supported; ✗ means not supported, ▼ indicates the relevant point is not applicable for the comparison, while ? indicates unknown. The following approaches were selected to represent the different categories: PAAM, a real-time focused scheduler; rCuda, as a remote GPU virtualization framework; Nvidia Triton, as an industry-oriented inference server; and direct application access to accelerators.

Multi-Node describes the ability of the approach to scale horizontally to multiple nodes. PAAM is the only approach that does not support multi-node

Table 2. Qualitative comparison between the presented concept and other solutions

Feature	Direct Access	PAAM	rCuda	Triton	Proposed
Multi-Node	✓	✗	✓	✓	✓
Hardware heterogeneity	✗	✓	✗	✗	✓
Failure Recovery	✗	✗	✗	✗	✓
System Lifecycle Management	✗	✗	✗	✗	✓
Edge Deployment Focus	✓	✓	✗	✗	✓
Single Access Accelerators	✗	✓	▼	▼	✓
Model Loading Time	✓	?	?	✓/✗	✗

acceleration, with NVIDIA Triton supporting horizontal scaling trough extensions, such as Seldon Core 2. This limits scalability in larger systems, where a single compute node is not sufficient for all tasks. In the case of direct access, multi-node scalability is given, but is limited to the availability of suitable nodes. The proposed concept, in contrast, is able to provide multi-node scalability through the separation of the runner into a standalone component. **Hardware heterogeneity** shows the approach's ability to interface with multiple different kinds of hardware accelerators. PAAM is the only other approach offering hardware heterogeneity; in contrast, rCuda and NVIDIA Triton are both limited to the acceleration of tasks through either CPU or NVIDIA accelerators. Direct access from applications is also typically restricted to a single hardware accelerator. No other approach has built-in **failure recovery** or the ability to recover from failing or unreachable hardware accelerators. The presented approach is able to recover from failed or degraded accelerators or even complete compute nodes. **System lifecycle management** has three different aspects to it: The model, accelerator, and scheduling algorithm lifecycle. While new accelerators of the same class can be introduced, e.g., NVIDIA accelerators in rCuda or NVIDIA Triton, or the model can be changed, these approaches are unable to add accelerators based on a different architecture during runtime. Direct access applications have no inherent lifecycle management and would require custom changes. PAAM does not mention how new models would be introduced. **Edge deployment focus** shows the approaches focus on edge deployment. Both rCUDA and Nvidia Triton have, due to the reliance on NVIDIA accelerators, their focus on HPC cluster use-cases with multiple high-power NVIDIA cards, which are untypical to edge systems, where power usage and size often play a critical role. The last comparison point is shared access to **single access accelerators**. Some accelerators, such as Google's TPUs, only allow a single application to access it at the same time. Therefore, multiple direct access applications running at the same time would be unable to share these accelerators. With hardware access moved to a shared layer, such as in PAAM or the proposed concept, parallel access is possible. As rCuda and NVIDIA Triton both only target multi-access accelerators, this comparison point is not applicable. One disadvantage for distributed solutions is the time from acceleration request until the model is ready for processing, or **Model Loading Time**. While direct access applications can immediately load the model, networked on-demand solutions have to first route the request to an appropriate accelerator and then load the model. NVIDIA Triton can mitigate this issue by pre-loading models, which in turn results in higher memory usage. The presented approach with multiple, different accelerators also has an inherent need for a more complex scheduler, delaying the initial assignment further.

5   Discussion and Conclusion

This work introduced a new concept for deploying and scheduling AI workloads in distributed, heterogeneous edge systems, resolving existing limitations of previous approaches such as PAAM and NVIDIA Triton. The proposed concept is based on separating access to hardware accelerators from applications. The management of hardware accelerators is split into three dedicated components: The model database, the scheduler, and the runners. Applications signal their AI acceleration needs to the central scheduler, which assigns the workload to a suitable runner. The runner then gets the model and future model updates from the model database. In case of failure or degradation of a runner, the scheduler moves the workload to a different runner.

The proposed concept addresses challenges in distributed edge AI acceleration through architectural solutions that were absent in prior work. Highlighted are five key advances enabled by these: **Control-data decoupling**: The control of AI accelerators is separated from the dataflow, enabling direct source, accelerator, and receiver data communication, removing additional data hops present in frameworks such as NVIDIA Triton. **ONNX and beyond**: while the approach fundamentally relies on ONNX as the base for model files, the support for artifacts extends the concept to accelerators, which are not able to directly execute ONNX models, while at the same time decreasing the startup time for some accelerators directly supported. **Cross-node hardware virtualization**, although PAAM enables access to non-shareable accelerators such as the Google Coral TPU, the proposed approach extends this functionality across distributed systems. **Edge lifecycle adaptability**, the modular design combined with the hardware registration mechanisms allows seamless integration of new accelerators without distribution of other active workloads, addressing the long lifecycle of edge systems. **Failure Recovery** as a core feature highlights another focus on edge systems, where there is a higher chance of single components failing or being unreachable for some time.

While this paper presents a conceptual framework, its full realization and application will require future research in several areas. A primary focus is the scheduling strategy itself. To take full advantage of the available heterogeneous hardware, such a scheduler must navigate complex trade-offs beyond a single allocation based on resource availability. For instance, it needs to be aware of the physical system topology, considering network latency, power consumption, and thermal constraints to make an optimal decision. On the resource management level, it must also prevent fragmentation, potentially by reallocating workloads. Furthermore, identifying the relevant telemetry data to accurately measure the impact of each model on each accelerator is another future challenge. Lastly, the presented concept assumes that model variants are trained in an offline preparation step. This hinders the introduction and quick adoption of new accelerators and models. Including this step would help in creating an evolving system. Addressing these areas will be crucial for moving this concept towards a robust, production-grade infrastructure. Furthermore, the scheduling strategy's effectiveness is based on rich telemetry. Future work should therefore focus on identifying and using granular metrics that accurately capture the impact of different models on specific hardware. Finally, to create a truly evolving and adaptable system, the current assumption of offline model preparation could be extended to include online model compilation and optimization, enabling the rapid adoption of new hardware and model architectures. Addressing these areas will be crucial for realizing a truly flexible and hardware-agnostic acceleration infrastructure.

Acknowledgments. This work was supported by the German Federal Ministry of Research, Technology and Space (BMFTR) with funding number 16ME0818.

References

1. onnx/onnx. https://github.com/onnx/onnx
2. SeldonIO/seldon-core. https://github.com/SeldonIO/seldon-core
3. Chen, T., et al.: TVM: an automated end-to-end optimizing compiler for deep learning, pp. 578–594 (2018). https://www.usenix.org/conference/osdi18/presentation/chen
4. Dos Santos, M.C., et al.: 14.5 A 12nm Linux-SMP-capable RISC-V SoC with 14 accelerator types, distributed hardware power management and flexible NoC-based data orchestration. In: 2024 IEEE International Solid-State Circuits Conference (ISSCC), vol. 67, pp. 262–264 (2024). https://doi.org/10.1109/ISSCC49657.2024.10454572
5. Enright, D., Xiang, Y., Choi, H., Kim, H.: PAAM: a framework for coordinated and priority-driven accelerator management in ROS 2, pp. 81–94. IEEE Computer Society (2024). https://doi.org/10.1109/RTAS61025.2024.00015
6. Griessl, R., et al.: Evaluation of heterogeneous AIoT accelerators within VEDLIoT. In: 2023 Design, Automation & Test in Europe Conference & Exhibition (DATE), pp. 1–6 (2023). https://doi.org/10.23919/DATE56975.2023.10137021
7. Hutt, G., Viswanathan, V., Nadolski, A.: Deliver high performance ML inference with AWS Inferentia. https://d1.awsstatic.com/events/reinvent/2019/REPEAT_1_Deliver_high_performance_ML_inference_with_AWS_Inferentia_CMP324-R1.pdf
8. Liu, H.I.C., Brehler, M., Ravishankar, M., Vasilache, N., Vanik, B., Laurenzo, S.: TinyIREE: an ML execution environment for embedded systems from compilation to deployment **42**(5), 9–16 (2022). https://doi.org/10.1109/MM.2022.3178068
9. NVIDIA: NVIDIA Triton Inference Server – NVIDIA Triton Inference Server. https://docs.nvidia.com/deeplearning/triton-inference-server/user-guide/docs/index.html

10. Sibanda, M., Bhero, E., Agee, J.: AI edge processing - a review of distributed embedded systems. In: 2023 31st Southern African Universities Power Engineering Conference (SAUPEC), pp. 1–6 (2023). https://doi.org/10.1109/SAUPEC57889.2023.10057624

11. Varghese, B., Prades, J., Reaño, C., Silla, F.: Acceleration-as-a-service: exploiting virtualised GPUs for a financial application. In: 2015 IEEE 11th International Conference on E-Science, pp. 47–56 (2015). https://doi.org/10.1109/eScience.2015.15

Define-ML: An Approach to Ideate Machine Learning-Enabled Systems

Silvio Alonso$^{(\boxtimes)}$, Antonio Pedro Santos Alves , Lucas Romao ,
Hélio Lopes , and Marcos Kalinowski

Pontifical Catholic University of Rio de Janeiro (PUC-Rio), Rio de Janeiro, Brazil
{smarques,apsalves,lromao,lopes,kalinowski}@inf.puc-rio.br

Abstract. [Context] The increasing adoption of machine learning (ML)
in software systems demands specialized ideation approaches that
address ML-specific challenges, including data dependencies, technical
feasibility, and alignment between business objectives and probabilistic system behavior. Traditional ideation methods like Lean Inception
lack structured support for these ML considerations, which can result
in misaligned product visions and unrealistic expectations. [Goal] This
paper presents Define-ML, a framework that extends Lean Inception with
tailored activities–Data Source Mapping, Feature-to-Data Source Mapping, and ML Mapping–to systematically integrate data and technical
constraints into early-stage ML product ideation. [Method] We developed and validated Define-ML following the Technology Transfer Model,
conducting both static validation (with a toy problem) and dynamic validation (in a real-world industrial case study). The analysis combined
quantitative surveys with qualitative feedback, assessing utility, ease of
use, and intent of adoption. [Results] Participants found Define-ML effective for clarifying data concerns, aligning ML capabilities with business
goals, and fostering cross-functional collaboration. The approach's structured activities reduced ideation ambiguity, though some noted a learning curve for ML-specific components, which can be mitigated by expert
facilitation. All participants expressed the intention to adopt Define-ML.
[Conclusion] Define-ML provides an openly available, validated approach
for ML product ideation, building on Lean Inception's agility while aligning features with available data and increasing awareness of technical
feasibility.

Keywords: Ideation · Machine Learning · ML-Enabled Systems

1 Introduction

As machine learning (ML) continues to permeate software products across
diverse sectors, pressure increases to ideate ML-enabled systems that are
both innovative and feasible. However, early-stage ideation for such systems
is uniquely challenging. ML features are inherently probabilistic, dependent on

© The Author(s), under exclusive license to Springer Nature Switzerland AG 2026
D. Taibi and D. Smite (Eds.): SEAA 2025, LNCS 16081, pp. 79–96, 2026.
https://doi.org/10.1007/978-3-032-04190-6_6

data quality and availability, and often misunderstood by stakeholders unfamiliar with the limitations of ML [14]. Without proper guidance, teams risk proposing solutions that are technically infeasible, misaligned with business objectives, or disconnected from the realities of the available data.

Despite the popularity of structured ideation approaches like Lean Inception [6], these methods were designed for traditional software product ideation and lack explicit support for ML-specific considerations. They do not offer explicit mechanisms to evaluate data readiness or to align feature ideas with ML capabilities. This is particularly important considering that managing customer expectations and aligning requirements with data are among the main pain points of engineering ML-enabled systems [2,12].

To address this gap, we introduce Define-ML, a framework that extends Lean Inception with three structured activities: Data Source Mapping, Feature-to-Data Source Mapping, and ML Mapping. These activities guide teams in grounding their ideation process in data realities, clarifying the technical feasibility of ML features, and fostering alignment between business stakeholders, domain experts, and ML practitioners.

Define-ML was developed and validated following the Technology Transfer Model [9]. We conducted a static validation using a simulated problem with industry practitioners and a dynamic validation through a real-world case study in the retail domain. In both settings, participants reported increased clarity, improved alignment, and strong intent to adopt the framework. Define-ML offers a structured approach to ideate ML-enabled systems, helping to connect business vision and ML feasibility from the beginning of product development.

The remainder of this paper is organized as follows. Section 2 presents the background and related work. Section 3 presents a description of the research methodology. Sections 4 presents the Define-ML approach. Sections 5 and 6 describe the static and dynamic validations. Section 7 discusses the results and threats to validity. Finally, Sect. 8 concludes the paper.

2   Background and Related Work

Several ideation approaches exist for software products, *e.g.*, Design Thinking [5], Design Sprints [3], Lean Startup [15], and Lean Inception [6]. We adopt Lean Inception as our foundation due to its structured yet flexible approach to product visioning and feature prioritization, qualities particularly valuable for ML-enabled systems, where technical feasibility must align with business goals. In this section, we provide the background on the Lean Inception workshop and review related work on ideating ML-enabled systems.

2.1   Lean Inception

Lean Inception is an ideation workshop that fosters teamwork and collaboration [6]. It involves assembling a cross-functional team, encompassing developers, designers, business analysts, and representatives of different stakeholders.

The process is conducted in a workshop format, usually spanning about a week, to ensure a concentrated and intensive period of discussion, brainstorming, and decision-making.

Creating a shared product vision is a significant outcome of the Lean Inception process. This vision becomes the guiding beacon for all subsequent activities and decisions. A central element of the approach is the deep understanding and prioritization of customer needs. This is achieved by identifying user personas and delving into their problems and challenges. This understanding is important to ensure that the project or product directly addresses user requirements. Alongside this, journey mapping is employed to visualize and understand the user's experience, identifying key features and interaction points.

An important result of a Lean Inception workshop is the prioritization of product features. The team works to identify the most critical elements for the initial product version, often termed the Minimum Viable Product (MVP), and decides what can be developed later.

2.2   Ideation of ML-Enabled Products

Jansen and Colombo [10] address the challenges designers face in integrating ML into their processes. They propose the *Mix & Match Machine Learning Toolkit*, which aims to support ML-enabled ideation by providing tangible and accessible ML knowledge. The toolkit consists of physical tokens that represent data types (*e.g.*, labeled/unlabeled audio, images, text) and ML capabilities (*e.g.*, categorize, recommend, generate), along with a web interface for exploring and combining elements. Leveraging Tangible User Interfaces (TUIs), the approach fosters exploration and collaboration among designers, making ML concepts more approachable without requiring deep ML expertise. Workshops with design students showed that the toolkit supported both learning and ideation. It helped participants grasp basic ML concepts and generate novel ideas by offering a structured approach. It also influenced their language and thinking, as they adopted ML-related terminology during ideation.

Yildirim *et al.* [18] address AI integration challenges through human-centered design, developing a resource catalog of 40 common AI features across domains. Their study revealed that moderate AI performance often delivers more practical value than high-performance solutions. The authors created a flexible design tool featuring examples and an AI capability grammar, which effectively expanded idea generation in design sessions. A complementary study [19] examined how practitioners use human-AI guidelines (more specifically, the *People+AI Guidebook*) when designing AI-enabled products. The findings emphasize the need for enhanced problem-framing tools to support initial design phases. Although the guidelines are valuable for education and communication, practitioners explicitly reported insufficient early-stage ideation support.

3   Research Methodology

We followed the seven steps proposed by the Technology Transfer Model [9] and describe them hereafter. Figure 1 presents how the steps interact with each other. The instruments and data collected in each conducted study are available in our open science repository[1].

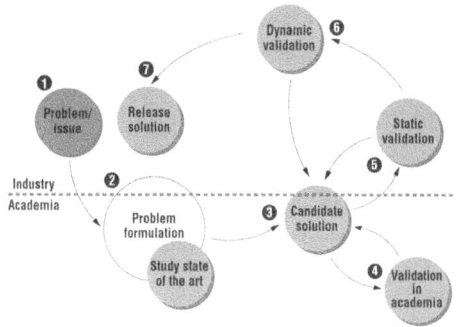

Fig. 1. Technology transfer model proposed by Gorschek *et al.* [9]

3.1   Step 1. Identify Problem Based on Industry Needs

The ideation and development of ML-enabled products pose unique challenges distinct from traditional software systems. A key difficulty is aligning requirements with available data, complicated by ML's non-deterministic nature [2]. Managing stakeholder expectations is also challenging, often due to limited AI literacy [14]. Communicating ML limitations and uncertainties [2], along with translating vague business goals into concrete functional requirements [14,17], further complicates the process.

Several MVP ideation practices, such as Lean Inception and Design Thinking, have been cataloged in a recent systematic mapping [1]. However, these approaches lack explicit support for ML-specific concerns–such as data dependencies, model feasibility, and the need to align ML capabilities with business goals and user needs [8]. While some recent efforts address ML component specification [10,18], they do not provide a comprehensive framework tailored to the ideation of ML-enabled systems. Our R&D experiences developing ML-enabled systems with industry partners [11,13] reinforce these observations of the literature from a practical perspective. We also found that traditional ideation approaches fall short when applied to ML-enabled systems, underscoring the need for adapted methods that explicitly address ML integration while preserving agility and user-centricity.

---

[1] https://doi.org/10.5281/zenodo.15277758.

3.2   Step 2. Formulate the Research Problem

Based on the issue described in the previous step, we defined our research problem as introducing and evaluating Define-ML, an approach that extends Lean Inception to support ML-enabled system ideation. Define ML includes tailored activities like Data Source Mapping, Feature-to-Data Source Mapping, and ML Mapping, helping teams identify necessary data sources and suitable ML capabilities, ensuring that the ideated ML capabilities are not only aligned with business goals but also technically feasible.

3.3   Step 3. Formulate a Candidate Solution

To better support the ideation of ML-enabled products, we propose an adaptation of the Lean Inception approach. The main change consists of introducing three new activities: *Data Source Mapping*, which aims at identifying and discussing the quality of available data sources; *Feature-to-Data Source Mapping*, which connects the features to the necessary data sources to implement them; and *ML Mapping*, an adaptation of the Mix and Match ML toolkit. The latter guides teams in selecting appropriate ML techniques by mapping problem requirements to feasible algorithmic solutions. These extensions address gaps in traditional Lean Inception workshops, which often overlook technical constraints and data dependencies critical to ML projects. The candidate solution is explained in detail in Sect. 4.

3.4   Step 4. Conduct Lab Validation

As an initial academic validation, a two-hour workshop was conducted to assess the Define-ML approach. The session took place at the ExACTa PUC-Rio lab and was attended by 18 participants (three professors, six Ph.D. students, six MS students, and three of the lab's hired professionals engaged in industry-academia collaborations). This group brought a wealth of experience, particularly in ideation workshops such as Lean Inception, as many participants had previously contributed to projects using the Lean R&D framework [11].

During the workshop, the first author gave a detailed presentation of the Define-ML approach, with a specific focus on the new proposed activities. The presentation aimed to provide a comprehensive understanding of the approach while inviting critical feedback from attendees. Participants were encouraged to share their perspectives on the strengths, limitations, and potential areas for refinement of the approach. The participants agreed with the (theoretical) suitability of the approach and offered constructive suggestions, which resulted in improvements in the artifacts before the studies involving industry partners. For example, the data source mapping artifact was refined to consider perceived quality.

3.5   Step 5. Perform Static Validation

The static validation consisted of a three-hour session at an industry partner, a prominent company in the Brazilian energy sector, in which they were introduced to the Define-ML approach and applied its new activities in practice to a toy problem. The goal was to validate the Define-ML approach with industry practitioners. The static validation and its results are explained in detail in Sect. 5.

3.6   Step 6. Perform Dynamic Validation

The dynamic (real-world) validation of our proposed approach involved conducting a three-day workshop facilitated by the research team and attended by practitioners (data intelligence team) from a multinational energy drink company. The demand from the business partner involved facilitating the ideation of a solution for retail demand forecasting. The workshop strictly followed the Define-ML approach, allowing for the gathering of additional insights on the practical applicability in real-world settings. We document this case study following Runeson *et al.*'s guidelines [16] and present it in detail in Sect. 6.

3.7   Step 7. Release the Solution

To facilitate the adoption of the Define-ML approach, the researchers released an open-access template in Miro[2] accompanied by detailed usage instructions. This template is supplemented with an online example demonstrating a common ML-enabled product use-case.

4   Candidate Solution

Define-ML is an adaptation of the Lean Inception approach, that despite providing a solid foundation for cross-functional alignment, lacks activities tailored to the data-specific requirements of ML products. The proposed approach introduces several adaptations to the Lean Inception methodology to better suit the needs of ML-enabled product ideation. A typical agenda for the Define-ML workshop is presented in Fig. 2. Recognizing that ML products require specialized knowledge and consideration of technical constraints, the approach includes the attendance of ML experts in the workshop sessions. These experts provide quick, valuable insights on technical feasibility and offer explanations about the limitations of ML, ensuring that ideas remain grounded in what is realistically achievable. Their presence helps the team make informed decisions early on, preventing potential misalignment between the product vision and ML capabilities.

Another adaptation involves replacing the traditional personas definition activity with a streamlined activity focused on identifying the key roles affected

---

[2] https://miro.com/miroverse/defineml-template/.

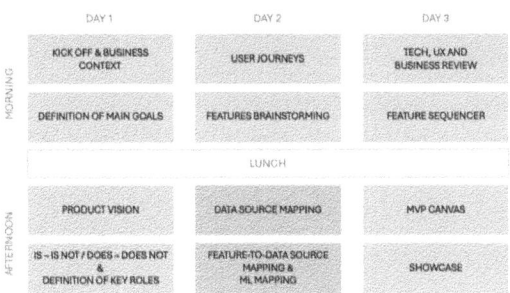

Fig. 2. Define-ML typical agenda

by the product. This simplification aims at saving time in the workshop without sacrificing essential context, allowing participants to focus on defining roles rather than detailed user characteristics.

The main adaptation of Define-ML concerns incorporating three new activities specifically designed to address the unique data and technical requirements of ML products: *Data Source Mapping*, *Feature-to-Data Source Mapping*, and *ML Mapping*. These activities are explained hereafter.

4.1 Data Source Mapping

The *Data Source Mapping* activity was designed to map the primary data sources used by the organization and the desired data sources relevant for the product. The board used for this mapping can be seen in Fig. 3.

The board is structured with two axes. The x-axis differentiates whether the data is public or private, helping the team quickly identify access restrictions and privacy considerations. The y-axis distinguishes whether the data is under corporate governance. For instance, data from an ERP system is managed under corporate governance, while a spreadsheet maintained by a specific individual within the organization may not be on corporate governance's radar. Data quality is also visually represented through circles representing three quality levels: high, medium, and low.

Additionally, the approach considers using differently colored post-its to differentiate between data sources the organization already possesses and data sources it wishes to organize or obtain. This allows participants to easily recognize gaps in data availability and identify strategic priorities for acquiring additional data sources necessary for the product.

4.2 Feature-to-Data Source Mapping

This activity aims to connect the features to the data sources deemed necessary for their development. This step serves to provide a foundational understanding of how data will support the feature's implementation. Step 1 presented in Fig. 4 shows an example of this connection.

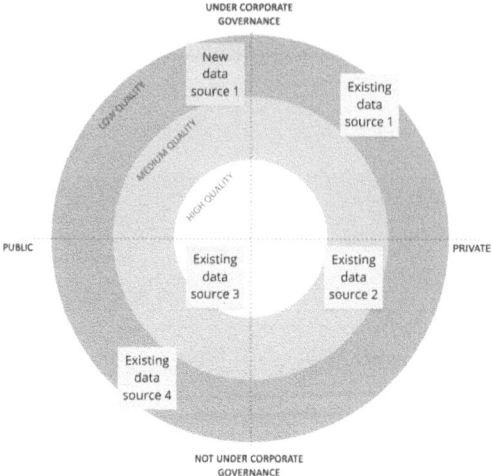

Fig. 3. Data source mapping board

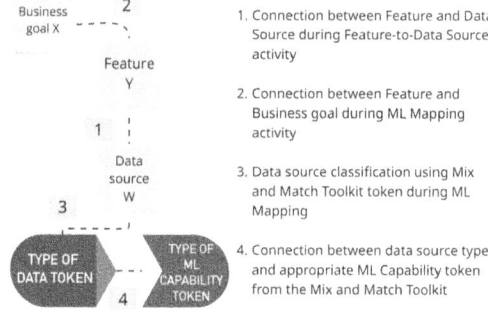

Fig. 4. Feature-to-Data Source Mapping and ML Mapping

4.3   ML Mapping

The *ML Mapping* activity starts with categorizing features into "ML-intensive" (*i.e.*, features that use ML) and "non-ML-intensive" features. Thereafter, a set of steps is performed for the ML-intensive ones. These steps were inspired by the *Mix & Match ML toolkit* proposed by Jansen and Colombo [10], which involves relating data types to ML capabilities as a way of making complex ML concepts more approachable.

Each ML-intense feature is linked to a business objective. This connection, presented as Step 2 in Fig. 4, addresses the common issue of misalignment between ML initiatives and business objectives, as highlighted by Nahar *et al.* [14], ensuring that each ML-intensive feature is purpose-driven and tied to measurable business outcomes.

Following this, the tokens proposed in the Mix and Match ML toolkit [10] are used, classifying the data sources according to the categories in the toolkit and matching them with appropriate model types. Steps 3 and 4 of Fig. 4 represent this classification and matching, respectively. This visual and interactive approach is designed to help participants grasp the technical possibilities, making the gaps between the available data and the desired ML capabilities explicit.

The ML Mapping activity provides a structured approach to align ML capabilities with business objectives, data availability, and ML model possibilities. The involvement of ML experts in this activity is essential, as they help to clarify what could realistically be achieved based on the intended business objectives and on the available data.

5   Static Validation

5.1   Goal and Research Questions

We defined the goal of the static validation using the Goal-Question-Metric (GQM) goal definition template [4] as follows: "*Analyze* Define-ML *for the purpose of* characterization *with respect to* perceived usefulness of the new activities and of the approach *from the point of view of* practitioners *in the context of* applying the approach to a toy problem."

Based on this goal, we defined the following Research Questions (RQs): **RQ1:** Is the Data Source Mapping activity perceived as useful for ideating ML-enabled systems? **RQ2:** Is the Feature-to-Data Source Mapping activity perceived as useful for ideating ML-enabled systems? **RQ3:** Is the ML Mapping activity perceived as useful for ideating ML-enabled systems? **RQ4:** Is the Define-ML approach perceived useful for ideating ML-enabled systems?

5.2   Validation Context

A three-hour session was conducted with a company from the Brazilian energy sector, integrated into their internal ideation training program. Eleven practitioners participated (IT, data analysis, and business strategy roles), where researchers presented the particularities of ideating ML-enabled systems and the Define-ML approach and its activities (one hour) and facilitated the practitioners in applying each of the three new activities (30 min for each) in practice on a toy problem. The toy problem concerned an intelligent banking system for loan approval. It is noteworthy that, as suggested by the *Technology Transfer Model* [9], the static validation did intentionally use a simulated context.

5.3   Data Collection and Analysis Procedures

After the session, the participants completed a printed questionnaire about their familiarity with ideation workshops, the perceived utility of the new activities and of Define-ML (using a five-point likert scale and open-text for feedback), and improvement suggestions.

5.4   Results

The participants demonstrated varied exposure to ideation methods, with 2 participants (18%) being highly experienced (three or more prior workshops), 6 (54%) moderately experienced (one to two workshops), and 3 (27%) first-time participants. All instruments and data are available in our open science repository. The quantitative analysis of the responses is presented in Fig. 5.

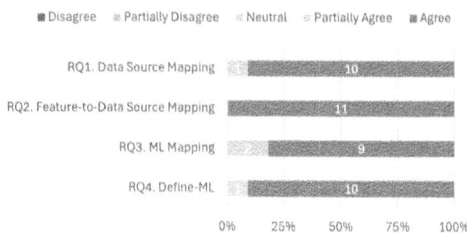

Fig. 5. Agreement frequencies on usefulness

RQ1: Data Source Mapping Perceived Usefulness. The majority of respondents (10 out of 11) agreed that the activity of mapping data sources is valuable for delineating ML-enabled system products. One participant partially agreed, indicating a minor divergence in opinion.

The feedback on the activity of mapping data sources was overwhelmingly positive. Participants emphasized that it is essential for understanding data architecture and that it plays a crucial role in enhancing the scope of solutions. The activity was noted as critical for comprehending data formats, maturity, and feasibility, which are key factors in ensuring the success of ML-enabled systems. Additionally, it was highlighted for promoting valuable discussions about data quality and its alignment with project expectations.

RQ2: Feature-to-Data Source Mapping Perceived Usefulness. All 11 respondents unanimously agreed on the usefulness of mapping features to the data sources. This highlights strong support for the activity's importance in the process.

The feedback on mapping features with data highlighted its significant role in facilitating a clear understanding of functional expectations based on data. Participants noted that this activity helps align functionality with data sources, which not only reduces the likelihood of scope changes but also ensures that deliverables are realistic and well-defined.

RQ3: ML Mapping Perceived Usefulness. Nine respondents agreed that classifying data and identifying ML techniques is a useful activity. However, two participants partially agreed, reflecting some concerns regarding its applicability.

The feedback on classifying data and ML techniques emphasized the importance of supporting technical solution analysis and ensuring the feasibility of ML-intensive features. Participants noted that this activity enables a deeper understanding of data types and provides clarity on how to effectively treat and classify them. However, some challenges were identified, as certain respondents found the discussion overly technical and less relevant to business stakeholders. Indeed, a suggestion was made to simplify the data classification process, making it more accessible and aligned with business needs.

RQ4: Define-ML Perceived Usefulness. Ten respondents expressed agreement on the Define-ML framework's usefulness for ideating ML-enabled system products. One participant partially agreed, indicating a minor divergence.

The feedback on the Define-ML framework highlighted its effectiveness. Participants appreciated the structured approach, which aids in aligning functionalities, data, and expectations to achieve cohesive outcomes.

6 Dynamic Validation

We report the dynamic validation as a case study following the guidelines suggested by Runeson *et al.* [16].

6.1 Goal and Research Questions

We followed the GQM goal definition template [4] to define the research goal as follows: "*Analyze* Define-ML *for the purpose of* characterization *with respect to* perceived usefulness of its activities and acceptance of the approach *from the point of view of* practitioners *in the context of* a real-world ML-enabled system product ideation."

Based on this goal, we defined the following RQs: **RQ1:** Is the Data Source Mapping activity perceived as useful for ideating ML-enabled systems? **RQ2:** Is the Feature-to-Data Source Mapping activity perceived as useful for ideating ML-enabled systems? **RQ3:** Is the ML Mapping activity perceived as useful for ideating ML-enabled systems? **RQ4:** How well is Define-ML accepted for the ideation of ML-enabled systems?

6.2 Validation Context

A three-day in-person Define-ML ideation workshop was scheduled and took place at the ExACTa PUC-Rio lab. The briefing provided to the ExACTa team set the context for the ideation session, explaining that the partner company, a large multinational energy drink manufacturer, sought to "enhance their demand prediction capabilities."

The workshop attendees included a diverse group of professionals. The workshop was facilitated by the last author with direct support from the first author. Five additional specialists from the ExACTa lab provided technical ML expertise. Additionally, eleven professionals from the partner company participated, bringing domain knowledge and practical insights into the company's business needs and operational challenges.

Throughout the sessions, technical experts from ExACTa and professionals from the partner company worked together in co-creation (Fig. 6). The activities were supported by printed templates of the Define-ML boards, and the participants collaborated by filling post-its and attaching them to the boards. The second author manually copied the physical boards to a digital board in Miro.

Fig. 6. Workshop sessions and the printed Define-ML boards being filled

6.3   Data Collection and Analysis Procedures

Participants were invited to complete a questionnaire via Google Forms, designed based on the Technology Acceptance Model (TAM) [7]. The questionnaire was developed to evaluate the research questions by capturing both quantitative and qualitative insights regarding participants' experiences and perceptions of the proposed ideation workshop framework.

To ensure ethical standards, the questionnaire provided information on the study's ethical considerations, specifically clarifying that all responses would remain anonymous and the identities of the participants would not be disclosed. This measure aimed to foster a sense of security and openness, encouraging honest and unbiased responses.

The questions concerned the participants' professional backgrounds and ideation workshop experience, TAM-based perceptions (utility, ease of use, intention to use) on Define-ML, and specific questions on the perceived usefulness of each new activity. Quantitative data from TAM-based measures (utility, ease of use, intention to use) were analyzed using descriptive statistics to identify participant acceptance trends. Qualitative responses underwent thematic analysis by the first author, with themes validated by the last author to ensure reliability.

6.4 Results

Filling out the questionnaire was not mandatory and only nine of the eleven business partner participants provided answers. Experience levels with ideation workshops varied significantly: six respondents (67%) had participated in three or more previous workshops (e.g., Design Thinking, Lean Inception), while two (22%) reported one prior experience, and one (11%) had no previous exposure. This distribution provided valuable perspectives from both ideation-experienced practitioners and first-time participants. The quantitative analysis of the responses is shown in Fig. 7.

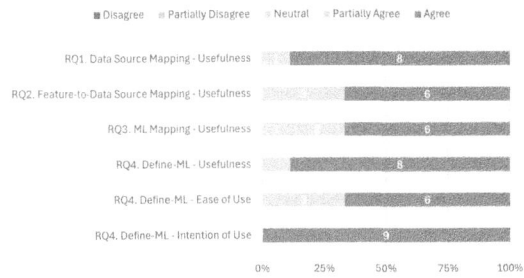

Fig. 7. Frequencies of the responses

RQ1: Data Source Mapping Activity. Quantitative analysis revealed that 8 out of 9 participants (89%) agreed on the usefulness of the Data Source Mapping activity, with one participant expressing partial agreement. The themes that emerged from the qualitative analysis follow.

Enhanced Data Understanding. Participants valued the activity's ability to clarify data complexity. One noted: *"Understanding all data sources and their qualities provided excellent clarity about current complexity."* Another highlighted how it revealed *"the volume of data processed by the company and the origin/utility of each source."*

Data Alignment. The visual mapping enabled teams to design unified data strategies: *"We easily created a blueprint for aligning data into a single source."* Another participant appreciated the *"visual artifact to group data and identify gaps to achieve product objectives."*

As an improvement opportunity, one participant suggested avoiding data quality assessment at this stage: *"Useful to show data complexity, but quality mapping felt inconsistent across stakeholders. Perhaps focus only on source identification without quality ratings."*. This indicates potential to streamline the activity while preserving its core value.

In practice, the activity successfully reduced ambiguity about data availability, fostered cross-functional alignment. The strong agreement confirms its utility as an important element of ML ideation.

RQ2: Feature-to-Data Source Mapping Activity. The Feature-to-Data Source Mapping activity also received strong endorsement from participants, with 6 out of 9 practitioners (67%) fully agreeing on its usefulness and 3 (33%) partially agreeing. The analysis revealed two key themes:

MVP Scope Definition. Participants recognized the activity's role in clarifying deliverables, with one noting: *"Necessary to understand the MVP's immediate benefit and the final product's value."* Another emphasized how it *"prevents creating features unsupported by available data."*

Data Impact Visualization. The mapping helped understanding data-product relationships: *"Useful to see how each data source impacts the product."* Others valued how it *"clarifies which data supports each feature for MVP prioritization."*

Participants who partially agreed mentioned two considerations. One regarding technical familiarity: *"Our team understands features well but needs more clarity on implementation paths and which data sources would be used."* and other regarding the short time: *"Because of the short ideation time... the task got a bit confusing."*

Hence, while *Feature-to-Data Source Mapping* was effective and recognized as useful to support precise scope definition and understand the impact of data, participants suggest allocating more time to maximize its effectiveness.

RQ3: ML Mapping Activity. The ML Mapping activity evaluation revealed mixed but generally positive perceptions among participants, with six out of nine practitioners (67%) agreeing on its usefulness, 2 (22%) partially agreeing, and 1 neutral (11%). The analysis revealed three key themes:

Technical Requirements Clarification. Participants valued the activity's role in scoping ML needs: *"Very useful to understand the ML process requirements for the final product."* Another noted it *"ensures chosen techniques align with specific product feature needs."*

Application Point Identification. The mapping helped teams locate optimal ML integration points: *"Useful to identify where ML model application would be valuable, considering data source limitations."*

Stakeholder Alignment. The activity bridged technical-business gaps: *"An opportunity for customer participation in typically technical discussions."*; *"Useful to align knowledge and expectations across the team."*

The participant who provided a neutral response justified: *"This was the artifact that confused me most."*. Another participant also recognized the complexity: *"A quick workshop about ML techniques could happen before the activity."*

Overall, we consider that the activity successfully introduced ML considerations into the ideation, but recognize that it requires careful facilitation to maximize its effectiveness across diverse stakeholder groups.

RQ4: Define-ML Acceptance. The evaluation of Define-ML's acceptance revealed strong agreement across all three TAM dimensions:

Perceived Usefulness. Eight out of nine participants (89%) agreed that the approach effectively supports ML-enabled systems product ideation. They highlighted benefits such as structured collaboration–"it helped us jointly design the product and its core benefits; the in-person format was crucial"–as well as value acceleration by structuring and prioritizing deliverables, and cross-functional alignment by unifying diverse needs into data-driven solutions.

Ease of Use. Six participants (67%) found the approach easy to use with proper facilitation, while three partially agreed. Participants noted that facilitators played a key role– *"we couldn't have done it independently"*–and acknowledged initial complexity for first-timers, which eased over time. Others emphasized that *"effective facilitation is needed to ensure productive contributions."*

Intention to Use. All nine participants (100%) expressed willingness to adopt Define-ML. They appreciated how it helps transform ideas into products and accelerates project outcomes. One participant noted, *"A really pleasant experience seeing ideas become concepts then products."* Another one mentioned that it *"brings together both sides interested in product development, improving knowledge exchange."*

7 Discussion and Threats to Validity

7.1 Discussion

The evaluation results indicate that Define-ML helps to bridge the gap between traditional product ideation and the requirements of ML-enabled systems. The approach's three core innovations–*Data Source Mapping*, *Feature-to-Data Source Mapping*, and *ML Mapping*–address critical challenges identified in prior work, particularly the alignment of technical capabilities with business objectives and the management of data dependencies in early-stage ideation.

Our findings support existing research on the importance of data-awareness in ML projects (*e.g.*, [2,14]) while introducing a structured approach to product-oriented ideation. The Data Source Mapping activity proved particularly valuable in making data visible and actionable early in the process, reducing the risk of later rework. Similarly, the Feature-to-Data Source Mapping gave practitioners a vision of what data sources need to be available to develop specific features. Finally, the ML Mapping activity successfully translated abstract ML concepts into practical product features.

Participants identified skilled facilitation (mentioned by 5 participants) as a critical element for successful adoption. They also praised the method's collaborative approach, which fostered inclusivity, alignment, and stakeholder engagement, aiding decision-making and consensus-building. Overall, results indicate acceptance of Define-ML, with a unanimous intent to adopt the framework, suggesting high potential for industry adoption.

Compared to existing solutions, Define-ML advances beyond toolkit approaches [10] by embedding ML considerations within a full product ideation workflow. While feature catalogs [18] can provide valuable inspiration, our framework offers systematic translation of features into implementable solutions through its integrated mapping activities.

7.2   Threats to Validity

Following Runeson *et al.* [16], we examine potential threats in four validity categories.

Construct Validity: Our approach combined quantitative surveys based on the TAM constructs with qualitative feedback. While TAM and qualitative feedback basically capture perceptions, we also triangulated these with the actual ideation outcomes (*i.e.*, the results of the conducted activities). However, future work could benefit from longitudinal tracking of Define-ML adoption and impact.

Internal Validity: Both validation settings included participants with varied levels of ML and ideation experience, which may have influenced responses. In addition, all workshops were facilitated by the researchers, which could introduce facilitator bias. To mitigate this, we collected anonymous feedback and included open-ended questions.

External Validity: We validated Define-ML with partners from two industry domains using a toy problem and a real-world case. The dynamic validation reflects a single application context and company culture. Broader replications across additional domains, team compositions, and project types are necessary to establish external validity more robustly.

Reliability: Qualitative analysis was conducted by the first author and reviewed by the last author, with consensus used to resolve discrepancies. Furthermore, we strengthened reliability through methodological triangulation (*e.g.*, comparing questionnaire data with actual workshop artifacts).

8   Conclusion

Define-ML provides a structured framework for addressing the unique challenges of ideating ML-enabled systems. By extending Lean Inception with targeted activities–*Data Source Mapping, Feature-to-Data Source Mapping*, and *ML Mapping*–the approach helps teams ground ideation in real data constraints, clarify ML feasibility, and align proposed features with business objectives.

Through static and dynamic validations with industry partners, Define-ML indicated strong perceived usefulness, ease of use when properly facilitated, and a clear practitioners' intent to adopt. The results suggest that Define-ML can help to effectively bridge gaps left by traditional ideation techniques. In contrast to existing toolkits or guidelines that focus on isolated aspects of ML design, Define-ML offers an end-to-end, workshop-based ideation approach that integrates data and model considerations into the collaborative sessions. These characteristics position Define-ML as a valuable contribution toward more actionable and feasible ML product definitions.

As future work, we aim to expand Define-ML's scope to accommodate emerging AI paradigms, such as Generative AI and intelligent agents.

Acknowledgments. We express our gratitude to CNPq (Grant 312275/2023-4), FAPERJ (Grant E-26/204.256/2024), Kunumi, and Stone Co. for their generous support.

References

1. Alonso, S., Kalinowski, M., Ferreira, B., Barbosa, S.D., Lopes, H.: A systematic mapping study and practitioner insights on the use of software engineering practices to develop MVPs. Inf. Softw. Technol. **156**, 107144 (2023)
2. Alves, A.P.S., et al.: Status quo and problems of requirements engineering for machine learning: results from an international survey. In: International Conference on Product-Focused Software Process Improvement, pp. 159–174 (2023)
3. Banfield, R., Lombardo, C.T., Wax, T.: Design Sprint: A Practical Guidebook for Building Great Digital Products. O'Reilly (2015)
4. Basili, V.R., Rombach, H.D.: The tame project: towards improvement-oriented software environments. IEEE Trans. Softw. Eng. **14**(6), 758–773 (1988)
5. Brown, T., et al.: Design thinking. Harv. Bus. Rev. **86**(6), 84 (2008)
6. Caroli, P.: Lean inception: how to align people and build the right product. Editora Caroli (2018)
7. Davis, F.D.: Perceived usefulness, perceived ease of use, and user acceptance of information technology. MIS Q., 319–340 (1989)
8. Ferreira, B., Marques, S., Kalinowski, M., Lopes, H., Barbosa, S.D.: Lessons learned to improve the UX practices in agile projects involving data science and process automation. Inf. Softw. Technol. **155**, 107106 (2023)
9. Gorschek, T., Garre, P., Larsson, S., Wohlin, C.: A model for technology transfer in practice. IEEE Softw. **23**(6), 88–95 (2006)
10. Jansen, A., Colombo, S.: Mix & match machine learning: an ideation toolkit to design machine learning-enabled solutions. In: Proceedings of the Seventeenth International Conference on Tangible, Embedded, and Embodied Interaction, pp. 1–18 (2023)
11. Kalinowski, M., et al.: Lean R&D: an agile research and development approach for digital transformation. In: Product-Focused Software Process Improvement: 21st International Conference, PROFES 2020, Turin, Italy, 25–27 November 2020, Proceedings 21. Springer, pp. 106–124 (2020)
12. Kalinowski, M., et al.: Naming the pain in machine learning-enabled systems engineering. arXiv preprint arXiv:2406.04359 (2024)
13. Kalinowski, M., et al.: Experiences applying lean R&D in industry-academia collaboration projects. In: 17th International Conference on Software Quality, Software Quality Days SWQD 2025, Munich, Germany, 20-22 May 2025, pp. 1–15 (2025)
14. Nahar, N., Zhang, H., Lewis, G., Zhou, S., Kästner, C.: A meta-summary of challenges in building products with ml components–collecting experiences from 4758+ practitioners. In: 2023 IEEE/ACM 2nd International Conference on AI Engineering–Software Engineering for AI (CAIN), pp. 171–183. IEEE (2023)
15. Ries, E.: The Lean Startup: How Today's Entrepreneurs Use Continuous Innovation to Create Radically Successful Businesses. Crown Currency (2011)
16. Runeson, P., Host, M., Rainer, A., Regnell, B.: Case Study Research in Software Engineering: Guidelines and Examples. Wiley (2012)
17. Villamizar, H., Kalinowski, M., Lopes, H., Mendez, D.: Identifying concerns when specifying machine learning-enabled systems: a perspective-based approach. J. Syst. Softw. **213** (2024)

18. Yildirim, N., et al.: Creating design resources to scaffold the ideation of AI concepts. In: Proceedings of the 2023 ACM Designing Interactive Systems Conference, pp. 2326–2346 (2023)
19. Yildirim, N., Pushkarna, M., Goyal, N., Wattenberg, M., Viégas, F.: Investigating how practitioners use human-AI guidelines: a case study on the people+ AI guidebook. In: Proceedings of the 2023 CHI Conference on Human Factors in Computing Systems, pp. 1–13 (2023)

MLTradeOps: Embedding Trade-Off Management into the MLOps Workflow

Vladislav Indykov[1]([✉]), Daniel Strüber[1,2], and Rebekka Wohlrab[1,3]

[1] Chalmers University of Technology and University of Gothenburg,
Gothenburg, Sweden
{indykov,danstru,wohlrab}@chalmers.se
[2] Radboud University, Nijmegen, The Netherlands
[3] Carnegie Mellon University, Pittsburgh, USA

Abstract. The unique nature of machine learning (ML) software systems, characterized by a high level of uncertainty and a crucial dependency on data, has led to challenges for traditional DevOps practices. As a result, a new domain entitled MLOps emerged, which considered these specifics. The evolution of MLOps is aligned with its specialization on certain quality attributes, such as security (*SecMLOps*) or reliability (*SafeMLOps*). However, due to their focus on one exclusive quality characteristic, such frameworks have limited applicability for production aimed at achieving multiple quality objectives at once (e.g., high reliability with the least resources consumed). Explicitly managing the trade-offs between different, potentially competing, quality objectives can help organizations by enhancing the flexibility and predictability of the MLOps workflow.

This vision paper presents a vision around the novel notion of *MLTradeOps*, focused on explicitly managing trade-offs during the MLOps workflow. It brings together the expertise of existing and emerging *DevOps* branches focused on specific quality attributes, and also ongoing monitoring and addressing of other general quality characteristics of in-production software systems. We envision a framework that makes trade-off management a core part of the decision-making process and contains a high-level cycle to make conscious trade-offs for the ML-enabled system, which are then reflected in lower-level decisions during the MLOps lifecycle. We supplement our vision with a roadmap for the potential formation of this framework.

Keywords: MLOps · Trade-offs · Software quality · Vision

1 Introduction

Over the last decades, the role of machine learning in industrial software production has become prominent and significant, since ML technologies allow organizations to reach results that are difficult to achieve through traditional solutions [16]. This fact caused the need for significant changes in common DevOps practices, since introducing machine learning into production comes with unique

D. Taibi and D. Smite (Eds.): SEAA 2025, LNCS 16081, pp. 97–112, 2026.
https://doi.org/10.1007/978-3-032-04190-6_7

challenges, such as fundamental dependency on data, other acceptable levels of uncertainty for the final results, and specific procedures of model training and testing [20], that could not be optimally addressed by existing DevOps vision. In response to this phenomenon, a new paradigm called *Machine Learning Operations (MLOps)* emerged in 2018 and attracted significant interest from the industry and researchers.

In this vision paper we operate with the broadest definition of *MLOps* given by Kreuzberger et al., who considered it as "a paradigm, including aspects like best practices, sets of concepts, as well as a development culture when it comes to the end-to-end conceptualization, implementation, monitoring, deployment, and scalability of machine learning products" [20]. This definition covers not only the production of ML pipelines but also the production of ML-enabled systems in general. The selection of MLOps interpretation is important for defining its scope and the possible challenges it may address. In other words, MLOps explores not only the behavior and characteristics of the model and data flows but also monitors the decisions and their consequences within the overall system architecture and production workflow.

The decisions can vary on different levels of abstraction and perspectives on the production, starting from the overall MLOps team setting, and ending with a small function added to a certain software component. What they have in common is the fact that every decision (even the most minor one) has the potential to significantly impact the quality of the final product. Such impacts regularly lead to a large set of potential *trade-offs*, since the process of decision-making is usually aligned with sacrificing resources (time, computational power, cost, etc.) to achieve a certain goal [25]. While several trade-offs relate to resource efficiency, some emerge between other quality attributes (e.g., a software architect may choose a less efficient ML algorithm in terms of accuracy if their primary goal is to introduce a highly explainable model [21]). These *trade-offs* require balancing or finding compromises between several quality attributes.

While trade-offs may appear in ML pipelines (e.g., between resource efficiency and model accuracy [24]), a systematic view of the overall architecture and production workflow of ML-enabled systems opens the horizon of complex trade-off mapping, which is far beyond the ones that appear in ML pipelines in isolation. We noticed that the existing MLOps paradigm includes trade-off management in certain phases [18]; however, it does not make their consideration fundamental for decision-making. It leads to the issue that, in certain cases, the final product is not optimal or even unsatisfactory from the perspective of certain quality characteristics. For example, if the MLOps team never balanced their decisions with ethical considerations, the final product may fail to meet the expectations of stakeholders and society [12].

Our vision makes trade-off management a core part of the decision-making process within the MLOps workflow. We believe that such an approach has the potential to make decisions more informed and conscious by estimating their impacts on quality attributes, and, at the same time, provide extra flexibility in the adaptation of MLOps practices specific to certain quality characteristics by

Table 1. Evolution of Operations in chronological order

Operations	Year of Emergence	Class	Description
DevOps	2007	Fundamental	Optimizing the production of software
DevSecOps	2012	Quality-oriented	Optimizing the security of software in production
DataOps	2014	Quality-oriented	Optimizing data transparency and maintainability within the software in production
AIOps	2016	Methodological	Optimizing processes within DevOps using AI
FinOps	2018	Quality-oriented	Optimizing computing, development, and maintenance costs of software in production (in SE)
MLOps	2018	Fundamental	Optimizing production of ML-enabled systems
ModelOps	2018	Type-oriented	Optimizing governance and life-cycle management of AI models
FLOps	2022	Type-oriented	Optimizing production of Federated Learning models
SecMLOps	2022	Quality-oriented	Optimizing the security of ML-enabled systems in production
LLMOps	2023	Type-oriented	Optimizing production of Large Language Models
SafeMLOps	2024	Quality-oriented	Optimizing the reliability of ML-enabled systems in production
IoTOps	2024	Type-oriented	Optimizing production of IoT systems (incl. devices, deep learning models, etc.)

embracing techniques from different quality-oriented MLOps frameworks (such as SecMLOps, SafeMLOps).

The remainder of this vision paper is structured as follows: Sect. 2 provides an analysis of the DevOps evolution and identifies trends in its development; Sect. 3 includes our vision as a way to address the issues of existing MLOps paradigm; Sect. 4 describes a roadmap for the potential formation of the proposed framework; Sect. 5 includes the discussion of future development and potential limitations of our vision; Sect. 6 concludes the paper.

2 Background

From the end of the 20th century, more and more companies started to produce software products, following waterfall or semi-agile approaches. The development process had become clearly not optimal as systems became more complex and, as a response to this, a completely new paradigm of *DevOps* was introduced [6] in

2007. Its wide adoption made the delivery of software faster, improved internal and external collaborations, and increased the reliability of the final products.

Over time, this paradigm has evolved and transformed. We collected the most significant milestones of DevOps evolution in Table 1. These milestones were divided into 4 classes. The first class is *"fundamental"*, which means that the transformation of DevOps was so significant that it emerged in a completely new paradigm with a set of unique approaches and priorities. The second one is *"quality-oriented"*. This class is characterized by the focus of the existing fundamental paradigm on certain quality attributes of the produced software (e.g., on security or reliability) and its possible extension with quality-specific techniques. The third class is *"type-oriented"*, which is characterized by the focus of the existing fundamental paradigm on a certain type of the produced software (e.g., IoT systems) or type of model in its core (e.g., Large Language Model) and its possible extension with type-specific techniques. Finally, the fourth class is *"methodological"*. It describes the changes in the existing paradigm due to newly emerged unique tools or methods that can be used to optimize the workflow. While there are several interpretations of the scope of each type of operation, we selected the most high-level ones. We observe that DevOps extensions emerged in different contexts: DevOps for security-critical systems (SecDevOps) [7] and the financial side of production, including cloud-based software production (FinOps) [27]. The growth of data volume caused the emergence of DataOps [3], requiring more maintainable and transparent data flows within the systems in production. AIOps came as an extension to DevOps and as a response to emerging AI tools and their potential usage to optimize the production processes [8].

While the year of MLOps' emergence is debatable, the most widespread version is that it was introduced in 2018 by several Big Tech companies [28]. The first implementations of MLOps dealt primarily with operationalization of model training, data versioning issues, and enhanced communications between data scientists and software engineers. The MLOps paradigm itself continued to evolve and be refined.

While there are several views on the taxonomy of MLOps and ModelOps, the most widely used one is that MLOps was extended by ModelOps, which covers a broader spectrum of operations connected to the AI models and ensures their reliability [15]. Further, different MLOps extensions arose, such as LLMOps [9] and IoTOps [22]. We are also witnessing the emergence of SecMLOps [31], which is the combination of SecDevOps and MLOps principles, SafeMLOps [30] prioritizing the reliability over other system qualities.

Summing up this investigation, we can state that DevOps and MLOps were the "game-changers" in the area of software production. Other types of *DevOps* are serving as their extensions to specify or expand the use of these 2 frameworks in different contexts:

1. Based on the specific issues that arise from prioritized quality attributes (SecDevOps, SecMLOps, SafeMLOps, FinOps)
2. Based on the specific issues that arise from different types of algorithms or models lying in the core of the systems in production (LLMOps, IoTOps)

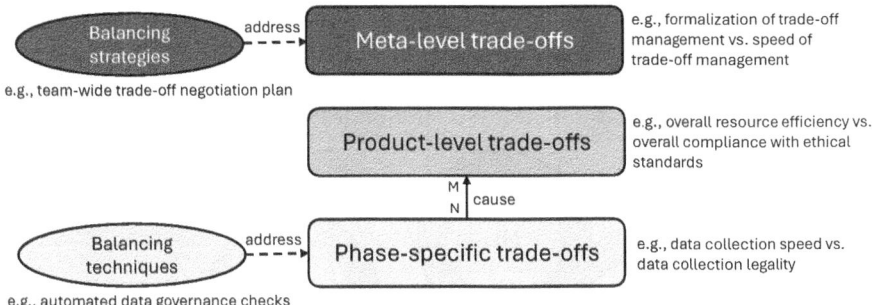

Fig. 1. Taxonomy of trade-offs in MLOps according to our vision

3. Based on the potential to optimize the existing paradigm with new, unique methods and tools (AIOps).

While quality-oriented extensions arise dynamically, providing useful insights on how to achieve specific quality objectives, none of them is optimized for achieving multiple quality objectives at the same time. Given the increasing complexity of software being produced and the dynamic growth of competition in the market, pursuing multiple quality goals is becoming an important vector of industry development, while prioritizing only one quality attribute in isolation from others may lead to non-optimal system performance, user dissatisfaction, or even critical vulnerabilities [5].

3   Vision

The core vision of *MLTradeOps* is to consider quality attributes in a holistic way, raising awareness of trade-offs and supporting MLOps teams in making principled, quality-oriented decisions. We propose to aggregate best practices from existing quality-oriented MLOps extensions, e.g., security-focused practices from SecMLOps, reliability-centered ones from SafeMLOps, methods of resource analysis from FinOps, as well as from emerging ones that are not fully formed yet but provide first promising solutions, e.g., based on environmental considerations in GreenMLOps. Quality attributes may generally conflict with each other. Therefore, to support decision-making, we suggest the development of a coherent framework that makes multi-level trade-off management a first-class citizen.

The proposed framework would enable industries to utilize suitable techniques from various quality-oriented types of MLOps, thereby achieving multiple quality goals simultaneously by striking a balance among them. For example, if a company is required to deliver security-critical products, but at the same time has to ensure high levels of resource efficiency, monitoring and managing this trade-off becomes essential at each phase of the MLOps life cycle. Moreover, other quality characteristics - such as fairness, reliability, functional suitability

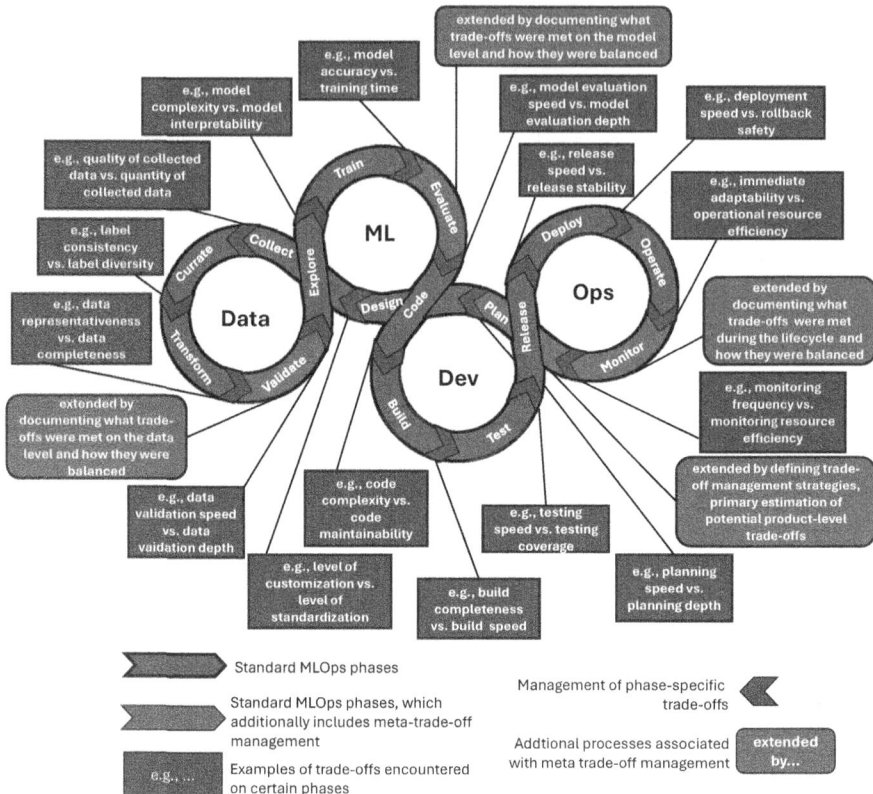

Fig. 2. Overview of MLTradeOps

- may need to be satisfied at least at a minimum acceptable level before the product is delivered. In existing MLOps workflows, mapping these qualities and trade-offs can become overly complicated.

We now explain our vision in detail, first introducing a taxonomy of trade-offs, and then suggesting activities for addressing them. Together, this leads to a framework of *MLTradeOps* building on the MLOps paradigm as a basis. According to the selected definition [20], MLOps covers best practices, sets of concepts, and developing culture in four main areas: data management, machine learning model production, system-level production, and operations associated with the deployed product.

Taxonomy of Trade-Offs. Our vision distinguishes three types of trade-offs, shown in the overview in Fig. 1: (i) *Phase-specific trade-offs*, emerging during a specific MLOps phase and involving low-level quality attributes associated with it (e.g., for the phase of data validation: data validation speed vs. data validation depth). These trade-offs can be balanced with certain balancing techniques (e.g., probabilistic data validation); (ii.) *Product-level trade-offs*, emerging at the level of the overall product and being the consequences of one or several phase-specific quality trade-offs (e.g., product resource efficiency vs. product security). Such trade-offs could not be solved in isolation from the phase-specific ones that caused them. Thus, product-level trade-offs serve primarily as signals for MLOps teams to take action. According to our vision, the only way to balance product-level trade-offs is to balance phase-specific one(s) that caused it; (iii.) *Meta-level trade-offs*, emerging on the meta-level of trade-off management. They involve teams' strategic goals in organizing trade-off management workflow (e.g., level of formalization of trade-off management vs. speed of trade-off management).

Table 2. Examples of potential product-level trade-offs caused by phase-specific ones

Phase	Phase-specific trade-off	Product-level trade-off	Description
Model Training	Model Accuracy vs. Training Time	Product Reliability vs. Product Resource Efficiency	Model training requires significant resources. If the model lies at the core of the product, the lack of resources invested in its training may cause issues with overall product reliability [11].
Coding	Code Complexity vs. Code Maintainability	Product Resource Efficiency vs. Product Maintainability	The proper and clear structuring of code requires efforts, however, when those efforts are insufficient, they lead to increased code complexity, reduced readability, and higher technical debt, which in turn reduces overall product maintainability [2].
Data Transformation	Data Representativeness vs. Data Completeness	Product Accuracy vs. Product Fairness	When the data is transformed to reflect the target distribution for the model (data representativeness), the performance of the algorithms that use it can be higher than when it operates with rawer data (data completeness). At the same time, the algorithms may further ignore rare cases or anomalies that affect minority users, decreasing the fairness of the overall product [23].

Addressing these trade-offs leads to a comprehensive set of activities that augment the regular MLOps process, shown graphically in Fig. 2. It adds new proposed steps to the standard MLOps schema and updates certain phases with extra logic. In our vision, the end of each phase of the MLOps workflow should be supplemented by a mandatory step of phase-specific trade-off management, while the phases of *"planning"*, *"data validation"*, *"model evaluation"* and *"monitoring"*, must be updated with the additional strategies for meta trade-off management.

Balancing Meta-level Trade-Offs. According to our vision, meta trade-off management should be conducted in addition to standard MLOps procedures at the phase of *"planning"*, and include mapping of the main quality priorities for the delivered product(s), trade-offs that may potentially be encountered further, and high-level approaches for balancing them. Quality priorities should be selected from a predefined catalog of quality attributes supported by the framework. The selection of priorities for the specific product should be conducted according to stakeholders' needs, governmental policies, and the developers' mission. Together with such priorities, the team has to define a minimal threshold for other quality attributes commonly used in the domain, which are proposed by *MLTradeOps* as well. At this phase, the team analyzes meta-level trade-offs and selects the overall workflow of trade-off management.

Balancing Phase-Specific Trade-Offs. Further, the team should estimate what main trade-offs it may encounter at different phases of the MLOps lifecycle. While the most widespread trade-offs will be described by *MLTradeOps*, teams will never be able to estimate all the possible cases on each step of the MLOps workflow in advance [18]. Therefore, the need for regular adjustments at the end of each phase arises, which is addressed by the phase-specific trade-off management.

The phase-specific trade-off management deals with the trade-offs arising from the decisions made on a certain phase and level of abstraction. For example, decisions made on the phase of data curation may cause trade-offs between data quality vs. resource efficiency (e.g., if the datasets are big but noisy, they require significant resources to be cleansed [1]), data relevance vs. data stability (the most up-to-date data can improve model relevance, but at the same time can lead to data drift [13]).

These trade-offs can be managed and balanced by applying certain techniques [4,14]. Such techniques are different for each trade-off as well as for each phase and level of abstraction. The *MLTradeOps* framework includes the most common ones.

Balancing Product-Level Trade-Offs. Decisions made at a given phase typically result in trade-offs between phase-level quality attributes; however, they may later lead to product-level trade-offs. For example, for the phase of model evaluation, the trade-off may occur between evaluation speed and evaluation depth (basic evaluation makes the phase quick; however, deeper evaluation provides more reliable performance estimates [29]). This trade-off appears exclusively on the model level at the evaluation phase, however, it may later cause a system-level trade-off between overall resource efficiency (how many resources were invested in the product in total) and overall reliability (how reliable the outputs of the product are). In Table 2, we take examples of phase-specific trade-offs from Fig. 2 and suggest which product-level trade-offs they may lead to.

According to our vision, the only way to balance product-level trade-offs is to balance phase-specific ones that caused them. On the phases of "data validation", "model evaluation" and "operational monitoring", in addition to standard MLOps procedures, the connection of certain phase-specific trade-offs, encountered in the associated layers (model layer, data layer, operational layer, respectively), to product-level ones should be investigated. We propose to add extra meta trade-off management activities associated with documenting the applied balancing techniques and their outcomes retrospectively. In parallel, management at these phases allows teams to re-balance meta-level trade-offs and adjust their strategies accordingly (e.g., to increase participation of stakeholders).

In this section, we provided the vision of how our framework may be used by MLOps teams. In the following section, we provide our vision on the possible formation of such a framework and the main artifacts it should contain.

4 Road Map

We present a roadmap for the formation of MLTradeOps, showing an overview in Table 3. This roadmap covers its entire development from initial conceptualization, systematic collection of necessary content, validation of the framework through production testing, and logic for regular updates. This structured process ensures that the framework is both practical and adaptable to the changing needs of ML-enabled systems in production environments.

MLTradeOps, like other quality-oriented MLOps frameworks, will be implemented as a set of best practices oriented on enhancing the quality of the delivered software products and associated workflow. While the application of *MLTradeOps* in the processes within companies is supposed to be fully agile-based, the formation of the framework follows more sequential logics and implies different interconnected steps of data collection. One of the main sources of data for its formation should be the most recent experience from the successful mature companies. The main attention should be paid to companies that successfully implemented certain quality-oriented MLOps extensions.

The formation of the framework starts with the planning step (*Step 1*). While this paper describes our high-level vision, Step 1 must include a deep investigation of potential conflicts and inconsistencies with the existing MLOps paradigm. The resource planning must also be included. The primary strategy involves a close collaboration between universities and industries. The academic environment promotes a systematic approach to the framework formation and consideration of existing scientific knowledge, while the industry is a provider of the experience that forms the main part of the framework content.

All the content included in *MLTradeOps* (including collected quality attributes, trade-offs, balancing strategies, and techniques) must satisfy the following criteria and be:

Table 3. Roadmap for the implementation of MLTradeOps.

Formal Step	Description
Step 1: Planning the embedding of the framework into the existing MLOps paradigm.	This step is associated with the conceptual design of the *MLTradeOps* framework and includes a deep investigation of existing MLOps implementations and theoretical integration of the framework into the MLOps paradigm with analysis of potential inconsistencies and conflicts. If the designed *MLTradeOps* concepts contradict existing MLOps principles, the designers should revise the framework to avoid this conflict or provide a solid analysis of the possible consequences of such a contradiction on the overall MLOps workflow.
Step 2: Collecting the most common product-level quality attributes of ML-enabled solutions	Product-level quality attributes describe the overall quality of the software in production. Additionally, they can consider the quality of the overall workflow, excluding the process associated with trade-off management. *Examples of the product-level quality attributes:* resource efficiency, reliability, security, maintainability.
Step 3: Collecting the most common trade-offs encountered on the product level in the production of ML-enabled solutions.	Product-level trade-offs are caused by one or several phase-specific trade-offs and affect the overall quality of delivered software. *Examples of the product-level trade-offs:* resource efficiency vs. reliability; system accuracy vs. system explainability; maintainability vs. security.
Step 4: Collecting the most common meta-level trade-offs.	Meta-level trade-offs describe possible dilemmas that arise when organizing the processes of trade-off management. *Examples of the meta-level trade-offs:* level of formalization of trade-off management vs. speed of trade-off management; degree of stakeholder involvement vs. speed of trade-off management.
Step 5: Collecting the most common meta trade-off balancing strategies.	Meta trade-off management strategies imply high-level decisions associated with the workflow and serve to address meta-level trade-offs. *Examples of the balancing strategies:* team-wide trade-off negotiation plan, methods of multi-objective optimization, stakeholder-driven prioritization.
Step 6: Collecting the most common quality attributes specific to all standard MLOps phases.	Phase-specific quality attributes describe the quality of processes within different MLOps phases. While the collection of all possible phase-specific quality attributes is unfeasible due to the unique architecture of each product, the list of attributes provided by the framework must operate with the most widely applicable ones. *Examples of the phase-specific quality attributes:* code complexity for coding phase; environment consistency for deploying phase; training speed for model training phase.
Step 7: Collecting the most common trade-offs that emerge between phase-specific quality attributes.	Phase-specific trade-offs come as consequences of the decisions made on certain phases and levels of abstraction. However, they may later evolve into dilemmas between product-level quality attributes. The framework must explicitly describe these connections. *Examples of the phase-specific trade-offs:* for the data collection phase: data collection speed vs. data collection legality (e.g., ensuring that data is collected strictly according to GDPR, HIPAA principles may sufficiently reduce the speed of data collection); for the design phase, the trade-offs may arise between phase-specific attributes: design scalability vs. design simplicity, which may later lead to a trade-off between product-level quality attributes: product maintainability vs. product reliability.

(continued)

Table 3. (*continued*)

Formal Step	Description
Step 8: Collecting the most common techniques to balance phase-specific trade-offs.	These techniques can be applied on different levels of abstraction according to the phase with which they are associated. *Examples of the balancing techniques*: data anonymization or automated data governance checks to deal with data collection speed vs. data collection legality; modularization or use of lightweight abstractions to balance design scalability vs. design simplicity.
Step 9: Assembling and formalizing knowledge into a single coherent framework.	Once all the best practices have been collected, they need to be combined into one coherent structure. At this stage, the framework is documented and formalized. An important task at this step is to ensure that all of the identified product-level trade-offs are connected to certain phase-specific ones.
Step 10: Testing the framework in industrial settings and conducting necessary updates.	Before the framework is presented to the public, it must go through wide testing in industrial settings. To obtain fair testing, collaboration with industrial partners of different sizes, domains, and maturity levels is required. If the results of testing require any changes in the designed framework, the updates are conducted accordingly at the appropriate step.
Step 11: Promoting the framework for industrial use.	On this step, the marketing strategies for framework distribution are designed and followed.
Step 12: Initiation of framework updates and return to *Step 1*.	The updates of the framework should be triggered by a certain event, which can be, for example, the end of a certain period (e.g., the framework remains up-to-date only for 1 year) or the emergence of new ML implementations. Since the development of new implementations is currently quite rapid, it is necessary to constantly monitor their emergence. However, before initiating updates and including the experience of such implementations into MLTradeOps, it is necessary to conduct certain checks, including checking the scope of implementation, the methodologies by which it was formed, the level of assessment of practices in industrial conditions to evaluate if the content of certain implementation corresponds to the requirements of MLTradeOps content. As soon as the time for updates comes, the process comes back to Step 1.

1. *Common*, i.e., combining the most widespread knowledge among different industries.
2. *Unified*, i.e., relevant for all types of delivered ML-enabled products (e.g., LLM-based software, deep learning systems).
3. *Up-to-Date*, i.e., regularly updated according to the recent developments of the industry.

The road map is cyclical. This was made to ensure that "up-to-date" criteria are satisfied and that the framework includes the logic for its constant updates. While the formal trigger for such updates will be defined on *Step 1*, since such a decision requires deep research into the dynamics of change in overall MLOps, we see a need for conducting such updates regularly. In parallel, we acknowledge the fact that balancing techniques may evolve much faster than balancing strategies, and possible phase-specific trade-offs may require specification and review more frequently than at the product or meta level. As a result, the framework updating process must be flexible and include only the necessary steps.

Product-Level Trade-Offs. Once the planning step is complete, the collection of common quality attributes at the product level begins. The studies conducted previously by the authors of this vision proposed a common quality model for ML-enabled systems based on the results of a systematic literature review and the evaluation of findings in industrial settings [16]. To be included in the framework, this quality model requires a broader evaluation within larger and more mature companies. The consideration of existing studies [26], standards, such as ISO-25059 [10], and, most importantly, documented experience of a wide range of industries is also required at this step.

Once the list of product-level quality attributes is formed, the collection of the most common trade-offs encountered on the product level begins. Previously, we conducted a study that collected trade-offs met by different industries on a product-level [17]. We believe that the methodology proposed by that study may be scaled and embrace the experience of a wider range of companies to be included in *MLTradeOps*.

Meta-level Trade-Offs. Step 4 involves identifying the most common meta-level trade-offs associated exclusively with the workflow of trade-off management, including the identification of the most widespread strategic goals and priorities.

Further, the most common strategies used by organizations to manage trade-offs on the meta level are identified. These high-level strategies serve as guiding principles for navigating quality concerns across the MLOps life cycle and are selected accordingly to balance meta-level trade-offs. To ensure wide applicability, only the strategies that have proven efficiency across multiple domains and organizational maturity levels must be considered for inclusion in the framework. The strategies must be augmented with potential use cases, constraints, and maturity indicators to guide their adoption.

Phase-Specific Trade-Offs. Once the high-level perspective is captured, the framework proceeds to collect quality attributes specific to individual MLOps phases. These phase-specific quality attributes provide a more granular view of quality and reflect the unique demands of each phase. Each attribute is defined in the context of its operational environment. While the exhaustive collection of all possible attributes is infeasible due to architectural variation across products, the framework focuses on identifying the most widely applicable ones through literature synthesis and industrial feedback.

After identifying the relevant phase-specific quality attributes, the investigation of the trade-offs that commonly emerge between them is conducted. These trade-offs typically emerge when optimizing one phase-specific attribute leads to the degradation of another. Initially localized in specific MLOps phases, such trade-offs can escalate to product-level ones. Therefore, understanding the cascading nature of these trade-offs is essential. The framework explicitly traces the evolution of phase-specific decisions into product-wide implications, thus promoting more holistic trade-off management.

To navigate these localized conflicts, the framework includes a catalog of balancing techniques tailored to specific phases. Phase-specific techniques are more granular and actionable than the balancing strategies identified previously, but like them, are annotated with use cases, constraints, and maturity indicators.

Validation and Dissemination. Once the fundamental elements (quality attributes, trade-offs, strategies, and techniques) are collected, assembling and formalizing this knowledge into a single coherent framework begins. At this stage, the framework from a conceptual collection of insights evolves into a structured and navigable model that can be applied in real-world settings. The formalization process includes defining relationships between the different elements, establishing a consistent taxonomy, and ensuring terminological clarity across components.

Following framework formalization, Step 10 involves rigorous testing in industrial settings. This validation phase is critical to ensure that the framework performs effectively across varying levels of organizational maturity, domain specificity, and scale of ML integration.

Once validated, Step 11 is dedicated to the promotion and dissemination of the framework for industrial use. This includes designing targeted marketing strategies, planning the presentations at diverse seminars and conferences, and developing scenarios of direct communications with the companies.

The roadmap represents our high-level vision of a possible framework formation. It can be updated and specified in the process, however, it is supposed to be used as the basis for further work. In the following section, we discuss potential limitations associated with our vision and with the proposed roadmap in particular.

5   Discussion

Embedding into Evolution of DevOps and MLOps. Based on the analysis of past DevOps development, we see several potential scenarios for its further evolution. Our vision could contribute to each of them:

Scenario 1. MLOps may evolve into new directions, such as the following three: First, extensions specialized in newly emerged types of ML models (e.g., self-optimizing models with a framework that could be called SOMLOps). Regular updates to our framework allow us to consider the specifics of such models and analyze the unique trade-offs they may lead to. Second, extensions specialized in quality attributes of emerging importance (e.g., GreenMLOps focused on sustainability). Experience from such extensions can be augmented by the consideration of other quality attributes, proposed by *MLTradeOps*.

Scenario 2. New DevOps extensions, not necessarily connected to ML, may appear (e.g., DevOps focused on ethical considerations - EthicOps). Fundamental concepts of *MLTradeOps* are flexible and may cover trade-off management of non-ML-enabled products by analyzing trade-offs specific to them.

Scenario 3. There may be another "game changer" that will fundamentally shift the paradigm of DevOps, like it was with the emergence of MLOps: e.g., Artificial General Intelligence with GIOps. We believe that new paradigms inevitably come with trade-offs. While the trade-offs and associated balancing strategies may differ, the need for their management remain relevant.

The vision at the core of our framework allows different teams to operate in the dimensions of several quality priorities, mitigating the need for new separate quality-oriented extensions of MLOps, but provoking the need to constantly update the proposed framework with the most recent knowledge in the industry. As a result, by applying *MLTradeOps*, the overall quality of delivered products increases, and the workflow becomes more predictable.

Justification of Assumptions. Our overall vision is based on a foundational assumption that product-level trade-offs arise as consequences of certain MLOps phase-specific ones. According to the Architecture Tradeoff Analysis Method (ATAM) [19], the analysis of trade-offs within the product is directly connected to the investigation of the trade-off points (parameters in the architecture to which several measurable quality attribute responses are highly correlated). Such points emerge as the result of decisions made on different levels of abstraction and different phases of the MLOps lifecycle. ATAM is compatible with our vision and can be leveraged to analyze cause-effect relationships and balance phase-specific trade-offs at the end of each phase.

Challenges. The execution of our vision may lead to a number of challenges. Considering the proposed road map, some steps take inspiration from the studies that rely on literature and limited-scale industrial evaluation. This fact may omit factors that only emerge at broader operational scales. Therefore, future iterations should include multiple independent methodological validations of each step, ideally performed by external researchers or practitioners not involved in the original design of this road map.

Our framework is supposed to operate with the most common experience, which means widely used practices in companies of different domains, sizes, and maturity levels. This introduces a threat that the content of the framework relies excessively on the chosen definition of such "commonality". To mitigate this, the analysis of how existing MLOps frameworks were formed methodologically should be done, and the formation of *MLTradeOps* must be aligned with that.

Although the framework is designed to be unified and common across various industries, differences in organizational maturity, team structures, regulatory environments, and ML deployment pipelines may be too significant. As a result, the applicability of the framework in certain contexts may be limited. For example, the most widespread quality trade-offs in heavily regulated domains (e.g., healthcare, autonomous vehicles) may differ from more flexible ones (e.g., marketing, retail sectors). Additionally, organizations at the early stages of MLOps adoption may find the full framework overwhelming or not directly applicable. Therefore, we see the need to customize our framework based on organizational maturity and domain-specific extensions where appropriate, in the future.

6   Conclusions

This vision paper provides our view on how the existing MLOps paradigm may be enhanced to obtain high-quality production in terms of several quality characteristics, while maintaining satisfactory levels of quality for the rest common quality attributes. The main difference of our framework from the existing MLOps paradigm is fundamental embedding of trade-off management on two levels: phase-specific ones, where certain balancing techniques are applied, and meta-level, where overall balancing strategies are defined, and applied decisions are documented and analyzed.

Acknowledgments. This work was partially funded by Vetenskapsrådet, project *SEMLA: Software Engineering for Machine Learning - Integrated Approach*, and the Wallenberg AI, Autonomous Systems and Software Program (WASP) funded by the Knut and Alice Wallenberg Foundation.

Disclosure of Interests. The authors have no competing interests to declare that are relevant to the content of this article.

References

1. Al-Sabbagh, K.W., Staron, M., Hebig, R.: Improving test case selection by handling class and attribute noise. JSS (2022)
2. Ardito, L., Coppola, R., Barbato, L., Verga, D.: A tool-based perspective on software code maintainability metrics: a systematic literature review. Sci. Program (2020)
3. Atwal, H.: Practical DataOps (2020)
4. Berander, P., Damm, L.-O., Eriksson, J., et al.: Software quality attributes and trade-offs. Blekinge Institute of Technology (2005)
5. Billeter, Y., et al.: MLOps as enabler of trustworthy AI. In: SDS. IEEE (2024)
6. Bou Ghantous, G., Gill, A.: DevOps: concepts, practices, tools, benefits and challenges. In: PACIS (2017)
7. Casola, V., De Benedictis, A., Rak, M., Salzillo, G.: A cloud SecDevOps methodology: from design to testing. In: QUATIC. Springer (2020)
8. Dang, Y., Lin, Q., Huang, P.: AIOps: real-world challenges and research innovations. In: ICSE. IEEE (2019)
9. Diaz-De-Arcaya, J., López-De-Armentia, J., Miñón, R., Ojanguren, I.L., Torre-Bastida, A.I.: Large language model operations (LLMOps): definition, challenges, and lifecycle management. In: SpliTech. IEEE (2024)
10. International Organization for Standardization: ISO/IEC 25059:2023 Software engineering - Systems and software Quality Requirements and Evaluation (SQuaRE) - Quality model for AI systems. Technical report, ISO (2023)
11. Gupta, S., Zhang, W., Wang, F.: Model accuracy and runtime tradeoff in distributed deep learning: a systematic study. In: ICDM. IEEE (2016)
12. Hanna, M., et al.: Ethical and bias considerations in artificial intelligence. Mod. Pathol. (2024)
13. Ryan Hoens, T., Polikar, R., Chawla, N.V.: Learning from streaming data with concept drift and imbalance: an overview. AI (2012)

14. Horcas, J.-M., Strüber, D., Burdusel, A., Martinez, J., Zschaler, S.: We're not gonna break it! Consistency-preserving operators for efficient product line configuration. IEEE TSE (2022)
15. Hummer, W., et al.: ModelOps: cloud-based lifecycle management for reliable and trusted AI. In: IC2E. IEEE (2019)
16. Indykov, V., Strüber, D., Wohlrab, R.: Architectural tactics to achieve quality attributes of machine-learning-enabled systems: a systematic literature review. JSS (2025)
17. Indykov, V., Wohlrab, R., Strüber, D.: Quality trade-offs in ML-enabled systems: a multiple-case study. In: SIGAPP SAC. ACM (2025)
18. John, M.M., Olsson, H.H., Bosch, J., Gillblad, D.: Exploring trade-offs in MLOps adoption. In: APSEC. IEEE (2023)
19. Kazman, R., Klein, M., Clements, P.: ATAM: Method for Architecture Evaluation. Carnegie Mellon University, USA (2000)
20. Kreuzberger, D., Kühl, N.: Hirschl, S.: Machine learning operations (MLOps): overview, definition, and architecture. IEEE Access (2023)
21. London, A.J.: Artificial intelligence and black-box medical decisions: accuracy versus explainability. Hastings Center Report (2019)
22. Melnikov, A., Birkholz, H.: IOT operations (2024)
23. Milanzi, E., Njagi, E.N., Bruckers, L., Molenberghs, G.: Data representativeness: issues and solutions. In: EFSA (2015)
24. Moshref, M., Minlan, Y., Govindan, R.: Resource/accuracy tradeoffs in software-defined measurement. In: SIGCOMM. ACM (2013)
25. Seale, D.A., Rapoport, A.: Sequential decision making with relative ranks. Organ. Behav. Hum. Decis. Process. (1997)
26. Siebert, J., et al.: Construction of a quality model for machine learning systems. In: SQ (2022)
27. Storment, J.R., Fuller, M.: Cloud FinOps. O'Reilly (2023)
28. Testi, M., Ballabio, M., Frontoni, E., Iannello, G., Moccia, S.: MLOps: a taxonomy and a methodology. IEEE Access (2022)
29. Varoquaux, G., Colliot, O.: Evaluating machine learning models and their diagnostic value. In: Machine Learning for Brain Disorders. Springer (2023)
30. Zeller, M., Waschulzik, T., Schmid, R., Bahlmann, C.: Toward a safe MLOps process for the continuous development and safety assurance of ML-based systems in the railway domain. AI Ethics (2024)
31. Zhang, X., Jaskolka, J.: Conceptualizing the secure machine learning operations (SecMLOps) paradigm. In: QRS. IEEE (2022)

Extracting Design Patterns from Mined Component Models of ML-Enabled Systems

Erik Eriksson[1], Joel Olausson[1], Vladislav Indykov[1(✉)], Daniel Strüber[1,2],
and Rebekka Wohlrab[1,3]

[1] Chalmers University of Technology and University of Gothenburg,
Gothenburg, Sweden
{indykov,danstru,wohlrab}@chalmers.se
[2] Radboud University, Nijmegen, The Netherlands
[3] Carnegie Mellon University, Pittsburgh, USA

Abstract. Machine Learning (ML) is increasingly integrated into software systems, introducing a set of recurring architectural challenges not commonly addressed in traditional development, such as managing data-driven components, uncertainty, and quality concerns specific to ML. While established software design patterns exist for conventional systems, a coherent set of patterns for ML-enabled architectures is still lacking. Such patterns would help guide recurring decisions and make their trade-offs more transparent to architects.

This paper presents 14 design patterns identified from a set of 49 component models of ML-enabled systems, which we compiled through a multivocal literature review covering both academic and grey literature sources. Each pattern captures a recurring architectural decision grounded in real-world practice. To assess their practical relevance and implications, we conducted interviews with 10 experts, focusing on how the identified patterns impact key quality attributes such as maintainability, reliability, explainability, and fairness. The resulting pattern collection supports software architects in reasoning about trade-offs in ML-based system design and provides a foundation for further research on architectural best practices.

Keywords: Software Architecture · Machine Learning · Component Models · Design Patterns

1 Introduction

Artificial intelligence (AI) is booming in various industries. With this increase in popularity, more and more software systems include AI components, often based on Machine Learning (ML). In an ML-enabled system, ML components typically make up only a small fraction [28]. Developing the vast infrastructure that surrounds the ML components leads to several distinct challenges, originating from aspects such as data handling and processing, data drift, and an

D. Taibi and D. Smite (Eds.): SEAA 2025, LNCS 16081, pp. 113–129, 2026.
https://doi.org/10.1007/978-3-032-04190-6_8

extended set of relevant quality attributes for ML systems, including aspects such as fairness [22]. Such concerns typically need to be addressed at the level of a software system's architecture [28].

Despite the massive uptake of ML research, which is often primarily focused on different model types and algorithms, research on the architecture of ML-enabled systems is only in its infancy and leaves various open challenges [20, 22, 24] that recur regularly in different projects [31]. Some of the most crucial challenges include a lack of architecture frameworks, processes, and evolution strategies for developing such systems [24]. Therefore, we notice the fundamental value of studying the whole system architectures rather than ML components or pipelines in isolation.

The most common high-level visualization of system architecture is the *component model*. Component models summarize the set of selected architectural decisions and highlight the most important parts of the system as well as the connections between them [25]. Such a source meets our intention to investigate how ML-enabled systems are produced in practice. Particularly, the analysis of several component models allows us to detect common decisions made in independent projects. By understanding which decisions are made recurrently, to address the same problems in the context of different projects, we identify *design patterns* for the engineering of ML-enabled software systems, whose systematic documentation can positively contribute to the evolution of ML-enabled software [36].

The implementation of design patterns generally affects the quality of the resulting system in multiple dimensions [36]. However, while some quality attributes can be effectively improved with certain design patterns, others can be affected negatively. Hence, to support the architect during their primary risk analysis, accounts of design patterns should be supplemented with an analysis of their impact on the general quality characteristics of the system [15]. By connecting design patterns to quality attributes, software architects can roughly estimate the consequences of pattern implementation and predict the associated quality attribute benefits or costs [3].

In this paper, we present 14 design patterns extracted from 49 component models of ML-enabled systems, which were identified through a multivocal literature review of 80 primary sources. These patterns were derived in a systematic manual process and address recurring architectural challenges. To evaluate their impact on software quality, we conducted interviews with 10 experts. The resulting pattern collection helps architects reason about trade-offs and supports future research.

2   Background

We now revisit the necessary background for our paper in three main directions: quality models for ML-enabled software, component models, and design patterns.

Quality Models for ML-Enabled Software. As we strive to contribute to the creation of high-quality software systems, *"comprehensive specification and* *evaluation of the software quality is a key factor"* [16]. The standard ISO-9126 for software engineering product quality [16] defines a quality model with quality attributes (QAs) to clearly outline where software systems may falter in quality.

Since machine learning relies heavily on data, "systems require consideration of several unique characteristics in addition to traditional ones" [14]. In our previous work [14], we performed a systematic literature review on quality attributes mentioned in the scientific literature on ML-enabled systems, and based on the results, created a quality model [14]. This quality model includes the following 14 quality attributes: functional suitability, resource efficiency, system accuracy, usability, reliability, security, maintainability, portability, explainability, fairness, data quality, and compatibility. Functional suitability is excluded from the empirical analysis due to its system-specific nature. More details on the model and attribute definitions can be found in the long version [8].

Component Models. According to Crnković, *"A component model defines standards for properties that individual components must satisfy and methods for composing components."* [6]. Component models are unique to the systems they represent since they depict how the specific components of that system are composed and assembled [21]. Another important aspect of component models is that they represent connections or relationships between different components within the systems [25].

While a component model may be non-visual, for the rest of this study, only visual component models (in the form of graphical figures) are considered. This decision significantly improves the reproducibility of findings. Component models may be visualized as *component diagrams*, standard notation for software architecture, and one of the 14 diagram types of UML. However, in this study, we use not only component diagrams, but also other visual representations of component models to cover more potential sources.

Design Patterns. *Design pattern* is an important term in software engineering. Gamma et al. define design patterns as *"general solution[s] to reoccurring problems in software"* [10]. The SWEBoK defines design patterns as *"essence[s] describing both higher-level architecture and organization of code as well as lower-level design and implementation details"* [4] We adopt the SWEBoK's broader view, focusing on patterns that affect system architecture as expressed in component models. This aligns with our goal of identifying reusable architectural solutions in ML-enabled systems.

3 Related Work

Design Patterns for ML-Enabled Systems. Design patterns have been investigated in software engineering for more than four decades [2]. Within AI specifically, design patterns for responsible AI (i.e. the ability of AI to behave ethically and responsibly) [23], and multi-agent systems (i.e. a subfield of AI involving the interaction of intelligent agents) [18] have also been studied for latest decade. There have been studies on design patterns for the Internet of Things [34] and microservices [30].

However, to our knowledge, only two secondary studies on design patterns for ML-enabled systems have been produced. Washizaki et al. conducted a multivocal literature review to find patterns for ML architecture and design, which they claimed was the first of its kind [35]. In total, they found 33 patterns and anti-patterns, with only two of them described in detail. Later, Washizaki et al. continued the work on these patterns and narrowed them down to 15, removing those that were vaguely defined or had questionable usefulness [33]. The identified patterns are either high-level architectural patterns (e.g., "Distinguish Business Logic from ML Models"), or more design-oriented (e.g., "Data Lake"). In 2023, Heiland et al. conducted an MLR with a similar purpose—identifying design patterns for AI systems [13]. They identified 70 patterns, 36 of which they classified as "traditional patterns", i.e., patterns that can be found in non-AI contexts but have been adapted to an AI context, and 25 architecture-relevant ones, which are particularly relevant for the present study. Unlike these previous studies, we used a mining methodology, based on component models of existing systems as a main source, while the previous work relies on available textual descriptions of patterns. The obtained lists of patterns are different and complementary to each other. We compare them in detail in the long version [8]. In addition, we supplement our list of design patterns with their evaluation by experts and investigation of their quality consequences.

Connection of Design Patterns to Quality Attributes. It is established that using design patterns correctly can significantly improve the quality of the overall system in a resource-efficient manner [36]. However, evaluating the connection of patterns to quality attributes remains a complicated task due to the context dependency, as stated by Mayvan et al. in a systematic mapping study on design patterns [2].

In our study, we strive to focus on generalizable insights leaving the specifics of certain systems behind and involve experts to get primary assessment of the impacts of design patterns on the common quality attributes.

4   Methodology

The aim of this study is to identify existing design patterns in ML-enabled software and explore their impacts on different system quality characteristics. We address and answer the following two research questions (RQs):

RQ1: What common design patterns can be derived from existing component models of ML-enabled software systems?

RQ2: What impact do design patterns have on the common quality attributes of ML-enabled systems?

Our research method for addressing these questions has the following main components: To answer RQ1, a multivocal literature review was conducted to extract component models, with further derivation of design patterns from them. The answer to RQ2 is based on interviews with experts to evaluate found patterns and identify the quality consequences of their application.

Multivocal Literature Review. To answer RQ1, we conducted a multivocal literature review (MLR) that combined peer-reviewed and grey literature, following the guidelines by Garousi et al. [11]. Our objective was to collect a broad and diverse set of architectural models of ML-enabled systems. We systematically searched six academic databases—ACM Digital Library, IEEE Xplore, SpringerLink, ScienceDirect, Scopus, and Wiley Online Library—and complemented this with grey literature from blogs, GitHub repositories using Google Search, and patent documentation using Google Patents. After deduplication, we screened 754 unique sources. We included sources that (1) described real-world systems, (2) contained component or architecture diagrams, and (3) involved ML components integrated into larger systems. We excluded purely conceptual papers, review articles, and sources focusing only on ML models without architectural context. This resulted in 49 selected component models, which span a variety of domains and development contexts. These models served as the foundation for identifying recurring architectural decisions. Full search strings, filtering stages, and protocol details are available in the long version [8].

Pattern Elicitation. To identify architectural design patterns, the first and second author independently analyzed all 49 component models from the literature review. Each model was printed and annotated on paper, marking component-level architectural decisions such as data flows, ML model placement, and supporting infrastructure. The authors then independently clustered recurring decisions observed across different systems, seeking to identify generalizable solutions to common problems. After the initial pass, their findings were compared and consolidated through iterative refinement in joint discussion with the remaining authors. This process led to a set of 14 patterns, each grounded in at least two independent source models. Where relevant, we compared these with the two prior pattern catalogs [13,33] to assess novelty. Each pattern includes a definition, the problem it addresses, a structural solution, and an illustrative example. More detail on the extraction process is provided in the long version [8].

Interviews. To evaluate the quality impacts of the identified patterns (RQ2), we conducted semi-structured interviews with 10 researchers who have experience in software architecture, ML pipelines, or AI-based systems. Participants were recruited from the joint home institutions of the authors, and were faculty members (assistant professor and upwards). Each interviewee was assigned 4âĂŞ6 design patterns, selected to balance familiarity and ensure full pattern coverage across the group. For each pattern, interviewees rated its impact on 13 predefined quality attributes using a 7-point Likert scale from -3 (strongly negative) to +3 (strongly positive), based on a quality model developed in prior work [14]. Quality attribute definitions were provided to ensure consistency. Interviews were conducted remotely, lasting between 45 and 60 min. Each session included open-ended questions to capture explanations and contextual reasoning. Interviews were recorded, transcribed, and coded independently by two authors using an inductive coding approach. This enabled both a quantitative and qualitative understanding of how patterns affect system-wide quality attributes. Further

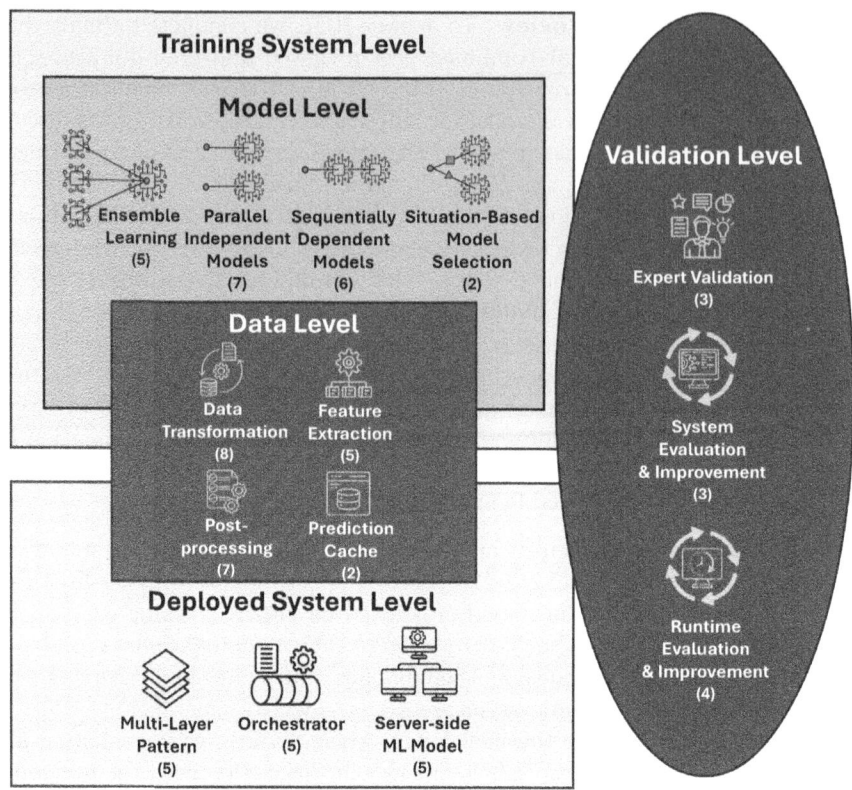

(x) – number of component models from which the design pattern was extracted

Fig. 1. Overview of our 14 identified design patterns in 4 groups

details, including the interview guide, participant profiles, and coding protocol, are provided in the long version [8].

5   Design Patterns

We now present the results of RQ1, on the identification of design patterns. Figure 1 presents an overview of the identified design patterns along with the frequency of occurrence of each pattern in the 49 considered component models. Each pattern occurred between 8 and 2 times, reflecting the notion that patterns are *reoccurring* solutions to problems. In total, we derived 14 design patterns from 49 component models, grouped into four overarching categories depending on the level of abstraction on which they are implemented: data-level, which describes data flows used both in *training system* (that primarily characterizes ML pipeline for training an ML model), e.g., training data, and *deployed system* (that primarily characterizes the executed system that includes a trained

ML model), e.g., real-time input data; model-level, which describes how several models can be organized in the training system; deployed system level, which represents high-level architectural design decisions of the deployed system and, as a cross-cutting concern, the validation level, which describes evaluation of processes in the training and deployed systems. Note that ML-enabled systems may embed the training system into the overall architecture to introduce continuous retraining and improvement based on new data [26]. However, in some cases, the training system can be independent.

We now present the patterns in detail, following the grouping as explained above. We introduce each pattern with a brief example and, in selected cases, visual illustrations. The long version [8] includes one example visual illustration for each pattern.

5.1   Model-Level Patterns

These patterns concern how a system can utilize multiple models in different ways to achieve different goals.

Pattern 1: Ensemble Learning

Definition: A system running multiple models, combining them into one prediction. This can either be done by multiple models running on the same data or different parts of the same data.

Problem to be solved: Individual machine learning models may make errors, but the errors might not always overlap.

Background: Ensemble learning is an established technique for combining the output of multiple models to increase model accuracy and resilience by studying the same problem from different angles [29].

Example: Figure 2 depicts a system trying to find *Botnet* domain names [32]. Botnet domains have names either of random characters or random words. The system looks for these features in parallel and then combines the answers from the two models to predict if it is a botnet domain.

Pattern 2: Parallel Independent Models

Definition: Running multiple independent models on the same input data to find different characteristics using different specialized models to get different outputs.

Problem to be solved: A need to differentiate between different types of information in the data within a frame of complex analysis.

Example: In image processing, differentiating between different types of objects can be tricky for an ML model. Therefore, it could be easier and more reliable to have multiple models searching for different things. For example, an image processing may search for traffic lights, lanes, and obstacles independently of the same input image.

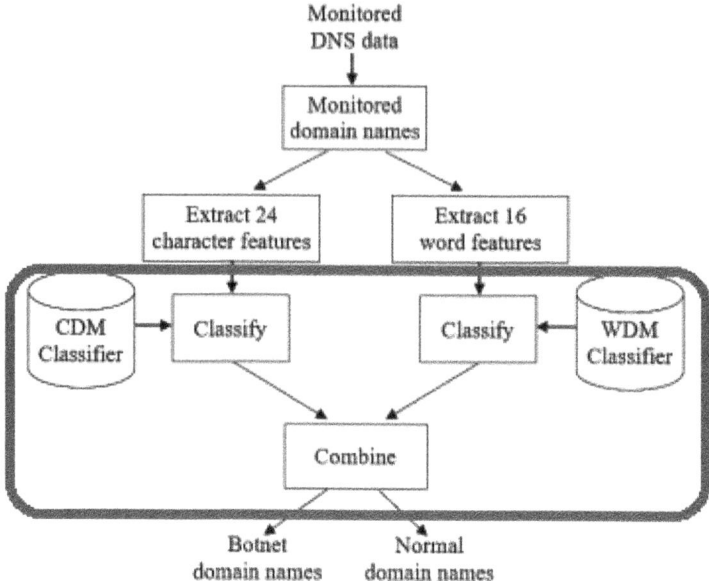

Fig. 2. Example of the ensemble pattern taken from [32] with the pattern circled in red (Color figure online)

Pattern 3: Sequentially Dependent Models

Definition: Running multiple ML models in sequence, each with a distinct responsibility of solving a smaller step in the process of solving a greater problem.

Problem to be solved: The need to break down a complex ML problem into a sequence of simpler sub-problems, where each model is responsible for its own sub-problem and uses the output of the previous model as input or corrects its errors.

Example: For example, a face detection model first extracts a face from an image; then a gender classification model processes the detected face to determine gender; finally, an age prediction model uses the face (and optionally the gender) as an input to estimate the person's age.

Pattern 4: Situation-Based Model Selection

Definition: When the system has multiple models to choose from, and picks one of them to use based on the situation.

Problem to be solved: A need to select the most efficient solution based on the specific characteristics of the problem, contextual environment, or certain conditions.

Background: This pattern can be seen as a specialized case of the strategy pattern [10]. The models are interchangeable and can be changed at runtime.

Example: An autonomous driving system may support different states that a car can be in, with tailored models for each state to predict the optimal trajectory.

5.2   Data-Level Patterns

These design patterns concern how training, testing, input, and output data are handled.

Pattern 5: Data Transformation
Definition: Data is transformed through a series of procedures, which produce incremental results to transform the data into the desired type of input for the model.
Problem to be solved: The raw data is not in the correct format for the ML model and needs to be broken down or changed so it fits the model.
Background: This pattern is related to the traditional *pipes and filters* pattern [13], which involves breaking down a system into a series of data processing steps, expressed as filters. A strict implementation of pipes and filters leads to particularly strong modularity by explicitly creating pipes through which transformation steps are performed, which allows for freely exchanging the filters running between them.
Example: A medical application that preprocesses MRI scans by normalizing image intensities, resizing images to a fixed resolution, and converting them into a tensor format suitable for input into an ML model. The transformation is first to find the blood vessels, and then extract the parts of the blood vessel that might be an aneurysm, which is done via image processing and not ML.

Pattern 6: Feature Extraction
Definition: When the input for the model first goes through a component that extracts a set of features, instead of using the raw data as input for the model.
Problem to be solved: A need to reduce the complexity of the model running on a dataset with large entries and improve its performance.
Background: Feature extraction is a well-established technique within machine learning [12] for decreasing the size of the feature space without losing information about the original feature space [19].
Example: A botnet detection algorithm that applies character-based and word-based feature extraction techniques to domain names of potential bots, and combines them in one model.

Pattern 7: Post-processing
Definition: If the output of the model is not in the format wanted by the system, it is fed into a component that processes the model output to the desired format.
Problem to be solved: The output from the model is in the wrong format, or some information or features need to be reconstructed since they can be lost in the model.
Example: Consider the case of a Bose Inc. patent [17]. After the ML component has filtered out background noise from a microphone input, a component is used to reconstruct the sound of the person speaking into the microphone. Thanks to the reconstruction component, the background noise is removed, but the sound of the speaker can be preserved.

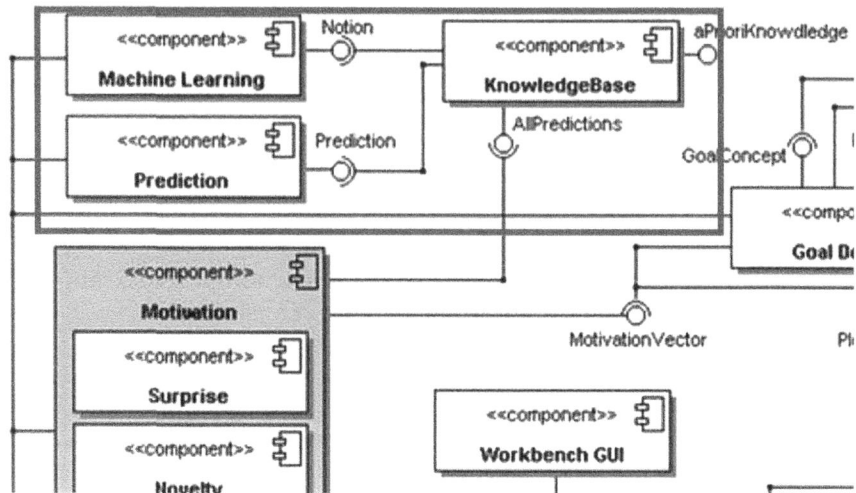

Fig. 3. Example of the prediction cache pattern taken from [1] with the pattern circled in red (Color figure online)

Pattern 8: Prediction Cache

Definition: The input and/or prediction is saved so that it can later be queried to see if it is unique.

Problem to be solved: A need to optimize resources when the input to the model is repeated multiple times and the same output is expected.

Example: In Fig. 3, we can see an example of the prediction cache pattern. This system takes real-time news and Twitter info and boils that info down to a simpler version. Since multiple sources can report the same event, there is a component at the end that saves each prediction, in this case, an event representation. These are then checked to see if any of the ones made before are close enough that they represent the same event to make sure the event feed is not flooded each time an event occurs.

5.3 Deployed System-Level Patterns

These patterns concern how components are structured and how they communicate with each other.

Pattern 9: Multi-Layer Pattern

Definition: The system is divided into different layers, which have clearly defined purposes, where each layer communicates only with its closest neighbors.

Problem to be solved: A need to introduce the *separation of concern* as well as *low coupling, high cohesion*.

Example: A system that creates an event feed from two input feeds, a Twitter-based one and a news one [27]. The first layer detects events from the raw input streams. The second layer applies filtering to remove irrelevant or low-quality

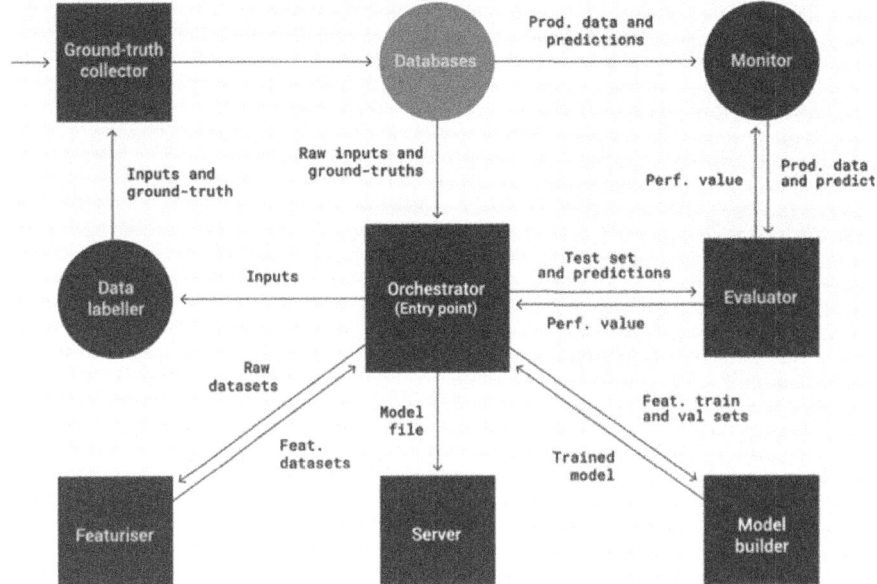

Fig. 4. Example of the orchestrator pattern taken from [7], where the orchestrator itself can be seen in the center

events (applied only for Twitter, due to its noisier nature). Each layer focuses on a single responsibility and communicates only with adjacent layers, following the principles of separation of concerns and low coupling.

Pattern 10: Orchestrator

Definition: A central component that handles and initiates communication between the machine learning-related components, including but not limited to data handling, training, evaluation, and prediction requests.

Problem to be solved: A need to efficiently manage interactions and data flows among diverse components within an ML-enabled system.

Background: This pattern is similar to the *mediator pattern* in the work by Heiland et al. [13]. But in contrast to the mediator pattern, the orchestrator is the initiator of the contact with the components, while in the mediator pattern, the components communicate with each other through a mediator. The problem they solve is therefore different, meaning they should be separate patterns.

Example: As seen in Fig. 4, the orchestrator connects all the components. It manages the different models that a model builder creates with the data supplied by the orchestrator, as well as evaluation, supplying models to the server, etc.

Pattern 11: Server-Side ML Model

Definition: One component has the role of server and allows components or subsystems to take the role of client, initiating a connection with the server to obtain a prediction from its model.

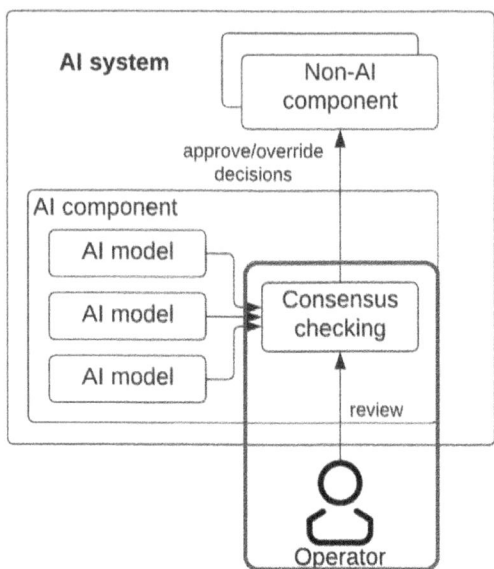

Fig. 5. Example of the expert validation pattern taken from [5] with the pattern circled in red (Color figure online)

Problem to be solved: A need to ensure efficient processing, scalability, and secure access to predictions for different clients.

Example: A central prediction service exposes an HTTP API used by both a web front-end and a mobile app to obtain classification results.

5.4   Validation-Level Patterns

These patterns concern validation within the systems in some way, either by evaluating an ML model directly or an application within a larger system to ensure their correctness, performance, or reliability. By having some form of validation in these ways, an improvement to key aspects of the system is intended.

Pattern 12: Expert Validation

Definition: A system where a human domain expert validates a critical step to ensure it fulfills certain criteria.

Problem to be solved: A need to ensure the reliability of model predictions, especially in scenarios with low error margins.

Example: An example of the expert validation pattern can be seen in Fig. 5, a simple component model depicting ensemble learning with expert validation. Here, the expert validates the consensus checking between the models.

Pattern 13: Runtime Evaluation and Improvement

Definition: A system that monitors and evaluates the deployed ML model, and makes improvements to it either by retraining, tweaking the model, or creating a new model with some changes.

Table 1. Connections between design patterns and quality attributes

Pattern	RE	U	R	S	M	P	E	SA	F	DQ	C
Ensemble learning	+		+		−	−		+	+		
Parallel independent models	−		+		±	−		+			
Sequentially dependent models	+		−		−		±	−	−		+
Situation-based model selection	+	+			+			+	+		
Data transformation	±			+	−	−	−	+	−		
Feature extraction	−		+	+			+	+	+		
Post-processing		±	+						+		+
Prediction cache	+		−	−		−					
Multi-layer pattern						+	+				
Orchestrator	+		−	+	+	+					+
Server-side ML model	−			±	+	+					+
Expert validation		+	+		+			+	±		
Runtime eval. and improvement			+		−					−	
System eval. and improvement	+		+	+	−						−

+Positive impact ±Balanced positive and negative impact −Negative impact

RE-Resource Efficiency *U*-Usability *R*-Reliability *S*-Security
M-Maintainability *P*-Portability *E*-Explainability *SA*-System Accuracy
F-Fairness *DQ*-Data Quality *C*-Compatibility

Problem to be solved: A need to avoid model drift and ensure high reliability of the model over time.

Example: An e-commerce platform monitors model performance on live recommendation data and retrains the model weekly using accumulated clickstream feedback to adapt to changing user behavior.

Pattern 14: System Evaluation and Improvement
Definition: A system that is monitored by an ML model to evaluate the system itself and to make iterative changes to the system based on the feedback from the model.

Problem to be solved: A need to continuously adapt and improve a system in response to changes in its environment, as detected by an ML-based evaluation mechanism.

Example: A cloud monitoring service uses an ML model to detect degraded system configurations and suggests architectural adjustments, such as redistributing services across nodes to improve latency.

6 Quality Attribute Impacts

To answer RQ2, we investigated how each of the 14 identified patterns impacts system-level quality characteristics. Our evaluation is based on 10 expert interviews conducted using the protocol described in Sect. 4. Experts rated each assigned pattern using a 7-point scale from -3 (strong negative impact) to +3 (strong positive impact) across 13 quality attributes derived from ISO-25010 and our previous work [14]. Ratings were only recorded if justified with clear motivation; unmotivated scores were discarded.

Table 1 provides an overview of the observed impacts for all defined patterns. *Positive impact* refers to patterns that were consistently described as beneficial by interviewees (e.g., Parallel independent models can improve reliability by enabling fault tolerance if individual model fail or produce inconsistent results). *Negative impact* indicates patterns that were generally perceived as problematic or harmful, creating confusion or inefficiencies in the context of certain quality attributes (e.g., Parallel independent models can harm resource efficiency by duplicating computations, increasing memory and processing overhead). *Balanced impact* captures patterns that had both advantages and disadvantages depending on context, user preferences, or implementation details (e.g., the impact of parallel independent models on maintainability is balanced because, on the positive side, their modular design allows individual models to be updated independently; however, on the negative side, maintaining multiple models introduces version management and re-training overhead). If no connection was reported by the interviewee(s), then the corresponding cell in the table remains empty. Below, we summarize major trends for all four pattern groups. Full pattern-by-pattern breakdowns and supporting quotes are included in the long version [8].

Model-level patterns were generally perceived as beneficial to *system accuracy, reliability*, and sometimes *fairness*, especially when models are composed to balance out individual weaknesses. However, several patterns (e.g., *ensemble learning*) were noted to have trade-offs in *resource efficiency* and *maintainability*, due to added complexity and redundancy.

Data-level patterns showed mixed results. Experts recognized improvements to *accuracy, fairness*, and *explainability* for patterns like *feature extraction*, but noted trade-offs in *portability* and *resource efficiency* due to added processing steps and infrastructure. Views on *security* varied by use case.

Deployed system-level patterns like *orchestrator* and *server-side model* were often praised for improving *security, portability*, and *maintainability*, yet posed risks to *reliability* or introduced bottlenecks due to the system context.

Validation-level patterns had the most positive and consistent scores, especially for *usability, reliability*, and *fairness*. Experts emphasized that runtime evaluation helps combat drift and that expert validation remains essential for trust in critical systems.

Overall, most patterns had both positive and potentially negative impacts, depending on implementation and context.

7   Discussion

Practical Usage. The identified design patterns can support software architects aiming to build trustworthy ML-enabled systems. They help select solutions aligned with quality goals while highlighting potential trade-offs. For instance, an orchestrator may improve maintainability or load balancing, but could introduce a single point of failure. The observed QA impacts can also act as architectural smells: if a pattern strongly undermines a required quality (e.g., maintainability), this may signal a mismatch between architecture and system goals. In practice, architects may use these patterns during early design phases or architecture reviews to guide structured discussions. Our pattern catalog may also support tooling for architecture documentation, automated design suggestions, or educational materials in architecture-centric ML engineering courses. Future work should validate and expand the catalog across domains and system sizes.

Pattern Comparison. We compared our results to two existing pattern catalogs. Seven of our 14 patterns – *Sequentially Dependent Models, Parallel Independent Models, Data Transformation, Feature Extraction, Post-processing, Server-side ML Model,* and *Orchestrator* – overlap with patterns identified by Heiland et al. [13]. None overlap with the patterns by Washizaki et al. [35]. A detailed comparison table is found in the long version [8]. The limited intersection is explained by differences in methodology: we mined visual component models, whereas prior works used textual pattern descriptions. Our results emphasize structural patterns that emerge from system architecture diagrams and reflect design practice more directly. These patterns may be particularly relevant for model-driven or architecture-first development approaches.

Threats to Validity. Internal validity may be affected by subjectivity in pattern extraction. This was mitigated by having the first and the second author analyze the models independently, followed by consensus-based consolidation. For QA impact assessment, construct validity is influenced by expert interpretations; while assignments were matched to areas of expertise, subjective judgment cannot be excluded. Still, the consistency observed in many ratings lends credibility to the aggregated findings. External validity is limited by the number and diversity of source models and interview participants. While we made efforts to cover different domains and roles, broader sampling could surface additional patterns or divergent quality views. To support transparency and future reuse, all component models and pattern definitions are included in our artifact [9].

8   Conclusion

We conducted a multivocal literature review of 754 sources and extracted 49 component models of ML-enabled systems. From these, we derived 14 recurring architectural design patterns, categorized into *model-, data-, deployed system-,* and *validation*-level patterns. To assess their quality impacts, we conducted expert interviews in which 10 domain experts rated the patterns on 13 quality attributes. This resulted in 71 positive, negative, or ambivalent connections between patterns and QAs. Our findings support practitioners in designing ML-enabled systems more systematically. Documenting recurring patterns, previously underrepresented in ML system design, can improve maintainability and enhance overall system quality.

Acknowledgments. This work was partially funded by Vetenskapsrådet, project *SEMLA: Software Engineering for Machine Learning - Integrated Approach*, and the Wallenberg AI, Autonomous Systems and Software Program (WASP) funded by the Knut and Alice Wallenberg Foundation.

Disclosure of Interests. The authors have no competing interests to declare that are relevant to the content of this article.

References

1. Awaad, I., León, B.: XPERSIF: a software integration framework and architecture for robotic learning by experimentation. Ph.D. thesis, Bonn-Rhein-Sieg High School (2008)
2. Mayvan, B.B., Rasoolzadegan, A., Yazdi, Z.G.: The state of the art on design patterns: a systematic mapping of the literature. JSS **125**, 93–118 (2017)
3. Bass, L., Clements, P., Kazman, R.: Software Architecture in Practice. Addison-Wesley Professional, Boston (2012)
4. Bourque, P., Fairley, R.E.: Guide to the Software Engineering Body of Knowledge (SWEBOK(R)): Version 4.0. IEEE Computer Society Press (2024)
5. Commonwealth Scientific and Industrial Research Organisation (CSIRO). Multi-model decision maker (2023)
6. Crnkovic, I., Sentilles, S., Vulgarakis, A., Chaudron, M.R.V.: A classification framework for software component models. IEEE Trans. Softw. Eng. **37**(5), 593–615 (2010)
7. Dorard, L.: 9 components of a real-world machine learning system (2020)
8. Eriksson, E., Olausson, J., Indykov, V., Strüber, D., Wohlrab, R.: Extracting design patterns from mined component models of ML-enabled systems: long version (2025). https://doi.org/10.6084/m9.figshare.29129027
9. Eriksson, E., Olausson, J., Indykov, V., Strüber, D., Wohlrab, R.: Supplementary artifact (2025). https://doi.org/10.6084/m9.figshare.28023146
10. Gamma, E., Helm, R., Johnson, R., Vlissides, J.M.: Design Patterns: Elements of Reusable Object-Oriented Software. Addison-Wesley Professional, Boston (1994)
11. Garousi, V., Felderer, M., Mäntylä, M.V.: Guidelines for including grey literature and conducting multivocal literature reviews in software engineering. Inf. Softw. Technol. **106**, 101–121 (2019)
12. Guyon, I., Gunn, S., Nikravesh, M., Zadeh, L.A.: Feature Extraction: Foundations and Applications. Springer, Berlin (2008)
13. Heiland, L., Hauser, M., Bogner, J.: Design patterns for AI-based systems: a multivocal literature review and pattern repository (2023)
14. Indykov, V., Strüber, D., Wohlrab, R.: Architectural tactics to achieve quality attributes of machine-learning-enabled systems: a systematic literature review. JSS (2025)
15. Indykov, V., Wohlrab, R., Strüber, D.: Quality trade-offs in ML-enabled systems: a multiple-case study. In: SIGAPP SAC. ACM (2025)
16. International Organization for Standardization (ISO). System and software quality models. International standard, ISO (2011)
17. Jain, A.D., Hera, C.M.: Noise reduction using ML (2018)

18. Juziuk, J., Weyns, D., Holvoet, T.: Design patterns for multi-agent systems: a systematic literature review. In: Shehory, O., Sturm, A. (eds.) Agent-Oriented Software Engineering, pp. 79–99. Springer, Heidelberg (2014). https://doi.org/10. 1007/978-3-642-54432-3_5

19. Khalid, S., Khalil, T., Nasreen, S.: A survey of feature selection and feature extraction techniques in machine learning. In: 2014 Science and Information Conference, pp. 372–378 (2014)

20. Kumeno, F.: Software engineering challenges for machine learning applications: a literature review. Intell. Decis. Technol. **13**, 463–476 (2020)

21. Lau, K.-K.: Software component models. In: ICSE, pp. 1081–1082 (2006)

22. Lewis, G.A., Ozkaya, I., Xu, X.: Software architecture challenges for ML systems. In: ICSME, pp. 634–638 (2021)

23. Lu, Q., Zhu, L., Xu, X., Whittle, J., Zowghi, D., Jacquet, A.: Responsible AI pattern catalogue: a collection of best practices for AI governance and engineering (2023)

24. Muccini, H., Vaidhyanathan, K.: Software architecture for ML-based systems: what exists and what lies ahead (2021)

25. United States Department of Defence. Component models. DODAF Report (2023)

26. Peldszus, S., Knopp, H., Sens, Y., Berger, T.: Towards ML-integration and training patterns for AI-enabled systems. In: International Conference on Bridging the Gap between AI and Reality, pp. 434–452. Springer, Cham (2023)

27. Petroni, F., et al.: An extensible event extraction system with cross-media event resolution. In: SIGKDD, pp. 626–635. ACM (2018)

28. Sculley, D., et al.: Hidden technical debt in machine learning systems. In: NeurIPS Press. MIT Press (2015)

29. Singh, A.: Comprehensive guide for ensemble models (2023)

30. Taibi, D., Lenarduzzi, V., Pahl, C.: Architectural patterns for microservices: a systematic mapping study. In: CLOSER (2018)

31. Thórisson, K.R.: Integrated AI systems. Minds and Machines (2007)

32. Vu, X.H., Hoang, X.D., Chu, T.H.H.: A novel model based on ensemble learning for detecting DGA botnets. In: KSE, pp. 1–6 (2022)

33. Washizaki, H., et al.: Software-engineering design patterns for machine learning applications. Computer 30–39 (2022)

34. Washizaki, H., Ogata, S., Hazeyama, A., Okubo, T., Fernandez, E.B., Yoshioka, N.: Landscape of architecture and design patterns for IoT systems. IoT **7**, 10091–10101 (2020)

35. Washizaki, H., Uchida, H., Khomh, F., Guéhéneuc, Y.G.: Studying software engineering patterns for designing machine learning systems. In: IWESEP, pp. 49–495 (2019)

36. Wedyan, F., Abufakher, S.: Impact of design patterns on software quality: a systematic literature review. IET Software (2020)

Quality by Prompt: LLM-Powered Transformation of Data Quality Requirements Into Great Expectations

Moamin Abughazala[1,2(✉)] ⦿, Motunrayo Ibiyo[1] ⦿, Henry Muccini[1] ⦿,
and Mohammad Sharaf[2]

[1] FrAmeLab, University of L'Aquila, L'Aquila, Italy
{moamin.abughazala1,henry.muccini}@univaq.it,
motunrayoosatohanmen.ibiyo@student.univaq.it
[2] CAP, An Najah National University, Nablus, Palestine
{m.abughazaleh,sharaf}@najah.edu

Abstract. Ensuring data quality is critical for reliable decision-making, analytics, and machine learning applications. Traditional data validation methods often depend on manually defining quality rules, a process that is time-consuming, error-prone, and difficult to scale. Great Expectations (GEs) is a widely adopted framework for data validation; however, crafting its rules manually introduces challenges in scalability, domain adaptability, and syntactic complexity. This study explores the use of Large Language Models (LLMs) to automate the conversion of natural language data quality requirements into structured GEs validation rules. We fine-tune the LLaMA-3.2-3B-bnb-4bit model using Low-Rank Adaptation (LoRA) on real-world datasets sourced from the telecommunications and IT sectors. To evaluate the effectiveness of this approach, we apply standard NLP metrics ROUGE, BLEU, METEOR, and BERTScore, alongside practical QA metrics such as rule completeness and manual effort reduction. Our results demonstrate that the fine-tuned LLM significantly outperforms generic models, generating rules with greater fluency, accuracy, and domain alignment.

Keywords: Data Quality · Data-Intensive Applications · LLM · Great Expectations

1 Introduction

Data validation is the process of determining whether a data point $(x, y) \in K \times D$, where x represents a key from a finite set K and y is a value from a domain D, satisfies a predefined set of criteria. Informally, data validation can be described as the process of assessing whether a data point meets a set of prior expectations or constraints [1]. This step is critical for ensuring the integrity and reliability of data before their use in decision-making, analytics, or machine learning applications. Poor data quality has been widely recognized as a source of

D. Taibi and D. Smite (Eds.): SEAA 2025, LNCS 16081, pp. 130–147, 2026.
https://doi.org/10.1007/978-3-032-04190-6_9

erroneous insights, financial losses, and operational inefficiencies across multiple domains [2]. Traditionally, data validation relies on manually defined quality rules, like Great Expectations rules, a method that is often labor-intensive, prone to human error, and challenging to scale across heterogeneous datasets [3].

Great Expectations (GEs) is an open-source data validation framework that helps organizations define, test, and manage data quality expectations [4]. However, manually creating GE rules comes with several challenges. Scalability is a key issue because writing validation rules for large and complex datasets can be time-consuming and resource-heavy. Additionally, different industries–such as healthcare, finance, and e-commerce–need customized validation rules to match their specific data characteristics [5]. Lastly, the framework's complexity can be a barrier since using it effectively requires understanding its syntax and structure, which can be difficult for new users.

Recent breakthroughs in Large Language Models (LLMs) have demonstrated remarkable capabilities in natural language understanding and structured data generation [6,7]. These advances present a compelling opportunity to automate the translation of data quality specifications into executable GE validation rules. However, realizing this potential requires overcoming substantial obstacles, such as ensuring the precision, consistency, and contextual appropriateness of automatically generated rules.

Despite ongoing efforts, manual validation remains inefficient and error-prone, while existing automated solutions exhibit limited generalizability and adaptability [8,9]. This study aims to bridge these gaps by harnessing the expressive power of LLMs to systematically automate the generation of robust and context-aware data validation rules, thereby advancing the state-of-the-art in scalable data quality assurance.

Specifically, this paper introduces **Quality by Prompt**[1], a novel framework for automating the generation of data quality validation rules leveraging fine-tuned Large Language Models (LLMs)[2]. Our primary contributions are as follows:

- We employ Low-Rank Adaptation (LoRA) to fine-tune the LLaMA-3.2-3B-bnb-4bit model, significantly enhancing its ability to generate accurate and domain-specific data validation rules [10].
- We conduct a comprehensive evaluation of the generated Great Expectations (GE) validation rules, assessing their accuracy, fluency, and coherence using established metrics including ROUGE, BLEU, METEOR, and BERTScore [11].

The rest of the paper is organized as follows: Sect. 2 reviews related work on data validation and LLM-based rule generation. Section 3 details the methodology, including dataset collection, data augmentation, model fine-tuning, and evaluation metrics. Section 4 presents the experimental results. Section 5 addresses threats to validity, and Sect. 6 discusses the findings. Finally, Sect. 7 concludes the study and outlines directions for future work.

---

[1] **UI**: https://huggingface.co/spaces/myexternal/GE-LLM-APP.
[2] **Model**: https://anonymous.4open.science/r/great-expectation_LLM-E536.

2   Background and Related Work

2.1   Data Validation Approaches

Ensuring data quality is a fundamental challenge in data engineering, analytics, and machine learning. Data validation is the process of defining rules that ensure data accuracy, completeness, and consistency before it is used in business or technical applications [12]. Traditional approaches to data validation can be categorized into manual rule definition and automated validation techniques.

Manual validation involves hand-coding rules using tools like SQL or Python, offering flexibility but lacking scalability and being error-prone [13]. Although this approach offers a high degree of customization, it presents several significant limitations [2]. Manual rule creation is resource-intensive, error-prone, and heavily reliant on domain expertise [8].

Additionally, manually created validation rules are prone to logical errors and inconsistencies, making the process susceptible to inaccuracies [14]. To address these issues, automated data validation techniques have gained traction. These techniques use predefined templates, machine learning (ML), and AI-based rule generation to improve efficiency [15].

Automated validation techniques using ML and AI can infer constraints via anomaly detection or template-based rule generation [16]. Large Language Models (LLMs) for rule generation have recently been studied for automating rule conversion and constraint inference, enabling the automatic extraction of validation rules from structured and semi-structured data [17].

2.2   Existing Data Quality Tools

Several open-source and commercial tools are available to support data validation and quality enforcement. Rule-based data validation tools play a crucial role in this process. Tools like Great Expectations [4], Deequ [18], and TensorFlow [19] Data Validation support rule-based validation at scale.

While these tools provide structured rule validation mechanisms, they still rely heavily on **manually defined expectations**. The integration of LLMs to automate the creation of these rules is an emerging area of research. These tools lack domain adaptability and often require significant manual effort [20,21].

2.3   LLM-Based Data Validation Approaches

The emergence of Large Language Models (LLMs) has opened new possibilities for automating data validation and quality rule generation. Recent advancements in LLMs have enabled the automatic generation of structured validation rules, thereby reducing human effort and improving scalability [22].

LLMs for Automated Data Validation. LLMs like GPT and LLaMA can interpret schema constraints and generate validation rules [23]. Recent studies have explored the use of LLMs in schema inference and data consistency validation, enabling automated detection of missing schema constraints and inconsistencies. They have also been applied to the automated transformation of business logic into structured validation rules, reducing the need for manual rule definition. Additionally, LLMs have shown effectiveness in anomaly detection within large datasets by identifying patterns and deviations that may indicate errors or inconsistencies. For instance, M. Zhang [23] examined how LLMs can be leveraged for enterprise data validation by automating schema detection and constraint enforcement.

LLMs for Automated Unit Test and Rule Generation. While software validation and unit test generation have traditionally relied on manual scripting, LLMs have demonstrated the potential to automate test case generation for data validation and error detection [24]. These models can automatically generate SQL-based validation rules, transforming natural language requirements into structured validation tests. They are also capable of detecting missing constraints in enterprise databases, enhancing the accuracy and completeness of data governance. Schafer et al. [24] explored how LLMs can improve enterprise-level data governance by generating structured unit tests and validation rules, thereby reducing the dependency on manual coding.

Despite their advantages, LLMs still face several challenges in automated data validation. Ensuring contextual accuracy remains a concern, as generated validation rules must align with specific industry standards to be effective [23]. Scalability is another challenge, as handling large-scale enterprise datasets while maintaining efficiency can be complex [24]. Additionally, bias and hallucination present risks, with LLMs sometimes generating syntactically correct but logically incorrect validation rules, necessitating human oversight to ensure reliability [22]. To our knowledge, no prior work has applied these techniques to the DQR-to-GE rule translation problem at scale. Our approach leverages LLMs to automate this process with broader domain adaptability and reduced manual effort.

Unlike prior efforts, our method fine-tunes a compact LLaMA model using domain data and evaluates both syntactic and QA metrics.

3   Methodology

This section describes the method to assess the effectiveness of using LLMs to automate the translation of natural language data quality requirements into structured GEs validation rules.

Figure 1 provides a high-level overview of the end-to-end workflow implemented in this study.

We discuss the study objective (Section III-A), the guiding research questions (Section III-B), the dataset composition–sourced from two industry partners in telecommunications and IT sectors (Section III-C), the end-to-end experimental workflow, including data augmentation and model fine-tuning (Section III-D), and the evaluation metrics employed to measure model performance across semantic and syntactic dimensions (Section III-E).

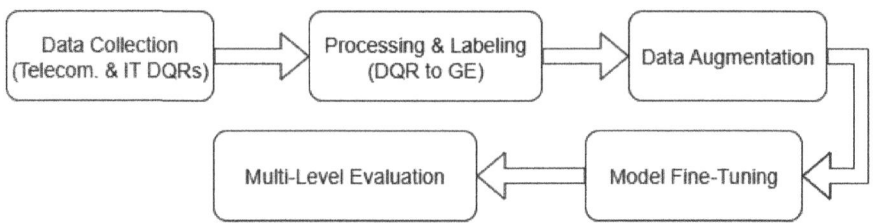

Fig. 1. Overview of the Quality by Prompt Framework. The pipeline includes: (1) data collection from industry contracts, (2) preprocessing and labeling of DQR-to-GE rule pairs, (3) data augmentation using GPT-4o-mini, (4) model fine-tuning using LoRA on LLaMA-3.2-3B, and (5) multi-level evaluation with NLP and QA-specific metrics.

3.1 Goal

The goal of this study is to develop and evaluate a methodology that leverages LLMs to automatically generate GEs validation rules from data contracts. This research focuses on improving the efficiency, scalability, and consistency of data quality enforcement by reducing manual rule-writing effort.

Using the Goal-Question-Metric (GQM) approach [25], we define our study goal as follows:

Use LLMs **to** automate the generation of GE data quality rules.

From the viewpoint of data engineers, data governance teams, and data architects

In the context of In the setting of data contracts collected from industry sources in telecommunications and IT

3.2 Research Question

To achieve this goal, we address the following three research questions (RQs):

– **RQ1**: How accurately can large language models (LLMs) generate GEs validation rules from descriptions of data quality constraints?
– **RQ2**: Do fine-tuned LLMs outperform generic models in GE rule accuracy and consistency?
– **RQ3**: How does the LLM-based rule generation approach compare to traditional manual rule-based methods in terms of efficiency, completeness, complexity handling, and required manual effort?

Each research question corresponds to a different experimental setup, ranging from zero-shot prompting to fine-tuned LLMs trained on domain-specific data.

3.3 Dataset Collection

Industry Data Collection. The dataset[3] used in this study was sourced from two industry partners in the telecom and IT sectors. Each company provided

---

[3] **Data**:https://anonymous.4open.science/r/great-expectation_LLM-E536/data/.

data contracts outlining structured Data Quality Rules (DQR) applicable to various types of contracts. These contracts specified a range of constraints, including schema, value, referential, and temporal constraints. In total, 75 DQRs were collected from the telecommunications company and 55 from the IT services provider.

Data Processing and Pre-processing. Fig. 2 shows a sample record used in the data set used for this study. After collecting the data, we processed the natural language descriptions of data validation rules through several steps. First, text parsing was performed to extract structured and semi-structured validation rules from data contracts. Next, standardisation was applied to format the extracted rules into a structured input suitable for LLMs. Finally, labeling was conducted to create pairs of natural language descriptions and their corresponding expected GEs rules for training and evaluation. Parsing and standardization were done using Python scripts and verified by QA engineers.

Data Quality Rule (Natural Language):
"The 'customer_id' column must be unique and cannot contain null values."
Expected GE Output:
expect_column_values_to_not_be_null("customer_id")
expect_column_values_to_be_unique("customer_id")

Fig. 2. Natural Language Data Quality prompt with Corresponding Great Expectation rule

3.4   Data Augmentation

To enhance the dataset for fine-tuning LLMs, we implemented a data augmentation strategy to automate the generation of DQRs and their corresponding GE, using a few-shot learning approach and GPT-4o-mini model. The first step in this augmentation process involved generating *data validation prompts expressed in natural language (English)* across multiple domains. This was achieved through an iterative process that began with the selection of an appropriate domain and a set of relevant DQR constraint categories. Based on these two inputs and some examples from the original dataset, the LLM generates natural language DQRs specific to the selected domains, effectively simulating a diverse range of real-world validation scenarios.

The next phase of data augmentation involved mapping the corresponding *GEs rules* for each DQR. This was also accomplished using well-defined few-shot prompts with GPT-4o-mini, ensuring adherence to predefined data quality expectations. Of the 14,062 augmented samples, approximately 700 (5%) were manually reviewed by domain experts. These reviews helped refine prompt strategies and informed filtering criteria for common generation errors. Although not all samples were manually validated, automated quality checks, including syntax validation and parameter completeness, were applied to minimize the risk of training on invalid rules. GPT-4o-mini served as a teacher model to guide the smaller LLaMA-3.2-3B via knowledge distillation.

3.5   Model Fine-Tuning

Fine-tuning large-scale language models enables researchers to adapt power-ful general-purpose models to specialised tasks without incurring the signifi-cant computational costs associated with training from scratch. In this study, we fine-tuned LLaMA-3.2-3B-bnb-4bit, a 3-billion-parameter language model, utilising Low-Rank Adaptation (LoRA) in combination with memory-efficient training techniques. The fine-tuning process was conducted using Google Colab infrastructure, specifically leveraging a Tesla T4 GPU with CUDA version 12.4, supported by 12.7 GB of system RAM and 15 GB of GPU memory.

The LLaMA-3.2-3B-bnb-4bit model was initialised using 4-bit quantisation to optimise GPU memory utilisation, with a maximum sequence length of 512 tokens per input instance. To further enhance computational efficiency, we employed the Unsloth library to implement Low-Rank Adaptation (LoRA) [10]. LoRA updates low-rank matrices while keeping most model weights frozen, enabling efficient fine-tuning.

This approach enables efficient fine-tuning on resource-constrained hardware without sacrificing model performance. The LoRA configuration was set to a scal-ing factor of two to balance adaptation efficiency and the following transformer modules "q_proj", "k_proj", "v_proj", "o_proj", "gate_proj", "up_proj", and "down_proj" were enabled for updates. This targeted fine-tuning approach ensures minimal memory overhead while preserving the model's ability to learn task-specific patterns.

Fine-tuning was performed using Supervised Fine-Tuning (SFT) combined with a structured set of optimisation techniques. The final training configura-tion was determined through a grid search procedure aimed at identifying the most effective hyperparameter settings. We employed the adamw_torch optimiser with a learning rate of 2×10^{-4} (2e-4), which provided a balance between conver-gence speed and training stability. A stepwise evaluation strategy was adopted to facilitate periodic assessments of model performance during training, enabling continuous monitoring and adjustment where necessary.

The training and evaluation datasets were preprocessed to conform to the ShareGPT format, a structured role-content format designed for fine-tuning chat-based models. The preprocessing steps included:

1. Data Standardization: this converts each prompt and instruction pair of the data set into a structured *role-content format*, in alignment with the Hug-gingFace nominal multiturn format.

```
<|start_header_id|>user<|end_header_id|>
<|start_header_id|>assistant<|end_header_id|>
```

2. Tokenization: the *LLaMA-3 tokeniser* was used to map raw text into token sequences.
3. Dataset Splitting: We split the dataset into two sets for testing and training in a 1:9 ratio. The training set was further divided in the ratio of 7:3 for the final training and training validation set.

3.6   Evaluation Metrics

We use two categories of evaluation metrics, *NLP-based generation metrics* for automated model comparisons, and *practical rule evaluation metrics* for assessing real-world QA workflows.

NLP-Based Generation Metrics. The evaluation of text generation in natural language processing (NLP) typically relies on a combination of complementary metrics rather than a single standard measure. In alignment with best practices in various literatures, our study adopts a multi-metric evaluation strategy incorporating ROUGE-1, BLEU, METEOR, and BERTScore.

ROUGE. (Recall-Oriented Understudy for Gisting Evaluation) [26] is a set of metrics developed to assess the quality of machine-generated summaries by comparing them to reference texts. In this study, we specifically employ ROUGE-1, which evaluates unigram (single word) overlap between generated and reference outputs. The choice of unigrams was to ensure that the GE rules which are in *snake_ case* format are adequately evaluated.

BLEU (Bilingual Evaluation Understudy) [27] is a precision-based metric widely used in the evaluation of machine translation. It measures the degree of n-gram overlap between generated text and reference sentences, providing insight into how closely the model's output approximates expected GE test cases.

METEOR. (Metric for Evaluation of Translation with Explicit Ordering) [28] addresses some of BLEU's limitations by considering synonymy, stemming, and word order in its alignment of candidate and reference texts. This makes it particularly effective for evaluating semantically equivalent variations in natural language DQR expressions. The use of METEOR scores helps to buttress the evaluation against exact matching of ROGUE and BLEU scores especially for contraints that involve the definition of JSON Schema, dates and datatype. For example, integer can also be expressed as int.

BERTScore [11] is an embedding-based evaluation metric that leverages contextualised representations from pre-trained BERT models to compute the semantic similarity between candidate and reference texts using cosine similarity. Given its ability to capture deep semantic relationships, BERTScore has demonstrated strong correlation with human judgement and is therefore used as the primary evaluation metric in this study.

Practical Rule Evaluation Metrics. These metrics assess performance in real-world QA scenarios, where correctness, effort, and generalizability are key:

– **Average Creation Time**, Time required to produce a GE rule from a DQR (Data Quality Requirement), recorded in minutes/seconds. Three QA engineers independently authored GE rules for fifty DQRs each (total = 150). Rule creation time was logged using an IDE-integrated timer. After writing each rule, engineers recorded their perceived effort level.
– **Completeness Score**, Binary reviewer rating for whether a rule satisfies all constraints. Each rule (manual and LLM-generated) was peer-reviewed by a different engineer to determine completeness. A binary score (1 = complete, 0 = incomplete) was assigned.
– **Manual Effort Rating** measures how much mental and technical effort a QA engineer needs to write a GE rule manually. It's based on a three-point scale: Low, Moderate, and High. In this study, manual rule creation was often rated as Moderate to High due to complexity and time demands, while the LLM-based approach required no manual effort, as rule generation was fully automated.

4   Results

In Sect. 2.3, we outlined key challenges associated with applying LLMs to automated data validation: (1) ensuring contextual accuracy, (2) handling large-scale datasets efficiently, and (3) mitigating risks of hallucinated or logically incorrect rules. The following sections present our empirical findings and examine how our fine-tuned model addresses these issues through domain-specific training, LoRA adaptation, and curated dataset augmentation.

This section presents the results and evaluation of fine-tuning the LLM in response to the research questions. To evaluate the capability of LLMs in generating GEs, we randomly selected 10% from the dataset and used the NL prompts as the static test set for evaluating all the LLMS.

Table 1. Evaluation Results of Base and Fine-tuned LLaMA-3.2-3B Models

Metric	Measure	B	FT-I	FT-A
ROUGE-1	Avg F1	0.1525	0.7352	0.7721
ROUGE-2	Avg F1	0.0433	0.6374	0.7345
ROUGE-L	Avg F1	0.1187	0.7112	0.7513
BLEU	-	0.0308	0.5586	0.6204
METEOR	-	0.1709	0.6115	0.6785
BERTScore	F1	0.7640	0.9465	0.8972

B: Base LLaMA-3.2-3B model without fine-tuning **FT-I**: LLaMA fine-tuned on the initial real-world dataset **FT-A**: LLaMA fine-tuned on the augmented dataset (real + GPT-generated)

4.1   RQ1: How Accurately Can LLMs Generate Great Expectations Validation Rules?

To address RQ1, we compared the performance of the base LLaMA-3.2-3B model and GPT-4o-mini in generating Great Expectations (GE) validation rules from natural language descriptions of data quality checks. GPT-4o-mini demonstrated the ability to produce outputs closely aligned with the expected syntax of GE rules. In contrast, the base LLaMA model struggled to replicate the correct format, often attempting to implement data validation logic using generic Python code instead of the GE framework. Figure 3 illustrates a sample comparison of the outputs generated by the base LLaMA-3.2-3B model and GPT-4o-mini.

We fine-tuned LLaMA-3.2-3B in two stages: using real-world data, then GPT-augmented samples for improved coverage (see Sect. 3.5). Evaluation used BLEU, ROUGE, METEOR, and BERTScore (see Sect. 3.6).

Table 1 presents the evaluation results, highlighting a substantial performance improvement after fine-tuning. Our dataset includes labeled DQR-to-GE pairs sourced from two industry partners, a telecommunications company and an IT services provider. While both domains contributed valuable domain-specific rules, we did not separate the evaluation by company. This was due to similar schema patterns and the goal of maximizing training diversity. Informal qualitative reviews indicated consistent model performance across both domains. Future work will include a formal per-domain evaluation to assess fine-tuning generalization more explicitly.

The model fine-tuned on the initial dataset exhibited substantial gains across all evaluation metrics: ROUGE-1, ROUGE-2, and ROUGE-L scores increased from 0.15, 0.04, and 0.12 to 0.74, 0.64, and 0.71, respectively. Fine-tuning enhanced the model's ability to match GE syntax and semantics. Furthermore, BLEU and METEOR scores improved significantly, increasing from 0.03 and 0.17 to 0.56 and 0.61, respectively, reflecting better syntactic coherence and n-gram precision at the phrase level.

Further fine-tuning using the augmented dataset yielded incremental improvements, most notably in the ROUGE-2 and BLEU metrics, indicating that the augmented data enhanced the model's generalization capabilities across diverse phrasings and domain-specific constructs. However, a slight decrease was observed in the BERTScore, which declined to 0.8972. This reduction reflects a subtle semantic drift, potentially attributable to the variability introduced by the synthetic data. While GPT-generated data helped diversify the training corpus, it also posed challenges. We noted a slight decrease in BERTScore (from 0.9465 to 0.8972) after training on synthetic data, indicating potential semantic drift. Manual reviews showed that some outputs lacked domain-specific constraints or misrepresented complex validations, risking compounding bias. Although 5% of generated pairs were validated by experts, we did not perform a formal variance analysis between real and synthetic samples, highlighting a limitation. Future work will focus on adversarial validation or embedding-based metrics to better quantifying this gap. Table 1 shows that while the base and fine-tuned LLaMA-3.2-3B models were evaluated, GPT-4o-mini also performed on the same static

M. Abughazala et al.

test set, achieving BLEU 0.7342, METEOR 0.7824, and BERTScore F1 0.9638–
slightly below the fine-tuned LLaMA model (BLEU 0.8165, BERTScore 0.9754).
This demonstrates that, although not fine-tuned, GPT-4o-mini performs well.
Moreover, our results indicate that a smaller, fine-tuned model like LLaMA-3.2-
3B can exceed this performance, making it a more practical choice for organizations with resource constraints.

Data Quality Rule (Natural Language):

Check that the `threat_level` column has values that are either
'Low', 'Medium', or 'High', ensuring uniqueness."

Response (Base LLaMa Model):

```
"You can use the following Python code snippet to check
for unique values in the 'threat_level' column.
```python
import pandas as pd

def check_threat_level(df, column, allowed_values):
    # Check if the column exists
    if column not in df.columns:
        raise ValueError(f""Column '{column}' does not
        exist in the DataFrame."")
        # Check if the column values are unique and
        #within the allowed values
    if not (df[column].unique().tolist() == allowed_values):
        duplicates = set(df[column].unique()) - set(
                                        allowed_values)
        if duplicates:
         print(f""Non-unique values found in the'{column}'column:"")
         print(duplicates)
        else:
         print(f""The '{column}' column values are unique,
        containing the following values:"")
         print(set(df[column]))

    # Ensure the column values match the allowed values
    if not (df[column].tolist() == allowed_values):
        print(""Column values do not match the allowed
        values."")
        return False

    return True
```

Response (GPT-4o-mini):

```
expect_column_values_to_be_in_set(column='threat_level',
                    value_set=['Low'; 'Medium'; 'High']),
expect_column_values_to_be_unique(column='threat_level')
```

Fig. 3. Output comparison between Base LLaMA and GPT-4o-mini on a data quality
prompt
```

Overall, these results confirm that fine-tuning large language models on curated, domain-specific datasets, even of modest size, can significantly improve their ability to generate structured, domain-compliant outputs like Great Expectations validation rules. In addition, augmenting training data with GPT-generated examples can further enhance syntactic conformity and lexical diversity.

Table 2. Category-Wise Distribution of DQRs with Low Sentence BLEU Score (Threshold 0.7)

S/N	Category	F-Q	F-%	MC-Q	MC-%
1	Table shape	46	11.76	34	73.91
2	Missing values, unique values, and types	112	28.64	101	90.18
3	Sets and ranges	173	44.25	125	72.25
4	String matching	45	11.51	37	82.22
5	DateTime parsing	84	21.48	65	77.38
6	JSON parsing	61	15.60	7	11.48
7	Aggregate functions	16	4.09	5	31.25
8	Distributional functions	9	2.30	1	11.11
9	Multi-column	**40**	**10.23**	13	32.50
10	File Data Asset	15	3.84	6	40.00

F-Q: Frequency Quantity (number of DQRs with low BLEU score in that category) **F-%**: Frequency Percentage **MC-Q**: Multiple Category Quantity (appeared with other categories) **MC-%**: Multiple Category Percentage

4.2 Error Analysis of BLEU Scores

To qualitatively analyze the performance of the fine-tuned model, we manually reviewed the responses from the fine-tuned model and evaluated the distribution of 391 data points that had a BLEU score of the sentence below 0.7000. Table 2 presents the distribution of these 391 data points, which had low BLEU scores. Among these instances, the most frequent DQR categories were *Sets and Ranges* (44.25%), followed by *Missing Values, Unique Values, and Types* (28.64%), and *Datetime Parsing* (21.48%). However, further analysis revealed that many prompts were associated with multiple categories, making it inaccurate to attribute errors solely to a single category.

In addition to the quantitative analysis described above, we conducted a manual review of the responses generated by both the GPT model and the LLaMA model fine-tuned with GPT-augmented data. Each model's outputs were evaluated qualitatively to determine which model produced more accurate and contextually appropriate Great Expectations validation rules. This manual assessment revealed a range of performance strengths and weaknesses for both models, which are detailed below.

1. **Rule Omission:** The fine-tuned LLaMA model frequently omitted enforcing data type validation rules (e.g., `integer`, `float`) when processing numeric prompts that involved range checks. Instead of specifying both type constraints and range constraints, LLaMA often focused solely on minimum and maximum value boundaries, neglecting the type verification component.
2. **Distribution Handling:** The LLaMA model exhibited notable challenges in handling distribution-related prompts, particularly those involving uniform and normal distributions. In contrast, GPT consistently applied the `parameterized_distribution_ks_test_p_value_to_be_greater_than` expectation effectively, demonstrating superior performance in this category.
3. **Multi-Column Relationships:** The LLaMA model faced significant difficulties in generating correct validation rules for prompts requiring comparisons between two columns, such as verifying that the values in one column were less than or greater than the values in another column. GPT handled these multicolumn relationships more reliably by correctly selecting and structuring the appropriate expectations. Example Prompt: *"Values in the 'Start_Date' column should always precede values in the 'End_Date' column when the 'Status' column equals 'Completed'."*

Despite these issues, LLaMa demonstrated particular strengths in certain areas like:

1. **Reference Prompts:** LLaMa excelled at understanding time reference-based prompts, such as prompts that check for dates using date references. For example, "dates within the last past year", "dates should be in the future", or "dates should be in the past or future". It performed better than GPT in these cases.
2. **Percentage and Range Prompts:** LLaMa was also more adept at interpreting prompts involving percentages or percentage change, particularly when the prompt specified column values that should reflect these changes.
3. **Maximum and Minimum Value Prompts:** GPT frequently struggled with prompts involving maximum and minimum values, often misapplying distribution rules. LLaMa excelled in these situations by interpreting the instructions more comprehensively and using range-based rules.
4. **JSON Schema Generation:** LLaMa demonstrated greater expressiveness, especially in generating JSON schemas, outperforming GPT in this area.

4.3 RQ2: Do Fine-Tuned LLMs Outperform Generic Models in GE Rule Accuracy and Consistency?

To improve the performance of the fine-tuned model and address the issues identified in Sect. 4.2, we conducted a final round of fine-tuning on the LLaMA model using an enhanced dataset. The dataset was refined by manually correcting the weaknesses observed in the GPT-generated responses. This additional fine-tuning stage was carried out to evaluate whether an open-source LLM, after targeted adaptation, could outperform closed-source LLMs in generating high-quality Great Expectations validation rules. We then compared the performance of the initial model (fine-tuned on GPT responses) against the final fine-tuned model using the same evaluation metrics described previously, as shown in Table 3.

Table 3. Performance metrics for Fine-Tuned LLM

Metrics	Measures	Fine-Tuned LLM Score	Improvement (%)
ROUGE-1	Average F1	0.8824	+14.3%
ROUGE-2	Average F1	0.8415	+14.5%
ROUGE-L	Average F1	0.8621	+14.7%
BLEU	-	0.8165	+31.6%
METEOR	-	0.8400	+23.8%
BERTScore	F1	0.9754	+8.7%

The new fine-tuning of the LLaMA model on the improved dataset resulted in substantial performance gains. The final fine-tuned model consistently outperformed the previous version across all evaluation metrics. Specifically, the BLEU score improved by 31.6%, increasing from 0.6204 to 0.8165, reflecting a higher degree of accuracy in generating GE rules. BERTScore F1 also improved, reaching 0.9754, indicating stronger semantic alignment with the reference expectations. Furthermore, the ROUGE scores increased by approximately 14%, demonstrating enhanced coherence, structural correctness, and completeness in the generated validation rules.

Table 4. Comparison of Traditional Rule-Based vs. LLM-Based Rule Generation

Metric	Traditional Rule-Based	LLM-Based (Fine-Tuned)
Average Creation Time	4.3 min/rule	less than 5 sec/rule
Batch Generation	One-by-one	Supported
Manual Effort Rating	Moderate–High	None (automated)

4.4 RQ3: Comparison with Traditional Rule-Based Rule Creation

This section presents the comparative results between the proposed fine-tuned LLaMA model and the traditional manual rule-based method conducted by a team of QA professionals (three Engineers). The comparison covers three key performance indicators aligned with the experimental protocol described in Sect. 3.6.

Table 4 presents a side-by-side comparison of the traditional manual rule-based method and the LLM-based (fine-tuned) approach across six key evaluation dimensions. The Average Creation Time metric reflects the efficiency of rule development, showing that manually writing a Great Expectations (GE) rule takes on average 4.3 min, while the LLM generates rules in under 5 s. This stark contrast highlights the time-saving potential of automation. The Batch Generation capability–absent in manual workflows–refers to the ability of the LLM to process and generate multiple rules simultaneously from a batch of prompts. This is especially beneficial in large-scale data environments, where hundreds of DQRs need to be translated at once.

Finally, the Manual Effort Rating captures the perceived cognitive and technical workload reported by QA engineers during manual rule creation. While the manual process was consistently rated as moderate to high effort, the LLM-based method requires virtually no manual intervention for rule generation, significantly lowering the barrier for adoption in production pipelines. Although our approach automates rule generation, it does not eliminate the need for manual validation. Around 5–20% of the generated rules still require correction, particularly in complex scenarios. This represents a major reduction compared to traditional workflows, which require full manual rule creation.

5   Threats to Validity

Despite the promising results, several threats to the validity of this study must be acknowledged. Internal validity may be affected by prompt phrasing or dataset bias, though we mitigated this by using standardized prompts and cross-metric evaluations. To mitigate this, we standardized the prompt-response format and conducted cross-metric evaluations to validate consistency across different rule types.

Our findings are derived from datasets in the telecommunications and IT sectors. Generalizing the approach to other domains, such as healthcare or finance, is reserved for future work. To address this limitation, upcoming iterations will involve fine-tuning and evaluating the model on datasets from diverse domains. This will enable us to assess the model's adaptability to varying schema structures, constraint vocabularies, and regulatory contexts. These efforts aim to provide a more comprehensive evaluation of the model's generalization capabilities across industries.

Construct validity concerns how well our metrics reflect the true quality of generated rules. While we used standard NLP metrics (BLEU, ROUGE, METEOR, BERTScore), they emphasize surface similarity and may miss logical accuracy. To mitigate this, we included expert reviews and completeness scoring, though these are subjective and limited in scope.

6 Discussion

Fine-tuned LLMs effectively automate GE rule generation, improving both accuracy and efficiency. The strong performance across semantic and syntactic metrics (BLEU, ROUGE, METEOR, and BERTScore) demonstrates the effectiveness of domain-specific fine-tuning.

However, this work also reveals critical challenges that limit its immediate applicability in industrial settings. The model encounters difficulties when handling prompts that involve multiple columns, statistical distributions, and aggregate validations. These limitations impact production data pipelines. Inaccurate multi-column validations risk invalid records and downstream failures, highlighting the need for human oversight in complex rules. Therefore, while the model automates much of the standard rule generation, complex relational logic still needs human review or post-processing to ensure integrity. Cross-domain applicability remains a future direction. Despite limitations, the approach offers immediate gains in standard validation tasks.

7 Conclusion and Future Work

This study demonstrates that fine-tuned LLMs, specifically LoRA-adapted LLaMA-3.2-3B models, can significantly improve the automation of data quality rule generation from natural language specifications. Our method improved rule accuracy and coverage via domain-specific fine-tuning.

Nonetheless, critical gaps remain. Handling complex multi-constraint rules, ensuring cross-domain generalization, and improving the explainability of generated rules must be addressed to realize the full potential of LLMs in production-grade data governance systems.

Future work will concentrate on refining the model through targeted fine-tuning, particularly on complex categories such as multicolumn constraints and statistical validations. Additionally, Future work includes evaluating cross-domain generalization in healthcare (e.g., HL7) and finance. These domain-expansion efforts are critical to making the system robust and broadly applicable across enterprise settings.

Our approach addresses contextual accuracy, scalability, and hallucination concerns through domain-specific fine-tuning and expert-reviewed augmentation.

These findings suggest that the proposed method–especially when combining LoRA-based fine-tuning and curated GPT augmentation–offers a practical and scalable path for overcoming key challenges in LLM-driven data validation.

Acknowledgments. This research was supported by the Behavior-enabled IoT (BeT) PRIN 2022 project (2022TEPX4R). The manuscript includes language refinements assisted by generative AI tools (e.g., Grammarly, ChatGPT); all content was subsequently reviewed and edited by the first author to ensure clarity, precision, and accuracy.

References

1. Van Der Loo, M.P., De Jonge, E.: Data validation, arXiv preprint arXiv: 2012.12028 (2020)
2. Redman, T.C.: The impact of poor data quality on the typical enterprise. Commun. ACM **41**(2), 79–82 (1998)
3. Pipino, L.L., Lee, Y.W., Wang, R.Y.: Data quality assessment. Commun. ACM **45**(4), 211–218 (2002)
4. G. Expectations Great expectations (2021). https://greatexpectations.io/
5. Madnick, S., Wang, R., Xian, X.: The design and implementation of a corporate householding knowledge processor to improve data quality. J. Manag. Inf. Syst. **20**(3), 41–70 (2003)
6. Achiam, J.., et al.: Gpt-4 technical report, arXiv preprint, arXiv: 2303.08774 (2023)
7. Touvron, H., et al.: Llama: Open and efficient foundation language models. arXiv preprint, arXiv: 2302.13971 (2023)
8. Batini, C., Cappiello, C., Francalanci, C., Maurino, A.: Methodologies for data quality assessment and improvement. ACM Comput. Surv. (CSUR) **41**(3), 1–52 (2009)
9. Sculley, D., et al.: achine learning: The high interest credit card of technical debt," In: ML: software engineering for machine learning (NIPS 2014 Workshop), vol. 8. Cambridge, MA (2014)
10. Hu, E.J., et al.: Lora: low-rank adaptation of large language models. ICLR **1**(2), 3 (2022)
11. Zhang, T., Kishore, V., Wu, F., Weinberger, K.Q., Artzi, Y.: Bertscore: Evaluating text generation with bert. arXiv preprint, arXiv: 1904.09675 (2019)
12. Strong, D.M., Lee, Y.W., Wang, R.Y.: Data quality in context. Commun. ACM **40**(5), 103–110 (1997)
13. Bertino, E., Sandhu, R.: Database security-concepts, approaches, and challenges. IEEE Trans. Dependable Secure Comput. **2**(1), 2–19 (2005)
14. Strimling, Y.: Beyond accuracy: what documentation quality means to readers. Tech. Commun. **66**(1), 7–29 (2019)
15. Abedjan, Z., et al.: Detecting data errors: where are we and what needs to be done? Proc. VLDB Endow. **9**(12), 993–1004 (2016)
16. Hellerstein, J.M.: Quantitative data cleaning for large databases (2013)
17. Bangad, N. et al.: A theoretical framework for ai-driven data quality monitoring in high-volume data environments, arXiv preprint, arXiv: 2410.08576 (2024)
18. A. Labs. Deequ - unit tests for data (2018). https://github.com/awslabs/deequ
19. TensorFlow Tensorflow data validation (2022). https://www.tensorflow.org/tfx/guide/tfdv
20. Halevy, A., Norvig, P., Pereira, F.: The unreasonable effectiveness of data. IEEE Intell. Syst. **24**(2), 8–12 (2009)
21. Song, J., He, Y.: Auto-validate: Unsupervised data validation using data-domain patterns inferred from data lakes. In: Proceedings of the 2021 International Conference on Management of Data, 2021, pp. 1678–1691
22. Raiaan, M.A.K., et al.: A review on large language models: architectures, applications, taxonomies, open issues and challenges. IEEE Access **12**, 26839–26874 (2024)
23. Zhang, M., Ji, Z., Luo, Z., Wu, Y., Chai, C.: Applications and challenges for large language models: from data management perspective. In: 2024 IEEE 40th International Conference on Data Engineering (ICDE), pp. 5530–5541 (2024)

24. Schäfer, M., Nadi, S., Eghbali, A., Tip, F.: An empirical evaluation of using large language models for automated unit test generation. IEEE Trans. Software Eng. **50**(1), 85–105 (2024)
25. Caldiera,V.R.B.G., Rombach, H.D.: The goal question metric approach. Encyclopedia Softw. Eng. 528–532 (1994)
26. C.-Y. Lin, "Rouge: A package for automatic evaluation of summaries," in *Text summarization branches out*, 2004, pp. 74–81
27. Papineni, K., Roukos, S., Ward, T., Zhu, W.-J.: Bleu: a method for automatic evaluation of machine translation. In: Proceedings of the 40th Annual Meeting of the Association for Computational Linguistics, pp. 311–318 (2002)
28. Banerjee, S., Lavie, A.: Meteor: an automatic metric for mt evaluation with improved correlation with human judgments. In: Proceedings of the acl Workshop on Intrinsic and Extrinsic Evaluation Measures for Machine Translation and/or Summarization, pp. 65–72 (2005)

ML Pipeline Insights Service for Rule-Based Assessment of Training Practices in Reinforcement Learning

Evangelos Ntentos[1]([⊠])[iD], Francesco Urdih[2][iD], and Uwe Zdun[1][iD]

[1] Faculty of Computer Science, Research Group Software Architecture,
University of Vienna, Vienna, Austria
{evangelos.ntentos,uwe.zdun}@univie.ac.at
[2] UniVie Doctoral School Computer Science (DoCS), University of Vienna,
Vienna, Austria
francesco.urdih@univie.ac.at

Abstract. As artificial intelligence continues to advance, Reinforcement Learning (RL) has established itself as a core approach for developing intelligent agents that make decisions over time. As RL systems grow in complexity, the need for standardized training practices becomes critical. This paper introduces a rule-based assessment approach to enforce best practices in RL training. We define a comprehensive set of architectural rules focused on RL pipeline practices, models versioning, multi-agents deployment and managing models in inference. Our methodology integrates Large Language Models (LLMs) and custom-based code detectors to ensure compliance with these best practices across diverse RL systems. We developed a *ML pipeline insights service* to automatically validate RL training practices directly from the source code. We validate our approach by applying it in a large-scale industrial case study and sixteen open-source case studies. Our evaluation showed that custom-based detectors achieved near-perfect precision and recall ($F_1 \approx 0.98$), while LLM-based detectors provided scalable validation with moderate F_1 scores (0.67–0.71), demonstrating the hybrid approach's strength in balancing accuracy and automation. The results demonstrate our tool's accuracy in identifying and enforcing best practices with high precision and recall rates, highlighting its practical applicability and automation feasibility.

Keywords: Reinforcement Learning · Best Practices · Machine Learning · Architecture Rules · Case Studies

1 Introduction

Reinforcement Learning has emerged as a major paradigm for training intelligent agents to make sequential decisions in the dynamic field of artificial intelligence and machine learning. As RL architectures become increasingly complex and scalable, practices regarding training strategies and their impact on software architecture grow more intricate. Several studies have aimed to document patterns and best practices in training strategies within RL architectures [1,9,11].

Reliable RL pipelines go beyond training, they require careful planning for development, management, and deployment [2]. Key stages include data collection, training, evaluation, and deployment, with automation ensuring efficiency and consistency. In

D. Taibi and D. Smite (Eds.): SEAA 2025, LNCS 16081, pp. 148–163, 2026.
https://doi.org/10.1007/978-3-032-04190-6_10

RL, frequent model updates make version tracking essential for reproducibility and collaboration.

Multi-agent reinforcement learning (MARL) adds complexity due to agent interactions. Developers address this with modular pipelines, communication strategies, and tools like graph neural networks for coordination and hierarchical frameworks for scalable learning [14, 21].

To address the complexities and variations in RL training practices, we propose a method, based on our previous approach [13], which investigates how well LLMs can identify patterns and practices, to automatically evaluate RL training-related practices directly from source code. This involves expanding our prior set of architectural rules to a comprehensive collection of thirty-two rules and the corresponding detectors. The framework is designed as an ML pipeline insights service, leveraging a service-based architecture to provide real-time insights into ML training and inference processes.

To validate our approach's applicability and the performance of the defined rules, we performed a large-scale industrial case study of applying RL in a cyber-physical system for production automation and sixteen open-source case studies of RL systems. The industrial case study uses the insights service to observe multiple CI/CD pipelines across production facilities. This comprehensive evaluation allows us to assess the practical implementation of our rules across diverse RL environments and training practices, demonstrating our approach's practical applicability and automation feasibility.

The paper is organized as follows: Sect. 2 introduces RL practices. The methodology and specifics of automatic rule checking are discussed in Sect. 3. Case studies are presented in Sect. 4. The quantitative evaluation and case study are discussed in Sect. 5. Section 6 interprets the results, while Sect. 7 addresses potential validity threats. Related work is reviewed in Sect. 8, and Sect. 9 concludes the paper.

2   Background on Reinforcement Learning Practices

This section provides background information on the RL practices in the focus of this work.

RL Pipeline Implementation. To ensure everything runs properly, it is important to follow a certain process: starting with collecting the right data, then training the model, testing its performance, and finally putting it into action. By following these steps, RL workflows are more scalable, easy to reproduce, and dependable [2]. One key part of building an effective pipeline is automating the repetitive tasks.

Model Versioning. A key practice is that in RL versioning models is used to ensure that experiments are reproducible, changes are traceable, and collaborative development runs smoothly [8]. Since RL models are frequently updated in response to new data or policy changes, having a structured way to track different versions becomes very important. Version control tools such as Git make it easier to log changes to models and training data, which is critical for comparing performance across different iterations [2].

Multi-agent Aspects and Deployment Practices. MARL adds an extra layer of complexity because it involves several autonomous agents interacting within the same environment. To make MARL work well in practice, it needs certain strategies for things such as coordination, communication, and scaling, especially since the environment can change over time and agents often do not have full visibility of it [21]. One of the biggest factors in successful MARL systems is strong communication between agents. Recent techniques using graph neural networks [12] have advanced the field by modeling how agents relate to each other, which helps improve cooperation in tasks like multi-agent collaborations.

Managing Models in Inference. Managing models efficiently during inference is critical when RL systems are deployed in the real world scenario. For maintaining speed and responsiveness, recent practices focus on reducing the computation, for instance, using sparse computation techniques [3]. These practices help RL models make quick decisions even when resources are limited. Another aspect that is important to understand is why a model makes a certain decision. This is relevant to interpretability. By linking RL with probabilistic inference frameworks, it can make the decision-making process more transparent [10].

3   Approach

This section describes the research methods followed in this study and our rule-based assessment approach to ensure best practices. The data used in and produced as part of this study have been made available online for reproducibility[1].

3.1   Research Methods

We initially reviewed various knowledge sources on RL-specific best practices, including practitioner books, blogs, scientific literature ([4,7,16,18,19]), and open-source repositories. Subsequently, we conducted a qualitative analysis using Grounded Theory (open and axial coding), to analyze the collected data and extract relevant practices. We then formulated thirty-two rules and developed two types of source code detectors, custom-based and LLM-based detectors, to automate compliance with each practice described in Sect. 2. Next, we selected a number of case studies, analyzed them, and used for evaluation. The main steps after analysis are:

Architectural Rule Definitions. We defined key rules to improve RL training reliability and performance across four areas: pipeline design, model versioning, multi-agent deployment, and inference. Pipeline rules ensure modularity and reproducibility. Versioning rules promote traceable, automated model management using registries and tools like Kubernetes or Helm. For multi-agent setups, rules address coordination, scalability, and conflict handling. Inference rules support versioned models, and real-time monitoring.

---

[1] https://doi.org/10.5281/zenodo.15487181.

Development of Detectors and Insights Service. In the next step, we developed a prototype tool with source code detectors and an insights service for automating the validation of RL training practices to be in compliance with the specified rules. This includes writing advanced code detectors that met the rules requirements. The detectors were integrated into the RL systems, enabling them to parse source code and generate outputs in JSON format with the detected patterns and compliance values.

Application to Case Studies and Validation. The final step of our approach involves the usage of the insights service for evaluating different RL systems. This involved thorough validation in different scenarios, including one industrial case study and sixteen open-source RL systems. This evaluation showed the weaknesses and strengths of the RL training practices.

3.2   Architecture of the ML Pipeline Insights Service

The *ML pipeline insights service* architecture consists of several key modules, each playing a crucial role in the analysis and validation process. The major components of the architecture are as follows: The *Service* orchestrates the analysis workflow by taking project source code as input and running rule-based detectors. These detectors, which check for best practices and issues in RL code, are split into two types: built-in rules for common patterns and custom rules tailored to specific project needs. Rule-based detectors are integrated in a *Code Analyzer*, which parses RL source code and checks for rule compliance. It identifies violations and passes the findings to the *Result Generation* component, which outputs detailed JSON reports.

Figure 1 provides an overview of the architecture of the ML pipeline insights service. The service runs within the *MLOps pipeline* of the ML project or as a standalone service. It provides its reports to the *Web-based Insights UI*, enabling a continuous feedback loop with the ML specialists and software architects working on the project.

3.3   Architecture of LLM-Based Detection Approach

The *LLM-based detection framework* is crafted as a modular and intelligent system for automating the discovery of best practices within RL-based software architectures. Figure 1 shows the architecture of the framework.

The main component of the system is the *LLM Code Flow Executor*, which runs full validation workflows or targeted checks. These workflows, defined in the *LLM Code Flows* module, specify rule-aligned detection steps. The *LLM* module abstracts different language models, while the *Conversation* class handles structured interactions, allowing detectors to query and interpret LLM responses within context. The interactions between the detection logic and the LLM are managed by the *Conversation* class within the *LLM* module. It maintains conversational state, enabling detectors to pose structured queries and interpret the LLM's contextual responses as part of the detection process. The *LLM-based Detectors* module implements the detection routines responsible for verifying the architectural rules. Each detector receives a shared Data Transfer Object, the *LLM Code Flow DTO*, which encapsulates critical context such as project metadata, source file paths, and accumulated validation results. As the object moves through the detector pipeline, it gradually builds a compliance report.

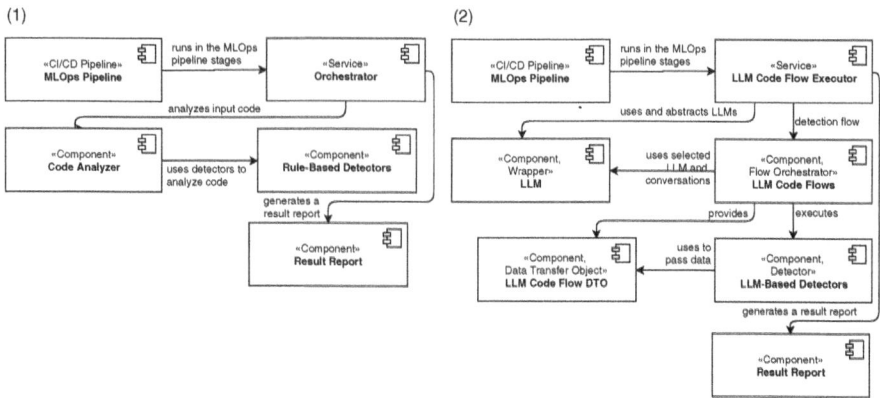

Fig. 1. (1): Architecture of the ML Pipeline Insights Service, (2): Architecture of the LLM-Based Detectors

3.4   Rules and Detectors

Rules. Tables 1, 2, 3 and 4 present a binary classification of architectural rules used in this study. A rule is considered true when the associated architectural principle is evidently implemented in the source code. Conversely, a rule is false if the implementation either contradicts or lacks the required elements.

For example, in the evaluation of CS11, the rule *R11: Maintain a centralized model registry* holds true because all trained RL models are saved in uniquely named directories, with comprehensive metadata including training level, mode, and performance logs, as implemented across files. Similarly, the rule *R13: Implement versioning semantics* is also supported: while semantic versioning is not explicitly used, the code applies a structured naming convention with incremental epoch tracking and level-based model restoration, ensuring backward compatibility and traceability.

Rule-Based Detectors. The rule-based detectors consist of specialized functions that analyze source code to determine rule compliance. These detectors use regular expressions, pattern matching, and parsing techniques to identify relevant implementation patterns.

Custom rule-based detectors directly analyze functional roles. For example, in CS12, detectors identify structured logging via `logging.debug()` and track evaluation callbacks like `EvalLogCallback`, while verifying modularity through the separation of classes and function responsibilities across independent files.

LLM-based detectors leverage LLMs to examine source code, identify patterns, and assess the adherence of these patterns to architectural rules. Unlike rule-based systems, these detectors are capable of flexible reasoning, allowing them to recognize relevant structures in the code even when they do not precisely conform to predefined syntactic patterns.

Our design emphasizes a high degree of modularity: Each LLM-based detector focuses on identifying a specific fragment of code that contributes to realizing a particular rule. Rather than attempting to assess an entire rule, each detector contributes

Table 1. RL Pipeline Implementation Rules

Rule	Description
R01	Maintain a dedicated configuration file specifying all RL pipeline parameters, including environment settings, agent hyperparameters, and training policies
R02	Ensure modular design by separating environment creation, agent design, training logic, and evaluation into distinct components
R03	Incorporate structured logging mechanisms to record events and metrics at each stage of the RL pipeline, including environment setup, training progress, reward trends, and evaluation outcomes
R04	Define consistent data formats (e.g., CSV, JSON) for storing training metrics, policy weights, and performance records to facilitate analysis and reproducibility
R05	Implement checks to ensure that trained agents are compatible with various versions of the environment before deployment
R06	Integrate hyperparameter optimization frameworks (e.g., Grid Search, Bayesian Optimization) to automate the tuning process
R07	Incorporate checkpointing strategies that save the model's state at regular intervals
R08	Regularly test policy generalization by evaluating the trained agent on variations of the environment
R09	Set fixed random seeds and track software/library versions to ensure that training experiments are reproducible
R10	Establish evaluation protocols that compare agent performance against baseline policies and predefined benchmarks

a single piece to the overall validation. This granularity has two distinct advantages: it enhances the precision and reliability of the LLM's responses, and it allows for transparent traceability between the rule and its concrete realizations in the source code.

The detection workflow follows structured steps: the LLM scans code for relevant elements, checks them against architectural rules, and links any violations to specific code lines. It works within a larger framework that manages data, settings, and reporting, ensuring reliable validation.

4   Case Studies

In this section, we describe the case studies used to evaluate our approach and test the performance of the rule detection. Table 5 summarizes the case studies.

4.1   Industrial Case Study

To test our rule-based assessment approach, we applied our *ML pipeline insights service* to a real industrial system. This system is a flexible framework for training both single-agent and multi-agent reinforcement learning (RL) models across different environments. It includes modules for managing agents, customizing training environments, and running both centralized and decentralized learning. The framework also supports advanced hyperparameter tuning and optimization to improve AI performance.

Table 2. RL Model Versioning and Lifecycle Management Rules

Rule	Description
R11	Maintain a centralized model registry to store all trained RL models along with comprehensive metadata (version ID, training environment conditions, hyperparameters, performance metrics)
R12	Interactions with the model registry or other system components (training pipelines, deployment orchestrators, inference services) should only occur via defined HTTP APIs
R13	Implement versioning semantics (e.g., semantic versioning or incremental numeric identifiers) consistently across all models stored in the registry
R14	Deployments of RL models should use Kubernetes manifests or Helm charts for scalability and controlled rollouts
R15	Implement automated rollback mechanisms triggered by threshold breaches or deployment errors
R16	Integrate a standardized model evaluation step within the pipeline, systematically comparing candidate RL models using predefined metrics
R17	Automate the selection and promotion of the optimal RL model candidate based on evaluation results
R18	Define and monitor key indicators (e.g., environment state changes, performance degradation) explicitly as automated triggers to initiate RL model retraining pipelines without manual intervention
R19	Use configurable threshold parameters for retraining triggers via YAML, JSON, or similar configuration files
R20	Implement structured logging of retraining events, capturing trigger reasons, timestamps, relevant metrics, and outcomes
R21	Store metadata such as training parameters, environment configurations, simulation settings, and performance metrics
R22	Upon successful training in simulation, automatically register the new model version in the model registry along with its metadata
R23	Ensure that deployment stages reference specific model versions from the registry
R24	Maintain separate stages (e.g., development, staging, production) with distinct model versions to facilitate safe testing and deployment. e.g. canary releases and A/B testing
R25	Incorporate small real-world testing of newly deployed models

Table 3. Multi-Agent System Deployment Rules

Rule	Description
R26	Utilize established messaging libraries or frameworks to facilitate inter-agent communication
R27	Employ frameworks that support dynamic agent management and scalability
R28	Implement logging mechanisms to monitor inter-agent interactions
R29	Implement conflict detection and resolution mechanisms within the agent framework

The platform is used to automate production tasks with AI and is designed to work smoothly in real factory settings. Our insights service is integrated into its MLOps pipeline, offering real-time feedback on training and inference to support best practices. Developed by a large team, the framework is being rolled out across factories worldwide. It helps standardize production processes and gives ML engineers and software architects clear insights into how training pipelines are built and maintained across projects. This case study shows our tool works well in a complex, real-world environment.

Table 4. Rules for Managing Models in Inference

Rule	Description
R30	Utilize frameworks that optimize resource usage during model inference
R31	Maintain a versioned repository of models to track changes
R32	Implement monitoring tools to evaluate model performance metrics in real-time

Table 5. Overview of Python-based systems and their functionalities

ID	Description
ICS	This system focuses on an advanced framework for single-agent and multi-agent RL. It enables thorough testing and optimization of AI policies in diverse environments (See Sect. 4.1 for details)
CS1	In this system, zombies originate at the top border of the screen and move downward along varying, unpredictable trajectories until they reach the bottom borderhttps://pettingzoo.farama.org/tutorials/sb3/kaz/
CS2	In this system, Waterworld, the simulation revolves around archaea organisms navigating their environment in a quest for survival. https://pettingzoo.farama.org/tutorials/sb3/waterworld/
CS3	This system is a Chess example. It uses the observation and action spaces similar to the AlphaZero method, with slight modifications https://pettingzoo.farama.org/tutorials/sb3/connect_four/
CS4	This system is a game that uses physics-based challenge where the objective is to guide a ball to the left wall of the game's boundary.https://pettingzoo.farama.org/tutorials/rllib/pistonball/
CS5	This system is a game where 2 players must connect four of their tokens vertically, horizontally, or diagonally. https://docs.agilerl.com/en/latest/tutorials/pettingzoo/dqn.html
CS6	This system is a classic Atari game, where there are two ships controlled by two players who are each trying to maximize their score. https://pettingzoo.farama.org/tutorials/agilerl/MADDPG/
CS7	This system trains AI agents to play Tic-Tac-Toe using the PettingZoo environment. https://github.com/Farama-Foundation/PettingZoo/blob/master/tutorials/Tianshou/3_cli_and_logging.py
CS8	In this system, there are two agents: the 'speaker' and the 'listener'. The 'speaker' agent possesses the ability to communicate verbally but lacks the capability to move autonomously.https://docs.agilerl.com/en/latest/tutorials/pettingzoo/matd3.html#matd3-tutorial
CS9	This system is also a classic Atari game similar to CS6 https://github.com/vwxyzjn/cleanrl/blob/master/cleanrl/ppo_pettingzoo_ma_atari.py
CS10	This system is similar to CS1. It trains agents in the "Knights-Archers-Zombies" environment using Black Death wrapper to handle agent deaths effectively. https://pettingzoo.farama.org/tutorials/sb3/kaz/
CS11	This system, HHMARL 2D, simulates hierarchical multi-agent air combat scenarios, where heterogeneous aircraft agents perform fight or escape maneuvers coordinated by a high-level commander policy. https://github.com/IDSIA/hhmarl_2D
CS12	This system, NFVdeep, applies deep reinforcement learning to dynamically orchestrate service function chains in network function virtualization environments. https://github.com/CN-UPB/NFVdeep
CS13	This system, IMIL (Infosys Model Inference Library), offers a unified, high-performance framework for loading and deploying machine learning models across diverse platforms and formats. https://github.com/Infosys/Infosys-Model-Inference-Library
CS14	This system implements a multi-agent concierge using LlamaIndex Workflows, where customizable agents equipped with tools collaboratively manage tasks and interact with users in a coordinated environment. https://github.com/run-Llama/multi-agent-concierge
CS15	This system applies distributed Proximal Policy Optimization (PPO) to manage multi-agent traffic light control in a SUMO-based urban grid, where each intersection acts as an independent reinforcement learning agent. https://github.com/maxbrenner-ai/Multi-Agent-Distributed-PPO-Traffc-light-control
CS16	This system, JAT (Jack of All Trades), is a multi-purpose transformer agent capable of handling diverse reinforcement learning and vision-language tasks using a unified architecture. https://github.com/huggingface/jat

5 Validation

In this section, we validate our approach by demonstrating how the defined rules support best practices in RL systems. Our evaluation uses three popular LLMs, OpenAI GPT-4o, Qwen2.5 72B, and Llama 3.3 70B. The OpenAI models were run on Microsoft Azure[2], while the five freely available models were deployed via OLlama[3] on a Cisco UCS C245 M6 server. We evaluated their effectiveness across diverse RL settings and addressed the following research questions.

This paper aims to answer the following research questions:

- **RQ1 Accuracy:** How accurately does the LLM-based rule checking mechanism ensure compliance with best practices for RL training compared to the custom-based rule checking mechanism?
- **RQ2 Automation:** How to automatically validate these architectural rules?

5.1 Validation Setup

The validation involved three main steps: defining architecture rules covering RL pipelines, model versioning, multi-agent setups, and inference; implementing a tool to automatically check code against these rules; and applying this tool in a case study to assess rule compliance in real RL systems.

To evaluate our rule-based detectors, we use three metrics: precision, recall, and F1-score. *True Positives (TP)* are correctly identified best practice cases, *False Positives (FP)* are incorrect detections, and *False Negatives (FN)* are missed valid cases. We exclude *True Negatives (TN)* since our ground truth only includes compliant code.

$$P = \frac{TP}{TP + FP} \quad R = \frac{TP}{TP + FN} \quad F_1 = \frac{2PR}{P + R}$$

Precision (P) shows how accurate the detections are, recall (R) shows how complete they are, and the F1-score balances both to give an overall performance measure. This focus helps us assess how well the method detects compliant code.

5.2 Results

This section presents the validation results, summarized in Tables 6 7 8 9, assessing the accuracy of the rule-based detectors.

5.3 Results on the Industrial Case Study

The *custom-based detectors* achieved consistently high performance across all categories, with perfect precision, recall, and F1 scores in most cases. These detectors were particularly effective at capturing the structure and logic of RL-specific patterns such as checkpointing, modular training loops, version control mechanisms, and agent-environment configuration.

---

[2] https://azure.com.
[3] https://oLlama.com.

All LLMs also performed strongly, especially for general RL pipeline rules and multi-agent setup, where they achieved perfect scores. These models reliably identified practices such as agent orchestration, modular environment definitions, and deployment-ready configurations. However, their recall dropped significantly in rules related to *model versioning and inference management*. While their precision remained high (1.0), indicating correct predictions when rules were found, the low recall (0.5) shows that they missed many relevant code instances. These suggest that while LLMs can identify well-known or syntactically explicit practices, they are less sensitive to subtler implementation patterns or project-specific naming conventions, especially in version control and inference flows.

The *N/A* in the tables indicate cases where no relevant rules were supported or detected within the system.

5.4   Results on the Open-Source Case Studies

RL Pipeline Implementation. The custom-based detectors demonstrated strong and consistent performance across all case studies, with F1 scores generally exceeding 0.90 and reaching 1.0 in systems such as CS6–CS9 and CS12–CS15. These detectors successfully identified best practices such as modular environment and agent creation, structured logging, and separation of training logic. In comparison, Qwen2.5 and Llama 3.3 also showed high precision but varied in recall. Qwen2.5, for instance, scored well in CS3 and CS7 (F1 = 0.91 and 0.89), but underperformed in CS4 and CS14 (F1 = 0.50 and 0.46). GPT-4o generally had lower recall, such as in CS6 and CS7, indicating it often failed to identify some rule occurrences even when predictions were accurate.

Model Versioning and Lifecycle Management. Custom detectors consistently achieved perfect scores across all systems (F1 = 1.0), showing strong capability in detecting practices such as checkpointing with metadata, rollback mechanisms, and version tracking. In contrast, all LLM-based detectors exhibited performance degradation in this category. Recall values were particularly low, resulting in low to moderate F1 scores. For example, in CS4 and CS9, Qwen2.5 and Llama had F1 scores as low as 0.12–0.13. GPT-4o showed relatively better recall in CS2 and CS5 (F1 = 0.75 and 0.60), but still fell short of the custom-based detector performance.

Multi-agent Aspects and Deployment. For this practice, custom-based detectors again performed optimally in all relevant systems, achieving perfect precision and recall. These detectors effectively recognized common multi-agent configurations, communication mechanisms, and environment setups. The LLM-based detectors showed variable performance. While Qwen2.5 had strong results in CS14 (F1 = 0.86), it performed poorly or failed entirely in systems like CS3, CS12–CS16. GPT-4o and Llama 3.3 achieved strong results in CS9 and CS14 (F1 = 0.80–0.86) but showed limited recall elsewhere. The inconsistencies suggest that multi-agent patterns that are not explicit or follow custom abstractions challenge the LLMs.

Managing Models in Inference. Inference rules performing models and their integration into evaluation scripts–were reliably captured by custom detectors in all applicable

Table 6. Results on Rules for RL Pipeline Implementation

Case Study	Custom-Based			Qwen 2.5			GPT-4o			LLaMA 3.3		
	Precision	Recall	F1 Score	Precision	Recall	F1 Score	Precision	Recall	F1 Score	Precision	Recall	F1 Score
ICS	1.00	0.89	0.94	0.90	1.00	0.95	0.89	0.89	0.89	0.90	1.00	0.95
CS1	1.00	0.80	0.89	1.00	0.60	0.75	0.56	1.00	0.71	0.83	1.00	0.91
CS2	1.00	0.80	0.89	1.00	0.60	0.75	0.50	0.60	0.55	0.67	0.80	0.73
CS3	1.00	0.80	0.89	0.83	1.00	0.91	0.50	0.80	0.62	0.50	0.80	0.62
CS4	1.00	0.75	0.86	0.38	0.75	0.50	0.50	0.50	0.50	0.33	0.75	0.46
CS5	1.00	0.89	0.94	0.86	0.67	0.75	0.88	0.78	0.82	0.88	0.78	0.82
CS6	1.00	1.00	1.00	0.56	0.83	0.67	1.00	0.17	0.29	0.60	1.00	0.75
CS7	1.00	1.00	1.00	0.80	1.00	0.89	0.50	0.12	0.20	0.80	1.00	0.89
CS8	1.00	1.00	1.00	0.60	1.00	0.75	0.60	0.50	0.55	0.56	0.83	0.67
CS9	1.00	1.00	1.00	0.44	1.00	0.62	0.40	0.50	0.44	0.44	1.00	0.62
CS10	1.00	0.80	0.89	0.67	0.40	0.50	0.50	0.80	0.62	0.67	0.80	0.73
CS11	1.00	0.88	0.93	0.80	1.00	0.89	0.78	0.88	0.82	0.80	1.00	0.89
CS12	1.00	1.00	1.00	0.70	1.00	0.82	0.62	0.71	0.67	0.70	1.00	0.82
CS13	1.00	1.00	1.00	0.50	1.00	0.67	0.44	0.80	0.57	0.50	1.00	0.67
CS14	1.00	1.00	1.00	0.30	1.00	0.46	0.12	0.33	0.18	0.30	1.00	0.46
CS15	1.00	1.00	1.00	0.60	1.00	0.75	0.62	0.83	0.71	0.60	1.00	0.75
CS16	1.00	0.83	0.91	0.60	1.00	0.75	0.60	1.00	0.75	0.60	1.00	0.75

systems. In contrast, LLMs struggled across most systems, with frequent N/A entries indicating no rule detections. When applicable, Qwen2.5 and Llama achieved moderate results (e.g., CS5–CS9 with F1 between 0.50–0.80). GPT-4o performed slightly better in CS9, CS11–CS13, but generally failed to detect rules in systems where inference handling was not explicitly coded or used unconventional naming.

6   Discussion

This section examines the research questions and discusses other lessons learned.

RQ1. Accuracy. The evaluation across the industrial case study and the sixteen open-source case studies confirms that the overall detection accuracy of the approach is high when using custom rule-based detectors. These detectors consistently achieved near-perfect scores across all rule categories (Precision: 1.0, Recall: 0.96, and F1-score: 0.98 on average), demonstrating their effectiveness in capturing full rule implementations, including practices like metadata tracking, inference-ready model handling, or agent orchestration.

LLM-based detectors showed promising results but exhibited variance across rule types and systems. Qwen2.5 achieved an average Precision of 0.71, Recall of 0.74, and F1-score of 0.69, with relatively strong performance in common RL pipeline configurations and multi-agent aspects but lower sensitivity for versioning and inference patterns. GPT-4o and Llama 3.3 performed similarly, with GPT-4o reaching an average F1 of 0.67 and Llama 3.3 achieving 0.68, both affected by recall drops in complex or less explicit code structures. These results indicate that LLMs can detect many true positives but still miss implicit or tightly coupled implementations.

RQ2. Automation. Both evaluated detection approaches support fully automated execution once configured. However, the degree of required *manual setup and adaptation*

Table 7. Results on RL Model Versioning and Lifecycle Management Rules

Case Study	Custom-Based			Qwen 2.5			GPT-4o			LLaMA 3.3		
	Precision	Recall	F1 Score	Precision	Recall	F1 Score	Precision	Recall	F1 Score	Precision	Recall	F1 Score
ICS	1.00	1.00	1.00	0.33	1.00	0.50	0.33	1.00	0.50	0.33	1.00	0.50
CS1	1.00	1.00	1.00	0.25	0.33	0.29	0.33	1.00	0.50	0.22	0.67	0.33
CS2	1.00	1.00	1.00	0.50	0.33	0.40	0.60	1.00	0.75	0.20	0.33	0.25
CS3	1.00	1.00	1.00	0.33	0.67	0.44	0.27	1.00	0.43	0.25	1.00	0.40
CS4	1.00	1.00	1.00	0.07	1.00	0.13	0.33	1.00	0.50	0.07	1.00	0.13
CS5	1.00	1.00	1.00	0.36	0.83	0.50	0.43	1.00	0.60	0.38	0.83	0.53
CS6	1.00	1.00	1.00	0.23	1.00	0.38	1.00	0.33	0.50	0.20	1.00	0.33
CS7	1.00	1.00	1.00	0.14	0.67	0.24	0.67	0.67	0.67	0.20	1.00	0.33
CS8	1.00	1.00	1.00	0.20	1.00	0.33	0.50	0.67	0.57	0.23	1.00	0.38
CS9	1.00	1.00	1.00	0.07	1.00	0.12	0.08	1.00	0.15	0.07	1.00	0.13
CS10	1.00	1.00	1.00	0.50	0.33	0.40	0.60	1.00	0.75	0.25	0.67	0.36
CS11	1.00	1.00	1.00	0.33	1.00	0.50	0.36	1.00	0.53	0.33	1.00	0.50
CS12	1.00	1.00	1.00	0.20	1.00	0.33	0.38	1.00	0.55	0.20	1.00	0.33
CS13	1.00	1.00	1.00	0.07	1.00	0.12	0.07	1.00	0.12	0.07	1.00	0.12
CS14	N/A	N/A	N/A	0.00	N/A	N/A	0.00	N/A	N/A	0.00	N/A	N/A
CS15	1.00	1.00	1.00	0.27	1.00	0.42	0.17	0.50	0.25	0.27	1.00	0.42
CS16	1.00	1.00	1.00	0.13	1.00	0.24	0.13	1.00	0.24	0.13	1.00	0.24

effort varies significantly. The custom detectors provide the highest accuracy across all rule categories but require rule-specific implementation tailored to the project context. This includes coding logic to trace rule-specific workflows, such as verifying inference-time model loading sequences.

In contrast, LLM-based detectors require no manual coding per rule but show varying performance across environments and rule types. They generalize well for common RL pipeline patterns, especially for modular design or agent orchestration, but struggle in accurately detecting rules that involve implicit logic or custom abstractions, such as lifecycle hooks or inference flow logic. These models offer a low-effort automation entry point but require post-hoc validation or fallback detection when full rule coverage is critical.

Further Lessons Learned. While LLMs provide flexibility and adaptability across projects and libraries without explicit reimplementation, their limitations in rule completeness and traceability remain evident. For example, in systems like CS4, CS13, and CS16, LLMs failed to detect rules that custom detectors handled precisely. This highlights the benefit of hybrid use: LLMs can quickly scan unfamiliar systems, whereas custom detectors should be employed when consistent detection or complete traceability is required. We recommend applying LLM-based detectors in early review phases for a broad but coarse overview, then refining findings with custom detectors where critical rules or complex code structures are involved. This staged use ensures scalability for ML observability pipelines, such as in CI/CD scenarios, while maintaining trust in detection accuracy.

7 Threats to Validity

In this section, we discuss the potential threats to the validity and the steps taken to mitigate these threats.

Table 8. Results on Multi-Agent Aspects and Deployment Rules

Case Study	Custom-Based			Qwen 2.5			GPT-4o			LLaMA 3.3		
	Precision	Recall	F1 Score	Precision	Recall	F1 Score	Precision	Recall	F1 Score	Precision	Recall	F1 Score
ICS	1.00	1.00	1.00	1.00	1.00	1.00	1.00	1.00	1.00	1.00	1.00	1.00
CS1	1.00	1.00	1.00	1.00	0.33	0.50	1.00	1.00	1.00	1.00	0.33	0.50
CS2	1.00	1.00	1.00	1.00	0.50	0.67	0.67	1.00	0.80	1.00	0.50	0.67
CS3	1.00	1.00	1.00	0.00	0.00	0.00	0.50	1.00	0.67	0.67	1.00	0.80
CS4	1.00	1.00	1.00	0.50	1.00	0.67	1.00	0.50	0.67	0.33	0.50	0.40
CS5	1.00	1.00	1.00	0.50	0.50	0.50	0.50	0.50	0.50	0.50	1.00	0.67
CS6	1.00	1.00	1.00	0.50	1.00	0.67	1.00	0.50	0.67	0.50	1.00	0.67
CS7	1.00	1.00	1.00	0.33	0.50	0.40	1.00	1.00	1.00	0.50	1.00	0.67
CS8	1.00	1.00	1.00	0.50	1.00	0.67	0.67	1.00	0.80	0.50	1.00	0.67
CS9	1.00	1.00	1.00	0.50	1.00	0.67	0.67	1.00	0.80	0.67	1.00	0.80
CS10	1.00	1.00	1.00	N/A	0.00	N/A	0.75	1.00	0.86	1.00	0.33	0.50
CS11	1.00	1.00	1.00	0.50	1.00	0.67	0.50	1.00	0.67	0.50	1.00	0.67
CS12	N/A	N/A	N/A	0.00	N/A	N/A	0.00	N/A	N/A	0.00	N/A	N/A
CS13	N/A	N/A	N/A	0.00	N/A	N/A	0.00	N/A	N/A	0.00	N/A	N/A
CS14	1.00	1.00	1.00	0.75	1.00	0.86	0.75	1.00	0.86	0.75	1.00	0.86
CS15	N/A	N/A	N/A	0.00	N/A	N/A	0.00	N/A	N/A	0.00	N/A	N/A
CS16	N/A	N/A	N/A	0.00	N/A	N/A	0.00	N/A	N/A	0.00	N/A	N/A

External validity refers to the generalizability of our findings. While our study includes one industrial and sixteen open-source case studies, broader testing across more domains is needed to strengthen generalizability. The current diversity helps mitigate threats, but future work will expand the dataset.

Internal validity ensures the accuracy of results and their attribution to the interventions. We maintained internal validity by rigorously defining and applying rules with our assessment framework. Detection algorithms were carefully implemented and manually verified to identify true positives and false negatives. Multiple researchers cross-checked the results to minimize biases, ensuring that did not introduce issues.

Construct validity checks if the study measures what it intends to. Our construct validity relies on accurately specifying and detecting RL training best practices. We mitigated threats by basing rule definitions on a thorough literature review and established practices. Acknowledging interpretations and expertise, we incorporated feedback from experts to refine the rules and ensure they reflect best practices accurately.

8   Related Work

In this section, we discuss related studies and compare them to our study.

Several studies explore various aspects of RL methodologies and applications. Lee et al. [9] analyze the evolution of RL algorithms, emphasizing the transition from single-agent to multi-agent systems, focusing on distributed optimization. Canese et al. [1] outline multi-agent algorithms, comparing them across key attributes essential for multi-agent RL applications such as non-stationarity, scalability, and observability.

A survey by Samsami and Alimadad [15] provides an overview of distributed RL techniques, discussing key challenges such as efficient data usage and the balance between exploration and exploitation. Similarly, Hoffman et al. [6] introduced Acme,

Table 9. Results on Managing Models in Inference Rules

Case Study	Custom-Based			Qwen 2.5			GPT-4o			LLaMA 3.3		
	Precision	Recall	F1 Score	Precision	Recall	F1 Score	Precision	Recall	F1 Score	Precision	Recall	F1 Score
ICS	1.00	1.00	1.00	0.33	1.00	0.50	0.33	1.00	0.50	0.33	1.00	0.50
CS1	N/A	N/A	N/A	0.00	N/A	N/A	0.00	N/A	N/A	0.00	N/A	N/A
CS2	N/A	N/A	N/A	0.00	N/A	N/A	N/A	N/A	N/A	0.00	N/A	N/A
CS3	N/A	N/A	N/A	N/A	N/A	N/A	0.00	N/A	N/A	0.00	N/A	N/A
CS4	1.00	1.00	1.00	0.33	1.00	0.50	N/A	0.00	N/A	0.33	1.00	0.50
CS5	1.00	1.00	1.00	1.00	0.50	0.67	1.00	0.50	0.67	0.67	1.00	0.80
CS6	1.00	1.00	1.00	0.33	1.00	0.50	N/A	0.00	N/A	0.33	1.00	0.50
CS7	1.00	1.00	1.00	0.67	1.00	0.80	N/A	0.00	N/A	0.67	1.00	0.80
CS8	1.00	1.00	1.00	0.33	1.00	0.50	N/A	0.00	N/A	0.33	1.00	0.50
CS9	1.00	1.00	1.00	0.50	0.50	0.50	0.67	1.00	0.80	1.00	1.00	1.00
CS10	N/A	N/A	N/A	0.00	N/A	N/A	0.00	N/A	N/A	0.00	N/A	N/A
CS11	1.00	1.00	1.00	1.00	1.00	1.00	1.00	1.00	1.00	1.00	1.00	1.00
CS12	1.00	1.00	1.00	0.67	1.00	0.80	1.00	0.50	0.67	0.67	1.00	0.80
CS13	1.00	1.00	1.00	0.33	1.00	0.50	0.33	1.00	0.50	0.33	1.00	0.50
CS14	N/A	N/A	N/A	0.00	N/A	N/A	0.00	N/A	N/A	0.00	N/A	N/A
CS15	1.00	1.00	1.00	0.67	1.00	0.80	1.00	0.50	0.67	0.67	1.00	0.80
CS16	1.00	1.00	1.00	1.00	1.00	1.00	1.00	1.00	1.00	1.00	1.00	1.00

a modular framework designed to simplify the implementation of scalable RL algorithms. In multi-agent RL settings, Zhu et al. [22] proposed MSRL, a training system that employs fragmented dataflow graphs to execute RL algorithms in a flexible and scalable manner. Liang et al. [11] developed RLlib, a library focused on making RL training more scalable by distributing computational tasks efficiently.

The complexities of MARL are addressed by Hernandez-Leal et al. [5] in their comprehensive survey, which tackles challenges such as non-stationarity and scalability in training multiple agents in dynamic environments. Zhang, Yang, and Basar [20] provide an overview of theories and algorithms in MARL, focusing on cooperative and competitive settings and emphasizing the need for robust training practices. While these studies provide theoretical and algorithmic insights into MARL, our work applies these concepts by defining specific rules for multi-agent training and validating their implementation through automated tools.

In automated code analysis and rule-based systems, Schneider et al. [17] discuss rule-based security analysis for microservices. Their work underscores the importance of automated rule checking to maintain best practices in software systems. Our work is similar in its goal of automating the enforcement of best practices, but it focuses specifically on RL training practices rather than security analysis.

9   Conclusions and Future Work

This paper introduced a rule-based assessment approach to automatically validate best practices in RL training pipelines. The approach was implemented as a modular pipeline insights service and evaluated using an industrial system and sixteen diverse open-source case studies. The key RL aspects assessed include RL pipeline practices, model versioning, multi-agent deployment and managing models in inference. The evaluation demonstrated that the *custom rule-based detectors* consistently achieved high accuracy across all systems and rule categories, with near-perfect precision and recall. In contrast, LLM-based detectors enabled fully automated, low-effort validation but showed variable recall. These findings show that while LLMs provide a scalable and adaptable first level of analysis, custom detectors are indispensable to achieve complete and reliable coverage of rule implementations. This hybrid detection setup allows fast insights in early development stages and deep validation when rules must be strictly enforced.

Future work will expand the rules to include distributed training and environment-specific patterns. We also plan to integrate rule checks into CI/CD pipelines for real-time validation, enhancing transparency of RL systems.

Acknowledgments. This work was supported by: FFG (Austrian Research Promotion Agency) project MODIS (no. FO999895431); Austrian Science Fund (FWF) project CQ4CD, Grant-DOI: 10.55776/I6510. For open access purposes, the authors have applied a CC BY public copyright license to any author accepted manuscript version arising from this submission.

References

1. Canese, L., et al.: Multi-agent reinforcement learning: a review of challenges and applications. Appl. Sci. **11**(11), 4948 (2021)
2. Dagster: Ml pipelines: 5 components and 5 critical best practices. Dagster Blog (2023)
3. Deng, Y., Dai, Q., Zhang, Z.: An Overview of Computational Sparse Models and Their Applications in Artificial Intelligence, pp. 345–369. Springer, Berlin (2013)
4. Eimer, T., Lindauer, M., Raileanu, R.: Hyperparameters in reinforcement learning and how to tune them. In: International Conference on Machine Learning, pp. 9104–9149 (2023)
5. Hernandez-Leal, P., Kartal, B., Taylor, M.E.: A survey and critique of multiagent deep reinforcement learning. Auton. Agent. Multi-Agent Syst. **33**(6), 750–797 (2019). https://doi.org/10.1007/s10458-019-09421-1
6. Hoffman, M.W., Oh, J., Andrychowicz, M., et al.: Acme: A research framework for distributed reinforcement learning. arXiv preprint arXiv:2006.00979 (2020)
7. Lakshmanan, V., Robinson, S., Munn, M.: Machine Learning Design Patterns. Inc, O'Reilly Media (2020)
8. Latendresse, J., Abedu, S., Abdellatif, A., Shihab, E.: An exploratory study on machine learning model management. ACM Trans. Softw. Eng. Methodol. **34**(1), 1–31 (2024)
9. Lee, D., He, N., Kamalaruban, P., Cevher, V.: Optimization for reinforcement learning: from a single agent to cooperative agents. IEEE Signal Process. Mag. **37**(3), 123–135 (2020)
10. Levine, S.: Reinforcement learning and control as probabilistic inference: Tutorial and review (2018). https://arxiv.org/abs/1805.00909
11. Liang, E., et al.: Rllib: Abstractions for distributed reinforcement learning. In: International conference on machine learning, pp. 3053–3062. PMLR (2018)
12. Liu, Z., et al.: Graph neural network meets multi-agent reinforcement learning: Fundamentals, applications, and future directions. IEEE Wireless Commun. (2024)
13. Ntentos, E., Warnett, S.J., Zdun, U.: Rule-based assessment of reinforcement learning practices using large language models. In: 4th International Conference on AI Engineering ? Software Engineering for AI (CAIN) (April 2025)

14. Pateria, S., Subagdja, B., Tan, A.H., Quek, C.Q.: Hierarchical reinforcement learning: a comprehensive survey. Artif. Intell. Rev. **55**, 3577–3621 (2022)
15. Samsami, M., Alimadad, A.: A survey of distributed reinforcement learning: Techniques and applications. arXiv preprint arXiv:2011.11012 (2020)
16. Samsami, M.R., Alimadad, H.: Distributed deep reinforcement learning: An overview. arXiv preprint arXiv:2011.11012 (2020)
17. Schneider, S., et al.: Automatic rule checking for microservices: Supporting security analysis with explainability. Available at SSRN 4658575 (2023)
18. Sharma, R., Davuluri, K.: Design patterns for machine learning applications. In: 2019 3rd International Conference on Computing Methodologies and Communication (ICCMC), pp. 818–821 (2019)
19. Washizaki, H., et al.: Software-engineering design patterns for machine learning applications. Computer **55**(3), 30–39 (2022)
20. Zhang, K., Yang, Z., Başar, T.: Multi-agent reinforcement learning: a selective overview of theories and algorithms. Handbook of Reinforcement Learning and Control, pp. 321–384 (2021)
21. Zhang, K., Yang, Z., Başar, T.: Multi-agent reinforcement learning: a selective overview of theories and algorithms. Appli. Sci. **11**(11), 4948 (2021). https://www.mdpi.com/2076-3417/11/11/4948
22. Zhu, J., Lu, Y., et al.: Msrl: A scalable and modularized multi-agent rl training system. arXiv preprint arXiv:2210.00882 (2022)

Reconsidering Requirements Engineering: Human–AI Collaboration in AI-Native Software Development

Mateen Ahmed Abbasi$^{(\boxtimes)}$, Petri Ihantola, Tommi Mikkonen, and Niko Mäkitalo

Faculty of Information Technology, University of Jyväskylä, Jyväskylä, Finland
{mateen.a.abbasi,petri.j.ihantola,tommi.j.mikkonen, niko.k.makitalo}@jyu.fi

Abstract. Requirement Engineering (RE) is the foundation of successful software development. In RE, the goal is to ensure that implemented systems satisfy stakeholder needs through rigorous requirements elicitation, validation, and evaluation processes. Despite its critical role, RE continues to face persistent challenges, such as ambiguity, conflicting stakeholder needs, and the complexity of managing evolving requirements. A common view is that Artificial Intelligence (AI) has the potential to streamline the RE process, resulting in improved efficiency, accuracy, and management actions. However, using AI also introduces new concerns, such as ethical issues, biases, and lack of transparency. This paper explores how AI can enhance traditional RE practices by automating labor-intensive tasks, supporting requirement prioritization, and facilitating collaboration between stakeholders and AI systems. The paper also describes the opportunities and challenges that AI brings to RE. In particular, the vision calls for ethical practices in AI, along with a much-enhanced collaboration between academia and industry professionals. The focus should be on creating not only powerful but also trustworthy and practical AI solutions ready to adapt to the fast-paced world of software development.

Keywords: Requirements Engineering (RE) · Artificial Intelligence (AI) · Natural Language Processing · Machine Learning · Predictive Analytics · Ethical Accountability · Ambiguity in Requirements · Transparency in AI

1 Introduction

Requirements engineering (RE) is the foundation of software development. During RE, stakeholders' needs are transformed into explicit system requirements [58]. The success of software project depends on the quality of the RE process [48]. This critical initial phase involves eliciting, analyzing, specifying, and validating the needs, constraints, and expectations of stakeholders to establish

D. Taibi and D. Smite (Eds.): SEAA 2025, LNCS 16081, pp. 164–180, 2026.
https://doi.org/10.1007/978-3-032-04190-6_11

a clear understanding of the software system [48,69]. It also requires understanding the problem context, modeling requirements, and reconciling conflicting demands [67]. However, RE faces persistent challenges, including ambiguity in requirements [11], conflicts among stakeholders, and the dynamic nature of software development [24]. Effective RE significantly reduces rework and improves project success [41].

AI is emerging as a transformative force in software engineering, particularly in RE [22], offering new opportunities to support or automate RE activities such as requirement elicitation, traceability, and task prioritization [17,38,44]. However, the integration of AI into RE also brings a new set of risks. The complexity and unpredictability of AI systems can introduce uncertainty into software projects [17], particularly when RE depends heavily on human understanding, context, and negotiation. Interpreting AI-generated recommendations becomes critical for aligning system behavior with stakeholder expectations.

In this paper, we focus on data-driven AI techniques, particularly Machine Learning (ML) and Generative AI approaches, and explore how they are shaping the future of RE. While these methods offer significant potential, they also raise challenges related to data quality, interpretability [28], and ethical concerns such as inherited bias in AI-generated outputs [30,40,54,70]. These shifts suggest that AI is not just improving RE tasks in isolation, but gradually transforming the way RE is practiced, how roles are defined, and how decisions are made throughout the development lifecycle.

This article contributes to this discussion by:

- Identifying long-standing RE challenges,
- Analyzing how AI is affecting and reshaping these challenges,
- Outlining future research directions aimed at mitigating AI-driven challenges in RE.

The rest of the paper is structured as follows. Section 2 describes the methodology. Section 3 discusses key RE challenges, the role of AI in addressing them, and new challenges introduced by AI. Section 4 explores potential solutions and directions for future research. Section 5 presents our conclusions.

2   Methodology

To examine how AI technologies are affecting the requirements engineering process, we conducted a structured (though not fully systematic) literature review designed to be transparent and reproducible. Drawing from established literature review practices, the process applied defined search strategies, relevance-based inclusion criteria, and thematic synthesis to ensure consistency and traceability across all phases. The research process followed three phases (I, II, and III) as explained below.

2.1   Phase I: Identifying Traditional RE Challenges

In Phase I, we conducted a literature review to identify the key challenges associated with traditional requirements engineering. Our search focused on databases including Google Scholar and Scopus. The search strings included terms such as "requirements engineering challenges", "common issues in RE", and "RE problem studies". We prioritize peer-reviewed publications and filtered out those that did not directly address RE challenges. Studies were screened according to the relevance of the title and abstract, followed by full text evaluation.

To group RE challenges into the five key themes discussed in Sect. 3, we used qualitative coding and thematic grouping. Each selected study was fully reviewed and relevant challenges were tagged and grouped based on recurrence and thematic similarity. For example, challenges related to vague requirements, inconsistent terminology, and stakeholder misunderstandings were grouped under "Ambiguity and Conflicting Requirements." The search was concluded upon reaching thematic saturation, meaning that additional articles no longer introduced new or substantially different categories of challenges. In total, approximately 35 peer-reviewed articles were reviewed in full for thematic synthesis.

Numerous challenges in traditional RE have been identified in previous studies, including difficulties in requirements elicitation [27,69], ambiguous and conflicting requirements [11], communication barriers [27,62], dynamic and volatile requirements [14,24,56], poor traceability [7,20,38], and issues with prioritization and stakeholder involvement [1,44]. Other important challenges include insufficient domain knowledge [15], feedback cycles in requirement validation [12], requirement reuse in inappropriate contexts, inadequate modeling of nonfunctional requirements [64], and evolving requirements during development [46].

The RE challenges discussed here were selected based on their prevalence, significance, and impact across RE practices. Our selection process involved:

- Reviewing peer-acknowledged literature frequently included in systematic reviews and key RE studies.
- Prioritizing research that explicitly analyzed major RE challenges.
- Ensuring coverage of challenges that remain critical across various RE methodologies (waterfall, agile, hybrid models).

After identifying the challenges from the following literature reviews [5,11, 62,66,68] and empirical studies [4,11,23,41,66] we synthesized the findings to form a comprehensive and balanced understanding of traditional RE challenges. The results have been introduced in Sect. 3.

2.2   Phase II: Review Process on AI in RE

In Phase II, we examined recent research exploring how AI techniques are applied within requirements engineering. We followed the following review process:

- Identification: To investigate how AI is applied to address RE challenges, we searched Google Scholar using the following query: "AI in Requirements Engineering" OR "Natural Language Processing for RE" OR "Machine Learning in RE" OR "AI for Requirement Prioritization" OR "Automated Requirement Traceability." This initial search yielded 136 results. Although Phase I used both Scopus and Google Scholar, Phase II relied solely on Google Scholar due to its broader coverage of recent and preprint literature, which is especially valuable in the rapidly evolving field of AI. We acknowledge that using a single source may introduce selection bias due to less curation compared to databases like Scopus. To mitigate this, we applied an iterative refinement strategy that included removing redundant entries, analyzing backward and forward citations from key articles, adjusting search keywords, and prioritizing the most recent peer-reviewed publications directly related to AI in RE. Title and abstract screening were used to exclude studies focusing solely on theoretical discussions or on non-functional requirements. We reviewed the full text of the remaining papers to ensure methodological relevance. This filtering process resulted in a curated set of studies that formed the basis for the analysis in Phase III.

- Eligibility: We focused on studies that proposed, evaluated, or discussed AI techniques such as Natural Language Processing (NLP), Machine Learning (ML), Deep Learning (DL), and Information Retrieval methods applied to RE tasks including requirement elicitation, ambiguity detection, traceability automation, conflict resolution, prioritization techniques, and ethical concerns such as bias mitigation and explainability.
- Inclusion: We selected studies that directly focused on the integration of AI techniques with RE for detailed analysis. These selected studies were supplemented by seminal papers frequently cited in RE research to ensure a comprehensive understanding of existing challenges, advancements, and gaps in AI-driven RE methodologies. These findings set the foundation for our later exploration of emerging AI approaches in Sect. 4.

2.3   Phase III: Analysis How AI Is Changing RE Challenges

In Phase III, we analyzed how AI techniques can help address specific RE challenges, based on insights from the literature. The evaluation criteria included:

- Accuracy and Reliability: How effectively AI models can identify, classify, and refine requirements.
- Scalability: The capacity of AI tools to manage large and evolving sets of requirements.
- Transparency and Explainability: The extent to which AI decisions can be interpreted by RE professionals.
- Ethical Considerations: How well the models mitigate bias and promote fairness.

While our review is not exhaustive, we focused on synthesizing the most influential and recent works from both theoretical and empirical perspectives to provide a balanced discussion on AI integration in RE processes.

From Phase I, we identified a broad range of traditional RE challenges. For structured analysis, we narrowed our focus to five recurring and thematically central challenges: (1) ambiguity and conflicting requirements, (2) dynamic and volatile requirements, (3) communication barriers, (4) poor traceability, and (5) prioritization and stakeholder involvement. These challenges were selected based on the frequency with which they appear in the literature and their relevance to AI-based solutions. In this phase, we examined how AI addresses these challenges and also identified new issues that AI introduces. Section 3 is structured accordingly.

While some concerns such as data bias or explainability are common in general AI applications, they are particularly impactful in RE due to the foundational role of requirements in shaping the entire software development lifecycle. Misinterpretations at this stage can propagate into critical downstream flaws.

3   RE Challenges and the Impact of AI

This section presents a unified analysis of key challenges in RE and examines how Artificial Intelligence (AI) techniques are influencing these areas. For each challenge, we explore the traditional difficulties faced in RE, how AI technologies have been used to address them, the new issues introduced through AI integration, and practical examples where applicable. This synthesis draws on findings from both classical RE literature and recent research on AI applications in RE.

3.1   Ambiguity and Conflicting Requirements

Ambiguity and conflicting requirements have been one of the major challenges in RE, due to vague stakeholder inputs and different interpretations [11,22]. Ambiguity and conflicting requirements arise when stakeholders provide ambiguous, incomplete, or inconsistent information [60,65], These problems generally occur due to differences in understanding and unclear requirements among stakeholders [26,60]. Different stakeholders may use different terminology or may have conflicting objectives, which makes requirements vague or inconsistent [52,57,68]. Ambiguous requirements increase the probability of errors in later development phases [64]. Stakeholders are usually unable to clearly articulate all their requirements during the early stages of a project, leading to incomplete requirements. As development proceeds, the missing requirements are realized during the system integration or testing phases [32].

How AI has Changed this Challenge: AI-based methods can handle large volumes of requirements and ensure consistency between artifacts [22]. LLMs act as conversational agents that can process domain-specific knowledge and generate structured requirements from unstructured data [8]. NLP-based tools such as CoreNLP, NLTK, and OpenNLP assist in detecting ambiguous phrases and inconsistencies in requirements [6]. However, resolving these ambiguities requires human expertise to ensure correctness and alignment with stakeholder expectations [6,31]. AI tools can assist in extracting requirements from various sources, such as emails, meeting notes, and documentation. This helps to resolve the issues of incomplete requirements, ensuring that no important details are missed [8].

What New Challenges AI has Introduced: While AI reduces ambiguity, it also introduces problems such as biases in language models. One key challenge is the need for large and high-quality datasets for training and evaluating AI models. The effectiveness of AI models in RE depends on the quality and diversity of the data used for training [35]. Additionally, prompt design plays a critical role in requirement extraction using LLMs since poorly constructed prompts may cause misinterpretation or amplify biases [8]. Collecting and preparing proper datasets for AI systems is resource-intensive and requires careful curation to ensure relevance and accuracy. If the data used to train the models is biased or incomplete, the AI might misunderstand stakeholders' requirements or fail to detect conflicts [30].

Example: AI-driven requirement prioritization can struggle when it comes to managing conflicting stakeholder needs, especially when requirements are ambiguous. For instance, an AI system focused on optimizing functional performance may deprioritize usability requirements, assuming they are less critical. However, stakeholders could have different opinions on the relative priority of performance versus user experience, leading to overlooked priorities and mismatched expectations.

3.2 Dynamic and Volatile Requirements

The ever-changing nature of requirements, often referred to as "requirements volatility," poses a significant challenge in software development [14]. Volatile requirements can disrupt project timelines, increase costs, lead to significant rework, and affect stability and consistency in the development process [14,24]. Traditional RE struggles with managing frequent requirement changes due to evolving business needs. Excessive change may also affect system design, project scope, and budget [34,56]. Another challenge arises due to stakeholders' shifting needs, which inevitably bring changes in requirements during the development process [3]. Dynamic and frequent changing requirements can derail the success of the project [68].

How AI has Changed this Challenge: ML algorithms can address the challenges of dynamic and volatile requirements through predictive analytics [5], which anticipate possible requirement changes based on past projects and stakeholder behavior [22,45]. AI solutions can help reduce the effects of requirement changes by offering better tools in areas like requirements elicitation, analysis, and change management [22].

What New Challenges AI has Introduced: AI may offer promising solutions, it also brings its own set of challenges [36]. AI models trained on historical data can assist in identifying the most important requirements by predicting how they will impact cost, time, and user satisfaction [43]. Predictive analytics relies on the quality of existing data. If the data is incomplete or outdated, the predictions might be incorrect or misleading [36]. Over-reliance on AI predictions might cause teams to overlook new factors that may not align with historical trends [2]. One significant challenge is that volatility, often driven by changing contexts or evolving user needs, cannot be entirely predicted or controlled through AI. Another limitation is the inherent complexity of AI models. AI models trained on biased datasets, tend to perpetuate the already existing biases in requirements elicitation and prioritization. The biggest concern is how fair an AI-driven RE process will be, especially in ensuring equitable treatment of stakeholders, while minimizing bias in interpretations [53]. AI systems should be held accountable for ethical norms governing biases and transparency [16].

Example: A development team working on an e-commerce platform uses predictive analytics to identify future needs in a fast-paced business area. However, as the user base of the platform evolves (e.g. demographics of the region), the training data no longer reflects the changing realities of the platform. The predictions become less accurate and start overemphasizing some historical trends while missing emerging ones (e.g., new payment methods or region-specific regulations).

3.3   Communication Barriers

Communication barriers arise when stakeholders and development teams face problems in sharing and understanding information [21], particularly during the elicitation of requirements, where misunderstandings and incomplete information are common. Differences in technical knowledge, language, and culture hinder communication between stakeholders and developers [27]. These differences can lead to incomplete or misinterpreted requirements, ultimately affecting project outcomes. Global teams often encounter cultural and language barriers that complicate collaboration [23,62].

How AI has Changed this Challenge: AI can enhance communication and collaboration in the requirements engineering process [6]. One of the primary way to reduce communication barriers is through language translation and NLP techniques [6,19]. AI-driven chatbots and virtual assistants significantly improve communications by providing standard responses to common queries and helping clarify requirements during discussions [19].

What New Challenges AI has Introduced: AI brings significant benefits in addressing communication barriers in RE, it also introduces several challenges that must be considered [22,36]. One major issue is bias within AI systems [63]. AI systems may inherit biases from training data and can skew the interpretations of requirements [53]. AI solutions for communication barriers can lead to over-reliance on automated translations, which may not be able to convey cultural nuances or context-specific meanings [47]. Moreover, misinterpretations by AI tools can even exacerbate rather than mitigate communication issues in high-stakes discussions [55].

Example: AI chatbots and NLP tools used to bridge communication gaps between technical and non-technical stakeholders can sometimes misunderstand special terms or cultural details. For example, in a global project, one stakeholder might say a "warehouse" means a main storage place, while another might mean a decentralized distribution hub. If the AI fails to recognize this context, it may generate specifications that don't align with expectations, exacerbating communication issues rather than solving them.

3.4   Poor Traceability

Requirement traceability is important to establish the connections between requirements, design, and implementation [7]. Poor traceability refers to the difficulty in establishing and maintaining the link between requirements and other development artifacts, such as design documents, code, and test cases [7,38]. Manual traceability is error-prone and labor-intensive, resulting in gaps in requirements management [20]. The lack of traceability complicates validation and verification, making it harder to ensure that the final product satisfies all requirements.

How AI has Changed this Challenge: Deep learning and NLP techniques can be used to automate traceability linking between requirements and other artifacts [37]. The integration of AI techniques into the RE process can provide benefits by enhancing traceability and reducing manual effort [20].

What New Challenges AI has Introduced: The quality and reliability of AI-generated traceability links are highly dependent on the quality of the training data. If the data is incomplete or biased, it may result in recommendations that would harm the overall traceability of the system [36]. Errors in AI-generated traceability links might go unnoticed if there is not enough human oversight, which could cause problems later in the development process [37]. Another key challenge is ensuring the traceability of AI itself, such as tracking the sources of training data and models, to promote transparency and accountability [50].

Example: If the AI automatically links requirements to code and test cases but incorrectly maps them, it could create false dependencies. For example, it might associate a requirement for "data encryption" with unrelated logging functions, leading to wasted effort in verifying irrelevant links. Also, relying too much on the AI's traceability suggestions might lower manual checks, increasing the likelihood of undetected errors.

3.5   Prioritization and Stakeholder Involvement

Prioritization ensures that the most critical features are addressed early in the software development process, prioritization and stakeholder involvement are critical to ensure essential requirements align with the project objectives to be delivered first [1,44]. It becomes challenging when stakeholders have conflicting interests, resources are limited, or some are not actively involved in the RE process [4,44]. Requirement prioritization is inherently subjective, as stakeholder interests often vary. Limited participation of stakeholders in RE phases may result in requirements that do not meet user expectations [44].

How AI has Changed this Challenge: The identification and involvement of the right stakeholders is crucial [44]. NLP and ML techniques can help by automating document analysis, user feedback, and other sources to identify key stakeholders and their needs [29,51]. AI techniques like utility-based recommendation, matrix factorization, and content-based recommendations can analyze requirements and support prioritization [29]. These AI techniques can automate the prioritization process, stakeholder preferences, requirement dependencies, and changing priorities over time [29,44]. Techniques such as utility-based recommendation and optimization approaches like Analytic Hierarchy Process (AHP) and Binary Search Tree [29,44] can be enhanced through modern ML algorithms such as Random Forests and Linear Programming for analyzing trade-offs between cost, time, and stakeholder needs to achieve optimal prioritization.

What New Challenges AI has Introduced: AI tools and techniques can enhance prioritization and stakeholder involvement, but it also raises issues such as bias, transparency, and ethical considerations [13,30,35,61]. As ML-based AI systems rely on historical data to improve prioritization, Such data often fail to capture the specific context of the project [61]. Moreover, AI-driven tools mostly work as black boxes [42], making it difficult for users to understand how decisions are made. This lack of transparency can lead to low trust in AI recommendations [9,25]. The use of AI in RE also raises ethical concerns related to accountability and decision-making. Ethical accountability is essential because AI systems might reinforce biases, unfairly prioritize requirements, or make choices that conflict with the real needs of the stakeholders [30]. Accountability in AI can improve trust and collaboration between stakeholders by clarifying decision processes [59], especially in large projects with many stakeholders [18]. It has to be ensured that AI recommendations comply with ethical standards and stakeholder values [33].

Example: AI tools that analyze and prioritize requirements might unintentionally favor stakeholders who provide more data or have more consistent feedback patterns. For example, in a project involving multiple teams, AI might prioritize features requested by the marketing department due to clearer documentation while neglecting crucial but less well-documented feedback from other stakeholders. Table 1 summarizes the key RE challenges, the ways in which AI addresses them, and the new challenges that AI introduces.

4   Discussion and Future Directions

This paper set out to examine how Artificial Intelligence is influencing Requirements Engineering at a broader level, not only by offering technical solutions, but by gradually reshaping the way RE is performed, who performs it, and how decisions are made throughout the process.

Our analysis shows that AI is no longer just assisting with individual RE tasks; it's starting to affect core aspects of the RE process, including ambiguity resolution, stakeholder prioritization, traceability, and adaptation to change. These shifts also raise important concerns about the role of human oversight, explainability of AI decisions, and the trust that stakeholders place in automated recommendations. Figure 1 illustrates how traditional RE challenges intersect

Table 1. Summary of Challenges and AI Impact

RE Challenge	How AI Addresses It	New Challenges Introduced by AI
Ambiguity and Conflicting Requirements	NLP tools and LLMs structure unstructured input and detect ambiguity.	Bias from training data, reliance on prompt engineering, and limited explainability
Volatile and Dynamic Requirements	Predictive analytics models forecast requirement changes and adjust priorities.	Overfitting to historical trends, difficulty capturing emerging needs
Communication Barriers	Chatbots and translators ease understanding across diverse teams.	Loss of context or nuance in translation, misinterpretation of domain-specific terms
Poor Traceability	Automates linking between requirements, code, and tests.	Errors in automated linking, lack of transparency in traceability logic
Prioritization and Stakeholder Involvement	ML-based ranking systems analyze feedback and optimize prioritization.	Bias favoring well-documented or dominant stakeholders, lack of transparency in decision-making

with AI-driven approaches, and how new challenges emerge as AI becomes more embedded in RE practices.

While issues such as dataset adequacy, over-reliance on AI-generated outputs, prompt engineering skills, bias and fairness concerns, and explainability and trust problems are broadly recognized in AI research, they manifest with particular importance in the context of Requirements Engineering. Unlike many other domains, RE heavily relies on nuanced, context-rich human inputs, where misinterpretations, biases, or lack of transparency during early stages can propagate into critical system specifications and significantly impact downstream development activities.

Moreover, our literature review revealed notable gaps: although various AI methods have been applied to traditional RE tasks, there remains limited exploration of emerging approaches such as retrieval-augmented generation (RAG), lightweight domain adaptation techniques, and dynamic prioritization using reinforcement learning. In this section, we discuss how AI techniques can help mitigate these challenges, and present our future research ideas and objectives.

4.1   AI Techniques for Enhancing RE

Retrieval-Augmented Generation (RAG): Retrieval-Augmented Generation (RAG) combines retrieval techniques with generative models to produce contextually relevant outputs [39]. In RE, RAG can be utilized to retrieve knowledge from requirement specifications, past project documentation, and knowledge bases of specified domains.

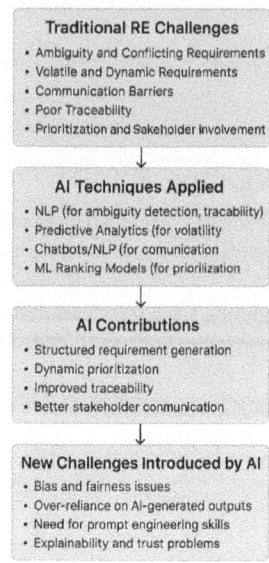

Fig. 1. Conceptual flow linking RE challenges, AI contributions, and new challenges introduced by AI integration.

- *Addressing RE Challenges:* RAG can help mitigating ambiguous and conflicting requirements by retrieving structured requirement statements from past projects, which reduces inconsistencies and improves clarity.
- *Future Research:* We are developing a RAG-based tool to help software development teams extract past requirements from project repositories in a systematic and reusable way for multiple projects. Then evaluate how RAG can help to resolve these issues.

Fine-Tuning Pre-trained Models: Fine-tuning involves modifying pre-trained language models to perform more effectively in particular domains by training them with domain-relevant datasets [49]. Fine-tuning large language models (LLMs) like BERT and GPT for RE activities can improve the accuracy in eliciting, classifying, and analyzing requirements. This can better handle domain-specific terminologies and stakeholder preferences by training on RE datasets.

Though fine-tuning can enhance model performance for RE tasks, it also presents challenges such as high computational costs, the risk of overfitting, and environmental concerns. Therefore, our future work will also explore more lightweight domain adaptation strategies, such as prompt optimization, adapter-based fine-tuning, and retrieval-augmented approaches, to balance domain specificity with practical deployment feasibility.

– *Addressing RE Challenges:* Fine-tuned models can improve requirement elicitation and traceability by generating more accurate and structured requirement documents.
– *Future Research:* We will explore different fine-tuning approaches and study how fine-tuned model can help tackling regulatory compliance challenges (e.g., HIPAA, GDPR) so that AI-driven requirements assistant produce requirements that are regulation compliant.

Reinforcement Learning (RL): In an software development project, a reinforcement learning (RL) system can continuously learn from feedback over sprints (rewards or penalties), and refine priority suggestions for requirements to align with changing user needs.

– *Addressing RE Challenges:* Reinforcement learning methods can help improve decision-making in RE by managing dynamic and volatile requirements and by learning from past requirements changes and predicting future changes to enable more adaptive and effective requirement management.
– *Future Research:* In future, we study how RL methods can be used to help with requirement prioritization by learning from feedback experience on previous projects. By defining reward functions in terms of cost, risk, and stakeholder satisfaction, RL agents can assist in changing requirement priorities as projects evolve [10].

4.2 Research Objectives

Empirical Testing of AI Models in RE Tasks: Our objective is to evaluate how efficient AI techniques such as RAG, fine-tuning, and RL can help mitigate the identified RE challenges. In future studies, we plan to conduct benchmarking the AI methods with traditional RE processes to measure improvements in efficiency, accuracy, and stakeholder satisfaction.

Comparative Analysis of AI-Driven vs. Traditional RE Processes: Our objective is to compare AI-assisted and manual RE processes to analyze where AI is most valuable and where human decision-making is still very pertinent. We plan to use surveys, controlled experiments, and performance analysis to compare the outcomes of each approach.

Developing a Concrete Integration Framework: Our final objective is the creation of a comprehensive framework to integrate AI into industrial RE practices. The framework will outline best practices for handling data, improving models, interpreting results, and incorporating human input into the process. It also needs to provide guidelines on how to balance automation with ethics and achieve transparency and accountability in AI-supported RE activities.

4.3 Implications for Practice and Theory

Implications for Practice: The findings of this article show how AI can be applied to real RE problems, such as using NLP tools to detect ambiguous requirements, ML models for prioritizing tasks, and reinforcement learning to adapt to changing needs. These techniques can help reduce manual work, improve accuracy, and make the RE process more manageable in practice. The discussion of current tools and emerging strategies can help guide the selection or development of AI-based RE solutions in real-world projects.

Implications for Theory: This work contributes to the ongoing research connecting AI with RE by pulling together current studies and identifying gaps, like explainability, ethical concerns, and data quality in AI-based RE tools. It also sets the stage for future studies that will experiment with how effective AI is in RE, especially through novel methods like RAG and reinforcement learning.

5   Conclusions

This paper presents a structured analysis of the evolving role of AI in RE, highlighting both its transformative potential and the new challenges it brings. Techniques like RAG, fine-tuning, and reinforcement learning offer promising approaches to address key RE challenges, including ambiguity, volatility, and prioritization. Integrating AI into RE processes can help organizations reduce time and costs while improving accuracy and reliability. However, despite these benefits, numerous issues like ethical concerns, algorithmic biases, transparency, and fairness arise.

Our findings suggest that AI should be considered as an augmentative tool, not a substitute for human decision-making in RE. AI can enhance efficiency, but its results should be interpretable, fair, and aligned with stakeholder needs. To address the new challenges AI introduces into RE, our future work will focus on exploring techniques to detect and reduce biases in AI-generated requirements, ensuring fairness in requirements prioritization and decision-making.

Acknowledgments. This work has been supported by FAST, the Finnish Software Engineering Doctoral Research Network, funded by the Ministry of Education and Culture, Finland.

Disclosure of Interests. The authors have no competing interests to declare that are relevant to the content of this article.

References

1. AbdElazim, K., Moawad, R., Elfakharany, E.: A framework for requirements prioritization process in agile software development. J. Phys: Conf. Ser. **1454**, 012001 (2020)
2. Aldoseri, A., Al-Khalifa, K.N., Hamouda, A.M.: Re-thinking data strategy and integration for artificial intelligence: concepts, opportunities, and challenges. Appl. Sci. **13**(12), 7082 (2023)
3. Almeida, F.: Challenges in migration from waterfall to agile environments. World J. Comput. Appl. Technol. **5**(3), 39–49 (2017)

4. Alqaisi, I.F.: The effects of stakeholder's engagement and communication management on projects success. In: MATEC Web of Conferences, vol. 162, p. 02037. EDP Sciences (2018)
5. Alsalemi, A.M., Yeoh, E.T.: A systematic literature review of requirements volatility prediction. In: 2017 International Conference on Current Trends in Computer, Electrical, Electronics and Communication (CTCEEC), pp. 55–64. IEEE (2017)
6. Alzayed, A., Al-Hunaiyyan, A.: A bird's eye view of natural language processing and requirements engineering. Int. J. Adv. Comput. Sci. Appl. **12**(5) (2021)
7. Antoniol, G., Cleland-Huang, J., Hayes, J.H., Vierhauser, M.: Grand challenges of traceability: the next ten years. arXiv preprint arXiv:1710.03129 (2017)
8. Arora, C., Grundy, J., Abdelrazek, M.: Advancing requirements engineering through generative AI: assessing the role of LLMs. In: Generative AI for Effective Software Development, pp. 129–148. Springer (2024)
9. Bach, T.A., Khan, A., Hallock, H., Beltrão, G., Sousa, S.: A systematic literature review of user trust in AI-enabled systems: an HCI perspective. Int. J. Hum. Comput. Interact. **40**(5), 1251–1266 (2024)
10. Bagherzadeh, M., Kahani, N., Briand, L.: Reinforcement learning for test case prioritization. IEEE Trans. Softw. Eng. **48**(8), 2836–2856 (2021)
11. Bano, M.: Addressing the challenges of requirements ambiguity: a review of empirical literature. In: 2015 IEEE Fifth International Workshop on Empirical Requirements Engineering (EmpiRE), pp. 21–24. IEEE (2015)
12. Bano Sahibzada, M., Zowghi, D.: Service oriented requirements engineering: practitioner's perspective. In: Service-Oriented Computing-ICSOC 2012 Workshops: ICSOC 2012, International Workshops ASC, DISA, PAASC, SCEB, SeMaPS, WESOA, and Satellite Events, Shanghai, China, 12–15 November 2012, Revised Selected Papers 10, pp. 380–392. Springer (2013)
13. Belani, H., Vukovic, M., Car, Ž.: Requirements engineering challenges in building AI-based complex systems. In: 2019 IEEE 27th International Requirements Engineering Conference Workshops (REW), pp. 252–255. IEEE (2019)
14. Biddle, M., Moritz, S.: 1.3. 2 context-based measurement of requirements instability. In: INCOSE International Symposium, vol. 16, pp. 119–132. Wiley Online Library (2006)
15. Birk, A., Heller, G.: Challenges for requirements engineering and management in software product line development. In: Sawyer, P., Paech, B., Heymans, P. (eds.) REFSQ 2007. LNCS, vol. 4542, pp. 300–305. Springer, Heidelberg (2007). https://doi.org/10.1007/978-3-540-73031-6_22
16. Boch, A., Hohma, E., Trauth, R.: Towards an accountability framework for AI: Ethical and legal considerations. Technische Universität München, Institute for Ethics in Artificial Intelligence, Technical report (2022)
17. Bosch, J., Olsson, H.H., Crnkovic, I.: Engineering AI systems: a research agenda. In: Artificial Intelligence Paradigms for Smart Cyber-Physical Systems, pp. 1–19 (2021)
18. Caliskan, A., Bryson, J.J., Narayanan, A.: Semantics derived automatically from language corpora contain human-like biases. Science **356**(6334), 183–186 (2017)
19. Chen, K., Shao, A., Burapacheep, J., Li, Y.: Conversational AI and equity through assessing GPT-3's communication with diverse social groups on contentious topics. Sci. Rep. **14**(1), 1561 (2024)
20. Cleland-Huang, J., Gotel, O., Zisman, A., et al.: Software and Systems Traceability, vol. 2. Springer (2012)

21. Connor, A.M., Buchan, J., Petrova, K.: Bridging the research-practice gap in requirements engineering through effective teaching and peer learning. In: 2009 Sixth International Conference on Information Technology: New Generations, pp. 678–683. IEEE (2009)
22. Dalpiaz, F., Niu, N.: Requirements engineering in the days of artificial intelligence. IEEE Softw. **37**(4), 7–10 (2020)
23. Damian, D.E., Zowghi, D.: An insight into the interplay between culture, conflict and distance in globally distributed requirements negotiations. In: Proceedings of the 36th Annual Hawaii International Conference on System Sciences, 2003, pp. 10–pp. IEEE (2003)
24. Dasanayake, S., Aaramaa, S., Markkula, J., Oivo, M.: Impact of requirements volatility on software architecture: how do software teams keep up with ever-changing requirements? J. Softw. Evol. Process **31**(6), e2160 (2019)
25. Doshi-Velez, F., Kim, B.: Towards a rigorous science of interpretable machine learning. arXiv preprint arXiv:1702.08608 (2017)
26. Dube, R.R., Dixit, S.K.: Process-oriented complete requirement engineering cycle for generic projects. In: Proceedings of the International Conference and Workshop on Emerging Trends in Technology, pp. 194–197 (2010)
27. de Farias Junior, I.H., de Azevedo, R.R., de Moura, H.P., da Silva, D.S.M.: Elicitation of communication inherent risks in distributed software development. In: 2012 IEEE Seventh International Conference on Global Software Engineering Workshops, pp. 37–42. IEEE (2012)
28. Felderer, M., Ramler, R.: Quality assurance for AI-based systems: overview and challenges (introduction to interactive session). In: Winkler, D., Biffl, S., Mendez, D., Wimmer, M., Bergsmann, J. (eds.) SWQD 2021. LNBIP, vol. 404, pp. 33–42. Springer, Cham (2021). https://doi.org/10.1007/978-3-030-65854-0_3
29. Felfernig, A.: AI techniques for software requirements prioritization. In: Artificial Intelligence Methods for Software Engineering, pp. 29–47 (2021)
30. Ferrara, E.: Fairness and bias in artificial intelligence: a brief survey of sources, impacts, and mitigation strategies. Science **6**(1), 3 (2023)
31. Ferrari, A., Esuli, A.: An nlp approach for cross-domain ambiguity detection in requirements engineering. Autom. Softw. Eng. **26**(3), 559–598 (2019)
32. Firesmith, D.: Common requirements problems, their negative consequences, and the industry best practices to help solve them. J. Object Technol. **6**(1), 17–33 (2007)
33. Floridi, L., et al.: AI4people-an ethical framework for a good AI society: opportunities, risks, principles, and recommendations. Mind. Mach. **28**, 689–707 (2018)
34. Galster, M., et al.: Variability and complexity in software design: towards a research agenda. ACM SIGSOFT Softw. Eng. Not. **41**(6), 27–30 (2017)
35. Ghaisas, S., Singhal, A.: Dealing with data for RE: mitigating challenges using NLP and generative AI. arXiv preprint arXiv:2402.16977 (2024)
36. Gjorgjevikj, A., Mishev, K., Antovski, L., Trajanov, D.: Requirements engineering in machine learning projects. IEEE Access (2023)
37. Guo, J., Cheng, J., Cleland-Huang, J.: Semantically enhanced software traceability using deep learning techniques. In: 2017 IEEE/ACM 39th International Conference on Software Engineering (ICSE), pp. 3–14. IEEE (2017)
38. Guo, J.L., Steghöfer, J.P., Vogelsang, A., Cleland-Huang, J.: Natural language processing for requirements traceability. arXiv preprint arXiv:2405.10845 (2024)
39. Gupta, S., Ranjan, R., Singh, S.N.: A comprehensive survey of retrieval-augmented generation (RAG): evolution, current landscape and future directions. arXiv preprint arXiv:2410.12837 (2024)

40. Hajian, S., Bonchi, F., Castillo, C.: Algorithmic bias: from discrimination discovery to fairness-aware data mining. In: Proceedings of the 22nd ACM SIGKDD International Conference on Knowledge Discovery and Data Mining, pp. 2125–2126, August 2016

41. Hall, T., Beecham, S., Rainer, A.: Requirements problems in twelve software companies: an empirical analysis. IEE Proc. Softw. **149**(5), 153–160 (2002)

42. Handelman, G.S., et al.: Peering into the black box of artificial intelligence: evaluation metrics of machine learning methods. Am. J. Roentgenol. **212**(1), 38–43 (2019)

43. Harman, M., Mansouri, S.A., Zhang, Y.: Search-based software engineering: trends, techniques and applications. ACM Comput. Surv. (CSUR) **45**(1), 1–61 (2012)

44. Hudaib, A., Masadeh, R., Qasem, M.H., Alzaqebah, A., et al.: Requirements prioritization techniques comparison. Mod. Appl. Sci. **12**(2), 62 (2018)

45. Iqbal, T., Elahidoost, P., Lucio, L.: A bird's eye view on requirements engineering and machine learning. In: 2018 25th Asia-Pacific Software Engineering Conference (APSEC), pp. 11–20. IEEE (2018)

46. Kasauli, R., Knauss, E., Horkoff, J., Liebel, G., de Oliveira Neto, F.G.: Requirements engineering challenges and practices in large-scale agile system development. J. Syst. Softw. **172**, 110851 (2021)

47. Kirkpatrick, K.: Natural language misunderstanding. Commun. ACM **63**(11), 17–18 (2020)

48. Konrad, S., Gall, M.: Requirements engineering in the development of large-scale systems. In: 2008 16th IEEE International Requirements Engineering Conference, pp. 217–222. IEEE (2008)

49. Liu, Y., Agarwal, S., Venkataraman, S.: AutoFreeze: automatically freezing model blocks to accelerate fine-tuning. arXiv preprint arXiv:2102.01386 (2021)

50. Lüthi, P., Gagnaux, T., Gygli, M.: Distributed ledger for provenance tracking of artificial intelligence assets. Privacy and Identity Management. Data for Better Living: AI and Privacy: 14th IFIP WG 9.2, 9.6/11.7, 11.6/SIG 9.2. 2 International Summer School, Windisch, Switzerland, 19–23 August 2019, Revised Selected Papers 14, pp. 411–426 (2020)

51. Maalej, W., Pham, Y.D., Chazette, L.: Tailoring requirements engineering for responsible AI. Computer **56**(4), 18–27 (2023)

52. Maiden, N., Gizikis, A., Robertson, S.: Provoking creativity: imagine what your requirements could be like. IEEE Softw. **21**(5), 68–75 (2004)

53. Mehrabi, N., Morstatter, F., Saxena, N., Lerman, K., Galstyan, A.: A survey on bias and fairness in machine learning. ACM Comput. Surv. (CSUR) **54**(6), 1–35 (2021)

54. Nazer, L.H., Zatarah, R., Waldrip, S., Ke, J.X.C., Moukheiber, M., Khanna, A.K., Mathur, P.: Bias in artificial intelligence algorithms and recommendations for mitigation. PLOS Digit. Health **2**(6), e0000278 (2023)

55. Nijiati, A., Karabulatova, I., Lin, Y., Sautieva, F.: Problems of cognitive distortions in cross-cultural communication when using automatic translation in the Russian Chinese dialogue. In: SHS Web of Conferences, vol. 88, p. 03004. EDP Sciences (2020)

56. Nurmuliani, N., Zowghi, D., Powell, S.: Analysis of requirements volatility during software development life cycle. In: Proceedings of the 2004 Australian Software Engineering Conference, pp. 28–37. IEEE (2004)

57. Nuseibeh, B., Easterbrook, S.: Requirements engineering: a roadmap. In: Proceedings of the Conference on the Future of Software Engineering, pp. 35–46 (2000)

58. Pohl, K.: Requirements Engineering: Fundamentals, Principles, and Techniques. Springer (2010)
59. Ribeiro, M.T., Singh, S., Guestrin, C.: "why should i trust you?" Explaining the predictions of any classifier. In: Proceedings of the 22nd ACM SIGKDD International Conference on Knowledge Discovery and Data Mining, pp. 1135–1144 (2016)
60. Sandhu, G., Sikka, S.: State-of-art practices to detect inconsistencies and ambiguities from software requirements. In: International Conference on Computing, Communication & Automation, pp. 812–817. IEEE (2015)
61. Santhanam, P.: Quality management of machine learning systems. In: Shehory, O., Farchi, E., Barash, G. (eds.) EDSMLS 2020. CCIS, vol. 1272, pp. 1–13. Springer, Cham (2020). https://doi.org/10.1007/978-3-030-62144-5_1
62. Schmid, K.: Challenges and solutions in global requirements engineering–a literature survey. In: Software Quality. Model-Based Approaches for Advanced Software and Systems Engineering: 6th International Conference, SWQD 2014, Vienna, Austria, 14–16 January 2014. Proceedings 6, pp. 85–99. Springer (2014)
63. Schwartz, R., Down, L., Jonas, A., Tabassi, E.: A proposal for identifying and managing bias in artificial intelligence. Draft NIST Special Publication 1270 (2021)
64. Shah, T., Patel, S., et al.: A review of requirement engineering issues and challenges in various software development methods. Int. J. Comput. Appl. **99**(15), 36–45 (2014)
65. Shah, U.S., Jinwala, D.C.: Resolving ambiguities in natural language software requirements: a comprehensive survey. ACM SIGSOFT Softw. Eng. Not. **40**(5), 1–7 (2015)
66. Shahbeklu, F.: Requirement elicitation from diverse sources for software projects: a literature review and interview study (2024)
67. Sommerville, I.: Software Engineering (ed.). Pearson Education Inc., America (2011)
68. Tukur, M., Umar, S., Hassine, J.: Requirement engineering challenges: a systematic mapping study on the academic and the industrial perspective. Arab. J. Sci. Eng. **46**, 3723–3748 (2021)
69. Umber, A., Naweed, M.S., Bashir, T., Bajwa, I.S.: Requirements elicitation methods. Adv. Mater. Res. **433**, 6000–6006 (2012)
70. Yarger, L., Cobb Payton, F., Neupane, B.: Algorithmic equity in the hiring of underrepresented it job candidates. Online Inf. Rev. **44**(2), 383–395 (2020)

Cyber-Physical Systems

Challenges of Virtual Validation and Verification for Automotive Functions

Beatriz Cabrero-Daniel[1,3]([✉]) [iD] and Mazen Mohamad[2,3] [iD]

[1] University of Gothenburg, Gothenburg, Sweden
beatriz.cabrero-daniel@gu.se
[2] RISE, Research Institutes of Sweden, Borås, Sweden
[3] Chalmers University of Technology, Gothenburg, Sweden

Abstract. Verification and validation of vehicles is a complex yet critical process, particularly for ensuring safety and coverage through simulations. However, achieving realistic and useful simulations comes with significant challenges. To explore these challenges, we conducted a workshop with experts in the field, allowing them to brainstorm key obstacles. Following this, we distributed a survey to consolidate findings and gain further insights into potential solutions. The experts identified 17 key challenges, along with proposed solutions, an assessment of whether they represent next steps for research, and the roadblocks to their implementation. While a lack of resources was not initially highlighted as a major challenge, utilizing more resources emerged as a critical necessity when experts discussed solutions. Interestingly, we expected some of these challenges to have already been addressed or to have systematic solutions readily available, given the collective expertise in the field. Many of the identified problems already have known solutions, allowing us to shift focus towards unresolved challenges and share the next steps with the broader community.

Keywords: Autonomous Driving · Simulation · Validation and Verification · Challenges

1 Introduction

Verification and Validation (V&V) of automotive functions is very challenging, mainly due to the huge amount of test scenarios to cover in order to ensure safety, which requires hundreds of years to perform in a physical setup [12]. Hence, an established practice in automotive is to use simulations for safety and for ensuring coverage [6]. However, achieving realistic and useful simulations is challenging. It is crucial to understand the limitations and obstacles in reaching this level of realism to effectively use simulations for V&V [22].

Reported literature in the field (both white and grey) have explored various approaches to utilizing synthetic data for verification and validation (V&V) in automotive testing [2]. However, a major issue remains: there are no universally

---

Supplementary Information The online version contains supplementary material available at https://doi.org/10.1007/978-3-032-04190-6_12.

D. Taibi and D. Smite (Eds.): SEAA 2025, LNCS 16081, pp. 183–200, 2026.
https://doi.org/10.1007/978-3-032-04190-6_12

accepted standards for testing vehicles or for developing and evaluating virtual toolchains. This lack of standardization leads to inconsistencies in how different organizations define, implement, and validate their simulation environments. Without common benchmarks and guidelines, it becomes difficult to ensure the reliability, accuracy, and comparability of simulation-based V&V processes across the industry.

The aim of this study is to collect insights from experts regarding the challenges and potential solutions for simulation-based verification and validation gathered during a 3 year-long research project. These experts were both academics and practitioners from the whole automotive value chain, with a large expertise on the topic at hand, from eight different organizations, that worked on a project focusing on Enabling virtual validation & verification for automotive functions by utilizing physical test and simulations. Their suggested solutions are then assessed for feasibility, helping to identify practical approaches that could enhance the accuracy, reliability, and applicability of simulations in automotive testing and validation. The research process began with a workshop that incorporated various brainstorming activities to encourage open discussion and idea generation among participants. This initial phase allowed experts to share their experiences, identify key challenges, and group these challenges together into challenge groups. A survey was then sent out to further consolidate the results of the workshop and to gather additional insights and potential solutions to the identified challenges. This enabled us to address the following research questions:

RQ1 What are the challenges of using simulations for validation and verification of driving functions?

RQ2 What solutions exist to address these challenges and what roadblocks exist that hinder these solutions?

RQ3 How common and generalizable are these challenges and how well known are the solutions?

The key takeaway from this study is the importance of sharing lessons learned from these types of projects. The industry can build upon past efforts and avoid repeatedly starting from scratch only by openly exchanging knowledge and experiences. This collaborative approach allows researchers and practitioners to stand on the shoulders of giants in the future and reach a higher technology readiness level for simulations for V&V. Without this collective contribution, valuable insights remain within individual organizations, preventing the cumulative growth of expertise in the field.

Section 2 gives an overview of the context of this study (the project), Sect. 3 provides related work, and 4 describes the research method for the study. Results are presented in Sects. 5 and 6, and the discussion is in Sect. 7. Finally, we conclude and discuss future work in Sect. 8.

2   Context

This study summarises the final activity of a research project, a workshop to reflect on the challenges faced during the project and gather lessons learned.

This section briefly presents the project to serve as context for the present report. The purpose of the research project at focus was to explore and develop V&V (validation and verification) strategies that balance feasibility and reliability of virtual test in a measurable way. The project considered both complementing and completely replacing traditional real-world data collection with simulated data. To effectively achieve this, the project conducted simulated and physical tests (in a test track) to quantify the gap between these two test environments. Being able to do so would enable systematic testing of software functions in vehicle systems before deployment.

Participation. Nine partners, both industrial and academic, participated in the project. The partners included four automotive companies with expertise in simulation environments, two academic partners, in charge of equipping and managing the test vehicle, a research institute, a company managing a physical test track facility for AD and ADAS, who acted as coordinator, and a company specialised on gathering and annotating real data. The coordinator chaired weekly follow-up meetings in which progress was discussed, developing shared terminologies and understanding.

Test Vehicle. A Volvo XC90 with computers operating with the open-source OpenDLV software, which allows data collection from multiple sources (sensors) and control of brake, throttle and steering. The data gathered from the physical tests performed was shared with all project partners.

Timeline. The first goal was to develop a common view on the best practices for gap analysis between simulated and real-world testing, as well as to understand each partners virtual toolchain and its maturity. Then, KPIs were discussed in a number of periodic workshops across the project. Five use cases were then distributed to the partners to perform physical and virtual tests using an open and transparent tool chain, which were used to compare the physical and virtual test and discuss the fidelity level achieved. In a final step, we organized a workshop (at the end of said project) to reflect on the challenges faced and lessons learnt, which are analysed in the present report, and to discuss their implications and potential solutions as of 2025. The workshop also helped the author structure the presentation of the findings.

3   Related Work

Testing is essential for the certification and safety of automotive functions. Therefore, it is essential to plan and design a V&V strategy for each technology used in AD. Standards like ISO 26262 (about functional safety) provide strategies to mitigate systematic failures in hardware and software, as well as faults during design, implementation, verification, validation, and monitoring phases [10]. Artifacts that are used for conformance with these standards can then be used as evidence to argue for the functional safety for the function to V&V.

However, the infinite combinations of factors in their environment makes it impossible to cover them in physical test environments [24]. Alternative strategies include testing in virtual environments: simulations are revolutionising testing in the automotive industry by enabling engineers to anticipate results, lowering costs and speeding up development [21]. Digital Twins (DTs) expand on this by acting as virtual real-time mirrors of the systems and the test tracks [1,2].

Simulations are based in models which provide mathematical representations of the systems under test [7]. The simulation models within the DT also mimic the behaviour of sensors such as cameras or LiDARs to capture the simulated environment [3], which should simulate realistic surroundings [4,23], road networks [14], diverse weather conditions [19,25], and dynamic obstacles [2].

Most DTs are typically built from scratch even though open-source software and tools exist to be reused [2,8] and to facilitate the integration of synthetic data into the V&V process [2]. By leveraging open-source tools, academic researchers can accelerate their research progress and contribute to the advancement of the field of DTs for V&V [2].

Even though simulations and DTs are already being used to avoid risking lives and valuable equipment in early stages of V&V [5,25], state-of-the-art virtual V&V tools are not considered to be trustworthy enough on its own [9]. This is not only due to technical challenges, but also organizational ones [17]. Requirements Engineering (RE) therefore plays a vital role in ensuring that the DT accurately represents the real world (e.g., the physical test track facility) and can therefore provide useful insights into the vehicle system under test [2].

Generating realistic data within a DT is as challenging as validating its accuracy [3]. The use of real-world data enables the assessment of the fidelity of the DT in replicating the real world environment and the behaviour of the real vehicle system [25]. By comparing the behaviour and performance of the DT with that of the actual vehicle, the virtual V&V may be verified and validated [2]. To achieve this, we need to establish appropriate standards to provide confidence in the reliability and safety of automotive features before testing in the real world [2].

Assurance cases have been used for a long time in various domains to reason about safety [20] and cybersecurity [16,18] and are explicitly required in various standards, e.g., ISO/SAE 21434 [11] and ISO 26262 [10]. The United Nations' "New Assessment/Test Methods for Automated Driving (NATM) [26] Guidelines for Validating Automated Driving System (ADS)." NATM requires that ADS manufacturers provide evidence of the credibility of virtual toolchains [26]. These documents would be used by relevant authorities to assess new automotive functions, formally V&V them.

4   Methodology

To comprehensively identify and understand the challenges encountered in the research project, we organized a collaborative in-person workshop. This workshop brought together partners representing the full automotive value chain, including: Original Equipment Manufacturers (OEMs), providers, sensor suppliers, test site operators, and academics. Following it, we conducted a survey[1] to identify potential solutions, gather additional insights, and deepen our understanding of the identified challenges. In the following sub-sections, we describe the activities conducted at the workshop and the survey and list the contributors in each activity.

4.1 Collaborative Workshop

The workshop brought together a diverse group of seven participants from five of the project partners (1 OEM, 3 test site operators, 1 academic, 1 sensor supplier, and 1 provider) as well as two moderators. We followed the *1-2-4-All* Liberating Structure approach [13] to engage everyone in generating ideas and discussions. The approach starts with giving every participant a short time to reflect by themselves (1 min), followed by a pair discussion (2 min) and lastly a group discussion (4 min). This is then done iteratively until a saturation is achieved. The total time of the workshop was 4 h. As a tool for collaboration, we used the built-in collaboration features which allowed us to visualize the challenges as post it notes in a collaborative whiteboard. The workshop consisted of three main activities:

Identification of Challenges. We started with asking each participant to individually list the challenges they had encountered during the project. This was followed by a pair and then a group discussion on these challenges. At the end of the activity, similar challenges were grouped together to streamline a list and identify patterns.

Voting on Importance. Once the challenges were organized, participants were asked to vote on the ones most important. Each participant was given 10 votes to distribute the challenges (max 1 vote per challenge). This activity helped highlighting the areas that required more focus or further discussion. On average, the participants used seven of their votes. As a result we got a list of ordered challenges based on their perceived importance for participants.

Categorization. In the final step, we asked the participants to categorize the challenges based on two dimensions: the degree of agreement among the project partners regarding the way to address the challenge; and the degree of certainty on whether results will be generated from it. The goal of this activity was to let participants reflect on the solutions for the identified challenges and their complexity. This activity was done in two groups followed by a joint discussion. As a result, challenges were categorized according to an Agreement-Certainty Matrix [13] into *simple*, *complex*, *complicated*, and *chaotic*. The Supplementary

---

[1] Details of the survey can be found in the Supplementary Materials: https://doi.org/10.5281/zenodo.15798639.

Materials include the categorization by each of the groups that was later used for discussion [15].

4.2   Survey to All Project Partners

To gain deeper insights into the collected challenges, we sent out a survey, published as Supplementary Materials [15], that included Likert and open-ended questions about the nature of the challenges, their possible solutions, and potential roadblocks of the solutions. Additionally, we asked the respondents, listed in Table 1, to select the challenges that should be the focus in upcoming projects, and we also asked if they wanted to add additional challenges.

Table 1. Focus of the organisations of the survey participants

Participant	Partner contribution
P1, P7	Academic
P2	Simulation, OEM
P3, P4, P6	Test site operator
P5, P9	Simulation
P8	Research institute
P10	Test vehicle provider

While the number of experts participants in the final workshop was relatively small, the authors would like to remind the reader that their insights reflect the work of the larger group, as well as the reality of the state of the art as of 2025.

5   Challenges and Proposed Solutions

The problems that occurred during the project were identified by the workshop participants and written in sticky notes. During the second half of the workshop, the participants merged them to reveal 17 distinct challenges. This section presents each of them as described by the workshop participants, addressing **RQ1**, and classified into: technical, resource-related, missing requirements, and organizational. Each is accompanied by the solutions proposed in the follow-up survey, addressing **RQ2**, as well as a discussion on the main roadblocks to achieve this solution, according to the experts.

5.1   Technical

C1. **Correlation between physical and simulated sensors** is important in some levels of testing. However, "inaccuracies have occurred in replicating a physical sensor" (P9). Idealizing sensors removes an important aspect when verifying functionalities, as "the behaviour of a system might end up being different" (P2), e.g., real-life sensors can malfunction or perform poorly. Moreover, "sensor models may not represent accurately the hardware's performance across weather conditions" (P7).

Solutions. Conducting "trial test runs to align simulation and measured sensor outputs" could be a solution (P6). Another approach involves using more accurate sensor models or "combining simulations with [hardware-in-the-loop strategies]" (P8). A practical step is to perform a "dry run to test out the whole pipeline" from data collection to processing (P4). Key actions are to use "concrete KPIs and standardization" (P2), clarifying "how detailed a model needs to be" and setting "limits on accuracy for specific tests" (P5).

Roadblocks. The "lack of high-fidelity sensor models from suppliers" (P6) makes it hard to adjust the sensor model to the needs of the tests as "correct sensor models could only be developed by each sensor supplier" (P8) and remain a "black box" for others (P2). This is mainly due to providers not revealing sensitive information, e.g., sensor limitations.

C2 . Unexplained distortions in sensors' log data happened during the project due to unpredictable factors such as "drift, weather, or terrain" (P6). This led to "inconsistent logs between experiments and unexpected values which could be correlated to other collected data" (P3).

Solutions. Avoiding distortions in logged datacould be achieved by repeating the tests multiple times to have redundant data (P6, P10, P7) together with "automated checks of the output logs to detect problems early could be some possibilities" (P3). This could involve booking "backup test track slots" in case issues or anomalies are detected (P6).

Roadblocks. P1 did however mention that "sensor glitches may only occur in data post-processing, when [workarounds] are not possible anymore." Moreover, said anomalies could be caused by many factors, and it might be impossible to find a general solution.

C3 . Sensor failures and malfunctions lead to missing data happened "due to lack of knowledge about the sensors lent [led to having] a plan that could not be performed" (P8), "wrong measurements, and a loss of valuable time" (P7). The workshop participants and survey respondents acknowledged how this became a challenge, given that the gathered data had "missing data points in different test cases and a significant reduction of test cases where all results were available, making analysis difficult and results less certain" (P3).

Solutions. Sensor failures or malfunctions could be mitigated, according to respondents, by preparing and testing the equipment better before running full-scale experiments (P3, P5) as well as taking these risks into consideration when planning the use of the test tracks (P8, P10), and "if possible, using redundant systems" to gather data (P3).

Roadblocks. While this was seen as solvable to a large extent, "malfunctions are inherent and inevitable in real-life testing," specially in early-development phases (P7, P10), and "tight deadlines and too little time leads to mistakes; [moreover, we always try to get as much as possible] so they are always stressful" (P3). This is mainly because it is often not possible to redo the experiments due to the limited resources (e.g., test track availability).

C4 . Parsing complex simulation data for analysis required a lot of time "due to different tool-chains [with] different outputs" (P6). The main challenge arises from processing simulated and real data measured in the test track to overlay them (P6, P9, P4, P10), since it might be otherwise difficult to compare "since they do not share the same time steps" (P4). However, using the terms of the workshop, P4 pointed out that this is a complex problem, rather than a complicated one, and P5 said it is "always part of the job."

Solutions. Common tools to parse and break down simulation and make it manageable were identified as the solution for fidelity and correlation analysis (P6, P8), and for model integration (P8). "Regarding the timing of the data," P4 suggested to "use the latest available data point" instead of interpolating and overlaying the simulated and real data.

Roadblocks. However, time, budget, and resources were identified as roadblocks (P6, P8, P10) to process the data appropriately, and better documentation was highlighted by P4 as needed "to understand on a high level how data preprocessing might affect the result."

C5 . Consistent time-stamping for synchronizing simulated and real data was one of the roots of C4. Experts agreed on the need to time-stamp data (P6, P8) to make two time series (simulated and real, or from two sensors) comparable (P4, P5). The difficulty lies in finding a good starting point to do the synchronization (P10, P7), "especially if [the signals] lead to the triggering of an actuator" (P7).

Solutions. Consistent time-stamping would be simple if "the logging was performed the exact same way in simulation as it is on the real vehicle" (P4). However, some partners had to combine data "in post processing" (P5) by interpolating points, which was described as an "engineering challenge that can be addressed by a proper system design" (P1). This could include time-sync devices, using a network time protocol, or marking starts for scenarios (P2, P7, P10). To achieve this, P8 stated that "more lopping and more testing" would be needed.

Roadblocks. Unfortunately, in projects there might be "sensor issues and a pressure to execute the measurements quickly" (P6). Thus, more time, budget, and documentation would be needed (P8, P9, P4), as well as "know-how regarding the setup of this kind of systems" (P7).

C6 . Test Cases and Simulation Results Must be Significant and Representative. Sampling real-world scenarios and measuring what "should be known" is a major issue (P1): there is a tendency to simulate every possible combination of input variables, which can result in an overwhelming number of test cases (P6). Instead, we need to define "what constitutes statistically significant" (P8), but the limited number of runs per scenario "makes it difficult to draw any statistically significant conclusions from the studies" (P4).

Solutions. Strategies to address this challenge include "Defining criticality levels for test case simulations - this is usually connected to the ASIL levels" (P6), "ensuring that the simulation is within a certain statistical thresholds generated from the real world scenario runs." (P4), and "making use of more drivers" to perform physical tests (P7).

Roadblocks. "Environmental and physical factors are hard to fully simulate" (P2). A major limitation is that "it will take more time to run the tests, and will cost more to keep the [physical test] track" (P4). Additionally, "different stakeholders have different opinions on what scenarios are most valuable" (P10).

5.2   Lack of Resources

C7. **Availability of physical test track time** was mentioned by all workshop participants. In the follow-up survey, P8 mentioned that the test track could be booked even before needs are elicited, and added that "the challenge is even bigger for research projects" due to funding. Due to these difficulties, scenarios were changed and "manual tweaks" were needed to adjust the simulations multiple times (P6, P10), which lead "to quick measurements with poor to no documentation" (P6).

Solutions. Better planning, including "booking extra slots (buffer days) in case issues arise" (P6, P8), was seen as the only solution for the scarce availability of the physical test tracks. Moreover, in order to cope with the frequent changes in the studied scenarios due to using alternative tracks, P10 suggested working with auto-generated scenarios, and P6 highlighted the need to "pre-align" the simulation and physical test environment before the tests.

Roadblocks. These solutions are expensive, particularly for research projects (P8). Moreover, no matter how much planning is done, "there will always be [last minute] changes" (P10) and "sensor issues in the real [test] car" (P6). These prevalent issues, that eat up the "buffer time," could "lead to less documentation due to lack of time" (P6).

C8. **The Gap Between Models and Real Sensor Data.** "It is hard to get a sensor model that accurately models the real physical sensor and creates similar results" (P9). Consequently, the used models are "ideal," which means they do not model sensor distortions and never fail to detect obstacles or traffic agents. This is due to prevailing intellectual property (IP) issues, and was an issue both when testing each model and in full-system testing (P8).

Solutions. To narrow the gap, experts agreed that realistic simulation models would be needed. In order to achieve this, "we need to decompose to lowest level of model" (P8) and "add different parameters until the results are good enough" (P9), by comparing them to to real data (P8, P10). The same should be done "to integrate several models" (P8).

Roadblocks. As for other solutions, partners identified time, funding, and access to resources, in this case high fidelity models, as the main roadblocks to achieve this solution. Other factors include the difficulty to settle on "KPIs to model and verify the level of realism" (P1), and the difficulty to parametrize the environment (P10).

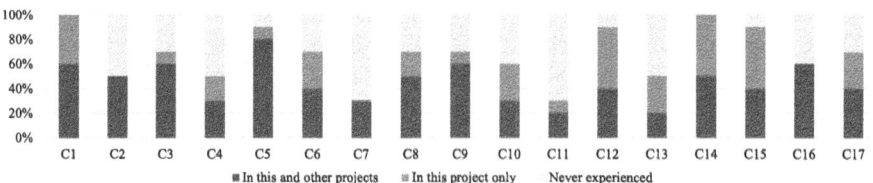

Fig. 1. Proportion of participants having experienced each of the challenges in this project (orange) and either in this or in other projects (blue). (Color figure online)

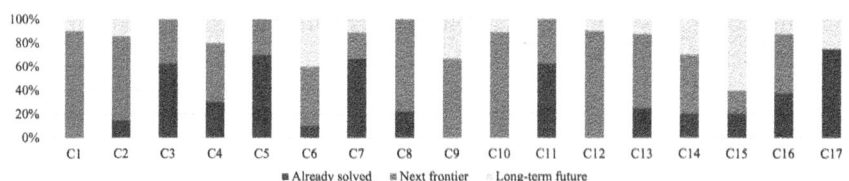

Fig. 2. Classification of solutions (into solved, next frontier, or long-term future) for each identified challenge, according to the survey respondents.

5.3   Lack of Requirements (Missing or Incomplete)

C9 . Accurate Full System Behaviour. This challenge is twofold. First, it is challenging to model complex vehicle systems with many components. Second, we need to assess the model's trustworthiness for debugging. Experts said that "it is always a challenge to define the fidelity to opt for" (P6) and to "know when it is good enough, as there is no standard way" (P4); it might depend on the vehicle (P10) and on the "status of the project" (P6): "at lower levels of testing, [there is no issue] because this will always be handled higher up in the [V&V] cycle and will be an internal OEM or TIER 1 discussion" (P8), while higher levels need external assessors.

Solutions. The respondents suggested external tests and assessment methods, in which clear expected outcomes, comprehensible acceptance criteria, and specific KPIs for realism are pre-determined (P1, P2, P6, P8). P6 suggested using "different levels of fidelity depending on requirements and feasibility," and P4 said "we should aim to reduce the complexity" and "make it easier to set thresholds for the [individual components'] simulation models."

Roadblocks. This challenge was identified as unsolved by the experts, as seen in Fig. 2. The main reason is that there is a "huge amount of models that need to be validated before the [full system] can be assessed" (P8) and that it is difficult to determine how each affect the overall results; for instance, P2 mentioned "understanding and accurately modelling all physical principles affecting sensor readings". It is worth noting that the experts also discussed, in the workshop and in the survey, that there is typically a lack of access to and knowledge about the full vehicle system.

C10 . Fidelity Needs Depend on Scope and Phase. The experts discussed at length the needs for simulation fidelity depending on project scope and phase within V model. P6 said that "due to different status of [virtual] and [physical testing] one should not expect the best correlation from the start." As the project advanced, different tests were planned conducted: from "simple unit testing or high level safety testing" to "the highest level of testing, [which] requires a higher fidelity model" (P4). However, it is difficult to assess which fidelity level is acceptable when the requirements are not explicitly defined, as discussed during the workshop.

Solutions. This challenge can be tackled with better planning and documentation, particularly regarding the needs and scope of work for each partner. Additionally, each phase of the v-model can have different a fidelity level and that needs to be traced back to the scope, requirements and tests of that particular phase. In this regard, P4 said that "a new research project to investigate the mapping from testing in the V[-model] to the required fidelity."

Roadblocks. Misunderstandings about the scope between partners led to this, which, according to P6, is "always a challenge" since requirements might evolve, and the physical vehicle and its digital twin might be at different stages of development and testing. Moreover, different partners might have different focus and goals, and hence different expectations of the needed fidelity.

C11 . Planning the use of sensors was difficult due to the lack of clear data requirements. As P3 pointed out in the survey: "requirements on data are difficult to define, and might not be available in time when data collection needs to be done, which means some guesswork will be involved."

Solutions. Clear data requirements to plan the use of sensors, and for what to record or measure would be needed (P6, P10). P8 suggested using "a checklist [while in the test track] and reviewing data live." P5 also pointed at routines and checklists, but stressed there are not "fail-safe."

Roadblocks. Once more, the respondents identified timing as a challenge to accomplish these solutions; for instance, P3 stated that "it is difficult to fully specify data requirements before you have attempted to analyse the data, but you need data to start analysing." Because of this, an iterative approach with evolving requirements was recommended.

C12 . **Determining the fidelity gap with meaningful metrics** is challenging, yet essential to achieve the goal of using simulations and DTs for V&V. P6 said we must "define what metrics will be reviewed and what is a good enough outcome." Therefore, there is a need quantify the gap and to reach a consensus for acceptable results among all partners.

Solutions. As a solution to this challenge, the participants suggested breaking down the system into smaller and more manageable components, which allows for an easier decision regarding the required fidelity gaps and metrics. For instance, P2 said we need to "break down a system into its components, following further down, and associating sensor outputs with metrics in combination with object properties." Finally, P5 said "it would be good to find some limits on fidelity for what is needed for certain tests."

Roadblocks. Lack of documentation and existing standards being too abstract and high-level. Additionally, there is a lack of established methods for credibility assessment of virtual tool chains along with KPIs to make sure that they are credible enough to perform V&V. For example, P3 said "there are proposed frameworks, e.g., in UNECE proposed NATM [but] leaves the question open of how to derive meaningful metrics and required fidelity thresholds for specific use cases."

C13 . **Whether to simulate a human driver or an AD** lead to a discussion on the challenges of modelling human behaviour. "There's a difference between the performance of an AD and a human," P7 wrote, as performance depends on the drivers, which "will lead to a [higher] variability." Partners had different views on whether it was necessary to simulate human driving, and P5 wrote: simulating "AD and human drivers answers different questions," so "both are important."

Solutions. Defining whether to simulate an AV or a human driver early on and planning accordingly was defined as key both during the workshop and in the follow-up survey. P4 said the "specific goals for the AV part of the study and for the human driver part of the study" needed to be made clear, and P7 connected setting such goals with the scope of the verification, which also needed to be defined earlier on.

Roadblocks. Workshop participants also discussed the difficulty of simulating human drivers, which relies on "including more subjective opinions and experiences" (P5).

5.4   Organizational

C14 . **Integrating proprietary formats,** still requires significant effort, despite industry standards. "Simulation tool chains use different formats" (P8) which need to be verified, but "documentation about data is sometimes missing or outdated" (P1), which is tedious. While standards exist, workshop participants said it is difficult to "manually tweak" them to fit the real test track

(P9, P10). "Scenario files [sometimes] need pre-processing work [to be imported] in commercial software" (P6, P4), which "always requires work than expected" (P5, P10), and "the existing set of standards and simulators is ever expanding," so "it will be impossible to unify them" (P4).

Solutions. Integrating data formats and platforms could benefit, according to the workshop and survey participants, from relying more on standards like ISO 26262 or the FMI standard, test catalogs like Euro NCAP, and agreeing on best practices (P6, P10, P2). P3 explained a solution is "creating a common platform for scenarios" even though there already exists "a number of existing tools using different open and [proprietary] file formats." Similarly, standard interfaces, APIs, and adapters should be provided (P8, P3); even though P3 points out that "a 1:1 mapping is often not possible."

Roadblocks. It is difficult to establish "the granularity in which the standards must be applied to the simulation," (P2) e.g., "how to deal with surrounding environment, trees, buildings and so on?" (P5), and NCAP scenarios were deemed too simple for their blank surroundings. P6 and P8 questioned who should lead the standardisation efforts, and pointed out the considerable effort needed to "establish one [format] that works consistently for all commercial software."

C15 . IP concerns are a recurrent challenge when sharing "sensitive highly detailed models [and] parametrizations" (P5) between organizations because "it could be possible to gain insight into how a AD stack works from them" (P4). P6 said: "IP frameworks vary across companies and resolving such discrepancies can take months or years." As a result, vehicle, sensor, and tire models were unlikely to be shared (P10, P7) or shared as a black-boxes to protect trade secrets (P3).

Solutions. "Simplifying the whole simulation model, or parts of it" (P4, P2), sharing only black boxes that can "used without compromising IP" (P7), or "normalizing results so that the absolute values of the models is never presented" (P4) were some of the suggestions. However, as seen in Fig. 2, solutions are considered long-term.

Roadblocks. The lack of agreement, e.g., on the level of abstraction to use (P2, P7) and how "good enough" should the shared models be (P5), was raised once more as a roadblock to achieving the proposed solutions. Thus, P3 said that these tasks will always be decided on a "case-to-case basis [and that] the issue largely remains for every new exchange." Moreover, P6 pointed out the "long time [needed] for legal alignment" and P3 added that "new legal frameworks continually makes sharing more difficult."

C16 . Lack of Detailed Sensor Specifications. IP concerns make it hard to get detailed sensor specifications, since only black box models are shared (P10) which makes it difficult to develop accurate simulations. Without knowing what is the output of physical sensors, it is difficult to "align the simulation accordingly" (P6) and simply defining "low, mid and high" fidelity levels is not enough (P8).

Solutions. Respondents P6 and P8 wrote that there should be a higher alignment between partners, including sharing models. P8 added that "sensor developers [must be] ready to take responsibility and clearly define fidelity gaps," but P3 thinks verification tasks need to be "redefined as there is no good way to obtain a good enough model."

Roadblocks. The workshop and survey participants acknowledged that IP restrictions, and the protection of trade secrets will always be a challenge: sensor suppliers will still "keep detailed performance characterization a secret" (P3).

C17 . Changes in Human Resources. The experts reflected on how [human] resources changed out during the project. When this happens "there is a loss of information" (P4) and delays in the project, since there is not enough hand-over and "ramp up time" (P6, P3) and some tasks might be started from scratch, "sometimes several times" (P3).

Solutions. Better sub-project management, work documentation, task handover, and planning were the solutions proposed by the survey participants. This, the respondents wrote, should be the responsibility of each partner. Moreover, the "project coordination could request a redundancy plan from each partner," P8 and P3 suggested.

Roadblocks. All the survey participants agreed that changes in human resources were to be expected; P10 even said "I see this as a risk in all projects." Moreover, they stated that documentation is hard to maintain and access, "due to specialized knowledge needed, and the limited available funded time" (P3). These issues were thus identified as roadblocks for these theoretical solutions in practice.

6   General Challenges and Known Solutions

As workshop and survey participants pointed out, many of the challenges listed in Sect. 5 can be seen as a "risk in all projects." This section moves on to discuss which of these challenges, are common in other projects, and how well-known are their potential solutions, addressing **RQ3**.

As seen in Fig. 1, all survey participants have experienced challenges C1 and C14, often in other projects too. Other challenges are almost as common: C5, C12, and C15 were also common, with 90% of the survey participants having experienced it. Challenges C3, C6, C8, C9, and C17 were also common across partners and projects, as seen in Fig. 1. Some others were not as common, as they are typically experienced by specific partners, e.g., C7 and C11, which are very related to the use of the physical test track.

Figure 2, gathers the opinion of experts on what is the next frontier for enabling virtual V&V of automotive functions. A take away from this analysis is that a number of the challenges are, according to experts, already solved. Meanwhile, other challenges are left for the long-term future. It is also worth noting that for some of the challenges, participants did not agree on whether the challenges were solvable.

7 Discussion

This study has identified 17 challenges for virtual V&V of automotive functions by asking representatives of the 10 partners of a research project, described in Sect. 2. These challenges were categorised into four groups: technical, organisational, managerial, and requirements-related. Several of these challenges, moreover, share common characteristics. For instance, the difficulties related with working with test vehicles, that the experts deem inevitable, as well as the "it works on my machine syndrome."

Technical challenges accounted for only 30% of the total identified challenges. The majority were related to organization, management, and requirements. For example, a common source of challenges was a lack of clarity that, according to experts, is unavoidable in early-stage development, but which could have been mitigated by establishing standard practices and verification requirements. Although doing so in early stages is universally challenging, a potential solution discussed was to periodically and systematically review and refine the requirements to prevent inconsistencies and conflicts as the project advances. Implementing a formal agile approach in research projects could facilitate them and support project management in guaranteeing the expected outcomes.

> The lack of resources was not identified as a major challenge, but it became evident when proposing solutions that they are a critical requirement for the continuation of this study, e.g., increased time, funding, personnel, redundancy, and standardised practices to adhere to.

Given the collective expertise in the field and the large body of work in the academic literature covering these challenges, one might expect not to have encountered these challenges in the project. This work however reflects the reality of the state of practice as of 2025 and aims to remind the reader about the necessity to focus on the particular areas here discussed. The striking result, rather than the concrete challenges, is that these challenges still exist. This is specially true given that the systematic solutions to these issues seemed to be well-understood and agreed among partners. However, many of these, as seen in Figs. 1 and 2, were identified as well-known yet long-term future challenges.

> This raises two important questions: first, why do these challenges persist despite previous experiences? Second, if a similar workshop had been conducted before the project start, would the partners have reached an agreement on the solutions to implement?

Despite the challenges encountered, the project successfully delivered valuable outcomes across all work packages, and will serve as a basis for a subsequent project focusing on the assessment of the virtual toolchains used for V&V of automotive functions. Based on the learnings in this project, we will encourage incorporating a structured challenge analysis in the initial planning activities. Similarly, we also encourage researchers and practitioners undertaking similar projects to share their challenges and insights, fostering a culture in which we can collectively advance knowledge.

7.1 Threats to the Validity of the Results

In terms of construct validity, we considered the risk of misunderstandings and misinterpretations by the participants in the workshop and survey. To mitigate this, we presented the purpose of the study and its context at the beginning of the workshop. In the second part of the workshop, participants discussed the identified challenges in detail. Moreover, this study is based on partners that have worked together for at least two years, developing shared terminologies and a common understanding of the subject matter.

For internal validity, we ensured a structured discussion during the workshop. Two moderators facilitated the session, ensuring that all participants shared their opinions without any dominating the conversation. Moreover, we employed the 1-2-4 technique [13], allowing participants to reflect individually before the group discussions, reducing bias. For the survey, we carefully filtered the quotes to balance contributions, ensuring that no perspective was overrepresented.

Regarding external validity, we asked participants whether they had previously encountered the identified challenges, but we could only rely on their subjective opinions. As a result, there is a risk that the findings may not be fully generalizable. However, our study involved experts from diverse organizations, spanning both academia and industry. The participants also had many years of expertise in the field and a strong understanding of the existing body of knowledge, which strengthens the credibility of our findings.

8 Conclusion and Future Work

The aim of this study was to collect insights from experts regarding the challenges and potential solutions for simulation-based verification and validation of automotive functions. These experts were both practitioners and academics from the organizations that worked on a project focusing on enabling virtual V&V for automotive functions by utilizing physical test and simulations. By doing this, we identified challenges, potential solutions, and roadblocks to achieve them. Moreover, we report expert opinions to understand how generalisable these are and whether they should be the next steps in research.

Future projects (academic and industrial) should build on these by providing systematic approaches to solve the "already solved" challenges, and focus on next frontier solutions. Specially, our experts stressed the need to establish a common framework for performing credibility assessments of virtual tool-chains and environments, which could promote virtual V&V to complement physical testing. Additionally, this will support the use of simulations in regulatory testing, type approval, and certifications such as EuroNCAP.

Acknowledgment. This work is supported by Sweden's innovation agency, Vinnova, under Grant No. 2021-05043 entitled "Enabling Virtual Validation and Verification for ADAS and AD Features (EVIDENT)".

References

1. Batty, M.: Digital twins. Environ. Plan. B Urban Anal. City Sci. (2018)
2. Cabrero-Daniel, B., Abdelkarim, A.Y., Broberg, A.: Digital twins for early verification and validation of autonomous driving features: open-source tools and standard formats. In: 2024 IEEE Intelligent Vehicles Symposium (IV), pp. 2477–2482. IEEE (2024)
3. Conti, M., Di Pietro, R., Mancini, L.V., Mei, A.: (new) distributed data source verification in wireless sensor networks. Inf. Fus. **10**(4), 342–353 (2009). https://doi.org/10.1016/j.inffus.2009.01.002. http://portal.acm.org/citation.cfm?id=1555009.1555162
4. Dosovitskiy, A., Ros, G., Codevilla, F., Lopez, A., Koltun, V.: CARLA: an open urban driving simulator. In: Proceedings of the 1st Annual Conference on Robot Learning, pp. 1–16 (2017)
5. European Union: Regulation (EU) 2024/1689 of the European Parliament and of the Council of 13 June 2024 laying down harmonised rules on artificial intelligence (Artificial Intelligence Act), June 2024. Official Journal of the European Union, L 1689/1. https://eur-lex.europa.eu/legal-content/EN/TXT/?uri=CELEX%3A32024R1689
6. Fadaie, J.: The state of modeling, simulation, and data utilization within industry: an autonomous vehicles perspective. arXiv preprint arXiv:1910.06075 (2019)
7. Guala, F.: Models, simulations, and experiments. In: Model-Based Reasoning: Science, Technology, Values, pp. 59–74. Springer (2002)
8. Hu, X., Li, S., Huang, T., Tang, B., Chen, L.: Sim2real and digital twins in autonomous driving: a survey (2023)
9. Inland Transport Committee: World Forum for Harmonization of Vehicle Regulations Framework document on automated/autonomous vehicles
10. International Organization for Standardization: ISO 26262:2018 (all parts). Road Vehicles - Functional Safety. Standard, International Organization for Standardization (2018)
11. International Organization for Standardization and Society of Automotive Engineers International: Road vehicles – Cybersecurity engineering, August 2021. iSO/SAE 21434:2021. https://www.iso.org/standard/70918.html
12. Kalra, N., Paddock, S.M.: Driving to safety: how many miles of driving would it take to demonstrate autonomous vehicle reliability? Transp. Res. Part A Policy Pract. **94** (2016)
13. Lipmanowicz, H., McCandless, K.: The Surprising Power of Liberating Structures: Simple Rules to Unleash a Culture of Innovation. Liberating Structures Press, Seattle, WA (2014), https://www.liberatingstructures.com/
14. Lu, Y., et al.: Smart manufacturing process and system automation – a critical review of the standards and envisioned scenarios. J. Manuf. Syst. **56**, 312–325 (2020). https://doi.org/10.1016/j.jmsy.2020.06.010. https://www.sciencedirect.com/science/article/pii/S027861252030100X

15. Mohamad, M., Cabrero Daniel, B.: Challenges of virtual validation and verification for automotive functions - supplementary materials (2025). https://doi.org/10.5281/zenodo.15798639
16. Mohamad, M., Jolak, R., Askerdal, O., Steghöfer, J.P., Scandariato, R.: CASCADE: an asset-driven approach to build security assurance cases for automotive systems. ACM Trans. Cyber-Phys. Syst. **7**(1) (2023). https://doi.org/10.1145/3569459
17. Mohamad, M., Steghöfer, J.P., Knauss, E., Scandariato, R.: Managing security evidence in safety-critical organizations. J. Syst. Softw. **214**, 112082 (2024)
18. Mohamad, M., Steghöfer, J.P., Scandariato, R.: Security assurance cases-state of the art of an emerging approach. Empir. Softw. Eng. **26**(4), 70 (2021)
19. Nvidia: Nvidia Announces Digital Twin Platform for Scientific Computing (2022). https://nvidianews.nvidia.com/news/nvidia-announces-digital-twin-platform-for-scientific-computing
20. Palin, R., Habli, I.: Assurance of automotive safety–a safety case approach. In: Computer Safety, Reliability, and Security: 29th International Conference, SAFECOMP 2010, Proceedings 29, 14–17 September 2010, pp. 82–96. Springer (2010)
21. Rasheed, A., San, O., Kvamsdal, T.: Digital twin: values, challenges and enablers from a modeling perspective. IEEE Access **8**, 21980–22012 (2020)
22. Sagmeister, S., Kounatidis, P., Goblirsch, S., Lienkamp, M.: Analyzing the impact of simulation fidelity on the evaluation of autonomous driving motion control. In: 2024 IEEE Intelligent Vehicles Symposium (IV), pp. 230–237. IEEE (2024)
23. Shah, S., Dey, D., Lovett, C., Kapoor, A.: AirSim: high-fidelity visual and physical simulation for autonomous vehicles. In: Hutter, M., Siegwart, R. (eds.) Field and Service Robotics, pp. 621–635. Springer, Cham (2018)
24. Siddique, U.: SafetyOps. arXiv preprint arXiv:2008.04461 (2020)
25. Ulbrich, S., Menzel, T., Reschka, A., Schuldt, F., Maurer, M.: Defining and substantiating the terms scene, situation, and scenario for automated driving. In: IEEE Conference on Intelligent Transportation Systems, Proceedings, ITSC 2015, October, pp. 982–988 (10 2015). https://doi.org/10.1109/ITSC.2015.164
26. United Nations Economic Commission for Europe: New assessment/test method for automated driving (NATM) guidelines for validating automated driving system (ADS) (2023). eCE/TRANS/WP.29/2023/44. https://unece.org/sites/default/files/2023-04/ECE-TRANS-WP.29-2023-44e.pdf

A Systematic Approach to Fault Injection Test Case Generation in Practice

Tiziano Munaro[1]([✉])[ID], Matko Turalija[2][ID], Simon Barner[1][ID],
and Marko Halak[2][ID]

[1] fortiss GmbH, Munich, Germany
{munaro,barner}@fortiss.org
[2] TTTech Auto AG, Osijek, Croatia
{matko.turalija,marko.halak}@tttech-auto.com

Abstract. The same failure mode, injected into the same component of the same Cyber-Physical System (CPS) may or may not reveal a residual fault depending only on the parametrization of the tested failure scenario: This is shown in Part 10, Clause 8 of the ISO 26262 standard. Hence, when performing Fault Injection (FI) testing to assess the functional correctness, accuracy, and timing of safety mechanisms, it is essential to determine the "worst-case" scenarios in a typically high-dimensional, unbounded, and continuous parameter space. These scenarios are commonly influenced by intricate interactions among system components and between the system and its environment, and are thus known to change with each modification to the system under test. As a result, manually created FI test suites tend to be error-prone, sub-optimal, and expensive to maintain. In contrast, automated FI Test Case Generation (TCG) approaches have already proven to be effective in identifying potentially unsafe behavior of CPS while significantly reducing manual effort. However, given the lack of systematic methodologies for the application of such techniques in real-world development environments, we set to understand how FI TCG can be applied in continuous development, integration, and testing processes. Based on our findings, we propose a methodology for encoding the generation of "worst-case" FI test cases as an optimization problem to which generic optimization approaches can be applied. We apply this methodology to assess two of the safety mechanisms safeguarding the TTTech Auto MotionWise automotive middleware. Using search-based TCG in a Hardware-in-the-Loop (HiL) setup, we demonstrate how it supports the identification of highly challenging FI test cases and increases confidence in the absence of residual faults with minimal manual effort.

Keywords: Software and system safety · Fault injection · Test generation · Continuous development

1 Introduction

To ensure safe and reliable execution and communication, Cyber-Physical Systems (CPS) such as modern vehicles typically implement *safety mechanisms*:

D. Taibi and D. Smite (Eds.): SEAA 2025, LNCS 16081, pp. 201–218, 2026.
https://doi.org/10.1007/978-3-032-04190-6_13

Software- and/or hardware-based solutions to "detect and mitigate or tolerate faults or control or avoid failures" [18] in any *operational situation*[1]. For example, replicating (and monitoring) a hardware component can allow a system to tolerate (or at least detect and mitigate) the loss of one of the redundant elements.

To assess not only the correct functional performance and accuracy but also the timeliness of safety mechanisms, the ISO 26262 standard highly recommends *Fault Injection* (FI) testing: A "method to evaluate the effect of a fault within an element by inserting faults, errors, or failures in order to observe the reaction" [18,19]. Crucially, FI testing shall "support the argumentation of completeness and correctness of a system architectural design with respect to faults" (cf. [19])—essentially requiring systematic coverage of not only failure modes but their potentially infinite manifestations as well. This is emphasized in [17] where, based on the example of a sensor affected by a *stuck-at* fault, the ISO 26262 standard illustrates how an FI test case may or may not reveal a *residual fault*[2]: The defect is detected only for certain combinations of physical values (determined by the operational situation) and measured values (affected by the FI).

In the automotive domain, each functional safety requirement is commonly associated with an FI test whose parameters defining the operational situation (e.g., the number and type of applications running on an Electronic Control Unit (ECU)) and the fault's manifestation (e.g., the discrepancy between two ECUs' clocks) are selected manually following *boundary testing* and experience-based *error guessing* approaches as suggested in [19]. At the same time, it is typically ensured that the selected parameters are sufficiently generic to be applicable to all possible hardware and software configurations. In contrast, safety-related time intervals such as the *Fault Detection and Fault Reaction Time Intervals* (FDTI and FRTI respectively),[3] are often derived analytically or estimated, and verified manually by selectively taking time measurements.

While the testing effort is notable, it is unlikely that the manually created test suites reliably pinpoint the potentially fault-revealing parameter combinations for all software/hardware configurations as the intricate interactions within complex CPS involving, e.g., hypervisors, middleware, schedulers, and non-deterministic communication media are increasingly difficult to fully comprehend [39]. Moreover, as these "worst-case" parameter combinations can change with each modification to the System Under Test (SUT) or its requirements, the effort of maintaining manually created test suites is prohibitive [13]. At the same time, the effectiveness of exhaustive FI TCG campaigns (typically applying random or uniform sampling of the parameter space, e.g., [35,42]) in identifying fault-revealing test cases is also questionable given the vast number of potential test cases resulting from the continuous and unbounded environments modern CPS operate in. Moreover, as discrete notions of states and transitions

---

[1] A scenario a system may encounter (e.g., following a vehicle at speed) [18].

[2] A potentially hazardous fault not covered by safety mechanisms [18].

[3] Combined, the FDTI and FRTI of a safety mechanism must not exceed the possibly situation-specific *Fault Tolerant Time Interval* (FTTI) [18].

do not capture the complexity of typical environments either, coverage-based approaches cannot be expected to perform better [15, 28].

Hence, automated FI TCG approaches able to systematically *optimize* test case parameters (by using, e.g., heuristic algorithms or machine learning [8, 38]) are seen as key to (1) effectively identifying parameter values with a high likelihood of revealing residual faults while (2) ensuring short feedback cycles as required in modern continuous development, integration, and testing (CX) processes.

1.1   Problem

Optimization algorithms applicable for automated TCG are typically generic, operate on abstract data structures, and require case-specific metrics for guidance. The heuristic algorithm applied in Sect. 4.3, e.g., optimizes the *genes* of *individuals* in a *population* and requires a *fitness* metric to determine its progress. Hence, to efficiently apply and effectively leverage automated TCG techniques in practice one must know how to **systematically** ...

... **encode the problem** of identifying FI test case parameters with a high likelihood of revealing residual faults such that generic optimization algorithms can be applied,

... **derive the inputs** required for the TCG including parametrized test scenarios, failure models and guidance metrics, and

... **process the output** generated by the typically hundreds of test cases to enable practitioners to effectively pinpoint potential defects in case of failures and judge the confidence in the absence of residual faults otherwise.

However, we not only observe a **lack of guidelines, methodologies, and processes covering these individual activities in practice** but also come across **unanswered questions on their *integration* into modern development processes** that guide our research: Which changes to the socio-technical CX process are required? Which activities must be performed manually and which ones can be automated as part of the CX pipeline? When shall the respective activities be executed? Will the qualification requirements for practitioners change?

1.2   Contribution

In the context of this work, we understand how to encode the problem of generating challenging FI test cases for the application of optimization algorithms, we identify the required inputs to apply such approaches and determine how to interpret the generated output to facilitate the estimation of the confidence in the absence of defects. These findings allow us to propose a **semi-automated end-to-end FI TCG methodology defining concrete artefacts and guided activities, designed to be implemented in the context of a real-world CX process.**

2   Related Work

Standards provide collections and taxonomies of typically informal fault and failure models lacking, however, any guidelines illustrating their systematic application for FI testing (cf., e.g., [2], [3, Sect. 6.3] and [20, Annex D]). Hence, in our previous work, we introduce a collection of parametrizable failure models for simulation-based FI providing executable behavior specifications [32]. While this work hints at the systematic application of the presented failure models in combination with TCG approaches, no concrete guidelines or best practices are provided.

The same can be said about state-of-the-art TCG frameworks: While, e.g., heuristic and machine learning-based testing approaches have proven to be cost-effective in identifying unsafe behavior in embedded systems by generating highly challenging edge cases (cf., e.g., [1, 4, 12, 23, 24, 28, 29, 31, 38, 39, 41–43]), the typically context-specific solutions do not address process-related questions such as *who* shall perform *which* activity and *when*. The following related work, however, is notable for taking steps towards a systematic application of TCG approaches in practice: [40] proposes a modular, open-source framework for search-based TCG providing practitioners with concise interfaces for all input and output artefacts, a library of optimization algorithms, and generic post-processing and visualization features. However, given the intentionally generic nature of the tool, neither its integration into development processes nor the elicitation of input models is covered. [14] partially addresses the derivation of inputs by proposing a practical approach for deriving fitness functions for heuristic TCG. [33] as well as [36, 37] provide examples for the integration of systematic safety verification approaches in continuous development processes. However, the approach in [33] is limited to state automata and the solution presented in [36, 37] to individual software components in a deterministic execution environment with register-level access. Therefore, neither approach can (1) be applied for system-level testing or integration testing of distributed real-time systems involving different hosts, networks, and operating systems such as the automotive middleware introduced in Sect. 4.2, and (2) detect any deviations in the *systemic* real-time behavior of CPS (as expressed by, e.g., control loops).

In contrast, real-world CX processes for distributed, safety-critical CPS such as the ones illustrated in [11] and [10], for example, depict very clearly how continuous development and testing with Model-, Software-, and Hardware-in-the-Loop test beds can be integrated into existing engineering, validation and certification processes, which activities must be performed, when and by whom. However, test selection is either not covered or it is manual and requirements-based.

In summary, we observe an abundance (1) of *normative documents* listing failure models for FI testing without a methodology illustrating their systematic application (e.g., [2]), (2) of *academic frameworks* for TCG lacking the necessary guidance for practitioners to adapt and integrate them into real-world development processes (e.g., [40]), and (3) of *industry publications* on continuous development, integration and testing for CPS which, however, either do not cover test selection or resort to the same manual, requirements-based approach mentioned in Sect. 1 (e.g., [11]). To address the resulting **research gap**, we propose a methodological framework enabling domain experts to systematically integrate existing optimization approaches to automatically generate system- and revision-specific "worst-case" FI tests into their CX process.

3 Approach

We introduce a systematic methodology for applying automated TCG for FI testing in an industrial context, thereby addressing the research gap delineated in Sect. 2. Wherever possible, the methodology combines existing, proven concepts (e.g., logical test cases [30], parametrized failure models [32], templates for guidance metrics [14], or TCG performance metrics [6]) into the systematic, semi-automated, end-to-end process depicted in Fig. 1. The circled numbers ① to ③ refer to the following subsections. For the sake of simplicity, examples typically refer to the case study presented in Sect. 4. Note however, that the methodology is agnostic to use cases and optimization engines and thus not limited to, e.g., genetic algorithms.

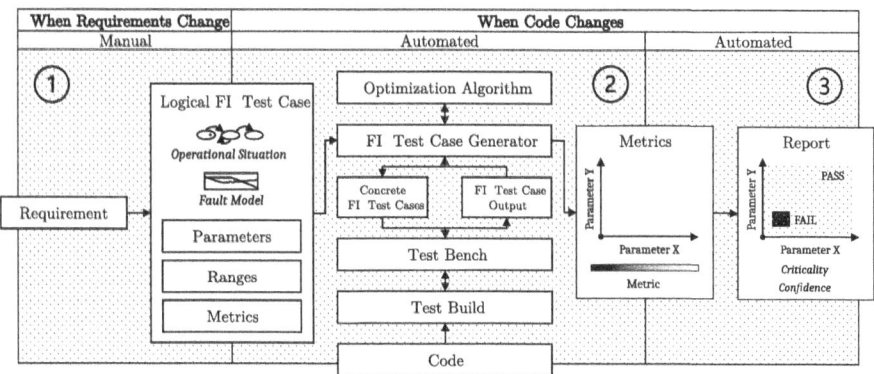

Fig. 1. Illustration of the proposed FI TCG process highlighting the required steps and artefacts. Note the column headers defining which activities must be performed manually and which ones can be automated, and recommending when to execute the activities.

① We introduce the concept of a **logical FI test case** which, similar to *logical scenarios* defined in [30], encodes a concrete, yet parametrizable *operational situation*. In contrast to the scenarios in [30], however, the logical test case also specifies an equally parametrizable *failure model* encoding, e.g., a delay, a bit-flip, or a signal loss (cf. [32]). Being essentially parametrizable FI test cases, logical FI test cases are derived following the same methods that are currently applied to manually define FI test cases. The ISO 26262, e.g., recommends analyses of both functional and non-functional **requirements**, interfaces, operational situations, boundary values, limit conditions, environmental conditions, functional dependencies, and failure modes. However, while the techniques are the same, with the presented process, practitioners are not required to manually derive the concrete, worst-case manifestation of the identified operational scenarios based on their understanding of the SUT and its environment. Hence, the proposed method leverages the human ability to comprehend and define high-level operational situations and combines it with the effectiveness of TCG approaches in identifying challenging parametrizations of said scenarios. Crucially, any factor identified by the aforementioned analyses which might impact the outcome of a test is a candidate to be defined as a **parameter** rather than being hardcoded. Given their focus on establishing the effect of certain variations in the system or its environment, the *guide word*-based analyses recommended in [21, Annex E] (e.g., Systems Theoretic Process Analysis (STPA) [26]) are particularly suitable to identify relevant parameters. For additional support to identify relevant failure models and their parameters, we refer to [32], a systematic literature study proposing a library of parametrized failure models for FI testing of CPS.

The parameters' **ranges** shall be defined to be either exhaustive or over-approximative. In other words, whenever a bounded range can be specified, it is recommended to do so. Otherwise, the lower and upper bounds of possible values shall be estimated generously: By applying test case optimization algorithms, regions of the combined parameter space where failures are unlikely, are expected to be identified efficiently. To systematically avoid such regions and approximate parameter combinations which are likely to reveal a residual fault, optimization algorithms commonly require a quantitative measure of how close a test case is to, e.g., violating a safety goal. These guidance **metrics** are typically derived by defining a distance measure in the dimension regulated by the requirement, calculated based on a test case's output, and either minimized or maximized in the TCG process. For the case study in Sect. 4, e.g., we seek to reveal violations of requirements limiting the FDTI of safety mechanisms. Hence, we select the FDTI (calculated by processing the logs included in the test case output) as guidance metric and choose to maximize it. Complex guidance metrics can be constructed by applying the templates introduced in [14]. Note that while, e.g., heuristic algorithms benefit from continuous metrics, other approaches such as the machine learning-based approach proposed in [38] only require a binary metric.

② Generic, state-of-the-art **optimization algorithms** operate on use case-agnostic data structures, oblivious to the semantics of the parameters to be optimized and of the metrics to be used for guidance. Moreover, they typically proceed iteratively. The heuristic algorithm applied in Sect. 4.3, for instance, requires the definition of a set of *genes* of *individuals* of a *population*, whose *fitness* is to be maximized over a series of *generations*. Hence, it is the **test case generator**'s task to (1) *encode* the problem of optimizing (a typically randomly initialized set of) **concrete test cases** using these data structures (translating, e.g., test case parameters into genes, concrete test cases into individuals, test suites into populations, and metrics to fitness values) and (2) *decode* the proposed optimization back into the domain of FI testing (updating the concrete FI test cases with parameter values derived from, e.g., the respective gene expressions).

Once generated, the concrete FI test cases are executed, and their output is processed to determine the values of the guidance metrics defined in the logical test case. These metrics are then encoded by the test case generator and forwarded to the optimization algorithm together with the respective parameter values. Based on this feedback, the optimization algorithm proposes new parameter values, which are then decoded again into concrete FI test cases. Iteratively repeating this process over the course of a TCG **campaign** leads to an approximation of those areas in the commonly multi-dimensional parameter space which lead to better values of the guidance metric—and potentially to a violation of the related requirement. As this methodology aims to be case-independent, the selection and configuration of specific optimization algorithms is out of this publication's scope. There are, however, existing comparisons to support and guide these activities (cf., e.g., [8,16]). As FI TCG campaigns may take several hours to execute (depending, e.g., on the size of the parameter space and the time required to execute each concrete test case), we generally recommend running them on a nightly basis while setting the total number of test cases to take full advantage of the time available.

Finally, the execution of FI test cases typically involves a **test bench**, which exercises the SUT (provided in form of a **test build**) and can take different forms, ranging from Model-in-the-Loop (MiL) to Hardware-in-the-Loop (HiL) setups. Crucially, both the test bench and the test build must provide the data required for the elicitation of the specified guidance metrics (e.g., the time stamps to derive the FDTIs for the case in Sect. 4.2).

③ Once completed, the test case generator provides a data set listing each executed test case (identified by its parameters) and the respective values of the elicited metrics. We propose the automatic generation of a human-readable **report** from this typically vast, purely numeric data set. Metric-based heat maps of the parameter space (or two-dimensional projections thereof) provide an initial impression of the results and serve as guidance for practitioners. To support the selection of representative test cases for analysis when numerous failures of similar nature have been found, the test cases are clustered and the ones closest to the centroids are identified [6]. To estimate the confidence in the absence of defects in cases where no failures have been found, the area of the test cases' convex hull in the parameter space and the standard deviation of the edge lengths of their Minimum Spanning Tree (MST) are combined to quantify which regions of the parameter space have been covered and at which granularity [6]. In addition, the report also contains the TCG campaign's metadata including references to the logical test case and the optimization algorithm, names and ranges of parameters, etc.

Note that the proposed process only requires manual intervention whenever the requirements change (to update the collection of logical test cases) while **no manual effort is required in case the code changes** as the FI test cases are automatically optimized for the updated SUT. Combined with the reduced manual effort of defining *logical* test cases rather than *concrete* ones, the overall reduction in manual effort is expected to be significant.

4   Case Study

This case study aims to demonstrate the *applicability* and *efficiency* of the semi-automated FI TCG methodology introduced in Sect. 3 in an industrial setting and provide practitioners with a real-world example. Hence, the approach is implemented in the CX environment of *MotionWise*: An automotive middleware for safety-critical applications developed by TTTech Auto. The resulting impact is assessed based on the feedback of test engineers and project managers collected by means of semi-structured interviews.

4.1   Design

Following the guidelines for conducting and reporting case study research in software engineering introduced in [5, 27, 34], we opted for a systematically derived questionnaire to assess the proposed contribution in the light of the problem delineated in Sect. 1.1. Hence, the questionnaire is systematically derived starting from the following goals by applying the Goal-Question-Metric (GQM) approach [5, 27]: (1) ANALYZE *two methodologies for FI testing* FOR THE PURPOSE OF *comparison* WITH RESPECT TO THEIR *effectiveness in identifying potential defects* FROM THE POINT OF VIEW OF *test engineers and project managers* IN THE CONTEXT OF *a continuous development process in an industry setting*. (2) ANALYZE *an FI testing approach* FOR THE PURPOSE OF *assessment* WITH RESPECT TO ITS *applicability* FROM THE POINT OF VIEW OF *test engineers and project managers* IN THE CONTEXT OF *a continuous development process in an industry setting*.

The goals are refined into the questionnaire listed in Table 1. Considering related work on assessing the effectiveness of testing methods (cf. [27]) and the applicability of methods in computer science (cf. [25]), the questions are designed to be compiled by using 5-value *Semantic Differential Scales (SDS)* (ranging from *Very Low (1)* to *Very High (5)*), 5-value *Likert Scales (LKS)* (ranging from *Disagree Completely (1)* to *Agree Completely (5)*), or by estimating a *Time Span in Hours (TSH)*. In addition, the rationale behind each answer shall be stated in one to two sentences. Note that, while the *proposed* method always refers to the approach described in Sect. 3, the *current* method is case-specific and thus introduced in Sect. 4.2. Moreover, as the understanding of manual effort may diverge, the answers to questions 1 and 2 will not be reported individually, but the relative difference *within subjects*.

Table 1. Systematically derived questionnaire used for the semi-structured interviews in the context of the case study. The question types are introduced in Sect. 4.1.

#	Question	Type
1.	*How much manual effort is required to parametrize FI test cases with the current method?*	TSH
2.	*How much manual effort is needed to define the input artefacts for the automated FI TCG with the proposed method?*	TSH
3.	*The automated TCG in case of code changes, enabled by the proposed method, significantly reduces the required manual effort for FI testing over the course of a project.*	LKS
4.	*What level of understanding of the system is required to create, parametrize, execute, and evaluate FI test cases with the current method?*	SDS
5.	*What level of understanding of the system is required to derive the input artefacts, execute the TCG, and evaluate the output artefacts following the proposed method?*	SDS
6.	*What level of knowledge about the FI testing method is required to create, execute, and evaluate FI test cases with the current method?*	SDS
7.	*What level of knowledge about the FI testing method is required to derive the input artefacts, execute the TCG, and evaluate the output artefacts following the proposed method?*	SDS
8.	*Applying the proposed method increases the number of detected defects.*	LKS
9.	*Applying the proposed method reveals different types of defects compared to the current method.*	LKS
10.	*The proposed method also reveals the defects identified by the current method and can thus replace the current approach rather than being used alongside it.*	LKS
11.	*The generated report facilitates the estimation of the "confidence in the absence of unintended functionality and properties" [21, Clause 9].*	LKS
12.	*The proposed method for deriving input artefacts and processing output artefacts facilitates the application of automated FI TCG approaches in an industry setting to the point where domain experts can apply them autonomously.*	LKS
13.	*The proposed method covers all aspects of the systematic application of automated FI TCG approaches in an industry setting and does not miss to specify any inputs, guidelines, or outputs.*	LKS

To cover both mentioned points of view, the questionnaire is compiled by test engineers and project managers following a live demonstration of the applied methodology including the derivation of all TCG inputs for the case described in Sect. 4.2, the specification of a TCG campaign (cf. Listing 1.1), and the generated TCG report. During the subsequent analysis, the numerical data collected from each question is validated using the rationales given by the practitioners and summarized using descriptive statistics. The number of test cases until the first failure and the maximum quality (based on the guidance metric) reached by TCG campaigns run in the context of this case study are also used to provide context to the discussion in Sect. 4.5 and validate the questionnaire's results. However, as the performance of the particular instantiation of the presented method described in Sect. 4.3 depends on the SUT, the optimization algorithm, and the definition of the input artefacts, a *quantitative* evaluation of its efficiency in detecting potential defects is out of this case study's scope. We refer the interested reader to [6] for such a performance-oriented evaluation of FI TCG.

4.2 Case

MotionWise is an automotive middleware designed to integrate and safely execute arbitrary software applications on different hardware platforms. To ensure controlled and safe execution of vehicle software components and reliable communication among them, MotionWise includes safety mechanisms encompassing, among others, task timing monitors (to handle, e.g., task overruns), communication timing monitors (to handle, e.g., loss or time out of messages), aliveness monitors (to handle, e.g., deadlocks, freezes, or crashes), and redundancy checks (to handle, e.g., data corruption) as well as error handling components (to coordinate the fault reaction). In the context of this evaluation, the here proposed methodology is applied to test the compliance of two of those safety mechanisms w.r.t. their FDTI requirements: The first one monitors the *time synchronization* between MotionWise hosts, the second one *task execution times*.

As middleware for potentially safety-critical software applications, MotionWise is subject to stringent functional safety requirements specified in, e.g., the ISO 26262 standard or in the AUTOSAR E2E Protocol Specification. Currently, each of these requirements is associated with one or more manually specified, *concrete* FI test cases. Following the reasoning delineated in Sect. 1, any of these test cases aiming to cover a worst-case scenario must be reassessed after each change to the system, its context, and its requirements. To ensure the validity of any time-related metrics (e.g., FDTIs), the test build is executed on a HiL test bench. The test case output is stored in a machine-readable report, allowing for automated parsing of the log files.

4.3 Execution

Starting from the **requirement** limiting the FDTI of both safety mechanisms to a concrete time budget, the relevant **logical test cases** are identified using the same systematic safety analysis methods as are currently applied for the manual specification of test cases: By means of, e.g., Fault Tree Analysis (FTA), Failure Mode and Effect Analysis (FMEA), and System-Theoretic Process Analysis (STPA) those failure modes (among the ones defined by standards such as the

AUTOSAR E2E Protocol Specification [3]) are identified, which could potentially lead to a violation of the FDTI requirement. For instance, the logical test case targeting the Time Synchronization Monitor (TSM) stipulates the deviation of the hardware clock of one of the two Systems-on-a-Chip (SoCs) jointly running the MotionWise middleware. In contrast, the logical test case exercising the Task Monitor (TM) introduces a task overrun in any of the monitored software components. In both cases, it shall be asserted that any deviation larger than a set threshold is detected and handled within the respective time budget. The logical test case for the TSM defines the injected *offset between the clocks* as a first **parameter** and the one targeting the TM the *extent of the task overrun* injected. In either case, an additional influencing factor is identified by means of an STPA of the error handling process: As excessive reporting of other errors may delay the reaction to the injected fault, the logical test cases' operational scenarios foresee the reporting of additional, unrelated errors. To modulate the stress on the error handling components, the *number of error reporters* and the respective *frequency of error reports* are defined as second and third parameters. The **ranges** of the clock offset, the task overrun, and the error reporting frequencies have been *over-approximated* by domain experts from -10 ms to 10 ms, from 0 ms to 10 ms, and from 1 Hz to 10.000 Hz respectively. The number of reporters, on the other hand, *exhaustively* covers the range from only one reporter to all software components defined in the test build. Notably, the logical test cases differ from a current, manually created FI HiL test case only in that the aforementioned parameters are not hardcoded, but can be given as arguments. Finally, the **metric** is defined following the reasoning that parameter combinations resulting in longer FDTIs are closer to violating the FDTI requirement. Correspondingly, given a **test case output** t, the guidance metric f is defined as follows and shall be *maximized*: $f(t) = t.FDTI$.

Given its modularity, open-source availability, and its integration of the pymoo library of Multi-Objective Optimization (MOO) algorithms (cf. [7]), we have adapted the OpenSBT framework for search-based testing to serve as **test case generator** [40]. The encoding of the FI TCG as a MOO problem is defined in a dedicated `FIProblem` subclass of OpenSBT's `Problem` class (cf. Listing 1.1): Here, a test suite with n test cases is encoded as a *population* with n *individuals*— each with a set of genes corresponding to the test case parameters to optimize. The *fitness* of an individual corresponds to its guidance metric (i.e., its FDTI). In addition to the `parameters`, `ranges`, and `fitness` arguments, the `FIProblem` also takes a `logical` test case and a reference to a function to `execute` concrete test cases as input: These are used to determine the guidance metrics by (1) decoding an individual using its genes as parameter values for the logical test case, (2) executing the respective concrete test cases on the test bench, and (3) evaluating the metrics determined based on the test case's output.

It is advisable to select the **optimization algorithm** by carefully considering the properties of the SUT and the environment it operates in, as well as the time and computational resources available [6]: E.g., while some approaches might be more *effective*, others might be more *efficient*. Given the promising

Listing 1.1. Pseudocode illustrating the main entry point of the FI test case generator implemented for the case study (cf. Sect. 4.3).

```
def campaign():
    logical = 'TSM_0100000.py'
    parameters = ["INTERVAL", "REPORTERS"]
    ranges = [(0.0001, 1), (0, 100)]
    fitness = metrics.fdti(trace)
    execution = bench.batch(tests)
    population, generations = 5, 10

    problem = FIProblem(
        parameters, ranges, fitness
        logical, execution)
    config = FIConfig(population, generations)
    results = NSGAII(problem, config).run()
    report(results)
```

results obtained in [6], we select the NSGA-II algorithm as optimization algorithm for the case at hand [9]. Moreover, as the FI TCG shall be evaluated in a continuous development context, we limit the total number of test cases such that the campaign can be executed as part of a nightly CX pipeline. As recommended in [16], the number of generations has been prioritized over the number of individuals: Testing the TSM, we configure the algorithm to optimize a population of 5 individuals over 10 generations. As the tests for the task monitoring requirement take twice the time to execute, the 5 individuals are optimized over 5 generations only. The **test bench** and the **test build** introduced in Sect. 4.2 remain unchanged as they already implement the FI and measurement capabilities required for the selected test scenarios. The FDTI is safely over-approximated by subtracting the timestamp taken at the moment of FI from the termination time stamp of the software component responsible for the fault detection.[4]

4.4   Results

Following the experiment design introduced in Sect. 4.1, the implementation of the proposed FI TCG methodology presented in Sect. 4.3 has been demonstrated to five test engineers and two project managers at TTTech Auto which have subsequently compiled the questionnaire listed in Table 1. The box-whisker plot on the left of Fig. 2 illustrates the practitioners' answers to the LKS- and SDS-type questions listed in Table 1. The plot on the right depicts the relative difference between each practitioner's estimates of the manual effort required for the

---

[4] An even more precise measurement can be taken by logging the time stamps when the exact line of code detecting the fault is executed. However, for this particular case study, the gain in precision does not outweigh the manual effort of identifying and annotating the respective lines of code for each fault and maintaining these annotations in view of frequent code changes.

current and the proposed approach. We also observe that in over 90 % of the campaigns executed in the context of the case study, the first potentially fault-revealing test case is found within the first 20 generated test cases, with FDTIs significantly exceeding the expected values.

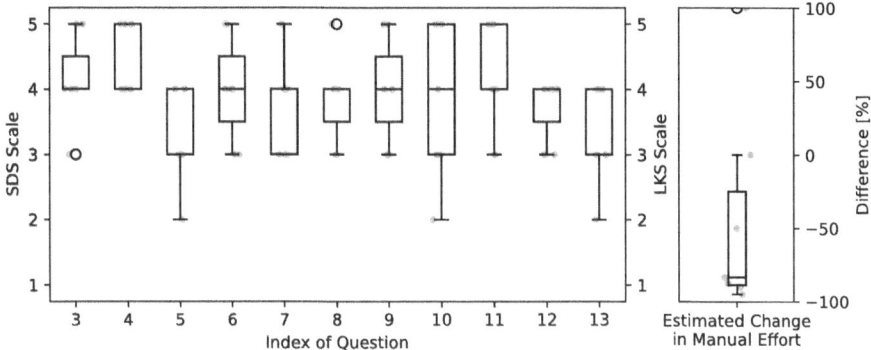

Fig. 2. The box-whisker plot on the left aggregates the answers to the LKS- and SDS-type questions in Table 1. The LKS and SDS scales are introduced in Sect. 4.1. The plot on the right depicts the relative, *within-subject* difference between the answers to questions 1 and 2. Hence, a value of, e.g., -50 % would indicate that the proposed approach is expected halve the manual effort. The unaggregated data is represented by the gray markers included in both plots.

4.5   Discussion

The demonstrated campaigns indicate that automated FI TCG is not only applicable in an industrial context by following the proposed method—it can also effectively identify highly challenging FI test cases for the targeted safety mechanisms. However, while the criticality of the identified test cases has been confirmed by TTTech Auto, the practitioners note that fault reactions are expected to be initiated sooner than the measured FDTIs indicate as multiple safety mechanisms are triggered along the injected fault's propagation. For example, the additional load on MotionWise's error handling components can lead to the TSM-related error processed not by the first scheduled instance of the responsible software component but by the one after that—resulting in a longer FDTI than expected. However, this also triggers an execution flow error, whose fault reaction is expected to intervene faster than the one triggered by the TSM.

In addition, the numerical answers to the questions listed in Table 1 combined with the rationales given by the practitioners indicate that the proposed FI TCG method reduces (1) the level of understanding of the system required to perform

FI testing (cf. questions 4 and 5), and (2) the manual effort for FI testing (with the reduction estimated at 43 % on average; cf. questions 1, 2, and 3). However, the required knowledge of the testing method is not expected to change with the proposed approach (cf. questions 6 and 7). Hence, while FI testing must likely still be performed by experienced test engineers, the proposed method significantly reduces the time required to get sufficiently familiar with the SUT. Moreover, while the practitioners agree that the proposed approach will detect *more* defects and *different* defects than the current approach (cf. questions 8 and 9), they are divided on whether the proposed approach is able to uncover the *same* defects as the current one (cf. question 10). Based on the provided rationales, the skepticism does not stem from a perceived shortcoming of the proposed approach but rather from the considerable resource requirements associated with the test case optimization, which may prevent the proposed approach from completely replacing the current method. Regarding the only moderately positive answers to the questions on the ease of deriving input artefacts and the completeness of the proposed method (cf. questions 12 and 13), practitioners point out (1) that the guidance for deriving test case metrics from requirements could be improved and (2) a lack of guidance for selecting those requirements, which benefit most from FI TCG. Finally, the respondents largely agree that the generated report facilitates the estimation of the confidence in the absence of defects (cf. question 11).

4.6   Validity

We followed state-of-the-art guidelines for case study research within the possibilities of the presented *in vivo* experiment. On the one hand, this case study's **external validity** is supported by meeting the criteria for relevant case studies mentioned in [22]: (1) The *subjects* shall be representative of the intended users (i.e., industry professionals rather than students), (2) the *setting* shall be representative of the intended usage (i.e., industrial settings rather than laboratory settings), (3) the *scale* of the applications shall be of realistic size (i.e., industrial-scale systems rather than toy examples), and (4) the *research method* shall be relevant for practitioners (i.e., case studies rather than conceptual analyses). On the other hand, the systematic derivation of metrics following the GQM approach underpins its **construct validity** while the **internal validity** is based on the involvement of multiple practitioners. However, as mentioned in [27], there is typically a trade-off between external and internal validity, with *in vivo* experiments providing high external validity at the cost of limited control and reduced internal validity. This is especially true when assessing multi-faceted properties such as applicability and effectiveness, whose quantitative (and especially statistical) evaluation would require the involvement of a significantly higher number of domain experts across different projects and organizations. Limited control also meant that multiple metrics which could, in theory, be determined objectively were determined subjectively. Also, a *quantitative* assessment of automated FI TCG in terms of effectiveness in finding defects was never the goal as this is highly dependent on the choice and configuration of the optimization algorithm [6].

5   Conclusion

We address the lack of guidance for the integration of FI TCG in modern development processes by proposing a semi-automated, end-to-end methodology. In particular, we highlight the required changes to the development process (cf. Fig. 1), define which activities must be performed manually and which ones can be automated (note the *"Manual"* and *"Automated"* annotations in Fig. 1), recommend when to execute the activities (illustrated by the *"When Requirement/- Code Changes"* annotations in Fig. 1), and investigate the effects on qualification requirements for practitioners (cf. Sect. 4.5). The applicability of the proposed FI TCG methodology is demonstrated in an industrial context by assessing the FDTI of two safety mechanisms of the TTTech Auto MotionWise automotive middleware. The qualitative evaluation by means of systematically derived, semi-structured interviews with industry professionals leads to the following observations: (1) Applying the proposed FI TCG method is estimated to require a lower level of understanding of the system under test and significantly less manual effort compared to manually parametrizing FI test cases. The approach is thus expected to support test engineers in efficiently assessing different systems or properties thereof after a shorter familiarization period. (2) The generated report and the contained metrics facilitate the estimation of the confidence in the absence of defects.

The case study also stipulates the direction of our future work, as practitioners call for better guidance for selecting those requirements that benefit most from TCG, and for deriving test case metrics from such requirements. These contributions shall be evaluated by means of a larger-scale case study providing the instrumentation for quantitative measurements and thus allowing more conclusive statistical analyses (e.g., hypothesis tests).

Disclosure of Interests. This study is based upon work supported by TTTech Auto AG in the TeFoSa project.

References

1. Abdessalem, R.B., Panichella, A., Nejati, S., Briand, L.C., Stifter, T.: Testing autonomous cars for feature interaction failures using many-objective search. In: Proceedings of the 33rd ACM/IEEE International Conference on Automated Software Engineering, pp. 143–154. ACM (2018). https://doi.org/10.1145/3238147. 3238192
2. AS-2C Architecture Analysis and Design Language: SAE Architecture Analysis and Design Language (AADL) Annex Volume 1: Annex A: ARINC653 Annex, Annex C: Code Generation Annex, Annex E: Error Model Annex (2015). https:// doi.org/10.4271/AS5506/1A

3. AUTOSAR: E2E Protocol Specification (2024). https://www.autosar.org/fileadmin/standards/R24-11/FO/AUTOSAR_FO_PRS_E2EProtocol.pdf
4. Bartocci, E., Mariani, L., Ničković, D., Yadav, D.: Property-based mutation testing. In: 2023 IEEE Conference on Software Testing, Verification and Validation (ICST), pp. 222–233. IEEE (2023). https://doi.org/10.1109/ICST57152.2023.00029
5. Basili, V.R., Caldiera, G., Rombach, H.D.: Goal Question Metric Approach, vol. 1, pp. 528–532. Wiley (1994)
6. Benkendorf, N., Ganahl, C., Munaro, T.: An ISO 26262-derived evaluation methodology for automated fault injection test case generators. In: 2025 IEEE Intelligent Vehicles Symposium (IV). IEEE (2025, in press)
7. Blank, J., Deb, K.: Pymoo: multi-objective optimization in python. IEEE Access **8**, 89497–89509 (2020). https://doi.org/10.1109/ACCESS.2020.2990567
8. Carpi, R.B., Picek, S., Batina, L., Menarini, F., Jakobovic, D., Golub, M.: Glitch it if you can: parameter search strategies for successful fault injection. In: Francillon, A., Rohatgi, P. (eds.) CARDIS 2013. LNCS, vol. 8419, pp. 236–252. Springer, Cham (2014). https://doi.org/10.1007/978-3-319-08302-5_16
9. Deb, K., Pratap, A., Agarwal, S., Meyarivan, T.: A fast and elitist multiobjective genetic algorithm: NSGA-II. IEEE Trans. Evol. Comput. **6**, 182–197 (2002). https://doi.org/10.1109/4235.996017
10. dSPACE GmbH: Sichere Legenden - Entwicklung und Absicherung von Regelsystemen für Hochleistungsaufgaben in ultimativen Supersportwagen. dSPACE Magazin, pp. 18–23 (2021). https://www.dspace.com/shared/data/pdf/2021/dSPACE-Magazin-2021-01_Bugatti_210507_D.pdf
11. dSPACE GmbH: SIL für eine frühe Validierung - Stellantis/FCA beschleunigt Software-Tests mit agilen Prozessen und Virtualisierung. dSPACE Magazin, pp. 30–35 (2021). https://www.dspace.com/shared/data/pdf/2021/dSPACE-Magazin-2021-01_FCA_Stellantis_210507_D.pdf
12. González, C.A., Varmazyar, M., Nejati, S., Briand, L.C., Isasi, Y.: Enabling model testing of cyber-physical systems. In: Proceedings of the 21th ACM/IEEE International Conference on Model Driven Engineering Languages and Systems - MODELS 2018, pp. 176–186. ACM Press, New York (2018). https://doi.org/10.1145/3239372.3239409
13. Hauer, F., Pretschner, A., Holzmuller, B.: Re-using concrete test scenarios generally is a bad idea. In: 2020 IEEE Intelligent Vehicles Symposium (IV), pp. 1305–1310. IEEE (2020). https://doi.org/10.1109/IV47402.2020.9304678
14. Hauer, F., Pretschner, A., Holzmüller, B.: Fitness functions for testing automated and autonomous driving systems. In: Romanovsky, A., Troubitsyna, E., Bitsch, F. (eds.) SAFECOMP 2019. LNCS, vol. 11698, pp. 69–84. Springer, Cham (2019). https://doi.org/10.1007/978-3-030-26601-1_5
15. Hellhake, D., Schmid, T., Wagner, S.: Using data flow-based coverage criteria for black-box integration testing of distributed software systems. In: 2019 12th IEEE Conference on Software Testing, Validation and Verification (ICST), pp. 420–429. IEEE (2019). https://doi.org/10.1109/ICST.2019.00051
16. Hort, M., Sarro, F.: The effect of offspring population size on NSGA-II. In: Proceedings of the Genetic and Evolutionary Computation Conference Companion, pp. 179–180. ACM (2021). https://doi.org/10.1145/3449726.3459479
17. International Organization for Standardization: ISO 26262-10:2018 - Road Vehicles - Functional Safety - Part 10: Guidelines on ISO 26262 (2018)
18. International Organization for Standardization: ISO 26262-1:2018 - Road Vehicles - Functional Safety - Part 1: Vocabulary (2018)

19. International Organization for Standardization: ISO 26262-4:2018 - Road Vehicles - Functional Safety - Part 4: Product development at the system level (2018)
20. International Organization for Standardization: ISO 26262-5:2018 - Road Vehicles - Functional Safety - Part 5: Product development at the hardware level (2018)
21. International Organization for Standardization: ISO 26262-6:2018 - Road Vehicles - Functional Safety - Part 5: Product development at the software level (2018)
22. Ivarsson, M., Gorschek, T.: A method for evaluating rigor and industrial relevance of technology evaluations. Empir. Softw. Eng. **16**, 365–395 (2011). https://doi.org/10.1007/s10664-010-9146-4
23. Jha, S., et al.: ML-based fault injection for autonomous vehicles: a case for bayesian fault injection. In: 2019 49th Annual IEEE/IFIP International Conference on Dependable Systems and Networks (DSN), pp. 112–124 (2019). https://doi.org/10.1109/DSN.2019.00025
24. Khosrowjerdi, H., Meinke, K.: Learning-based testing for autonomous systems using spatial and temporal requirements. In: Proceedings of the 1st International Workshop on Machine Learning and Software Engineering in Symbiosis - MASES 2018, pp. 6–15. ACM Press, New York (2018). https://doi.org/10.1145/3243127.3243129
25. Leszczyna, R.: Aiming at methods' wider adoption: applicability determinants and metrics. Comput. Sci. Rev. **40**, 100387 (2021). https://doi.org/10.1016/j.cosrev.2021.100387
26. Leveson, N., Thomas, J.P.: STPA Handbook (2018). https://psas.scripts.mit.edu/home/get_file.php?name=STPA_Handbook.pdf
27. Lott, C.M., Rombach, H.D.: Repeatable software engineering experiments for comparing defect-detection techniques. Empir. Softw. Eng. **1**, 241–277 (1996). https://doi.org/10.1007/BF00127447
28. Matinnejad, R., Nejati, S., Briand, L.C., Bruckmann, T.: Effective test suites for mixed discrete-continuous stateflow controllers. In: Proceedings of the 2015 10th Joint Meeting on Foundations of Software Engineering, pp. 84–95. ACM (2015). https://doi.org/10.1145/2786805.2786818
29. Matinnejad, R., Nejati, S., Briand, L.C., Bruckmann, T.: Test generation and test prioritization for simulink models with dynamic behavior. IEEE Trans. Software Eng. **45**(9), 919–944 (2019). https://doi.org/10.1109/TSE.2018.2811489
30. Menzel, T., Bagschik, G., Maurer, M.: Scenarios for development, test and validation of automated vehicles. In: 2018 IEEE Intelligent Vehicles Symposium (IV), pp. 1821–1827. IEEE (2018). https://doi.org/10.1109/IVS.2018.8500406
31. Moradi, M., Gomes, C., Oakes, B.J., Denil, J.: Optimizing fault injection in FMI co-simulation through sensitivity partitioning. In: SummerSim 2019: Proceedings of the 2019 Summer Simulation Conference, pp. 1–12 (2019)
32. Munaro, T., Muntean, I., Pretschner, A.: A failure model library for simulation-based validation of functional safety. In: Ceccarelli, A., Trapp, M., Bondavalli, A., Bitsch, F. (eds.) SAFECOMP 2024. LNCS, vol. 14988, pp. 18–32. Springer, Cham (2024). https://doi.org/10.1007/978-3-031-68606-1_2
33. Oertel, M., Kacimi, O., Böde, E.: Proving compliance of implementation models to safety specifications. In: Bondavalli, A., Ceccarelli, A., Ortmeier, F. (eds.) SAFECOMP 2014. LNCS, vol. 8696, pp. 97–107. Springer, Cham (2014). https://doi.org/10.1007/978-3-319-10557-4_13
34. Runeson, P., Höst, M.: Guidelines for conducting and reporting case study research in software engineering. Empir. Softw. Eng. **14**, 131–164 (2009). https://doi.org/10.1007/s10664-008-9102-8

35. Saraoglu, M., Morozov, A., Janschek, K.: MOBATSim: MOdel-based autonomous traffic simulation framework for fault-error-failure chain analysis. IFAC-PapersOnLine **52**, 239–244 (2019). https://doi.org/10.1016/j.ifacol.2019.08.077

36. Schirmeier, H., Borchert, C., Spinczyk, O.: Rapid fault-space exploration by evolutionary pruning. In: Bondavalli, A., Di Giandomenico, F. (eds.) SAFECOMP 2014. LNCS, vol. 8666, pp. 17–32. Springer, Cham (2014). https://doi.org/10.1007/978-3-319-10506-2_2

37. Schirmeier, H., Hoffmann, M., Dietrich, C., Lenz, M., Lohmann, D., Spinczyk, O.: FAIL*: an open and versatile fault-injection framework for the assessment of software-implemented hardware fault tolerance. In: 2015 11th European Dependable Computing Conference (EDCC), pp. 245–255. IEEE (2015). https://doi.org/10.1109/EDCC.2015.28

38. Sedaghatbaf, A., Moradi, M., Almasizadeh, J., Sangchoolie, B., Acker, B.V., Denil, J.: DELFASE: a deep learning method for fault space exploration. In: 18th European Dependable Computing Conference (EDCC 2022) (2022). https://doi.org/10.1109/EDCC57035.2022.00020

39. Sini, J., Violante, M.: An automatic approach to perform FMEDA safety assessment on hardware designs. In: 2018 IEEE 24th International Symposium on On-Line Testing And Robust System Design (IOLTS), pp. 49–52. IEEE (2018). https://doi.org/10.1109/IOLTS.2018.8474217

40. Sorokin, L., Munaro, T., Safin, D., Liao, B.H.C., Molin, A.: OpenSBT: a modular framework for search-based testing of automated driving systems. In: Proceedings of the 2024 IEEE/ACM 46th International Conference on Software Engineering: Companion Proceedings, pp. 94–98. ACM (2024). https://doi.org/10.1145/3639478.3640027

41. Svenningsson, R., Vinter, J., Eriksson, H., Törngren, M.: MODIFI: a MODel-implemented fault injection tool. In: Schoitsch, E. (ed.) SAFECOMP 2010. LNCS, vol. 6351, pp. 210–222. Springer, Heidelberg (2010). https://doi.org/10.1007/978-3-642-15651-9_16

42. Tahmasebi, K.N., Chen, D.: A fault injection tool for identifying faulty operations of control functions in automated driving systems. In: Lecture Notes in Networks and Systems, LNNS, vol. 484, pp. 340–349. Springer, Cham (2022). https://doi.org/10.1007/978-3-031-06746-4_33

43. Uriagereka, G.J., Lattarulo, R., Rastelli, J.P., Calonge, E.A., Ruiz Lopez, A., Espinoza Ortiz, H.: Fault injection method for safety and controllability evaluation of automated driving. In: 2017 IEEE Intelligent Vehicles Symposium (IV), pp. 1867–1872. IEEE (2017). https://doi.org/10.1109/IVS.2017.7995977

Counterfactual Self-adaptation in Cyber-Physical Systems

Ehsan Elahi[1]([✉])[iD], Matteo Camilli[2][iD], and Raffaela Mirandola[1][iD]

[1] Karlsruhe Institute of Technology, Karlsruhe, Germany
{ehsan.elahi,raffaela.mirandola}@kit.edu
[2] Politecnico di Milano, Milan, Italy
matteo.camilli@polimi.it

Abstract. Cyber-physical systems (CPS) operate in dynamic and uncertain environments, where maintaining operational objectives without manual intervention is critical. Self-adaptive systems (SAS) have emerged as a promising solution, leveraging machine learning (ML) models within feedback control loops to make runtime adaptation decisions. However, the black-box nature of these models poses challenges related to transparency and efficiency, particularly in safety-critical domains. This paper introduces CSA-Φ, a counterfactual-based self-adaptation approach that integrates model-agnostic interpretable ML into the adaptation loop. CSA-Φ includes two main components: an offline pre-processor with pre-trained classifiers for requirement evaluation, and an online opportunistic adaptation engine that uses counterfactual explanations to guide adaptation decisions efficiently. By bridging the gap between explainability and actionable adaptation, CSA-Φ enhances decision-making while reducing adaptation cost. Experimental results show that CSA-Φ achieves significant improvements in execution efficiency and provides adaptation decisions that are both effective and interpretable, outperforming selected baseline approaches.

Keywords: Explainability · Counterfactual explanations · Cyber-physical systems · Self-adaptive systems

1 Introduction

Cyber-physical systems (CPS) are software-intensive systems that tightly integrate computational processes with physical components. These systems typically operate in dynamic environments where uncertainty arises from changing or unpredictable conditions. As CPS and software systems become increasingly prevalent in critical domains, ensuring they can continuously maintain their operational objectives without requiring manual intervention or system redeployment is essential.

To address these challenges, self-adaptive systems (SAS) [10] have emerged as a promising solution. These systems are designed to autonomously adjust

D. Taibi and D. Smite (Eds.): SEAA 2025, LNCS 16081, pp. 219–236, 2026.
https://doi.org/10.1007/978-3-032-04190-6_14

their behavior in response to environmental changes or internal anomalies, making them well-suited for managing uncertainty in real-time [29]. Central to the architecture of SAS is an adaptation layer, which monitors system behavior and triggers adjustments when necessary through a feedback control loop. This loop operates by observing the current state, analyzing deviations, planning corrective actions, and executing adaptations–often leveraging machine learning (ML) techniques to handle complex decision-making tasks [15,21,31].

Supervised learning methods such as neural networks [27] and ensemble models [14] are commonly employed to build predictive models within the feedback loop encapsulating decision logic for adaptation. While ML-based adaptation offers benefits like learning from past behavior, it also poses transparency challenges. ML models are often black boxes, making it difficult for system engineers or administrators to understand adaptation decisions. This lack of interpretability can undermine trust in the system and lead to risks in safety-critical domains. In response to these concerns, the concept of explainability has gained traction in the context of self-adaptive systems [24]. Explainability aims to make the decision-making process more transparent and understandable to human stakeholders. Recent works [7,18,32] demonstrate how integrating explainability into the adaptation loop can enhance user trust, support debugging, and guide more informed adaptation strategies.

Beyond transparency, efficiency is another critical consideration when using black-box models for runtime adaptation. These models often need to explore large, complex solution spaces involving multiple, sometimes conflicting objectives (e.g., performance, reliability, energy efficiency). Exhaustive search in such spaces is computationally infeasible, highlighting the need for efficient optimization strategies. Explainability can also contribute here by revealing meaningful relationships between system parameters and objectives, thereby reducing the search space, guiding adaptation, and accelerating convergence toward high-quality solutions [7,15].

In this paper, we explore the use of counterfactual explanations [28]–a model-agnostic, interpretable machine learning technique–in the context of self-adaptive systems. Being model-agnostic, counterfactual explanations can be consistently applied to any machine learning model without assuming anything about the specific underlying model. Building on prior work [25] that employs post hoc explanation methods such as Partial Dependence Plots (PDP) [13] to enhance system interpretability, we introduce CSA-Φ^1, a novel counterfactual-based self-adaptation approach. CSA-Φ aims to bridge the gap between explainability and actionable adaptation strategies by leveraging counterfactual reasoning to support informed, interpretable, and effective adaptation decisions. The core objective is to demonstrate how counterfactual explanations can enhance the transparency of adaptive behavior while ensuring that multiple system requirements are satisfied efficiently and reliably.

The main components of CSA-Φ are *i*) an *offline pre-processor*, which includes a set of pre-trained classifiers, each specifically tailored to evaluate a distinct sys-

---

[1] CSA-Φ stands for Counterfactual Self-Adaptation in cyber-PHYsical systems.

tem requirement. These classifiers label the satisfaction of each requirement as either *true* (satisfied) or *false* (violated); and *ii*) an *online opportunistic adaptation engine*, which operates at runtime to generate and utilize explanations in order to guide and refine the selection among potential adaptation options.

The main contributions of this work are given as follows:

– We propose CSA-Φ, an automated approach that integrates model-agnostic interpretable machine learning into the feedback control loop to steer adaptation decisions while satisfying multiple system requirements.
– We conduct extensive experiments to evaluate the performance of CSA-Φ, demonstrating its efficiency and effectiveness in comparison to selected baseline approaches.
– We illustrate the usefulness of counterfactual explanations in enhancing the quality of adaptation decisions, by providing actionable insights into why certain adaptations are preferable.

The rest of this paper is organized as follows: Sect. 2 describes the illustrative example leveraged in our work. In Sect. 3, some background knowledge is introduced to help the readers. The proposed approach CSA-Φ is illustrated in Sect. 4, while empirical evaluation is discussed in Sect. 5 of this paper. In Sect. 6 threats to validity are discussed whereas Sect. 7 throws some light on the recent literature. Section 8 has the conclusion of the work.

2   Illustrative Example

As a running example, we consider the search-and-rescue robotic system, which is widely used in the literature [12]. In this example, there is a robotic system to discover and rescue people in dangerous situations such as fire, earthquake, hurricane, etc. This robotic system consists of appropriate abstractions for the physical interfaces such as sensors and actuators, as well as it incorporates the essential functions of rescuing such as navigation, human and/or obstacle detection, and avoidance. Since the robotic system has to operate in uncertain situations with different changes in the environment and resource variability at runtime, therefore, its components are designed to be configured at runtime. It is an adaptation layer, which is equipped with the feedback control loop, that enacts these configuration changes to meet the adaptation goals. Examples of the adaptation goals could be the safety requirements such as *"the probability that rescue robot maintains the protective distance from humans while moving must be greater than 0.90"* (R2) or it could be *"the probability that rescue robot does not crash into an obstacle must be greater than 0.90"* (R4). Inside the control loop, there are pre-trained classifiers (each trained for different requirements) that predict the requirements not satisfied based on the operating conditions and then, accordingly, steer the changes in the configuration so that the probability of satisfying the requirements can be increased, as per the operating conditions.

The operating conditions consist of configuration dimensions and environment dimensions. In the configuration dimension, there are features that the system can change to increase the likelihood of satisfying requirements, therefore also known as controllable features (CFs). On the other hand, environment dimensions are those that can only be observed as they are related to the environment, therefore also known as observable features (OFs). In Table 1, CFs (i.e., cruise speed, image resolution, illuminance, and controls responsiveness) and OFs (i.e., power, smoke intensity, obstacle size, obstacle distance, firm obstacle) are presented, which collectively form the semantic space [8].

Table 1. Semantic space of the self-adaptive system

Feature	Dimension	Type	Range
cruise speed	CF	continuous	[0, 5] m/s
image resolution	CF	categorical	{low, mid, high}
control responsiveness	CF	continuous	[10, 50] Mbit/s
illuminance	CF	continuous	[40, 120000] lux
power	OF	integer	[0, 100] %
smoke intensity	OF	categorical	{none, thin, thick}
obstacle size	OF	continuous	[0, 2] m^3
obstacle distance	OF	continuous	[0, 10] m
firm obstacle	OF	boolean	Yes/No

3   Background

In this section, we introduce background concepts to make the paper self-contained. Specifically, we describe the concepts of a self-adaptive system, supervised and interpretable machine learning.

3.1   Self-adaptive System

Self-adaptive systems adjust their behavior in response to changes in the environment in which they are deployed or in the system itself. The conceptual model of a self-adaptive system [29] has four elements: environment, managed system, adaptation goals, and feedback loop.

The environment is the external world, including both virtual and physical entities and users, where the system operates. It is not controlled by the system and can only be sensed or influenced through sensors and effectors, leading to some uncertainty. The managed system is the application software that serves users and can be adapted via its sensors and effectors. It is controllable and subject to adaptation. Adaptation goals are the managing system's quality concerns for the managed system, represented as uncertainties to address during operation. The managing system consists of adaptation goals and a feedback loop (MAPE-K: Monitor, Analyze, Plan, Execute, Knowledge) [17], which monitors and adapts the managed system and its environment to achieve these goals.

3.2 Supervised Machine Learning

In the context of machine learning, classification is a predictive task of antici-pating the class or label y of the given data point or instance x, having multi-ple feature values. Supervised learning techniques are used for the classification task for predicting either binary or multiclass labels. In other words, we have an instance x which consists of different features having some specific value x_j for each given feature j. A classifier is a supervised learning technique that performs the classification task of predicting the class labels.

In supervised learning, there is training data having class labels for each instance; it is the training set on which the classifier is trained (learning from the data). Once the classifier is trained, it predicts the testing data, which it has not seen earlier. Hence, it is evaluated on how accurately it can predict the unseen data. In supervised machine learning, there are many different classifiers for different problems. Some of them are simple models having predictions easy to understand and to explain, such as linear regression. On the other hand, there are some complex predictive models that are not inherently explained and therefore known as black box models, e.g., neural networks.

3.3 Interpretable Machine Learning

Interpretable simply refers to the extent of understanding of some phenomenon by humans. Similarly, Interpretable ML [24] is the process of extracting useful insights from the machine learning model, i.e., predictions, so that they can be well understood by humans as to why the particular decision has been made [2]. According to Miller [23], we make use of the terms *explainable* and *interpretable* interchangeably in this work. Interpretability can be global or local. Global inter-pretability gives a holistic view of the model and, therefore, explains the average behavior of the model. On the other hand, local interpretability explains the single prediction.

Counterfactual explanations, which come under the umbrella of local inter-pretability, demonstrate the causal situation by giving insights into the occur-rence of the prediction. For example, "if X had not happened, Y would not have happened". Here, X is the input instance that causes the Y output. To describe it in mathematical form:

$$f(X) = Y \quad \text{(Original Output)}$$
$$f(X') = Y' \quad \text{(Desired Output)}$$

where X' is obtained by slightly (minimally) modifying X.

If, for example, the robot is operating in darkness, then it may need to increase its camera resolution and illuminance to better detect and classify the obstacle and/or humans. The possible scenario of counterfactual explanation could be to slightly change the controllable feature values, such as *image reso-lution* and *illuminance*, so that the output of satisfying the system requirement is flipped from *False* to *True*. It is important to note that the counterfactual should be as close as possible to the original values and change as minimum features as possible for the given instance.

Figure 1 describes visually how counterfactual explanations work for the given model's decision boundary. For example, in the Fig. 1, the original input actually falls into the class label, *False*, the insights gained from counterfactuals guide the change in the value of the input feature *cruise speed*, so that the system requirement is satisfied by having the class label *True* (desired class).

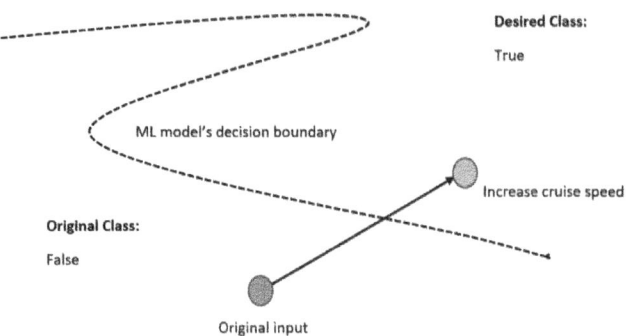

Fig. 1. Illustration of counterfactual explanation in a machine learning model.

4   Proposed Approach

This section presents our CSA-Φ approach that embeds counterfactual explanations into the MAPE-K loop, thus transforming insights into actionable adaptation configurations. It enables the system to not only reason about why an adaptation is necessary but also to answer what changes are needed to have the adaptation that satisfies the requirements. The knowledge component of the MAPE-K loop integrates the set of predictive models. As CSA-Φ relies on a model-agnostic, interpretable ML technique, it adds flexibility in using any underlying predictive model consistently and smoothly. Moreover, we have trained separate predictive models for each requirement to support multi-requirements scenarios, as well as to handle the trade-offs among requirements. This enables requirements-aware explainable systems, e.g., safety-critical systems in which adaptation may have competing priorities.

CSA-Φ has two components: an offline preprocessor and an online opportunistic approach. These components work in two different phases of the system. Offline pre-processor works before the system is deployed in its working environment. The online opportunistic approach is executed along with the MAPE-K control loop when the system is deployed in its running environment. Figure 2 shows the high-level view of the CSA-Φ approach and how it is incorporated into the MAPE-K control loop. An in-depth discussion of these aspects is given in the following sections.

4.1 Offline Pre-processor

This component is designed to preprocess the imbalanced data and train the models offline to enable the self-adaptive system to be computationally efficient and explainable. Algorithm 1 describes the overall working of the pre-processor component. Given as input controllable features CFs, system requirements $reqs$, and the balance ratio $balance\_ratio$, the offline pre-processor outputs the resampled data, as well as a set of trained models, to be utilized in the online phase. Algorithm 1 has four steps, as follows.

Step 1: The first step involves finding similar (nearby) data instances for a given test input. To achieve this, we employ the k-nearest neighbors (KNN) algorithm [9], which is used to identify instances that are close in the feature space. Using KNN ensures that the generated counterfactuals are both feasible and realistic, as they are based on actual data points rather than arbitrary perturbations. This step is implemented in Lines 2–4 of Algorithm 1.

Step 2: In this step, we compute the class distribution for each requirement by counting the number of instances labeled as true and false. The minority class is identified by comparing these counts. Based on the imbalance, a sampling strategy is defined using a balance ratio, which determines the extent to which the minority class should be oversampled. This step enables us to control the number of synthetic samples generated for the minority class. Refer to Lines 5–9 of Algorithm 1.

Step 3: To address class imbalance, we apply Borderline-SMOTE [16], a resampling technique that focuses on generating synthetic instances near the decision boundary. It interpolates new samples between borderline minority instances and their nearest neighbors in the feature space. Since each requirement may have a different degree of class imbalance, a customized sampling strategy is applied for each one. Refer to Lines 10–15 of Algorithm 1.

Step 4: In the final step, a separate neural network model is trained for each requirement using the balanced dataset. For instance, if we have four distinct requirements, four corresponding models are trained. These models are later used in the online phase of the system, allowing for efficient reuse and reduced computational overhead during runtime adaptation. See Lines 16–23 of Algorithm 1 for implementation details.

4.2 Online Opportunistic Engine

This component is responsible for determining the optimal values of controllable features, thereby guiding the adaptive behavior of the system to ensure that all specified requirements are satisfied. The objective is to identify an effective adaptation strategy that brings the system back into a compliant state. The overall functionality of the online opportunistic component is described in Algorithm 2. We assume that this component is integrated into the Plan phase of the MAPE-K control loop. Accordingly, when the predictive model outputs a negative label—indicating that one or more requirements are currently violated—the

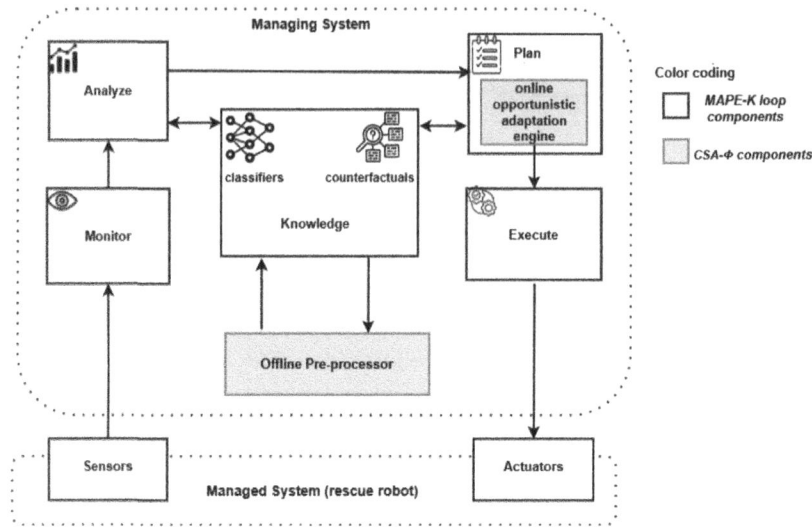

Fig. 2. CSA-Φ: Integrating explainability into the self-adaptive system.

Analyze phase of the loop activates the Plan phase. At this point, the online opportunistic engine is invoked to compute a suitable adaptation.

Algorithm 2 consists of the following three main steps:

Step 1: This step begins with exploring nearby instances in the feature space to generate a set of potential adaptations. Initially, the current system state serves as the baseline adaptation, which is incrementally refined as the algorithm progresses. To identify similar instances, the KNN algorithm is employed. For each neighbor identified, counterfactual examples are generated–these provide guidance on how to adjust the controllable feature values in order to satisfy system requirements. Each counterfactual corresponds to a potential adaptation, and these are collected into a candidate pool. This process is outlined in Lines 2–11 of Algorithm 2.

Step 2: In this step, a subset of controllable features is selected for modification based on the goal of minimizing confidence loss for the given requirement. Features that contribute least to the confidence degradation are prioritized for modification. These selected features are then updated using values suggested by the counterfactuals. After applying the changes, the model predicts the new confidence level for the requirement. If the updated state still fails to satisfy the requirement, the adaptation is rolled back to maintain system stability. See Lines 12–27 of Algorithm 2.

Step 3: Finally, the best adaptation, denoted as S_{opt}, is selected from the pool of potential adaptations. The selection criterion is based on the highest predicted confidence with respect to the system requirements. This ensures that the chosen adaptation not only satisfies the requirements but also does so with the greatest level of assurance. The final adaptation leverages insights from coun-

Algorithm 1.Offline Pre-processing

Input: Input features X; Outcome labels y; Controllable features $CF = \{CF_1, \ldots, CF_m\}$; System requirements $reqs$; Balance ratio $balance\_ratio$.
Output: Trained models $models = \{M_1, \ldots, M_n\}$; Resampled datasets ($X\_resampled\_list$, $y\_resampled\_list$).

1: Initialize empty lists: $X\_resampled\_list \leftarrow \emptyset$, $y\_resampled\_list \leftarrow \emptyset$
2: **Step 1: Train KNN Model**
3: $knn \leftarrow$ KNearestNeighbor()
4: knn.fit(X, num_neighbors = 0)
5: **Step 2: Class Distribution Analysis**
6: **for** each requirement req in $reqs$ **do**
7:    $y_{req} \leftarrow$ extract_labels(y, req)
8:    $minority\_class \leftarrow$ identify_minority_class(y_{req})
9:    $sampling\_strategy \leftarrow$ calculate_sampling_strategy($minority\_class$)
10:    **Step 3: Data Resampling**
11:    $sampler \leftarrow$ BorderlineSMOTE($sampling\_strategy = sampling\_strategy$)
12:    ($X_{resampled}$, $y_{resampled}$) $\leftarrow$ sampler.fit_resample(X, y_{req})
13:    $X\_resampled\_list$.append($X_{resampled}$)
14:    $y\_resampled\_list$.append($y_{resampled}$)
15: **end for**
16: **Step 4: Model Training**
17: Initialize $models \leftarrow \emptyset$
18: **for** each req in $reqs$ **do**
19:    $model \leftarrow$ NeuralNetwork()
20:    $model$.train($X\_resampled\_list[req]$, $y\_resampled\_list[req]$)
21:    $models$.append($model$)
22: **end for**
23: **Return** ($models$, $X\_resampled\_list$, $y\_resampled\_list$)

terfactual explanations to adjust the system's controllable features. This step corresponds to Lines 28–30 of Algorithm 2.

5 Evaluation

In this section, an empirical evaluation of our CSA-Φ approach is presented, considering multiple requirements. Table 2 presents the requirements that are considered in this study. In our experiments, the simulation environment allows us to monitor all variables in the semantic space (Table 1) to determine the unsatisfied requirements in the simulated scenario. The experimental results answer the following research questions.

RQ1: What is the computational cost of CSA-Φ with respect to the selected baselines?

RQ2: How effective is the counterfactual-guided self-adaptive system compared to the baselines?

We conduct a series of experiments to evaluate the effectiveness and efficiency of CSA-Φ, comparing it against two baseline methods: i) XDA [25], an explanation-driven approach designed to guide adaptation decisions based on interpretability insights; and ii) NSGA-III [11], a multi-objective metaheuristic optimization technique that relies on predictions from black-box models. To address RQ1, we measure the execution time (in seconds) for CSA-Φ and both baselines to assess their computational efficiency. To address RQ2, we evaluate the satisfaction likelihood, defined as the probability that a specific requirement is fulfilled under the current operating conditions, as estimated by the black-box

---

Algorithm 2. Online Opportunistic Approach

Input: Current system state S; Set of controllable features CF; Trained models $models =$ $\{M_1, ..., M_n\}$; Set of nearest neighbors N.
Output: Opportunistic adaptation S_{opt}.

1: **Initialize** $S_{opt} \leftarrow S$
2: **Step 1: Select Neighboring Adaptations**
3: $neighbors \leftarrow$ Find nearest instances from N
4: $adaptations \leftarrow \{S\}$
5: **for** $neighbor \in neighbors$ **do**
6:      Generate counterfactuals $counterfactuals \leftarrow counterfactual[neighbor]$
7:      **for** $f \in counterfactuals$ **do**
8:          Generate candidate adaptation S'
9:          $adaptations \leftarrow adaptations \cup \{S'\}$
10:     **end for**
11: **end for**
12: **Step 2: Opportunistic Loop:**
13: **for** $S' \in adaptations$ **do**
14:     $excludedFeatures \leftarrow \emptyset$, $tempExcludedFeatures \leftarrow \emptyset$
15:     **while** number of excluded features $<$ total controllable features **do**
16:         Select features to modify based on minimizing confidence loss
17:         Modify feature value within bounds
18:         Update confidence C'
19:         **if** C' does not satisfy requirements **then**
20:             Revert to the previous adaptation
21:             $tempExcludedFeatures \leftarrow tempExcludedFeatures \cup \{feature\}$
22:         **else**
23:             $tempExcludedFeatures \leftarrow \emptyset$
24:         **end if**
25:     **end while**
26:     Compute confidence $\mathcal{F}(S')$
27: **end for**
28: **Step 3: Select Best Adaptation**
29: $S_{opt} \leftarrow$ adaptation with highest $\mathcal{F}(S')$
30: **Return** S_{opt}

---

predictive model. For all experiments, a neural network model for each requirement is embedded within the managing system to serve as a runtime predictor.

5.1 Evaluation Subject

We consider the search and rescue robot illustrated in Sect. 2, and focus on a scenario where a rescue robot is navigating in a low-visibility environment to rescue injured persons. The camera mounted on the robot is trying to correctly classify the objects, such as obstacles and humans. Consider the following example. Due to the low-visibility environment, the robot's camera misclassified 20% of obstacles, which, in turn, increased the risk of collisions. Given these operating conditions, the predictive model anticipates the possible violation of R1. Thus, the analysis phase of the MAPE-K loop triggers the plan phase, which is responsible for the online opportunistic approach. The counterfactual is retrieved, suggesting a slight modification in the features, such as *cruise speed* from 4.5 m/s $\rightarrow$ 4.2 m/s and the *image resolution* from mid (720p) $\rightarrow$ high(1080p). The effect of this explainable adaptation is that the probability of classifying obstacles correctly increases from 80% $\rightarrow$ 87%, thus satisfying *R1*.

5.2   Testbed

All the experiments have been conducted on a commodity laptop running Windows 11 Home (Version 10.0, Build 22631). The hardware configuration includes an Intel Core i5-10300H processor (8 CPUs, 2.50 GHz) and 8 GB of RAM.

Table 2. Description of requirements

#	Requirements
R1	The rescue robot must correctly classify obstacles with a probability greater than 0.85.
R2	The rescue robot must maintain a safe distance from humans while in motion with a probability greater than 0.90.
R3	The rescue robot must avoid unwanted contact with humans with a probability greater than 0.95.
R4	The rescue robot must avoid collisions with obstacles with a probability greater than 0.90.

5.3   Results

Computational Cost (RQ1). CSA-Φ and the selected baselines are executed with the initial configurations and the assignment of controllable features in the semantic space. Each of these initial configurations of features indicates the operating conditions for which adaptation is needed. In our evaluation, we have a total of 200 assignments of features. So, to answer RQ1, we calculate the execution time of CSA-Φ and the selected baselines. It is the time taken by the plan phase of the MAPE-K loop when the system is actually deployed in its environment. Once calculated, we compare the distribution of execution time taken by CSA-Φ and baselines.

Results: Fig. 3 presents the execution time distribution of CSA-Φ and the two baseline methods using box plots (log scale). The results show that CSA-Φ exhibits minimal variability, indicating consistent performance and computational efficiency. The median execution times for CSA-Φ, XDA, and NSGA-III are 0.24, 0.52, and 13.26 s, respectively. When compared with NSGA-III, XDA has a lower median execution time, but its performance shows high variability, as evidenced by multiple outliers. This suggests that XDA may incur significant computational overhead in certain cases, affecting its reliability in time-sensitive scenarios. To assess the statistical significance of CSA-Φ's execution time compared to the baselines, we conducted a Mann-Whitney U test [22], with the results summarized in Table 3. The extremely low p-values and large z-scores reported in the table indicate that the differences in execution time are statistically significant and unlikely to be due to random variation. White-box approaches like CSA-Φ and XDA are less computationally expensive than

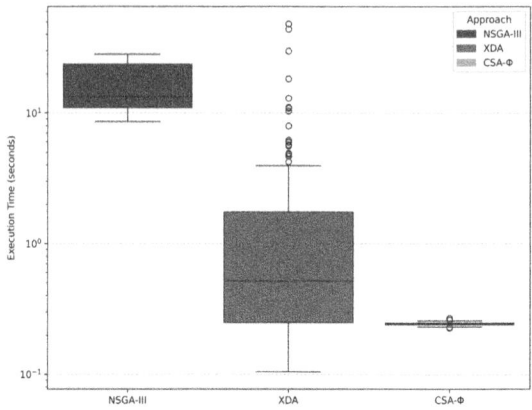

Fig. 3. Comparison of execution times in seconds (lower is better)

black-box methods such as NSGA-III, as shown in the evaluation results. Additionally, CSA-Φ exhibits a lower variance (i.e., a smaller interquartile range) compared to XDA, indicating more stable and consistent performance across different instances.

Table 3. Statistical significance for execution time

	p-value	z-score
XDA vs. CSA-Φ	2.45e−10	6.33
NSGA-III vs. CSA-Φ	2.56e−34	17.29

RQ1 summary: CSA-Φ demonstrates higher efficiency in execution time than baseline methods, consistently completing tasks faster with minimal variability. In contrast, NSGA-III incurs 87.25% higher computational cost on average.

Effectiveness (RQ2). To address RQ2, we executed CSA-Φ using the same initial configurations and controllable feature assignments within the semantic space as used in RQ1. In total, 200 distinct feature assignments were evaluated to ensure statistical robustness and eliminate the possibility of results being influenced by chance. Additionally, we applied the Mann-Whitney U test to assess whether the observed differences in performance are statistically significant.

Two key metrics are used to evaluate the effectiveness of the approach: satisfaction likelihood, which measures the predicted probability that a requirement is satisfied under given operating conditions, and success rate, which quantifies how often the system successfully satisfies all requirements after adaptation.

Satisfaction likelihood is the probability, as given by the black box model, for the class label to be *true*. The mathematical formula for satisfaction likelihood is as follows:

$$SL(R_i) = P_{M_i}\left(y = \text{true} \mid (\hat{CF}, \hat{OF})\right)$$

where P_{M_i} is the predicted probability of the given black-box model M_i, for the class label y, which represents whether the requirement is satisfied; $\hat{CF}$ represents the adaptation decision applied to controllable features; and $\hat{OF}$ is the current state of the observable features.

Success rate is defined as the number of instances in X that satisfy the requirement R_i under the given operating conditions $(\hat{CF}, \hat{OF})$, such that the probability estimation of the class label to be *true* is greater than the threshold (which is set to 0.8). The mathematical formula for success rate is as follows:

$$SuccessRate(R_i) = \frac{n_{\text{success}}(R_i)}{|X|}$$

where $n_{\text{success}}(R_i)$ indicates the number of successful cases in which the requirement R_i is satisfied. $|\cdot|$ represents cardinality (count), so in this context, it essentially means the number of elements in X.

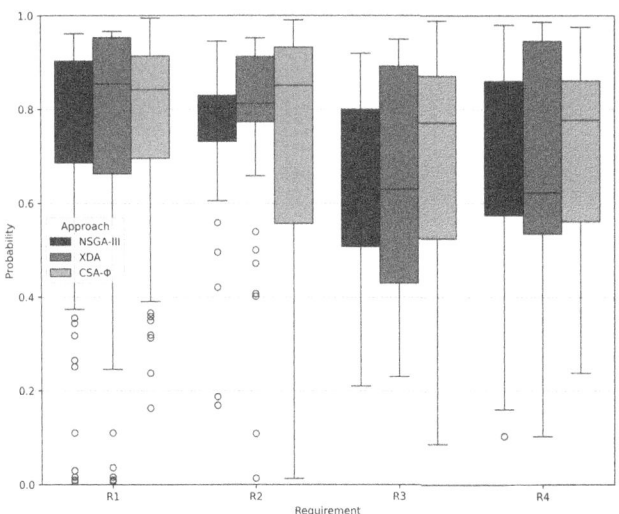

Fig. 4. Satisfaction likelihood (higher is better)

Results: Figure 4 presents a box plot comparing the satisfaction likelihood (ranging from 0 to 1) across all system requirements. For requirement R2, CSA-Φ exhibits a wider distribution, indicating higher variance in satisfaction likelihood. In the cases of R1 and R2, all approaches display outliers below the lower

Table 4. Statistical significance for satisfaction likelihood

	Requirements	p-value
XDA vs. CSA-Φ	R1	1.715e$-$1
	R2	6.190e$-$1
	R3	2.892e$-$2
	R4	2.883e$-$1
NSGA-III vs. CSA-Φ	R1	2.502e$-$1
	R2	3.289e$-$1
	R3	9.51e$-$3
	R4	4.469e$-$2

whiskers, representing extreme data points that deviate from the general trend. Except for R1, the median satisfaction likelihood values achieved by CSA-Φ are slightly higher than those of XDA and NSGA-III. This suggests that CSA-Φ is at least as effective as traditional optimization methods in satisfying requirements, particularly when evaluated through the lens of satisfaction likelihood.

To assess the statistical significance of these results, we performed the Mann-Whitney U test. Table 4 summarizes the outcomes, comparing CSA-Φ against both XDA and NSGA-III. As shown in the table, statistical significance is not consistent across all requirements; however, it is evident in several cases, which are specifically highlighted.

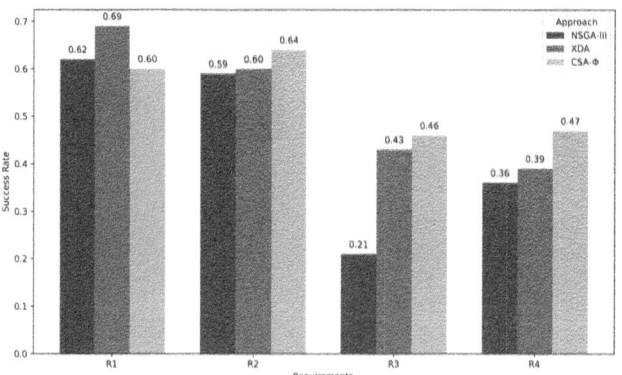

Fig. 5. Success rate (higher is better)

Figure 5 compares the success rate across all requirements for CSA-Φ and the baseline methods. As shown in the figure, CSA-Φ achieves a higher success rate in most cases—specifically for requirements R2, R3, and R4—when compared to both NSGA-III and XDA. This demonstrates CSA-Φ's consistency and effectiveness in fulfilling system requirements. The relative improvement over NSGA-III ranges from 0.032 to 0.543, highlighting a significant advantage in several scenarios. In comparison to XDA, the relative difference ranges from 0.063 to 0.170. These variations in relative success rates indicate that CSA-Φ provides substantial improvements over traditional black-box optimization techniques like NSGA-III and performs comparably (if not slightly better) than explanation-driven approaches such as XDA.

RQ2 summary:
CSA-Φ shows no statistically significant differences in satisfaction likelihood compared to baselines, though slightly higher medians suggest it is comparable to existing methods. It matches XDA in success rates while outperforming NSGA-III, demonstrating reliable adaptation compared to traditional black-box methods.

---

6   Threats to Validity

One possible threat to internal validity arises from the counterfactual generation process, which may emphasize changing certain features while overlooking others. To address this, CSA-Φ selects features for modification based on confidence loss, rather than relying on random or arbitrary changes. This ensures that feature selection is guided by meaningful impact on the satisfaction of requirements.

To mitigate construct validity concerns, we compared CSA-Φ against two established baselines, ensuring that the evaluation is grounded in meaningful and relevant metrics.

Regarding external validity, our experiments were conducted in a simulated environment where full control over both controllable and observable features was assumed. This setup allows for consistent and repeatable evaluation. We also repeated each simulation 200 times to improve the robustness and generalizability of the results. Additionally, we used the Mann-Whitney U test to validate statistical significance, strengthening result reliability.

7   Related Work

Although the concept of explainability originated within the field of artificial intelligence, it has become an increasingly important non-functional quality when designing systems that rely on black-box models [1]. As AI components are increasingly integrated into software systems, explainability is now also gaining prominence in the domain of software engineering [26]. For instance, MAB-EX [4] enables systems to monitor their environment and internal behavior, identify situations requiring explanation, and construct human-understandable responses using internal models. This enhances the granularity of system explanations and the user collaboration through the integration of runtime models and reasoning capabilities.

Similarly, the Explainable Self-Adaptation (XSA) framework [7] aims to increase the transparency of self-adaptive systems by explicitly explaining adaptation decisions. Integrated into the feedback control loop, XSA improves both user trust and the engineer's ability to interpret and debug runtime decisions. Köhl et al. [19] further emphasized explainability as a non-functional requirement, highlighting the importance of systematically eliciting explainability requirements to guide the development of trustworthy systems.

The self-adaptive systems research community focuses on building systems capable of operating under uncertain conditions—or gracefully degrading when this is not possible. SafeX [20], for example, incorporates various explainable AI techniques to enhance safety and trust in autonomous systems. It supports real-time assessment and debugging by structuring explanations while preserving the reliability of AI components.

Weyns et al. [30] proposed a hybrid approach that integrates the MAPE loop, control theory, and machine learning to achieve robust adaptation. In this model, the MAPE loop governs high-level decision-making, control theory manages real-time system metrics, and machine learning contributes adaptive capabilities. Calinescu et al. [5] also underscored the importance of runtime learning, proactive adaptation, and formal guarantees to manage uncertainty in SAS effectively.

To support human-in-the-loop adaptation, stochastic models have been employed to explain system behavior under uncertainty [6]. In robotics, explanation-driven approaches are increasingly being adopted to help both engineers and end-users understand the rationale behind operational decisions, thus fostering trust [3].

8   Conclusion

In this paper, we introduced CSA-Φ, a novel approach that integrates model-agnostic counterfactual explanations into the feedback control loop of self-adaptive systems. By embedding explainability directly into the adaptation process, CSA-Φ provides meaningful insights that help steer adaptation decisions while reducing the computational cost typically associated with optimization in white-box models. We conducted an empirical evaluation to assess both the efficiency (measured by execution time) and effectiveness (measured by satisfaction likelihood and success rate) of CSA-Φ. The results demonstrate that CSA-Φ significantly outperforms the baselines in terms of execution time while achieving comparable performance in terms of satisfaction likelihood and success rate.

Acknowledgment. This work was supported by funding from the pilot program Core Informatics at KIT (KiKIT) of the Helmholtz Association (HGF) and supported by the German Research Foundation (DFG) - SFB 1608 - 501798263 and KASTEL Security Research Labs, Karlsruhe.

References

1. Angelov, P.P., Soares, E.A., Jiang, R., Arnold, N.I., Atkinson, P.M.: Explainable artificial intelligence: an analytical review. Wiley Interdiscip. Rev. Data Min. Knowl. Disc. **11**(5), e1424 (2021)
2. Bersani, M.M., Camilli, M., Lestingi, L., Mirandola, R., Rossi, M., Scandurra, P.: A conceptual framework for explainability requirements in software-intensive systems. In: 2023 IEEE 31st International Requirements Engineering Conference Workshops (REW), pp. 309–315 (2023)
3. Bersani, M.M., Camilli, M., Lestingi, L., Mirandola, R., Rossi, M., Scandurra, P.: Towards better trust in human-machine teaming through explainable dependability. In: 2023 IEEE 20th International Conference on Software Architecture Companion (ICSA-C), pp. 86–90. IEEE (2023)
4. Blumreiter, M., Greenyer, J., et al.: Towards self-explainable cyber-physical systems. In: 2019 ACM/IEEE 22nd International Conference on Model Driven Engineering Languages and Systems Companion (MODELS-C), pp. 543–548. IEEE (2019)
5. Calinescu, R., Mirandola, R., Perez-Palacin, D., Weyns, D.: Understanding uncertainty in self-adaptive systems. In: IEEE International Conference on Autonomic Computing and Self-organizing Systems (ACSOS), pp. 242–251 (2020)
6. Cámara, J., Silva, M., Garlan, D., Schmerl, B.: Explaining architectural design tradeoff spaces: a machine learning approach. In: European Conference on Software Architecture, pp. 49–65. Springer (2021)
7. Camilli, M., Mirandola, R., Scandurra, P.: XSA: explainable self-adaptation. In: Proceedings of the 37th IEEE/ACM International Conference on Automated Software Engineering, pp. 1–5 (2022)
8. Camilli, M., Mirandola, R., Scandurra, P.: Enforcing resilience in cyber-physical systems via equilibrium verification at runtime. ACM Trans. Autonom. Adapt. Syst. **18**(3), 1–32 (2023)
9. Cover, T., Hart, P.: Nearest neighbor pattern classification. IEEE Trans. Inf. Theor. **13**(1), 21–27 (1967)
10. De Lemos, R., et al.: Software engineering for self-adaptive systems: a second research roadmap. In: Software Engineering for Self-Adaptive Systems II: International Seminar, Dagstuhl Castle, Germany, pp. 1–32. Springer (2013)
11. Deb, K., Jain, H.: An evolutionary many-objective optimization algorithm using reference-point-based nondominated sorting approach, part i: solving problems with box constraints. IEEE Trans. Evol. Comput. **18**(4), 577–601 (2013)
12. Esfahani, N., Malek, S.: Uncertainty in self-adaptive software systems. In: Software Engineering for Self-Adaptive Systems II: International Seminar, Dagstuhl Castle, Germany, 24–29 October 2010 Revised Selected and Invited Papers, pp. 214–238. Springer (2013)
13. Friedman, J.H.: Greedy function approximation: a gradient boosting machine. Ann. Stat., 1189–1232 (2001)
14. Gheibi, O., Weyns, D.: Lifelong self-adaptation: self-adaptation meets lifelong machine learning. In: Proceedings of the IEEE/ACM SEAMS, pp. 1–12 (2022)
15. Gheibi, O., Weyns, D., Quin, F.: Applying machine learning in self-adaptive systems: a systematic literature review. ACM TAAS **15**(3), 1–37 (2021)
16. Han, H., Wang, W.Y., Mao, B.H.: Borderline-smote: a new over-sampling method in imbalanced data sets learning. In: International Conference on Intelligent Computing, pp. 878–887. Springer (2005)

17. Kephart, J.O., Chess, D.M.: The vision of autonomic computing. Computer **36**(1), 41–50 (2003)
18. Khalid, N., Qureshi, N.A.: Towards self-explainable adaptive systems (SEAS): a requirements driven approach. In: REFSQ Workshops (2021)
19. Köhl, M.A., et al.: Explainability as a non-functional requirement. In: 2019 IEEE 27th International Requirements Engineering Conference (RE), pp. 363–368. IEEE (2019)
20. Kuznietsov, A., Gyevnar, B., Wang, C., Peters, S., Albrecht, S.V.: Explainable AI for safe and trustworthy autonomous driving: a systematic review. IEEE Trans. Intell. Transp. Syst. (2024)
21. Langford, M.A., Cheng, B.H.: "know what you know": predicting behavior for learning-enabled systems when facing uncertainty. In: Proceedings of IEEE/ACM SEAMS, pp. 78–89 (2021)
22. Mann, H.B., Whitney, D.R.: On a test of whether one of two random variables is stochastically larger than the other. Ann. Math. Stat., 50–60 (1947)
23. Miller, T.: Explanation in artificial intelligence: insights from the social sciences. Artif. Intell. **267**, 1–38 (2019)
24. Molnar, C.: Interpretable machine learning. lulu.com (2020)
25. Negri, F.R., Nicolosi, N., Camilli, M., Mirandola, R.: Explanation-driven self-adaptation using model-agnostic interpretable machine learning. In: Proceedings of IEEE/ACM SEAMS, pp. 189–199 (2024)
26. Tantithamthavorn, C.K., Jiarpakdee, J.: Explainable AI for software engineering. In: 2021 36th IEEE/ACM International Conference on Automated Software Engineering (ASE), pp. 1–2. IEEE (2021)
27. Vapnik, V.N.: An overview of statistical learning theory. IEEE Trans. Neural Netw. **10**(5), 988–999 (1999)
28. Wachter, S., Mittelstadt, B., Russell, C.: Counterfactual explanations without opening the black box: automated decisions and the GDPR. Harv. JL Tech. **31**, 841 (2017)
29. Weyns, D.: An Introduction to Self-adaptive Systems: A Contemporary Software Engineering Perspective. Wiley (2020)
30. Weyns, D., et al.: Towards better adaptive systems by combining MAPE, control theory, and machine learning. In: Proceedings of IEEE/ACM SEAMS, pp. 217–223 (2021)
31. Weyns, D., Gheibi, O., Quin, F., Van Der Donckt, J.: Deep learning for effective and efficient reduction of large adaptation spaces in self-adaptive systems. ACM TAAS **17**(1–2), 1–42 (2022)
32. Wohlrab, R., Cámara, J., Garlan, D., Schmerl, B.: Explaining quality attribute tradeoffs in automated planning for self-adaptive systems. J. Syst. Softw. **198**, 111538 (2023)

Exploring Explainability Requirements for Self-adaptive Systems

Cong Wang[1], Ali Torbati[2], and Verena Klös[2]($\boxtimes$)

[1] LASR Lab, Technische Universität Dresden, Dresden, Germany
cong.wang@tu-dresden.de
[2] Carl von Ossietzky Universität Oldenburg, Oldenburg, Germany
{ali.torbati,verena.kloes}@uni-oldenburg.de

Abstract. The growing prevalence of self-adaptive systems (SASs) in cyber-physical environments, and their close interactions with human operators and end-users increase the need for understanding and explaining their system behavior. However, explainability requirements for SASs are scarcely discussed in the literature. To identify aspects that need to be considered when designing explanations for SASs, we collected insights from literature and analyzed explainability requirements of several SAS exemplars from different domains. We identified the necessity, content, and characteristics of explanations across various stakeholder groups by utilizing five guiding questions for a systematic analysis. The results show that many existing exemplars would most likely profit from integrating context- and stakeholder specific explanations in order to increase their understanding for developers and end-users.

Keywords: self-adaptive systems · cyber-physical systems · requirements engineering · explainability

1 Introduction

Cyber-physical systems (CPS) are increasingly embedded in dynamic environments that are constantly evolving, due to changes and uncertainties in the system, its surrounding environment, and user behavior. To handle such changes and uncertainties CPS need to be able to adapt themselves. Such self-adaptive systems (SASs) have been extensively researched and can increasingly deal with uncertainties [1]. A self-adaptive system is able to monitor the software system and its environment at runtime, and correspondingly make decisions and take actions in a timely manner [2]. Adaptive decisions and actions often occur rapidly, in ways that may be difficult for users to understand, leading to a lack of trust [3]. With the growing influence of self-adaptive systems, there is a pressing need to consider human-centered software design and development, emphasizing the importance of understanding and explaining system behavior to align self-adaptive systems more closely with human needs and expectations, and to improve human-machine collaboration.

Explaining system behavior can improve users' understanding and trust in the system [4]. Explainability has gained increasing attention recently in the

D. Taibi and D. Smite (Eds.): SEAA 2025, LNCS 16081, pp. 237–253, 2026.
https://doi.org/10.1007/978-3-032-04190-6_15

area of *Explainable Artificial Intelligence* (XAI), with the aim of developing techniques that enable human users to better understand and trust the decisions made by machine learning models [5]. Since software systems are becoming increasingly complex and opaque, explainability has also garnered interest in the field of *Software Engineering* (SE) and *Requirements Engineering* (RE), where explainability is viewed as an important Non-Functional Requirement (NFR) indicative of system quality [6,7].

Since SASs have numerous runtime adaptations which can be confusing and potentially eroding human trust, explainability emerges as an essential consideration. While some recent studies have addressed the explanation of SASs [8–10] there are no systematic analyses of requirements or systematic engineering approaches for explainable SASs, and explainability of SASs still is a niche area of research [11]. This work aims to provide an overview of relevant aspects that need to be considered when eliciting explainability requirements for SASs and to analyze several existing exemplars in order to get preliminary answers to the following research questions:

RQ1. Would stakeholders of existing SASs exemplars profit from explainability?
RQ2. Do explanation needs differ for different application domains, stakeholder groups and contexts of adaptations?

To this end, we first collect relevant aspects for explainability requirements from literature in Sect. 3 and derive five guiding questions that we subsequently use for systematically analyzing several exemplars in Sect. 4. We discuss our findings and their implications for future work in Sect. 5 and conclude in Sect. 6. Our analysis reveals various explanation needs of different stakeholders and emphasizes the importance of explainability for SASs. To the best of our knowledge, this is the first work systematically reviewing explainability requirements of self-adaptive systems.

2   Related Work

Explaining Self-adaptive Systems. Only a few works explored explainability in SASs. Li *et al.* characterized explanations based on content, effect and cost. They proposed a probabilistic model checking approach to determine when explanations should be used to improve the overall system utility [10,12]. Camili *et al.* described different levels of explainability with corresponding meta-requirements, and demonstrated human-understandable explanations with robotic examples [9]. Feit *et al.* presented a technique for explaining deep reinforcement learning for SASs [8]. Wohlrab *et al.* address the problem of explaining the underlying tradeoffs between quality attributes and how their weighting in utility functions influence adaptation planning to developers and decision makers [13]. However, none of these addressed the problem of deriving explanation requirements or systematically characterized explanation needs in SASs.

XAI. The methodologies and insights from XAI are crucial in addressing the explainability challenges inherent in the complex and dynamic nature of self-adaptive systems. Over the last decade, XAI has been extensively researched to allow people to better understand black-box machine learning algorithms [14]. Arrieta *et al.* [15] enhanced the definition of explainability in machine learning, by showing that the concept of *audience* plays a crucial role in determining the contents and effects of explanations. They pointed out that both the content and the effect of explanations are completely dependent on the presented audience. The concept of audience is often more precisely referred to as *stakeholders.* Human stakeholder (e.g., users, developers, regulators) is a crucial concept in explainability, since a main aim of explainability approaches is to satisfy human stakeholders' desiderata [16]. Ribera and Lapedriza pointed out a new explainability pipeline, taking into account different types of stakeholders and different goals [17]. M. Langer *et al.* [16] distinguished five primary classes of stakeholders in XAI: users, developers, affected parties, deployers, and regulators. *Affected parties* refer to people who are in the scope of a system's impact but do not use it, they are often unaware of being affected. *Deployers*, who decide where to employ certain systems, are also referred to as *"AI Managers"* in some research [18]. *Regulators* refer to the class of stakeholders who monitor the whole process of systems regarding legal and ethical norms. Given the wide range of stakeholders involved, it is critical to ensure that these stakeholders from diverse backgrounds can effectively comprehend these complex systems.

Explainability in Software Engineering. Building upon the foundals of XAI, the field of explaining software systems has similarly garnered significant interest among researchers. Nunes *et al.* provided a systematic review and taxonomy of explanations in advice-giving software systems [19]. They investigated the purpose, generation, communication and evaluation of these explanations. Chazette *et al.* presented a quality framework for explainability requirements, integrating dependencies, characteristics, and evaluation methods [20]. Köhl *et al.* provided a conceptual analysis which unifies different notions of explainability and the corresponding demands [7].

3   Explanation Needs in SASs

In order to analyze explanation requirements for SASs, we first need to define when a self-adaptive system needs to explain its adaptations. To this end, we analyzed existing definitions that characterize explainability in software systems.

Köhl *et al.* pointed out that the need for an explanation originates in the lack of understanding of some phenomenon with respect to some aspects [7], and that it is important to consider the *aspect*, since the explanation depends on that. Chazette *et al.* expanded the definition of explainability by introducing the variable *addressee* that receives the explanation [21], further enriching the understanding of how explainability can be tailored to different stakeholders. We transferred their definition to self-adaptive systems:

Definition 1. *In a self-adaptive system S, an explanation E becomes necessary if and only if certain stakeholder groups G can observe an adaptation A, and require information I to understand A with respect to aspect X in context C.*

The above definition synthesizes the crucial factors that identify the need for explanations in a self-adaptive system. Following the work of stakeholder categorization in [16], we consider three primary stakeholder groups for our purposes: developers, users, and affected parties. An explanation E is deemed necessary within a self-adaptive system S, only if certain stakeholder groups G can observe an occurring adaptation A, and they require more information I to understand relevant aspects X of it. Ideally, the information I is the substance or content that an explanation E carries.

Aspects X of A can be seen as questions that stakeholders G may have for understanding an adaptation A. For some stakeholders, aspects X might not exist if they find the adaptation A easy to understand or irrelevant to their interests. Then, explanations E are not necessary for them.

Context C significantly influences the explanation E. Firstly, it determines the goals of the explanation E. Sameket *et al.* pointed out that the primary goals of XAI are verification of the system, improvement of the system, learning from the system, and compliance with legislation [22]. For our selected stakeholders, we combine verification and improvement under the term *system refinement* and refine learning from the system to *action requirement*, which means that the explanation E aims to enable certain stakeholders to perform actions. The legislation goal is mainly relevant for regulators. Secondly, the context dictates the constraints of the explanation E. The constraints are the factors that have an influence or limitations on the explanation E, such as time, technologies, modalities, etc. Our study concentrates on the constraint time imperative, which represents the time-criticality of the explanation, *i.e.*, how critical it is that the explanation E should occur within a specified time. In our work, we categorize three different levels of time imperative: *routine* (explanations are available for periodic inspection but not in a timely manner, e.g., as a report every week), *moderate* (explanations are needed in the situation but their computation may take some time, e.g., up to a minute), and *critical* (explanations should be available within seconds as they might be needed for choosing critical actions). The time imperative depends on the goal of the explanation, i.e., whether it should enable the explainee to perform some immediate actions.

Consider the following example. A car is equipped with a self-adaptive driving system S. The system can help navigate the car to its destination and make adaptations based on the current traffic situation. The assistant driver in the car, who is a non-expert in the field of self-adaptive systems, belongs to the user stakeholder group G_u. At one moment, S alters the planned route (adaptation A) to optimize traffic flow in the urban area. G_u is required to follow the instruction of S and change the route (goal: action requirement) within a certain time (time imperative τ). In this situation, G_u needs clear information I to understand the rationale (aspect X) of A. Therefore, explanations E_u are necessary for G_u. In this scenario, S may reroute more cars through areas typically dominated by pedestrians, whom belong to the stakeholder group of affected parties G_a. S should provide explanations E_a for G_a to better understand the reasons behind A. Explanations E_d are also necessary for the developer stakeholder group G_d, as they need technical information I of each A in S for regular maintenance and enhancing the system (goal: system refinement).

Definition 1 extends the foundation work of Köhl *et al.* [7] and Chazette *et al.* [21] in order to pinpoint when explanations are necessary and to guide the determination of their content and key characteristics. We derive the following *guiding questions*:

Q1. Which stakeholder group G can observe the occurring adaptation?
Q2. Which stakeholder group G requires further information to understand specific aspects of the observed adaptation?
Q3. What is the goal (*system refinement* or *action requirement*) of the explanation?
Q4. What is the time imperative level τ (*critical, moderate, routine*) of the explanation?
Q5. What information need to be included in the explanation?

Q1 aims to identify which stakeholder groups are able to observe the adaptation. However, certain stakeholders may not require additional information to understand the adaptation, if the changes are self-evident or easily comprehensible within their scope of understanding. In this case, explanations are not necessary for those stakeholders. Consequently, Q2 seeks to ascertain whether the observing stakeholders actually need further explanations from the system.

Q3 and Q4 focus on identifying the aforementioned goals and constraints of the explanation. They aim to evaluate the urgency and practical implications of the explanation, covering both immediate action requirements and long-term system refinements. Inadequately addressing the urgency and goals of explanations can significantly impair system responsiveness and hinder stakeholders' capacity to perform actions. Moreover, failing to deliver prompt and effective explanations in critical situations may also jeopardize user safety.

The last question Q5 aims to clarify what information needs to be included and ties back to the earlier questions, as different stakeholder groups might require diverse information related to specific aspects of the adaptation. Furthermore, the content of the explanation depends on the constraints and goals. In urgent situations, explanations should be concise to enable quick comprehension by stakeholders.

Utilizing these five guiding questions, we can now systematically review several SAS exemplars in the following section. Our aim is to analyze the necessity, contents, and properties of explanations for different stakeholder groups within these self-adaptive systems.

4   Analyzing of Exemplars

We systematically analyze explainability requirements of several SAS exemplars from a public database[1] to identify where explanations would help in the scenarios modeled by the exemplars (RQ1) and how explanation needs differ between different stakeholders, application scenarios and contexts (RQ2).

4.1   Methodology

Database. We chose the collection of self-adaptive system exemplars from this database because it provides a large collection of reviewed artifacts from different application areas, mostly in the area of CPS, that describe different types of adaptation in different contexts.

Exclusion Criteria. Since our aim is to explain observable adaptations within self-adaptive systems, we excluded papers in which adaptations are not specifically defined or not observable by humans, and those designed as evaluation systems for self-adaptive systems.

Analysis Process. We categorized the remaining 11 exemplars into five groups of application types: *Web Service, Traffic Management, Healthcare, Unmanned Vehicles*, and *IoT Applications*. These categories were selected based on the distinct use-cases, similar contexts and stakeholder groups. We analyzed the exemplars by sequentially answering our guiding questions Q1 to Q5. To limit the subjectivity of our answers, all questions were independently answered by two researchers and the findings were discussed in the group of all authors. Although many exemplars provide simulations without real "users" or "affected parties", our review considers potential implementations of these exemplars in real-world scenarios to analyze the full spectrum of explainability requirements in the proposed application scenarios.

4.2   Analysis of Exemplars

We introduce each exemplar and provide the analysis results in the following subsections. The answers to Q1 to Q4 are also summarized in Table 1.

Web Service. *Znn.com* [23] is a news service that provides its consumers with multimedia news content. It is a web-based client-server system that utilizes an N-tier architecture. In this system, server pool size and content presentation mode dynamically adapt in response to user activity. As client activity increases, the system not only expands its server pool size, but also switches content to a

---

[1] https://www.hpi.uni-potsdam.de/giese/public/selfadapt/exemplars/,   exemplars from 2024 were not yet available when we performed the analysis.

more resource-efficient textual mode. The primary goal is to deliver news content promptly while managing server costs effectively.

These adaptations are fully observable by system developers (G_d). Users (G_u), on the other hand, may not directly notice server adjustments but will experience varying content modes, from full multimedia to static text. G_d requires detailed technical information about the adaptations to verify and refine the system effectively. G_u requires information to understand the reasons for content switching. Based on these needs, we classify τ_d as *routine* and τ_u as *moderate*, due to the direct impact on user experience. Explanations E_d should encompass an overview of the number of users and the types of content presented across various periods. Meanwhile, E_u should include the reason behind content switching, such as high user demand. Ideally, E_u should also include an estimated time-frame for returning to the multimedia content mode.

Table 1. Answers of questions Q1 to Q4 for each exemplar.

Category	Exemplar	Q1	Q2	Q3	Q4
Web Services	Znn [23]	G_u G_d	G_u G_d	*refinement* (G_d)	moderate (τ_u) routine (τ_d)
Traffic Management	DeeCo [24]	G_u G_a	G_u	*action* (G_u)	moderate (τ_u)
	TRAPP [25]	G_u G_a	G_u	*action* (G_u)	moderate (τ_u)
	Platooning LEGOs [26]	G_u G_a	G_u G_a	*action* (G_u)	moderate (τ_u) moderate (τ_a)
HealthCare	TAS [27]	G_u G_d	G_u G_d	*action* (G_u) *refinement* (G_d)	critical (τ_u) routine (τ_d)
	BSN [28]	G_u G_d	G_u G_d	*action* (G_u) *refinement* (G_d)	critical (τ_u) routine (τ_d)
Unmanned Vehicles	UNDERSEA [29]	G_u	G_u	*action* (G_u) *refinement* (G_u)	moderate (τ_u)
	Dragonfly [30]	G_u G_a	G_u G_a	*action* (G_u) *refinement* (G_u)	moderate (τ_u) moderate (τ_a)
	DARTSim [31]	G_u G_a	G_u G_a	*action* (G_u) *refinement* (G_u)	critical (τ_u) critical (τ_a)
IoT Applications	DeltaIoT [32]	G_d	G_d	*refinement* (G_d)	routine (τ_d)
	DingNet [33]	G_d	G_d	*refinement* (G_d)	routine (τ_d)

G_d, G_u and G_a represent stakeholder groups of developers, users and affected parties, respectively; τ_d, τ_u, τ_a are time imperative levels of explanations for these stakeholder groups; *refinement* represents that the goal of explanations aims at system refinement; *action* represents the goal of requiring corresponding stakeholders for performing actions; The relevant aspects for stakeholders of *Q2* are discussed in the corresponding exemplar analyses.

Traffic Management. In the following exemplars, we assume that there is an assistant driver in each automated or self-adaptive vehicle, which can be seen as a member of G_u.

Distributed Emergent Ensembles of Components (DeeCo) [24] utilizes architectural abstractions to model a dynamic, self-adaptive cooperative parking reservation system. Each vehicle is represented as an autonomous component, and nearby vehicles dynamically compose an ensemble so that vehicles can exchange their knowledge about the available parking capacity. Vehicles detect and collect the information of nearby vacant parking spaces and exchange this information with each other when they are within a certain range. A vehicle searching for the nearest parking space adapts its planned route based on this updated information via vehicle-to-vehicle communication. As this vehicle navigates to its designated parking space, it reserves this space and shares this information with other vehicles through communication.

Such route adaptation is observable by this vehicle (G_u) and the other nearby vehicles (G_a). Although G_u and G_a can observe these adaptations, they typically do not need further information since there are no aspects X that need to be understood. However, in situations where a visually unoccupied parking space is actually reserved by another vehicle, and therefore G_u must navigate to a more distant destination, G_u requires additional information to understand the situation. The goal of explanations E_u is to let G_u perform actions, *i.e.* changing route, and we classify τ_u as *moderate*. E_u should encompass details of possible parking spaces and their reservation status. E_u should also indicate the reasons for navigating to specific parking spaces, such as the distance to these parking spaces and the timestamp of the last update of their reservation status.

The *Traffic Reconfigurations via Adaptive Participatory Planning* (TRAPP) [25] framework aims to optimize the dynamic traffic flow in a decentralized and participatory way. Within TRAPP, vehicles adapt their routes to their destinations based on the following adaptation strategies: load-balancing, avoiding overloaded streets, and tuning planning frequency. Specifically, these strategies aim to evenly distribute cars across the traffic network, avoid routing cars through congested streets, and optimize the frequency of route adjustments, respectively. These adaptations will affect the planned routes for certain vehicles, perhaps leading them through a more distant or unfamiliar route.

These route adaptations are observable by the involved vehicles G_u and nearby traffic participants G_a. G_u will need additional information to understand the rationale behind these adaptations. For G_a, we do not see any relevant aspects X. G_u need to adapt and alter their route, necessitating explanations for action performance, with *moderate* τ_u. Explanations E_u should provide the rationale for the system's adaptive routing decisions, *e.g.*, that the adaptation is made because an overloaded street appears in the original route. Furthermore, E_u could provide an estimated time change for the new route, and if feasible, provide several alternative routes.

Platooning LEGOs [26] describes a platoon of vehicles heading to the same destination that collaborate to reduce fuel consumption and road occupancy [34].

In such a platoon, vehicles adapt their velocities, lanes, or distances between each other to overcome environmental uncertainties. The leading vehicle adapts the driving lane and velocities based on its sensor information and communicates these decisions to the following vehicles.

The above mentioned adaptations can be observed by the assistant drivers (G_u) in the following vehicles of this platoon, and the affected traffic participants (G_a) in the nearby environment. G_u could have questions about these adaptations and need more information to obtain a comprehensive understanding, as they do not access the same information as the platoon leader. G_a also needs information on the reasons for the adaptations of the platoon, which impact the overall flow of traffic. G_u needs to take actions aligned with the platoon's behavior. Although G_a does not share this necessity, a prompt explanation can be beneficial for their traffic plan. Therefore we classify both τ_u and τ_a as *moderate*. Explanations E_u should encompass a detailed rationale for these adaptations, along with the corresponding sensor information. For example, if the length of the current platoon exceeds a threshold, the system decides to reduce the overall travel speed, consequently reducing the necessary safety distances between vehicles and, therefore, reducing the overall road occupancy. As a further result of these adaptations, the platoon also needs to switch to a slower driving lane. Instead of a technical rationale that E_u should include, E_a should convey to G_a the purpose of these observed adaptations, for instance, explaining that an adaptation aims to minimize road occupancy. Additionally, E_a should contain that this platoon currently has no plans for further lane changes.

In summary, the analysis of explainability requirements within these exemplars in the field of traffic management highlights that we should consider the other traffic participants as the stakeholder group *affected parties*. However, it is important to emphasize that explanations are not universally necessary for these affected parties. When analyzing explainability requirements, it is essential to investigate which adaptations can be confusing to these affected parties, alongside the aspects that they need to understand and the information they require. Therefore, explanations provided to these affected parties should contain the reasoning behind such confusing adaptations and solve their concerns. Such explanations can make adaptations in traffic management more transparent and comprehensible for all traffic participants.

Healthcare. *Tele Assistance System* (TAS) [27] is a service-based system that supports elderly individuals who need health support in the convenience of their households. It combines wearable sensors and third-party remote services to monitor patients' vitals and analyze their health. When a service failure occurs or a variation in service response time is detected, the system adapts by switching to an equivalent service or simultaneously invokes several services for idempotent operation. Additionally, the system integrates new services or changes the workflow architecture to meet new performance requirements while balancing the costs of service invocation.

Based on the aim of third-party service providers to develop services and analyze patient data, we classify them together with system developers as members of the stakeholder group G_d, as they both possess the capabilities and responsibilities in the development. While G_d can observe all adaptations, patients (G_u) may only notice service changes. G_d needs information to understand the rationale behind adaptations and their effects, enabling them to evaluate the services' quality and refine the system. Concealing service switches from users to prevent confusion might be prudent, however G_u needs to understand the reasons for service changes and take actions, such as replacing devices or calling for emergency help. Given these needs, τ_d is classified as *routine*, while τ_u is *critical*, due to the system's significant impact on user health. Explanations E_d should provide system developers the rationale and evaluation data of adaptations, such as metrics of the overall failure rates and response times before and after a service change. Additionally, E_d should offer service providers the rationale for replacing their service, *e.g.,* inadequate analysis of patient data or unreliable performance. Explanations E_u should provide the reasoning behind the change of a specific service, especially when it is related to the user's health status. For example, the system might adopt a new alarm service that is more sensitive and collects health data more frequently, due to a recent deterioration of the user's health. Furthermore, because of this change, the user may need to pay attention to charging the wearable device more often.

Body Sensor Network. (BSN) [28] is designed to monitor and analyze the health status of different individuals in real time within the context of healthcare self-adaptive cyber-physical systems. BSN adapts by adjusting the central hub service time rate, fine-tuning sensor sampling rates, and deactivating unnecessary sensors based on the managed system aiming to analyze the vital signs and detect the emergencies. These vital signs are periodically collected through a set of distributed sensors and forwarded to the central hub unit. Hereby, the central hub must fuse the collected data to classify the overall patient health status. The overall goal is to keep the reliability level while managing energy consumption.

These adaptations are fully observable by the system designers G_d. Contrarily, users G_u may not directly notice the adaptations regarding central hub and sensor sampling rates but will discover sensor deactivation over time. G_d requires detailed sensor information to dig into the system's adaptations aiming to evaluate the system's capability over time and introduce further refinements. G_u is in need of further information regarding sensor deactivation to understand whether these adaptations impact the system performance. Based on these commitments, τ_d is classified as *routine* while τ_u as *critical*, considering the system's effect on users' health. Explanations E_d should encompass an overview of the central hub and sensor settings, as well as information on resulting battery consumption over time. Meantime, explanations E_u should include reasoning behind observable decisions, such as deactivating the unnecessary sensors, and its effects in overall. Furthermore, a summary of the user's monitored health status should be considered in E_u, assuring the user's peace of mind.

In summary, our findings emphasize the importance of providing explanations to patients. Adaptations in response to uncertainties like device failures or delays can have critical consequences for patients. However, a lack of explanations in these urgent situations can significantly affect patient safety. In the healthcare domain, explanations provided to users must always consider critical time constraints. Therefore, the content of these explanations should be both concise and comprehensive, equipping patients with the necessary information to promptly perform the required actions.

Unmanned Vehicles. In this category, operators of these unmanned vehicles (UVs) possess advanced expertise and the capability to access and enhance the systems' effectiveness. Furthermore, they have the responsibility to perform actions in certain circumstances. Their role combines both stakeholder groups G_d and G_u. In this work, we classify them as members of the stakeholder group G_u, emphasizing their active role in remotely piloting UVs and performing actions.

UNDERSEA [29] is a simulated Unmanned Underwater Vehicle (UUV) designed for environmental surveillance missions. This UUV is equipped with several individually controllable sensors. It adapts its speed and sensor configuration due to the unpredictable underwater environment to achieve different requirements including performance, reliability, and energy use. It will change the set of active sensors, switch on additional/alternative sensors, or switch off degraded/energy-intensive sensors when needed.

G_u can observe these adaptations, and given our assumption of no other UUVs underwater, we do not consider G_a. G_u needs technical information from sensors to assess the performance of the UUV, enabling them to perform actions such as manually sending commands, and refine the adaptation plans to enhance the UUV's operational efficiency. We therefore classify τ_u as *moderate*. Explanations E_u should contain the rationale for adaptations and corresponding velocity and sensor information, such as the accuracy or the degradation level of the corresponding sensors.

Dragonfly [30] simulates drone behaviors under different conditions, covering both normal and exceptional situations. Within the Dragonfly framework, a drone dynamically adapts its flying mode on the way to its destination. It can adapt the flying mode between flying and gliding modes, considering various factors, such as the battery level, remaining distance, and environmental conditions like wind strength or flying over water. Additionally, in cases where it loses signal connectivity or receives a return command from the user, it starts initiating a protocol to return to its origin.

As G_u remotely tracks the drone's movement, they can observe adaptations of its flying pattern. Moreover, when drones fly near residential areas, other stakeholders G_a may also notice these adaptations, especially sudden turns, which can be confusing to them. G_u needs detailed information to verify and comprehend the behaviour of the drone, whereas G_a only needs clarifications to understand what to expect from the drone, *i.e.*, whether it might harm anyone. The goal of E_u is to enable G_u to take actions such as sending a return command or manually adjusting flying conditions, but also provides insights that can be used for optimizing planned routes for the drones in future tasks. We thus categorize τ_u and τ_a as *moderate*. E_u should encompass the detailed rational information when the drone adapts its flying conditions, *e.g.* the corresponding battery level, the remaining distance to the destination, and the environmental conditions. E_a should provide G_a with the reasons for the drone's approach, for example the drone moving to this residential area to avoid hazards like strong winds. Additionally, E_a can include an estimated time of departure.

DARTSim [31] implements a high-level simulation of a team of unmanned air vehicles (UAVs) performing a reconnaissance in a hostile and unknown environment. These UAVs adapt their altitude levels and detection modes to optimize target identification and mitigate risks in this environment. Although DARTSim is primarily intended for military applications, which we generally exclude from our research, our emphasis is on its use in search-and-rescue missions within hazardous and unexplored environments, such as in a forest fire scenario. These UAVs adjust altitudes and detection modes to identify rescue targets efficiently in the fire. They lower altitudes to approach targets and rise in perilous environments. G_u, serving as the rescue team, oversees the drones and is notified when the drones identify rescue targets (G_a).

The adaptations of altitude levels are observable to both G_u and G_a. G_u requires information to comprehend the environmental situation and the situation of rescue targets, and G_a should be informed about the rescue management, particularly if the drones' movements are unclear to them. The goal of E_u is to enable G_u to take corresponding actions, *i.e.*, rescuing the targets. E_a could also instruct G_a to take actions, *i.e.*, moving to a secure location. Due to this life-critical scenario, we classify both τ_u and τ_a as *critical*. E_u should provide G_u the rationale and potential consequences of the adaptations, particularly regarding the hazards and the rescue targets. For example, UAVs cannot fly lower in a certain location because of the fire, therefore increasing the likelihood of overseeing rescue targets. E_a aims to provide a sense of hope and calm to G_a, ensuring that they feel supported and reassured throughout the rescue. Additionally, E_a can facilitate cooperation between G_a with G_u. For instance, it may involve instructing G_a to move to a safe location, thereby enabling a more efficient rescue by G_u.

In summary, our analysis of explainability requirements for self-adaptive unmanned vehicles reveals a significant need for providing explanations. Since such UVs are designed to perform specific tasks, integrating explanations into these systems can be beneficial for operators to adjust strategies and issue necessary commands. Therefore, explanations can enhance the success rates of such tasks. One additional finding is that explanations should also be considered to affected parties, particularly when these UVs unexpectedly emerge in residential areas. As affected parties typically possess limited knowledge about unmanned vehicles, such as drones, they need additional information to understand the behaviors of these unmanned vehicles and to assess whether they are harmless.

IoT Applications. *DeltaIoT* [32] is a platform to assess and compare methods and tools for self-adaptation within the Internet of Things (IoT) domain. It employs multi-hop communication in IoT, where each IoT mote must have a path towards the gateway along other motes. The focus is on adapting network settings like transmission power, spread factor settings, or modifying traffic routes to reduce energy consumption of the motes while still guaranteeing high packet delivery performance. Since the system is adapting to different scenarios, such as sudden changes in traffic load, by adjusting the IoT network settings in different motes, these adaptations are only observable by system designers G_d. Because explanations are only required to understand reasons and effects of adaptations, τ_d is considered *routine*. Explanations should contain information about the monitored network state and fulfilment of adaptation goals before and after adaptations as well as assumptions made for selecting adaptations to enable a detailed understanding of adaptation decisions and their results.

DingNet [33] serves as a reference implementation designed to facilitate research in the field of self-adaptation within large-scale IoT systems with mobile devices. It offers a simulator that maps directly to a physical IoT setup that is deployed in Leuven, Belgium. DingNet solutions should adapt the communication settings (e.g. power settings, spreading factor adjustments for motes, changes in sampling rates for motes, resource management within the network, and the coordination of gateways) to achieve reliable and energy efficient communication. The described adaptations are either based on signal strength or distance of the mote to the closest gateway.

These adaptations are only observable by G_d, who require explanations for transparency and inspection to gain valuable insights that can be used for system refinement. Moreover, as no explanation is necessary to perform an action in the system, τ_d is considered *routine*. Explanations in this exemplar have similar requirements as described for the *DeltaIoT* exemplar. They have to provide information about monitored data, adaptation decisions, and adaptation effects.

5 Discussion

Our analysis of existing exemplars revealed interesting findings. First of all, we found that our guiding questions were very helpful to elicit explainability requirements in a systematic way. In our results, we identified at least one stakeholder group in each exemplar that would profit from getting explanations about the adaptation behavior - answering RQ1 and showing the importance of explicitly considering explainability as a nonfunctional requirement in SAS design. We also revealed explanation needs of the stakeholder group *affected parties* (e.g., in traffic management and unmanned vehicle exemplars), which are often not in the focus of developers.

When comparing the results over all exemplars, we can identify the following general findings regarding RQ2:

- developers usually need explanations for system refinement that provide information on the context, the reasons for choosing an adaptation and resulting effects

- affected parties usually possess limited knowledge about the system, therefore non-technical explanations about the system behavior are required
- users usually require explanations to gain sufficient understanding of the current system behavior to perform informed actions. They can also profit from explanations to optimize future interactions with the system

Thus explanation needs differ for different stakeholder groups. Additionally, we found that explanation goals and timing requirements differ between application types (i.e., categories of exemplars) and context.

5.1 Limitations and Threats to Validity

Our analysis provides valuable preliminary insights into which explanations would be required to satisfy explanation needs of various stakeholders, but has some limitations. First, we only considered three stakeholder groups, excluding, for example, *regulators*, which might require explanations to *check compliance* with legislation. Second, we did not fully include the goal *learning from the system*, which implies more detailed explanations for novices and fewer details for experienced stakeholders. Furthermore, we did not address design facets of explanations (e.g., presentation format) or evaluation aspects (e.g., evaluation metrics). For this, we refer to the reference model of Chazette *et al.* [21], which outlines key factors for explainability requirements for software systems. The answers to our analysis questions, i.e., time imperative and goal, can help to choose design options like format or tone from their reference model.

Our analysis results are subject to some threats to validity: The conception of the definition and the analysis questions was based on information extracted from the literature and personal experience in self-adaptive system design. The answers to the analysis questions are based on our understanding of the roles and needs of different stakeholders in similar applications. We did not conduct any interviews with stakeholders. Therefore, we can assume a given level of subjectivity. To mitigate this, the analysis questions were independently answered by and all findings were discussed between at least two researchers.

6 Conclusion

Explainability is an important nonfunctional property for complex systems like CPS that can serve as a means to achieve transparency, increase understanding, calibrate trust and improve human-machine collaboration. In order to analyze the necessity for explanations, relevant stakeholders and their information needs in SASs, we have studied characteristics that constitute explanation needs. By analyzing several existing SAS exemplars, we have identified situations and operator tasks that would profit from stakeholder specific explanations.

Our *Guiding Questions* provide a first means to systematically elicit explainability requirements. In future work, we aim to develop methods to provide stakeholder- and context-specific explanations for observable adaptations in

CPS. Furthermore, it would be interesting to evaluate our findings by conducting interviews with real stakeholders and by implementing explanations into selected exemplars and evaluate them in a user study.

Acknowledgements. Partially funded by the German Research Foundation (DFG, Deutsche Forschungsgemeinschaft) as part of Germany's Excellence Strategy – EXC 2050/1 – Project ID 390696704 – Cluster of Excellence "Centre for Tactile Internet with Human-in-the-Loop" (CeTI) of Technische Universität Dresden.

Disclosure of Interests. The authors have no competing interests to declare that are relevant to the content of this article.

References

1. Weyns, D.: Software engineering of self-adaptive systems. In: Handbook of Software Engineering, pp. 399–443 (2019). https://doi.org/10.1007/978-3-030-00262-6_11
2. Salehie, M., Tahvildari, L.: Self-adaptive software: landscape and research challenges. ACM Trans. Auton. Adaptive Syst. (TAAS) **4**(2), 1–42 (2009). https://doi.org/10.1145/1516533.1516538
3. Sawyer, P., Bencomo, N., Whittle, J., Letier, E., Finkelstein, A.: Requirements-aware systems: a research agenda for RE for self-adaptive systems. In: 18th International Requirements Engineering Conference, pp. 95–103. IEEE (2010). https://doi.org/10.1109/re.2010.21
4. Lim, B.Y., Dey, A.K., Avrahami, D.: Why and why not explanations improve the intelligibility of context-aware intelligent systems. In: Proceedings of the SIGCHI Conference on Human Factors in Computing Systems, pp. 2119–2128 (2009). https://doi.org/10.1145/1518701.1519023
5. Gunning, D., Aha, D.: Darpa's explainable artificial intelligence (xai) program. AI Mag. **40**(2), 44–58 (2019). https://doi.org/10.22541/au.163699841.19031727/v1
6. Chazette, L., Karras, O., Schneider, K.: Do end-users want explanations? analyzing the role of explainability as an emerging aspect of non-functional requirements. In: 27th International Requirements Engineering conference (RE), pp. 223–233. IEEE (2019). https://doi.org/10.1109/re.2019.00032
7. Köhl, M.A., Baum, K., Langer, M., Oster, D., Speith, T., Bohlender, D.: Explainability as a non-functional requirement. In: 27th International Requirements Engineering Conference (RE), pp. 363–368. IEEE (2019). https://doi.org/10.1109/re.2019.00046
8. Feit, F., Metzger, A., Pohl, K.: Explaining online reinforcement learning decisions of self-adaptive systems. In: International Conference on Autonomic Computing and Self-Organizing Systems (ACSOS), pp. 51–60. IEEE (2022). https://doi.org/10.1109/acsos55765.2022.00023
9. Camilli, M., Mirandola, R., Scandurra, P.: Xsa: explainable self-adaptation. In: 37th International Conference on Automated Software Engineering, pp. 1–5. IEEE (2022). https://doi.org/10.1145/3551349.3559552
10. Li, N., Cámara, J., Garlan, D., Schmerl, B.: Reasoning about when to provide explanation for human-involved self-adaptive systems. In: International Conference on Autonomic Computing and Self-Organizing Systems (ACSOS), pp. 195–204. IEEE (2020). https://doi.org/10.1109/acsos49614.2020.00042

11. Straub, R., Sihler, F., Torbati, A., Wang, C., Groner, R., Klös, V., Tichy, M.: Explainability in Self-Adaptive Systems: A Systematic Literature Review. In: 51st Euromicro Conference on Software Engineering and Advanced Applications (SEAA). Springer (2025)

12. Li, N., Adepu, S., Kang, E., Garlan, D.: Explanations for human-on-the-loop: a probabilistic model checking approach. In: 15th International Symposium on Software Engineering for Adaptive and Self-Managing Systems, pp. 181–187. IEEE (2020). https://doi.org/10.1145/3387939.3391592

13. Wohlrab, R., Cámara, J., Garlan, D., Schmerl, B.: Explaining quality attribute tradeoffs in automated planning for self-adaptive systems. J. Syst. Softw. **198**, 111538 (2023). https://doi.org/10.1016/j.jss.2022.111538

14. Suman, R.R., Mall, R., Sukumaran, S., Satpathy, M.: Extracting state models for black-box software components. J. Object Technol. **9**(3), 79–103 (2010). https://doi.org/10.5381/jot.2010.9.3.a3

15. Arrieta, A.B., et al.: Explainable artificial intelligence (xai): concepts, taxonomies, opportunities and challenges toward responsible ai. Information fusion **58**, 82–115 (2020). https://doi.org/10.1016/j.inffus.2019.12.012

16. Langer, M., et al.: What do we want from explainable artificial intelligence (xai)?-a stakeholder perspective on xai and a conceptual model guiding interdisciplinary xai research. Artif. Intell. **296**, 103473 (2021). https://doi.org/10.1016/j.artint.2021.103473

17. Ribera, M., Lapedriza García, À.: Can we do better explanations? a proposal of user-centered explainable ai. CEUR Workshop Proceedings (2019)

18. Meske, C., Bunde, E., Schneider, J., Gersch, M.: Explainable artificial intelligence: objectives, stakeholders, and future research opportunities. Inf. Syst. Manag. **39**(1), 53–63 (2022). https://doi.org/10.1080/10580530.2020.1849465

19. Nunes, I., Jannach, D.: A systematic review and taxonomy of explanations in decision support and recommender systems. User Model. User-Adap. Inter. , 393–444 (2017). https://doi.org/10.1007/s11257-017-9195-0

20. Chazette, L., Klös, V., Herzog, F., Schneider, K.: Requirements on explanations: a quality framework for explainability. In: 30th International Requirements Engineering Conference (RE), pp. 140–152. IEEE (2022). https://doi.org/10.1109/re54965.2022.00019

21. Chazette, L., Brunotte, W., Speith, T.: Explainable software systems: from requirements analysis to system evaluation. Requirements Eng. **27**(4), 457–487 (2022). https://doi.org/10.1007/s00766-022-00393-5

22. Samek, W., Wiegand, T., Müller, K.R.: Explainable artificial intelligence: Understanding, visualizing and interpreting deep learning models. arXiv preprint arXiv:1708.08296 (2017)

23. Cheng, S.W., Garlan, D., Schmerl, B.: Evaluating the effectiveness of the rainbow self-adaptive system. In: ICSE Workshop on Software Engineering for Adaptive and Self-Managing Systems, pp. 132–141 (2009). https://doi.org/10.1109/SEAMS.2009.5069082

24. Bures, T., Gerostathopoulos, I., Hnetynka, P., Keznikl, J., Kit, M., Plasil, F.: Deeco: an ensemble-based component system. In: Proceedings of the 16th International ACM Sigsoft Symposium on Component-based Software Engineering, pp. 81–90 (2013). https://doi.org/10.1145/2465449.2465462

25. Gerostathopoulos, I., Pournaras, E.: Trapped in traffic? a self-adaptive framework for decentralized traffic optimization. In: 14th International Symposium on Software Engineering for Adaptive and Self-Managing Systems (SEAMS), pp. 32–38. IEEE (2019). https://doi.org/10.1109/seams.2019.00014

26. Shin, Y.J., Liu, L., Hyun, S., Bae, D.H.: Platooning legos: an open physical exemplar for engineering self-adaptive cyber-physical systems-of-systems. In: 2021 International Symposium on Software Engineering for Adaptive and Self-Managing Systems (SEAMS), pp. 231–237 (2021). https://doi.org/10.1109/seams51251.2021.00038

27. Weyns, D., Calinescu, R.: Tele assistance: a self-adaptive service-based system exemplar. In: 10th International Symposium on Software Engineering for Adaptive and Self-Managing Systems, pp. 88–92. IEEE (2015). https://doi.org/10.1109/SEAMS.2015.27

28. Gil, E.B., Caldas, R., Rodrigues, A., da Silva, G.L.G., Rodrigues, G.N., Pelliccione, P.: Body sensor network: a self-adaptive system exemplar in the healthcare domain. In: International Symposium on Software Engineering for Adaptive and Self-Managing Systems (SEAMS), pp. 224–230 (2021). https://doi.org/10.1109/SEAMS51251.2021.00037

29. Gerasimou, S., Calinescu, R., Shevtsov, S., Weyns, D.: Undersea: an exemplar for engineering self-adaptive unmanned underwater vehicles. In: 12th International Symposium on Software Engineering for Adaptive and Self-Managing Systems (SEAMS). pp. 83–89. IEEE (2017). https://doi.org/10.1109/seams.2017.19

30. Maia, P.H., Vieira, L., Chagas, M., Yu, Y., Zisman, A., Nuseibeh, B.: Dragonfly: a tool for simulating self-adaptive drone behaviours. In: 14th International Symposium on Software Engineering for Adaptive and Self-Managing Systems (SEAMS), pp. 107–113. IEEE (2019). https://doi.org/10.1109/seams.2019.00022

31. Moreno, G., Kinneer, C., Pandey, A., Garlan, D.: Dartsim: an exemplar for evaluation and comparison of self-adaptation approaches for smart cyber-physical systems. In: 14th International Symposium on Software Engineering for Adaptive and Self-Managing Systems (SEAMS), pp. 181–187. IEEE (2019). https://doi.org/10.1109/seams.2019.00031

32. Iftikhar, M.U., Ramachandran, G.S., Bollansée, P., Weyns, D., Hughes, D.: Deltaiot: a self-adaptive internet of things exemplar. In: 12th International Symposium on Software Engineering for Adaptive and Self-Managing Systems (SEAMS), pp. 76–82. IEEE (2017). https://doi.org/10.1109/SEAMS.2017.21

33. Provoost, M., Weyns, D.: Dingnet: A self-adaptive internet-of-things exemplar. In: 14th International Symposium on Software Engineering for Adaptive and Self-Managing Systems (SEAMS), pp. 195–201. IEEE (2019). https://doi.org/10.1109/SEAMS.2019.00033

34. Bergenhem, C., Shladover, S., Coelingh, E., Englund, C., Tsugawa, S.: Overview of platooning systems. In: Proceedings of the 19th ITS World Congress, Oct 22-26, Vienna, Austria (2012) (2012)

Ethics-Based Requirements for Engineering Cyber-Physical Systems: A Literature Study

Yelyzaveta Kurkchi$^{(\boxtimes)}$ ⓘ and Catia Trubiani ⓘ

Gran Sasso Science Institute, L'Aquila, Italy
{yelyzaveta.kurkchi,catia.trubiani}@gssi.it

Abstract. The increasing adoption of complex systems, such as Cyber-Physical Systems (CPS), in daily activities poses novel research challenges that need to be tackled, and ethics comes into play as a crucial requirement for engineering and assuring the quality and trust of modern CPS. The goal of this paper is to elicit the requirements when foreseeing ethics-based principles fully intertwined in CPS. Our literature study builds upon the grounded theory methodology to grasp knowledge on ethical aspects in the domain of CPS, thus deriving a set of requirements that need to be considered when engineering these systems. We select 56 papers as relevant for our scope, and results are represented in a catalog that shows ethics-based requirements and their interdependencies. Within the catalog, we derive 58 ethics-based concerns and 156 dependencies, thus contributing to shed light on the complexity of handling ethics as a first-class concern when engineering CPS. The main contribution of this paper is the elicitation of a various set of ethics-based requirements that emerge in the literature, thereby reporting their diversity and discussing their interdependencies. Our study highlights that *Privacy, Security, Transparency, Fairness,* and *Trust* represent the main ethics-based concerns, hence engineering CPS calls for the development of methodologies that make an attempt to handle such concerns.

Keywords: Ethics-Based Requirements · Cyber-Physical Systems · Literature Study

1 Introduction

Cyber-Physical Systems (CPS) have been defined in the literature as an evolution of embedded systems, mostly due to a novel interplay between software and hardware components that fosters new research challenges [30,44]. Increasingly often, CPS are being deployed in real-world critical infrastructures (such as warehouse logistics and production monitoring [28,79], but also hospitals and farmhouses [40]) therefore their behavior is of key relevance for our daily lives.

Recently, there were a series of serious real-life incidents that strongly demonstrate the need to consider *ethics* in CPS. For instance, robots were capturing and sharing intimate moments of individuals, hence exhibiting privacy breaches [25], while cyber assistants such as Siri [31] and Alexa [48] have exposed private

D. Taibi and D. Smite (Eds.): SEAA 2025, LNCS 16081, pp. 254–272, 2026.
https://doi.org/10.1007/978-3-032-04190-6_16

information, thereby violating data confidentiality. These scenarios pose serious questions about consent, privacy, and the responsible use of technology in our daily activities. In essence, it is well understood that the ethical aspects of the CPS are not only theoretical, but they have a deep influence on humans, therefore reflecting on society.

Ethical aspects of CPS are also considered by the European Parliament [16] to provide insights into the related and unintended impacts of the possible evolution of CPS technology. The integration of CPS into various aspects of our daily lives raises important ethical considerations regarding issues such as privacy, security, transparency, accountability, and fairness, thus contributing to societal impact [16]. Ethics-based concerns in CPS involve ensuring that these systems are designed with respect for individuals' rights. The ethical guidelines must address potential risks in data collection and ensure informed consent, data protection, and privacy safeguards. Both the research community and software development companies share the responsibility to reflect such guidelines, hence engineering CPS calls for protecting human rights while reducing the possibility of biases and discrimination [54].

This paper inherits the considerations pointed out by the Scientific Foresight study of the European Parliament [16] and focuses on understanding how moral-based principles have been expressed in the context of CPS. A key factor for these systems is represented by the trade-off between the humans' willingness and machines' autonomy, since CPS are in charge of deciding when a machine should take action, but the humans may intervene in an unpredictable way, with the risk of interfering. Behind these trade-off decisions, we foresee a complex process of responsibility that finds its roots in the sound specification of ethics-based requirements. To address this challenge, our research focuses on understanding which ethics-based concerns are expressed in the literature and how they are connected to each other, thereby aiming to provide support for engineering CPS. We make use of the grounded theory methodology [75] to elicit from the literature which ethics-based requirements (and their connections, if any) are defined in the context of CPS. We do acknowledge that the very same definition of *Ethics* is indeed not unique, but we stick to a comprehensive description that presents it as being represented by accepted beliefs guiding human behavior [43]. Our literature study highlights several facets of ethics: we consider 56 papers from which we derive 58 ethics-based requirements, connected by 156 identified interdependencies, thus providing evidence on the complexity of pursuing ethics in engineering CPS. We think this literature study represents the primary step towards identifying actionable recommendations for engineering CPS.

In summary, the main contributions of this paper are: (i) a literature study that captures the diversity of defying ethics in CPS; (ii) the development of a catalog that reports a various set of ethics-based requirements along with their interdependencies. The goal is to support software engineers in understanding which requirements need to be considered towards foreseeing ethics as a first-class concern in CPS. Replication data are publicly available [41].

2   Related Work

Recent European initiatives and studies have highlighted the importance of incorporating ethical requirements into the design of CPS to ensure human-centered development [16, 36]. As anticipated in Sect. 1, a key challenge in CPS lies in addressing the trade-off between human intent and machine autonomy. CPS must determine when a machine should take an action while still allowing human intervention, which may, however, introduce the risk of interference and unintended harm. Despite growing attention, the complexity and interconnection of ethical principles in CPS are frequently underexplored. This indicates the need for a thorough investigation into how ethical requirements are defined in the literature and if there exist dependencies among such requirements.

Kwan et al. [43] conduct a relevant study that explores how to build trust in software through transparency and ethics. While ethics is addressed as a standalone concept in their analysis, the primary focus remains on trust as the central concern. This work recognizes ethical principles relevant to trustworthy software, but it does not intend to extract or relate ethical requirements. Cysneiros et al. [14] propose a core set of Non-functional requirements (NFRs) that should be considered while aiming to develop socially responsible software. They identify trust, ethics, privacy, safety, security, and transparency as key NFRs. While this study provides valuable insights into ethical concerns and their interdependencies, it primarily focuses on general-purpose software rather than cyber-physical systems, and its conceptual foundation is grounded in the Corporate Social Responsibility (CSR) literature. Rahman and Adaji [57] conduct a systematic literature review to investigate factors influencing the ethical perception of persuasive technologies across many application domains. This study identifies factors as autonomy, consent, data privacy, transparency, and addictive design strategies as having a significant impact on users' ethical judgments. While the paper provides a valuable list of ethical concerns, it does not explicitly address CPS or investigate the interdependencies between the identified factors.

Summarizing, to the best of our knowledge, existing studies (i) focus on other concepts, e.g., trust, or (ii) rely on domain-specific foundations like CSR or persuasive technologies, or (iii) consider ethical concerns without examining their interdependencies. This paper makes an effort to extract ethics-based requirements and reasoning on their interdependencies within the specific context of CPS, thus addressing a relevant gap in the literature.

3   Research Methodology

Our research method aims to collect a body of knowledge to facilitate the understanding of ethics-based concerns in CPS. In the following, we describe the research questions and the adopted research approach. The results and their reproducibility are guaranteed by a replication package [41], thus enabling the inspection of all the methodological steps.

3.1 Research Questions

Our literature study is mainly driven by two research questions. **RQ1:** *what are the ethics-based requirements in CPS?* **RQ2:** *which interdependencies can arise among these requirements when engineering CPS?* The motivation for focusing on the requirements is that they represent what humans expect from CPS, hence they need to be handled in the software development process. As a consequence, software developers need to be aware of such requirements and their possible interactions when engineering these systems.

3.2 Research Approach

We make use of the *Grounded Theory Literature Review Method* [6,73,75], i.e., a systematic review approach that generates theories from qualitative data without preset hypotheses [6]. In the context of requirements engineering, Grounded Theory proves particularly advantageous due to its capacity for discovering patterns and facilitating the elicitation of concepts [75]. For instance, the grounded theory research approach has been recently adopted in [43] to study how to achieve trust in software systems. One of the main benefits is that this research methodology offers a structured and traceable approach for generating theory directly from unstructured qualitative data sources.

We refer to Wolfswinkel et al. [73] that propose the *Grounded Theory Literature Review Method* in five iterative stages: (1) *Define*—identifying data sources, search terms, and inclusion/exclusion criteria; (2) *Search*—conducting a literature search; (3) *Select*—refining studies through reading titles, abstracts, scanning, and full reading for review; (4) *Analyze*—using open, axial, and selective coding activities to build dependencies among the identified concepts; and (5) *Present*—synthesizing findings into a coherent overview with key insights and decisions made during the review process. In the following, we detail the listed operational steps.

Define. We gather literature studies by identifying IEEE Xplore and Scopus as relevant data sources, since they have been used by similar studies [43,57]. The search string is defined as follows:

(ethics *OR* ethical *OR* "moral principle") *AND* (requirement *OR* concern) *AND* ("cyber-physical" *OR* "cyber physical")

We define the following inclusion/exclusion criteria for our literature study.
Inclusion Criteria:

✓ The paper is written in English;
✓ The paper has been peer-reviewed;
✓ The paper includes the specification of ethical requirements in the context of CPS;

✓ The paper includes a discussion that can be exploited to establish interdependencies among ethical requirements in the context of CPS.

Exclusion Criteria:

✗ The publication year is older than 2014;
✗ The paper is a duplicate one, or it is a shorter version of already included publications;
✗ The full text of the paper is not available;
✗ The paper is out of topic (i.e., the search terms are used for other purposes).

Search. The literature search has been performed in September 2024, and the initial set of studies was constituted of 196 papers.

Select. We consistently apply the inclusion and exclusion criteria across a three-stage selection process. In the first stage, we screen the title and abstract of each paper. In the second stage, we perform a quick scan of the full paper to assess its overall relevance. In the third stage, we conduct a thorough full-text reading to ensure the study meets all the stated criteria. Conflicts during the review process were resolved through collaborative discussions between the authors. One author conducted the search and initial selection, while the other provided supervision, oversight, and resolved any disagreements regarding inclusion to ensure consistency and relevance in the final selection. As a result, 56 papers were included for analysis, specifically [2–5, 8–13, 17–24, 26, 27, 29, 32–35, 37–39, 42, 45–47, 49–53, 55, 56, 58–65, 67–71, 74, 76, 77, 80].

Analyze. We review each paper, noting relevant findings and insights. We perform *open coding* [73] by analyzing text for key concepts, which we interpret in our context as ethical requirements, and categorizing them systematically.

Table 1. Open Coding Matrix (partial)

Article	Concept				
	Ethics	*Privacy*	*Transparency*	*Fairness*	...
[4]	x		x	x	
[51]	x	x	x	x	
[61]	x	x			
[3]			x		

Each concept's association with its respective paper was recorded in a matrix. Table 1 reports some of the considered articles, the columns show an excerpt of the concepts we derived from the literature study, e.g., *Ethics*, *Privacy*, *Transparency*, and *Fairness*. It is worth remarking that it is a partial matrix for illustration purposes only, the full information is reported in the replication package [41].

Let us describe the reasoning behind the open coding matrix. Ambritta et al. [4] highlight the importance of ethics, transparency, and fairness in human-centered systems. Ethics is presented as a complex concept since it involves different cultures, societies, and beliefs. We do share the statement that there is no unique way to look at and explain ethics. Transparency emerges as the measure that supports the verification of the decision-making process while taking into account the reasons that contribute to the decisions. Fairness instead refers to the goal of providing predictions and classifications that are not affected by biases. As another example, Mezgar et al. [51] include many concepts in their study, emphasizing a large number of requirements (e.g., privacy, accountability, safety and security, transparency and explainability, fairness and nondiscrimination, human control of technology, professional responsibility, and promotion of human values) in the context of collaborative robot (cobot) cells. These ethical requirements are considered essential for guiding the transition from experimental setups to industrial applications, ensuring that cobots operate responsibly within Cyber-Physical Enterprises. Serpanos [61] primarily focuses on the technical, legal, and societal challenges posed by CPS. The author indicates several concepts that are safety, security, privacy, reliability, and legal liability (see replication package [41]). In Table 1 we report privacy (besides ethics) that emerges from the discussion in [61] on safeguarding data and ensuring dependable system behavior.

Summarizing, we are aware that building the open coding matrix is a tedious and error-prone process, and this represents a threat to validity of our research methodology. However, it is also a way to capture a broad set of ethics-based requirements that find their roots in various domains and applications.

Table 2. Axial and Selective Coding Matrix (partial)

Concept	Contribution Type	Severity	Target	Source
Ethics	Positive	Help	Trust	[4,51]
Transparency	Positive	Help	Fairness	[32,74]
Manipulation of Sensor Data	Negative	Hurt	Reliability	[53]
Sanctionability	Positive	Make	Responsibility	[77]

Axial coding [73] is defined in the literature as the activity by which new concepts are identified and linked to one another, as well as to those from open coding, to build a deeper understanding of the phenomenon under investigation, in our case—Ethics in CPS. *Selective coding* [73] involves integrating concepts identified during open and axial coding with a central goal, which in our study is Ethics. Each interdependency is annotated with its contribution type (positive or negative) and its level of severity (help, make, or hurt). Table 2 presents an excerpt from our axial and selective coding matrix. Let us explain the reasoning behind it. Mezgar et al. [51] emphasize that *Ethics* is essential for building *Trust*, particularly in the context of human-robot collaboration, where humans have to trust the machines. Similarly, another study [4] notes that ethics supports building trust by ensuring that advanced technologies operate safely, respect privacy, prevent discrimination, and comply with legal standards. As another example, Table 2 illustrates a positive dependency between *Transparency* and *Fairness*. Woolley et al. [74] indicate that transparency helps promoting fairness by allowing stakeholders to clearly understand how decisions are made, thereby addressing concerns related to inclusion, accuracy, privacy, and trust. Moreover, integrating explainable AI into CPS strengthens transparency by making system decisions more understandable and accessible to users. This increased transparency helps identify and reduce biases in automated processes, thereby supporting more fair and equitable outcomes [32]. Table 2 also reports a negative contribution, i.e., the *Manipulation of Sensor Data* contradictory affects the *Reliability* of the perception process, which degrades the performance of the navigation and planning layers, and ultimately affects the behaviors of robotic systems [53].

Summarizing, similarly to the open coding matrix, we are aware that building the axial and selective coding matrix is an error-prone process, and this represents a threat to validity of our research methodology. However, it is also a way to establish dependencies among the identified ethical requirements, thus supporting software developers in the task of understanding which design strategies or solutions might be more appropriate when engineering CPS.

Present. For presentation purposes, we build a catalog whose legend is reported in Table 3. Concepts are depicted as nodes, while interdependencies are captured through edges. The connections between concepts elicited from either axial or selective coding are mapped to the interdependencies (graphically represented as arrows) between the nodes of the catalog. These connections can be either positive or negative,

Table 3. Catalog Legend

Element	Description
	Concept
⎯⎯⎯⎯→	Help Contribution
⎯⎯⎯⎯→	Make Contribution
⎯⎯⎯⎯→	Hurt Contribution

and their severity can be one of two: help/hurt (+/- arrows) and make (++ arrow). The help/hurt severity denotes that the concept has a significant positive or negative contribution to the target, respectively. The make severity indicates that the concept contributes to enforce the parent concept.

4   Results

The results of our literature study include a high-level catalog constituted by 58 concepts and 156 interdependencies. Given the complexity of reporting on such identified concepts, in the following we provide an overview with the goal of highlighting the most relevant findings. We recall that the complete data is publicly available [41].

4.1   Overview

The graphical representation of results is in a graph-based notation, specifically the identified ethical requirements (extracted from the reviewed papers) represent the nodes of the graph, whereas the outlined dependencies (i.e., help, make, and hurt) are showed by edges labeled with a symbol that reflect the type of the dependency, see Table 3.

Our initial open coding stage has been performed by identifying 16 concepts. Through the axial and selective coding stage, we do have the opportunity to

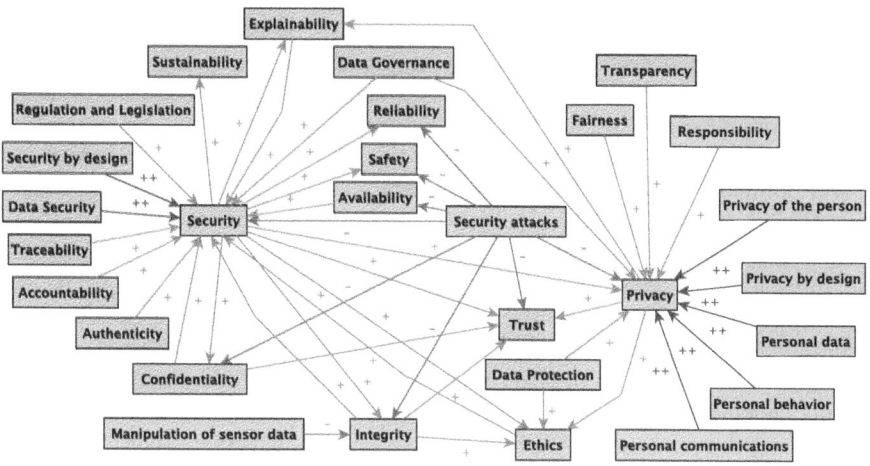

Fig. 1. Privacy and Security Detailed Catalog.

expand this set, and we come out with 58 concepts showing 156 interdependencies. To represent the results of our analysis, we applied hierarchical clustering to a concept co-occurrence matrix derived from the open coding phase. This matrix captured how often each pair of requirements appeared together, allowing us to group concepts based on their contextual dependencies. The data processing has been performed through a Jupyter Notebook including Python code that makes use of the SciPy clustering package, specifically the *fcluster* functionality[1]. For further technical details, please refer to the replication package [41]. The resulting clusters reveal this grouping: (i) Privacy and Security; (ii) Transparency, Fairness, and Trust; (iii) Regulation and Legislation, Safety, and Responsibility; (iv) Sustainability, Dignity, Equality, Autonomy, Reliability, Accountability, Awareness, and Beneficence. We use four clusters, as this number produced the most comprehensive grouping of concepts without leaving any isolated.

4.2 Privacy and Security

Privacy is a core ethical factor that protects individuals' rights while also promoting responsible and respectful treatment of sensitive information [20,22,55]. In the context of CPS, one example of privacy is described in [68] where sensor data processing triggers the need to involve individuals to control or have some influence over data since humans are interested in protecting the information about themselves.

As shown in Fig. 1, this concept has many dimensions, covering the protection of *personal behavior*, *personal communications*, *personal data*, and *privacy of the person* [63,68]. There are some further declarations of privacy, for instance *privacy by design* translates into the introduction of mechanisms that guaran-

---

[1] https://docs.scipy.org/doc/scipy/reference/generated/scipy.cluster.hierarchy.fcluster.html.

tee privacy at the level of the system design. It is an architectural solution to address privacy concerns by structuring a data collection system that incorporates privacy considerations from its foundational stage [11, 18, 52, 68]. As another example, *privacy of the person* (on Fig. 1 annotated with "++") is extracted from [63] since it emerges the need to preserve the person itself. Moreover, Vallez et al. [70] pointed out that implementing security protocols for Wi-Fi communications helps to provide privacy (as highlighted on Fig. 1 with "+" symbol).

Security must address not only traditional concerns, such as confidentiality and integrity, but also prioritize authenticity and availability, given the system's direct interactions with the physical world and the risks associated with these connections [27]. In the literature, risk mitigation is addressed by some approaches that make use of observation techniques [27], and our catalog shows interdependencies with safety, security, and resilience.

CPS may be exposed to different threats, particularly given their close interactions with humans and the sensitive nature of collected data. *Security attacks*, such as Denial-of-Service (DoS), Poisoning, Adversarial or Inference attacks, hurt (as highlighted in Fig. 1 with the arrow labeled with "−" symbol denoting a negative impact) both privacy and security [4, 53, 61]. For instance, in a DoS attack, a barrage of random packets leads to a high number of requests that the target system is not able to handle, thus generating delays [29].

4.3   Transparency, Fairness, and Trust

Transparency is instrumental in fostering ethical practices through providing visibility into decision-making and actions [2, 63, 76]. Open and transparent processes help to build an ethical culture by allowing stakeholders to make informed decisions. Transparency in CPS refers to the extent to which systems disclose the processes or parameters related to their functioning, thus understanding how a system behaves [34].

Explainability refers to the ability of a system to make its processes and decisions understandable by addressing both who the explanation is intended for and what specific information or reasoning is being conveyed [4]. CPS shall employ explainable methods that ensure understandable and tailored explanations, i.e., suited to the needs of various humans [32]. However, the explainability requirement is not uniform across all CPS. It may vary depending on the severity of potential failures and the application domain [32].

Fairness in digital and technological contexts refers to the equitable treatment of all stakeholders, framed by societal and cultural norms and guided by moral and ethical principles [74]. It considers both contextual factors, such as users' diverse backgrounds, and technological fairness metrics, which govern resource allocation and interactions within digital systems to ensure access and usability for all members of society.

Our catalog [41] shows that *Bias* hurts fairness since it can lead to unfair predictions, underscoring the critical need for diverse training data [50]. In some application domains, such as healthcare, bias can cause misdiagnoses, inappropriate treatments, or overlooked symptoms, disproportionately affecting certain groups of patients and perpetuating existing inequalities [37].

Trust is essential in promoting ethical concerns in CPS, particularly in ensuring that systems support user well-being [8,45,53]. Mezgare et al. [51] note that ethics and trust are in close reciprocal connection. A high-trust environment encourages to build better ethics, while ethical behavior supports trust building.

Trust in CPS is considered contingent upon the reliable and safe actions of core functions [29,62]. To increase ethical trust, Cioroaica et al. [13] propose using predictive simulation when evaluating ethical outcomes in a virtual setting. This proactive strategy allows for the early appraisal of ethical judgments, contributing to CPS's ethical functioning.

4.4 Regulation and Legislation, Safety, and Responsibility

Regulation, also referred to as legislation, represents a crucial instrument for CPS since laws may play an essential role in capitalizing on the benefits of systems, e.g., for environmental sustainability by regulating emissions and intelligent decision-making in various industries, therefore reducing ecological harm [21].

Implementing *Safety* measures supports ethical principles in CPS by promoting responsible behavior, mitigating risks, and ensuring individuals' well-being [55,65,71,76]. Integrating these measures into ethical considerations demonstrates a commitment to prioritizing stakeholders' well-being and protection across diverse contexts. For medical robotics, ethical principles guide the development of these systems to ensure patient's safety, privacy, and equitable access [53]. Furthermore, several studies underscore non-maleficence as a core aspect of ethically designed systems, aiming to avoid harm while supporting societal benefits [8,27,46,51].

Various factors, including failures, can lead to the loss of safety [11] (as highlighted in our catalog [41] with the arrow labeled with the "−" symbol denoting a negative impact). This inevitability underscores the significance of proactively avoiding breakdowns, especially for critical systems. Security attacks such as adversarial and poisoning harm the safety of AI and CPS [32,53,58]. Salhab et al. [58] also identify out-of-distribution inputs as a significant risk factor for machine learning models, especially in unsupervised learning.

Responsibility is fundamental to ethics in the field of CPS, and identifying the responsibilities of each stakeholder involved in their development and use poses a challenge. Embedding a sense of moral responsibility and self-understanding into these systems emphasizes the importance of responsibility in fostering ethical behavior [8,23,55,69]. For instance, Thekkilakattil and Dodig-Crnkovic [67] pointed out that the responsibility of software agents must be considered in formulating effective policies regarding the ethical aspects of CPS. Responsibility encompasses various notions, including *blameworthiness*, *accountability*, and *sanctionability* [77]. These include *collective responsibility* [67] and both *ethical and legal responsibility* [34] (as shown in our catalog [41] with "++" denoting make a contribution).

4.5 Sustainability, Dignity, Equality, Autonomy, Reliability, Accountability, Awareness, and Beneficence

Sustainability is an essential consideration in the ethical design of CPS. To align with ethical principles, smart systems should integrate sustainability as a core characteristic [8,46]. In healthcare systems, this means the ongoing ability of systems to incorporate and benefit from technologies, avoiding causing unintended consequences [37]. For software agents, social sustainability depends on ethical responsibility, underscoring the interdependence of responsibility and sustainability within CPS [67]. Laws also play an essential role in capitalizing on the benefits of technologies for environmental sustainability by establishing emissions regulating systems and intelligent decision-making in various industries, therefore reducing ecological harm [21]. As outlined in our catalog [41], sustainability also strengthens trust by balancing the common and specific interests of individual members of the social collaborative environment, ensuring ongoing, mutually beneficial collaboration that fosters lasting trust among members [8].

Autonomy of users has been recognized as foundational to ethical practice, especially in CPS [8,19,24]. For instance, in healthcare, patients should be empowered with deeper insights and accurate information, thereby enhancing their ability to make informed and autonomous decisions [37].

Dignity also needs to exhibit in intelligent systems [8,19,46], along with accessibility [53], equality [19,35,53] and promotion of human values [51] to be accomplished with ethical aspects. Javed et al. [37] highlight that ensuring broad access prevents the exacerbation of existing healthcare disparities caused by economic barriers, geographical disparities, and technological divides. Protecting human dignity within these systems also fosters trust (see catalog in [41]), as it ensures that technology respects individual values, creating a foundation for trusted interactions in different contexts [8,37].

Reliability minimizes the likelihood of system failures [58], which is essential for maintaining user confidence. A highly reliable system is expected to instill user confidence, thus enhancing overall trustworthiness. Our catalog [41] shows that the *Manipulation of Sensor Data* affects the reliability of the perception process. Besides degrading the performance of the navigation and planning layers, this influences the behavior in the control layer of robotic systems [53].

Accountability involves the responsibility for tasks that are not adequately fulfilled, emphasizing the assessment of whether an agent or group of agents failed to fulfill an assigned task despite their capability to do so. System decisions and actions need to be explained and justified to stakeholders, thus building a responsible development process [69].

As outlined in our catalog (see [41]), *Awareness* is strictly related to explainability and transparency [49], given that transparency provides insight into information sharing among agents, while explainability clarifies the reasoning behind system actions, enabling users to better anticipate and respond to system behavior. Establishing the ethical sensitivity of such decisions can be done by estimating the average user awareness based on the different aspects of the decision process [46,65], and this emphasizes the role of awareness.

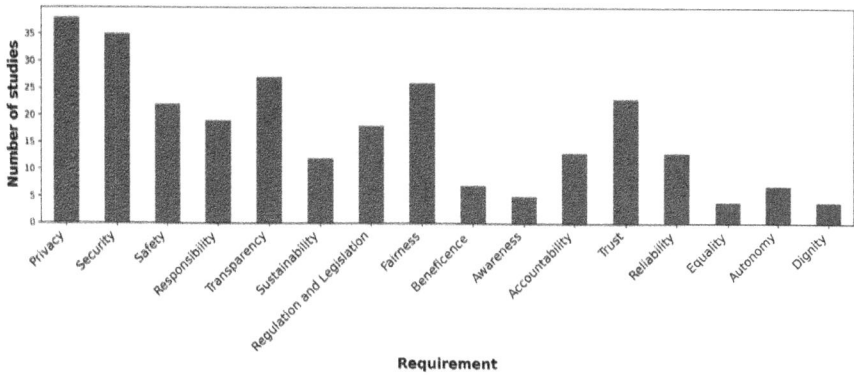

Fig. 2. Main ethics-based requirements identified in the reviewed studies.

Beneficence is meant to contribute to societal well-being by fostering fairness and inclusivity while promoting mental autonomy and equal opportunity. These principles highlight the relevance of ethical principles prioritizing positive impacts on individuals and society [52]. In the context of intelligent monitoring systems, ensuring economic benefits, welfare contributions, and positive social impact are crucial elements that align with the principle of beneficence [63].

5 Discussion

This section discusses the main lessons learned and threats to validity of our literature study. We also argue on the attempt of making use of our results in the process of engineering CPS, thus supporting software researchers and practitioners interested in future directions within this domain.

5.1 Lessons Learned

Complexity of the Elicitation Process. Our literature study highlights that eliciting ethics-based requirements for CPS is indeed not trivial. Our results confirm that in the literature, there exists a widespread range of ethics-based concepts (58) and their interdependencies (156). This indicates that several facets have been expressed as ethics-based requirements in the context of CPS, and these aspects are intertwined with positive and/or negative consequences. This paper makes an effort to highlight such complexity, thus raising attention to the need for introducing design strategies that take into account the effect of such requirements while engineering CPS.

Main Ethics-Based Requirements. Figure 2 shows an excerpt of the identified concepts (16 out of 58) and their frequency of occurrence in the selected studies. We can notice that *Privacy, Security, Transparency, Fairness,* and *Trust* represent the main ethics-based requirements, since they respectively appear in 38,

35, 27, 26, and 23 of the selected studies. Besides, *Privacy* and *Security* show a large overlap, in fact, 26 papers mention both these two requirements. This finding has its roots in the CPS domain since there is a need to guarantee privacy and security in data gathered by sensors, which is indeed a crucial aspect of CPS. The acquisition of data, the processing, the manipulation, and the access should be regulated by the involved stakeholders, thus empowering humans in decision-making and reflecting their willingness.

Concrete Examples of Ethics-Based Requirements. Among all the selected studies, one paper only [24] presents a few concrete examples of requirements in the domain of self-driving cars. *Non-maleficence* and *Beneficence* requirements are argued as follows. *Non-maleficence*: (i) the car should adopt a defensive driving behavior so that passengers do not feel nervous; (ii) the car should slow down when it gets around 20 m in the rear of a nearby car, thus avoiding hitting other cars; (iii) the car should turn off the motor every time it stops, thus avoiding environmental pollution. *Beneficence*: (i) the car should choose a quicker route towards the destination, thus passengers arrive on time; (ii) the car should stop before the crosswalk, and pedestrians have priority to cross it.

Integration of Elicited Requirements within CPS Life-Cycle Models. A recent systematic mapping study [7] points out that the agile approach is more prominent than waterfall and V-model methodologies due to its flexibility in supporting iterative development cycles and handling changes in requirements. This paper elicits ethics-based requirements that show the peculiarity of involving humans in reasoning and expressing their willingness; the capability of managing changes is of paramount importance. The agile methodology presents a stage for *requirements analysis* that is suitable for integrating the ethics-based concerns. We think this is the most appropriate stage, as identified errors are significantly less costly to fix compared to later phases, it is well assessed that correction costs increase exponentially throughout the development lifecycle [66].

5.2   Threats to Validity

Internal threats [72]. Our research methodology builds upon the grounded theory [73], including a set of decisions that may generate some biases. First, data sources, search terms, and inclusion/exclusion criteria might be questionable or performed differently. Second, the analysis process relies on judgment when extracting the concepts and their interdependencies. To smooth this process, we carefully read the full text of selected studies with the aim of collecting all the requirements they indicate. However, we do acknowledge that there might be some biases. There exist some established ethical frameworks to structure and classify the reviewed papers, for instance we can refer to the European AI Act [15] and IEEE's Ethically Aligned Design [1]. The reason for adopting grounded theory is to inductively capture how ethical requirements are represented in CPS literature without being constrained by predefined categories. This bottom-up approach aims to provide insights into how ethics is actually conceptualized by researchers, thereby reflecting the literature's actual discourse. While this may risk overlooking some formalized terms, we view our results as complementary to top-down frameworks [1,15] and plan to explore their integration as part of our future work. Furthermore, our methodology consists of presenting the findings in the form of illustrative catalogs capturing the collected basic elements, i.e., the concepts and their (help, make, and hurt) contributions. As future work, we plan to explore formal modeling techniques, such as ontologies or semantic graphs [78], to study different representations for the interdependencies among the elicited requirements. *External threats* [72]. The generalizability of our results can be limited as the study includes scientific papers only. To smooth this threat, a future mitigation plan consists of conducting a gray literature study that takes into account non-scientific literature such as industrial reports. *Construct validity* [72]. The derived findings may be biased by our analysis of the literature; to smooth this point the catalog is publicly available [41]. Software researchers and practitioners can check the analyzed papers and even perform further investigations that have not been considered in our study. For instance, we do acknowledge that our current investigation does not examine how ethical requirements have evolved over time, thus capturing a dynamic perspective of such requirements in CPS development. This may reveal the temporal evolution of technological advancements, policy changes, and societal values influencing the formulation of such requirements. A further aspect is represented by the connection of ethical requirements with different CPS domains, such as healthcare, transportation, and agriculture, where various stakeholders and domain-specific risks necessitate differentiated ethical guidance.

5.3   Implications of Analysis Results

For Researchers. We share a catalog that includes 58 ethics-based requirements and 156 interdependencies. This is the result of analyzing a collection of 56 scientific papers that may represent a valuable starting point for researchers interested in developing new methodologies when engineering CPS with the primary objective of pursuing ethics-based concerns.

For Software Practitioners. Our results showcase the need to manage a large set of ethics-based concerns when developing CPS. Given that privacy, security, transparency, fairness, and trust emerge as fundamental aspects to be considered, the recommendation is to empower CPS with design strategies that can support humans in deciding their own policies, thus fostering human-centered rules in the management of data.

6   Conclusion and Future Work

This paper proposes a literature study to shed light on ethics-based requirements for cyber-physical systems. Our results consist of a collection of 58 ethic-based requirements and 156 interdependencies that are established as relevant in the context of CPS. *Privacy, Security, Transparency, Fairness,* and *Trust* emerge as the most prominent ethics-based requirements that call for the development of methodologies addressing them. Besides, we learned that a crucial point is represented by the involvement of stakeholders in the decision-making process, given that humans differently perceive ethics; both researchers and practitioners have the challenge of empowering CPS with human-centered solutions.

As future work, besides addressing the threats to validity, we also plan to consider industrial case studies, thus understanding how to operationalize these requirements, i.e., modeling and analyzing the system behavior that emerges as the actual application of ethics-based concerns. Ultimately, we aim to gather design solutions that address the identified requirements, thereby providing actionable recommendations to practitioners. For instance, *encryption* mechanisms can be helpful in targeting the data protection requirement, as sensitive information is transformed into an unreadable format, thereby protecting it from unauthorized access. As a further design strategy, we can refer to *noise injection* which also aims to address data protection by adding random perturbations, thereby obscuring critical data [81]. This way, we can more concretely support software engineers in the task of quantitatively evaluating the evolution of CPS, thus contributing to improve the process of engineering these systems.

Acknowledgments. We would like to thank the anonymous reviewers for their valuable feedback. This work has been partially funded by the MUR-PRIN project DREAM (20228FT78M), MUR Department of Excellence 2023–2027 for GSSI, and MUR-PNRR project VITALITY (ECS00000041).

References

1. Ethically Aligned Design - A Vision for Prioritizing Human Well-being with Autonomous and Intelligent Systems, pp. 1–294 (2019). https://ieeexplore.ieee.org/document/9398613
2. Agbese, M., et al.: Governance of ethical and trustworthy al systems: research gaps in the ECCOLA method. In: International Conference on Requirements Engineering Workshops (REW), pp. 224–229 (2021)
3. Amaral, G., et al.: Trustworthiness requirements: The pix case study. In: Conceptual Modeling, pp. 257–267. Springer (2021)
4. Ambritta, P.N., et al.: Explainable AI for human-centric ethical IoT systems. IEEE Trans. Comput. Soc. Syst. **11**(3), 3407–3419 (2024)
5. Arlat, J., et al.: Towards resilient cyber-physical systems: the ADREAM project. In: International Conference on Design & Technology of Integrated Systems in Nanoscale Era (DTIS), pp. 1–5 (2014)
6. Badreddin, O.: Thematic review and analysis of grounded theory application in software engineering. Advances in Soft, Eng (2013)
7. Banerjee, A., Choppella, V.: Control software engineering approaches for cyber-physical systems: a systematic mapping study. ACM Trans. Cyber-Phys. Syst. **9**(1), 1–33 (2025)
8. Bangui, H., Buhnova, B., Ge, M.: Social Internet of Things: ethical AI principles in trust management. Procedia Comput. Sci. **220**, 553–560 (2023)

9. Bhati, R., Mittal, S.: The role and impact of artificial intelligence in attaining sustainability goals. In: International Conference on Advanced Computing and Communication Systems (ICACCS). vol. 1, pp. 2455–2458 (2023)

10. Boltz, N., et al.: Human empowerment in self-adaptive socio-technical systems. In: International Symp. on Software Engineering for Adaptive and Self-Managing Systems, pp. 200–206 (2024)

11. Calvin, C.: Architecture requirements for ethical, accurate, and resilient unmanned aerial personal remote sensing. In: International Conference on Unmanned Aircraft Systems (ICUAS), pp. 1–8 (2014)

12. Chituc, C.M.: Interoperability standards in the IoT-enabled future learning environments: an analysis of the challenges for seamless communication. In: International Conference on Communications, pp. 417–422 (2020)

13. Cioroaica, E., Buhnova, B., Tomur, E.: Towards trusting the ethical evolution of autonomous dynamic ecosystems. In: International Workshop on Software Engineering for Responsible AI, pp. 13–16 (2022)

14. Cysneiros, L.M., do Prado Leite, J.C.S.: Non-functional requirements orienting the development of socially responsible software. In: International Conference on Business-Process and Information Systems, pp. 335–342 (2020)

15. European Parliament: EU AI Act: first regulation on artificial intelligence. https://www.europarl.europa.eu/topics/en/article/20230601STO93804/eu-ai-act-first-regulation-on-artificial-intelligence (2023)

16. European Parliamentary Research Service: Scientific Foresight Unit - Ethical Aspects of Cyber-Physical Systems (2016). https://www.europarl.europa.eu/RegData/etudes/STUD/2016/563501/EPRS_STU(2016)563501_EN.pdf

17. Feng, N., et al.: Towards a formal framework for normative requirements elicitation. In: International Conference on Automated Software Engineering (ASE), pp. 1776–1780 (2023)

18. Fosch-Villaronga, E., et al.: Cloud services for robotic nurses? Assessing legal and ethical issues in the use of cloud services for healthcare robots. In: International Conference on Intelligent Robots and Systems (IROS), pp. 290–296 (2018)

19. Fosch-Villaronga, E., Millard, C.: Cloud robotics law and regulation: challenges in the governance of complex and dynamic cyber–physical ecosystems. Robot. Autonom. Syst. 77–91 (2019)

20. Gao, X., et al.: Assistance from the Ambient Intelligence: cyber-physical system applications in smart buildings for cognitively declined occupants. Eng. Appl. Artif. Intell. **123**, 106431 (2023)

21. Ge, S., et al.: The use of intelligent vehicles and artificial intelligence in mining operations: ethics, responsibility, and sustainability. IEEE Trans. Intell. Veh. **8**(2), 1021–1024 (2023)

22. Gračanin, D., et al.: Next generation smart built environments: the fusion of empathy, privacy and ethics. In: International Conference on Trust, Privacy and Security in Intelligent Systems and Applications (TPS-ISA), pp. 260–267 (2019)

23. Grady, C., Rajtmajer, S., Dennis, L.: When smart systems fail: the ethics of cyber-physical critical infrastructure risk. IEEE Trans. Technol. Soc. **2**(1), 6–14 (2021)

24. Guizzardi, R., et al.: Eliciting ethicality requirements using the ontology-based requirements engineering method. In: International Conference on Enterprise, Business-Process and Information Systems Modeling, pp. 221–236 (2022)

25. Guoarchive, E.: A Roomba recorded a woman on the toilet. How did screenshots end up on Facebook? MIT Technology Review (2022). https://www.technologyreview.com/2022/12/19/1065306/roomba-irobot-robot-vacuums-artificial-intelligence-training-data-privacy/

26. Hanna, M.J., Kimmel, S.C.: Current us federal policy framework for self-driving vehicles: opportunities and challenges. Computer **50**(12), 32–40 (2017)
27. Harkat, H., et al.: Cyber-physical systems security: a systematic review. Comput. Ind. Eng. **188**, 109891 (2024)
28. Hästbacka, D., et al.: Dynamic edge and cloud service integration for industrial IoT and production monitoring applications of industrial cyber-physical systems. IEEE Trans. Ind. Inf. **18**(1), 498–508 (2022)
29. He, H., et al.: The challenges and opportunities of human-centered AI for trustworthy robots and autonomous systems. IEEE Trans. Cogn. Dev. Syst. **14**(4), 1398–1412 (2021)
30. Hehenberger, P., Vogel-Heuser, B., Bradley, D., Eynard, B., Tomiyama, T., Achiche, S.: Design, modelling, simulation and integration of cyber physical systems: Methods and applications. Comput. Ind. **82**, 273–289 (2016)
31. Hern, A.: Apple contractors 'regularly hear confidential details' on Siri recordings. The Guardian (2019). https://www.theguardian.com/technology/2019/jul/26/apple-contractors-regularly-hear-confidential-details-on-siri-recordings
32. Hoenig, A., et al.: Explainable AI for cyber-physical systems: issues and challenges. IEEE Access **12**, 73113–73140 (2024)
33. Holzinger, A., et al.: Human-centered AI in smart farming: towards agriculture 5.0. IEEE Access **12**, 199–214 (2024)
34. Houghtaling, M.A., et al.: Standardizing an ontology for ethically aligned robotic and autonomous systems. IEEE Trans. Syst. Man Cybern. Syst. **54**(3), 1791–1804 (2023)
35. Hu, Y., et al.: Industrial Internet of Things intelligence empowering smart manufacturing: a literature review. IEEE Internet Things J. **11**(11), 19143–19167 (2024)
36. Inverardi, P.: The European perspective on responsible computing. Commun. ACM **62**(4), 64–64 (2019)
37. Javed, H., et al.: Impact of AI and dynamic ensemble techniques in enhancing healthcare services: opportunities and ethical challenges. IEEE Access **12**, 141064–141087 (2024)
38. Kanak, A., et al.: A review and strategic approach for the transition towards third-wave trustworthy and explainable AI in connected, cooperative and automated mobility (CCAM). In: International Conference on Communications (APCC), pp. 108–113 (2022)
39. Karim, H., Rawat, D.B.: Tollsonly please -homomorphic encryption for toll transponder privacy in internet of vehicles. IEEE Internet Things J. **9**(4), 2627–2636 (2021)
40. Kuntke, F., Romanenko, V., Linsner, S., Steinbrink, E., Reuter, C.: LoRaWAN security issues and mitigation options by the example of agricultural IoT scenarios. Trans. Emerg. Telecommun. Technol. **33**(5), e4452 (2022)
41. Kurkchi, Y., Trubiani, C.: Ethics-Based Requirements for Engineering Cyber-Physical Systems: a Literature Study — Replication Data (2025). https://doi.org/10.5281/zenodo.15847952
42. Kuru, K.: TrustFSDV: framework for building and maintaining trust in self-driving vehicles. IEEE Access **10**, 82814–82833 (2022)
43. Kwan, D., Cysneiros, L.M., do Prado Leite, J.C.S.: Towards achieving trust through transparency and ethics. In: International Conference on Requirements Engineering (RE), pp. 82–93 (2021)
44. Lee, E.A., Seshia, S.A.: Introduction to embedded systems: A cyber-physical systems approach. MIT Press (2016)

45. Lee, G., et al.: Security and privacy of things: Regulatory challenges and gaps for the secure integration of cyber-physical systems. In: International Conference on Information and Communication Technology (ICICT), pp. 1–12 (2019)
46. Leitão, P., Karnouskos, S.: The emergence of ethics engineering in Industrial Cyber-Physical Systems. In: International Conference on Industrial Cyber-Physical Systems (ICPS), pp. 1–6 (2022)
47. Li, X., Li, R.: A comprehensive review for four-dimensional trust management in distributed IoT. IEEE Internet Things J. **10**(24), 21738–21762 (2023)
48. Lynskey, D.: Alexa, are you invading my privacy? The dark side of our voice assistants. The Guardian (2019). https://www.theguardian.com/technology/2019/oct/09/alexa-are-you-invading-my-privacy-the-dark-side-of-our-voice-assistants
49. Maathuis, C.: Trustworthy human-autonomy teaming for proportionality assessment in military operations. In: International Conference on Applied Artificial Intelligence (ICAPAI), pp. 1–8 (2024)
50. Madichetty, S., et al.: Deep learning defined power electronic converters. IEEE Power Electron. **10**(4), 39–46 (2023)
51. Mezgár, I., et al.: Transforming experimental Cobot cell to industrial realization-an ethical AI approach. IFAC-PapersOnLine **56**(2), 7335–7341 (2023)
52. Milossi, M., et al.: AI ethics: algorithmic determinism or self-determination? The GPDR approach. IEEE Access **9** (2021)
53. Neupane, S., et al.: Security considerations in AI-robotics: a survey of current methods, challenges, and opportunities. IEEE Access **12**, 22072–22097 (2024)
54. Ozkaya, I.: Ethics is a software design concern. IEEE Softw. **36**(3), 4–8 (2019)
55. Patil, R., et al.: Medical cyber-physical systems in society 5.0: are we ready. IEEE Trans. Technol. Soc. **3**, 1–1 (2022)
56. Ponce, P., et al.: Smart cities using social cyber-physical systems driven by education. In: European Summit on Technology and Engineering Management, pp. 155–160 (2021)
57. Rahman, P., Adaji, I.: Ethics in persuasive technologies: a systematic literature review. In: International Conference on Mobile and Ubiquitous Multimedia, pp. 106–118 (2024)
58. Salhab, W., et al.: A systematic literature review on AI safety: identifying trends, challenges and future directions. IEEE Access **12**, 131762–131784 (2024)
59. Schoitsch, E.: Beyond smart systems-creating a society of the future (5.0) resolving disruptive changes and social challenges. Innovation and Transformation in a Digital World, pp. 4–7 (2019)
60. Seeam, A., et al.: Threat modeling and security issues for the Internet of Things. In: International Conference on Next Generation Computing Applications (NextComp), pp. 1–8 (2019)
61. Serpanos, D.: The cyber-physical systems revolution. Computer **51**(3), 70–73 (2018)
62. Shahraki, A., Haugen, Ø.: Social ethics in Internet of Things: an outline and review. IEEE Ind. Cyber-Phys. Syst. (ICPS) 509–516 (2018)
63. Shang, K., et al.: The development of ethically informed standards for intelligent monitoring systems of electric machines. In: International Conference on Computer Software and Applications, pp. 1598–1605 (2022)
64. Sibai, F.N.: AI crimes: a classification. In: International Conference on Cyber Security and Protection of Digital Services, pp. 1–8 (2020)
65. Šljivo, I., et al.: Agent-centred approach for assuring ethics in dependable service systems. In: Conference on Services, pp. 51–58 (2017)

66. Stecklein, J.M., Dabney, J., Dick, B., Haskins, B., Lovell, R., Moroney, G.: Error cost escalation through the project life cycle. In: 14th Annual International Symposium. No. JSC-CN-8435 (2004)
67. Thekkilakattil, A., Dodig-Crnkovic, G.: Ethics aspects of embedded and cyber-physical systems. In: International Conference on Computer Software and Applications (COMPSAC). vol. 2, pp. 39–44 (2015)
68. Torresen, J., et al.: Machine excellence tradeoffs to ethical and legal perspectives. In: International Conference on Artificial Intelligence (CAI), pp. 237–240 (2023)
69. Vakkuri, V., et al.: Ethically aligned design: an empirical evaluation of the RESOLVEDD-strategy in software and systems development context. In: Euromicro Conference on Software Engineering and Advanced Applications (SEAA), pp. 46–50 (2019)
70. Vallez, N., et al.: Eyes of things. In: International Conference on Cloud Engineering (IC2E), pp. 292–297 (2017)
71. Winfield, A.F., et al.: Machine ethics: the design and governance of ethical AI and autonomous systems. Proc. IEEE J. 107(3), 509–517 (2019)
72. Wohlin, C., Runeson, P., Höst, M., Ohlsson, M.C., Regnell, B.: Experimentation in Software Engineering. Springer (2012)
73. Wolfswinkel, J.F., Furtmueller, E., Wilderom, C.P.: Using grounded theory as a method for rigorously reviewing literature. Eur. J. Inf. Syst. 22(1), 45–55 (2013)
74. Woolley, S., et al.: Compounding barriers to fairness in the digital technology ecosystem. In: International Symp. on Technology and Society (ISTAS), pp. 1–5 (2021)
75. Würfel, D., Lutz, R., Diehl, S.: Grounded requirements engineering: an approach to use case driven requirements engineering. J. Syst. Softw. 117, 645–657 (2016)
76. Xu, Q.A., et al.: Artificial intelligence ethics and applications. In: International Conference on Industrial IoT, Big Data and Supply Chain (IIoTBDSC), pp. 322–328 (2022)
77. Yazdanpanah, V., et al.: Different forms of responsibility in multiagent systems: sociotechnical characteristics and requirements. IEEE Internet Comput. 25(6), 15–22 (2021)
78. Zahid, F., Tanveer, A., Kuo, M.M., Sinha, R.: A systematic mapping of semi-formal and formal methods in requirements engineering of industrial cyber-physical systems. J. Intell. Manuf. 33(6), 1603–1638 (2022)
79. Zhang, Y., Guo, Z., Lv, J., Liu, Y.: A framework for smart production-logistics systems based on CPS and industrial IoT. IEEE Trans. Ind. Inform. 14(9), 4019–4032 (2018)
80. Zhou, Z., et al.: Multiagent reinforcement learning: methods, trustworthiness, applications in intelligent vehicles, and challenges. IEEE Trans. Intell. Veh. 1–23 (2024)
81. Zhu, Y., Cheng, Y., Zhou, H., Lu, Y.: Hermes attack: steal DNN models with lossless inference accuracy. In: USENIX Security Symposium (2021)

Robot Mission Adaptation
with Quantitative Guarantees

Qi Zhang[1]([✉]) [iD], Ioannis Stefanakos[1] [iD], Javier Cámara[2] [iD],
and Radu Calinescu[1] [iD]

[1] Department of Computer Science, University of York, York, UK
{qi.zhang,ioannis.stefanakos,radu.calinescu}@york.ac.uk
[2] ITIS Software, Universidad de Málaga, Málaga, Spain
jcamara@uma.es

Abstract. Numerous cyber-physical systems must self-adapt in order
to satisfy complex functional and non-functional requirements despite
the uncertainty and change present in their operational environments.
Recent advances in Reinforcement Learning (RL) have enabled efficient
decision-making for self-adaptation. However, these approaches often suffer from learning bias, potentially leading to sub-optimal or even infeasible adaptations. Conversely, quantitative verification (QV) techniques
offer strong guarantees for individual requirements but are computationally costly. Hybrid RL-QV approaches have demonstrated promise, but
currently focus exclusively on quality requirements. Our paper proposes
a novel framework that integrates QV with RL, enabling decision-making
that optimizes the satisfaction of diverse requirements, including temporal event ordering and quality constraints. We validate our approach in
an assistive-care robotics scenario, where a robot must achieve multiple
goals in a specific sequence while avoiding obstacles and the supported
user. The experimental results demonstrate that our approach achieves
a balanced trade-off between safety and efficiency, converging faster to
near-optimal solutions than a Q-learning baseline.

Keywords: Cyber-physical systems · quantitative verification ·
reinforcement learning · assistive-care robotics

1 Introduction

Many cyber-physical systems operate in environments characterized by high levels of uncertainty and change, which must be handled through self-adaptation
aimed at avoiding the violation of their complex functional and non-functional
requirements [15]. Approaches to self-adaptation based on machine learning, particularly reinforcement learning (RL), offer effective decision-making capabilities
for adaptation due to their ability to learn optimal policies through interaction with the environment [10] in cyber-physical systems. However, RL methods may suffer from learning bias, potentially resulting in suboptimal or even
infeasible adaptations in safety-critical environments [31]. In contrast, decision-
making based on quantitative verification (QV) techniques, such as probabilistic

© The Author(s), under exclusive license to Springer Nature Switzerland AG 2026
D. Taibi and D. Smite (Eds.): SEAA 2025, LNCS 16081, pp. 273–289, 2026.
https://doi.org/10.1007/978-3-032-04190-6_17

model checking (PMC) [19], provides probabilistic guarantees regarding whether a system satisfies specific properties expressed in formal languages like Probabilistic Computation Tree Logic (PCTL) [19]. Despite their strong theoretical foundations, QV techniques face scalability challenges when applied to complex systems [9]. A third class of solutions that integrate RL and QV predominantly focuses on optimizing Quality of Service (QoS) levels (e.g., [22]). These approaches often fail to address other critical requirements, particularly those involving temporal ordering and safety aspects.

In this paper, we present a method for decision-making in cyber-physical systems that bridges the gap between RL and QV. Our method is capable of addressing both quantitative and temporal ordering requirements, as well as combinations thereof. This approach simultaneously handles functional requirements (such as task sequence) and non-functional requirements (such as collision avoidance). To achieve this, RL is informed by the verification of formalized requirements, expressed as temporal logic properties, which is performed during the learning process. This allows the agent to adjust its policy dynamically based on verification results. With this integrated framework, we provide a decision-making approach that optimizes the satisfaction of heterogeneous requirements, mitigating issues related to potentially infeasible adaptations generated by RL. We demonstrate the effectiveness of our approach through a motivating example in the domain of assistive care robotics. The results show an improvement in satisfying diverse requirements compared to a baseline Q-learning controller.

2   Motivating Example

In the domain of assistive care, robots are increasingly being deployed to support individuals with daily tasks, such as fetching objects, monitoring health parameters, or providing companionship [12]. These robots must operate safely and efficiently in dynamic and unpredictable home environments, where obstacles (e.g., furniture) often change position, and space is shared with humans. We consider an assistive care robot deployed to aid an elderly person (i.e., the *user*). The robot's tasks include fetching items from different rooms, delivering medications, and responding to emergencies, such as detecting a fall or health anomaly. The dynamic nature of the environment demands advanced navigation capabilities to ensure safety while maintaining efficiency. The robot must interact seamlessly with humans, respecting their space and preferences, to foster trust and usability.

a) Operation Environment: The operational environment is represented as a grid S of $N \times N$ cells, where each cell $s \in S$ incorporates a time-dependent variable that represents whether the cell contains an obstacle ($O : S \to \mathbb{B}$). We assume a discrete timeline, and for simplicity, we represent the obstacle presence in a cell at time instant $t \in [0, T]$ as $O_t(s)$.

b) Items: The environment contains a set of common household items (e.g., TV remote, cups) designated by $I = \{i_1, \ldots, i_n\}$ in different locations. A function $L_I : S \to \mathbb{P}(I)$ maps cells in the environment grid to the set of items it contains.

Table 1. Mission requirements for the assistive care robot.

Id	Description
R1	**Task Assistance Success.** The robot should respond to assistance requests by fetching in order the requested items from their locations and delivering them to the user, ensuring that the tasks are completed within acceptable time. **Formalization:** Our temporal logic formalization is adapted from the probabilistic maximization of the *sequenced visit pattern* (cf. [23, 24]): $$P_{\geq \rho_1}[\mathsf{F}^{\leq d}(p(i_1) \wedge \mathsf{F}(p(i_2) \wedge \ldots \mathsf{F}(p(i_m) \wedge \mathsf{F}(r.s = s_d))))]$$ with $\rho_1 \in [0,1]$. We assume that there is a single active request at a time (i.e., the user can request a set of items in a single request and has to wait for them to be delivered before issuing another request). There is a deadline $d \in [0,T]$ to deliver all the items grouped in a request $\{i_1, \ldots, i_m\} \subseteq I$ to location $s_d \in S$.
R2	**Collision avoidance.** The robot should avoid colliding with obstacles at all times. **Formalization:** $P_{\geq \rho_2}[\mathsf{G} \neg O(r.s)]$, with $\rho_2 \in [0,1]$.

Hence, the set of contents of a cell s at time t is designated by $L_{It}(s)$. We note that $\forall t : [0,T], \ \forall s, s' : S \bullet s \neq s' \Rightarrow L_{It}(s) \cap L_{It}(s') = \emptyset$ (an item can be in only one location at a time), and $\forall t : [0,T], \ \forall s : S \bullet O_t(s) \Rightarrow L_{It}(s) = \emptyset$ (items cannot be placed in grid cells occupied by an obstacle).

c) *User:* The user moves freely in the operational environment and issues assistance requests to the robot. The user is characterized by a pair $u = (s, A)$, where $u.s \in S$ is the position of the user in the environment, and the set of actions consists in moving to adjacent cells in four directions, and issuing requests for items. For simplicity, we designate a request by the set of requested items. Hence, the set of actions for the user corresponds to $u.A = \{up, down, left, right\} \cup \mathbb{P}(I)$.

d) *Robot:* We model the robot as a tuple $r = (s, I, A)$, where $r.s \in S$ is its position in the operation environment, $r.I \subseteq I$ is the set of items it is carrying, and A is the set of actions that it can execute, which consists of moving to adjacent cells in four directions, as well as picking items up and releasing them. Hence $r.A = \{up, down, left, right\} \cup \{p(i) \mid i \in I\} \cup \{r(i) \mid i \in I\}$, where $p(i)$ and $r(i)$ designate the pickup and release of item i, respectively. Granted, a precondition that applies to the execution of $p(i)$ is that the robot should be in the position where i is located ($\exists s' : S \bullet r.s_t = s' \wedge i \in L_{It}(s')$), whereas its execution entails that the object is removed from that position and transferred to the robot (i.e., $L_{It+1}(r.s_t) = L_{It}(r.s_t) \backslash \{i\} \wedge r.I_{t+1} = r.I_t \cup \{i\}$). The release of i can only be performed when the item is in possession of the robot ($i \in r.I_t$) and entails its incorporation into the delivery location ($L_{It+1}(r.s_t) = L_{It} \cup \{i\} \wedge r.I_{t+1} = r.I_t \backslash \{i\}$).

e) *Mission Requirements:* During operation, the robot should satisfy the set of requirements captured in the Table 1. Requirement **R1** specifies that the robot must carry out assistance tasks in a specific order and within certain time constraints. Requirement R2 emphasizes safe requirement by ensuring that the robot avoids cells with obstacles.

We note that some requirements in this scenario (such as R1), are relatively simple to express in temporal logic, but difficult to capture by a reward function that can be exploited in reinforcement learning. Indeed, obtaining a reward function able to combine multiple requirements of this nature (such as the ones provided in Table 1), further complicates matters.

3   Related Work

While the integration of formal verification is recognized as crucial for ensuring safety and quality of service (QoS) in self-adaptive cyber-physical systems, from manufacturing robots [30] and autonomous drones [27] to IoT systems [4], many current systems still do not apply these methods. For instance, the Navigation 2 [21] system demonstrates practical self-adaptation through its behavior tree-based architecture that enables autonomous navigation and recovery in dynamic environments. SUAVE [29] proposed two-layered self-adaptive systems through a ROS-based autonomous underwater vehicle implementation. However, both systems lack formal vitrifaction that would be beneficial for the safety of the systems.

By combining ML with QV techniques, specifically PMC, the authors of [4] show more reliable adaptation decisions while maintaining formal guarantees of system behavior, compared to using RL or QV independently. However, the approach only addresses quality requirements. A study demonstrates how self-adaptive systems can handle complex relationship between adaptation and task planning through formal methods and quantitative verification without using RL [3]. While a recent work [5] integrated MAPE-K feedback loops with adaptive controllers and digital twins to create an architecture for robotic manipulators, enabling dynamic control mode switching based on environment changes, it does not employ formal verification methods to validate the adaptation rules. While ML (and in particular, RL) encompasses a broad field of research, our focus is on integrating RL with formal verification, an area that has gained increasing attention in the field of self-adaptive systems research. A comprehensive survey on safe RL is presented in [8], which highlights methods that incorporate safety constraints into the learning process. The survey discusses techniques such as constrained Markov decision processes and the use of Lyapunov functions to ensure safety. However, these methods often require modifications to the RL algorithms or make assumptions about system dynamics, which may limit their practicality in certain scenarios. In this area, the authors proposed a Q-Learning based approach for online planning in self-adaptive software architecture [18], but it did not provide formal verification or guarantees about the learned adaptation policies. By using feature models to give structure to the system's adaptation space and thereby leverage additional information to guide exploration in RL, the authors [25] proposed a faster learning for large adaptation spaces. But there is no verification of safety properties during learning. Furthermore, several studies have investigated the integration of Limit Deterministic Büchi Automaton (LDBA) within reinforcement learning frameworks to enforce formal specification during the learning process [2,14,32,35]. For instance, the approach in [6] focuses on guiding RL algorithms using Linear temporal logic (LTL) specifications. This approach uses automata derived from LTL formulas to shape the reward function, ensuring that the learned policy adheres to specified temporal properties. However, it primarily guides the learning process and does not offer formal verification of the resulting policy.

The study in [26] explores robust RL by incorporating risk-sensitive control into the learning process. This approach adjusts the agent's behavior to account for uncertainties, aiming to improve the robustness of learned policies. While it addresses risk and uncertainty, it does not employ formal verification to provide guarantees about policy performance.

The MOSAIC framework [1] introduces a post-training verification approach. It first trains the RL controller fully and then verifies it through policy extraction and abstraction. Unlike methods that integrate verification into the learning process, MOSAIC adopts a sequential process. It constructs finite-state abstractions of the trained policy and uses probabilistic model checking to establish safety guarantees across different regions of the state space. A method for verifying stochastic RL policies is proposed in [11], focusing on post-training verification using PCTL formulas. The approach follows a structured three-step process: training the RL policy, converting the trained policy into a discrete-time Markov chain (DTMC) model, and verifying safety properties through model checking. This post-hoc verification strategy ensures safety properties are validated after the policy is fully trained, instead of being incorporated into the training.

Several studies, such as [7,16,33,34], have explored the use of reward machines to address formal language requirements in the learning process. However, these approaches lack rigorous formal verification methods, hampering the provision of guarantees about the learning outcomes.

To the best of our knowledge, this is the first approach to integrated a formal method, specifically in the form of probabilistic model checking of discrete-time Markov chains (DTMC) [19], into the reinforcement learning process to guide training. Compared to the Limit Deterministic Büchi Automaton (LDBA) approach, it enables a more flexible integration of formal language specifications to guide the training process.

4   Background

RL agents learn optimal policies by interacting with their environment and optimizing cumulative rewards based on feedback received. Standard RL techniques, such as Q-learning, focus on maximizing expected returns without explicitly considering safety constraints or the potential risks associated with certain actions. This limitation poses significant challenges when deploying RL agents in safety-critical applications, such as automotive or healthcare, where unsafe actions can lead to catastrophic outcomes. One of the primary concerns in applying RL to real-world scenarios is ensuring that the learned policies do not result in unsafe behaviors. RL methods inherently lack formal guarantees regarding an agent's behavior under all possible circumstances.

Probabilistic model checking [20] is a formal verification technique that can be used to analyze stochastic systems modeled as probabilistic state machines, such as a DTMC, which can be defined as a tuple $D = (S, P, \mathcal{AP}, L)$, where S represents a finite set of states, the transition probability function $P : S \times S \to [0, 1]$ specifies the probability of transitioning from one state to another, satisfying $\sum_{s' \in S} P(s, s') = 1$ for all $s \in S$, the set $\mathcal{AP}$ contains atomic propositions, and the labeling function $L : S \to 2^{\mathcal{AP}}$ assigns to each state the set of atomic propositions that are true in that state.

PMC allows for quantitative evaluation of system properties under aleatoric uncertainty. Properties to be verified are often specified in temporal logics, such as PCTL [13]. PCTL serves as a formal specification language for expressing properties of probabilistic systems, which can be interpreted over DTMCs and consist of state formulas ϕ and path formulas ψ. In the context of RL verification, PCTL enables us to formally express various safety and performance requirements. Considering $\mathbf{F}$ means "eventually" something will happen in the future, and $\mathbf{G}$ means always something holds at every point of time, a possible instantiation of R1 from Table 1 can be defined as:

$$P_{\geq 0.98}[\mathbf{F}(p(i_1) \wedge \mathbf{F}(p(i_2) \wedge \mathbf{F}(r.s = s_d)))] \tag{1}$$

Here, $P_{\geq 0.98}[...]$ denotes that the probability of the enclosed sequence of events occurring must be at least 98%. Similarly, R2 from the same table, can be expressed instanced as:

$$P_{\geq 0.95}[\mathbf{G} \neg O(r.s)] \tag{2}$$

This formal property expresses that the robot will operate safely with 95% probability, avoiding obstacles throughout its entire operation.

5   Approach

The proposed framework aligns with MAPE-K loop principles [17], providing a structured foundation for self-adaptive systems to operate effectively under uncertainty while addressing complex requirements. Its architecture, shown in Fig. 1, integrates RL and QV to ensure robust decision-making balancing effectiveness and safety.

The *Monitor* component observes the system's performance and environment, continuously collecting data that is archived in the *Knowledge base* (history) for future reference and learning. This historical data, combined with current-state run-time observations, informs the *Analyze & Plan* components, where models and policies are iteratively refined to meet temporal and quality constraints. The *Model Building* process generates and updates models based on domain requirements. The *Verification Engine* enhances adaptation policies

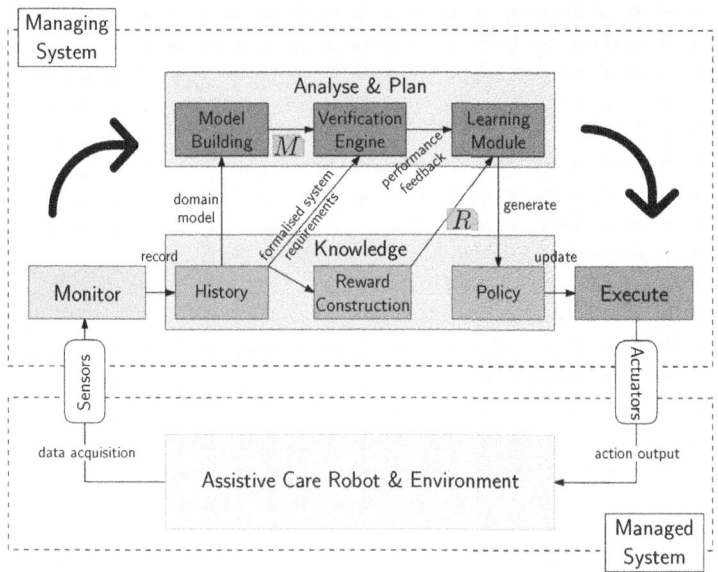

Fig. 1. Architecture diagram of the RL-QV framework.

to comply with formalized requirements. The *Learning Module*, leveraging RL, receives performance feedback to enable the adaptive optimization of policies. The *Execute* component translates validated policies into actions performed by actuators, ensuring adaptive responses to dynamic environmental conditions.

5.1 Reward Construction

Before proceeding with training, we need to define a set of reward functions that quantify the satisfaction of formalized system requirements in PCTL (as described in Sect. 2), enabling the RL approach to guide the robot's behavior effectively. For instance, the robot is required to follow a sequential ordering of tasks: visiting G_1[1], followed by G_2, and finally G_3 while avoiding obstacles. This sequential requirement can be formally expressed using PCTL as follows:

$$P_{\geq \rho}[\mathbf{F}(G_1 \wedge \mathbf{F}(G_2 \wedge \mathbf{F}(G_3)))] \tag{3}$$

For sequential goal achievement, the reward incorporates three predefined static reward components: R_{base1}, R_{base2}, R_{base3}. Each of these terms represents the base reward allocated when reaching the corresponding goal:

$$R_{\text{seqgoal}} = \begin{cases} R_{\text{base1}} \cdot (1 + P_{\text{goal1}}), & \text{if } (x, y) = G_1, \\ R_{\text{base2}} \cdot (1 + P_{\text{goal2}}), & \text{if } (x, y) = G_2, \\ R_{\text{base3}} \cdot (1 + P_{\text{goal3}}), & \text{if } (x, y) = G_3 \end{cases} \tag{4}$$

---

[1] For convenience, we use the shorthand $G_1 \equiv r.s = G_1$, $O_1 \equiv r.s = O_1$, etc. in the remainder of the paper.

If a goal is reached out of sequence, a penalty is applied. The penalty is calculated as:

$$Penalty = \min(P_{seq1}, P_{seq2}, P_{seq3}) \tag{5}$$

The probabilities for sequence violations, P_{seq1}, P_{seq2}, and P_{seq3}, are represented as follows:

$$P_{seq1} \equiv P_{=?}[\neg G_2 \ \mathbf{U} \ G_1]$$
$$P_{seq2} \equiv P_{=?}[\neg G_3 \ \mathbf{U} \ (G_1 \wedge (\neg G_3 \ \mathbf{U} \ G_2))] \tag{6}$$
$$P_{seq3} \equiv P_{=?}[(\neg G_2 \ \mathbf{U} \ G_1) \wedge (\neg G_3 \ \mathbf{U} \ (G_1 \wedge (\neg G_3 \ \mathbf{U} \ G_2)))]$$

Similarly to the sequence order construction, the obstacle avoidance property calculates the probability that the agent successfully avoids obstacles during a given period, such as 20 steps of its execution. This probability, referred to as the obstacle avoidance probability, can be defined as:

$$P_{obstacle} \equiv P_{=?}[\mathbf{G}_{\leq 20}\neg(O_1 \vee O_2)] \tag{7}$$

The agent is penalized for hitting obstacles and rewarded for avoiding them, with both penalties and rewards dynamically adjusted based on the obstacle avoidance probability during training. This hierarchical reward structure guides the agent's behavior by combining sequential rewards for reaching goals in the correct order, penalties for deviations from the goal sequence or collisions, and rewards for successfully avoiding obstacles. By integrating these elements, the framework encourages the robot to follow the desired goal sequence while discouraging deviations and promoting safe navigation.

5.2 Model Building

Employing QV requires constructing a probabilistic model of the domain that captures both the RL module's decision-making and the environment's dynamics. This model serves as the basis for verifying properties against formalized requirements. To this end, we encode our grid-world scenario as a DTMC model using the probabilistic model checker PRISM [19]. The model includes information about the robot's position, available actions, and labels indicating whether specific positions have been visited or if obstacles are present at certain locations. Due to space constraints, we omit an example of this model. However, technical details are available in our GitHub repository[2].

5.3 Verification

The integration of RL and QV combines the adaptability of learning algorithms with the rigor and assurance provided by formal verification. In this approach, QV-derived safety constraints are integrated into the learning process by restricting the agent's action space or modifying policy update rules. The framework

---

[2] https://github.com/DSDSEAA/PRISM-Guided-Learning.

Algorithm 1. PRISM-Guided Counterfactual Q-Learning

Require: Q-table Q, PRISM verifier P_{PRISM}, Exploration Rate ϵ, Learning Rate α, Discount Factor γ, maximum Experience Weighting K, Training Episodes T, Verification Interval Ω, Property P

1: **for** episode $= 1$ to T **do**
2:    $s \leftarrow s_0$, $k \leftarrow initial$ ▷ e.g. k=1
3:    **if** episode $\mathrm{mod}\,\Omega = 0$ **then**   ▷ Trigger Verification
4:       $M \leftarrow$ GENERATEMODEL(Q)
5:       $P_{PRISM} \leftarrow$ VERIFYPROPERTIES(M, P)
6:       $\varepsilon, \alpha \leftarrow$ ADAPTPARAMS($P_{\mathrm{PRISM}}, \varepsilon, \alpha$)
7:    **end if**
8:    **while** not $Env.done$ **do**
9:       $a \leftarrow \varepsilon\text{-greedy}(Q[s,:])$
10:      $(s', r) \leftarrow$ STEP(s, a)
11:      $C \leftarrow$ GENERATECOUNTERFACTUALS(s, a, s')
12:      **for** (s_c, a, s'_c) in $\{(s, a, s')\} \cup C$ **do**
13:         $r_c \leftarrow$ SHAPEREWARD($s_c, s'_c, r, P_{PRISM}, k$)
14:         $Q[s_c, a] \leftarrow Q[s_c, a] + \alpha \cdot (r_c + \gamma \cdot \max(Q[s'_c, a_c])$
                                   $-Q[s_c, a])$
15:      **end for**
16:      $s \leftarrow s'$
17:      $k \leftarrow \min(k + 1, K - 1)$ if $r > 0$ else k
18:    **end while**
19: **end for**
20: **return** $\pi(s) = \arg\max(Q[s,:])$

---

establishes a feedback loop, where the results of the verification phase directly guide the subsequent learning phase (cf. Fig. 1). This iterative process allows the agent to continuously refine its policy, striking a balance between achieving mission objectives and meeting safety requirements. This concept is realized through the PRISM-guided Q-learning algorithm (Algorithm 1), which integrates QV-based safety guarantees into the RL process.

Algorithm 1 enhances the agent's learning process by combining Q-learning with verification-based policy refinement. It details the specific steps for integrating formal verification and reward shaping within the Q-learning framework. The algorithm starts by initializing the agent's state s_0, which includes agent's spatial coordinates and a set of Boolean flags tracking goal achievements (line 2). It needs a PRISM verifier to formally verify temporal logic properties of generated policy. The hyperparameters include an exploration rate ϵ, a learning rate α, and a discount factor γ. Additionally, the method requires a maximum experience weighting K, a total number of training episodes T, and a verification interval Ω that determines how frequently formal verification is triggered, and a property specification P from PRISM that defines the logic constraints to be verified.

At each time step (line 3) within the training loop, the algorithm performs a verification step at intervals (line 3) determined by Ω. During this step:

- The generated model undergoes formal verification using PRISM (line 5). This process evaluates multiple temporal properties, including goal reachability, sequential orders, and obstacle avoidance probabilities.
- The results of verification feed into the parameters' adjustment (line 6). Parameters like the exploration rate are dynamically updated based on the agent's performance as reflected in the verification outcomes.

Next, the algorithm selects an action using an ϵ-greedy policy and executes it (line 9), transitioning to a new state while receiving an environmental reward r (line 10). From the real transition, GENERATECOUNTERFACTUALS produces a set C of hypothetical transitions to expand the agent's learning process (line 11). For both the real transition and the counterfactual transition in C, r_c is calculated based on the combination of baseline environmental feedback with weighted factors derived from the probabilities obtained through PRISM, including sequence satisfaction and obstacle avoidance metrics (line 13). Q-Value is updated (line 14), which is explained in detail in Sect. 5.4. Then, the current state is updated to the next state (line 16). Considering maximum counterfactual experience weighting K (line 17), episode terminate upon reaching terminal states through completing T episodes. The final policy π, returned at the end of the process provide a satisfaction of both sequential goal-reaching and obstacle avoidance requirements (line 20).

5.4   Learning Module

For the learning process, we use counterfactual Q-learning, in addition to regular Q-learning, which has demonstrated better performance in existing studies (e.g. [35]) to enhance the effectiveness of sequential ordering. Both of counterfactual learning and Q-Learning utilize the Temporal Difference update equation, which is a well-established off-policy method [28]. In our work, the process of updating the Q-table's values is enhanced with risk probability awareness derived from PMC. In other words, the agent learns a policy based on probabilistic quantitative rewards. Following is temporal difference update with formal verification capturing the reward-shaping and Q-update mechanism:

$$Q(s_t, a_t) \leftarrow Q(s_t, a_t) + \alpha \left[\underbrace{r_c(s_t, a_t, s_{t+1})}_{\text{Shaped Reward}} + \gamma \max_a Q(s_{t+1}, a) - Q(s_t, a_t) \right] \quad (8)$$

Here, the reward function $r(s, a)$ is formulated as a composite structure incorporating both immediate state-action rewards and temporal logic satisfaction metrics. Specifically, it is computed as a weighted sum of base navigational costs, obstacle avoidance penalties, goal achievement bonuses, and sequence violation penalties, which is achieved by incorporating the PRISM-verified sequential satisfaction probabilities.

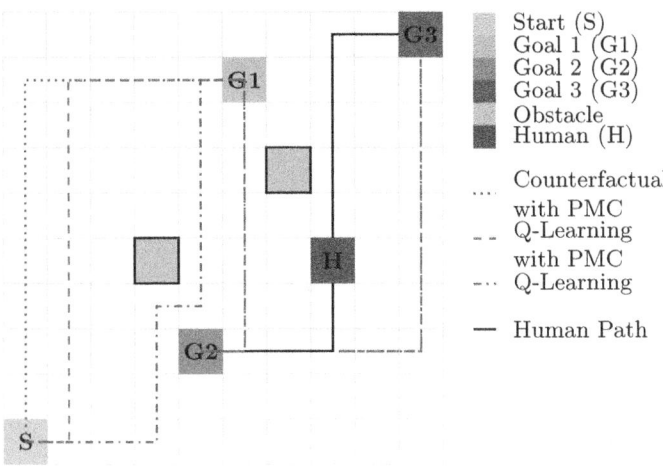

Fig. 2. Grid world model showing the agent's starting position (S), goal locations (G_1, G_2, and G_3), obstacles, and optimal paths generated by Counterfactual Learning with PMC, Q-Learning with PMC, and Q-Learning methods. Human path is represented by thick black line.

6   Evaluation

This study addresses two fundamental research questions:

- **RQ1: Effectiveness analysis.** Does our method demonstrate better performance in balancing safety and efficiency compared to the baseline method?

- **RQ2: Implementation Cost.** What is the cost of integrating PMC compared to methods without it?

6.1   Evaluation Methodology

To ensure fair comparisons between different methods, we maintained the same training parameters across all experiments. The evaluation process examined three approaches: Q-Learning with PMC, Counterfactual Learning with PMC, and Q-Learning. Each method was evaluated under identical conditions, including the number of training episodes, learning rate, discount factor, and initial exploration rate. In the first experiment, the setup utilized a 10×10 grid world environment, where a robotic agent was tasked with following an ordered sequence of visits to various locations while avoiding obstacles, as shown in Fig. 2. The robotic agent must follow a specific sequence: first moving to cupboard G1, then to cupboard G2, and finally to the kitchen cooking area (G3). This experiment enabled us to evaluate the general behavior of the different decision-making mechanisms in a static environment. In the second experiment as shown in Fig. 2, a human-robot collaboration scenario in a kitchen environment is considered comprising multiple locations. Both the robot agent and the human have to accomplish specific task sequences. The human's task sequence requires: (i) navigation to the second cupboard (G2); (ii) then movement to the kitchen (G3). Simultaneously, the robotic agent needs to execute the same sequence as previously established. This experiment aims at assessing the ability of the agent in carrying out the designated tasks while collaborating with the human and avoiding collision. Our study focused on exploring the two key research questions introduced earlier, specifically addressing the effectiveness of the three methods in achieving objectives such as adherence to sequential order and obstacle avoidance, as well as their computational cost under identical conditions.

6.2   Experimental Results

Figure 2 illustrates the multi-goal navigation paths generated by three distinct learning approaches in the grid environment. The visualization demonstrates that both Counterfactual Learning and Q-Learning with PMC generate trajectories that maintain a safe distance from obstacles while navigating between target locations. In contrast, the standard Q-Learning algorithm, operating without verification guidance, exhibits more aggressive path planning behavior, selecting trajectories that pass in close proximity to obstacles. This distinct difference in path characteristics highlights the impact of incorporating safety verification mechanisms into the learning process.

Figure 3 presents the results from Experiment I, which compared the performance of the three approaches. Figure 3acompares episode rewards across the three methods. While all methods converge to similar reward levels after training, this suggests comparable final performance in terms of reward maximization. The learning stability results (Fig. 3b) illustrate that all three methods demonstrate rapid initial convergence within the first $0.6 - 0.8$ normalized episode progress, followed by a stabilization phase. Regarding obstacle avoidance performance (Fig. 3c), both Q-Learning with PMC and Counterfactual Learning with PMC rapidly converge to optimal performance. In contrast, the standard Q-Learning approach shows lower performance, converging to approximately 0.97. This result underscores the effectiveness of PMC-guided learning in enhancing the agent's ability to avoid obstacles effectively. As illustrated in Fig. 3d) reveals that learning with PMC outperforms the standard Q-learning approach. In Fig. 3, all methods ultimately converge to their optimal performances in the complete sequence $(G_1 \rightarrow G_2 \rightarrow G_3)$ obstacle avoidance experiment, albeit with different learning trajectories. Counterfactual Learning with PMC exhibits the highest final learning rates, reaching a 0.98 completion rate by approximately 0.6 normalized episode progress. In contrast, Q-Learning with PMC shows a more gradual learning curve. The performance differences are most evident in the final learning phases.

Table 2 shows the differences in performance between the PMC-augmented methods and Q-Learning without PMC across multiple evaluation metrics for

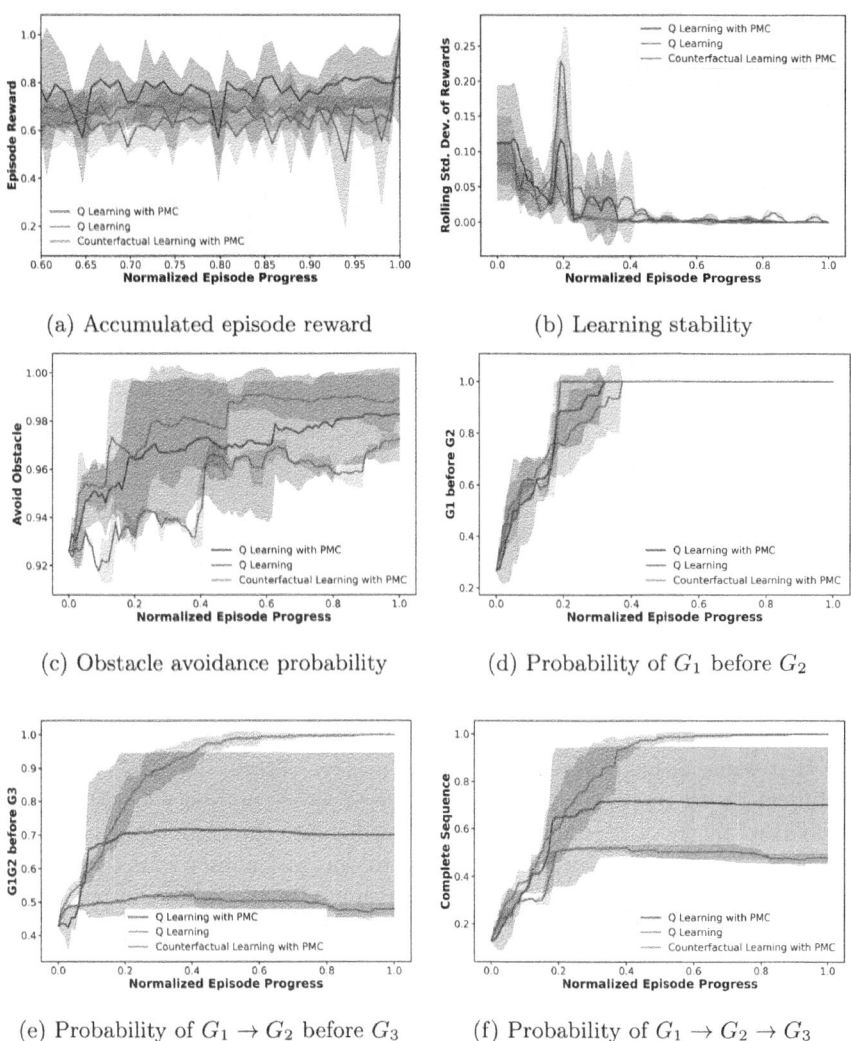

(a) Accumulated episode reward

(b) Learning stability

(c) Obstacle avoidance probability

(d) Probability of G_1 before G_2

(e) Probability of $G_1 \rightarrow G_2$ before G_3

(f) Probability of $G_1 \rightarrow G_2 \rightarrow G_3$

Fig. 3. Performance evaluation results for Experiment I: Q-learning (green color —), Q-learning with PMC (blue color —), and counterfactual learning with PMC (red color —). (Color figure online)

the Experiment II. Counterfactual Learning with PMC demonstrates a better performance, achieving higher scores (1.0000 ± 0.0000) for the G_1 before G_2 metric and high performance in obstacle avoidance (0.9942 ± 0.0012). Both PMC-based approaches show similar results for sequential tasks completion ($G_1 \rightarrow G_2$ before G_3 and $G_1 \rightarrow G_2 \rightarrow G_3$), with the Counterfactual Learning method showing slightly better results and reduced variance, indicating more consistent performance across experimental runs. Regarding stability, the data shows a

Table 2. Performance comparison of counterfactual learning with PMC (CFL–PMC), QL with PMC (QL–PMC) and QL learning methods.

Metrics	CFL–PMC	QL–PMC	QL
Performance			
$P_{seq1} \equiv P_{=?}[\neg\, G_2\ \mathbf{U}\ G_1]$	1.0000 ± 0.0000	0.9337 ± 0.1482	0.4299 ± 0.0349
$P_{seq2} \equiv P_{=?}[\neg\, G_3\ \mathbf{U}\ (G_1 \wedge (\neg\, G_3\ \mathbf{U}\ G_2))]$	0.5863 ± 0.0058	0.5835 ± 0.0085	0.5815 ± 0.0107
$P_{seq3} \equiv P_{=?}\big[(\neg\, G_2\ \mathbf{U}\ G_1) \wedge$			
$\quad (\neg\, G_3\ \mathbf{U}\ (G_1 \wedge (\neg\, G_3\ \mathbf{U}\ G_2)))\big]$	0.5863 ± 0.0058	0.5467 ± 0.0797	0.2654 ± 0.0198
$P_{obstacle} \equiv P_{=?}[\mathbf{G}_{\leq 20}\neg(O_1 \vee O_2)]$	0.9942 ± 0.0012	0.9924 ± 0.0021	0.8252 ± 0.0129
Time to Stable Convergence			
$P_{seq1} \equiv P_{=?}[\neg\, G_2\ \mathbf{U}\ G_1]$	$57.5\% \pm 9.2\%$	$47.1\% \pm 33.7\%$	$13.2\% \pm 7.9\%$
$P_{seq2} \equiv P_{=?}[\neg\, G_3\ \mathbf{U}\ (G_1 \wedge (\neg\, G_3\ \mathbf{U}\ G_2))]$	$24.6\% \pm 11.2\%$	$34.1\% \pm 20.6\%$	$17.2\% \pm 2.1\%$
$P_{seq3} \equiv P_{=?}\big[(\neg\, G_2\ \mathbf{U}\ G_1) \wedge$			
$\quad (\neg\, G_3\ \mathbf{U}\ (G_1 \wedge (\neg\, G_3\ \mathbf{U}\ G_2)))\big]$	$57.5\% \pm 9.2\%$	$56.6\% \pm 29.2\%$	$15.9\% \pm 5.7\%$
$P_{obstacle} \equiv P_{=?}[\mathbf{G}_{\leq 20}\neg(O_1 \vee O_2)]$	$4.6\% \pm 1.5\%$	$5.0\% \pm 2.2\%$	$2.8\% \pm 1.7\%$
Stability			
$Stability Metric(RewardStd.)$	8.0851 ± 0.8496	7.9684 ± 0.9014	46.6731 ± 3.1969

clear difference in reward patterns during the final learning phase. The PMC-augmented methods shows more stable reward results (8.0851 ± 0.8496 and 7.9684 ± 0.9014, respectively) compared to Q Learning without PMC, suggesting that PMC guidance helps stabilize policy behavior. The convergence metrics show that while Q-Learning without PMC achieve certain behaviors quickly, it has difficulties to guarantee the performance of more complex sequential tasks, as evidenced by the percentages showing how far into the training process. This improved performance may be attributed to the probability guidance mechanism that can avoid human movement, resulting in more stable and predictable interaction patterns.

6.3   Discussion

While Counterfactual Learning and Q-Learning with PMC demonstrate superior performance in sequence ordering tasks, they come with certain trade-offs. The learning stability graph indicates that the Counterfactual Learning method exhibits higher variance during the middle stages of the learning process in the Experiment I. This suggests that its improved logic performance may come at the cost of learning stability. This trade-off highlights the importance of balancing logic-based performance optimization with overall system reliability.

The decomposition of temporal logic into sequential sub-goals (G_1 before G_2, $G_1 \rightarrow G_2$ before G_3, and the complete sequence) introduces potential logical redundancy in the guidance mechanism. While this multi-level temporal specification approach enhances learning performance—as evidenced by improved convergence rates—it may also lead to increased computational overhead and conflicting guidance signals.

In terms of computational time, incorporating PMC guidance into Counterfactual Learning and Q-Learning introduces additional overhead compared to Q-Learning with PMC verification alone. Specifically, computation time increases by approximately 8.5% for Counterfactual Learning with PMC and 6.2% for Q-Learning with PMC in the Experiments. This overhead stems from integrating PMC guidance throughout the learning process, rather than limiting it to post-verification. Counterfactual Learning with PMC requires slightly more time than Q-Learning with PMC, with an additional 2.5% increase, due to the computational cost of counterfactual reasoning. Despite these increases, the additional computational cost remains modest, making PMC-guided learning a practical approach to improving safety and reliability.

7 Conclusion and Future Work

We presented a novel framework combining RL with QV for adaptive mission planning in robotic systems, enabling decision-making that optimizes temporal event ordering and quality constraints. The experimental results show an improved performance of the temporal logic requirements in the learning process. Moreover, PMC-guided methods outperform standard Q-Learning in adhering to task sequences and avoiding obstacles. Additionally, our approach has a better stability during learning processes in human-robot interaction scenarios. Future research directions include optimizing temporal logic formulations to minimize redundancies, balancing expressiveness and system performance, and exploring the interaction of multiple temporal properties in guided learning. We also plan to extend the scenario to a real robotic environment with realistic obstacles and objectives, in order to further evaluate the robustness and adaptability of our framework.

Acknowledgment. This work was funded by the Assuring Autonomy International Programme and the University of York's Centre for Assuring Autonomy.

References

1. Bacci, E., Parker, D.: Probabilistic guarantees for safe deep reinforcement learning (2020). https://arxiv.org/abs/2005.07073
2. Cai, M., Zhou, Z., Li, L., Xiao, S., Kan, Z.: Reinforcement learning with soft temporal logic constraints using limit-deterministic generalized büchi automaton. Journal of Automation and Intelligence (2024)
3. Cámara, J., Schmerl, B., Garlan, D.: Software architecture and task plan co-adaptation for mobile service robots. In: SEAMS, pp. 125–136 (2020)
4. Cámara, J., Muccini, H., Vaidhyanathan, K.: Quantitative verification-aided machine learning: A tandem approach for architecting self-adaptive iot systems. In: 2020 IEEE International Conference on Software Architecture (ICSA), pp. 11–22 (2020)

5. Edrisi, F., Perez-Palacin, D., Caporuscio, M., Giussani, S.: Adaptive controllers and digital twin for self-adaptive robotic manipulators. In: IEEE/ACM 18th Symposium on Software Engineering for Adaptive and Self-Managing Systems (SEAMS), pp. 56–67 (2023)

6. Fu, J., Topcu, U.: Probably approximately correct mdp learning and control with temporal logic constraints (2014). https://arxiv.org/abs/1404.7073

7. Furelos-Blanco, D., Law, M., Jonsson, A., Broda, K., Russo, A.: Hierarchies of reward machines. In: Proceedings of the 40th International Conference on Machine Learning, vol. 202, pp. 10494–10541 (2023)

8. García, J.: Fern, o Fernández: A comprehensive survey on safe reinforcement learning. J. Mach. Learn. Res. **16**(42), 1437–1480 (2015)

9. Gerasimou, S., Calinescu, R., Banks, A.: Efficient runtime quantitative verification using caching, lookahead, and nearly-optimal reconfiguration. In: 9th International Symposium on Software Engineering for Adaptive and Self-Managing Systems, pp. 115–124. ACM (2014)

10. Ghanadbashi, S., Safavifar, Z., Taebi, F., Golpayegani, F.: Handling uncertainty in self-adaptive systems: an ontology-based reinforcement learning model. J. Reliable Intell. Environ. **10**(1), 19–44 (2024)

11. Gross, D., Spieker, H.: Probabilistic model checking of stochastic reinforcement learning policies (2024). https://arxiv.org/abs/2403.18725

12. Hamilton, J., Stefanakos, I., Calinescu, R., Cámara, J.: Towards adaptive planning of assistive-care robot tasks. In: Proceedings Fourth International Workshop on Formal Methods for Autonomous Systems. EPTCS, vol. 371, pp. 175–183 (2022)

13. Hansson, H., Jonsson, B.: A logic for reasoning about time and reliability. Formal Aspects Comput. **6**(5), 512–535 (1994)

14. Hasanbeig, M., Kroening, D., Abate, A.: Deep reinforcement learning with temporal logics. In: Formal Modeling and Analysis of Timed Systems: 18th International Conference, p. 1–22. Springer-Verlag, Berlin, Heidelberg (2020)

15. Hezavehi, S.M., Weyns, D., Avgeriou, P., Calinescu, R., Mirandola, R., Perez-Palacin, D.: Uncertainty in self-adaptive systems: A research community perspective. ACM Trans. Autonomous Adaptive Syst. **15**(4) (2021)

16. Jothimurugan, K., Bansal, S., Bastani, O., Alur, R.: Compositional reinforcement learning from logical specifications. In: Advances in Neural Information Processing Systems, vol. 34, pp. 10026–10039. Curran Associates, Inc. (2021)

17. Kephart, J., Chess, D.: The vision of autonomic computing. Computer **36**(1), 41–50 (2003)

18. Kim, D., Park, S.: Reinforcement learning-based dynamic adaptation planning method for architecture-based self-managed software. In: 2009 ICSE Workshop on Software Engineering for Adaptive and Self-Managing Systems pp. 76–85 (2009)

19. Kwiatkowska, M., Norman, G., Parker, D.: Prism 4.0: Verification of probabilistic real-time systems. In: Computer Aided Verification, pp. 585–591 (2011)

20. Kwiatkowska, M.Z., Norman, G., Parker, D.: Stochastic model checking. In: Formal Methods for Performance Evaluation, 7th International School on Formal Methods for the Design of Computer, Communication, and Software Systems. LNCS, vol. 4486, pp. 220–270. Springer (2007)

21. Macenski, S., Martín, F., White, R., Clavero, J.G.: The marathon 2: A navigation system. In: IEEE/RSJ International Conference on Intelligent Robots and Systems (IROS), pp. 2718–2725 (2020)

22. Mason, G., Calinescu, R., Kudenko, D., Banks, A.: Assurance in Reinforcement Learning Using Quantitative Verification, pp. 71–96. Springer (2018)

23. Menghi, C., Tsigkanos, C., Askarpour, M., Pelliccione, P., Vazquez, G., Calinescu, R., García, S.: Mission specification patterns for mobile robots: providing support for quantitative properties. IEEE Trans. Software Eng. **49**(4), 2741–2760 (2022)

24. Menghi, C., Tsigkanos, C., Pelliccione, P., Ghezzi, C., Berger, T.: Specification patterns for robotic missions. IEEE Trans. Software Eng. **47**(10), 2208–2224 (2019)

25. Metzger, A., Quinton, C., Mann, Z.A., Baresi, L., Pohl, K.: Realizing self-adaptive systems via online reinforcement learning and feature-model-guided exploration. Computing **106**(4), 1251–1272 (2022)

26. Morimoto, J., Doya, K.: Robust reinforcement learning. Neural Comput. **17**(2), 335–359 (2005)

27. Ryan, P., Shahbeigi, S., Zou, J., Stefanakos, I., Molloy, J.: A dynamic assurance framework for an autonomous survey drone. In: Computer Safety, Reliability, and Security: 43rd International Conference, pp. 285–299. Springer (2024)

28. Shao, J., Qu, Y., Chen, C., Zhang, H., Ji, X.: Counterfactual conservative q learning for offline multi-agent reinforcement learning (2023). https://arxiv.org/abs/2309.12696

29. Silva, G.R., Pasler, J., Zwanepol, J., Alberts, E., Tarifa, S.L.T., Gerostathopoulos, I., Johnsen, E.B., Corbato, C.H.: SUAVE: An Exemplar for Self-Adaptive Underwater Vehicles. In: SEAMS. pp. 181–187 (2023)

30. Stefanakos, I., Calinescu, R., Douthwaite, J., Aitken, J., Law, J.: Safety controller synthesis for a mobile manufacturing cobot. In: Software Engineering and Formal Methods: 20th International Conference, pp. 271–287. Springer-Verlag (2022)

31. Tambon, F., Laberge, G., An, L., Nikanjam, A., Mindom, P.S.N., Pequignot, Y., Khomh, F., Antoniol, G., Merlo, E., Laviolette, F.: How to certify machine learning based safety-critical systems? A systematic literature review. Autom. Softw. Eng. **29**(2), 1–74 (2022). https://doi.org/10.1007/s10515-022-00337-x

32. Tian, D., Fang, H., Yang, Q., Yu, H., Liang, W., Wu, Y.: Reinforcement learning under temporal logic constraints as a sequence modeling problem. Robot. Auton. Syst. **161**, 104351 (2023)

33. Toro Icarte, R., Klassen, T.Q., Valenzano, R., McIlraith, S.A.: Reward machines: exploiting reward function structure in reinforcement learning. J. Artif. Intell. Res. **73**, 173–208 (2022)

34. Voloshin, C., Le, H., Chaudhuri, S., Yue, Y.: Policy optimization with linear temporal logic constraints. In: Advances in Neural Information Processing Systems, vol. 35, pp. 17690–17702. Curran Associates, Inc. (2022)

35. Voloshin, C., Verma, A., Yue, Y.: Eventual discounting temporal logic counterfactual experience replay (2023). https://arxiv.org/abs/2303.02135

Symbolic Runtime Verification and Adaptive Decision-Making for Robot-Assisted Dressing

Yasmin Rafiq[1] , Gricel Vázquez[2(✉)] , Radu Calinescu[2] ,
Sanja Dogramadzi[3] , and Robert M. Hierons[4]

[1] Department of Computer Science, University of Manchester, Manchester, UK
yasmeen.rafiq@manchester.ac.uk
[2] Department of Computer Science, University of York, York, UK
{gricel.vazquez,radu.calinescu}@york.ac.uk
[3] School of Electrical and Electronic Engineering, The University of Sheffield,
Sheffield, UK
s.dogramadzi@sheffield.ac.uk
[4] School of Computer Science, The University of Sheffield, Sheffield, UK
r.hierons@sheffield.ac.uk

Abstract. We present a control framework for robot-assisted dressing that augments low-level hazard response with runtime monitoring and formal verification. A parametric discrete-time Markov chain (pDTMC) models the dressing process, while Bayesian inference dynamically updates this pDTMC's transition probabilities based on sensory and user feedback. Safety constraints from hazard analysis are expressed in probabilistic computation tree logic, and symbolically verified using a probabilistic model checker. We evaluate reachability, cost, and reward trade-offs for garment-snag mitigation and escalation, enabling real-time adaptation. Our approach provides a formal yet lightweight foundation for safety-aware, explainable robotic assistance.

Keywords: Robot-Assisted Dressing · Symbolic Runtime Verification · Probabilistic Model Checking · Human-Robot Interaction · Adaptive Control

1 Introduction

As assistive robots become more integrated into daily life, ensuring safety and reliability during physical human-robot interaction (pHRI) remains a critical challenge [5,7,9,12]. In tasks such as Robot-Assisted Dressing (RAD) [4,14], the robot must perform close-contact assistance in coordination with a human, where garment dynamics, force disturbances, and user motion introduce runtime uncertainty. While low-level control strategies (e.g., force thresholds, compliant motions, and speed modulation) can mitigate immediate issues, they operate reactively and lack long-term task-level reasoning. This motivates the need for

© The Author(s), under exclusive license to Springer Nature Switzerland AG 2026
D. Taibi and D. Smite (Eds.): SEAA 2025, LNCS 16081, pp. 290–308, 2026.
https://doi.org/10.1007/978-3-032-04190-6_18

high-level control strategies that reason over future states and adapt using runtime feedback.

This paper presents a high-level control framework for safety-critical human-robot interaction, combining symbolic verification with runtime adaptation. While demonstrated through Robo-Assisted Dressing (RAD), the approach is methodological and generalisable to other uncertain human-in-the-loop systems.

We propose a high-level control framework that integrates parametric discrete-time Markov chains (pDTMCs) [13], Bayesian inference [2], and symbolic runtime verification [17]. Safety and performance requirements, derived from a hazard analysis [8], are formally specified using probabilistic computation tree logic (PCTL) [6]. Symbolic expressions for these requirements are precomputed using the probabilistic model checkers PRISM [16] and PARAM [13], and are evaluated at runtime using parameters updated via Bayesian inference.

The main contributions of our paper are:

- A high-level formal verification framework using a pDTMC model guided by hazard analysis.
- Integration of runtime Bayesian inference to update model parameters using sensory data and user feedback.
- Symbolic runtime verification using closed-form expressions generated with PRISM and PARAM.
- Symbolic evaluation of safety, cost, and reward properties to support dynamic adaptation and decision-making.

The RAD case study serves to ground our contribution in a real-world safety-critical setting, illustrating how the proposed framework supports runtime verification and decision-making under uncertainty. The rest of the paper is structured as follows. Section 2 reviews related work. Section 3 describes the system architecture. Section 4 defines the pDTMC model and its formal requirements, and Sect. 5 presents its symbolic analysis. Section 6 discusses practical insights and limitations. Section 7 summarises our results and outlines future work.

2   Related Work

This section reviews research at the intersection of probabilistic verification, runtime adaptation, and uncertainty quantification in robotics, particularly under pHRI settings.

Probabilistic Verification and Model Checking. Probabilistic model checking has been widely applied in robotics to provide formal guarantees over safety, reachability, and performance requirements under uncertainty. Tools such as PRISM [16] support the analysis of Discrete-Time Markov Chains (DTMCs) and verification of requirements specified in PCTL [6].

Zhao et al. [22] applied probabilistic verification to autonomous systems in extreme environments, but their approach focused on offline analysis without runtime adaptation. Similarly, Gleirscher et al. [10, 11] verified safety controllers for collaborative robots but did not incorporate runtime feedback or symbolic reasoning in human-interactive scenarios.

Bayesian Inference for Uncertainty Quantification. Bayesian learning has been used to adapt robot behaviour based on noisy perception and dynamic environments. Zhao et al. [21] proposed a framework that combines Bayesian inference with formal verification to improve robustness in autonomous systems. Similarly, Calinescu et al. present a tool for the verification and Bayesian-learned parameter inference of probabilistic world models [3]. However, they did not consider symbolic runtime evaluation or human-in-the-loop feedback.

Runtime Monitoring and Adaptive Control. Runtime monitoring techniques are often used for anomaly detection or logging, whereas runtime verification aims to formally check execution traces against temporal specifications. Kirca et al. [15] proposed a runtime monitoring framework for anomaly detection using logs, but without safety property verification. Li et al. [18] introduced a probabilistic motion planning approach that models human uncertainty, but it lacks continuous verification of safety requirements during task execution.

Our Contribution in Context: In contrast to the above, our work integrates probabilistic model checking, runtime Bayesian inference, and hazard-driven safety property verification in a human-in-the-loop context. We introduce a pDTMC model whose transition probabilities are updated at runtime using Bayesian learning. Precomputed symbolic expressions for PCTL properties are evaluated on-the-fly through parameter substitution, enabling lightweight runtime verification without re-invoking the model checker. Our framework bridges the gap between high-assurance probabilistic verification and adaptive human-aware control. It enables formal safety reasoning in real time while responding to user input, physical interaction events and task-level uncertainty during robot-assisted dressing.

3   System Overview and Modelling Framework

3.1   Robot-Assisted Dressing Context

Robot-Assisted Dressing (RAD) involves a robotic manipulator physically assisting a user in donning garments (e.g., jacket). The task is inherently collaborative, requiring safe human-robot interaction, real-time trajectory execution, and continuous hazard monitoring to ensure comfort and prevent failure. Dynamic factors such as user movement, garment deformation, and variable force profiles can lead to hazards including garment snagging or user discomfort. A robust RAD system must detect such events and respond appropriately.

In our setup, a validated low-level control system is responsible for executing motion trajectories, monitoring contact forces, and responding to user-issued verbal feedback (e.g., reports of pain). These behaviours will be detailed in a companion paper on reactive control strategies.

This paper focuses on the high-level control framework that operates above the low-level controller. It models the dressing task as a probabilistic discrete-time Markov chain (pDTMC), enabling symbolic runtime verification of safety and performance requirements. The high-level system continuously updates beliefs about task state using Bayesian inference, substitutes these into pre-computed symbolic expressions, and adaptively refines robot decision-making.

Together, this layered architecture supports both proactive and reactive responses to runtime uncertainty, advancing safe and adaptive human-robot collaboration in dressing assistance.

3.2   Low-Level Control Strategy Overview

The low-level control strategies implemented in our RAD system serve as the foundational layer for real-time hazard mitigation. These strategies were developed and validated through physical dressing trials involving simulated garment snags and user-reported discomfort. Full implementation and evaluation details are provided in our comparison study [19] The two primary strategies are:

- **Garment Snagging Control:** When excessive interaction forces are detected via integrated force sensors, the system triggers one of three responses: (a) prompt the user for assistance through a Rasa-based chatbot interface, (b) initiate autonomous recovery by adjusting the robot's trajectory, or (c) abort the task safely if mitigation fails.
- **User Discomfort Mitigation:** Enables users to express pain or discomfort through natural language commands. The robot responds by progressively reducing speed and, if needed, aborting the task.

These low-level mechanisms are essential for reactive safety during dressing and were experimentally validated across multiple dressing trials, showing effective mitigation of hazards in both user-assisted and autonomous recovery modes.

The high-level control strategies introduced in this work are designed to complement these reactive behaviours by offering predictive, symbolic reasoning capabilities through pDTMC-based runtime verification. Together, the combined architecture ensures both proactive and reactive safety handling in robot-assisted dressing.

The high-level control strategy presented in this paper focuses on symbolic reasoning and runtime verification based on the pDTMC abstraction. While the low-level controller plays a critical role in reactive execution (e.g., force compliance and trajectory recovery), it is validated through extensive experimental dressing trials but not formally verified here. A detailed account of the low-level control mechanisms and their empirical evaluation is provided in our companion study [19]. Formal verification of continuous low-level dynamics is out of scope for this work, which concentrates on symbolic guarantees and adaptive decision-making at the task level.

3.3   High-Level Control Architecture

Figure 1 illustrates the runtime-adaptive control architecture for the RAD system. The architecture integrates low-level sensor processing with high-level symbolic reasoning to support safe and responsive operation under uncertainty.

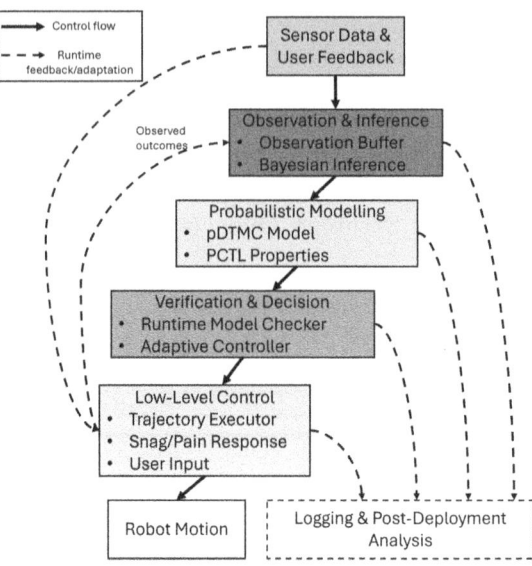

Fig. 1. High-level control architecture showing runtime adaptation via symbolic verification. Sensor inputs inform both high-level inference and low-level control actions.

At the top of the pipeline, the system receives continuous inputs from sensors (e.g., force, trajectory deviation) and verbal user feedback. These inputs are processed by an *Observation and Inference* module that maintains a buffer of recent events and uses Bayesian inference with observation ageing [1,2] to update runtime estimates of key transition probabilities (e.g., snag detection, recovery success).

These updated probabilities are injected into a symbolic *Probabilistic Model* comprising a parametric Discrete-Time Markov Chain (pDTMC) and a set of PCTL-specified safety and reliability requirements. The model is evaluated by the *Verification and Decision* layer using closed-form expressions obtained via PRISM+PARAM [13], enabling rapid runtime checks without re-invoking the model checker.

The output of this layer informs the *Adaptive Controller*, which adjusts system behaviour based on the verification results. If a safety threshold is violated (e.g., escalation risk exceeds 0.5), the system proactively transitions to compliant or abortive behaviour. Otherwise, it proceeds with recovery or continues execution.

Finally, the *Low-Level Control* layer executes trajectory plans, responds to snag and pain feedback, and integrates real-time user input. These behaviours are conditionally triggered based on the decisions verified in the upper layers. Together, this architecture ensures that the RAD system adapts at runtime to user-specific conditions while maintaining conformance with formal safety constraints. The pDTMC abstraction enables runtime introspection and supports explainability in decision-making.

3.4 Hazard Analysis and Safety Constraints

The pDTMC model and associated evaluation requirements were informed by a structured hazard analysis conducted during system design [8]. This analysis identified the following safety requirements related to task failure, user discomfort, and mitigation breakdowns, and derived constraints that the system must satisfy to maintain safe and reliable operation:

- **Limit the risk of task abortion.** The system should minimise the likelihood of entering an abort state due to unresolved snags or escalation failures.
- **Ensure reliable task completion.** The dressing task should succeed in a high proportion of executions, even under varying user behaviour and environmental noise.
- **Bound the expected cost of silent failures.** Escalations that go undetected should not incur high expected penalties, motivating prompt detection and mitigation.
- **Avoid prolonged or delayed recovery.** Mitigation pathways should resolve issues efficiently, avoiding excessive retries or delays in user or autonomous responses.

These constraints are later formalised in PCTL, and evaluated via symbolic expressions over transition parameters. This ensures that the RAD system maintains compliance with safety and comfort requirements—even in uncertain and dynamic execution contexts.

4 Snagging Model and Formal Verification

To verify safety-critical behaviour in robot-assisted dressing, we formalise the high-level control strategy as a pDTMC. This model captures task progression, garment-snag escalation, and recovery pathways as probabilistic transitions, abstracting from the robot's low-level motion control.

Model Description. The pDTMC models 10 abstract task states (Fig. 2). The initial dressing task begins in state s_0 (dressingProcess), progressing towards s_3 (dressingComplete). Potential snags are detected in s_1 (potentialSnag) or escalated undetected to s_2 (undetectedEscalation). If mitigation is required, the system enters s_4 (mitigationStrategy), choosing between human assistance s_5 (requestHRI) or autonomous resolution s_6 (autonomousResolution). Successful mitigation reaches s_7 (snagMitigated); failure results in task abortion s_8 (abortTask). All outcomes eventually transition to s_9 (moveHome) before resetting.

Formal Definition. The pDTMC is defined as a tuple $\mathcal{M} = (S, s_0, P, \mathcal{L}, \rho)$, where:

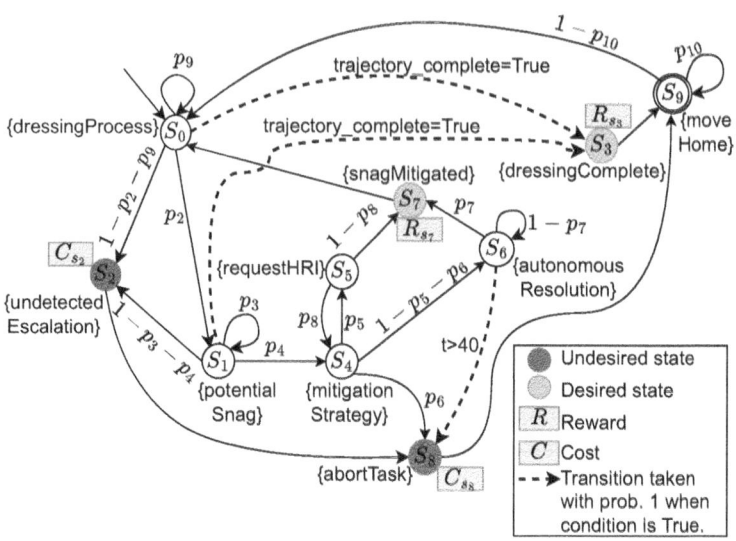

Fig. 2. Abstraction of the pDTMC RAD model. Transition probabilities $(p_{[.]})$ govern state transitions. Timeout conditions (e.g., $t = \texttt{MAX\_TIME}$ in s_6) ensure escalation resolution. Rewards $(R_{[.]})$ and costs $(C_{[.]})$ are linked to outcome states.

- S is the finite set of states. Each state is represented by:

$$s' = (s,\ t,\ \texttt{time\_step},\ \texttt{trajectory\_complete})$$

  where:
  - $s \in [0,9]$ is the current task stage.
  - $t \in [0, \texttt{MAX\_TIME}]$ tracks time in s_6 (autonomous retries).
  - $\texttt{time\_step}$ tracks progress in s_0, s_1 until trajectory completion.
  - $\texttt{trajectory\_complete}$ is a Boolean flag signalling task end.
- s_0 is the initial state: the dressing process starts with all timers at zero.
- $P : S \times S \to [0,1]$ is the parametric transition matrix governed by symbolic parameters p_1 to p_{10}, representing task observations and control uncertainties. All model transitions are defined by the PRISM model in Appendix A of the full version of this paper on arXiv [20].[1]
- $\mathcal{L} : S \to \mathcal{AP}$ labels each state with atomic propositions (e.g., **dressing Complete**), enabling property specification such as $P_{\leq 0.1}[F\ \textbf{abortTask}]$.
- $\rho : S \to \mathbb{R}_{\geq 0}$ assigns rewards and costs to terminal states, capturing success and failure outcomes. These are:
  - $R_{s_3} = BASE\_REWARD\_S3 = 20$ - base reward constant for successful dressing (used in symbolic analysis).

---

[1] For each state $s \in S$, the outgoing transition probabilities are either mutually exclusive or explicitly normalized to ensure that the total probability of leaving a state does not exceed 1. This guarantees that $\sum_{s' \in S} P(s,s') \leq 1$, preserving the validity of the DTMC semantics.

- $R_{s_7} = R\_S7 = 10$ for snag mitigation.
- $C_{s_2} = C\_S2 = 10$ for undetected escalation.
- $C_{s_8} = C\_S8 = 5$ for task abortion.

In our symbolic analysis, R_{s_3} is set to 20 as previously described; however, in the simulation, we further examine the effect of time by modelling this reward as a decayed value, as detailed below.

Reward Decay. Although cumulative reward properties are not symbolically supported by PRISM+PARAM, we model a decaying reward in the PRISM simulation model to discourage long delays in dressing completion:

$$R_{s_3} = e^{-\texttt{DECAY\_RATE}\cdot\texttt{time\_step}} \cdot BASE\_REWARD\_S3$$

with DECAY_RATE set to 0.5. This decay reward is applied during simulation-based evaluation only and is excluded from the symbolic analysis in Sect. 5, which uses the constant BASE_REWARD_S3.

Model Features. The pDTMC supports runtime verification and adaptive reasoning through:

- **Symbolic transitions:** Parametric probabilities capture runtime uncertainty in detection, recovery, and escalation.
- **Progress tracking:** trajectory_complete and time_step govern dressing task duration and allow symbolic evaluation of task timing.
- **Reward/cost abstraction:** Terminal states encode outcomes for reward-guided or risk-sensitive control.
- **Time-bounded retries:** Timeout in s_6 prevents infinite loops in autonomous recovery.

This model provides the formal basis for the symbolic evaluation in Sect. 5, and is structured to support runtime adaptation via parameter updates (see Discussion, Sect. 6).

4.1   Specification of Safety and Reliability Requirements

The safety and performance requirements identified through hazard analysis (Sect. 3.4) are formalised using Probabilistic Computation Tree Logic (PCTL) [6]. These requirements are used to evaluate the symbolic pDTMC model and guide runtime decision-making.

PCTL enables the specification of probabilistic reachability, time-bounded, and reward-bounded behaviours in discrete-time systems. For example, $P_{\leq 0.1}[F\,s = 8]$ specifies that the probability of eventually aborting the task should be no greater than 10%. Although PRISM+PARAM currently supports only reachability requirements in symbolic form, we approximate cost-based constraints using reachability proxies (see Sect. 5.3).

Finally, the following requirements formalise the core constraints derived from the hazard analysis [8]:

- **(H1) Limit the risk of task abortion**

$$P_{\leq 0.1}[F \, s = 8] \tag{1}$$

"The probability of reaching the task abort state $s = 8$ must remain below 10%."
- **(H2) Ensure reliable task completion**

$$P_{\geq 0.9}[F \, s = 3] \tag{2}$$

"The dressing task should complete successfully in at least 90% of executions."
- **(H3) Bound undetected escalation cost**

$$ExpectedCost_{s2} = C_{S2} \cdot P_{=?}[F \, s = 2] \leq MAX\_C2 \tag{3}$$

"The expected cost of undetected escalation (reaching $s = 2$) must remain within limit set by the maximum cost allowed MAX_C2." This is evaluated symbolically via a proxy expression.
- **(H4) Timely mitigation success reward**

$$ExpectedReward_{s7} = R_{S7} \cdot Pmax_{=?}[F \, s = 7] \tag{4}$$

"The system should maximise the probability of successfully mitigating snags." The expected reward is derived symbolically based on p_7 and p_8.
- **(H5) Encourage time-bounded completion**

$$P_{\geq 0.95}[F_{\leq \texttt{MAX\_TIME\_TRAJ}} \, s = 3] \tag{5}$$

"The dressing task should complete within the designated trajectory time in at least 95% of cases." This is used in simulation.

These formal specifications provide a rigorous basis for symbolic evaluation and runtime adaptation. Requirements (H1)–(H4) are fully captured by symbolic expressions derived via `PRISM+PARAM`, enabling lightweight verification through parameter substitution. Time-bounded and cumulative reward constraints are approximated or evaluated using proxy expressions where symbolic support is unavailable.

Parameter Value Ranges. The symbolic expressions for reachability and reward properties are defined over symbolic parameters p2–p10, which represent key transition probabilities within the pDTMC. For the purpose of symbolic analysis and heatmap visualisation, these parameters were evaluated over plausible ranges informed by system design, empirical dressing trials, and prior work [19]. These ranges are summarised in Table 1, and provide a safe operating envelope for runtime adaptation. During execution, these probabilities are dynamically updated using Bayesian inference, allowing the system to respond to real-time sensor data and user feedback.

Table 1. Parameter Ranges Used in Symbolic Evaluation

Parameter	Description and Range
p_2	Probability of detecting a potential snag. Range: $[0.0, 1.0]$
p_3	Probability of remaining in escalation monitoring without triggering mitigation. Range: $[0.0, 1.0]$
p_4	Probability of escalation after a detected snag. Range: $[0.4, 0.9]$
p_5	Probability of selecting human-assisted recovery. Range: $[0.5, 1.0]$
p_6	Probability of selecting autonomous recovery. Range: $[0.0, 0.5]$
p_7	Success probability of autonomous recovery. Range: $[0.0, 1.0]$
p_8	Failure probability of human intervention. Range: $[0.0, 1.0]$
p_9	Probability of escalation failure leading to task abort. Range: $[0.0, 0.3]$
p_{10}	Probability of returning to idle/home state. Range: $[0.9, 1.0]$

4.2 Symbolic Model Checking Using PRISM+PARAM

We perform symbolic verification of the pDTMC model using the `PRISM+PARAM` toolchain [13]. This enables closed-form algebraic expressions to be extracted for PCTL reachability requirements such as $P_{=?}[F\, s = 2]$ and $P_{=?}[F\, s = 7]$. These symbolic expressions are parametrised over key transition probabilities (e.g., p_2, p_3, p_7, p_8), enabling analysis of system behaviour under uncertainty and variable conditions. Each expression captures the probability of reaching a safety-critical or goal state as a function of the system's current configuration. In our evaluation (Sect. 5), these expressions are visualised over bounded parameter ranges to assess risk and performance.

While the symbolic engine supports reachability queries, cumulative reward properties of the form $P_{=?}[C \leq T]$ are not currently supported. To address this, we reformulate cost and reward analysis using proxy expressions—multiplying the reachability probability by a fixed reward or cost scalar (e.g., see Eq. 3).

4.3 Runtime Verification Using Bayesian Learning

To enable adaptive decision-making, the RAD system performs runtime verification by updating the transition probabilities of the pDTMC using Bayesian learning. This approach applies *observation ageing* [1,2], giving more weight to recent observations while discounting older data, allowing the system to respond to changes in user behaviour or task context.

The updated estimate of transition probability $p_{ij}^{(k)}$ after k observations is computed as:

$$p_{ij}^{(k)} = \frac{c_0}{c_0 + k} p_{ij}^{(0)} + \frac{k}{c_0 + k} \cdot \frac{\sum_{l=1}^{k} w_l \cdot x_{ij}^{(l)}}{\sum_{l=1}^{k} w_l} \qquad (6)$$

Here, $p_{ij}^{(0)}$ is the prior estimate, c_0 controls the influence of the prior, and $w_l = \alpha^{-(t_k - t_l)}$ applies exponential ageing to past observations. The decay factor $\alpha \geq 1$ controls how quickly older data are discounted. The variable $x_{ij}^{(l)}$ denotes the observed occurrence (typically binary: 1 for a transition observed from state i to j at time step l, and 0 otherwise). The symbolic expressions derived offline for reachability and reward properties (e.g., $P_{=?}[F \, s = 7]$) are evaluated at runtime by substituting dynamically updated probabilities (e.g., p_7, p_8). This enables lightweight, real-time runtime verification to guide decision-making during dressing without invoking a model checker.

4.4   How the Adaptation Mechanism Operates

During execution, the RAD framework monitors real-time sensor data (e.g., garment force feedback, joint velocities) and user responses to update transition probabilities within the symbolic pDTMC model. These updated probabilities are substituted into precomputed symbolic expressions for key safety and performance requirements, allowing the framework to assess evolving risk and make informed decisions at runtime.

If a safety threshold is violated—e.g., the probability of task abortion exceeds a bound—the framework responds on two levels:

1. **Low-Level Control Actions**: The controller immediately enters a compliant mode, reducing speed and applied force or halting movement to mitigate user discomfort or mechanical risks.
2. **High-Level Adaptation**: The symbolic pDTMC model is used to track evolving task context. Bayesian learning updates transition probabilities (e.g., likelihood of snag, success of user or autonomous recovery), enabling dynamic substitution into symbolic expressions (e.g., $P_{=?}[F \, s = 2]$). This supports real-time risk evaluation without rechecking the model.

For example, if repeated snagging is observed under specific motion trajectories, the estimated probability of transitioning from s_0 (dressingProcess) to s_1 (potentialSnag) increases. Similarly, success rates of user-assisted or autonomous mitigation are reflected in the transition probabilities to s_5 and s_6. Rather than storing full execution histories, the Bayesian update loop maintains a compact belief over transition likelihoods. This integration of symbolic runtime evaluation and adaptive control ensures that the framework responds promptly to immediate safety threats while gradually improving high-level decision-making in dynamic, user-specific contexts.

5   Evaluation

To assess the robot-assisted dressing system under uncertainty, we adopt a symbolic evaluation approach using the PRISM+PARAM toolchain. Our evaluation focuses on three core aspects: (i) the reachability of critical failure or success-ful mitigation states, (ii) the expected cost of failure, and (iii) the expected reward of mitigation success. Rather than relying on simulation-based numeri-cal experiments, we symbolically evaluated the parametric DTMC model across key parameters that influence the system's decision-making behaviour—such as the reliability of snag detection, human and autonomous recovery, and escala-tion outcomes. These symbolic expressions allow for offline design analysis and enable runtime reasoning via parameter substitution. Each symbolic property is visualised using annotated heatmaps and contour plots.

5.1   Symbolic Analysis of Snag Mitigation

We analysed the probability of successfully mitigating a snag (i.e., reaching state $s = 7$) in the pDTMC model (Fig. 2) using PRISM+PARAM. The property of inter-est is the symbolic reachability expression $P =?[F\ s = 7]$, which quantifies the probability of eventually reaching the successful mitigation state under varying system conditions.

A closed-form symbolic expression was derived, capturing the joint influence of snag detection, escalation, and recovery through both autonomous and human intervention. To aid interpretability, we introduce the following terms:

- $\alpha = p_2.p_4$—snag detection and escalation,
- $\beta = p_5.p_8$—failed recovery attempts via human mitigation,
- $\delta_k = p_7^k$—recursive retries of autonomous recovery (limited to 40 steps).

A simplified excerpt of the symbolic expression extracted using PRISM+PARAM is shown below. This highlights the compound effects of detection ($\alpha = p_2 \cdot p_4$), human failure ($\beta = p_5 \cdot p_8$), and recursive autonomous retries ($\delta_k = p_7^k$):

$$P_{s=7} = \cfrac{10000\,\beta^2 \cdot \alpha^2 - 20000\,\beta \cdot p_5 \cdot \alpha^2 + \cdots + 100\,\beta \cdot \delta_2 \cdot \alpha^2 + \cdots + 10\,\delta_1 \cdot \alpha + \cdots}{10000\,\beta^2 \cdot \alpha^2 - 20000\,\beta \cdot p_5 \cdot \alpha^2 + \cdots + 200\,\beta^2 \cdot p_5^2 \cdot p_2 + \cdots + 40\,p_2 + 1} \tag{7}$$

The symbolic expression captures nested recovery paths and enables com-parison of mitigation effectiveness. The full expression is provided in Appendix B of the arXiv version [20].

Figure 3 shows the evaluated symbolic expression over a range of human and autonomous recovery capabilities. A safety threshold contour at $P = 0.5$ distinguishes high-risk scenarios (top-left) from safer operating regions (bottom-right). The *Safe Zone* is defined where the probability of reaching sate $s = 7$ (snag mitigation) exceeds 0.6. This typically occurs when the autonomous

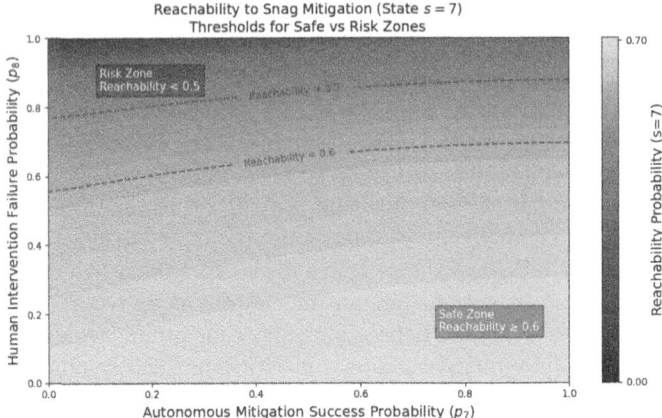

Fig. 3. Probability of successful mitigation (s_7) varying autonomous mitigation success probability (p_7) and human failure probability (p_8). Lighter regions indicate higher success.

mitigation success probability (p_7) is high, or the human intervention failure probability (p_8) is low.

The results highlight an important compensation effect: strong performance in one recovery pathway (human or autonomous) can offset weaknesses in the other. For example, even when p_7 is low, maintaining a low p_8 (i.e., reliable human intervention) preserves high overall success rates. Conversely, increasing p_7 improves robustness against human failure.

> Our findings reinforce the benefit of hybrid, adaptive recovery strategies in which human-in-the-loop support and autonomous recovery dynamically compensate for each other. Our symbolic reachability analysis provides both an interpretable quantitative basis for design decisions and an analytical foundation for runtime adaptation.

5.2   Symbolic Analysis of Snag Escalation Failure

We now analyse the second key reachability property of interest $P_{=?}[F \ s = 2]$. This property quantifies the probability of reaching state s_2, representing an undetected escalation of a detected snag—a critical failure scenario in the robot-assisted dressing task.

Using `PRISM+PARAM`, we symbolically evaluated this property while varying two key parameters: (1) the probability of detecting a potential snag, p_2, and (2) the probability of remaining in the monitoring state without triggering mitigation, p_3. These directly govern the likelihood of silent escalation, with all other transitions held constant to isolate their effect.

The symbolic expression extracted from `PRISM+PARAM` was algebraically simplified and normalised. It captures both direct and indirect contributions to s_2

reachability via recursive monitoring cycles. A normalised version was evaluated over a grid of p_2 and p_3 values, revealing the influence of detection and monitoring performance.

The simplified symbolic expression is given by:

$$P = \frac{100\,P_3 \cdot P_2 + 98\,P_2 - 99}{88\,P_2 - 100} \tag{8}$$

This captures the trade-off between detection (p_2) and monitoring (p_3). While the numerator increases linearly with p_2 and p_3 the denominator introduces a non-linear effect governed solely by p_2. As p_2 improves, the denominator approaches zero from below, causing a steep drop in failure probability—a clearly reflected in the heatmap gradient (Fig. 4). The PRISM+PARAM-generated expression is valid for $88p_2 - 100 > 0$; outside this range, results are clipped to $[0, 1]$ for validity.

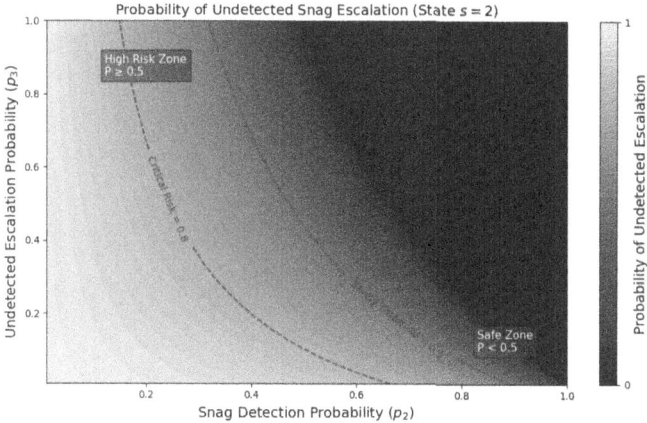

Fig. 4. Reachability probability of undetected snag escalation (s_2) as a function of detection probability p_2 and undetected escalation probability p_3. Lighter regions indicate higher failure probability. Dashed contour lines highlight key risk thresholds: $P = 0.5$ (Safety Threshold) and $P = 0.8$ (Critical Risk). Annotated zones mark high-risk and safe regions.

Figure 4 illustrates the reachability landscape for undetected snag escalation, based on the symbolic property $P_{=?}[F\ s = 2]$. The heatmap shows how the failure probability varies over a grid of snag detection probabilities (p_2) and escalation persistence probabilities (p_3).

The *"Safe Zone"* $(P < 0.5)$ occurs in the lower-right corner, where detection is strong $(p_2 \rightarrow 1)$ and escalation is unlikely $(p_3 \rightarrow 0)$. The *"High Risk Zone"* $(P \geq 0.5)$ appears in the upper-left corner, where detection is weak $(p_2 \rightarrow 0)$ and escalation is persistent $(p_3 \rightarrow 1)$.

The red dashed contours highlight two thresholds: the safety threshold at $P = 0.5$, and the critical risk boundary at $P = 0.8$, making conditions where the likelihood of silent failure is dangerously high. Notably, the steep gradient along the p_2 axis reveals that even modest gains in detection capability can substantially reduce failure risk.

> These findings highlight the system's high sensitivity to snag detection accuracy and provide actionable insights for both formal verification and runtime adaptation. Prioritising high p_2 values can significantly lower the probability of silent escalation, thereby improving overall safety.

5.3 Proxy Cost Analysis of Undetected Snag Escalation

To evaluate the cost implications of undetected snag escalation, we adopt a proxy formulation based on the symbolic reachability expression for state $s = 2$ (undetected escalation). Specifically, we compute Eq. 3, where C_{S2} is a fixed penalty associated with entering the failure state. This formulation provides a lightweight approximation of the impact by scaling the symbolic reachability with the defined failure cost. It enables efficient evaluation during runtime and captures the increasing cost of failure under unsafe parameter regimes.

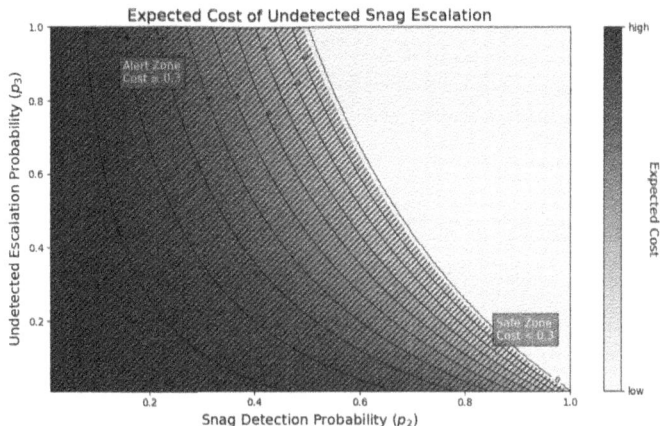

Fig. 5. Expected cost of undetected snag escalation, computed as $C_{S2} \cdot P_{=?}[F\ s = 2]$, over varying detection probability (p_2) and escalation persistence (p_3). The *Alert Zone* (Cost ≥ 0.3) highlights failure-prone conditions; the *Safe Zone* (Cost < 0.3) reflects robust detection and recovery.

Figure 5 visualises this cost landscape. The *"Alert Zone"* (Cost ≥ 0.3) arises when snag detection is weak ($p_2 \to 0$) and the likelihood of persistent, undetected escalation is high ($p_3 \to 1$). The hatched area clearly marks this high-risk region.

Conversely, the *"Safe Zone"* (Cost < 0.3) occupies the lower-right corner of the heatmap, where effective detection significantly reduces escalation risk and associated penalty. Compared to the raw reachability view in Fig. 4, this proxy formulation adds interpretability by contextualising risk in cost terms.

> Our proxy formulation allows the system to perform low-overhead runtime checks against unsafe conditions using a single symbolic expression and supports proactive adaptation in safety-critical human-robot interactions.

5.4   Symbolic Analysis of Mitigation Success

This analysis focuses on the expected reward associated with successful snag mitigation, represented by reaching state s_7 in the pDTMC model. Since cumulative reward properties cannot currently be symbolically evaluated in PRISM+PARAM, we compute the expected reward using a scaled reachability formulation from Eq. 4, where R_{S7} is a fixed reward assigned to successful mitigation. The symbolic reachability expression $P_{=?}[F\ s = 7]$ was derived in Sect. 5.1 and captures the combined effect of detection, escalation, and mitigation strategies (both human and autonomous).

To examine reward trade-offs, we fix parameters $p_2 = 0.9$, $p_4 = 0.7$, and $p_5 = 0.65$, and vary:

- p_8: the failure probability of human intervention,
- p_7: the success probability of autonomous recovery.

The symbolic expression is evaluated over this 2D parameter space, and the expected reward is computed accordingly.

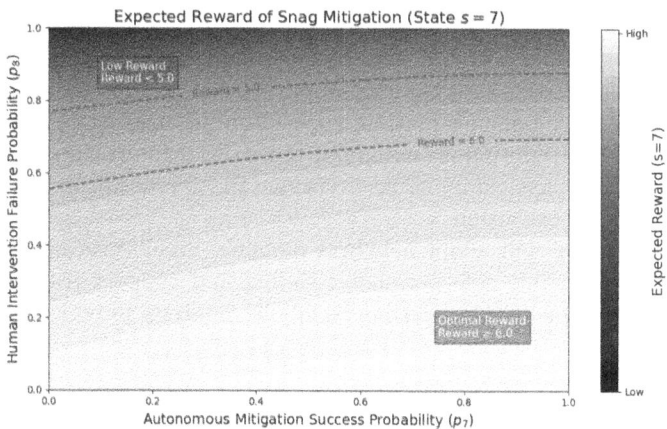

Fig. 6. Expected reward for mitigation success ($s = 7$) evaluated from the symbolic expression over human intervention failure (p_8) and autonomous recovery success (p_7). The *Optimal Reward* zone arises when both modalities are reliable; *Low Reward* emerges when both pathways are likely to fail.

Figure 6 illustrates the resulting expected reward surface. A clear *"Optimal Reward"* zone emerges in the bottom-right corner ($p_8 \to 0$, $p_7 \to 1$), where both mitigation pathways are highly effective. In contrast, the *"Low Reward"* region appears when both autonomous and human strategies are likely to fail ($p_7 \to 0$, $p_8 \to 1$). Contour lines at reward thresholds $R = 5.0$ (Lower Bound) and $R = 6.0$ (Optimal Reward) delineate these regions.

> These findings reinforce the hybrid design principle: strong performance in either the human-in-the-loop or autonomous recovery pathway can compensate for the other's limitations, enabling robust, reward-aware adaptation in safety-critical scenarios.

6   Discussion

Our approach demonstrates how hazard-informed modelling, symbolic verification, and Bayesian adaptation can be combined to support safe, adaptive decision-making in human-robot collaboration. The symbolic evaluation presented in this work offers several critical insights into the safety and adaptability of RAD systems operating under uncertainty. It also shows how requirements like snag escalation and mitigation success can be interpreted as algebraic functions of runtime-updated parameters such as p_2, p_3, p_7, and p_8, from our model example. Analysis of such functions allow the controller to identify and avoid unsafe regions of the parameter space proactively. Our approach addresses a fundamental challenge in pHRI: managing runtime uncertainty with provable safety assurances.

A key benefit is that runtime verification does not require re-running a model checker. Once symbolic expressions are precomputed, parameter substitution enables real-time evaluation with minimal computational overhead. This facilitates explainable decision-making and supports runtime assurance. One current limitation is that symbolic evaluation is based on an abstract model that does not fully capture the continuous dynamics of low-level controllers. Further work will integrate these physical dynamics to bridge the gap between symbolic guarantees and physical execution.

Future validation will adopt a hybrid pipeline. Simulators such as Gazebo or Isaac Sim will enable safe parameter tuning and support transfer learning for physical deployment. Our current symbolic analysis provides a feasibility baseline.

7   Conclusion and Future Work

This paper introduced a high-level control framework for safety-critical human-robot interaction that integrates symbolic verification with runtime adaptation. Although we demonstrated the framework using a Robot-Assisted Dressing (RAD) scenario, the contribution is methodological in nature and applicable to a wide range of human-in-the-loop systems with probabilistic behaviour and runtime uncertainty.

Our pDTMC-based framework enables fast runtime evaluation of PCTL properties using precomputed symbolic expressions and dynamically updated transition probabilities via Bayesian inference. This supports real-time adaptation and safety assurance. Results identify safe parameter regimes and alert zones requiring mitigation.

Future work includes closer integration of the symbolic model with low-level control. Due to RAD's complexity, we focus on snagging mitigation, but full assurance requires broader scenario modelling. We will explore a multi-model RAD world [3] to support system-level verification. The framework can extend to robot-assisted undressing (RAUD), which may involve different constraints (e.g., constrained-to-unconstrained transitions) and hazards (e.g., visibility or balance loss), requiring adapted models and PCTL properties. Finally, our approach can generalise to pHRI systems with inherent uncertainty and variability. Future work will focus on validating its generality and effectiveness through extensive case studies and experimental evaluations.

Acknowledgment. This work was funded by the EPSRC projects EP/V026747/1 'UKRI Trustworthy Autonomous Systems Node in Resilience' and EP/V026801/2 'UKRI Trustworthy Autonomous Systems Node in Verifiability'.

Disclosure of Interests. The authors declare that they have no conflict of interest relevant to the content of this work.

References

1. Calinescu, R., Johnson, K., Rafiq, Y.: Using observation ageing to improve Markovian model learning in qos engineering. In: Proceedings of the 2nd ACM/SPEC International Conference on Performance Engineering, pp. 505–510 (2011)
2. Calinescu, R., Rafiq, Y., Johnson, K., Bakır, M.E.: Adaptive model learning for continual verification of non-functional properties. In: Proceedings of the 5th ACM/SPEC international conference on Performance engineering. pp. 87–98 (2014)
3. Calinescu, R., Yaman, S.G., Gerasimou, S., Vázquez, G., Bassett, M.: Verification and external parameter inference for stochastic world models. arXiv preprint arXiv:2503.16034 (2025)
4. Chance, G., Jevtić, A., Caleb-Solly, P., Dogramadzi, S.: A quantitative analysis of dressing dynamics for robotic dressing assistance. Front. Robot. AI **4**, 13 (2017)
5. Christoforou, E.G., Avgousti, S., Ramdani, N., Novales, C., Panayides, A.S.: The upcoming role for nursing and assistive robotics: opportunities and challenges ahead. Front. Digital Health **2**, 585656 (2020)
6. Ciesinski, F., Größer, M.: On probabilistic computation tree logic. Validation of Stochastic Systems: A Guide to Current Research pp. 147–188 (2004)
7. Cooper, S., Di Fava, A., Vivas, C., Marchionni, L., Ferro, F.: Ari: the social assistive robot and companion. In: 2020 29th IEEE International Conference on Robot and Human Interactive Communication (RO-MAN), pp. 745–751. IEEE (2020)

8. Delgado Bellamy, D., Chance, G., Caleb-Solly, P., Dogramadzi, S.: Safety assessment review of a dressing assistance robot. Front. Robot. AI **8**, 667316 (2021)
9. Erickson, Z., Gangaram, V., Kapusta, A., Liu, C.K., Kemp, C.C.: Assistive gym: A physics simulation framework for assistive robotics. In: 2020 IEEE International Conference on Robotics and Automation (ICRA), pp. 10169–10176. IEEE (2020)
10. Gleirscher, M., Calinescu, R.: Safety controller synthesis for collaborative robots. In: 2020 25th International Conference on Engineering of Complex Computer Systems (ICECCS), pp. 83–92. IEEE (2020)
11. Gleirscher, M., Calinescu, R., Douthwaite, J., Lesage, B., Paterson, C., Aitken, J., Alexander, R., Law, J.: Verified synthesis of optimal safety controllers for human-robot collaboration. Sci. Comput. Program. **218**, 102809 (2022)
12. Gu, D., Andreev, K., Dupre, M.E.: Major trends in population growth around the world. China CDC weekly **3**(28), 604 (2021)
13. Hahn, E.M., Hermanns, H., Wachter, B., Zhang, L.: PARAM: A model checker for parametric Markov models. In: Computer Aided Verification: 22nd International Conference, CAV 2010, Edinburgh, UK, July 15-19, 2010. Proceedings 22, pp. 660–664. Springer (2010)
14. Jevtić, A., Valle, A.F., Alenyà, G., Chance, G., Caleb-Solly, P., Dogramadzi, S., Torras, C.: Personalized robot assistant for support in dressing. IEEE Trans. Cognitive Dev. Syst. **11**(3), 363–374 (2018)
15. Kirca, Y.S., Degirmenci, E., Demirci, Z., Yazici, A., Ozkan, M., Ergun, S., Kanak, A.: Runtime verification for anomaly detection of robotic systems security. Machines **11**(2), 166 (2023)
16. Kwiatkowska, M., Norman, G., Parker, D.: PRISM 4.0: Verification of probabilistic real-time systems. In: 23rd International Conference on Computer Aided Verification (CAV'11), pp. 585–591 (2011)
17. Kwiatkowska, M., Norman, G., Parker, D.: Probabilistic symbolic model checking with prism: A hybrid approach. Int. J. Softw. Tools Technol. Transfer **6**(2), 128–142 (2004)
18. Li, S., Figueroa, N., Shah, A., Shah, J.A.: Provably Safe and Efficient Motion Planning with Uncertain Human Dynamics. In: Proceedings of Robotics: Science and Systems. Virtual, July 2021. https://doi.org/10.15607/RSS.2021.XVII.050
19. Rafiq, Y., James, B.A., Xu, K., Hierons, R.M., Dogramadzi, S.: Hybrid control strategies for safe and adaptive robot-assisted dressing (2025). https://arxiv.org/abs/2505.07710
20. Rafiq, Y., Vázquez, G., Calinescu, R., Dogramadzi, S., Hierons, R.M.: Symbolic runtime verification and adaptive decision-making for robot-assisted dressing (2025). https://arxiv.org/abs/2504.15666
21. Zhao, X., Gerasimou, S., Calinescu, R., Imrie, C., Robu, V., Flynn, D.: Bayesian learning for the robust verification of autonomous robots. Commun. Eng. **3**(1), 18 (2024)
22. Zhao, X., Robu, V., Flynn, D., Dinmohammadi, F., Fisher, M., Webster, M.: Probabilistic model checking of robots deployed in extreme environments. In: Proceedings of the AAAI Conference on Artificial Intelligence, vol. 33, pp. 8066–8074 (2019)

Configurable Abstraction of Signals Using Signal Temporal Logic

Ulrike Engeln[✉][iD] and Sibylle Schupp[iD]

Institute for Software Systems, Hamburg University of Technology,
Hamburg, Germany
{ulrike.engeln,schupp}@tuhh.de

Abstract. Abstractions of signals help to avoid cognitive and storage overload, especially in systems with many signals such as cyber-physical systems (CPS). For assessing trends and reconstructing behavior, it often suffices to have a rough understanding how signals evolve, e.g., whether their behavior is monotonic or periodic. This work provides a configurable abstraction of signal behavior, where signals are described by a sequence of oscillation and linear patterns. We formalize templates of both behaviors in parameterized signal temporal logic (PSTL) and provide an algorithm that abstracts signals in terms of those patterns. The templates are configurable such that they allow for choosing the level of abstraction, e.g., by limiting the approximation error or the minimal oscillation frequency. For segmentation of the signal, we solve an optimization problem using a modified version of TeLEx. The evaluation demonstrates that configuration of the patterns is suitable to define the level of abstraction. Further, on control output from the ARCH wind turbine benchmark and flow data from medical ventilation, it demonstrates that the abstraction method can be applied to real-world signals.

Keywords: time series · signal temporal logic (STL) · temporal formula learning · pattern-based abstractions

1 Introduction

Modern cyber-physical systems (CPS) record large amounts of signals, e.g., sensor values, internal calculation results, or events. The data are required for several applications as debugging or analysis of environmental conditions. However, interpreting and storing all data is a difficult task. One way to ease interpretability and reduce storage need is to abstract the data and provide or store a reduced version of the original values.

We propose a novel technique for a configurable abstraction of signals that describes them by predefined patterns. Existing works on piecewise approximation, e.g., linearization for path compression [13], provide such abstractions in terms of polynomial patterns. However, for real-world signals with oscillations as the controller output sketched in Fig. 1, piecewise polynomial approximation is not effective as it would result in many small segments. For analysis, it often

D. Taibi and D. Smite (Eds.): SEAA 2025, LNCS 16081, pp. 309–326, 2026.
https://doi.org/10.1007/978-3-032-04190-6_19

suffices to know whether a signal evolves monotonically or oscillates. Therefore, in this work, we decide to cover monotonic and periodic behavior, and abstract signals in terms of oscillations and linear functions. By those patterns, the signal from Fig. 1 can be abstracted into three instead of five segments, which would result from linear approximation. Since such high-level abstraction is not adequate for all applications, we further introduce configuration parameters, which allow for definition of the abstraction level.

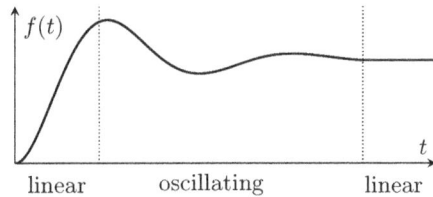

Fig. 1. Segmentation of a simple, settling signal.

Signal temporal logic (STL) [15] is a logic for formal specification of temporal properties of signals. It is both understandable by humans and suited for automatic monitoring. STL is thus an adequate choice for detecting patterns from signals for configurable abstractions. Figure 2 illustrates the complete abstraction process. Based on pattern templates defined in PSTL, we perform a segmentation of the signal such that we can abstract the segments in terms of the provided patterns. For reduction of the signal, the goal of the segmentation is to reduce the signal to a small number of segments

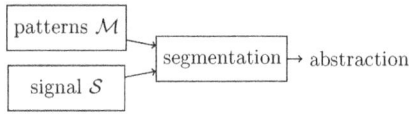

Fig. 2. Framework for abstraction

that can be abstracted to the provided patterns. We find such segmentation through STL formula learning. Existing work on STL formula learning, e.g., TeLEx [10], focuses on learning formulae that optimize the distance to the traces. In our work, we define base patterns that inherently guarantee an upper bound on the deviation between specification and signal. For the optimization problem the distance is not of interest. Instead, for finding a segmentation with few segments, our goal is to find formulae that globally hold for a segment of maximal length.

The main contributions of this paper are:

- Formal introduction of simple, parameterizable patterns that allow for abstraction of signals. We introduce an oscillation and a linear pattern in parameterized signal temporal logic (PSTL).
- A configurable, piecewise abstraction of signals using STL formula learning. The abstraction, of which the abstraction level is configurable, describes the signal in terms of generic signal patterns. Through an optimization problem, we find segments of maximal length that satisfy general PSTL patterns.

– An evaluation that shows configurability of the abstraction and demonstrates its application to real-world examples.

The first two contributions form the abstraction procedure from Fig. 2. The PSTL abstraction patterns contain parameters that are used to configure the level of abstraction. To abstract a given signal in terms of the introduced patterns, we reformulate the optimization problem of STL formula learning from [10] and introduce an iterative algorithm that generates abstractions of signals in terms of the introduced patterns. For solving the optimization problem, we apply a modified version of TeLex [10]. We evaluate the proposed configurable abstraction method on a controller step response and show that the configuration parameters allow for definition of the abstraction level. Further, we perform abstractions of real-world signals, namely wind turbine controller output [20] and a ventilation curve [1].

The remainder of this paper is structured as follows: In Sect. 2, we provide the necessary definitions of temporal logic. Section 3 summarizes related work in the fields of STL formula learning, piecewise signal abstraction, and hybrid system identification. In Sect. 4, we present our approach to configurable abstractions of signals by linear and oscillation segments. We evaluate the approach in Sect. 6 and finally summarize it in Sect. 7.

2 Preliminaries

2.1 Signals

A signal is a mapping $\mathbb{T} \mapsto \mathbb{R}$ from a time domain, $\mathbb{T} \subset \mathbb{R}^+$, to a value domain that describes evolution of a system over time. A discrete trace of a signal $\mathcal{S} = \{s_k \in \mathbb{R} | k \in [\![0, n]\!]\}$ is a sequence of values sampled from the signal at frequency f where the kth value is sampled at time $t_0 + \frac{k}{f}$ and the double brackets ($[\![,]\!]$) denote an interval of natural numbers.

2.2 Signal Temporal Logic

Signal temporal logic (STL) [15] is a logic for definition of properties on real-valued signals. In this work, we deal with discrete signal traces, $\mathcal{S}$, and thus employ a discrete-time version of STL. An atomic proposition in STL, μ, is an inequality on a signal $\mathcal{S}$ and a constant, $c \in \mathbb{R}$, in the form $\mathcal{S} \sim c$ with $\sim \in \{=, \leq, <, >, \geq\}$. In addition to conjunctions and disjunctions of propositions, STL allows for temporal specifications through the operator "until", $\mathbf{U}_{[t_1, t_2]}$ with $t_1, t_2 \in \mathbb{R}^+$ and $t_2 > t_1$. The grammar of STL is given by

$$\varphi := \top | \mu | \neg \varphi | \varphi_1 \wedge \varphi_2 | \varphi_1 \mathbf{U}_{[t_1, t_2]} \varphi_2.$$

We use the shorthand $\mathbf{F}_{[t_1, t_2]} \varphi$ for "eventually" and $\mathbf{G}_{[t_1, t_2]} \varphi$ for "globally", which can be expressed using the operator "until" by $\top \mathbf{U}_{[t_1, t_2]} \varphi$, and $\neg(\top \mathbf{U}_{[t_1, t_2]} \neg \varphi)$, respectively.

The semantics of STL over a signal trace, $\mathcal{S}$, are as follows:

$$
\begin{aligned}
\mathcal{S} &\models \mu && \text{iff } \forall s \in \mathcal{S} : s \text{ satisfies } \mu \\
\mathcal{S} &\models \neg\varphi && \text{iff } \mathcal{S} \not\models \varphi \\
\mathcal{S} &\models \varphi_1 \wedge \varphi_2 && \text{iff } \forall s \in \mathcal{S} : s \models \varphi_1 \text{ and } s \models \varphi_2 \\
\mathcal{S} &\models \varphi_1 \mathbf{U}_{[t_1,t_2]}\varphi_2 && \text{iff } \exists t' \in [t_1, t_2] : s_{f \cdot t'} \models \varphi_2 \\
& && \text{and } \forall t'' \in [0, t'[: s_{f \cdot t''} \models \varphi_1
\end{aligned}
$$

The signal trace is valid w.r.t. an STL formula φ iff for all samples of $\mathcal{S}$, φ is valid. Note that in the operator "until", the index of the signal values is given by $f \cdot t$, time and frequency.

Parameterized signal temporal logic (PSTL) [2] is an extension of STL that allows for parameter variables, π and τ, in addition to concrete times and constants, t and c. A parameter valuation θ that maps variables (π, τ) to concrete values (c, t) transforms a PSTL formula back to an STL formula. We write φ_θ for the STL formula that results from mapping valuation θ to the PSTL formula φ.

3   Related Work

STL Formula Learning. Learning STL formulae from examples is an active research area. Formula learning deduces an STL formula based on a set of example signal traces, e.g., for mining requirements of the system [11], or learning of classifiers for anomaly detection [12]. The formula is learned by optimizing the robustness of the signals to the formula, i.e., the minimal distance a signal has from violation of the formula. There exist approaches to learning parameterization and structure of STL formula, e.g., using decision trees [6], using a subset of STL that allows for organization of formulae in a directed acyclic graph [12], or discovering possible formula structures [17].

The idea of our work is to learn from provided PSTL formulae. One advantage of learning from predefined formulae is interpretability since the general shape of the pattern is defined manually. There exist approaches that pursue a counterexample-guided method and learn from good and bad traces [4,11]. However, as in this work, negative examples or testing mechanisms do not always exist.

In [9], a set of STL specifications is learned from positive examples only and used for anomaly detection, where an anomaly is assumed if more than a defined percentage of the specifications is violated. [7] also learns from positive traces but assumes that there exists an underlying optimization problem in the trace. Most relevant to this work is the work by Jha et al. In [10], the authors introduce TeLEx, a framework that learns parameterizations of predefined PSTL formulae based on a given set of traces. The authors introduce a tightness metric and formulate an optimization problem that optimizes tightness of the formula for the given traces. This work uses TeLEx but adapts the optimization target from tightness to length of the interval for which the formula holds true.

For further references, [5] provides a survey on STL specification mining.

Piecewise Linear Approximation. A common method to abstract data is piecewise linear approximation. There exist multiple approaches to offline linear approximation from the field of cartographic generalization, such as the Douglas-Peucker algorithm [8]. More recent work in this field concentrates on online path compression, which is an active field of research in the maritime context [14]. There exist several sliding [23,24] and opening window [16,21] approaches.

Similarly to piecewise linear approximation, this work provides piecewise abstraction in terms of predefined patterns. It complements linear approximation by an oscillation pattern that allows for more efficient and less detailed abstraction of signals with oscillations.

Hybrid System Identification. Hybrid systems are widely used to model CPS. They have a finite set of continuous modes that are controlled by discrete dynamics. The goal of hybrid system identification is to identify the continuous and discrete dynamics based on traces of the system. Most approaches first perform a segmentation of the provided traces, then cluster the segments, and identify dynamics of the clusters. For segmentation, e.g., changes in slope or value [22], a loss-based method [19], or optimization problems [3,18] are applied. Mode clustering and identification can, for example, base on symbolic regression [19], or linear matrix inequalities [22].

The methods for hybrid system identification are similar to our work in that they also provide a segmentation of signals based on different modes. As opposed to our work, modes are generally not known beforehand. Most related to our approach is [3], where modes are restricted to linear shapes.

4   Abstraction of Signals by Configurable Segments

In this section, we describe our method to generate a piecewise abstraction of a signal. We first formalize the problem in 4.1. In 4.2, we formally introduce the patterns in terms of which we abstract the signals. Subsection 4.3 defines the optimization problem and provides an iterative algorithm for the generation of abstractions.

4.1   Formalization of Signal Abstraction

Our goal is to find an abstract representation for a one-dimensional signal trace $\mathcal{S} = \{s_k \in \mathbb{R} | k \in [\![0, n]\!]\}$ of length $n + 1$, for which we assume constant interpolation. We call a subset $\mathcal{S}_I = \{s_k \in \mathbb{R} | k \in I\}$ with $I = [\![k_1, k_2]\!]$ and $k_1 < k_2 < n$ a segment of $\mathcal{S}$ with length $|\mathcal{S}_I| = k_2 - k_1 + 1$ and duration $\frac{|\mathcal{S}_I|}{f}$, where f is the sample frequency of the signal. Further, we define a segmentation $\{\mathcal{S}_0, .., \mathcal{S}_k\}$ of the signal as partition of $\mathcal{S}$ into segments $\mathcal{S}_i$ such that segments do not overlap, $\bigcap_i \mathcal{S}_i = \emptyset$, and cover the whole signal, $\bigcup_i \mathcal{S}_i = \mathcal{S}$.

The core idea of this work is to find a segmentation of the signal, where every segment can be abstracted by a predefined pattern, $m \in \mathcal{M}$. Those patterns describe signal behavior, e.g., oscillations, in a general, parameterized form. We say that a segment, $\mathcal{S}_I$, can be abstracted by a pattern if

$$\exists m \in \mathcal{M}, \theta : \mathcal{S}_I \models m_\theta, \tag{1}$$

i.e., if there exists an abstract pattern, m, and corresponding valuation, θ for the parameters of m such that the segment satisfies the pattern m_θ.

4.2   Formal Description of Signal Patterns

A central element for the segmentation of a signal into abstract patterns is the definition of those patterns. Along with the signal, the patterns are required as input to the segmentation problem from Fig. 2. This subsection provides a formal description of two patterns, namely oscillating and linear behavior, in PSTL.

Oscillation. An oscillation is a periodic variation of a signal. One way to identify such variations is to analyze the first derivative, $\mathcal{S}'$, of a signal, $\mathcal{S}$, where an oscillation shows as periodic change of sign. We first formulate this behavior in PSTL by implications where a negative derivative implies that it will eventually get positive and vice-versa:

$$(s' \leq 0 \implies F_{[0,t_f]}(s' > 0)) \wedge (s' \geq 0 \implies F_{[0,t_f]}(s' < 0)). \tag{2}$$

In words, Eq. 2 signifies that if the signal is constant or decreasing, within time t_f, it will increase. If it is constant or increasing, it will eventually decrease within t_f. Note that inclusion of equivalence to zero in the first part of the subformulae and exclusion in the later part is important, otherwise a constant signal, where $\forall t : s' = 0$, would satisfy the pattern since the premise of the implication would never be true. The upper limit, t_f, of the operator "future" is a configuration parameter, which limits the minimal frequency of the oscillation to $f_{min} = \frac{1}{2t_f}$.

In this work, in order to distinguish oscillations from local extrema, we consider a signal as oscillating if it contains at least two changes of sign in the first derivative. In PSTL we express this by a nested operator "future" in the implication, extending the PSTL oscillation pattern to

$$(s' \leq 0 \implies F_{[0,t_f]}(s' > 0 \wedge F_{[0,t_f]}(s' < 0))) \wedge$$
$$(s' \geq 0 \implies F_{[0,t_f]}(s' < 0 \wedge F_{[0,t_f]}(s' > 0))). \tag{3}$$

If the signal is constant or decreasing, there is a sample within time t_f, in which the signal increases and where it decreases within t_f. If it is constant or increasing, the same properties hold with inverted comparison symbols.

Figure 3 illustrates the difference between Eqs. 2 and 3. While the formula from Eq. 2 remains valid until t_2, that from Eq. 3 becomes invalid at t_1 since after t_1 only one change of sign in the signal remains.

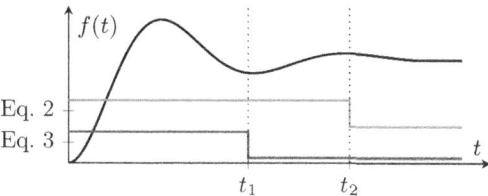

Fig. 3. Exemplary oscillating signal and the validity of the STL formulae from Eqs. 2 (——) and 3 (——).

Equation 3 is problematic for real-world signals, where approximately constant behavior results in s' being close to zero but not strictly zero. Such behavior shall not be identified as oscillation. We introduce a threshold, σ, on the derivative as second configuration parameter and replace $s'\{>,\geq\}0$ and $s'\{<,\leq\}0$ from Eq. 3 by $s' > \sigma$ and $s' < -\sigma$, respectively. To avoid that the premise of the implication is always false, we further add the term

$$F_{[0,t_f]}(s' > \sigma \lor s' < -\sigma). \tag{4}$$

The final oscillation pattern, m_{osci}, is thus a conjunction of Eq. 3 with 0 replaced by $\pm\sigma$ and Eq. 4:

$$
\begin{aligned}
m_{osci} = F_{[0,t_f]}(s' > \sigma \lor s' < -\sigma)\land \\
(s' < -\sigma \implies F_{[0,t_f]}(s' > \sigma \land F_{[0,t_f]}(s' < -\sigma)))\land \\
(s' > \sigma \implies F_{[0,t_f]}(s' < -\sigma \land F_{[0,t_f]}(s' > \sigma))). \quad (5)
\end{aligned}
$$

Linear. The characteristic of linear behavior is that the signal evolves at a constant rate. One way to formalize linear behavior in PSTL is the constraint

$$s' == c, \tag{6}$$

which requires equality of the first derivative, s', to some constant, c. In real signals, because of noise and disturbances, strict equality is not applicable. Extending c to some range around c makes the formula applicable to real-world signals. One problem about such formula is that it does not guarantee a constant bound on the error between signal and abstraction. All signals within the dashed corridor from Fig. 4a would satisfy such formula. With increasing segment length, the possible error increases.

For meaningful abstractions, we require that the original signal is in a range of $\pm\varepsilon$ from its abstraction. Figure 4b shows such error constraint. A signal that is abstracted by the black line from Fig. 4b must lie within the corridor that is restricted by the dashed lines. There exists no natural way to define that property in PSTL, since it requires comparing the signal to a non-constant, linearly evaluating value. To overcome this gap, we introduce a counter signal,

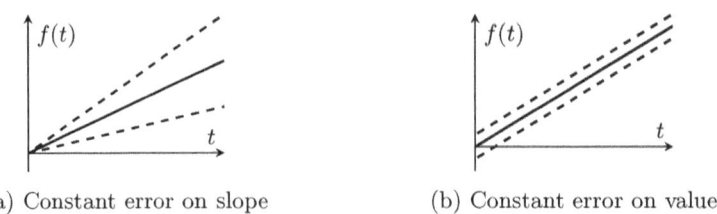

(a) Constant error on slope   (b) Constant error on value

Fig. 4. Exemplary linear function and error bounds $(\text{-}\text{-}\text{-})$ of the formula.

C, which is incremented by $\frac{1}{f}$ with each timestep. We formalize the final linear pattern as

$$m_{lin} = (\pi_1 \cdot C + \pi_2 < s + \varepsilon) \wedge (\pi_1 \cdot C + \pi_2 > s - \varepsilon), \tag{7}$$

where π_1, π_2 are parameters for slope and offset, respectively and ε is a configuration parameter that binds the maximal linear approximation error.

4.3   Optimization Problem for Signal Abstraction

As stated in Subsect. 4.1, our goal is to find a segmentation of the signal where each segment can be abstracted by at least one of the patterns from the prior subsection according to Eq. 1. One naïve approach to finding such segmentation is to divide the signal into segments of length 1 and abstract them linearly. However, such abstraction neither increases interpretability nor reduces the amount of information, which both improve if the signal is divided into fewer segments. In this subsection, we introduce an approach to find a segmentation with few long segments.

Therefore, for each pattern, $m \in \mathcal{M}$, we search for the longest possible segment in the signal $\mathcal{S}$ that starts at time i and satisfies m. We define the search as an optimization problem. We add the PSTL operator $G_{[\frac{i}{f},\frac{\pi_l}{f}]}$ to the description of the pattern, which defines that the pattern must hold globally within the segment $\mathcal{S}_{[\![i,\pi_l]\!]}$. The resulting optimization problem is

$$opti(\mathcal{S}_{[\![i,n]\!]}, m) = \max_{\theta, \pi_l} \pi_l$$
$$\text{s.t. } \mathcal{S} \vDash \mathbf{G}_{[\frac{i}{f},\frac{\pi_l}{f}]}(m_\theta), \tag{8}$$

where $(\pi_l - i)$ is the length of the maximal segment of mode m with optimal parameterization θ.

We apply the iterative greedy search algorithm presented in Algorithm 1 to find a segmentation of the entire signal. Starting from the first sample of the signal, i.e., $i = 0$, for all patterns, $m \in \mathcal{M}$, we solve the optimization, $opti(\mathcal{S}_{[\![i,n]\!]}, m)$. The optimization searches for l and θ, the length and parameterization of the longest possible segment that starts at the sample s_i and satisfies the pattern (here Eqs. 5 or 7).

We use the pattern m_θ of maximal length, l, as abstraction for the segment $\mathcal{S}_{[\![i,\pi_l]\!]}$ and repeat the procedure starting from s_{i+l+1} until $i+l+1 \geq n$, i.e., the end of the signal is reached.

Algorithm 1 Greedy search algorithm for abstraction of signals into interpretable segments

---

Require: Input: signal $\mathcal{S} = \{s_0, .., s_n\}$, list of patterns $\mathcal{M} = [m_{lin}, m_{osci}]$
1: $i = 0$
2: **while** $i \leq n$ **do**
3:     length $= 0$
4:     **for all** $m \in \mathcal{M}$ **do**
5:         $\theta, l = \text{opti}(\mathcal{S}_{[\![i,n]\!]}, m)$
6:         **if** $l >$ length **then**
7:             length $= l$
8:             abstr $= m_\theta$
9:         **end if**
10:     **end for**
11:     segments.append($(m_\theta,$ length$)$)
12:     $i = i + l + 1$
13: **end while**

Properties of the Abstraction. The abstraction according to Algorithm 1 guarantees *existence* of a *unique* abstraction for every signal trace by construction:

- Every signal trace can be abstracted by a piecewise linear function, where the linear pieces always connect two consecutive samples, i.e., segments are of length $\frac{1}{f}$. Thus, an abstraction is guaranteed to exist.
- The *for loop* of the algorithm searches for the approximation segment of maximal length. In case of equal length of oscillation and linear segment, the linear segment is chosen. The abstraction it hence unique.

Optimality of the abstraction w.r.t. a minimal number of segments is not guaranteed. As Fig. 3 shows, oscillation segments end before the identified oscillation by design since they require two following changes of sign in the slope. An optimal identification of oscillations requires redefinition of m_{osci}.

5   Mode Detection Using TeLEx

This section describes the adaptions we made to TeLEx and our defined patterns for implementation of the optimization problem that finds the longest possible segment that matches a specific pattern, i.e., line 5 of Algorithm 1.

5.1   Reformulate Patterns

For implementation of oscillation detection according to Eq. 5, we need the derivative of the signal, which is not directly available in TeLEx. We calculate the derivative, s'_k, at time step k as the difference between the signal value and its prior value scaled with the sample frequency, f,

$$s'_k = f \cdot (s_k - s_{k-1}). \tag{9}$$

The derivative of the first sample, s'_0, is set to zero.

For implementation of linear pattern detection, we reformulate Eq. 7 according to the grammar of TeLEx, where each side of a constraint either contains a signal or a parameter. For linear behavior, the slope, π_1, is the parameter. The signal, s, and the introduced counter, C, are signals, where C is zero at time step k_0, the beginning of the interval, and increases by $\frac{1}{f}$ with every timestep. The offset, π_2, is set to s_{k_0}, the first signal value of the interval that shall be approximated. Thus, the pattern is guaranteed to be valid at time k_0. The pattern detection needs to ensure that it still is from time k_1 on. We obtain

$$\mathbf{G}_{[\frac{k_1}{f}, \frac{\pi_l}{f}]}\left(\left(\pi_1 < \frac{s - \pi_2 + \varepsilon}{C}\right) \wedge \left(\pi_1 > \frac{s - \pi_2 - \varepsilon}{C}\right)\right) \tag{10}$$

as linear pattern for TeLex with error threshold ε.

5.2   Adaption to the Optimization Objective

The optimization target of TeLEx is to find a parameterization of a PSTL formula such that the formula tightly fits the provided traces. As stated in Subsect. 4.3, in our work, we are not interested in a tight formula but in one that maximizes $l = (\pi_l - i)$, the length of the interval in which the pattern globally holds. We thus adapt the scoring function ρ of the optimization problem in TeLEx as follows:

$$
\begin{aligned}
&\rho(\top, t) = 1, \rho(\bot, t) = -1 \\
&\rho(\varphi_1 \wedge \varphi_2, t) = \min(\rho(\varphi_1, t), \rho(\varphi_2, t)) \\
&\rho(\varphi_1 \vee \varphi_2, t) = \max(\rho(\varphi_1, t), \rho(\varphi_2, t)) \\
&\rho(\mathbf{F}_{[t_1, t_2]}\varphi) = \sup_{t' \in [t_1, t_2]} \rho(\varphi, t') \\
&\rho(\mathbf{G}_{[t_1, t_2]}\varphi) = \frac{2}{1 + e^{-0.1 l}} \inf_{t' \in [t_1, t_2]} \rho(\varphi, t') \\
&\rho(\varphi_1 \mathbf{U}_{[t_1, t_2]}\varphi_2) = \sup_{t' \in [t_1, t_2]} (\min(\rho(\varphi_2, t'), \inf_{t'' \in [t_1, t'[} \rho(\varphi_1, t''))).
\end{aligned}
\tag{11}
$$

The scoring function is defined recursively. All formulae except those that include the operator "globally" have score 1 if the formula is satisfied and -1 else. The score of the operator "globally" is the minimal score of φ in its defined interval $[t_1, t_2]$, weighted with a factor that increases with the length $l = t_2 - t_1$ of the interval according to $\frac{2}{1 + e^{-0.1 l}}$ as proposed in [10].

6   Evaluation

For evaluation of the proposed abstraction framework, we first test its configurability on artificially generated step responses of a closed-loop controller. In
a second step, we demonstrate the application to real-world problems on control output from the ARCH wind turbine benchmark [20] and medical ventilator
signals [1].

6.1   Configurability of the Abstraction

To assess the configurability of the abstraction method, we simulate output
signals of a simple closed-loop controller as shown in Fig. 5. On the oscillating
output signal, we show that through the choice of parameters in the patterns,
we can achieve different levels of abstraction.

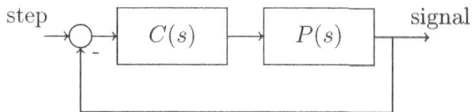

Fig. 5. Closed-loop controller for trace generation

System. In the control loop, we apply a PID controller, C, to control the output
of a plant, P. As signal for evaluation of the configurability, we use the closed-
loop step response of the control loop, i.e., its output when a change from 0 to 10
is applied as input. The transfer function, $C(s)$, of the controller with complex
Laplace variable s is

$$C(s) = 50 + \frac{1}{s} + 0.01\frac{1}{1 + \frac{1}{s}}, \tag{12}$$

and the plant is a simple second order system defined by

$$P(s) = \frac{1}{s^2 + s + 1}. \tag{13}$$

We sample the control output over 15 s at 10 Hz. Figure 6 shows the resulting
signal. During the first second, it is constant zero. At 1 s, it increases to approximately 17.8 and then shows a decaying oscillation around the value 10. The
oscillation period is between 8.5 s and 9 s.

Experiments and Results. To evaluate the configurability, we target abstraction of the signal from Fig. 6 at two different abstraction levels:

- A high-level abstraction representing the signal as sequence of linear functions and oscillations.
- A more detailed low-level abstraction that approximates the oscillations by linear segments.

To achieve the different abstractions, we configure the parameters for maximal oscillation period, $2t_f$, and minimal oscillation slope, σ, of oscillating segments (Eq. 5) and the maximal approximation error, ε, of linear segments (Eq. 7).

For the *high-level abstraction*, the oscillations of the signal must match the general form defined in Eq. 5. Therefore, the maximal oscillation period, $2t_f$, must be at least the maximal oscillation period of the signal, which is 9 s. We hence choose t_f to 4.5 s. We set σ to a small value of 0.01 for capturing oscillations with small slopes. Further, we limit the linear approximation error to 2% of the maximal signal value, 17.8, which gives $\varepsilon = 0.35$. Figure 7 shows the resulting abstraction.

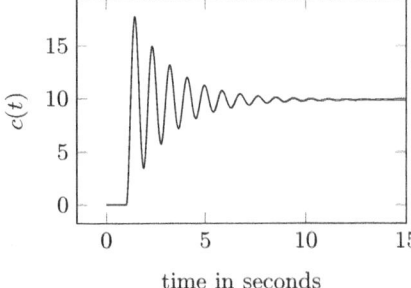
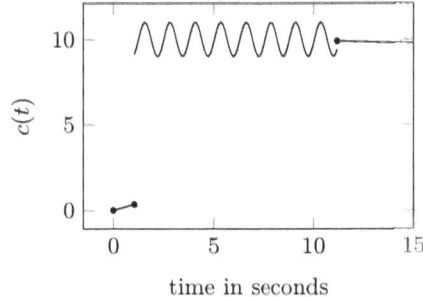

time in seconds   time in seconds

Fig. 6. Control loop output to a step of 10. The signal shows a decaying oscillation around the value 10.

Fig. 7. High-level abstraction of the controlled signal with $2t_f = 9$ s.

The signal is abstracted to 3 segments, whereof the first and last are linear and the middle is oscillating. The oscillation ranges from 1.05 s to 11.1 s.

The *low-level abstraction* aims at representing details of the oscillations. We thus set the parameter t_f down to 1 s, which is less than half of the minimal oscillation period. By that choice, we do not expect the abstraction to capture oscillation segments. Hence, the choice of σ has no impact on the result. We keep it at 0.01. We compare two choices of ε, namely a maximal error of 2 % and of 5 % of the maximal signal value. This gives $\varepsilon = 0.35$ and $\varepsilon = 0.9$, respectively. The abstraction results are shown in Fig. 8.

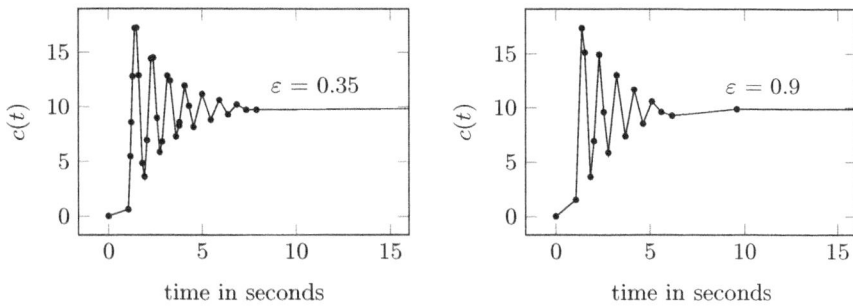

Fig. 8. Low-level abstraction of the controlled signal (from Fig. 6) with $2t_f = 1$ for different linear approximation error thresholds.

Both abstractions consist of linear segments only. While the abstraction with a maximal error of 0.35 results in 31 linear segments, the abstraction with maximal error of 0.9 results in 17 segments.

Table 1 summarizes the results of the performed experiments. They show that with the configuration parameters, the level and degree of detail of the abstraction can be set.

Table 1. Summary of configuration experiments

	t_f	σ	ε	# segments (# oscillation segments)
High-level	4.5 s	0.01	2 % (0.35)	3 (1)
Low-level I	1 s	0.01	2 % (0.35)	31(0)
Low-level II	1 s	0.01	5 % (0.9)	17(0)

We remark that for an adequate choice of parameters for the desired level of abstraction, general information about the signal, e.g., its maximal and minimal oscillation period must be known. With the presented patterns, the only way to distinguish between oscillation and linear segment is the maximal period, which is sufficient for the presented example. For higher configurability of the abstraction, further criteria as, for example, a maximal oscillation amplitude can be introduced by extension of the pattern in future work.

6.2 Demonstration on Real-World Examples

We demonstrate the proposed abstraction on two real-world examples, flow curves from a ventilated patient [1], and controller output signals of a wind turbine example from the ARCH benchmark suite [20].

Medical Ventilation. We use flow data recorded by a medical ventilator during volume-controlled ventilation to demonstrate real-world application of the abstraction. The black curve from Fig. 9 shows 100 s of the recorded data. We can either look at the ventilation curve from a high-level perspective, where it is an oscillation around zero with a period of approximately 5 s, or at a low-level perspective for analyzing the shape of the curves, e.g., maximal and minimal flow, or the inspiration to expiration ratio.

In an experiment, we demonstrate a high-level abstraction of the flow curve. To achieve such abstraction, we choose the maximal period to 10 s, σ to $0.15\,\mathrm{L\,min^{-1}\,s^{-1}}$, and the maximal linearization error to $0.8\,\mathrm{L\,min^{-1}}$. Note that the period is chosen as twice of the value that we observed in the curves. This allows for an oscillation abstraction even though the duration of inspiration and expiration are not of equal length.

The abstraction result is depicted by the colored curve from Fig. 9. It consists of an oscillation segment of length 97.3 s (blue) followed by 6 linear segments (orange).

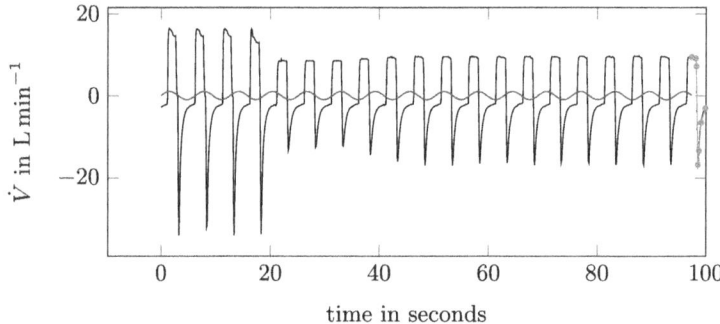

Fig. 9. Ventilation curve and its high-level abstraction (colored). (Color figure online)

As expected, the abstraction framework is able to capture the oscillation and abstracts the whole ventilation as oscillation. However, as described in Subsect. 4.3, the end of the oscillation is not properly captured. The last period of the oscillation (orange part in Fig. 9) is not included in the oscillation but abstracted by linear segments.

Wind-Turbine Controller. We perform a similar experiment to demonstrate the applicability of the designed abstraction to controller output of a wind turbine example.

The wind turbine from the ARCH benchmark suite [20] consists of a nonlinear model of a wind turbine and two controllers that control the generator torque of the turbine and the pitch angle of its blades. The control target of the pitch angle controller is to set the angle θ_d such that the turbine rotates at constant angle velocity. The velocity of the turbine further depends on the generator torque and the wind speed. We evaluate the abstraction of the pitch angle controller output sampled over 600 s at 1 Hz for two scenarios: unsteady and constant wind.

In reality, wind is *unsteady*, which results in unsteady control output as depicted in Fig. 10a. For the control output, we create a high-level abstraction with maximal linear approximation error of 5 % of the maximal signal amplitude, i.e. 0.015 rad. We further set σ to 0.005 rad s^{-1} and the maximal oscillation period, $2t_f$, to 20 s. The abstraction results in Fig. 10b show a mixture of linear and oscillation segments.

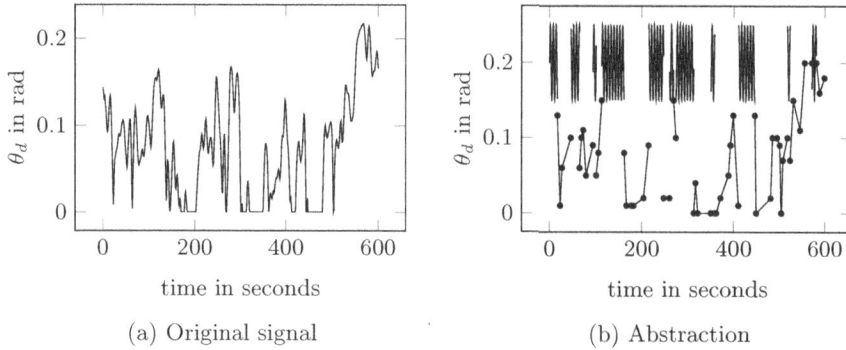

(a) Original signal   (b) Abstraction

Fig. 10. Wind turbine controller output for unsteady wind and its abstraction.

We modify the example such that the wind is *constant* at 12 m s^{-1} and the target angle velocity varies between 123 rad s^{-1} and 143 rad s^{-1} with a step every 100 s. The resulting controller output is shown in Fig. 11a. With every step in the target velocity, the pitch angle oscillates for about 30 s and then settles at 0.8 rad until the next step in the target leads to a new oscillation. To achieve a high-level abstraction, we choose t_f to 10 s, σ to 0.005 rad s^{-1}, and the maximal linear approximation error, ε, to 5 % of the maximal amplitude, i.e., 0.015 rad.

The abstraction results in Fig. 11b show that such regular behavior suits much better for abstractions. The abstraction shows 6 repetitions of the sequence oscillation, decreasing linear segment, increasing linear segment, constant linear segment. We get an abstraction of 24 segments, whereof 6 are oscillations and 18 linear.

The results from the wind turbine examples illustrate that an abstraction in terms of linear and oscillation segments is not applicable for all signals but only if there are recognizable patterns as in the constant wind examples. For unsteady data as in the realistic wind example, even for humans, it is impossible to find concise abstractions and segmentations. Hence, the proposed method is not able to generate meaningful abstractions for such signals. In the abstraction of the steady wind example, as in the ventilation example, we observe that the oscillation segment ends before the actual oscillation. The last period of the

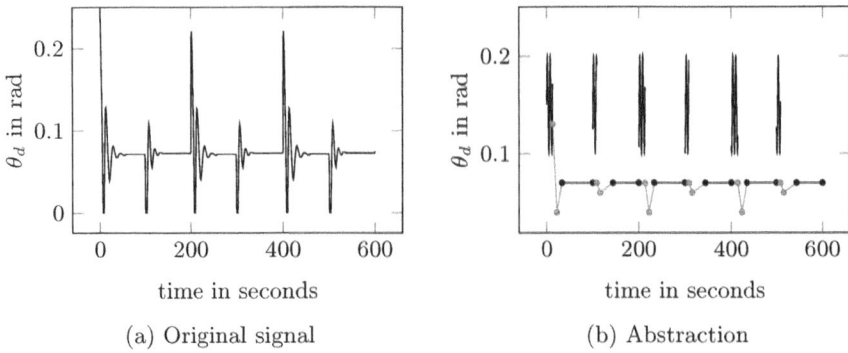

(a) Original signal   (b) Abstraction

Fig. 11. Wind turbine controller output for constant wind and changing speed target and its abstraction.

oscillation is abstracted by linear segments (orange part in Fig. 11b) instead of belonging to the oscillation segment. In general, the abstraction of the signal by linear and oscillation segments is appropriate but a redefinition of the oscillation pattern that includes the whole oscillation would, particularly for short oscillations as in this example, result in more concise abstractions.

7   Conclusion

In this work, we have presented a novel approach to configurable signal abstraction using temporal logic. We have defined linear and oscillation pattern templates in PSTL and provided a mechanism to abstract signals in terms of these patterns, where the range of applicable parameters in the patterns is configurable. The abstraction mechanism is based on an optimization problem, which provides a segmentation of the signal that consists of segments of maximal length. We use a modified version of the STL formula learning tool TeLEx for solving the optimization problem. The evaluation shows that our approach to signal abstraction is configurable and allows for high- and low-level abstractions. The chosen patterns are applicable to signals with steady, regular behavior, whereas for unsteady signals, the generated abstractions are not meaningful.

Future work includes further evaluation and comparison to existing methods from hybrid system identification as well as improvement in robustness when dealing with noisy signals. The problem of properly detecting the end of oscillations should be addressed and new patterns, e.g., exponential behavior may be introduced. We further envision reporting of identified parameters of the patterns (e.g., slope) and a systematic approach for identification of configuration parameters. We intend to introduce an online method for pattern-based abstraction of signals and using the abstractions for explanations of signals, i.e., by detecting repeating pattern sequences and visualizing the signal as automaton.

Acknowledgments. This work has been funded by the Deutsche Forschungsgemeinschaft (DFG, German Research Foundation) project no. 513623283 as part of the Research Training Group CAUSE.

Disclosure of Interests. The authors have no competing interests to declare that are relevant to the content of this article.

References

1. private communication with an industrial partner. unpublished
2. Asarin, E., Donzé, A., Maler, O., Nickovic, D.: Parametric identification of temporal properties. In: Runtime verification, pp. 147–160. Lecture Notes in Computer Science (2012). https://doi.org/10.1007/978-3-642-29860-8_12
3. Bartocci, E., Deshmukh, J., Gigler, F., Mateis, C., Nickovic, D., Qin, X.: Mining shape expressions from positive examples. IEEE Trans. Comput.-Aided Design Integr. Circ. Syst. **39**(11), 3809–3820 (2020). https://doi.org/10.1109/TCAD.2020.3012240
4. Bartocci, E., Manjunath, N., Mariani, L., Mateis, C., Ničković, D.: CPSDebug: automatic failure explanation in CPS models. Int. J. Softw. Tools Technol. Transfer **23**(5), 783–796 (2020). https://doi.org/10.1007/s10009-020-00599-4
5. Bartocci, E., Mateis, C., Nesterini, E., Nickovic, D.: Survey on mining signal temporal logic specifications. Inf. Comput. **289**, 104957 (2022). https://doi.org/10.1016/j.ic.2022.104957
6. Bombara, G., Belta, C.: Offline and online learning of signal temporal logic formulae using decision trees. ACM Trans. Cyber-Phys. Syst. **5**(3), 1–23 (2021). https://doi.org/10.1145/3433994
7. Chou, G., Ozay, N., Berenson, D.: Explaining multi-stage tasks by learning temporal logic formulas from subimal demonstrations. Robotics: Sci. Syst. (2020). https://doi.org/10.48550/arXiv.2006.02411
8. Douglas, D.H., Peucker, T.K.: Algorithms for the reduction of the number of points required to represent a digitized line or its caricature. Cartographica: The Int. J. Geograph. Inform. Geovisualization **10**(2), 112–122 (1973). https://doi.org/10.3138/FM57-6770-U75U-7727
9. Indri, P., Bartoli, A., Medvet, E., Nenzi, L.: One-shot learning of ensembles of temporal logic formulas for anomaly detection in cyber-physical systems. In: Medvet, E., Pappa, G., Xue, B. (eds.) Genetic Programming, Lecture Notes in Computer Science, vol. 13223, pp. 34–50. Springer International Publishing, Cham (2022). https://doi.org/10.1007/978-3-031-02056-8_3
10. Jha, S., Tiwari, A., Seshia, S.A., Sahai, T., Shankar, N.: TeLEx: learning signal temporal logic from positive examples using tightness metric. Formal Methods in System Design **54**(3), 364–387 (2019). https://doi.org/10.1007/s10703-019-00332-1
11. Jin, X., Donzé, A., Deshmukh, J.V., Seshia, S.A.: Mining requirements from closed-loop control models. IEEE Trans. Comput.-Aided Design Integr. Circ. Syste. **34**(11), 1704–1717 (2015). https://doi.org/10.1109/TCAD.2015.2421907
12. Kong, Z., Jones, A., Belta, C.: Temporal logics for learning and detection of anomalous behavior. IEEE Trans. Autom. Contr. **62**(3), 1210–1222 (2017). https://doi.org/10.1109/TAC.2016.2585083

13. Lin, M.H., Carlsson, J.G., Ge, D., Shi, J., Tsai, J.F.: A review of piecewise linearization methods. Math. Probl. Eng. **2013**, 1–8 (2013). https://doi.org/10.1155/2013/101376

14. Makris, A., Kontopoulos, I., Alimisis, P., Tserpes, K.: A comparison of trajectory compression algorithms over AIS data. IEEE Access **9**, 92516–92530 (2021). https://doi.org/10.1109/ACCESS.2021.3092948

15. Maler, O., Nickovic, D.: Monitoring temporal properties of continuous signals. In: Formal Techniques, Modelling and Analysis of Timed and Fault-Tolerant Systems, pp. 152–166 (2004). https://doi.org/10.1007/978-3-540-30206-3_12

16. Meratnia, N., de By, R.A.: Spatiotemporal compression techniques for moving point objects. In: Bertino, E. (ed.) Advances in database technology, Lecture Notes in Computer Science, vol. 2992, pp. 765–782. Springer-Verlag, New York (2004). https://doi.org/10.1007/978-3-540-24741-8_44

17. Mohammadinejad, S., Deshmukh, J.V., Puranic, A.G., Vazquez-Chanlatte, M., Donzé, A.: Interpretable classification of time-series data using efficient enumerative techniques. In: Ames, A. (ed.) Proceedings of the 23rd International Conference on Hybrid Systems: Computation and Control, pp. 1–10. ACM Digital Library, Association for Computing Machinery, New York,NY,United States (2020). https://doi.org/10.1145/3365365.3382218

18. Monier, Y., Denis, B., Faraut, G., Anwer, N.: A new global imization for hybrid automaton Identification. IFAC-PapersOnLine **58**(1), 252–257 (2024). https://doi.org/10.1016/j.ifacol.2024.07.043

19. Plambeck, S., Schmidt, M., Fey, G., Subias, A., Travé-Massuyès, L.: Dynamics-based identification of hybrid systems using symbolic regression. In: 2024 50th Euromicro Conference on Software Engineering and Advanced Applications (SEAA), pp. 64–71 (2024). https://doi.org/10.1109/SEAA64295.2024.00019

20. Schuler, S., Daher Adegas, F., Anta, A.: Hybrid modelling of a wind turbine. In: Goran Frehse and Matthias Althoff (ed.) Applied Verification for Continuous and Hybrid Systems, pp. 18–8. EPiC Series in Computing, EasyChair (2017). https://doi.org/10.29007/tf1p

21. Trajcevski, G., Cao, H., Scheuermanny, P., Wolfsonz, O., Vaccaro, D.: On-line data reduction and the quality of history in moving objects databases. In: Chrysanthis, P.K. (ed.) MobiDE 2006, pp. 19–26. ACM Press, New York, NY (2006). https://doi.org/10.1145/1140104.1140110

22. Yang, X., Beg, O.A., Kenigsberg, M., Johnson, T.T.: A framework for Identification and validation of affine hybrid automata from input-output traces. ACM Trans. Cyber-Phys. Syst. **6**(2), 1–24 (2022). https://doi.org/10.1145/3470455

23. Zhang, T., Wang, Z., Wang, P.: A method for compressing AIS trajectory based on the adaptive core threshold difference Douglas-Peucker algorithm. Sci. Rep. **14**(1), 21408 (2024). https://doi.org/10.1038/s41598-024-71779-4

24. Zhao, L., Shi, G.: A method for simplifying ship trajectory based on improved Douglas-Peucker algorithm. Ocean Eng. **166**, 37–46 (2018). https://doi.org/10.1016/j.oceaneng.2018.08.005

Model-Driven Engineering
and Modeling Languages

Meta-Metamodel-Independent Model Transformations

Philipp Zech[1]([⊠])(iD), Christopher Kelter[1], Sascha Hammes[2](iD),
Judith Michael[3](iD), and Ruth Breu[1]

[1] Department of Computer Science, University of Innsbruck, Tyrol, Austria
{philipp.zech,christopher.kelter,ruth.breu}@uibk.ac.at
[2] University of Innsbruck, Unit for Energy Efficient Buildings, Tyrol, Austria
sascha.hammes@uibk.ac.at
[3] University of Regensburg, Programming and Software Engineering, Regensburg, Germany
judith.michael@ur.de

Abstract. Model-driven engineering efficiently manages complexity through high-level abstractions and model transformations, progressively refining models into executable code. However, current approaches require models to adhere to the same meta-metamodel, limiting their applicability to isolated ecosystems like Eclipse/Ecore or UML. The adoption of Building Information Modeling (BIM) has highlighted the need for transforming models across various life cycle phases. Yet, the fractured modeling landscape of BIM poses challenges as of existing solutions' restriction on complying to the same meta-metamodel and supported modeling formalisms (e.g., Eclipse/Ecore or UML). We introduce a novel *meta-metamodel-independent* model transformation formalism, accompanied by a domain-specific modeling language for declaring transformation rules at the meta-model level. Our approach leverages a formalism-independent *core language* for on-the-fly establishment of meta-models, enabling *meta-metamodel-independent* model transformations. We validate our proposal through case studies in construction and software engineering, demonstrating its feasibility and generalizability.

Keywords: Model Transformations · Domain-specific Modeling Languages · Building Information Modeling

1 Introduction

The adoption of Building Information Modeling (BIM) has revolutionized the construction industry by introducing digital representations of built assets, supporting virtually integrated design, construction, and operation (ViDCO) [32, 35, 41]. However, diverse modeling formalisms, i.e., Industry Foundation Classes (IFC) [4] and Green Building XML (gbXML) [10], create a fractured landscape that hinders collaboration and tool interoperability at the model level [3, 41].

Model transformations are pivotal in model-driven engineering (MDE), enabling automated translation and manipulation of models for system refinement, analysis, optimization, and interoperability [5, 7, 13, 15, 17, 29]. Despite

D. Taibi and D. Smite (Eds.): SEAA 2025, LNCS 16081, pp. 329–348, 2026.
https://doi.org/10.1007/978-3-032-04190-6_20

their importance, current frameworks are constrained by the requirement for models to conform to the same meta-metamodel, limiting their applicability across different domains [13,16]. This limitation is particularly evident in BIM, where models must often be transformed across various life cycle phases and formalisms [41]. The aforesaid required conformity to the same meta-metamodel restricts the application of existing solutions (cf. Sect. 2) in environments like BIM, where diverse meta-metamodels are prevalent.

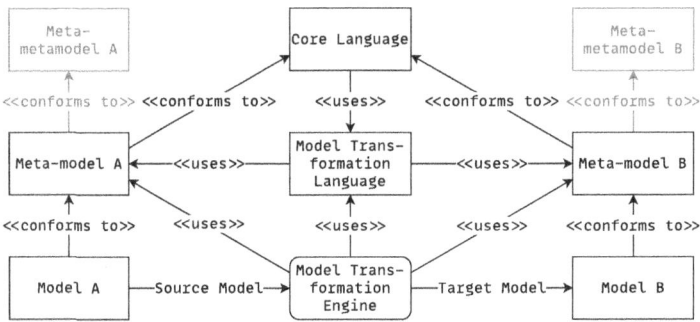

Fig. 1. Proposed model transformation framework. Source models may conform to meta-model A which in turn conforms to meta-metamodel A. Target models however may conform to a completely different modeling formalism i.e., B, which by definition is not compatible with A. Our framework enables model transformation between two such distinct modeling formalisms by generating meta-models *in-place*, capitalizing on the *core language* for *formalism-independent* representation of meta-models yielding *meta-metamodel-independence* (indicated by grayed-out meta-metamodels).

To address these challenges, we propose a *meta-metamodel-independent* model transformation framework. Our approach utilizes a domain-specific modeling language (DSML) to declare transformation rules at the meta-model level, enabling seamless transformations between models conforming to distinct meta-metamodels as outlined in Fig. 1. Inspired by the LLVM compiler infrastructure, our framework employs an intermediate representation based on a *core language* (cf. Fig. 1) to bridge different modeling formalisms, as illustrated in Fig. 2. LLVM serves as a compiler framework designed to optimize program code during compile-time, link-time, run-time, and even idle time between runs [23]. It enables optimizations and transformations to be applied consistently across different source languages, and then translated into machine code for various architectures [23]. By mimicking this architecture, our framework allows for a shared intermediate representation that multiple modeling languages can "compile" to and from, thus facilitating interoperability and extensibility. This approach supports the evolving needs of BIM and software solutions where different modeling formalisms have to get in touch, e.g., Digital Twins [8,12,24,25,38,40,43], by enhancing interoperability and collaboration across diverse engineering disciplines.

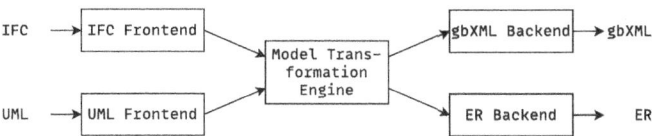

Fig. 2. LLVM-like infrastructure [23] of our proposal. Input models are parsed by frontends into an intermediary representation for subsequent transformation by a *Model transformation engine* and finally emitted in their novel representation using backends.

Our solution capitalizes on a formalism-independent core language for on-the-fly establishment of meta-models, facilitating model transformations across diverse ecosystems. This is achieved by resolving meta-metamodel incompatibilities at the syntactical layer of the implementation language, as depicted in Fig. 3. Given that two meta-metamodels are implemented in the same implementation language, a *DSML for model transformations* (cf. *model transformation language* in Fig. 1) capitalizing on concepts formalized in the *mutual* implementation language can be defined. Consequently, transformation rules between two models *A* and *B* that conform to distinct meta-metamodels *A* and *B* (cf. Fig. 1) can be implemented in such a DSML. We validate our proposal through case studies in construction and software engineering, demonstrating its feasibility and generalizability.

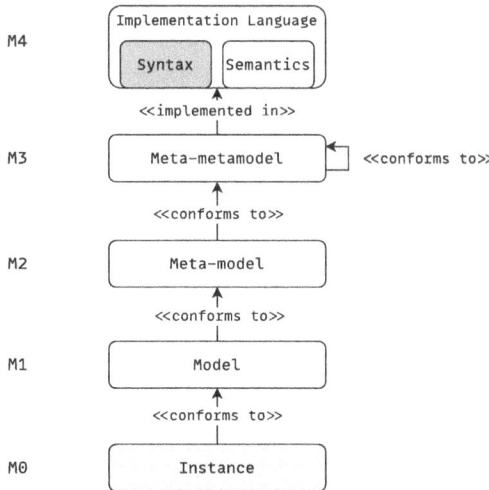

Fig. 3. Conceptual extension of the standard modeling infrastructure by an additional layer *M4*, viz. the *Implementation Language*. By choosing *syntactical conformity*, model translations between two models *A* and *B* that conform to contrary meta-metamodels *A* and *B* become practically feasible.

Organization. Section 2 discusses related work. Section 3 outlines the research problem, challenges, and contributions. Sections 4, 5, 6 introduce our meta-metamodel-independent model transformation formalism and its accompanying DSML. Section 7 evaluates our proposal in BIM and software engineering domains. Finally, Sect. 8 concludes our work.

2   Related Work

Model transformations have garnered significant attention, particularly in the early 2000s, as part of the growing interest in MDE for managing the complexity of systems and software engineering. Stevens assessed the landscape of bidirectional model transformations within Model-driven Architecture [31]. Kappel et al. provided the first comprehensive overview of model transformations, categorizing them into *endogenous* (same meta-model) and *exogenous* (distinct meta-models) approaches [16]. Their survey highlighted the reliance on a common meta-metamodel as a limitation that remains unaddressed.

Kahani et al. conducted the most extensive survey on model transformations and related tool support, examining both model-2-model and model-2-text transformations [14]. They classified these transformations into various dimensions, such as *relational*, *imperative*, *graph-based*, and *hybrid* for model-2-model, and *template-based*, *visitor-based*, and *hybrid* for model-2-text. Despite advancements, model transformations have primarily been explored within software engineering ecosystems like UML and Eclipse/Ecore, with limited application elsewhere [26]. Kahani et al. also noted the lack of long-term availability of model transformation tools, often due to frequent changes in language specifications requiring constant updates. Existing languages for translating between Ecore-based models often rely on compile-time Ecore structures, which restricts their use in dynamic environments where runtime flexibility is essential, such as when independence from an underlying modeling formalism is required. Our proposal addresses this by introducing meta-metamodel-independence at the syntactical layer of the implementation language, effortlessly capturing changes to a meta-metamodel.

Recent research has advanced model transformation techniques, such as the abstract mapping syntax $\mathcal{TL}$ for specifying bidirectional transformation rules [20,21], and formalizing model transformation patterns using Z notation [27]. Eisenberg et al. explored the use of reinforcement learning for optimizing rule application during in-place model transformations [6]. These proposals do not address the reliance on a common meta-metamodel, which however requires immediate attention for broader application in domains like construction engineering.

Sánchez Cuadrado et al. [28] introduced generic model transformation templates aimed at enhancing transformation reusability by defining templates over meta-model concepts. This allows for flexible binding to different meta-models, addressing structural heterogeneities. However, while it promotes reusability within similar contexts, it does not address the need for transformations between models conforming to different meta-metamodels.

The most related work to our proposal is Kovse and Härder [19], who proposed a framework for generic model transformations in UML-based models using XSLT, focusing on the implementation language rather than the modeling formalism. Their work, however, was limited to transformations within a single formalism (UML). Our approach extends beyond this restriction by enabling transformations among models from different formalisms (cf. Sect. 4).

3 Problem Context, Challenges and Contributions

The practical introduction of BIM in the construction sector demarcates a turning point in the planning and execution of construction projects. Whereas previously, 2D/3D drawings were the basis for planning and execution, BIM introduces a tool-supported process for the creation and management of digital representations of physical and functional characteristics of built assets along their life cycle [33]. Importantly, BIM postulates the use of structured, object-based models as a central unit of collaboration throughout the complete building life cycle. Consequently, the construction industry is transforming from its established rigid, plan-based project execution (cf. *Design-Bid-Build*) towards more agile, life cycle-oriented approaches that capitalize on the close collaboration of all stakeholders throughout the entire building life cycle (cf. *Design-Build*) [39, 42]. With the BIM model as the central unit of collaboration, model transformations are inevitable to (i) transform models within and between life cycle phases, (ii) accompanying representations conforming to distinct meta-metamodels (cf. IFC and gbXML), and (iii) for integrating additional tools in the design, engineering, and operations phases.

Commensurate with our previous discussions that highlight the current shortcomings of existing model transformation frameworks as to their formulation atop a single meta-metamodel, we thus address the following challenges:

1. Lacking support for model transformations among models conforming to distinct meta-metamodels.
2. Lacking general support for model transformations outside the software engineering domain.
3. Lacking support for model transformations on large and complex building models (cf. larger and more complex than the commonly used textbook examples in software engineering).

In resolving these challenges, we deliver the below contributions to execute model transformations among models conforming to distinct meta-metamodels and thus make model transformations accessible in other domains (e.g., construction engineering):

- Meta-metamodel-independent model transformations that support distinct meta-metamodels.
- A model transformation DSML for specifying declarative transformation rules with support for in-place operations.

– A scalable, rule-based model transformation engine with support for in-place operation evaluation.

Our contribution follows Design Science Research (DSR) [36] and provides artifacts to both facilitate meta-metamodel-independent model transformations and enable model transformations in other domains than software engineering, e.g., construction engineering. We start with requirements elicitation (cf. Sect. 4) and conclude with prototyping and experimentation (cf. Sect. 7). Our artifacts [37] are deployed as a solution to the following design science problem [36]:

> **Improve** *model transformations* (context)
> **by designing** *a scalable model transformation engine with*
> *an accompanying model transformation language* (artifact)
> **that satisfies** *meta-metamodel independence* (requirement)
> **to enable** *model transformations outside software engineering*
> *(e.g., construction engineering).* (goal)

4   Meta-Metamodel-Independent Model Transformations

To systematically derive the requirements for our meta-metamodel-independent model transformation framework, we followed the principles of DSR [36]. We grounded our requirements elicitation in both domain-specific challenges (e.g., interoperability limitations in BIM) and a critical review of related literature on model transformation frameworks (cf. Sect. 2). Key sources that guided our formulation include the classification of transformation tools by Kahani et al. [14] and the meta-metamodel constraints emphasized by Kappel et al. [15], both of which reveal gaps in supporting heterogeneous model ecosystems. This dual grounding—literature-based and problem-driven—ensures that our requirements reflect both theoretical rigor and practical relevance. Table 1 (see p. 7) outlines the requirements for our approach.

4.1   Solution Proposal

As presented in Figs. 1 and 2, we propose a model transformation formalism that is independent of the meta-metamodel where this *independence* refers to supporting distinct meta-metamodels w.r.t. source and target models, cf. *A* and *B* in Fig. 1. Specifically, we propose an architecture that is conceptually similar to the LLVM compiler infrastructure [23], which comprises a central optimizer (cf. the model transformation engine in our case) which is connected to different frontends (cf. IFC or UML frontends in our case) and different backends (cf. gbXML or ER in our case). We also employ an intermediary representation of models based on a core language (cf. Sect. 5.1) on which we run transformations and emit the target models. However, whereas LLVM capitalizes on a *common textual* representation of programs, our proposal primarily relies on *common XML-based* (and akin dialects like XMI) representation of models and meta-models (cf. Fig. 3). Given that a meta-model and a model are formalized using XML (and akin dialects), our proposal supports both parsing meta-models and models and emitting models that conform to distinct meta-metamodels. Figure 4 outlines this idea conceptually.

Table 1. Requirements for our proposed framework.

Req.	Description
[R1]	Existing model transformation approaches are constrained by the need for models to adhere to the same meta-metamodel, limiting their applicability. The construction industry requires transformations that bridge disparate modeling ecosystems, such as IFC and gbXML, making meta-metamodel independence a central requirement
[R2]	Achieving meta-metamodel independence necessitates representing meta-models independently of their underlying formalism. This requires a formalism-independent core language (cf. Fig. 1) for on-the-fly generation of meta-model implementations, defining the domain of possible model transformations expressed in the transformation language (cf. [**R6**])
[R3]	Modern BIM-based construction projects require frequent model and data exchange between tools (e.g., design vs. simulation) which often employ different geometric representations. Support for in-place expressions (e.g., value conversions or arithmetic operations) that are dynamically evaluated during transformations are essential
[R4]	Endogenous transformations, which rely on the same meta-model, are relatively straightforward as they use the same language for source and target models. Exogenous transformations, however, are more complex as they involve distinct meta-models. Our proposal introduces a third category, *isogenous* transformations, inspired by the Greek word $\iota\sigma o\gamma\varepsilon\upsilon\eta\zeta$, meaning "equal in kind or nature." This refers to transformations between models conforming to distinct meta-metamodels through a mutual implementation language (cf. Fig. 3). By design, our framework supports endogenous, exogenous, and isogenous transformations, allowing models to adhere to the same or different meta-metamodels seamlessly
[R5]	BIM models are substantially larger than software models, encompassing all design and execution information for construction projects. Our framework must scale to handle large models, particularly in infrastructure engineering, and manage the number of associated transformation rules efficiently
[R6]	The model transformation language (MTL; cf. Fig. 1) is crucial for defining the functional space of our proposal [18]. It must support various transformation types, including model-2-model and model-2-text transformations, and in-place expressions. Additionally, it should be extensible for custom rules and modular for reuse in composite transformations, promoting maintainability and reusability

The following sections provide a detailed discussion of our core language (Sect. 5.1), the model transformation language (Sect. 5), the underlying model transformation engine (Sect. 6), and necessary front- and backends (Sect. 6.2).

5   Transformation DSML

Before discussing our transformation DSML, we first introduce the necessary core language atop which our solution capitalizes.

5.1   Core Language

To perform transformations between source and target models, an efficient representation of these models is essential. This allows the transformation engine to systematically process and map data from the source to the target model using defined rules. As with meta-metamodel-dependent solutions, the structure of the source and target models by their meta-models is required.

The core language is central to our proposal, enabling meta-metamodel independence (cf. Fig. 4). It governs how meta-models of source and target models are processed and stored, defines the interface for frontends and backends, and specifies how to parse and emit models. Additionally, it determines the structure and application of transformation rules. Our approach relies on a formalism-independent, minimalist *core language* (CL; cf. Fig. 4) to represent meta-models independently of any formalism.

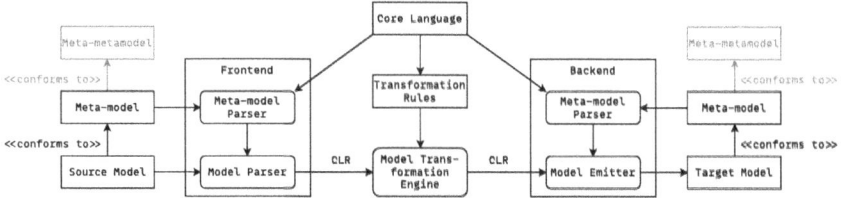

Fig. 4. Overview of the workings of our proposal. The *model transformation engine* receives an input model in the *core language representation* (CLR) (based on the core language, see Sect. 5.1) which is then subjected to the specified transformation rules. After all rules have been applied, the core representation of the model is emitted in the target language via the backend. Meta-metamodels are grayed out to indicate independence from them.

Ecore, provided by the Eclipse Foundation, represents such a core language [11]. As part of the Eclipse Modeling Framework (EMF), Ecore offers the necessary entities to represent meta-models and instantiate models accordingly. Using Ecore leverages existing tooling infrastructures, reducing the implementation effort for parsing and emitting models (i.e., frontends and backends). We refer to Gronback [11] for a detailed description. Observe that KM3 [2,34], another viable candidate, is no longer maintained and has been archived by the Eclipse Foundation.

5.2   A DSML for Rule-Based Model Transformations

Our *STructured RUle-based Model transformation Language* (STRUML; see Fig. 5 for the syntax diagram) is designed to be accessible to users with minimal programming experience. We opt for a declarative approach over an operational one, as it emphasizes the "what" rather than the "how," allowing users to focus on defining transformations without worrying about implementation details, which are handled by our transformation algorithm (cf. Sect. 6).

With STRUML, users define transformation `Rules`, specifying the `source` and `target` types involved in a `mapping`. The transformation process is governed by mapping `Rules` that dictate how values from the source model, such as `AssignmentValues`, are converted into suitable values in the target model, represented by `AssignmentTarget`. These values can be `AssignmentSourceValues` from the source model, default values, or in-place expressions evaluated during transformation (cf. `AssignmentExpression` and Sect. 5.2). Crucially, `AssignmentSourceValue` allows for the specification of additional element `properties` (e.g., attributes or methods) to be employed and evaluated during transformation, e.g., to query an elements type like `ifc_type = i.relatedObjects.ifcRoot.!0.?type`. Additionally, STRUML includes preconditions to ensure that transformations are executed under well-defined conditions, enhancing clarity and efficiency in managing complex model transformations.

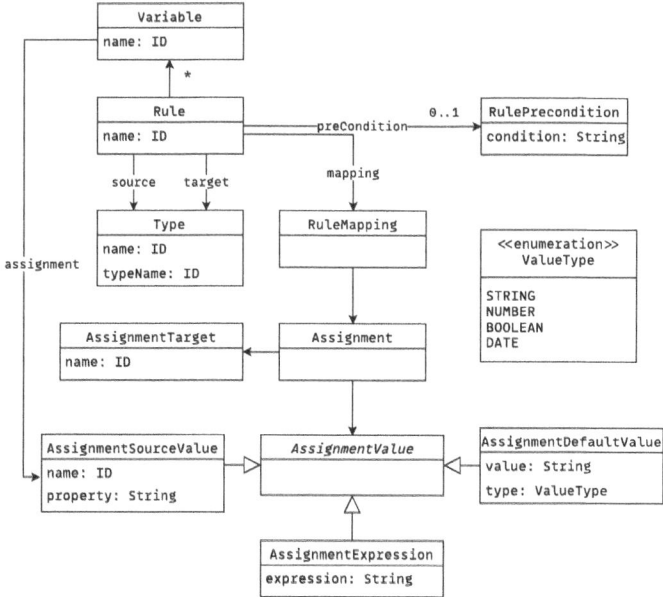

Fig. 5. Syntax Diagram of STRUML, our rule-based DSML for model transformations.

Listing 1 provides an example of a simple rule to convert an `IfcProperty` to a gbXML `UserDefinedField`.

In-Place Expressions

STRUML supports in-place expressions for dynamic evaluation during model transformations. A `Rule` can define `Variables` identified by a `name`, holding values from the source model for use in `AssignmentExpressions`. Currently, STRUML supports simple computational operations, such as value conversions or basic arithmetics, which are particularly relevant when converting between different modeling standards like IFC and gbXML. Listing 2 illustrates a mapping using in-place expressions, which are indicated by $\${"\dots"}$.

6   Artifact Implementation

In the following, we detail our artifact's implementation, which uses Java 21 and builds atop Eclipse Xtext [1] for DSML engineering (cf. Sect. 5). We further employ Ecore [30] for efficient in-memory model management using our CLR (cf. Sect. 5.1) and model emitting, and Apache Commons JEXL for evaluating in-place expression (cf. Sect. 5.2) [9].

6.1   Transformation Engine

Algorithm 1 outlines our model transformation engine, which systematically converts a source model S into a target model T using predefined mapping rules R and meta-models M_S and M_T. The `Transform(S,R)` function (l.4) initializes an empty target model T and iterates over each root element in S. For each element, it identifies the appropriate transformation rule by invoking `TransformElement(s,R)` (l.12). If a matching rule r is found, a new target element t is constructed using the structure defined in M_T and inserted into T. Elements are skipped if no rule is found or preconditions are not met, preventing invalid mappings. The transformed model T is returned as the output.

```
rule PropertyToAttribute {                                          1
    source type x: IfcProperty                                      2
    target type y: UserDefinedField                                 3
                                                                    4
    mapping {                                                       5
        y.name = x.name                                             6
        y.type = x.type.name                                        7
    }                                                               8
}                                                                   9
```

Listing 1: A rule to map an `IFCProperty` to a gbXML `UserDefinedField`.

```
 1   mapping {
 2       g.surfaceType = "InteriorWall":STRING
 3       g.id = ${"'_' + id"}
 4       g.constructionIdRef = ${"'_' + construction_id"}
 5       g.name.!0 = i.name
 6       g.rectangularGeometry.!0.height.!0.value = ${"height"}
 7       g.rectangularGeometry.!0.width.!0.value = ${"width"}
 8       g.rectangularGeometry.!0.cartesianPoint.!0.coordinate.!0.value = ${"x"}
 9       g.rectangularGeometry.!0.cartesianPoint.!0.coordinate.!1.value = ${"y"}
10       g.rectangularGeometry.!0.cartesianPoint.!0.coordinate.!2.value = ${"z"}
11       g.rectangularGeometry.!0.tilt.!0 = "90": NUMBER
12       g.rectangularGeometry.!0.azimuth.!0 = "0": NUMBER
13       g.opening.!0 = i.@RelatedElementsType1.ifcProduct.!1
14   }
```

Listing 2: A mapping of a complex transformation rule using in-place expressions (cf. ${"..."}) to convert IFC's rectangular, geometry-based object representation of a wall to gbXML's point-based representation by mapping from an IfcWallStandardCase (i) to gbXML's Surface (g).

The MapFields(s,t,r,R) function (l.21) is crucial for ensuring accurate field transfer. It uses a rule r to map primitive fields directly and handles associations by recursively resolving referenced elements and transforming them using TransformElement(x,R) (l.12). This preserves object relationships and hierarchical dependencies. MapFields(s,t,r,R) also evaluates in-place expressions using Apache Commons JEXL, enabling dynamic logic execution.

Our algorithm provides a scalable framework for model transformations through modular design, rule-based processing, and recursive reference resolution. It is applicable to various scenarios, including converting UML models to database schemas or transforming domain-specific models like building models. The complexity of Algorithm 1 is $O(n)$ for best-case flat models, $O(n \cdot m)$ for average cases with moderate recursion, and $O(n^2)$ for worst-case fully connected models, depending on the number of elements (n), fields (m), and recursion depth.

6.2 Frontend and Backend

Following our LLVM-inspired design (cf. Fig. 2), our model transformation engine requires respective front- and backends for parsing meta-models and models into our CLR, and for emitting models from the CLR, respectively.

The frontend initially parses a meta-model in XML to establish its internal representation in our CLR. This process is parameterized by a configuration that specifies how XML elements are interpreted, including type information, node representation, and enumeration handling within the CLR. The resulting meta-model is then processed by the Model Parser, which instantiates its defined types while parsing the source model, also encoded in XML.

Algorithm 1. Model Transformation Algorithm.

```
1: Global: meta-model M_S, M_T
2: Input: Source model S, Mapping rules R
3: Output: Target model T

4: function Transform(S,R)
5:     Initialize target model T
6:     for each root element s ∈ S do
7:         t ← TransformElement(s, R)
8:         Insert target element t in T
9:     end for
10:     return T
11: end function

12: function TransformElement(s,R)
13:     Find matching transformation rule r ∈ R for s
14:     if r exists and s ⊢ r.preCondition then
15:         Create target element t from M_T
16:         MapFields(s,t,r,R)
17:         return t
18:     end if
19:     return ∅
20: end function

21: function MapFields(s,t,r,R)
22:     for each field f ∈ s do
23:         if f is a primitive type then
24:             Map f from s to t according to r
25:         else if f is an association a then
26:             x ← a.end                              ▷ a.end: referenced type
27:             y ← TransformElement(x,R)
28:             Map y to t according to r
29:         end if
30:     end for
31: end function
```

Similar to the `Metamodel Parser`, the `Model Parser` is configured to handle model loading, including resolving model element IDs, processing attributes or fields (cf. Algorithm 1), and optionally adding a fake root element when necessary (e.g., for IFC models as to their flat structure). This fake root element ensures that the transformation engine has a main entry point for rule application. An example configuration for parsing an IFC model is shown in Listing 3. Finally, the `Model Parser` emits the source model in our CLR, serving as an intermediary representation for applying meta-metamodel-independent model transformations.

```
 1   {
 2     "idTag": "id",
 3     "refTag": "ref",
 4     "loadReferences": true,
 5     "attributeIgnoreCase": true,
 6     "attributePrefix": "exp:",
 7     "attributeCamelCaseSeparator": "-",
 8     "defaultValueAttribute": "value",
 9     "fakeRoot": "IfcModel",
10     "addidtionalTypeInfo": false
11   }
```

Listing 3: Example frontend configuration for parsing an IFC model. The entries command the parsing process of an IFC input model, e.g., how to resolve element IDs and references, whether to ignore case, load additional type information, insert a fake root, etc.

Contrary to the frontend, the backend is responsible for emitting models after transformations have been applied, and does not require a configuration or a meta-model. All relevant information pertaining types' structures, which is relevant for emitting a target model readily can be inferred from the CLR-based representation of the target model. The examples discussed in the next section both employ the same frontend and backend, where the former is parameterized for the respective modeling formalisms employed (cf. Sect. 7), showcasing the versatility of our proposal.

7   Results and Discussion

We evaluate our proposal on two examples, (i) transforming an IFC model into its corresponding gbXML representation, and (ii) transforming a UML class diagram into an ER model formalized using Ecore. Our artifact with examples (input models, meta-models, parser configurations, and transformation rules, as well as output models) is available for download and experimentation [37].

7.1   IFC to gbXML

The IFC and gbXML are two well-known and established open standards for BIM-based modeling, with the former focusing on a general-purpose representation and the latter focusing on building energy and performance analysis. Figure 6a shows an IFC models (version 2x3, exported from Autodesk Revit using *In-session settings* and *Bounding Box* export) of a room with four walls, one window and a door. Given STRUML, we formulated the necessary transformation rules (cf. Listings 1 and 2). After defining the necessary configurations, we instrumented our artifact with these inputs (e.g., meta-models of the IFC and of gbXML, the actual IFC model, the mapping rules, and the configurations) to produce the gbXML-based model (version 6.01). The source and the target model are available in our artifact repository [37].

 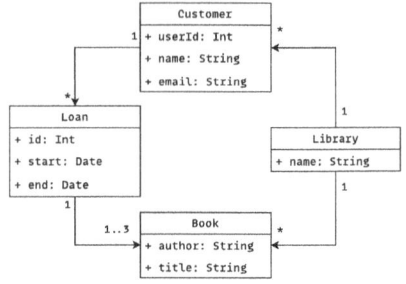

(a) IFC model of a room with 4 walls, a window and a door.   (b) UML model of a simple library management system.

Fig. 6. Input models (IFC and UML) used during our expriments.

7.2   UML to ER

To demonstrate the versatility of our proposal, we also applied it to a common use case from software engineering, viz. transforming a UML class diagram into its ER-based representation for database modeling. Figure 6b shows our input model (UML version 2.5.1) describing a simple library management system. Analogously to the case of transforming an IFC to a gbXML model, we defined the necessary transformation rules and configurations, instrumented our artifact with the relevant inputs (e.g., meta-models of the UML and our Ecore-based ER meta-model, the actual UML model, the mapping rules and the configurations) to produce an ER diagram (EMF version 2.41.0). The source and the target model are available in our artifact repository [37].

7.3   Performance Evaluation

During our experiments, we also established measurements to investigate performance-related aspects of our implementation (see Table 2). For the IFC to gbXML transformation, the framework efficiently processed 4131 source elements into 101 target elements in approximately 1.097 s. This demonstrates the framework's capability to handle large and complex models, which is crucial for applications in construction engineering. The time was distributed across parsing the source meta-model (0.66 s), the target meta-model (0.075 s), the source model (0.342 s), executing the transformation (0.082 s), and emitting the target model (0.004 s).

Table 2. Performance measurements (in seconds) for our experiments from Sects. 7.1 and 7.2.

Example	$|M_S|$	$|M_T|$	$|S|$	$|T|$	$|Ref_{M_S}|$	$|Ref_S|$	$|R|$	t_{M_S}	t_{M_T}	t_S	t_{Tr}	t_E	t_{Total}
IFC to gbXML	1473	256	4131	101	93	374	13	0.66	0.075	0.342	0.082	0.004	1.05
UML to ER	242	9	36	44	459	30	4	7.173	0.025	0.066	0.092	0.006	7.362

$|M_S|$: Number of elements in source meta-model; $|M_T|$: Number of elements in target meta-model; $|S|$: Number of elements in source model; $|T|$: Number of elements in target model; $|R|$: Number of rules applied; $|Ref_{M_S}|$: Number of references in source meta-model; $|Ref_S|$: Number of references in source model; $|R|$ Number of transformation rules; t_{M_S}: Processing time source meta-model (in secs.); t_{M_T}: Processing time target meta-model (in secs.); t_S: Processing time source model (in secs.); t_{TT}: Transformation time in secs.; t_E: Time to emit target model (in secs.); t_{Total}: Total duration (in secs.)

In contrast, the UML to ER transformation involved a smaller source model with 36 elements and a target model with 44 elements, taking about 7.362 s. The longer duration is attributed to the complexity of the UML meta-model. This highlights the impact of meta-model complexity on processing time.

Overall, the results indicate that the framework shows promise in scalability and efficiency, with the ability to handle transformations across various domains and model complexities. The performance insights suggest that although the framework performs reliably for large-scale transformations, there is room for improvement in optimizing the handling of complex meta-models to potentially enhance its efficiency further.

7.4 Discussion

In addressing the outlined requirements from Table 1, our framework effectively delivered all necessary capabilities to support meta-metamodel-independent model transformations. By leveraging a formalism-independent core language and a robust transformation engine, we ensured seamless interoperability between diverse modeling formalisms (**R1**). The successful transformation of models from IFC to gbXML and from UML to ER highlights the framework's ability to manage both the intricacies and the scale required in construction and software engineering domains (**R5**). STRUML facilitates the specification of declarative transformation rules with in-place expressions, supporting dynamic evaluations during transformations (**R3**, **R6**). This adaptability and performance enhance model transformation processes, meeting the evolving needs of various engineering disciplines, and fulfilling the initial requirements of scalability, flexibility, and applicability across domains (**R2**, **R4**).

The case studies and performance evaluation underscore the feasibility and generalizability of the proposed meta-metamodel-independent model transformation framework. The transformation from IFC to gbXML effectively demonstrates the framework's capability to manage large and complex models, a critical requirement for applications in construction engineering. This capability is essential for integrating diverse tools and workflows across the building life cycle,

344   P. Zech et al.

from design to operation. The UML to ER transformation further highlights the framework's versatility, showcasing its ability to handle models from different domains with varying complexities. This adaptability is crucial for broader adoption in software engineering and other fields where model transformations are essential for system integration and data interoperability.

Our findings align with existing research that emphasizes the need for flexible model transformation frameworks. Previous studies, such as those by Kahani et al. [14] and Kappel et al. [16], have highlighted the limitations of current approaches that rely on a common meta-metamodel, which restricts their applicability across different domains. Our framework addresses these limitations by introducing meta-metamodel independence at the syntactical layer, thereby enhancing interoperability and collaboration across diverse engineering disciplines.

Our, evaluation also reveals several challenges and areas for improvement. One significant issue is the potential for information loss during transformations, particularly when converting between different modeling standards like IFC and gbXML. This loss can be mitigated by caching the lost information for reintegration in subsequent transformations or by supplementing missing data from online sources or large language models. The necessity of bidirectional transformations without information loss depends on practical requirements and will be addressed incrementally in future iterations of the framework.

Scalability is another critical aspect. While our framework efficiently handles large models, as seen in the IFC to gbXML case, the complexity of meta-models significantly impacts performance. This is evident in the UML to ER transformation, where parsing the complex UML meta-model was more time-consuming. Future work will thus also focus on optimizing the handling of complex meta-models to enhance overall efficiency. Additionally, the framework's current implementation does not address error handling and debugging capabilities which are crucial for practical deployment. Generating frontends and backends dynamically could further streamline the transformation process, reducing the need for manual configuration and increasing flexibility.

While our framework demonstrates promising capabilities, its scalability in handling large-scale, real-world BIM projects requires further empirical validation. Future work will focus on conducting comprehensive tests with BIM models of various sizes and levels of detail [22] to substantiate our scalability claims. Additionally, we recognize the potential benefits of introducing higher-order transformations to automate the front-end step, which could further streamline the transformation process and enhance efficiency. Finally, to ensure the practical applicability of STRUML, we plan to conduct user studies with architects and BIM engineers to evaluate the framework's usability and its ability to capture domain semantics effectively. These studies will provide valuable insights into the framework's accessibility and inform improvements to better meet the needs of industry practitioners.

In utilizing Ecore as our CL, we acknowledge the benefits of tapping into a well-established ecosystem, although this choice inherently links our runtime to the EMF/Java environment. This strategic decision was made to enhance reusability and integrate seamlessly with existing tooling, rather than developing a new CL with necessary tooling from scratch. While our current implementation assumes XML-based model serialization, we recognize the importance of supporting non-XML formats in the future, possible through adaptable front and backend plugins (cf. Fig. 2), e.g., JSON or set theory-based representations [44]. Our reliance on Ecore does not affect meta-metamodel independence.

Although our current work does not delve into a deeper formalization of transformation semantics or guarantees which are crucial for model transformations-future work in this area is essential to build confidence in STRUML. Additionally, further clarification on the boundaries of mapping scenarios it handles, particularly in complex transformation situations, would enhance the understanding of STRUML's application scope.

In summary, while the proposed framework shows promise in facilitating model transformations across diverse domains, addressing these challenges is key to enhancing its robustness, applicability, and acceptance in practice.

8   Conclusion

Our work introduces a novel framework for meta-metamodel-independent model transformations, which addresses the ongoing challenge of integrating disparate modeling formalisms in disciplines such as BIM. We have effectively demonstrated the feasibility and efficacy of our approach through two case studies, including transformations from IFC to gbXML (BIM) and UML to ER (SE) models, by employing a core language (cf. Ecore) and STRUML, e.g., a custom DSML for defining model transformation rules. Our results emphasize the potential of our framework, which provides acceptable scalability and flexibility in model transformations. Our proposal promotes greater interoperability and collaboration among a variety of engineering disciplines.

In synopsis, our research not only resolves a critical technical challenge but also establishes new opportunities for innovation in BIM and related technologies, e.g., Digital Twins. By removing the barriers of incompatible meta-metamodels, we establish a more efficient and integrated approach to the model-driven design and management of complex systems.

References

1. Bettini, L.: Implementing domain-specific languages with Xtext and Xtend. Packt Publishing Ltd. (2016)
2. Bézivin, J., Brunette, C., Chevrel, R., Jouault, F., Kurtev, I.: Bridging the generic modeling environment (gme) and the eclipse modeling framework (emf). In: Proceedings of the Best Practices for Model Driven Software Development at OOPSLA, vol. 5 (2005)
3. Boje, C., Guerriero, A., Kubicki, S., Rezgui, Y.: Towards a semantic construction digital twin: directions for future research. Autom. Constr. **114**, 103179 (2020)

4. buildingSMART International: Industry Foundation Classes (IFC) Specification (2018)
5. Bézivin, J., Büttner, F., Gogolla, M., Jouault, F., Kurtev, I., Lindow, A.: Model transformations? transformation models! In: Nierstrasz, O., Whittle, J., Harel, D., Reggio, G. (eds.) MODELS 2006. LNCS, vol. 4199, pp. 440–453. Springer, Heidelberg (2006). https://doi.org/10.1007/11880240_31
6. Eisenberg, M., Pichler, H.P., Garmendia, A., Wimmer, M.: Towards reinforcement learning for in-place model transformations. In: 2021 ACM/IEEE 24th International Conference on Model Driven Engineering Languages and Systems (MODELS), pp. 82–88 (2021)
7. Felderer, M., Fiedler, F., Zech, P., Breu, R.: Flexible test code generation for service oriented systems. In: 9th International Conference on Quality Software (QSIC 2009). IEEE (2009)
8. Ferko, E., Berardinelli, L., Bucaioni, A., Behnam, M., Wimmer, M.: Towards interoperable digital twins: integrating sysml into aas with higher-order transformations. In: 2024 IEEE 21st Int. Conf. on Software Architecture Companion (ICSA-C), pp. 342–349. IEEE (2024)
9. Foundation A.S: Apache commons jexl - java expression language (2025). https://commons.apache.org/proper/commons-jexl/, Accessed Jan 04 202
10. gbXML Organization: Green Building XML Schema (gbXML) Specification (2023). https://www.gbxml.org, version 6.01
11. Gronback, R.C.: Eclipse modeling project: a domain-specific language (DSL) toolkit. Pearson Education (2009)
12. Hauer, M., et al.: Integrating digital twins with bim for enhanced building control strategies: A systematic literature review focusing on daylight and artificial lighting systems. Buildings 14(3), 805 (2024)
13. Kahani, N., Bagherzadeh, M., Cordy, J.R., Dingel, J., Varró, D.: Survey and classification of model transformation tools. Softw. Syst. Model. 18, 2361–2397 (2019)
14. Kahani, N., Bagherzadeh, M., Cordy, J.R., Dingel, J., Varró, D.: Survey and classification of model transformation tools. Softw. Syst. Model. Softw. Syst. Model. 18(4), 2361–2397 (2019)
15. Kappel, G., Langer, P., Retschitzegger, W., Schwinger, W., Wimmer, M.: Model transformation by-example: a survey of the first wave. Conceptual Modelling and Its Theoretical Foundations: Essays Dedicated to Bernhard Thalheim on the Occasion of His 60th Birthday, pp. 197–215 (2012)
16. Kappel, G., Langer, P., Retschitzegger, W., Schwinger, W., Wimmer, M.: Model transformation by-example: a survey of the first wave. In: Düsterhöft, A., Klettke, M., Schewe, K.-D. (eds.) Conceptual Modelling and Its Theoretical Foundations. LNCS, vol. 7260, pp. 197–215. Springer, Heidelberg (2012). https://doi.org/10.1007/978-3-642-28279-9_15
17. Kapsammer, E., Reiter, T., Schwinger, W.: Model-based tool integration-state of the art and future perspectives. In: Proceedings of the 3rd International Conference on Cybernetics and Information Technologies, Systems and Applications (CITSA 2006) (2006)
18. Kosar, T., Bohra, S., Mernik, M.: Domain-specific languages: a systematic mapping study. Inf. Softw. Technol. 71, 77–91 (2016)
19. Kovse, J., Härder, T.: Generic XMI-based UML model transformations. In: Bellahsène, Z., Patel, D., Rolland, C. (eds.) OOIS 2002. LNCS, vol. 2425, pp. 192–198. Springer, Heidelberg (2002). https://doi.org/10.1007/3-540-46102-7_24

20. Lano, K., Fang, S., Kolahdouz-Rahimi, S.: *TL*: an abstract specification language for bidirectional transformations. In: 23rd ACM/IEEE Int. Conf. on Model Driven Engineering Languages and Systems: Companion Proc, pp. 1–10 (2020)
21. Lano, K., Kolahdouz-Rahimi, S., Fang, S.: Model transformation development using automated requirements analysis, metamodel matching, and transformation by example. ACM Trans. Softw. Eng. Methodol. **31**(2) (2022)
22. Latiffi, A.A., Brahim, J., Mohd, S., Fathi, M.S.: Building information modeling (bim): exploring level of development (lod) in construction projects. Appl. Mech. Mater. **773**, 933–937 (2015)
23. Lattner, C., Adve, V.: LLVM: A compilation framework for lifelong program analysis & transformation. In: International Symposium on Code Generation and Optimization, CGO 2004, pp. 75–86. IEEE (2004)
24. Michael, J., et al.: Integrating models of civil structures in digital twins: State-of-the-Art and challenges. J. Infrastructure Intel. Resilience **3**(3) (2024). https://doi.org/10.1016/j.iintel.2024.100100
25. Muctadir, H.M., Manrique Negrin, D.A., Gunasekaran, R., Cleophas, L., van den Brand, M., Haverkort, B.R.: Current trends in digital twin development, maintenance, and operation: an interview study. Softw. Syst. Model., 1–31 (2024)
26. Platenius-Mohr, M., Malakuti, S., Grüner, S., Schmitt, J., Goldschmidt, T.: File- and API-based interoperability of digital twins by model transformation: an IIoT case study using asset administration shell. Futur. Gener. Comput. Syst. **113**, 94–105 (2020)
27. Rouhi, A., Kolahdouz Rahimi, S., Lano, K.: Formalizing model transformation patterns. J. Softw. Evolut. Process **34**(2) (2022)
28. Sánchez Cuadrado, J., Guerra, E., de Lara, J.: Generic model transformations: *write once, reuse everywhere*. In: Cabot, J., Visser, E. (eds.) ICMT 2011. LNCS, vol. 6707, pp. 62–77. Springer, Heidelberg (2011). https://doi.org/10.1007/978-3-642-21732-6_5
29. Sebastián, G., Gallud, J.A., Tesoriero, R.: Code generation using model driven architecture: a systematic mapping study. J. Comput. Lang. **56**, 100935 (2020)
30. Steinberg, D., Budinsky, F., Merks, E., Paternostro, M.: EMF: eclipse modeling framework. Pearson Education (2008)
31. Stevens, P.: A landscape of bidirectional model transformations. In: Generative and Transformational Techniques in Software Engineering II, vol. 5235 (2008)
32. Succar, B.: Building information modelling framework: a research and delivery foundation for industry stakeholders. Autom. Constr. **18**(3), 357–375 (2009)
33. Succar, B., Sher, W., Williams, A.: Measuring BIM performance: five metrics. Architect. Eng. Design Manag. **8**(2), 120–142 (2012)
34. Tisi, M., Jouault, F., Fraternali, P., Ceri, S., Bézivin, J.: On the use of higher-order model transformations. In: Paige, R.F., Hartman, A., Rensink, A. (eds.) ECMDA-FA 2009. LNCS, vol. 5562, pp. 18–33. Springer, Heidelberg (2009). https://doi.org/10.1007/978-3-642-02674-4_3
35. Turk, Ž: Ten questions concerning building information modelling. Build. Environ. **107**, 274–284 (2016)
36. Wieringa, R.J.: Statistical Difference-Making Experiments. In: Design Science Methodology for Information Systems and Software Engineering, pp. 295–317. Springer, Heidelberg (2014). https://doi.org/10.1007/978-3-662-43839-8_20
37. Zech, P.: Meta-metamodel-independent model transformations (2025). https://doi.org/10.5281/zenodo.15501693

38. Zech, P., Clark, T., Breu, R.: An empirical analysis of digital twin adoption. In: 58th Hawaiin International Conference on System Sciences (HICSS'58), pp. 6253–6262 (2025)
39. Zech, P., Goldin, E., Hammes, S., Geisler-Moroder, D., Pfluger, R., Breu, R.: Model-based auto-commissioning of building control systems. In: Proceedings of the 26th International Conference on Enterprise Information Systems (ICEIS 2024), pp. 121–128 (2024)
40. Zech, P., Hammes, S., Goldin, E., Geisler-Moroder, D., Breu, R., Pfluger, R.: From bim to digital twin: a transformation process through advanced control modeling and automated commissioning using daylight and artificial lighting as examples. Energy Build. **329**, 115184 (2025)
41. Zech, P., Jäger, A., Fröch, G., Pfluger, R., Breu, R.: Agile, continuous building energy modeling and simulation. SIMULATION **101**(3), 241–265 (2025)
42. Zech, P., Jäger, A., Schneiderbauer, L., Exenberger, H., Fröch, G., Flora, M.: Agile construction digital twin engineering. Buildings **15**(3), 386 (2025)
43. Zech, P., Nardin, C., Ristov, S., Flora, M., Breu, R.: Digital-twins-as-a-service in construction engineering. In: 2024 IEEE 20th International Conference on Automation Science and Engineering (CASE), pp. 3004–3010. IEEE (2024)
44. Zech, P., Vangheluwe, H., Breu, R.: A theoretical framework for model-based life cycle engineering of simulation models. In: 2025 Annual Modeling and Simulation Conference (ANNSIM), pp. 1–13. IEEE (2025)

Investigating the Role of LLMs Hyperparameter Tuning and Prompt Engineering to Support Domain Modeling

Vladyslav Bulhakov, Giordano d'Aloisio$^{(\boxtimes)}$, Claudio Di Sipio ,
Antinisca Di Marco , and Davide Di Ruscio

DISIM Department, University of L'Aquila, L'Aquila, Italy
vladyslav.bulhakov@student.univaq.it,
{giordano.daloisio,claudio.disipio,antinisca.dimarco,
davide.diruscio}@univaq.it

Abstract. The introduction of large language models (LLMs) has enhanced automation in software engineering tasks, including in Model Driven Engineering (MDE). However, using general-purpose LLMs for domain modeling has its limitations. One approach is to adopt fine-tuned models, but this requires significant computational resources and can lead to issues like catastrophic forgetting.

This paper explores how hyperparameter tuning and prompt engineering can improve the accuracy of the Llama 3.1 model for generating domain models from textual descriptions. We use search-based methods to tune hyperparameters for a specific medical data model, resulting in a notable quality improvement over the baseline LLM. We then test the optimized hyperparameters across ten diverse application domains.

While the solutions were not universally applicable, we demonstrate that combining hyperparameter tuning with prompt engineering can enhance results across nearly all examined domain models.

Keywords: domain modeling · large language models · MDE

1 Introduction

The interplay of Model Driven Engineering (MDE) and large language models (LLMs) has recently gained popularity, leading to different applications in several modeling tasks, including model completion [12], model generation [5,13], and specification of software architectures [1]. Nevertheless, full automation in modeling tasks is far from being reached [10], especially in domain modeling tasks, where human expertise is pivotal [33]. Moreover, general-purpose LLMs exhibit limitations in assisting modelers in completing or generating domain models [13]. One practical solution is represented by fine-tuning processes when an LLM can be specialized for a particular task [30]. While this method has been proven to be effective in domain modeling [15], it requires high-quality datasets that need to be collected, pre-processed, and encoded to train the model. Moreover, fine-tuned models can suffer from the so-called catastrophic forgetting [14], i.e., a

© The Author(s), under exclusive license to Springer Nature Switzerland AG 2026
D. Taibi and D. Smite (Eds.): SEAA 2025, LNCS 16081, pp. 349–366, 2026.
https://doi.org/10.1007/978-3-032-04190-6_21

significant drop in performance on previously learned tasks. Alternatively, the overall performance of a deep learning model can be increased by relying on the hyperparameter tuning technique [17], which is focused on finding the best combination of hyperparameters without additional training phases.

In this paper, we investigate the effect of hyperparameter tuning and prompt engineering on a notable LLM i.e., Llama 3.1 [31] when employed in a very specific task, i,e., domain modeling. First, we exploit the NSGA-II algorithm to find an initial set of hyperparameters for a specific application domain, i.e., medicine, using one single domain model, i.e., related to the LIFEMap project.[1] Afterward, a grid search is performed to refine the set of hyperparameters aiming at reaching a trade-off between semantic and syntactical correctness. In addition to the hyperparameter tuning, we experiment with three notable prompt techniques, i.e., zero-shots, few-shots, and chain-of-thoughts, as they have been successfully used in domain modeling [13].

To evaluate our approach, we compare models generated by Llama 3.1 with optimal configurations to those produced by Llama 3.1 using default hyperparameters, both utilizing the LIFEMap domain model as input. The performed experiments confirm that the models generated by the LLM with optimal configurations are significantly better than the baseline, motivating the need for hyperparameter tuning. Then, we assess the generalizability of the optimal solutions. To this end, we run the Llama 3.1 model using the identified list of hyperparameters on ten different application domains and collect the results for each prompt technique. Again, we compare the obtained results with a baseline model with default hyperparameters. While our results show that hyperparameter tuning alone is insufficient to achieve adequate automation in different domains, the combination with prompt technique helps mitigate this issue, achieving better results in most of the analyzed domains. These results again motivate the need for LLM's hyperparameter tuning to support domain model generation. In particular, hyperparameter tuning does not require a large set of modeling artifacts to be conducted, offering a valuable alternative when fine-tuning is not applicable. In future work, we plan to extend this analysis to other notable LLMs - like GPT, BERT, or DeepSeek - to assess if hyperparameter tuning is also effective with different models.

The main contributions of the paper are: *i)* a rigorous study on hyperparameter tuning on LIFEMap domain; *ii)* an extensive evaluation with 10 state-of-the-art domain models to assess to what extent our approach is generic; *iii)* a replication package to foster research in this domain [9].

2   Motivation and Related Work

Motivating Example: Through domain modeling, formal representations typically specified in class diagrams are conceived out of textual requirements. Although several approaches have been developed to assist modelers in domain modeling, the process is still challenging due to the complexity of peculiar

---

[1] https://www.thelifemap.it/.

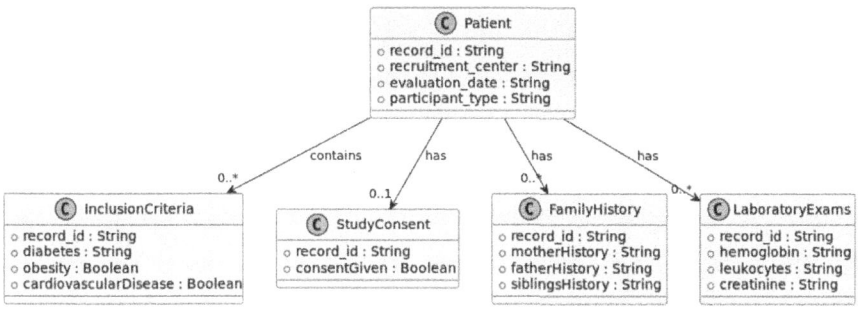

Fig. 1. Excerpt of the LIFEMap domain model

domains. Figure 1 depicts an excerpt of the LIFEMap model, which represents a medical Case Report Form (CRF) for patients under specific treatments. In particular, a `Patient` has a `FamilyHistory` that may affect the treatment and the corresponding `LaboratoryExams`. It is worth mentioning that the discussed model is only an excerpt of the whole domain model,[2] which contains 31 classes, 291 attributes, and 48 relationships.

To produce domain models, modelers must manually inspect huge textual documents to extract relevant concepts. Relying on automated techniques, like intelligent modeling assistants [32], requires curated and large modeling datasets [29]. Moreover, documents might contain sensitive data that cannot be disclosed, as modeled by the entity `StudyConsent`, thus limiting training data to perform advanced training techniques, e.g., fine-tuning or retrieval augmented generation (RAG) [3,28]. To overcome such limitations, in this paper, we leverage the hyperparameter tuning strategy by providing a set of hyperparameters that can support the usage of LLMs in this peculiar domain.

Related Work: DoMoBOT [34] combines NLP and a supervised ML model to automatically retrieve domain models from textual contents using the spaCy tool.[3] After the pre-processing phase, the predictive component uses the encoded sentences to retrieve similar model entities and generate the final domain model.

In [6], authors exploit the NSGA-II algorithm to retrieve partial metamodels. The system first searches a list of candidates given inputs relevant to the considered task. Then, several similarity criteria are selected as additional optimization objectives to support model completion.

Chaaben *et al.* [12] supports model completion using GPT-3 equipped with using semantic mapping, i.e., embedding the model elements as structured text in the prompt. Preliminary results computing traditional accuracy metrics on 30 models extracted from the ModelSet dataset [29] show that the few-shot approach can help modelers complete static UML models. In [8], the authors

---

[2] The complete model is available in the online appendix [9].
[3] https://spacy.io/.

exploited the GPT-3 model with a few-shots prompt technique to translate textual requirements in domain-specific modeling language (DSL) specifications in the context of Advanced Driver Assistance Systems (ADAS). Starting from unstructured textual requirements, they derive formal rules used in the DSL specification.

Camara *et al.* [11] explored the capability of GPT3.5 to automate domain modeling tasks, including OCL rule generation. The conducted experiment, considering 40 models belonging to 8 different domains, shed light on limitations in model generation.

Mutagene [20] is a custom GPT-4 model to support the development of DSMLs that relies on a dedicated knowledge base, including the Xtext syntax, examples, and documentation to support a specific use case, i.e., modeling mutation. Similarly, ModelMate [15] relies on fine-tuned LLM to assist modelers in three different DSL-related tasks, i.e., identifier suggestion, line completion, and block completion. In particular, three different LLMs have been fine-tuned, i.e., GPT-2, Code Parrot, and Code-Gen, to support three tasks, showing superior accuracy compared to traditional techniques considering the three examined tasks. A conceptual framework to integrate LLMs with graphical DSML has been proposed in [7]. First, the high-level concepts are extracted from the current literature. Then, a proof-of-concept using ChatGPT is discussed, i.e., the proposed framework is used to design a simple traffic light DSML for individuals with color blindness.

The most related work to ours is [13], where the authors experimented with GPT-3.5 and GPT-4 using different prompt engineering methods and conducted a detailed comparative evaluation with precision, recall, and F1-measure, plus a manual comparison using a tailored correctness metric. While we rely on the same dataset to evaluate our approach, we cannot directly compare the obtained results as *i)* we rely on a smaller LLM, i.e., Llama 3, and *ii)* we adopt Cosine and BERT scores as similarity functions in the hyperparameter tuning as they provide proper integration with the NSGA-II algorithm.

3   Methodology

This section outlines the procedures used to identify the optimal hyperparameter configurations for the LLM, as well as the prompt engineering strategies that were implemented on the considered LLM, i.e., Llama 3.1.

3.1   Hyperparameter Tuning

Figure 2 reports an overview of the hyperparameter tuning process. We start from an initial search space of hyperparameters and possible value combinations. Next, we employ a global search strategy - namely NSGA-II [17] - to reduce the space of possible solutions. From this reduced search space, we perform an exhaustive grid search process to evaluate each potential solution. From this search process, we derive a set of optimal solutions that achieve the best

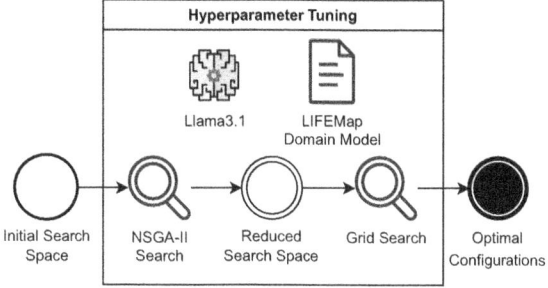

Fig. 2. Hyperparameter tuning methodology

Table 1. Hyperparameters search space

Hyperparameter	Value Range
Temperature	$[0.5, 2]$ with step size of 0.1
Top-k	$[0, 100]$ with step size of 10
Top-p	$[0.5, 1.0]$ with step size of 0.1
Repetition penalty	$[1.0, 2.0]$ with step size of 0.1
Max new tokens	$\{512, 1024, 2048, 3072, 4096, 8192\}$

semantical and syntactical correctness trade-off of the generated models. As mentioned above, the whole search process is performed using Llama3.1 as the base LLM. In particular, we ask the LLM to generate an Ecore metamodel of the LIFEMap textual domain model outlined in Sect. 2.

Search Space. In our study, we fine-tune the following hyperparameters of Llama3.1, which have been shown to be the most influential on the quality of the generated content [4]:

➤ **Temperature:** Influences output randomness; lower values (close to 0) make it deterministic, while higher values (≥ 1) increase randomness.
➤ **Top-k:** Determines the number of high-probability tokens to consider for text generation. Lower values (1–10) result in more deterministic behavior; higher values increase randomness.
➤ **Top-p:** Used with top-k to select tokens based on cumulative probability. Lower values (0.1–0.3) create a smaller set for selection, making the output more deterministic, while higher values (0.8–0.9) expand the selection set.
➤ **Repetition penalty:** Limits excessive repetition in output. Values close to 1 allow repetition; values (≥ 1.8) discourage it.
➤ **Max new tokens:** Sets the maximum number of tokens that can be generated in response to a prompt, with higher values leading to longer responses.

Since there is no agreement on which range of hyperparameter values is more suited for model generation tasks [4,13], we explore a wide range of values that spans from low to high settings. The search space is reported in Table 1.

Given the size of the search space and the high computational complexity of generative models, performing an exhaustive search of this space is infeasible. Thus, we rely on an advanced multi-objective search strategy to refine this space, as discussed in the next section.

Search Strategies. We employ a combination of two search strategies to explore the search space described in Sect. 3.1. The objective of our search task is to identify hyperparameter configurations within the search space that allow the LLM to produce models with the highest levels of semantic and syntactic correctness compared to a ground truth model. Thus, this task can be defined as a multi-objective search problem where we maximize both the semantic and syntactic correctness of the generated models.

First, we rely on a global search strategy to refine the search space. Secondly, starting from the reduced search space, we perform a comprehensive grid search of all the possible combinations. Eventually, the search process returns the solutions that achieve the best trade-off of semantic and syntactical correctness for the generated models.

Global Search. The global search strategy employed in our work is the NSGA-II algorithm [17]. It is an evolutionary algorithm that has been shown to be widely efficient and effective for multi-objective problems [24,25,36]. It follows the general behavior of genetic evolutionary algorithms, where an initial population of individuals progressively evolves following Darwin's theory of biological evolution [22].

The algorithm starts with an initial population of N randomly generated individuals, and the quality of each individual is assessed following a given *fitness* function. Next, the evolution process begins. First, the best individuals from the population are selected following a given *selection* strategy, creating an offspring population O_t. This new population is evolved using specific *crossover* and *mutation* strategies under specific probabilities p_c and p_m, respectively, and the quality of the new individuals is again evaluated. The new offspring population O_t is merged with the population of the t generation P_t to create a temporary population P'. The individuals from P' are sorted based on a non-dominated sorting strategy. Finally, the first N individuals are selected from P' to create the new population P_{t+1}. This process is repeated until the maximum number of generations G is reached and the final population P^* is returned.

In our use case, each individual in the search is represented as a dictionary of hyperparameters and related values, and the population size is 30. The number of generations is set to 10. The *selection* strategy is a *Tournament Selection* based on dominance between two individuals. The number of individuals selected is equal to the population size. The *crossover* function is a *Single Point Crossover* operator [27] with 90% of probability. The *mutation* strategy is a Uniform Mutation operator where all hyperparameters are randomly mutated. The mutation

Table 2. Reduced search space

Hyperparameter	Value Range
Temperature	$[1.0, 1.3]$ with step size of 0.1
Top-k	$\{0, 50\}$
Top-p	$[0.9, 1.0]$ with step size of 0.1
Repetition penalty	$\{1.0, 1.1, 1.2\}$
Max new tokens	$\{512, 1024, 2048, 3072, 4096\}$

probability is 20%. Finally, the quality of each individual is evaluated using two fitness functions for syntactical and semantic similarity against a ground truth model. Concerning syntactic similarity, we employ the widely adopted **Cosine Similarity** score [35]. This metric measures the similarity of two documents as the cosine of their angle in their term-frequency vector representation. If two documents are syntactically equal, then their cosine similarity is one. Instead, we use the **BERTScore** metric for semantic similarity. This metric evaluates the quality of a generated text by computing the similarity between the BERT embeddings of two documents [42]. As for the Cosine Similarity, the optimal value of this metric is one.

The choice for those metrics is driven by their employment in previous works related to domain modeling [19, 39]. While we acknowledge that there are more specific metrics to assess the similarity of modeling artifacts, e.g., EMFCompare[4], they do not provide an API to be used as a fitness function of the NSGA-II algorithm.

As stated above, we employ this global search strategy to reduce the search space of possible solutions. In particular, we ran the above mentioned algorithm ten times and identified the range of values for each hyperparameter in the final populations. Notably, we obtained a smaller set of hyperparameters, which made it suitable to perform an exhaustive grid search. The reduced space of solutions is reported in Table 2.

Grid Search. Starting from the reduced space of solutions returned by NSGA-II, we performed an exhaustive grid search by evaluating each possible hyperparameter setting in the search space. We conducted this additional search to evaluate all possible configurations and identify the optimal settings that could be reused for all domain modeling generation tasks.

The final outcome is the Pareto front of the solutions with respect to BERT Score and Cosine Similarity. The Pareto front solutions are those that are not dominated by any other solution in the search space - i.e., they are better than all solutions in at least one fitness score and no worse in all the others [23]. In particular, we identified six different configurations, which are the subject of our evaluation. The whole search process (i.e., NSGA-II search plus Grid

---

[4] https://github.com/eclipse-emf-compare/emf-compare.

Table 3. Optimal solutions and Llama default configuration

	Configuration
S0	{Temperature: 0.6, Top-k: 50, Top-p: 1.0, Max New Tokens: 4096}
S1	{Temperature: 1.0, Top-k: 0, Top-p: 1.0, Max New Tokens: 2048}
S2	{Temperature: 1.1, Top-k: 50, Top-p: 0.9, Max New Tokens: 3072}
S3	{Temperature: 0.8, Top-k: 50, Top-p: 0.9, Max New Tokens: 4096}
S4	{Temperature: 1.1, Top-k: 50, Top-p: 0.9, Max New Tokens: 3072}
S5	{Temperature: 1.1, Top-k: 50, Top-p: 0.9, Max New Tokens: 4096}
Llama Default	{Temperature: 0.7, Top-k: 50, Top-p: 0.9, Max New Tokens: 4096}

search) took around ten days of machine execution over a CentOS HPC cluster equipped with 32 Intel(R) Xeon(R) Gold 6140M CPUs and two Nvidia A100 and A30 GPUs. The optimal configurations are reported in Table 3.

3.2 Prompt Engineering

In this work, we analyze the three most adopted prompt engineering strategies for software engineering tasks. The choice of those strategies is also motivated by previous work on the adoption of LLMs for domain modeling [13]. In the following, we summarize each adopted prompt strategy, while the complete prompts are reported in our replication package [9].

Zero-Shot. This strategy is our baseline and has been employed during the hyperparameter tuning phase. An excerpt of the prompt employed is reported in Listing 1.1. In general, with a zero-shot prompt, the LLM is fed only textual instructions on the task to be performed and the input file to process. In our case, we give the LLM a textual description of the LIFEMap domain model and ask it to extract all entities, attributes, and relations from it. We ask the LLM to behave as a domain modeling expert and generate the output as an Ecore model.

```
You are a domain modeling expert.
Identify all entities in the text.
Identify all attributes and data types.
Identify all relationships among entities.
Generate the output as an Ecore model.
$<$textual LIFEMap domain model$>$
```

Listing 1.1. Excerpt of Zero-shot prompt

Few-Shot. Few-shot prompting extends the zero-shot strategy by including examples of the output that the LLM has to generate. In our case, we append two examples of Ecore models to the end of the prompt. An excerpt of the prompt is given in Listing 1.2.

```
<Zero-Shot prompt>
<example ecore model 1>
<example ecore model 2>
<textual LIFEMap domain model>
```

Listing 1.2. Excerpt of Few-shot prompt

Chain-of-Thought. Chain-of-Thought (CoT) is an extension of the few-shot strategy that includes reasoning steps in addition to the examples provided to the LLM [38]. The reasoning steps link the examples provided with the task that the LLM has to solve. In particular, in addition to the two examples of Ecore models, we feed the LLM with textual descriptions of those example domain models and the steps to follow to define Ecore models from those textual descriptions. An excerpt of this prompt is given in Listing 1.3.

```
<Zero-Shot prompt>
<textual description of example 1>
<steps to derive ecore model for example 1>
<example ecore model 1>
<textual description of example 2>
<steps to derive ecore model for example 2>
<example ecore model 2>
<textual LIFEMap domain model>
```

Listing 1.3. Excerpt of Chain-of-Thought prompt

Concerning the examined model, we focus on the `Llama-3.1-8B-Instruct` model available in the HuggingFace repository.[5] By the time of this paper, Llama 3.1 is among the latest releases of the family of Llama language models that exploit optimized transformer architecture and reinforcement learning with human feedback. Thus, the model is widely adopted for many tasks, including code-related tasks [18,21].

4 Evaluation

4.1 Reseach Questions

- **RQ$_1$**: *To what extent an optimal hyperparameter setting is effective for different domain models?* This research question evaluates whether optimal hyperparameter configurations can be generalized across different domain models without prompt engineering. We begin with a sanity check using the LIFEMap model to verify that the improved hyperparameters enhance the semantic and syntactic quality of generated models. We then apply these hyperparameters across various domain models using an existing dataset [13]. If the models are semantically and syntactically correct, we conclude that hyperparameter tuning can be done once, allowing for generalization without additional prompt engineering.

---

[5] https://huggingface.co/meta-llama/Llama-3.1-8B-Instruct.

- **RQ$_2$**: *How the combination of hyperparameter tuning and prompt engineering techniques can improve the quality of models generated for different domains?* To answer this question, we experiment with advanced prompt engineering strategies, i.e., Few-Shot, and CoT. Specifically, suppose the LLM, configured with a particular hyperparameter setting and employing a specific prompt engineering strategy, effectively generates models that are both semantically and syntactically correct across various domains. In that case, we can conclude that hyperparameter tuning can be performed once, and the optimal settings can be applied for multiple domain models when using that prompt engineering strategy.

4.2   Dataset

To assess the generalizability of the optimal solutions, we evaluate the semantical and syntactical correctness of domain models generated for the use cases employed in [13]. In particular, the dataset includes ten heterogeneous domain models: **BTMS:** *transportation* domain; **H2S:** *food delivery* domain; **Lab-Tracker:** *health* domain; **CeIO:** *social* domain; **TSS:** *sport* domain; **SHAS:** *IoT* domain; **OTS:** *teaching* domain; **Block:** *game* domain; **Tile-O:** *game* domain; **HBMS:** *management* domain.

A more detailed description of these domain models is available in [13]. However, it is worth noting that they have different degrees of complexity regarding the number of classes, attributes, and relations. The number of entities ranges from 7 to 23. The attributes span from 11 to 43, whereas the number of relationships ranges from 9 to 27. Nevertheless, none of them is comparable with the LIFEMap model in terms of size as discussed in Sect. 2.

4.3   Prompt Engineering and Metrics

For answering RQ$_1$, we use a zero-shot prompting strategy, maintaining the same structure as illustrated in Sect. 3.2 that represents our baseline model. To answer RQ$_2$, we utilize prompts designed with few-shot and chain-of-thought strategies, adhering to the structures detailed in Sects. 3.2 and Sect. 3.2, respectively. Note how, for RQ$_2$, the prompt engineering strategies are also used by the baseline LLM with default hyperparameters.

As mentioned in Sect. 3, the syntactic correctness is evaluated by computing the Cosine Similarity between the generated models and a ground truth consisting of a domain model manually created [35]. The semantic similarity is instead assessed by computing the BERTScore [42] between the generated models and the ground truth. These metrics are employed in both RQs.

Finally, to account for the randomness of LLMs in output generation, following previous works [13,16], for each RQ, we repeat the model generation process 20 times for each prompt and hyperparameter setting. In addition, we perform the one-sided non-parametric Wilcoxon test to assess if there is a statistically significant difference in the results obtained for each RQ [41]. Following common methodology [40], if the test's p-value is ≤ 0.05, then we can reject the null hypothesis and assess, with a statistical significance, that the Cosine Similarity and BERT Score of the domain models generated by the LLM with optimal configurations are higher (i.e., better) than the baseline. We chose this test instead of the paired t-test because, being non-parametric, it makes no assumption on the data distribution [41].

In addition, again following established standards [2], when the p-value is ≤ 0.05, we complement the results obtained by the Wilcoxon test with the Vargha-Delaney A_{12} effect size [37] to assess the size of the obtained difference. This test measures the proportions of items whose difference is higher than zero. Following previous work [36], we consider the effect size *large* if $A_{12} \geq 0.72$, *medium* if $0.64 < A_{12} < 0.72$, and *small* if $A_{12} \leq 0.64$.

5   Results

In this section, we discuss the results of our empirical evaluation. For all RQs (apart from $RQ_{1.1}$, which is a sanity check on the LIFEMap domain model), we counted the number of times in which each optimal configuration provided models that are syntactically and semantically better than the baseline. In particular, following previous empirical work [26], we use the so-called *Win / Tie / Loss* strategy. We count the number of times a solution scored a Wilcoxon's $p$value< 0.05 (Win), $p$value> 0.99 (Loss), and $0.05 \leq p$value ≥ 0.99 (Tie). In addition, we count the number of times the obtained A_{12} effect size is *large/medium/small* for each *Win* case.

Table 4a reports the statistics for each optimal solution, while Table 4b reports the results for each domain model. Note how, in Table 4b, the effect sizes are not reported since they are the same as in Table 4a. In both tables, we highlight cases where the number of wins is higher than losses.

5.1   RQ₁: Zero-Shot Prompting

$RQ_{1.1}$: **Sanity check.** Figure 3 reports the distribution of Cosine Similarity and BERT Score of models generated by Llama3.1 for the LIFEMap domain model. The left-most blue boxes show the results obtained by Llama3.1 with the optimal configurations, while the right-most orange boxes show the results obtained by the baseline model with default hyperparameters. As shown in the plot, the syntactical and semantical quality of domain models generated by the LLM with optimal hyperparameters significantly overcomes the results obtained by the baseline. This outcome is confirmed by the results of the Wilcoxon test and the A_{12} effect size, which reported a large significant difference.

The results obtained motivate the need for tuning the LLM's hyperparameter for domain modeling generation. Next, we investigate how the obtained results can be generalized to different domain models.

Table 4. Win / Tie / Loss between optimal solutions and the baseline model

(a) Comparison between any optimal solution and the baseline model in all domain models.

	RQ$_{1.2}$: Zero-Shot		RQ$_{2.1}$: Few-Shot		RQ$_{2.2}$: CoT	
	Cosine	BERT	Cosine	BERT	Cosine	BERT
S0	4 / 0 / 6	2 / 2 / 6	5 / 0 / 5	5 / 1 / 4	7 / 1 / 2	4 / 0 / 6
S1	1 / 0 / 9	2 / 1 / 7	8 / 0 / 2	4 / 0 / 6	6 / 1 / 3	1 / 0 / 9
S2	1 / 1 / 8	1 / 0 / 9	6 / 1 / 3	4 / 2 / 4	6 / 0 / 4	1 / 0 / 9
S3	3 / 0 / 7	1 / 2 / 7	9 / 0 / 1	2 / 0 / 8	8 / 0 / 2	5 / 0 / 5
S4	1 / 1 / 8	0 / 0 / 10	6 / 1 / 3	3 / 0 / 7	6 / 2 / 2	3 / 0 / 7
S5	4 / 0 / 6	3 / 3 / 4	7 / 0 / 3	3 / 0 / 7	7 / 0 / 3	2 / 1 / 7
A_{12}	14 / 0 / 0	9 / 0 / 0	41 / 0 / 0	21 / 0 / 0	40 / 0 / 0	16 / 0 / 0

(b) Comparison between all optimal solutions and the baseline model in each domain model.

	RQ$_{1.2}$: Zero-Shot		RQ$_{2.1}$: Few-Shot		RQ$_{2.2}$: CoT	
	Cosine	BERT	Cosine	BERT	Cosine	BERT
HBMS	3 / 1 / 2	3 / 0 / 3	4 / 0 / 2	3 / 1 / 2	5 / 0 / 1	1 / 1 / 4
OTS	0 / 0 / 6	0 / 1 / 5	3 / 0 / 3	0 / 0 / 6	4 / 0 / 2	2 / 0 / 4
SHAS	1 / 0 / 5	1 / 0 / 5	3 / 0 / 3	3 / 0 / 3	1 / 2 / 3	0 / 0 / 6
BTMS	2 / 0 / 4	3 / 2 / 1	3 / 1 / 2	2 / 0 / 4	4 / 0 / 2	4 / 0 / 2
LabTracker	1 / 0 / 5	0 / 0 / 6	6 / 0 / 0	4 / 1 / 1	5 / 0 / 1	2 / 0 / 4
CelO	5 / 0 / 1	0 / 2 / 4	6 / 0 / 0	3 / 0 / 3	5 / 0 / 1	3 / 0 / 3
TileO	0 / 0 / 6	0 / 1 / 5	2 / 1 / 3	0 / 0 / 6	3 / 1 / 2	0 / 0 / 6
H2S	2 / 1 / 3	2 / 1 / 3	6 / 0 / 0	1 / 0 / 5	5 / 0 / 1	2 / 0 / 4
TSS	0 / 0 / 6	0 / 1 / 5	5 / 0 / 1	5 / 0 / 1	4 / 1 / 1	2 / 0 / 4
Block	0 / 0 / 6	0 / 0 / 6	3 / 0 / 3	0 / 1 / 5	4 / 0 / 2	0 / 0 / 6

RQ$_{1.2}$: Solutions Generalizability. The results reported in Table 4a for Zero-Shot show how no configuration achieved more wins than losses. This result is confirmed for both Cosine Similarity and BERT Score. However, we also observe how, for the winning cases, the effect size is always *large*. Thus, when the LLM with optimal configurations generates better models, they are significantly better.

Instead, we observe in Table 4b a disagreement in the syntactical and semantical quality of the generated domain models. In fact, under Cosine Similarity (i.e., syntactical quality), there are two domain models with more wins than losses - namely **HBMS** and **CelO**. These domains pertain to *Hotel Booking Management* and *Celebration Organization*, respectively, and have an average number of classes, attributes, and relations compared to the other domain models. Thus, we found no particular pattern among these use cases and with the LIFEMap domain model. Instead, under the BERT Score (i.e., semantical quality), we found no domain models with more wins than losses.

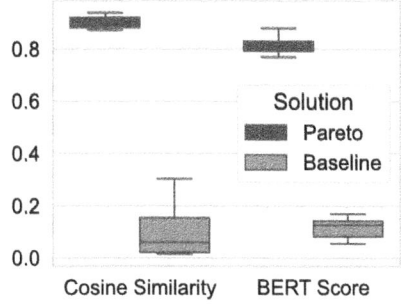

Fig. 3. $RQ_{1.1}$: Distribution of Cosine Similarity and BERTScore of models generated by Llama3.1 using the optimal configurations and with standard hyperparameters

In general, this evaluation may lead us to conclude that the optimal solutions returned by our search can not be generalized to different domain models. This result again motivates our next research question, which involves including prompt engineering strategies in the analysis.

Answer to RQ_1: The combination of identified optimal solutions and zero-shot prompting can significantly improve the quality of models generated for the training domain. However, the optimal solutions can not be generalized to different domain models.

5.2 RQ_2: Prompt Engineering

$RQ_{2.1}$: **Few-Shot.** From the statistics in Table 4a, we observe a discrepancy between the syntactical and semantic similarities of the generated models. Five out of six solutions have a higher count of wins concerning syntactical similarity. In contrast, we identified only one solution that had more wins with respect to the BERT Score. Notably, this solution is also the only one that did not have more wins in terms of Cosine Similarity. This finding may suggest a systematic disagreement between these two metrics when evaluating the quality of domain models. As for the RQ_1, we observe how the effect size for the winning cases is always large.

By looking at the statistics for each domain model in Table 4b, we observe how the number of domain models with more wins than losses increases compared with $RQ_{1.2}$. In addition, note how the two winning domain models from $RQ_{1.2}$ - i.e., **HBMS** and **CelO** - are also winning here.

It is worth noting that the two metrics are concordant in **LabTracker**, **HBMS**, and **TSS** domain models. On the one hand, this is quite expected in the first case since the **LabTracker** domain is the closest to the LIFEMap model, i.e., both are tailored for the medical domain even though the latter is more complex. On the other hand, **HBMS** and **TSS** are completely different from the medical concepts, even though both contain a lot of generalizations for representing different types of travelers and players, respectively.

RQ$_{2.2}$: Chain-of-Thoughts. By looking at the Win/Tie/Loss scores in Table 4a, we can see how all optimal solutions provide more wins than losses concerning Cosine Similarity. On the contrary, no solution achieves more wins concerning BERT Score. Again, this result may suggest a disagreement of those metrics.

By instead observing the stats for domain models in Table 4b, the number of domain models in which more optimal solutions are better than the baseline increases in Cosine Similarity while decreasing in BERT Score. Remarkably, only the **BTMS** model achieves the agreement between the two metrics. Our intuition is that the reasoning steps introduced in the CoT prompt lead to this result, thus allowing the usage of hyperparameter tuning in completely different domains.

From this evaluation, we may conclude that few-shot prompting is preferred to increase both syntactical and semantical similarity. At the same time, chain-of-thought may be suggested to obtain the best syntactical similarity of the generated models.

Answer to RQ$_2$: Adding hyperparameter tuning to prompt engineering strategies significantly improves the quality of generated models. Few-shot prompting is suggested to increase both syntactical and semantical similarity. On the contrary, optimal hyperparameters and chain-of-thought prompting obtained the best syntactical similarity of generated models.

6   Threats to Validity

This section discusses threats that may hamper the results of our study and the adopted mitigations.

Threats to internal validity concerns two aspects of our experiment, i.e., hyperparameter tuning and the employed prompt engineering techniques. Concerning the first aspect, we followed the state-of-the-art process adopted in operational research. In addition, we perform a sanity check to validate the results obtained from the global and local search. Concerning the second, we acknowledge that prompting can introduce unexpected variability during the generation of the domain models. To mitigate these issues, we compute well-known similarity functions to compare the generated domain models with the real ones. In addition, we used the Win/Tie/Loss test to confirm the outcomes of our study.

External validity is related to the generalizability of our results to other domains or LLMs. On the one hand, the results show that the hyperparameter tuning is not enough to generalize the results obtained with Llama 3 if different domains are considered. On the other hand, well-founded prompt engineering techniques can contribute to limiting this issue. Another issue is related to the used LLMs, i.e., Llama 3 may not be suitable for modeling tasks. In this respect, we opt for using the most popular open-source model even though we plan to extend our study to additional models with different architecture, e.g., DeepSeek, Claude, or GPT models.

7 Conclusion and Future Work

Motivated by the lack of previous studies in hyperparameter tuning for Large Language Models (LLMs) for supporting the generation of domain models, this paper introduced a novel approach that combines hyperparameter tuning and prompt engineering for supporting domain modeling using a single domain model. To this end, we leveraged the NSGA-II and grid search algorithm to identify a list of optimal hyperparameters for a specific LLM, namely Llama 3, and then employed it to generate ten different domain models. Although the results show that the hyperparameter tuning does not achieve adequate results in all the considered domains, the usage of prompt engineering techniques, especially few-shots, contributes to limiting this effect, thus opening future research in this direction. In future work, we plan to study in detail each hyperparameter, e.g., temperature or Top-p, to understand their impact during the model generation. In addition, we plan to experiment with additional LLMs (e.g., GPT or BERT) and similarity metrics to understand their impact on domain modeling. Finally, we can enlarge the dataset to different domain applications to further study the generalizability of the proposed methodology.

Acknowledgments. This work has been partially supported by Territori Aperti (a project funded by Fondo Territori, Lavoro e Conoscenza CGIL CISL UIL), by "LIFEMAP-Dalla patologia pediatrica alle malattie cardiovascolari e neoplastiche nell'adulto: mappatura genomica per la medicina e prevenzione personalizzata" Traiettoria 3 "Medicina rigenerativa, predittiva e personalizzata" - Linea di azione 3.1 "Creazione di un programma di medicina di precisione per la mappatura del genoma umano su scala nazionale" of the Italian Ministry of Health, by the MOSAICO project (Management, Orchestration and Supervision of AI-agent COmmunities for reliable AI in software engineering) that has received funding from the European Union under the Horizon Research and Innovation Action (Grant Agreement No. 101189664) and Project PRIN 2022 PNRR "FRINGE: context-aware FaiRness engineerING in complex software systEms" grant n. P2022553SL.

Disclosure of Interests. The authors have no competing interests to declare that are relevant to the content of this article.

References

1. Ahmad, A., Waseem, M., Liang, P., Fahmideh, M., Aktar, M.S., Mikkonen, T.: Towards human-bot collaborative software architecting with ChatGPT. In: Proceedings of the 27th International Conference on Evaluation and Assessment in Software Engineering, pp. 279–285. EASE '23, Association for Computing Machinery, New York, NY, USA (Jun 2023). https://doi.org/10.1145/3593434.3593468, read_Status: New Read_Status_Date: 2024-07-17T07:38:55.084Z
2. Arcuri, A., Briand, L.: A practical guide for using statistical tests to assess randomized algorithms in software engineering. In: Proceedings of the 33rd International Conference on Software Engineering, pp. 1–10. ICSE '11, Association for Computing Machinery, New York, NY, USA (May 2011). https://doi.org/10.1145/1985793.1985795,
3. Ardimento, P., Bernardi, M.L., Cimitile, M.: Teaching UML using a rag-based LLM. In: 2024 International Joint Conference on Neural Networks (IJCNN), pp. 1–8 (2024). https://doi.org/10.1109/IJCNN60899.2024.10651492
4. Arora, C., Sayeed, A.I., Licorish, S., Wang, F., Treude, C.: Optimizing large language model hyperparameters for code generation (2024). https://arxiv.org/abs/2408.10577
5. Arulmohan, S., Meurs, M.J., Mosser, S.: Extracting domain models from textual requirements in the era of large language models. In: 2023 ACM/IEEE International Conference on Model Driven Engineering Languages and Systems Companion (MODELS-C), pp. 580–587. IEEE, Västerås, Sweden (Oct 2023). https://doi.org/10.1109/MODELS-C59198.2023.00096, https://ieeexplore.ieee.org/document/10350787/
6. Batot, E., Sahraoui, H.: A generic framework for model-set selection for the unification of testing and learning MDE tasks. In: Proceedings of the ACM/IEEE 19th International Conference on Model Driven Engineering Languages and Systems, pp. 374–384. MODELS '16, Association for Computing Machinery, New York, NY, USA (2016). https://doi.org/10.1145/2976767.2976785
7. Ben Chaaben, M., et al.: Toward intelligent generation of tailored graphical concrete syntax. In: Proceedings of the ACM/IEEE 27th International Conference on Model Driven Engineering Languages and Systems, pp. 160–171. MODELS '24, Association for Computing Machinery, New York, NY, USA (2024). https://doi.org/10.1145/3640310.3674085, https://doi.org/10.1145/3640310.3674085
8. Bertram, V., et al.: Neural language models and few shot learning for systematic requirements processing in mdse. In: Proceedings of the 15th ACM SIGPLAN International Conference on Software Language Engineering, pp. 260–265. SLE 2022, Association for Computing Machinery, New York, NY, USA (2022). https://doi.org/10.1145/3567512.3567534
9. Bulhakov, V., d'Aloisio, G., Di Sipio, C., Di Marco, A., Di Ruscio, D.: LLama Ecore Study (Jan 2025). https://github.com/VPLEV23/ER_LLM
10. Burgueño, L., Di Ruscio, D., Sahraoui, H., Wimmer, M.: Automation in model-driven engineering: a look back, and ahead. ACM Trans. Softw. Eng. Methodol. (Jan 2025). https://doi.org/10.1145/3712008, just Accepted
11. Cámara, J., Troya, J., Burgueño, L., Vallecillo, A.: On the assessment of generative AI in modeling tasks: an experience report with ChatGPT and UML. Softw. Syst. Model. **22**(3), 781–793 (2023). https://doi.org/10.1007/s10270-023-01105-5
12. Chaaben, M.B., Burgueño, L., Sahraoui, H.: Towards using few-shot prompt learning for automating model completion. In: Proceedings of the 45th

International Conference on Software Engineering: New Ideas and Emerging Results, pp. 7–12. ICSE-NIER '23, IEEE, IEEE Press, Melbourne, Australia (Sep 2023https://doi.org/10.1109/ICSE-NIER58687.2023.00008, https://dl.acm. org/doi/10.1109/ICSE-NIER58687.2023.00008

13. Chen, K., Yang, Y., Chen, B., Hernández López, J.A., Mussbacher, G., et al.: Automated domain modeling with large language models: a comparative study. In: 2023 ACM/IEEE 26th International Conference on Model Driven Engineering Languages and Systems (MODELS), pp. 162–172 (Oct 2023). https://doi.org/10. 1109/MODELS58315.2023.00037, https://ieeexplore.ieee.org/abstract/document/ 10344012

14. Chen, P.H., Wei, W., Hsieh, C.J., Dai, B.: Overcoming catastrophic forgetting by bayesian generative regularization. In: Meila, M., Zhang, T. (eds.) Proceedings of the 38th International Conference on Machine Learning. Proceedings of Machine Learning Research, vol. 139, pp. 1760–1770. PMLR (18–24 Jul 2021), https:// proceedings.mlr.press/v139/chen21v.html

15. Costa, C.D., López, J.A.H., Cuadrado, J.S.: Modelmate: A recommender for textual modeling languages based on pre-trained language models. In: Proceedings of the ACM/IEEE 27th International Conference on Model Driven Engineering Languages and Systems, pp. 183–194. MODELS '24, Association for Computing Machinery, New York, NY, USA (2024). https://doi.org/10.1145/3640310.3674089

16. d'Aloisio, G., Fortz, S., Hanna, C., Fortunato, D., Bensoussan, A., Mendiluze Usandizaga, E., Sarro, F.: Exploring LLM-driven explanations for quantum algorithms. In: Proceedings of the 18th ACM/IEEE International Symposium on Empirical Software Engineering and Measurement, pp. 475–481 (2024)

17. Deb, K., Agrawal, S., Pratap, A., Meyarivan, T.: A fast and elitist multiobjective genetic algorithm: NSGA-II. IEEE Trans. Evol. Comput. **6**(2), 182–197 (2002)

18. Deroy, A., Maity, S.: Code generation and algorithmic problem solving using llama 3.1 405b. arXiv preprint arXiv:2409.19027 (2024)

19. Di Rocco, J., Di Ruscio, D., Di Sipio, C., Nguyen, P.T., Pierantonio, A.: Memorec: a recommender system for assisting modelers in specifying metamodels. Softw. Syst. Model, 1–21 (2022)

20. Di Sipio, C., Rubei, R., Di Rocco, J., Di Ruscio, D., Iovino, L.: On the use of LLMs to support the development of domain-specific modeling languages. In: Proceedings of the ACM/IEEE 27th International Conference on Model Driven Engineering Languages and Systems, pp. 596–601. MODELS Companion '24, Association for Computing Machinery, New York, NY, USA (2024). https://doi.org/10.1145/ 3652620.3687808, https://doi.org/10.1145/3652620.3687808

21. Fan, L., Liu, J., Liu, Z., Lo, D., Xia, X., Li, S.: Exploring the capabilities of LLMs for code change related tasks. ACM Trans. Softw. Eng. Methodol. (2024). https:// doi.org/10.1145/3709358

22. Forrest, S.: Genetic algorithms. ACM Comput. Surv. (CSUR) **28**(1), 77–80 (1996)

23. Giagkiozis, I., Fleming, P.J.: Pareto front estimation for decision making. Evol. Comput. **22**(4), 651–678 (2014). https://doi.org/10.1162/EVCO_a_00128

24. Gong, J., et al.: Greenstableyolo: optimizing inference time and image quality of text-to-image generation. In: International Symposium on Search Based Software Engineering, pp. 70–76. Springer Nature Switzerland Cham (2024)

25. Hamdani, T.M., Won, J.-M., Alimi, A.M., Karray, F.: Multi-objective Feature Selection with NSGA II. In: Beliczynski, B., Dzielinski, A., Iwanowski, M., Ribeiro, B. (eds.) ICANNGA 2007. LNCS, vol. 4431, pp. 240–247. Springer, Heidelberg (2007). https://doi.org/10.1007/978-3-540-71618-1_27

26. Hort, M., Moussa, R., Sarro, F.: Multi-objective search for gender-fair and semantically correct word embeddings. Appl. Soft Comput. **133**, 109916 (Jan 20). https://doi.org/10.1016/j.asoc.2022.109916, https://www.sciencedirect.com/science/article/pii/S1568494622009656

27. Kora, P., Yadlapalli, P.: Crossover operators in genetic algorithms: a review. Int. J. Comput. Appl. **162**(10) (2017)

28. Lewis, P., et al.: Retrieval-augmented generation for knowledge-intensive NLP asks. In: Proceedings of the 34th International Conference on Neural Information Processing Systems. NIPS '20, Curran Associates Inc., Red Hook, NY, USA (2020)

29. López, J.A.H., Cánovas Izquierdo, J.L., Cuadrado, J.S.: Modelset: a dataset for machine learning in model-driven engineering. Softw. Syst. Model. 1–20 (2021)

30. Ma, X., Wang, L., Yang, N., Wei, F., Lin, J.: Fine-tuning llama for multi-stage text retrieval. In: Proceedings of the 47th International ACM SIGIR Conference on Research and Development in Information Retrieval, pp. 2421–2425 (2024)

31. Meta: Meta LLama3. https://llama.meta.com/llama3/ (2024)

32. Mussbacher, G., et al.: Opportunities in intelligent modeling assistance. Softw. Syst. Model. **19**(5), 1045–1053 (2020). https://doi.org/10.1007/s10270-020-00814-5

33. Rumbaugh, J., Jacobson, I., Booch, G.: Unified Modeling Language Reference Manual, The (2nd Edition). Pearson Higher Education (2004)

34. Saini, R., Mussbacher, G., Guo, J.L.C., Kienzle, J.: Domobot: A bot for automated and interactive domain modelling. In: Proceedings of the 23rd ACM/IEEE International Conference on Model Driven Engineering Languages and Systems: Companion Proceedings. MODELS '20, Association for Computing Machinery, New York, NY, USA (2020). https://doi.org/10.1145/3417990.3421385

35. Salton, G., Buckley, C.: Term-weighting approaches in automatic text retrieval. Inform. Process. Manage. **24**(5), 513–523 (1988)

36. Sarro, F., Petrozziello, A., Harman, M.: Multi-objective software effort estimation. In: Proceedings of the 38th International Conference on Software Engineering, pp. 619–630. ICSE '16, Association for Computing Machinery, New York, NY, USA (May 2016). https://doi.org/10.1145/2884781.2884830

37. Vargha, A., Delaney, H.D.: A critique and improvement of the cl common language effect size statistics of Mcgraw and Wong. J. Educ. Behav. Stat. **25**(2), 101–132 (2000)

38. Wei, J., et al.: Chain-of-thought prompting elicits reasoning in large language models. Adv. Neural. Inf. Process. Syst. **35**, 24824–24837 (2022)

39. Weyssow, M., Sahraoui, H., Syriani, E.: Recommending metamodel concepts during modeling activities with pre-trained language models. Softw. Syst. Model. pp. 1–19 (2022)

40. Wohlin, C., Runeson, P., Höst, M., Ohlsson, M.C., Regnell, B., Wesslén, A.: Experimentation in software engineering. Springer Berlin Heidelberg, Berlin, Heidelberg (2012). https://doi.org/10.1007/978-3-642-29044-2. http://link.springer.com/10.1007/978-3-642-29044-2

41. Woolson, R.F.: Wilcoxon signed-rank test. Encyclopedia of Biostatistics **8** (2005)

42. Zhang, T., Kishore, V., Wu, F., et al.: Bertscore: evaluating text generation with bert. arXiv preprint arXiv:1904.09675 (2019)

Towards Modeling Human-Agentic Collaborative Workflows: A BPMN Extension

Adem Ait[1]([⊠])[iD], Javier Luis Cánovas Izquierdo[2][iD], and Jordi Cabot[1,3][iD]

[1] University of Luxembourg, Esch-sur-Alzette, Luxembourg
[2] IN3 - UOC, Barcelona, Spain
`jcanovasi@uoc.edu`
[3] Luxembourg Institute of Science and Technology, Esch-sur-Alzette, Luxembourg
`adem.ait@uni.lu, jordi.cabot@list.lu`

Abstract. Large Language Models (LLMs) have facilitated the definition of autonomous intelligent agents. Such agents have already demonstrated their potential in solving complex tasks in different domains. And they can further increase their performance when collaborating with other agents in a multi-agent system. However, the orchestration and coordination of these agents is still challenging, especially when they need to interact with humans as part of human-agentic collaborative workflows. These kinds of workflows need to be precisely specified so that it is clear who is responsible for each task, what strategies agents can follow to complete individual tasks or how decisions will be taken when different alternatives are proposed, among others. Current business process modeling languages fall short when it comes to specifying these new mixed collaborative scenarios. In this paper, we extend a well-known process modeling language (i.e., BPMN) to enable the definition of this new type of workflow. Our extension covers both the formalization of the new modeling concepts required and the proposal of a BPMN-like graphical notation to facilitate the definition of these workflows. Our extension has been implemented and is available as an open-source human-agentic workflow modeling editor on GitHub.

Keywords: LLM Agent · Collaborative Workflow · BPMN Extension

1 Introduction

In our current information-rich society, the integration of agents, especially agents powered by Large Language Models (LLMs), is becoming more and more important to quickly perform many tasks [17]. Agents can interact with the environment, make their own decisions, and learn from the received feedback. Moreover, often, agents do not work in isolation but as part of Multi-Agent Systems (MAS) where agents cooperate (or compete) to achieve a common goal [6]. This collaborative process is known as an agentic system. These systems have already demonstrated their superior performance against single-agent solutions [6].

© The Author(s), under exclusive license to Springer Nature Switzerland AG 2026
D. Taibi and D. Smite (Eds.): SEAA 2025, LNCS 16081, pp. 367–382, 2026.
https://doi.org/10.1007/978-3-032-04190-6_22

While agentic systems are performant in many tasks, complex scenarios require the participation of humans [16]. Therefore, there is a need to precisely define this collaboration and how each participant interacts with each other. Unfortunately, we argue that current process modeling languages, such as BPMN, lack the modeling constructs to specify this collaboration between humans and agentic systems as new primitives to define the confidence of the agents, the strategies they can use to perform a task, or the process to reach a decision. Furthermore, frameworks targeting the implementation of agentic workflows, such as LANGGRAPH[1], minimize the participation of humans in the process and therefore are not expressive enough to model the human-agent interaction beyond very simple cases.

The goal of this paper is to enable the precise definition of human-agentic workflows. To this aim, we study how the Business Process Model and Notation (BPMN), one of the most well-known modeling languages for workflows, could be used to represent this new type of workflow, and then, based on the identified limitations, we propose a BPMN extension to enable their definition in BPMN. Note that our approach can serve as a blueprint for extending other workflow languages, as the conceptual elements we identify are largely notation-independent. This extension has been implemented in an open source modeling tool available on GITHUB.

BPMN was chosen for several key reasons: (1) widespread adoption, BPMN is the *de facto* standard for business process modeling with broad industrial and academic support; (2) expressivity, BPMN already provides comprehensive constructs for modeling workflows involving human participants; (3) extensibility, BPMN offers an extension mechanism that enables domain-specific additions while maintaining compliance with the standard; (4) execution capabilities, BPMN models can be directly executed by business process engines, making the transition from conceptual models to implementation easier; and (5) integration with existing processes, many organizations already use BPMN, making it easier to incorporate agent-based elements into existing business processes.

The rest of the paper is structured as follows. Section 2 provides the background and a running example. Section 3 shows the mapping of agentic concepts to BPMN, while Sect. 4 presents the extension to the BPMN to overcome the limitations found. Section 5 and 6 provide the extension definition and the proof of concept, respectively. Section 7 presents the related work. Finally, Sect. 8 concludes the paper and presents the roadmap.

2   Background and Running Example

In this section, we briefly describe BPMN, the language we aim to extend; and present the main concepts of agentic systems. We end the section with a running example.

---

[1] https://www.langchain.com/langgraph.

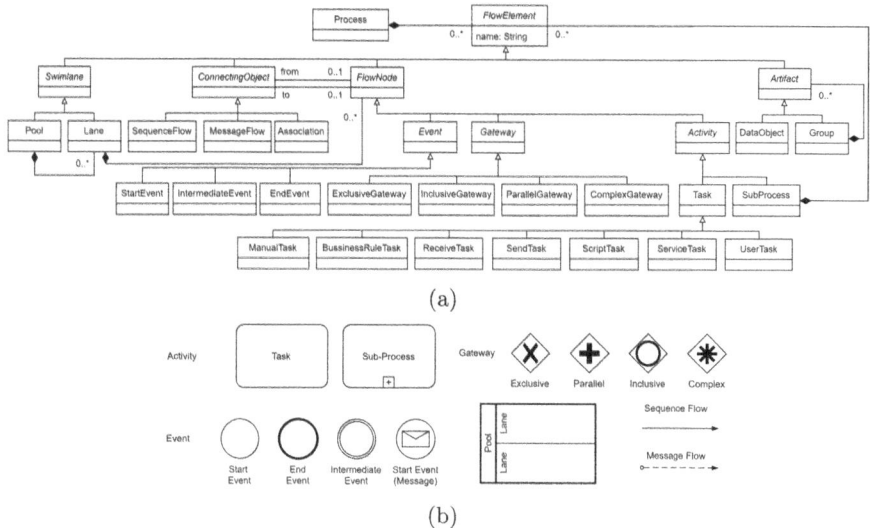

(a)

(b)

Fig. 1. Simplified (a) metamodel of BPMN and the corresponding (b) notation

2.1 BPMN

Business Process Management (BPM) studies how work is performed in an organization to ensure consistent outcomes and to take advantage of improvement opportunities [3]. BPM is about managing entire chains of events, activities, and decisions (called business processes) that ultimately add value to the organization and its customers. Thus, the formal representation of such process facilitates the orchestration, monitoring, and improvement of an organization's workflow.

BPMN [11] has become the de-facto standard for business processes diagrams. It is defined by the Object Management Group (OMG) and specified as ISO standard (ISO/IEC 19510:2013). BPMN provides a metamodel and a notation to define and visualize business process models. It provides an extension mechanism to allow modeling domain-specific elements not included in the specification. In particular, BPMN 2.0 extension mechanism enables the approach of extension by addition, which consists of attaching new domain-specific elements to the predefined elements of the language.

Figure 1(a) shows a simplified metamodel of BPMN. The different *FlowElements* compose the *Process*. The *Swimlane* is used to organize the *Process*, which can be either *Pool*, or *Lane*. *Pools* can be formed by several *Lanes*. *FlowObject* can be: (1) *Events*, which are used as triggers (e.g., timers); (2) *Activities*, the work unit, which can be atomic (i.e., *Tasks*) and non-atomic (i.e., *Sub-Process*); and (3) *Gateways* for controlling the flow. *ConnectingObject* is used to specify the order of *FlowElements* which is divided into: (1) *SequenceFlow*, to establish the flow within pools, which can also be conditional (i.e., the flow will continue if a condition is fulfilled); (2) *MessageFlow*, to communicate between pools; and (3) *Association*, used to connect user-defined text (an *Annotation*) with *Flow*

Nodes. Artifact describes the *DataObject* shared in the process and *Group*, a visual mechanism to group elements of a diagram informally. Figure 1(b) shows the notation of the main elements described.

2.2 Agentic Systems

LLMs excel at multiple tasks [15], but creating specialized LLMs instances to target specific tasks has shown promising results. These specialized LLMs are typically known as agents [17]. LLM-based agents use the potential of LLMs, facilitating sophisticated interactions, decision-making, tool-use capabilities, and in-context learning through memory [6].

However, LLMs exhibit non-deterministic behavior. To alleviate this, reflection strategies have been proposed to refine their answers [13], namely: (1) **self-reflection**, where agents generate feedback on the plan and reasoning process to refine themselves; (2) **cross-reflection**, where the feedback is provided by other agents; and (3) **human-reflection**, where humans provide the feedback.

To tackle more complex problems, a common approach is to increase the number of agents, forming what is known as a LLM-based MAS, or, more recently, rebranded as agentic systems, to emphasize the cooperation of the agents in the MAS which has already been proven to outperform single-agent solutions [6]. A key aspect in agentic systems is how agents work collaboratively to solve tasks, leveraging their interactions with the environment or other agents. The works by Guo et al. [6] and Liu et al. [9] introduce the first attempts at characterizing how agentic systems work.

Agentic systems can adhere to different types of cooperation patterns. The core ones are: (1) **voting-based**, where agents independently propose alternative solutions and reach consensus by voting; (2) **role-based**, where each agent, or group of agents, has assigned a role, thus making the decision according to such roles; and (3) **debate-based**, where agents submit and receive feedback to adjust the thoughts until a consensus is reached. Furthermore, an additional scenario is **competition-based** collaboration, where agents, instead of cooperating, compete and the fastest (or the most reliable output) is selected.

All these agentic aspects will need to be part of the process modeling language if we want to model in detail human-agentic collaborations as, for instance, in the scenario we use as running example.

2.3 Running Example

To illustrate our proposal, we will use a running example based on a simple resolution process for bug reports in a software project. The example process comprises five participants, two humans and three agents.

The humans are a user, who reports the bug; and a maintainer, who reviews the final change proposal and resolves the bug. The agents are responsible for solving the bug by implementing change proposals and deciding together the best option. There are three agents, one is used as a reviewer and the other two are specialized coding agents. Each agent comes with a level of uncertainty

Table 1. Partial mapping of human-agentic workflow concepts to BPMN elements.

HUMAN-AGENTIC WORKFLOW CONCEPT	VARIETY	BPMN ELEMENT
Agent	Single-agent	Pool or Lane
	Multi-agent	Multi-instance pool
Reflection	Self-reflection	Extra loop activity
	Cross-reflection	Loop with gateways and activities
	Human-reflection	Loop with gateways and activities
Agent Collaboration	All	Group or message flow
Merging Collaboration Efforts	All	Complex gateway or message flow

regarding the quality of all its actions. This value could be derived from the underlying LLM and/or the agent setup.

Once the reviewer agent validates the bug definition, using a reflective strategy to double-check on the first assessment, the two coding agents are in charge of proposing a solution to the bug. They both work independently in parallel and, following a role-based cooperation strategy, is the agent with the reviewer role who has the final decision, also considering the uncertainty of each coding agent in case of discrepancies.

3   Using BPMN to Model Human-Agentic Workflows

In this section, we study the current support of BPMN to model human-agentic workflows. The characteristics of agentic systems we aim at covering are the ones that concern the reflection and cooperation, while also addressing their non-deterministic behavior. Table 1 shows a possible mapping of BPMN elements to model human-agentic workflows. Note that this mapping is partial, as the current support of BPMN for this type of workflow is very limited, as we show in this section.

Agents could be represented as pools or lanes, depending on the process context. When agents are part of a project process, lanes could be used, but if they represent external contributors, pools could be used instead. Sets of agents could be represented as multi-instance pools. Information about the non-deterministic behavior of the agents could only be represented via text annotations.

Reflection strategies cannot be represented in standard BPMN. We could simulate them using additional activities and gateways. Self-reflection could be represented as a loop activity that follows the activity to be refined. For cross- and human-reflection, the feedback loop could be represented as several gateways and activities to keep refining the answer until the desired output is obtained.

To model the collaboration between agents, we consider two scenarios, depending on whether agents are located in lanes of the same or different pool/s (i.e., collaboration diagram). When located in the same pool, gateways could be used to route the flow towards multiple lanes, and groups could be utilized to set the collaboration strategy. If located in different pools, message flows could

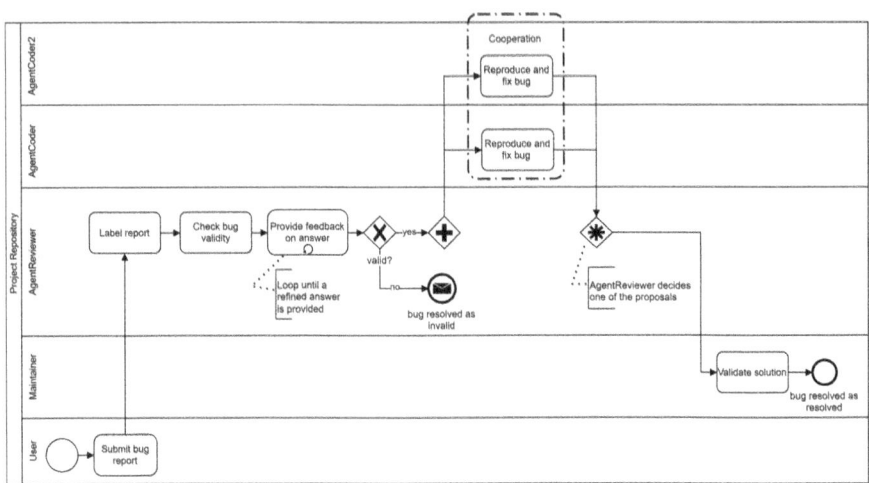

Fig. 2. Running example with standard BPMN.

be used, but text annotations should be added to describe the strategy. For merging collaborations, in the first scenario we could use a complex gateway and specify the desired merging strategy as an annotation, while in the second scenario we could specify the strategy as an annotation in the incoming message flow. Note the need to use text annotations to describe the behavior. BPMN also offers additional collaboration mechanisms such as choreographies (formalized coordination of interactions between participants), but these still require supplementary descriptions for agent-specific behaviors since their focus is on the exchange of information rather than the orchestration of their work.

Figure 2 shows the BPMN model for the running example. As can be seen, we used five lanes to represent the different actors. The *User* and *Maintainer* are the humans reporting the bug and validating the final proposed solution, respectively. The *AgentReviewer* is the agent designated to solve the bug, while *Agent-Coder* and *AgentCoder2* represent specialized coding agents that will help with coding tasks. To apply self-reflection on the *Check bug validity* activity, we define an extra loop activity (see *Provide feedback on answer*) with a loop condition defined in natural language to not stop until a refined answer is provided. Once we obtain a reliable answer, we proceed to fix the bug if the report is valid. To illustrate the cooperation, we use a group (see *cooperation*). Then, as a merging gateway, we use a complex gateway to define our own condition through an annotation, which is decided by *AgentReviewer*. Thus, only the selected solution will be the one delivered to the next activity.

Representing human-agentic workflows in BPMN is challenging, as the standard BPMN does not provide specific elements to model agents or their interactions. In the running example, we cannot set uncertainty to determine the agents' reliability or identify lanes or pools as agents. We can partially represent the collaboration and reflection strategies. We rely on natural language to describe the collaboration and reflection strategies, which can lead to ambiguity

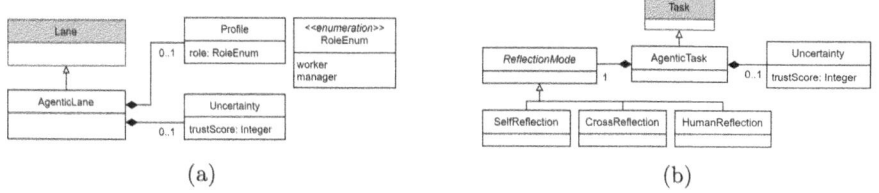

(a)   (b)

Fig. 3. Domain model of the (a) *AgenticLane* and the (b) *AgenticTask*.

and misinterpretation. Furthermore, the intricate process of representing reflection can hinder the readability and understandability of the model.

Despite the identified limitations, we believe that BPMN still provides a good starting point compared to alternative modeling languages. While languages like UML Activity Diagrams or YAWL could potentially be extended in similar ways, BPMN's widespread usage in industries means that practitioners are already familiar with its core concepts, reducing the learning curve for our extended notation.

In the next section, we propose an extension to BPMN that introduces formalized syntax for defining collaboration and reflection strategies, rules for merging collaborative outcomes, and agents' profiling (i.e., role and trustworthiness).

4   Extending BPMN to Model Human-Agentic Workflows

To address the limitations identified for modeling human-agentic workflow concepts in BPMN, we propose an extension to the BPMN specification. In particular, we propose to extend the following elements: lane, task, message flow, and parallel and inclusive gateways. In the following, we describe each extension point, showing the domain models of the extended BPMN elements. When illustrating the extension, classes of the BPMN 2.0 metamodel will be highlighted in gray. Note that, without loss of generality, we describe our extension as a BPMN extension, but a similar approach could have been used to extend other process modeling languages, as they offer a largely overlapping set of concepts.

4.1   Agent Profiling

Agent profiling requires modeling (1) the role of the agents in collaboration scenarios, as it is how an LLM is initialized as an agent; and (2) the reliability of the agent's output, or trust score, to address the non-deterministic nature of agents behavior. As shown in Sect. 3, in standard BPMN, representing agents as lanes or pools overlooks these aspects: (1) when having multiple lanes, each representing specialized agents, only lane names can be specified; and (2) there is no way to specify uncertainty for agent's output.

Figure 3a shows the domain model of the extension to address agent profiling. We differentiate between regular participants and *agentic* participants (see *Lane* and *AgenticLane*). The *Pool* element is the graphical representation of a participant. However, we decided to extend the *Lane* class rather than the *Pool* class to allow setting a profile for each agent within a pool. This way, a group of agents can be represented as a pool, where each agent can have different trust scores since they would be represented as lanes of the pool.

To represent the role and the trust score, we define the attributes in the *Profile* and *Uncertainty* classes, respectively. The role value distinguishes between manager and workers, but the corresponding enumeration could be extended to fulfill further roles (e.g., coder). When set to manager, the agent represented by the lane is the one in charge of selecting the valid output in role-based or debate-based cooperation. The trust score parameter is a percentage value (i.e., 0–100) of the trustworthiness of a particular agent.

4.2   Agent Reflection

Reflection is key in agentic systems, enabling agents to evaluate their actions and adapt their behavior accordingly. Although standard BPMN can model loops and decision points, it lacks the constructs to formally define and enforce self-reflection, cross-reflection, or human-reflection processes.

Figure 3b shows the domain model of the extension to address agent reflection. We extend the *Task* BPMN element, defining the *AgenticTask*, which can be associated to one of the three reflection strategies. We model the identified reflection strategies from the literature into three classes (see *SelfReflection*, *CrossReflection*, and *HumanReflection* classes), which are subclasses of the *ReflectionMode* class. Depending on the degree of reliability and the resources available, one could define the reflection as human-reflection, to avoid undesired outputs. However, if one wants a completely automated task, but also ensure some degree of reliability, one could use self-reflection or cross-reflection strategies, where the latter would be more expensive, since it requires instances of other agents, but it might provide better results.

Furthermore, tasks can have attached a trustworthiness score (see *Uncertainty*), used to represent the reliability of the task output. This trust score can be further used in the workflow to decide the next steps.

4.3   Agent Collaboration

In standard BPMN, collaboration between agents could be represented as groups, which allows for a basic depiction of collaborative efforts, but falls short in specifying the cooperation (and merging) strategies employed by the agents.

Figure 4 shows the domain model of the collaboration types along with their merging strategies, and how they are related to the extended *Gateway* and *MessageFlow* classes. The collaboration will be enclosed between diverging and merging gateways. The former specifies the collaboration strategy, while the latter indicates the merging strategy.

We model the *CollaborationMode* as the root of the hierarchy of collaboration modes, which can be either cooperation or competition, the former being the

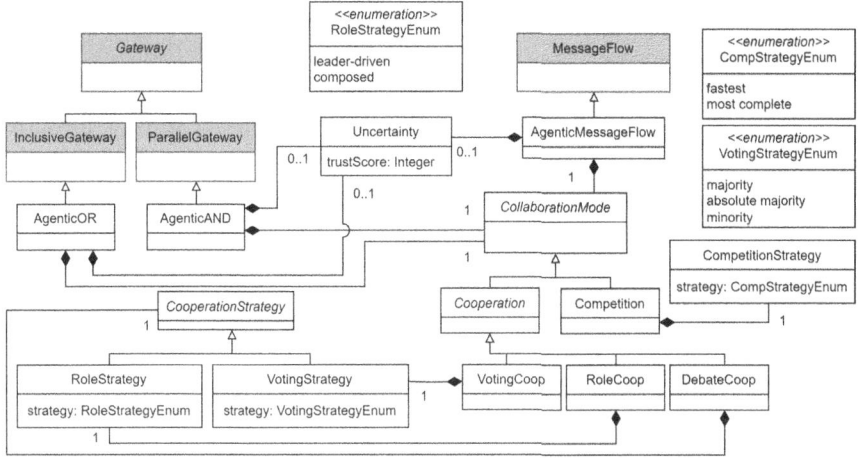

Fig. 4. Domain model of the *AgenticOR*, *AgenticAND* and *AgenticMessageFlow*.

root of three types of cooperation (i.e., voting, role and debate). We extend both the inclusive and parallel gateways (see *AgenticOR* and *AgenticAND*, respectively), which also set the collaboration strategy (see *CollaborationMode* association). The inclusive gateway allows specifying a condition so that only specific agents are activated, while the parallel gateway diverges the flow to all its outputs, which is desired when all the participants from the diverged flow are required to collaborate. Since agentic gateways are intended to represent collaboration, we only extend these two gateways. We do not consider the exclusive gateway, since the flow is allowed only to one output.

The merging strategies set how to decide the solution to select in collaboration scenarios. When competing, the *CompetitionStrategy* class indicates the merging strategy. Regarding the cooperation strategies, the merging strategies are represented in the *CooperationStrategy* class. *VotingStrategy* is used when the decision is made through voting, while *RoleStrategy* is used when the merging is taken by a manager role or by the inherent roles of the agents (e.g., specialized agents proposing each part of the output). While voting-based and role-based cooperation have explicit merging strategies because of their description, the debate-based cooperation might leverage from one of the two strategies.

The gateways allow the collaboration within pools, but if the set of agents is represented as another pool, message flows should be used (see *MessageFlow*). We extend the message flow, rather than choreography tasks, since it allows for an elementary depiction of the collaboration. Like done for gateways, the outgoing message flow sets the collaboration strategy, while the incoming message flow sets the desired merging strategy.

Finally, the agentic gateways and message flow are also associated with a trust score. In gateways, it can be used as a decision point, while in message flows can be used to understand the reliability of the received token.

4.4   BPMN Notation Extension

According to the BPMN specification, extensions notation must not alter the notation of its elements, and must be as close as possible, in terms of look and feel, to it [11]. Our extension introduces four new elements (see Table 2) with a graphical representation close the BPMN element being extended.

When choosing these elements, we also aimed to stick to the principles for effective visual notations by Moody [10]. For instance, to be compliant with the semiotic clarity principle, we maintain a 1:1 correspondence between semantic constructs and graphical symbols, with each agentic concept (lane, task, gateway, message flow) having its own distinct visual representation (see Table 2).

To identify the extended elements, we use a marker representing an agent. Our agent marker follows the perceptual discriminability principle, since it clearly distinguishes agentic elements from standard BPMN elements, while maintaining the basic shape of the original BPMN symbols to preserve familiarity. Furthermore, the agent icon intuitively suggests intelligence and automation being semantically immediate, following the semantic transparency principle.

On the other hand, we minimize the introduction of new symbols by using a consistent agent marker with letter modifiers rather than creating entirely new shapes, following the graph economy and dual coding principle (i.e., use both graphical elements and textual annotations to enhance cognition).

The agentic lane is identified with the agent marker centered below the name for vertical lanes, or centered at the right of the name for horizontal lanes. The trust score is set between the name of the lane and the agent marker, following the position of the text. The role is set as a letter below the marker, where "w" stands for worker and "m" for manager.

The agentic task is represented with the agent marker in the top-left corner, as it is done with specific tasks (e.g., *ManualTask*). The reflection and collaboration strategies are indicated with a marker at the bottom of the shape. The reflection strategy is set as a letter inside the marker, where "s" stands for self-reflection, "c" for cross-reflection, and "h" for human-reflection. Note that the notation shown in Table 2 the "x" is used as a placeholder.

The agentic gateways are represented with the agent marker at the top-left side, without disturbing the shape of the gateway. The diverging gateway contains the collaboration marker in the bottom-right corner. This way the visual distance between symbols is greater [10]. The same principle has been applied for the remaining notations. The collaboration strategy is set as a letter below the marker, where "c" stands for competition, "d" for debate cooperation, "r" for role cooperation, and "v" for voting cooperation. The merging gateway must contain the merging marker in the bottom-right corner. The merging strategy is represented with two sets of letters below the marker, the first as the strategy class and the second as the merging strategy type. Thus, for voting strategies are "v-ma" for majority, "v-a" for absolute majority, and "v-mi" for minority; for role-based strategies are "r-l" for leader-driven and "r-c" for composed; while for competition strategies are "c-f" for fastest, and "c-mc" for most complete.

Table 2. Graphical notation of the extended elements.

EXTENSION ELEMENT	NOTATION	EXTENSION ELEMENT	NOTATION
Agentic lane	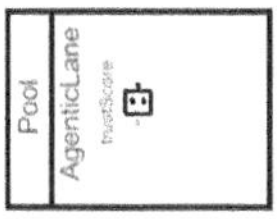	Agentic task	
Diverging agentic gateway		Merging agentic gateway	
Outgoing agentic message flow	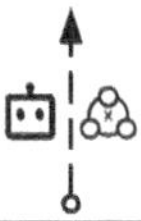	Incoming agentic message flow	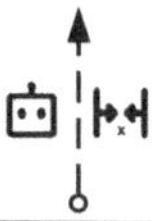

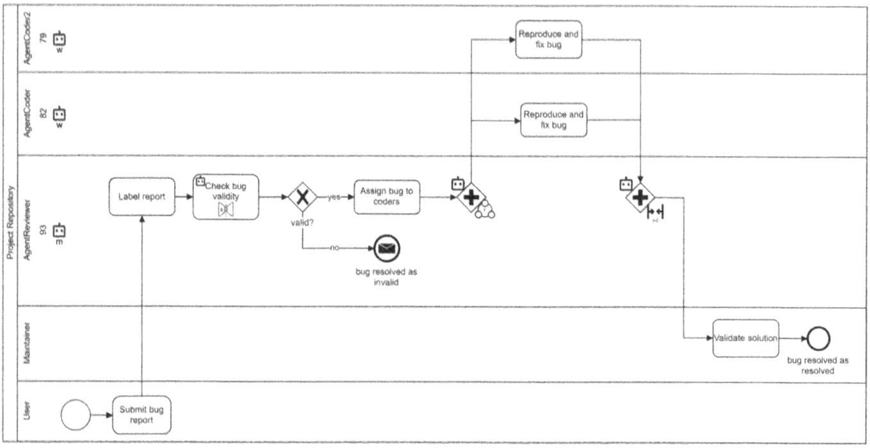

Fig. 5. Running example with our extension notation.

The agentic message flow is represented with the agent marker centered on the left side, if the message flow is vertical, or centered above the message flow, if it is horizontal. The collaboration or merging strategy is set with a marker on the right side, if the message flow is vertical, or centered below the message flow, if it is horizontal. As with the agentic gateway, the outgoing message flow must contain the collaboration strategy, while the incoming message flow must contain the merging strategy.

4.5 Using Our Extension to Model the Running Example

Figure 5 shows the running example using our extension. The different agents are denoted with *agentic lanes*, and have a trust score attached (see three top lanes). The second task (see *Check bug validity*) is an *agentic task* that applies self-reflection to the output.

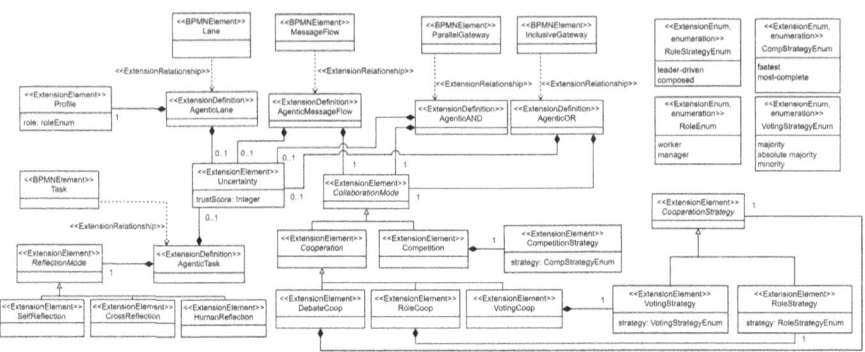

Fig. 6. Extension model.

To represent the collaboration between agents, we use the *agentic gateway*, since agents are represented as lanes of the same pool. The collaboration strategy applied is *role cooperation*, as denoted by the notation. After stating the collaboration strategy, the flow is divided towards the agents that collaborate. All flows from this collaboration are merged into an *agentic gateway* following the *leader-driven* strategy, as denoted by the notation. The remaining elements are compliant to standard BPMN.

5   Our Extension as a Standard BPMN Extension Definition

BPMN provides an extension mechanism to allow modeling domain-specific elements not included in the specification.

Nevertheless, there is a lack of methodological guides to develop and publish specific extensions. Stroppi et al. [14] define a method (called BPMN+X) to transform a domain model into a BPMN-compliant extension by using UML profiles, which is the typical approach used in the UML world to define lightweight extensions[2] to the language. Given a BPMN extension defined as a profile, the BPMN+X method uses mapping rules and automated model transformations to generate an XML Schema Extension Definition Document conforming to the official BPMN extension mechanism.

We follow this approach to redefine our extended BPMN metamodel as a BPMN extension. To this purpose, Fig. 6 shows the metamodel from Figs. 3a, 3b and 4 defined as a profile.

---

[2] The term lightweight extension is used to denote language extensions that are compatible with language semantics and that can be expressed using the own language extension mechanisms, enabling the direct use of the extension in any tool that supports the language. This is in contrast to heavyweight extensions that offer more complex extensions that enable richer semantics for the extension but require dedicated tooling support.

6   Proof of Concept

As a proof-of-concept of the proposal, we have implemented a modeling editor that enables any developer to use our extended BPMN language and notation.

The extension has been implemented using Sirius[3], an Eclipse project which allows you to easily create your own graphical modeling workbench by leveraging Eclipse Modeling technologies such as EMF and GMF. Aconite [12], a tool that helps produce Sirius-based graphical notations, has been used to automatically generate the Sirius-based implementation. Figure 7 shows a screenshot.

The tool repository[4] includes the files that use the Aconite annotations and the examples illustrated in this paper. The tool includes a main view of the diagram and a palette to allow the user to drag and drop the elements into the diagram. The palette contains the basic representation of BPMN, plus the extension elements proposed in this paper. Furthermore, the repository also includes several examples from the literature to illustrate the use of the extension.

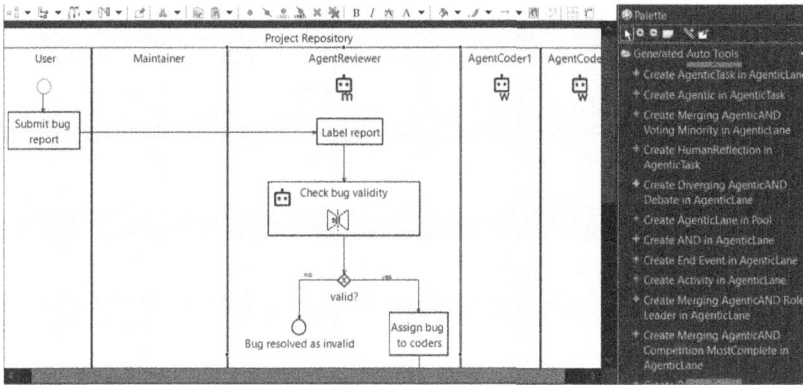

Fig. 7. Platform-independent implementation.

7   Related Work

We classify the related work into two groups: proposals that try to model agents in general process modeling languages and agent-specific tools that may include a language to orchestrate agentic workflows.

In the first group we have Küster et al. [8] that combine agent-oriented software engineering with business process design. Nevertheless, they do not extend BPMN and therefore suffer from the limitations stated in Sect. 3. Endert et al. [4] propose a mapping of BDI agents to business processes. However, while this proposal provides ways of mapping agent-specific concepts following the BDI paradigm to BPMN, they do not cover advanced aspects of the current generation of agents such as reflection strategies.

---

[3] https://eclipse.dev/sirius/overview.html.
[4] https://github.com/BESSER-PEARL/agentic-bpmn.

Other BPMN approaches partially cover uncertainty concerns. Ceballos et al. [2] propose a BPMN Business Process Diagram (BPD) normal form based on Activity Theory [5] that can be used for representing the dynamics of a collective human activity from the perspective of a subject. Herbert and Sharp [7] proposed a BPMN extension introducing the uncertainty in sequence flows. The extension includes probabilistic flows and rewards associated to the execution of tasks. Note that the uncertainty is determined in the sequence flows rather than in the participant or activity BPMN element. Our proposal introduces uncertainty at the participant level, then propagating to all the other elements. Both types of uncertainty could be combined.

Regarding specific tools to create agentic systems, some include the graphical modeling of the process. Three representative examples are LANGGRAPH[5] that allows modeling the action flow of an agent (or a set of agents) using cyclic graphs, FLOWISE[6], an open-source low-code tool for orchestrating LLM agents, and N8N[7], a workflow automation platform that includes the definition of agents. In all cases, the workflows are purely focused on agent collaborations. Humans can only trigger the actions but are not supposed to collaborate with the agent to accomplish them. In contrast, our extension considers humans as active participants and enables representing complex human-agent interactions.

8   Conclusions and Further Work

We have presented a BPMN extension to model human-agentic workflows. Our extension enables the modeling of complex collaboration patterns between humans and agents, including specifying the agents' reflection strategies. While we focused on BPMN due to its widespread adoption, the extension is notation-independent and could serve as a blueprint for extending other workflow modeling languages. Note that the dynamic and evolving nature of agent capabilities means that this extension will require future refinements as new collaboration patterns emerge. The modular design of our extension facilitates such evolution.

As further work, we plan to provide a sublanguage to specify in detail the governance and decision-making strategies as part of the merging nodes for agents' collaboration efforts (e.g., should decisions be based on consensus? voting strategies...). We will also propose an uncertainty propagation mechanism that, given the overall uncertainty of the agents and their confidence in the result of a given task, assigns an overall uncertainty of the task, which should then be propagated also to the consecutive tasks.

Additionally, we plan to work on code generators aimed at producing an executable representation of the model, including the governance aspects and the uncertainty propagation mechanisms to make operational the modeled workflows. The generators could target, potentially, a combination of BPEL engines

---

[5] https://www.langchain.com/langgraph.

[6] https://github.com/FlowiseAI/Flowise.

[7] https://n8n.io/.

and agentic platforms, where the BPEL engine would take care of the global orchestration and delegate to the agentic platform the task execution.

Finally, we plan to empirically evaluate our extension and explore its application in industrial use cases. In particular, to ensure the cognitive effectiveness of our notation, we plan to conduct a metric-based assessment based on the alignment with Moody's principles for visual notations [10], following our previous work on collaborative modeling notation evaluation [1].

Acknowledgments. This work is part of the project TED2021-130331B-I00 funded by MCIN/AEI/10.13039/501100011033 and European Union NextGenerationEU/PRTR; and BESSER, funded by the Luxembourg National Research Fund (FNR) PEARL program, grant agreement 16544475.

Disclosure of Interests. The authors have no competing interests to declare that are relevant to the content of this article.

References

1. Brambilla, M., Cabot, J., Izquierdo, J.L.C., Mauri, A.: Better call the crowd: using crowdsourcing to shape the notation of domain-specific languages. In: International Conference on Software Language Engineering, pp. 129–138 (2017)
2. Ceballos, H.G., Flores-Solorio, V., Garcia, J.P.: A probabilistic BPMN normal form to model and advise human activities. In: Baldoni, M., Baresi, L., Dastani, M. (eds.) EMAS 2015. LNCS (LNAI), vol. 9318, pp. 51–69. Springer, Cham (2015). https://doi.org/10.1007/978-3-319-26184-3_4
3. Dumas, M., Rosa, M.L., Mendling, J., Reijers, H.A.: Fundamentals of Business Process Management. Springer (2013)
4. Endert, H., Küster, T., Hirsch, B., Albayrak, S.: Mapping BPMN to agents: an analysis. Agents, Web-Serv. Ontologies Integrated Methodol., 43–58 (2007)
5. Engeström, Y., Miettinen, R., Punamäki-Gitai, R.L.: Perspectives on activity theory. Cambridge University Press (1999)
6. Guo, T., et al.: Large language model based multi-agents: A survey of progress and challenges. In: International Joint Conference on Artificial Intelligence, pp. 8048–8057 (2024)
7. Herbert, L., Sharp, R.: Precise quantitative analysis of probabilistic business process model and notation workflows. J. Comput. Inf. Sci. Eng. **13**(1) (2013)
8. Küster, T., Lützenberger, M., Heßler, A., Hirsch, B.: Integrating process modelling into multi-agent system engineering. Multiagent Grid Syst. **8**(1), 105–124 (2012)
9. Liu, Y., et al.: Agent design pattern catalogue: a collection of architectural patterns for foundation model based agents. J. Syst. Softw. **220**, 112278 (2025)
10. Moody, D.: The "physics" of notations: toward a scientific basis for constructing visual notations in software engineering. IEEE Trans. Software Eng. **35**(6), 756–779 (2009)
11. OMG: Business process model and notation (bpmn) 2.0.2 specification (Jan 2014). https://www.omg.org/spec/BPMN, Accessed July 2024
12. Richardson, N., Kolovos, D., Garcia-Dominguez, A.: Aconite: towards generating sirius-based graphical editors from annotated metamodels. In: International Conference on Software Language Engineering, pp. 16–28 (2024)

13. Shinn, N., Cassano, F., Gopinath, A., Narasimhan, K., Yao, S.: Reflexion: language agents with verbal reinforcement learning. In: Conference on Neural Information Processing Systems (2023)
14. Stroppi, L.J.R., Chiotti, O., Villarreal, P.D.: Extending BPMN 2.0: method and tool support. In: Dijkman, R., Hofstetter, J., Koehler, J. (eds.) BPMN 2011. LNBIP, vol. 95, pp. 59–73. Springer, Heidelberg (2011). https://doi.org/10.1007/978-3-642-25160-3_5
15. Wei, J., et al.: Emergent abilities of large language models. Trans. Mach. Learn. Res. **2022** (2022)
16. Wu, Q., et al.: Autogen: Enabling next-gen LLM applications via multi-agent conversation framework. CoRR abs/arXiv: 2308.08155 (2023)
17. Xi, Z., et al.: The rise and potential of large language model based agents: a survey. Sci. China Inf. Sci. **68**(2), 121101 (2025)

An Automated Diagram Generator of Reference Solutions for Modeling Educators

Giacomo Garaccione[(✉)] [iD], Riccardo Coppola[iD], and Luca Ardito[iD]

Politecnico di Torino, Turin, Italy
{Giacomo.Garaccione,Riccardo.Coppola,Luca.Ardito}@polito.it

Abstract. UML class diagrams are a relevant modeling language in Software Engineering education since they can be used to teach students how to visualize and display the different entities that compose a system, with their functionalities and relationships. The definition of modeling exercises and their evaluation can be time-consuming for educators due to the need to consider possible semantic variations and alternative representations of the same system requirements. To facilitate teachers in this process, we present TIGRE (auTomated dIagram Generator of REFerence solutions), an online editor for the definition of UML modeling exercises where teachers can define reference solutions in the form of both diagrams and detailed structures to be used for automated evaluation. The tool is enhanced by the interaction with recent Large Language Models for the automated generation of reference solutions starting from text, facilitating the creation of early drafts. A proof-of-concept case study has been performed by having TIGRE generate reference solutions for two exercises: most of the relevant concepts have been represented correctly, but issues emerged in the form of unnecessary classes being included and incorrect understanding of associations.

Keywords: UML Class Diagrams · Software Modeling · Large Language Models · Education

1 Introduction

Software modeling plays a pivotal role in Software Engineering (SE) education, as it allows students to develop critical thinking and the ability to represent real-world problems in an easily understandable visual form.

Among the various modeling types, conceptual modeling is particularly relevant, as it lets students learn how to visualize the different entities involved in a system, their functionalities, and the relationships among them.

One of the most commonly used notations in SE education is the Unified Modeling Language (UML), which provides several diagram types (e.g. class, use case, activity, deployment). UML class diagrams are considered to be one of the most suitable notations for conceptual modeling activities thanks to their ability to represent the different concepts involved in a system, their characterizing attributes and methods, and different relationship types.

© The Author(s), under exclusive license to Springer Nature Switzerland AG 2026
D. Taibi and D. Smite (Eds.): SEAA 2025, LNCS 16081, pp. 383–392, 2026.
https://doi.org/10.1007/978-3-032-04190-6_23

Learning UML usually requires students to solve exercises in the form of textual assignments, where a given system is described and the goal is to produce a satisfying model [1]. It is possible for students to produce solutions that differ from the original one envisioned by the teacher, either due to different element names or representing concepts in an equivalent (but still correct) way. Several tools and methodologies exist to perform UML modeling exercises [2], although some issues are presented such as tools not being available for use, creating and evaluating exercises being a time-consuming process that is rarely assisted by dedicated tools, and the inability to provide individual feedback to students.

To facilitate the evaluation process of UML class diagrams, and assist teachers in the definition of modeling exercises, we present TIGRE (auTomated dIagram Generator of REference solutions), an intelligent web-based platform that enhances the creation of diagrams by providing a modeling canvas where teachers can draw references, and the ability to interact with recent Large Language Models (LLMs) for the creation of preliminary sketches. The tool supports the definition of reference data structures for evaluating the students' diagrams, as one such structure contains the list of required elements, together with synonyms to ensure enough variability in the solution space is covered.

In this paper, TIGRE is presented as a prototype and its capabilities are assessed with a preliminary proof-of-concept example: by using the tool, we generated the solutions for two modeling exercises and then compared them with the original reference solutions; the evaluation showed that the most relevant concepts could be represented, although some issues were encountered in the form of unnecessary elements being added, incorrect representation of associations, and a tendency to represent associations as separate classes.

The remainder of the paper is structured as follows: Sect. 2 presents the background information with regards to the current state of the art, Sect. 3 describes the tool architecture, its functionalities, and the intended usage scenarios of the tool. In Sect. 4 we then describe the proof-of-concept example and discuss our findings and, lastly, we draw our conclusions and describe our future plans for TIGRE in Sect. 5.

2   Background and Related Work

There are various examples of tools for the automatic generation of class diagram exercises in literature. One such example is Wodel-EDU [3,6], a modeling tool built on the domain-specific language (DSL) Wodel [5]; through Wodel, teachers can define diagram constraints for an exercise and then have a student-produced solution be automatically evaluated to see how many constraints are respected. Wodel-EDU exploits the DSL by supporting several diagram types and, through a meta-model of a diagram and the corresponding graphical representation, allows for the generation of mutants that can be considered variations of a base diagram.

AutoER, proposed by Foss et al. [4], is a question-generation system for UML database design exercises that provides all requirements of a problem whose parts students can select to add new constructs to a diagram. This diagram is then compared with a teacher-defined diagram to identify matching names for entities, attributes, keys, and associations. Visual Narrator [7] is a tool built on a custom algorithm that exploits natural language processing techniques to convert user stories into conceptual models. The algorithm identifies concepts, relationships, attributes, and cardinalities.

Saini et al. [8] describe an approach built on machine learning and NLP techniques through a bot that receives textual input and continuous user feedback to generate and iteratively improve a class diagram: this is done by selecting decision points in the text and producing variations based on them, which the user can then choose as starting points for continuous improvement.

Yang et al. [9] describe a similar approach, where a textual description is processed by classifying sentences to identify classes, attributes, and associations, with grammar-based rules to then compose the various elements that make up a diagram. An evaluation performed on the tool yielded low precision and recall scores, painting the solution as inaccurate and unable to handle synonyms, ambiguities, and complex phrases.

The proposed approaches appear to be effective in some scenarios (with some being more effective than others) but are not completely generalizable. Moreover, none of the existing solutions appear to offer full support for editing diagrams directly, but instead rely on textual specifications, thus reducing the ability for users to define models with ease.

The use of LLMs for the creation of UML class diagrams has been explored in recent years by some preliminary studies [10–12] that highlight the potential of using such an approach for assisting teachers in the definition of class diagram exercises and references. To the best of our knowledge, no tools exist yet that directly integrate the LLM functionality in a modeling tool, as the aforementioned studies all make use of OpenAI's ChatGPT to produce the diagrams. Our aim is to provide an editor where the diagrams produced by an LLM can be edited with ease, rather than adopting strategies such as PlantUML that rely on text editing to make changes to a diagram. The same editor is intended to be used by students, providing them an easy interface for solving exercises. Additionally, with the definition of a reference structure, we intend to provide a replicable and reliable approach for the evaluation of class diagrams, without relying on one specific strategy to represent a diagram.

3   Tool Features

TIGRE is currently under development as a React-based web application that uses Apollon [13], an open-source online modeling editor that supports UML class diagrams. The application exploits HuggingFace's API services, allowing users to select the model they prefer to use. For this preliminary proof of concept, we selected DeepSeek's R1-Distill-Qwen-32B [14] as the model to use; we chose this model due to it showing good performance in reasoning while being, at the time of writing the article (April 2025), one of the most recent open-source LLMs.

In its current implementation, TIGRE allows SE teachers to define modeling exercises by providing a unique title and the textual description that accompanies the assignment. Reference solutions can then be defined for each existing exercise, and are identified by two objects, a *model* and a *structure*.

A *model* object contains all the information needed to draw a diagram and make it compatible with the Apollon modeler: it lists all classes present in the diagram, with their attributes and eventual methods, together with the graphical details needed to draw each class (e.g. width, height, position in the canvas); relationships are also included and are characterized by their type, the names of the two connected classes, the cardinality, and graphical details such as the starting points on each class and the relative position of the target class to the source.

A *structure* object, instead, is detached from the graphical representation of a class diagram and is intended to be used as a list of necessary elements that a student-produced diagram is expected to include when solving an exercise. Each structure object has the following attributes:

- A list of necessary classes. Each class has a unique name, a list of synonyms, a weight that expresses the importance of the class, a list of attribute names that the class cannot have, and a list of expected attributes. For each attribute, the following details are known: its name, its list of synonyms, its weight, and a list of accepted types.
- A list of necessary associations. Each association specifies the source and target class, a name, a list of synonyms, its type, and its weight. For both the source and target class, the class name, the eventual role that the class plays in the association, and a list of allowed multiplicities for the class are known.
- A list of necessary enumerations. Enumerations are similar to classes in terms of known attributes since they also have a unique name, a list of synonyms, a weight, and a list of literals. Literals are a special case of attributes, with the only difference being the list of allowed types, which is hard-coded to be an empty and unmodifiable array.
- A list of associations between an enumeration and a class. These associations specify the enumeration and the class, without adding the additional information specified by regular associations.
- A list of names that cannot be used to represent a class.
- A list of pairs of class names, with each item representing two classes that cannot be connected by an association.

Teachers can choose to create a new reference solution for an exercise by either drawing it on the modeling canvas, specifying directly the classes and their associations in an easily displayed and editable manner or through a dedicated form where, for each list of the structure object, it is possible to add a new item of the corresponding type or edit one of the existing items.

Additionally, both functionalities can also be enhanced through the interaction with the LLM: instead of drawing an entire diagram, it is possible to send the textual description of the exercise to DeepSeek and receive as an answer the list of expected elements that should be included. The answer is parsed and converted into a *model* object that can be displayed directly on the canvas, thus creating a preliminary sketch that teachers can use as a starting point for the full solution. The same can also be done for the creation of a starting *structure*: the answer given by DeepSeek is converted into a structure object that is set as the starting data for the form. Any time a reference is saved, no matter if it is a model or structure, a new object of the other type is also created with the same exact data, ensuring full compatibility between the two representations. Additionally, it is possible to enhance a structure object by passing it to DeepSeek and generate a list of synonyms for each named element, which teachers can then edit and validate; these synonyms can be easily revised through a dedicated form and removed from a structure in case they are not suitable. This aims to produce variation in the possible solution space, a goal that is further strengthened by the tool letting teachers define multiple alternative solutions (either by themselves or with the LLM's assistance) for a single exercise.

4   Proof-of-Concept Case

We present a proof-of-concept case study to test TIGRE's initial capabilities, identify potential issues and improvement areas, and define future development goals. Our objective is to evaluate TIGRE's integration with LLMs for editing UML class diagrams, focusing on the effectiveness of its automated diagram generation. We tested TIGRE by generating two class diagrams from textual requirements and analyzed the results.

The exercise requirements were sourced from past exams of the Information Systems course at Politecnico di Torino, where conceptual modeling is taught as a course topic. We used teacher-defined reference solutions to evaluate TIGRE's diagrams, using the same input descriptions given to the students during the exam. The exercises are labeled *Hackathons* and *Ski Passes*. The full text of the two exercises, the reference solutions, the generated diagrams, the results of our evaluation, and the prompt used for the generation of class diagrams are all available as an online resource[1].

We evaluated the diagrams using the method by Nikiforova et al. [15], which compares UML diagrams based on semantic similarity in four categories: classes, attributes, methods, and relationships. Matching elements are paired by human judgment and a similarity score is assigned to each pair; the distance scores among all pairs are used to create an Euclidean distance vector that yields the final distance score between two diagrams. The smaller the score, the higher the similarity, with 0 meaning two equivalent diagrams.

The comparison followed these steps: i) We matched each reference class with the most semantically similar generated class (and vice-versa), according to

---

[1] https://doi.org/10.6084/m9.figshare.28574861.

the best combination of name, attributes, and associations; unmatched classes received a distance score of 1 and enumerations were treated as classes and matched following the same criteria. ii) For attributes, we first checked pairs of matching classes, and matched their attributes according to name and type; unmatched attributes, and attributes of unmatched classes scored 1. Enumeration literals followed similar criteria, and were matched by name only. iii) Associations were matched if both classes were matched and the type (e.g. regular association, inheritance) and cardinality were equal; links between classes and enumerations were also considered associations and scored accordingly. iv) Once all elements were compared, we calculated the individual distances for classes, attributes, and associations, and we then computed the overall diagram distance based on them. This procedure was performed by one author of the paper; the remaining two authors then reviewed independently the evaluation, leading to the three authors converging their interpretations of the results into the final version.

Given the small sample size, we opted for qualitative analysis over statistical methods. Figures 1 and 2 display the two diagrams generated by the LLM, while Table 1 reports all evaluation metrics: counts of elements and computed distances for each exercise.

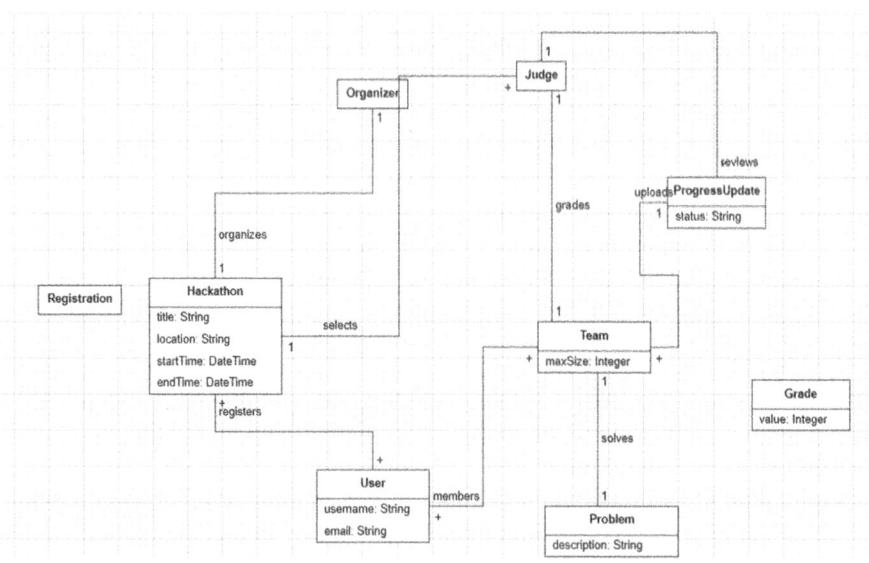

Fig. 1. Generated solution for the *Hackathon* exercise

Class distance scores were relatively low in both exercises, indicating somewhat good class generation capabilities. In *Hackathon*, 7 generated classes matched the reference, though 3 had name mismatches and 2 were unnecessary, with one representing an irrelevant concept and the other replacing an

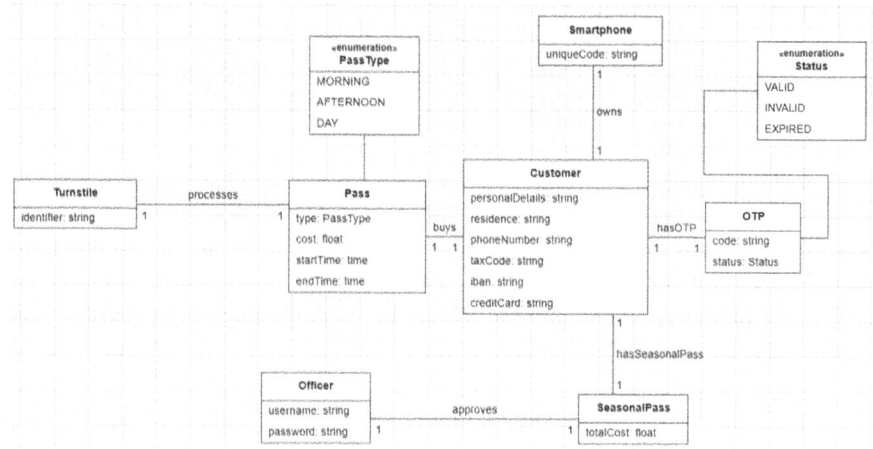

Fig. 2. Generated solution for the *Ski Passes* exercise

Table 1. Summary metrics for the two exercises

Metric	Hackathons	Ski Passes
Reference Classes	10	7
Reference Attributes	19	26
Reference Associations	14	6
Generated Classes	9	9
Generated Attributes	10	22
Generated Associations	8	8
Class Distance	2.40	2.96
Attribute Distance	4.58	5.83
Association Distance	3.87	3.16
Diagram Distance	6.46	7.26

attribute. In *Ski Passes*, only 4 out of 7 reference classes had matches, and the generated diagram included 5 unnecessary classes that would replace attributes or represent irrelevant content.

Attributes were the elements with the highest distance scores. In *Hackathon*, only 7 of 19 reference attributes had matches, and only 2 were exact matches with both name and type. *Ski Passes* showed similarly low results: 9 of 26 reference attributes had matches, with 2 attributes and 3 literals being exact. The second exercise also had 9 unmatched generated attributes and an unnecessary enumeration, compared to 4 unnecessary attributes in *Hackathon*.

Despite having relatively low distance scores, association generation also had some issues. In *Hackathon*, 6 of 14 reference associations had a matching name but only one also had the correct cardinality. This issue was more prominent in

Ski Passes where, although 3 reference associations had a match, all generated associations used incorrect 1-1 cardinalities, showing a flawed understanding of the problem to represent.

Overall, the generated diagrams appear to have captured the most relevant concept in both exercises and can offer a good starting point for defining modeling exercises' solutions. However, some limits such as introducing unnecessary elements, placing attributes in wrong classes, using classes for concepts that should be attributes, and focusing on one-to-one cardinalities are present and reduce the overall correctness.

The integration of LLMs in the diagram drawing process is not intended to fully replace human intervention, meaning that the produced diagrams are not supposed to be used as final output, but rather templates with the basic information that can then be edited and improved, since the textual answer is already parsed and converted in an easily editable class diagram. The ability to remove/edit unnecessary elements with a simple interaction offer more flexibility compared to the existing works in the literature, where the output was only textual or in PlantUML format, making it less flexible to edit.

5   Conclusions and Future Work

In this paper, we described TIGRE, a prototype web application that enhances the definition of UML modeling exercises through interaction with LLMs and the definition of dedicated reference structures for the evaluation of student-produced diagrams (both manual and automated). We performed a proof-of-concept test by generating the solutions to two exercises using the tool and then compared them with the original solutions: results were on the mixed side, since while the produced diagrams contained most of the required elements, the LLM also included different unnecessary elements and had trouble representing associations correctly.

These issues are however mitigated by the implementation of the UML modeler: rather than being simple textual content, the answers given by the LLM are automatically converted in an easily editable class diagram, facilitating the creation of reference solutions. The presence of a form where solution structures can be edited directly after creating a diagram also ensures that synonyms and semantic variations are covered, especially thanks to the integration with the LLM for this functionality.

Our future plans for the development of TIGRE include a refinement of the prompting strategies and the development of an evaluation engine that uses the reference structures as the base for assisting students by providing direct feedback through automated diagram comparisons. Lastly, we envision the extension of all functionalities (automated diagram creation, reference solutions, automated evaluation) to other diagram types such as process and use case diagrams.

References

1. Huber, F., Hagel, G.: Work-in-Progress: towards detection and syntactical analysis in UML class diagrams for software engineering education. In: 2020 IEEE Global Engineering Education Conference (EDUCON), pp. 3–7 (2020)
2. Huber, F., Hagel, G.: Tool-supported teaching of UML diagrams in software engineering education - a systematic literature review. In: 2022 45th Jubilee International Convention on Information, Communication and Electronic Technology (MIPRO), pp. 1404-1409 (2022)
3. Gómez-Abajo, P., Guerra, E., Lara, J.: Automated generation and correction of diagram-based exercises for Moodle. Comput. Appl. Eng. Educ. **31**, 1845-1866 (2023). https://onlinelibrary.wiley.com/doi/abs/10.1002/cae.22676
4. Foss, S., Urazova, T., Lawrence, R.: Automatic lof UML database design diagrams. In: Proceedings of the 53rd ACM Technical Symposium on Computer Science Education - Volume 1, pp. 626–632 (2022). https://doi.org/10.1145/3478431.3499376
5. Gómez-Abajo, P., Guerra, E., Lara, J. Wodel: a domain-specific language for model mutation. In: Proceedings of the 31st Annual ACM Symposium on Applied Computing, pp. 1968-1973 (2016,4). https://dl.acm.org/doi/10.1145/2851613.2851751
6. Gómez-Abajo, P., Guerra, E., Lara, J.: A domain-specific language for model mutation and its application to the automated generation of exercises. Comput. Lang., Syst. Struct. **49** 152–173 (2017,9). https://www.sciencedirect.com/science/article/pii/S147784241630094X
7. Robeer, M., Lucassen, G., Werf, J., Dalpiaz, F., Brinkkemper, S. Automated extraction of conceptual models from user stories via NLP. In: 2016 IEEE 24th International Requirements Engineering Conference (RE), pp. 196-205 (2016,9). https://ieeexplore.ieee.org/document/7765525,ISSN:2332-6441
8. Saini, R., Mussbacher, G., Guo, J., Kienzle, J.: Machine learning-based incremental learning in interactive domain modelling. In: Proceedings of the 25th International Conference on Model Driven Engineering Languages And Systems, pp. 176–186 (2022). https://dl.acm.org/doi/10.1145/3550355.3552421
9. Yang, S., Sahraoui, H.: Towards automatically extracting UML class diagrams from natural language specifications. In: Proceedings Of The 25th International Conference On Model Driven Engineering Languages And Systems: Companion Proceedings, pp. 396–403 (2022,11). https://dl.acm.org/doi/10.1145/3550356.3561592
10. De Bari, D., Garaccione, G., Coppola, R., Torchiano, M., Ardito, L.: Evaluating large language models in exercises of UML class diagram modeling. In: Proceedings of the 18th ACM/IEEE International Symposium On Empirical Software Engineering And Measurement, pp. 393–399 (2024). https://dl.acm.org/doi/10.1145/3674805.3690741
11. Shehata, M., Lepore, B., Cummings, H., Parra, E.: Creating UML class diagrams with general-purpose LLMs. In: 2024 IEEE Working Conference On Software Visualization (VISSOFT), pp. 157–158 (2024,10). https://ieeexplore.ieee.org/abstract/document/10794946, ISSN: 2832-6555
12. Wang, B., Wang, C., Liang, P., Li, B., Zeng, C.: How LLMs Aid in UML modeling: an exploratory study with novice analysts. In: 2024 IEEE International Conference On Software Services Engineering (SSE), pp. 249–257 (2024,7). https://ieeexplore.ieee.org/abstract/document/10664407/references
13. Krusche, S., Frankenberg, N., Reimer, L., Bruegge, B.: An interactive learning method to engage students in modeling. In: Proceedings of the ACM/IEEE 42nd

International Conference On Software Engineering: Software Engineering Education And Training, pp. 12-22 (2020). https://dl.acm.org/doi/10.1145/3377814.3381701

14. DeepSeek-AI DeepSeek-R1: Incentivizing Reasoning Capability in LLMs via Reinforcement Learning (2025). https://arxiv.org/abs/2501.12948, _eprint: 2501.12948

15. Nikiforova, O., Gusarovs, K., Kozacenko, L., Ahilcenoka, D., Ungurs, D.: An Approach to Compare UML Class Diagrams Based on Semantical Features of Their Elements. (2015,11)

Adopting the C4 Model for Lightweight Architecture Modeling - An Experience Report

Robbert Jongeling[1]([✉]) [iD], Niels Jørgen Strøm[2], Lars Peter Torp Nissen[2], Martin Kitchen[2], and Jan Carlson[1] [iD]

[1] Mälardalen University, Västerås, Sweden
{robbert.jongeling,jan.carlson}@mdu.se
[2] Grundfos, Bjerringbro, Denmark
{njstroem,lnissen,mkitchen}@grundfos.com

Abstract. This paper reports on experiences of migrating to a new way of documenting software architecture for embedded software development at a company developing software-intensive systems. A lightweight modeling approach using the C4 model for software architecture was adopted, where the architecture diagrams were expressed in PlantUML and stored within Markdown files alongside the code. We describe the problem context and the new approach, and report on a questionnaire survey among the software engineers to elicit their experiences and opinions two years after the introduction of this way of working. The majority of the 48 respondents reported being successful in using the new way of working and see benefits in terms of the better organization of the documentation as stored alongside the code, a clearer process of documenting, better alignment with the code, and ease of use. Engineers report a manageable learning curve but foresee challenges in maintenance and communication of changes across teams working on embedded software, hardware and electronics.

Keywords: Software architecture modeling · C4 model · Adoption in practice

1 Introduction

Organizations rely on various ways to document their software architecture, and these ways are not uncommonly guided by convenience and legacy. When change to the architecture documentation practice is needed, it may be challenging to choose an appropriate method among the many available options. In this paper, we provide an experience report of such a change at a company, not claiming a definitive best solution to a problem, but contributing to the body of knowledge that may support decisions about documenting architecture in similar situations.

This research was supported by Software Center www.software-center.se.

D. Taibi and D. Smite (Eds.): SEAA 2025, LNCS 16081, pp. 393–409, 2026.
https://doi.org/10.1007/978-3-032-04190-6_24

The context of this research is a long-running collaboration with the partner company, in which we have been working on ways to improve their software architecting practice. This paper reports on a change in the way of working implemented by the company two years ago, we describe the change and survey various stakeholders to map their experiences. The company develops cyberphysical systems and embedded software for these systems. Due to an increase in the required capabilities of these systems and a growth of variants of the products the company offers, the number of development teams in the company has also increased. Consequently, the previous ways of capturing the software architecture were deemed no longer sufficient. To address the shortcomings, the company has adopted a hierarchy of documenting the architecture following the C4 model for software architecture by Simon Brown [1]. This model consists of four layers: Context, Containers, Components, and Code. Entities at each layer are contained in entities in the above layers. The context level captures systems and people, the containers level shows the containers that constitute a software system of interest, and so on. In addition to adopting this hierarchy, the company has established new modeling guidelines for the various software engineering teams to create documentation in Markdown files, including PlantUML or "draw.io" diagrams, and store them alongside the code in the same repositories.

We report on experiences of this solution two years after its introduction. We gather feedback in discussions with the responsible architects and through a questionnaire among the software engineers. We find that the engineers perceive benefits in standardizing the way of working, in the structure provided by the C4 model, and by having the documentation alongside the source code. Reported challenges include a learning curve (although manageable), layout issues with PlantUML, and specific challenges encountered during the migration to the new way of working. Foreseen challenges for the future relate to maintenance.

The remainder of this paper is organized as follows. Section 2 describes the previous state of practice at the company and the need for adopting a new approach for documenting the architecture. Section 3 briefly mentions prior work exploring the same problem space as discussed in this paper. Section 4 describes the process of making the changes to the new way of working, and presents details of the chosen lightweight modeling to documenting the architecture, following the C4 model for architecture and PlantUML diagrams embedded in text files. Section 5 presents the results of an evaluative questionnaire answered by 48 software engineers in the company. Section 6 provides a discussion and reflection on the experiences reported on in this paper. Section 7 concludes.

2   Problem Context

The company in which we performed our study develops several products containing embedded software. This software is developed by approximately 150 software engineers, divided over eight platform teams and nine product teams that focus on specific products. Additionally, there are teams working on mobile and cloud applications, but these are not the focus of this experience report, which is limited to the domain of embedded software development. We have worked closest together with one central architecture team, responsible (among other things) for establishing the way of working with software architecture documentation. In particular, we focus on the way in which the software architecture and design are documented. We briefly describe the previous way of working here and the new way of working in Sect. 4.

The prior way of documenting the architecture was done through a combination of various loosely coupled artefacts. To describe features, a feature model was expressed in Pure::Variants [2]. Textual requirements were captured in IBM Doors, and an implementation in C code. The architecture was documented in Office documents stored in SharePoint, disconnected from the code. Feature definitions were strictly linked to requirements, but no strict linking was present between feature definitions and their implementation and verification artefacts. This was handled manually.

This way of working had several challenges, as identified by the architects and software engineers. The architecture and design documentation was difficult to. locate. Consequently, it was heavy to maintain these artefacts. Moreover, these artefacts were non-uniform, with potential big differences across teams. This was partly due to the informal nature of the architecture description and partly due to the design process, which did not explicitly include any modeling requirements as part of the documentation effort. The lack of a more guided way of working meant that changes to the implementation could be made without corresponding changes in the documentation, and this would potentially go unnoticed. Such inconsistencies then extended to other artefacts too, e.g., the feature model. These challenges impacted both the platform and the product teams. Therefore, the architecture team decided to implement changes in the way the architecture was documented across the teams working on embedded software development.

3   Related Work

In this paper, we report on experiences of modeling the architecture in textual (PlantUML) models that are created in a regular text editor and not in a dedicated modeling tool. The models have underlying semantics and the way they are expressed enables some degree of automated support for, e.g., consistency checking. Diagrammatic representations of these PlantUML models are automatically rendered and included in the documentation. This situates the modeling practices between informal diagramming and canonical modeling [3]. The considerations that the company made when introducing the practices relates to the question of "how much modeling is enough" [4]. Some modeling is needed for having an accurate documentation of the system, but complete modeling of the entire software has not enough benefits to be worth the cost. Hence, this in-between solution was chosen.

Software architecting is a continuous activity [5]. A consequence is that the architecture is subject to change throughout development, due to, e.g., new

incoming requirements. A common challenge in practice is then the maintenance effort of the architecture and ensuring its alignment with the source
code [6]. These consistency problems are common and not new. Indeed, the
established approach of inconsistency tolerance [7] is still relevant [8].

We mention three experience reports on architecting of software-intensive
systems that are relevant to this paper. The first focuses on re-use of architecture
decisions and finds that this is done ad-hoc [9]. This is relevant in our setting too
because of the shared embedded software domain and platform-product setup.
A second experience report is on using the C4 model in education [10], where
the C4 model is also used in conjunction with UML modeling. Experiences from
practice are more readily found in the gray literature than in research papers.
The third experience report we mention states that using diagrams at all four
levels is not necessary and it is better to pick and choose which ones are relevant
in the particular setting [11].

4   From the Previous to the New Way of Working

During 2021, the architecture team has identified the challenges discussed in
Sect. 2. One of the challenges was how to deal in particular with consistency
checking between the source code and the architecture, which at that time was
captured only in informal diagrams. During their early work, the team concluded
that there was a lack of documentation at the lower levels of abstraction. In
particular, besides an overview of the whole system, there was a need to capture
the design of individual components and their interfaces. Initial work in this
direction revealed the need to delimit more clearly what a software component
entails.

4.1   Characterizing a Software Component

The effort of clarifying what a software component is has resulted in the following description of its characteristics. A software component defines the level of
reusability and is captured at the C4 components level. To ensure it can be used
independently, a component must have high cohesion and low coupling. Moreover, components of the embedded software shall be built into an executable
which is deployed on a single ECU. Executables cannot be distributed across
multiple ECUs, and therefore neither can components.

Software components are a crucial element in the hierarchical definition of the
systems under development. At the highest level, there is a family of products.
Features are defined in a software product line context in a feature modeling
tool (Pure::Variants). Each feature is implemented by a single software component. Software components are grouped using the same structure as the features.
Naming conventions are in place to amplify alignment between the diagrams and
the source code.

4.2   Goals for the New Way of Working

The following goals for the new way of working with documentation were formulated by the company:

1. To have one holistic approach to architecture and design documentation;
2. For the documentation to be easy to locate, easy to produce, and easy to maintain;
3. To obtain more uniform documentation across development teams;
4. To use standard diagrams.

The new way of documenting comprises a textual documentation of the architecture in Markdown files, which will be stored alongside the source code and placed under version control. The Markdown files contain PlantUML definitions of diagrams, following the modeling semantics of UML. Detailed system aspects and connection to other (software) domains are currently captured partly outside this framework. This is a challenge which is discussed in Sect. 5.

4.3   C4 Model Adoption

After establishing the definition of software component, the architects have also provided guidelines of what and how to model at each of the C4 levels. These guidelines for each level are included in brief below.

C4 - Context. The intent of diagrams at this level is to identify the software systems that are built and delivered, in addition to who are using these systems. Moreover, they document how software systems interface with the existing environment. The context diagrams are described for each product instance. Stakeholders are product specialists, software engineers, and other product development engineers. The diagrams represent a static view of the context of the system and interactions with other software systems or people. In some cases, dynamic views are needed, for which scenario views are defined. These contain the same elements and are represented using UML sequence diagrams or communication diagrams.

C4 - Containers. The intent of diagrams at this level is to identify software containers that are built and delivered. The diagrams shall show how software containers are deployed on hardware elements, and how software containers interact with other containers or external systems. At this level, one view is required: a deployment view, which is a static view of the software containers deployed on hardware elements. A container in this context represents a software program developed by the company. Containers can be considered executables or deployables, too. Versioned releases of containers are published internally.

The deployment view comprises containers and their interactions with external systems. The container diagrams are created for each product instance. Stakeholders are product specialists, software engineers, and other product development engineers. Also at this level, sometimes dynamic scenario views are defined, using UML sequence diagrams or communication diagrams.

C4 - Components. Inside a container, we find components. One mandatory view that is created for each product instance shows the software components and their relations. This view is derived from a "150%" diagram (a single view including the union of the components used in the all product variants [12]), by excluding components that are not used in the product. Sometimes, new components can be added, to both this diagram and the "150%" diagram. The intent of diagrams at this level is to identify which software components are available and which are going to be included in the build of the instance. Moreover, the diagrams are used to illustrate how the software components interact.

Diagrams showing the component view are separated into two drawings, one for the basic layer and one for the application layer on top of the basic layer. Due to the stringent definition of software component, the component view for the application layer can be automatically generated for both the platform and product instances. Stakeholders are software engineers. For the basic layer, due to legacy and the importance of the graphical layout (visual placement of boxes) for conveying information about groupings and the relationships between components, component view diagrams are created using a drawing tool (draw.io). The drawing tool is preferred in this case over PlantUML, since the latter by design does not allow fine-grained control over layout of graphical elements.

Finally, dynamic views may be created that show scenarios using UML sequence, collaboration, communication, or activity diagrams.

C4 - Code. The intent of diagrams at this level is to serve as a manual or user guide for users of the component, to be a reference manual for the public interface of the component, and to capture the internal design of the component to facilitate maintenance. Diagrams at the code level describe modules and classes, and how they are related. Component documentation must explain how a user of the component shall instantiate and configure it. It must be clear how to reuse the component, connect to other components it depends on, scale it, and activate its functionality.

Internal design documentation could be represented by state machines. For dynamic scenarios, sequence or communication diagrams can be used. Component documentation is created at platform level, written in PlantUML in Markdown files stored alongside code in the same folder. Stakeholders are software engineers working on development of the embedded software.

4.4   Process Changes

In addition to adoption of the C4 model, there are some other changes to the way of working. For example, a gold-silver-bronze medal incentive system is introduced to motivate teams to create higher documentation coverage and to be able to monitor progress in the refactoring effort. The main purpose of these incentives if to increase alignment between feature model and code base.

5   Findings and Insights

In this section, we present insights gathered through discussions with the architecture team and through a questionnaire sent out to software engineers within the company. The architecture team that was responsible for initiating the changes to the way of working, reports five perceived benefits and three open challenges from their perspective.

5.1   Expert Opinions from the Architecture Team

Experienced Benefits of the New Way of Working. The first experienced benefit is a closer connection between the documentation and the code. The lightweight way of modeling, i.e., easy to produce and read but still having a defined semantics, allows for modeling to be a natural part of the design work. Moreover, the documentation is now co-located with the code, which makes it more accessible for software engineers to view. Producing documentation models is also made easier, since it is integrated in the daily work environment of software engineers, through tools they are already using (Visual Studio Code and BitBucket). These benefits are thus seen in readily available documentation and an easier process by which to produce and maintain it.

A second experienced benefit is in the ability to identify changes without heavy tooling. Most tooling that is needed was already established. The architecture is now expressed in a textual format and stored under version control, allowing easy identification of changes using text comparison. In addition, some new tooling is required for rendering the PlantUML diagrams, but this can be done within Visual Studio Code, that was already used, in combination with browser extensions for viewing the documents in BitBucket.

Benefits of following the C4 model for architecture are also reported. Modeling at the C4 *Components* level has allowed for the automatic generation of static views showing the included and excluded components for particular products. In addition, a dynamic view describes behavior belonging to the platform level, and these aspects are not expected to change in a product instance. Diagrams at the higher levels of the C4 model, specifically *Context* and *Containers* were found useful for communication with non-software stakeholders. These benefits are thus related to the choice to follow the C4 model for the various levels of abstraction at which the architecture is expressed.

Open Challenges. Despite the change in way of working, a persisting challenge is monitoring the consistency between various artefacts. While in the new way of working, the process of updating the documentation is closer to the software development, and the documentation is placed closer to the code, no automated means are in place to check the alignment between documentation and implementation. Thus the teams rely on manual means, e.g., code reviews to ensure that when code changes are made, the relevant documentation is also updated. This consistency is nevertheless important, especially when other teams rely on the models as an accurate reflection of the current state of a component.

At the higher levels in the C4 hierarchy, such as *Context* and *Containers*, the models are relevant also to other teams creating other systems. These other teams are mostly interested in the external interfaces offered by components, and in changes to those. To smoothen this cross-team collaboration, it may be valuable to eventually model these levels in a more formal way rather than the informal PlantUML diagrams that are currently used and that may provide limited abilities for automated analysis.

For the same reason, there may be benefits from more formal modeling when connecting the development of embedded software more to systems engineering. The goal is then to integrate the development of the embedded software closer to the other departments in the company, that develop the hardware and electronics of the products. Currently, the documentation effort for new and existing software components has priority and it is not yet a priority to expand these efforts. However, a company-wide Product Lifecycle Management effort is running in parallel, which includes a possibility of cross-domain modeling. Within this initiative there is an opportunity to create an environment of joint modeling for the different software domains such as cloud, handhelds and embedded as well as with the non software domains of mechanics and electronics.

5.2   Feedback from the Software Engineers (Quantitative)

We sent out a questionnaire survey by email to all (to limit selection bias) software engineers for embedded software at the company. A reminder was sent after 2 weeks. We got 48 responses from the complete sampled population of about 150 software engineers, a response rate of about 30%.

We structured the questionnaire as follows. First, we asked basic demographic questions: years of employment, role, and type of team. The years of employment are important to distinguish the responses from engineers that have experienced the way of working also before the changes were rolled out two years ago. The opinions of the newer employees on the new way of working are still interesting, even when these employees cannot compare their experience to a previous way of working. Second, we included questions on the frequency with which diagrams at the various C4 levels were created, edited, and viewed. Third, we included other questions about experiences working with C4. In particular, we inquired about mental load of using the way of working, the degree of success that engineers had with performing their tasks and the effort in terms of hard work and time spent. We repeated the similar question to ask those engineers familiar with the prior way of working to compare these task load aspects between the two ways of working. Fourth, we included open questions about experienced benefits, challenges, and foreseen challenges in the future. The complete questionnaire instrument is available as supplementary material [13]. To limit threats to construct validity, the questionnaire was created in several iterations with feedback from the architecture team. We now discuss the answers to each of the parts of the questionnaire.

Demographics. Most (35) of the respondents have been employed at the company for more than 2 years, and thus have experienced both ways of working. All but two of the respondents are software engineers; one is a product owner and another a software tester. The respondents are almost equally divided among the types of teams: product (24) and platform (23), one respondent replied "other."

Creating/Editing/Viewing C4 Diagrams. Before asking their concrete experiences with the C4 diagrams, we are interested to know how often engineers interact with them. Therefore, we asked respondents to grade on a 7-point scale the frequency with which they (i) create new diagrams, (ii) edit existing diagrams, and (iii) view existing diagrams at each of the C4 levels. The responses are aggregated in Fig. 1.

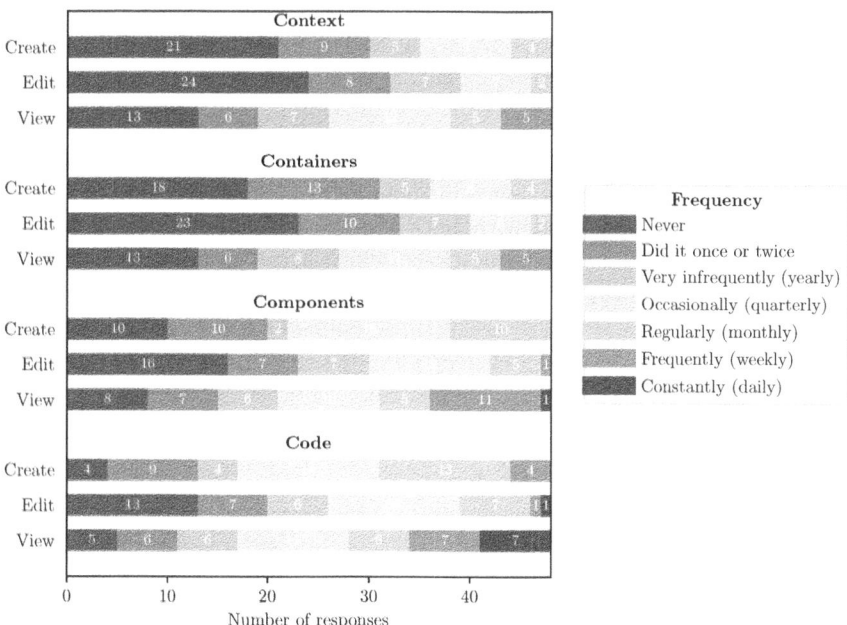

Fig. 1. Summarized overview of frequency of creating, editing, and viewing diagrams at the different C4 levels, as indicated by survey respondents

Viewing is the most common way to interact with the diagrams, which is expected. Respondents indicate creating new diagrams with slightly higher frequency than editing existing diagrams. Due to the relatively short time since the introduction of the new way of working, the engineers are mostly engaged in creating new documentation for components that are missing it, rather than updating documentation to reflect changes to the implementation. There are a total of 466 features to be documented, but only 42 components currently have a C4 code level document. Hence, most effort at this point is spent on filling this gap by creating new documentation.

A general trend that can be read from Fig. 1 is that the engineers most frequently interact with diagrams at the lower C4 levels. The diagrams at the higher levels see very infrequent use, with a third of the respondents even indicating to never view diagrams at context and containers levels. Both these results follow our expectations that software engineers would indeed most often need the information expressed in the code level diagrams. Moreover, this observation shows that the high-level architecture of the system is stable, few changes are needed to its documentation.

Task Load of New Way of Working. To elicit experiences with this new way of working, we selected relevant questions from the NASA Task Load Index [14] and adapted them to make them suitable for our context. We asked two questions and for each of them four sub-questions on the same topics. The two questions asked respondents to (i) indicate their experiences with the new way of working, and (ii) indicate their perceived difference with the previous way of working. These two are referred to as 'Absolute' and 'Relative' respectively in Fig. 2. For the 'Relative' question, we only include the answers from those respondents that answered the questions and indicated more than 2 years of employment, since they have worked with both approaches. The bold text labels in the figure indicate the four sub-questions, which asked respondents to rate (i) the mental load of working with the C4 model, (ii) how successful they were in accomplishing what they are asked to do, (iii) how hard they had to work to accomplish the required level of performance, and (iv) how much time they spent on accomplishing the documenting tasks using the C4 model.

Figure 2 shows a rather diverse experience with the new way of working. Note that for mental load, hard work, and time effort, lower values are generally more positive than higher values but not necessarily so. Since the previous practice (that the engineers are asked to compared to) for some of the respondents was to not document at all, some respondents will have marked a higher effort. Almost half the respondents indicate a lower mental load, and about a third think it is more difficult to work with the new way of working. Half the respondents indicate being more successful in accomplishing what they are asked to do using the new way of working compared to previously, a quarter think they are less successful. We now look at the answers to the open questions to further interpret these quantitative results.

5.3   Feedback from the Software Engineers (Qualitative)

To complement the previously presented quantitative data, we included open questions in the questionnaire to gather qualitative data, too. We asked three questions about (i) benefits, (ii) challenges, and (iii) foreseen future challenges of the new way of working. A final question was included to gather any other

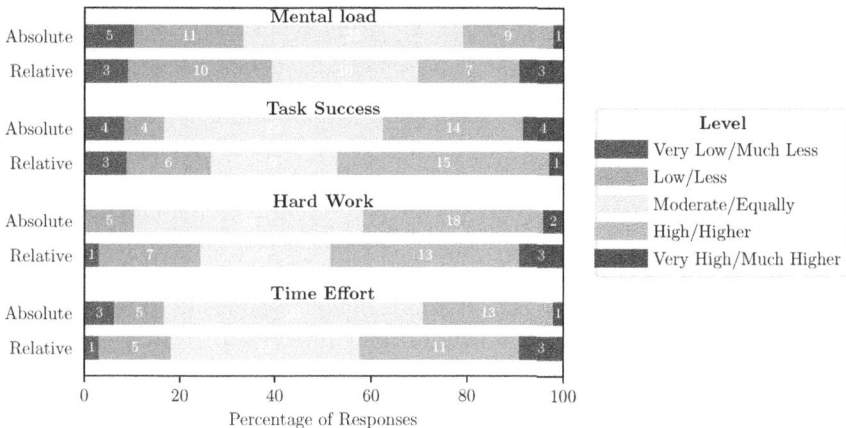

Fig. 2. For the four questions about task load, we are plotting the number of responses to the two questions about the absolute task load and the relative comparison to the previous way of working. The size of the bars indicates the percentage, the numbers inside the bars indicate the number of responses.

feedback for the architecture team or the researchers. To those last four questions, we gathered 32, 33, 28, and 19 answers, respectively. We now summarize the responses to each open question and include some supporting statements from the responses in *italics*.

Experienced Benefits. A categorized overview of the experienced benefits, and the number of answers they are mentioned in, is shown in Table 1.

Table 1. Categorized benefits as mentioned in the 32 responses, answers have been assigned to one or more categories.

Category of response	#
Documenting structure and well-defined process	15
Documentation located close to the code	13
Lightweight, fast, or otherwise easy to use	7
Improved understanding of implementation	6
No benefits seen	3

Most mentioned benefits (15 of the 32 responses to this question mention this) are in the improved organization of the documentation and an improved process of documenting. Very related to that, having the documentation close to the code is mentioned as a benefit in 13 of the responses. As an example of both, one respondent noted: *"It is very nice to have the architecture work standardized,* so you know what to do, and you know where to find the documentation. I like that code and documentation are in the same repository." The benefit of co-locating documentation and code is mostly seen in a better alignment of the documentation to the code: "It is a good thing as it ensures alignment of code and documentation. It streamlines the naming and structure of components."

Related to the specific way of working, 7 respondents explicitly mention ease of use and speed as benefits. In particular the textual notation and inclusion of pictures is appreciated for its simplicity: "Markdown is great for documentation because you are only allowed to write text, and put in pictures. Nothing fancy, so you have to make clear documentation." One respondent confirms that it remains important that the new way of working provides a: "better visualization of what we are trying to achieve." The learning curve for PlantUML is mentioned but experienced as manageable.

The better organization of the documentation and the process of document-ing the architecture also leads to easier understanding of the code, both for existing developers and newcomers, as mentioned in 6 responses. For example, they indicate an improved understanding of code behavior, dependencies, and interfaces. The new common understanding of the requirements for documenta-tion has benefits in both creating and reading documentation: "We now have a common understanding of the required amount of documentation and a standard to follow for creating/editing it. This makes it much easier to read existing doc-umentation and it is also great to know how much to do when documenting – even if the workload is then a bit bigger. This bigger workload is easily compen-sated for by the earlier mentioned benefits." This answer also indicates that the higher workload noticed in Fig. 2 is not per se experienced negatively. Overall, these answers align with the experienced benefits as mentioned by the team of architects.

Experienced Challenges. A categorized overview of the experienced chal-lenges, and the number of times they are mentioned, is shown in Table 2.

Table 2. Categorized challenges as mentioned in the 33 responses, answers have been assigned to one or more categories.

Category of response	#
Learning curve and time spent	11
Limited control over diagram layout	7
High effort and sometimes low value	6
Migrating to new way of working	5
Granularity of C4	2

The most mentioned challenge (in 11 responses to this question) is related to learning the new way of working and taking time to adopt the new process.

As with any new way of working, some new learning is required, so this is not a very surprising result. Moreover, one response puts this in challenge perspective of the lack of alternative: *"Learning PlantUML 'coding'. . . but hey – better than working with, e.g., Visio."* Responses also indicate that respondents experienced good support from the architecture team, created guides, and online resources to adopt the new way of working and learn the PlantUML syntax.

Since PlantUML diagrams are automatically rendered, there is limited control (by design) over the exact graphical layout of the diagrams. This is mentioned as a challenge by 7 respondents and can be exacerbated when the complexity of the diagrams grows: *"Diagram output is hopeless when complexity increases, lot of time spent on getting diagrams being readable"*

Some reported challenges related to the migration to the new way of working and the expected content of the documentation. As mentioned by 5 respondents, one challenge is in knowledge management of the features: *"Creating new C4 is easy but otherwise, knowledge about the feature and its purpose is needed but hard to get from previous owner."* This indicates a challenge of communication between the teams and other stakeholders. It then is also important that the teams document in the same way, to make it easier to understand documentation by anyone. One respondent experiences this challenge: *"Among teams it's very different how C4 is interpreted, hence the C4 artifacts are on very different quality levels."* Lastly, challenges are experienced in maintenance of the new documentation: *"In case of updating an existing feature for a new product, the time to convert to C4 considering backward compatibility is very high."*

Two responses mention challenges related to the granularity of the documentation. One specifically mentions the gap between containers and components, and seeks an intermediate breakdown. There are also some negative responses (6), that indicate experiencing little value of the new way of working, but at the same time a high effort in terms of time spent.

Foreseen Future Challenges. A categorized overview of the anticipated future challenges, and the number of times they are mentioned, is shown in Table 3.

Table 3. Categorized challenges as mentioned in the 28 responses, answers have been assigned to one or more categories.

Category of response	#
Maintenance effort and overhead	8
Quality assurance	6
No foreseen challenges	5
Alignment with feature model	4

Since the new way of working was rolled out two years ago, we considered that there may be challenges that are foreseen by the engineers but not yet encountered. This question anticipates challenges related to maintenance and indeed that was the most frequently recurring theme in the answers (8 mentions). Respondents expect future challenges in keeping the documentation aligned with the implementation in an efficient way: *"Keeping the documentation aligned with the code. However, I feel, that the C4 documentation interacts with the code in a way that will make such an alignment easier – or more likely to happen – than it has been in the past."*

Moreover, 6 responses mention that the quality of documentation needs to be high to ensure future maintenance effort is limited: *"We should make sure everybody is on the same level, and perhaps have a bit more governance around C4 to make sure generated artifacts are on the same (high quality) level."*

Another aspect of maintenance (mentioned 4 times) is related specifically to the way of working at the company, where also a feature model is created and maintained: *"Alignment with the feature model needs to be done."* Further challenges are mentioned related to the alignment with the feature model and communication between different teams: *"Communicating design and interfaces may need some work. If one is not present during the inception of the work, it is very difficult to deal with the interface and understand documentation. That is, you need to know the person that wrote the document to use the document for some modules."*

Some (5) responses do not foresee any challenges, or expect that the new way of working will help them in overcoming them: *"None. Much easier to find documentation and edit – also in the future."*

Other Feedback. In the last question, any other feedback could be shared. Some respondents shared their concerns about the approach being of high cost and low value, albeit without much supporting argumentation: *"C4 is a kind of white elephant"*. Others are specifically missing the value of the context and containers levels: *"the two top levels are more or less something we create because it is required, but I have yet to see the benefits of these two levels."* Some question the need for extensive documentation and find the software components simple enough to be understood without it: *"Only maybe 10% of software components needs documentation; 90% of the components are too simple so there is no need to spend time on making documentation (especially specious C4)."* The structure that the C4 model provides is appreciated under some conditions: *"C4 is a reference. For certain implementation, we may need a 'C5' or 'C6' or say 8 levels of decomposition to explain everything."*

6   Lessons Learned

In this section, we discuss lessons learned during the process of adopting the new way of working and its evaluation.

6.1 Defining the Concept of Software Component Is Important

The definition of what a software component comprises has been a crucial enabler for the new way of working. Previously, there was no such stringent definition and consequently, different interpretations existed across teams. This limited the abilities for reuse and made the initial efforts for homogenized documentation more difficult. The software component definition has proven to be instrumental in the refactoring efforts to achieve an architecture exhibiting high cohesion and low coupling. Moreover, the concrete definition of software component was a prerequisite for aligning the code-base with the feature model, the requirements structure, and the other aspects of the system design. Formulating a definition of software component was thus absolutely necessary for the successful adoption of the new way of working.

6.2 Documentation Close to Code is Experienced Positively

Keeping documentation close to code is experienced positively across the respondents and architecture team. The specific perceived benefits of this practice are accessibility and an increased ability to keep the documentation synchronized with the source code. These benefits are independent of the C4 model and could thus also be achieved with other paradigms to structure the documentation.

6.3 Drawing Is Still Needed Sometimes

The way of working rolled out at the company recommends the use of PlantUML and provides templates and guides to use it in combination with Markdown. However, sometimes PlantUML is not enough to capture everything that the engineers want to express, for example when it remains vital to have complete control over the layout for some diagrams. This is due to semantics that are implicitly captured by, e.g., positioning components close to each other or aligned to indicate local groupings or dependencies cross layers. It is thus crucial that the engineers are enabled to still use informal diagramming to express their designs. The new way of working supports this, and some diagrams are still created using "draw.io". Completely changing this approach into a modeling approach with strict adherence to a modeling language seems not of interest to these engineers, partly because the software engineers themselves do not experience benefits from expressing these diagrams in the form of models and partly because of the convenience of using the informal diagrams they are used to: *"For example, I am plotting a sequence diagram, where I would like to add some blocks of a flow diagram or decision making blocks for the sake of better understanding. But this is not possible to do in C4 diagrams, whereas we can do with office tools."* The C4 model paradigm is notation independent. It was the decision of the architect team to use UML at the lower documentation levels, because it has defined semantics which are particularly well suited for those levels, e.g., class diagrams.

6.4   Benefits and Challenges

Working with the C4 model is providing a good structure for the documentation, which the engineers appreciate. In addition, the engineers report benefits from the textual representation, especially as compared to the office tools as were in use previously to create informal diagrams. The engineers also scrutinize the new way of working as they perceive it to cost too much effort for too little perceived value. That is put into perspective by others, who mention the additional effort is worth it due to the better state of the documentation. Our results can thus not be unequivocally attributed to the C4 model, but in large part are related to simply having a more systematic means of documenting the architecture.

Overall, the use of the C4 model thus yielded mixed responses, some criticism citing an increase of effort with little perceived value, and at the same time a majority of respondents indicates they are successful in achieving what they are asked to do with the new way of working. In parallel with the roll-out of the new way of documenting, a large refactoring effort has been initiated to remove architectural technical debt. This refactoring has included some conversion of old documentation and the creation of missing documentation. In some cases, developers have found this work redundant, which may have affected the answers.

As future work, we plan to a follow-up of the questionnaire we performed in this study. Establishment of all the missing documentation is a currently on-going process and doing so for all software components will take more time to complete. We expect that a follow-up in two years would be appropriate to investigate if a higher coverage of the documentation is indeed achieved and what the experiences with the C4 Code level documents are by then.

7   Conclusion

In this paper, we have shared experiences of a company's adoption of a new way of working for documenting their software architecture. We described the reasons to change, the details of their practice, including lightweight modeling following the C4 model for software architecture. Moreover, we describe the crucial importance of the formulation of a definition of software component for the company. Two years after initiating the change in way of working, we performed a questionnaire survey among engineers working on the embedded software at the company. The results indicate that they interact mostly with the diagrams at the lower C4 levels (components and code). Compared to the previous way of working with very little architecture documentation and mostly use of informal diagrams, there is an understandable increase in time effort and hard work reported. This additional effort is not per se bad, as the structure the new approach brings is appreciated, and having the documentation next to the code is also appreciated by the software engineers.

We do not claim that these results are generalizable to all industry contexts, but we hope that this experience report can provide input to practitioners with similar considerations on how they can change their software architecture modeling and documentation practices.

References

1. Brown, S.: Software architecture for developers. LeanPub (2013)
2. PTC. Pure Variants. https://www.ptc.com/en/products/pure-variants
3. Jongeling, R., Ciccozzi, F.: Flexible modeling: a systematic literature review. J. Object Technol. **23**(3) (2024)
4. Bucchiarone, A., Cabot, J., Paige, R.F., Pierantonio, A.: Grand challenges in model-driven engineering: an analysis of the state of the research. Softw. Syst. Model. **19**(1), 5–13 (2020). https://doi.org/10.1007/s10270-019-00773-6
5. Martini, A., Bosch, J.: A multiple case study of continuous architecting in large agile companies: current gaps and the CAFFEA framework. In: 2016 13th Working IEEE/IFIP Conference on Software Architecture (WICSA), pp. 1–10. IEEE (2016)
6. Tian, F., Liang, P., Babar, M.A.: Relationships between software architecture and source code in practice: an exploratory survey and interview. Inf. Softw. Technol. **141**, 106705 (2022)
7. Balzer, R.: Tolerating inconsistency. In: Proceedings of the 13th International Conference on Software Engineering, pp. 158–165. IEEE Computer Society Press (1991)
8. Stevens, P.: Maintaining consistency in networks of models: bidirectional transformations in the large. Softw. Syst. Model. **19**(1), 39–65 (2020)
9. Manteuffel, C., Avgeriou, P., Hamberg, R.: An exploratory case study on reusing architecture decisions in software-intensive system projects. J. Syst. Softw. **144**, 60–83 (2018)
10. Vázquez-Ingelmo, A., García-Holgado, A., García-Peñalvo, F.J.: C4 model in a software engineering subject to ease the comprehension of UML and the software. In: 2020 IEEE Global Engineering Education Conference (EDUCON), pp. 919–924. IEEE (2020)
11. Reyes, I.: C4 Model. My experience + Example. https://itzareyesmx.medium.com/c4-model-my-experience-example-fbcf50def540
12. Czarnecki, K., Antkiewicz, M.: Mapping features to models: a template approach based on superimposed variants. In: Glück, R., Lowry, M. (eds.) GPCE 2005. LNCS, vol. 3676, pp. 422–437. Springer, Heidelberg (2005). https://doi.org/10.1007/11561347_28
13. Jongeling, R.: Questionnaire survey instrument used in the paper "adopting the C4 model for lightweight architecture modeling – an experience report (Jun 2025). https://doi.org/10.5281/zenodo.15736948
14. Hart, S.G., Staveland, L.E.: Development of NASA-TLX (Task Load Index): results of Empirical and Theoretical Research. In: Hancock,P.A., Meshkati, N. (eds.) Human Mental Workload, ser. Advances in Psychology, vol. 52, pp. 139–183. North-Holland (1988)

Author Index

The manufacturer's authorised representative in the EU is Springer
Nature Customer Service Centre GmbH, Europaplatz 3, 69115 Heidelberg,
Germany. If you have any concerns regarding our products, please
contact ProductSafety@springernature.com

Printed and bound by CPI Group (UK) Ltd, Croydon, CR0 4YY

28/04/2026

02098524-0009